CULTURE AND PERSONALITY

CULTURE AND PERSONALITY

Contemporary Readings

edited by
ROBERT A. LeVINE
University of Chicago

 ALDINE PUBLISHING COMPANY, Chicago

ABOUT THE EDITOR

Robert A. LeVine received his B.A. and M.A. from the University of Chicago, and his Ph.D. in social anthropology from Harvard. He also graduated from the Chicago Institute for Psychoanalysis and was a Fellow of the Center for Advanced Study in the Behavioral Sciences. He is Professor of Anthropology, Psychiatry and Human Development at the University of Chicago. Professor LeVine has published numerous works on personality and child rearing and has also written extensively on theory and method in the comparative study of human behavior. He has recently authored *Culture, Behavior, and Personality* (Aldine, 1973), an introduction to the comparative study of psychosocial adaptation.

First published 1974 by
Aldine Publishing Company
529 South Wabash Avenue
Chicago, Illinois 60605

ISBN 0-202-01121-6 clothbound edition
      0-202-01122-4 paperbound edition

Library of Congress Catalog Number 79-169515

Printed in the United States of America

To the memories of
William Caudill and S. G. Lee
Pioneers in Culture and Personality Research

CONTENTS

CULTURE AND PERSONALITY

INTRODUCTION

THIS BOOK IS A SELECTION from among the best culture and personality studies done in recent years by anthropologists and other behavioral scientists. My purpose in editing it has been to present an updated picture of research in a field that, having attracted widespread attention and controversy by its earlier efforts, has continued to grow, diversify, and develop standards and sophistication to match the intrinsic interest and significance of its subject matter. As publications in this area multiply in the journals and books of several disciplines, it becomes necessary to bring together a representative selection, that students may see where the frontiers of contemporary work in culture and personality lie. My book, *Culture, Behavior, and Personality* (1973), is devoted to consideration of what lies beyond those frontiers and how to design a scientific vehicle for getting there; it omits detailed examination of the ground already covered. The present volume offers views of that terrain through a series of studies that illuminate specific aspects of the landscape.

The study of culture and personality is an interdisciplinary field of inquiry within the social and behavioral sciences, defined primarily by its attention to behavioral differences between populations, the development in the individual of psychological dispositions accounting for such differences, and their relationships to social and cultural environments. With its roots in major trends of twentieth century thought in the social sciences, psychology, and psychiatry, the field now has a history of its own that

I am grateful to the Center for Advanced Study in the Behavioral Sciences, Stanford, California, to the Center for Psychosocial Studies, Chicago, and to the University of Chicago for facilities and services involved in preparing this manuscript for publication.

1

goes back almost half a century. Its first 25 years, 1927-1952, were devoted largely to pioneering theoretical statements and exploratory research efforts. Personality, normal and abnormal, and its development in the individual, were found to vary from one culture to another and to pose serious problems of reliable assessment. In other words, the earlier efforts indicated that individuals of diverse cultures differed in their psychological functioning and early experience, but they did not result in a consensus on how to demonstrate either these differences or their relationships to social and cultural institutions. Amidst the growing recognition that these research problems were more difficult than had been anticipated, anthropological research and writing in this area became the province of specialists in either comparative child psychology or comparative psychopathology who communicated as much with psychologists or psychiatrists as they did with other anthropologists.

The greater specialization of investigators in culture and personality since 1953 has been facilitated by an increasing interest of developmental psychologists and psychiatrists in cross-cultural studies. The psychocultural relativism advanced by Ruth Benedict, Margaret Mead, Edward Sapir, Abram Kardiner and others during the 1930s began having its major impact on psychology and psychiatry in the 1950s, when air travel, the increased availability of research funds, and the development of colleagues in many parts of the world allowed American and European investigators in those fields to think of field work abroad as a real possibility. This convergence of intellectual influence and practical considerations was first prominent in the psychiatric literature and can be seen in the establishment of new journals such as the *International Journal of Social Psychiatry* and the *Transcultural Psychiatric Review*. Somewhat later, beginning in the 1960s, academic psychologists in considerable numbers became involved in cross-cultural studies; this, too, is manifest in the published literature of the period and in new journals such as the *International Journal of Psychology* and the *Journal of Cross-Cultural Psychology*. Cross-cultural research is now established and thriving in both psychiatry and psychology.

Culture and personality research draws upon and contributes to the growing specialties of cross-cultural psychology and transcultural psychiatry, but it is not reducible to them. Its distinctiveness, now as in the past, resides in its focus on continuities and complementarities between (a) the normal and abnormal, (b) childhood and adulthood, (c) the personality system and the social and cultural systems, and on the connections between (a), (b), and (c). Its province, though not sharply bounded, may be defined as the interrelations between the life cycle, psychological functioning and malfunctioning, and social and cultural institutions. That is the definition embodied in the works of its foremost contemporary investigators such as John W. M. Whiting, William Caudill, Melford E. Spiro, George DeVos, and Anne Parsons. And that is the definition that guided the selection of readings for this book.

Guided by such a definition, the readings I have included represent primarily the integrating anthropological perspective on culture and personality rather than the narrower topical foci of cross-cultural psychology and psychiatry. The student must consult other publications for cross-cultural studies of discrete psychological functions such as perception, memory, concept formation, and learning, and for accounts of deviant behavior, diagnosis, and treatment in other cultures. The studies in this book use knowledge of discrete psychological functions but focus on their organization as personality dispositions in development, pathology, and adaptive functioning in social roles. Many selections touch on psychiatric problems but relate them to the cultural contexts of normal behavior. These are studies in environmental psychology, emphasizing the relationships of patterns of ecology, social interaction, and cultural meaning—as analyzed by social anthropologists—to the subjective experience of the individual and the growth and maintenance of his psychic organization. They are also readings in psychological anthropology, in which maintainance and change in social and cultural institutions are shown to depend on the private motives of those who participate in them.

The book has five parts. Part I, containing studies largely by psychologists and psychiatrists, deals with the old problem of psychological universals in the contemporary perspective of research on human biology, communication, and development. The universals of organismic capacity and adaptive requirement in the human species operate as constraints on variation across human populations. The readings in Part II show how much cross-population variation in psychological aspects of the life cycle —occurring in response to cultural values—is possible within these constraints. Part III illustrates selectively how cultural categories embodying such values penetrate the subjective experience of the individual, in the ideational content of his emotions, dreams, inner controls, and fantasies. Part IV takes up some of the ecological and economic determinants of cross-cultural variations in early experience, values, and personality characteristics. In Part V, the emphasis is reversed; these studies show how individuals in diverse cultures translate their motives, conscious and unconscious, into selective social behavior that affects patterns of mate selection, religion and law. I believe these five parts represent the major trends of contemporary research on culture and personality.

The methods used in these studies are diverse, ranging across ethnographic, clinical, and statistical approaches. Their methodological sophistication resides in the appropriateness of their methods for the problems they were attempting to study. Taken as a whole, they illustrate my contention that the field of culture and personality needs all these approaches, each in the place where it can most effectively contribute scientific understanding. The reader of this book should be able to learn not only what questions have been asked about culture and personality, and what evidence we have to answer them, but also how different investigators go about seeking the answers.

I. PSYCHOSOCIAL UNIVERSALS

MAN'S ADAPTIVE BEHAVIOR varies more widely from one population to another within the species than that of other animals; but this variability is limited by the structure of the human nervous system and its maturational schedule, by the human reproductive cycle, and by other species-wide characteristics that represent our evolutionary heritage. There can be no doubt that these characteristics of all human organisms operate as constraints on human behavioral variability, but the tightness of the constraints, the ways in which they operate, and their relationships with the ecology of the earliest *Homo sapiens* population—these are matters not yet resolved by scientific research.

These matters are of interest in the comparative study of culture and personality because of its focus on behavioral differences between populations and their basis in psychological development. The more we learn about the invariants that give structure to human functioning in all environments, the better we can fit the ways in which we observe behavior to the processes we investigate. If we know what limits are set on behavioral variation by universals of the human condition, we can frame our comparative observations accordingly, rather than making arbitrary assumptions about what is variable and what its range is. In the past, theoretical formulations in culture and personality and social anthropology were often based on arbitrary assumptions about the limits on human variation. A frequent form of explicating these assumptions was to make lists of universals of human nature and society, provided as axioms from which the comparative study of variation could proceed. Many of these universals, such as "the helplessness of infants," were based on common observation; others, like the incest taboo, were inductively derived from ethnographic data. Few were solidly anchored in a biological conception of human functioning, and most were of such broad generality that they could be, and usually were, ignored in field research.

In recent years, bio-psycho-social universals have become objects of investigation, as the readings in this section amply demonstrate. Informed by modern biology and the evolutionary perspective in which it places human communication and the human life cycle, psychologists and psychiatrists have begun to examine their familiar data for evidence of universals and to seek new data from diverse populations around the globe. Every hypothesis they generate about what is pan-human contains important implications for the study of cross-cultural variation—in perception, cognition, and psychosocial adaptation.

Since culture and personality research is primarily concerned with the last, I have selected works of greatest relevance to the psychosocial area and titled this section accordingly. My omission of studies dealing with universals of language and language development and sequences of cognitive development—not to mention universals of perception and memory—can be challenged. All of these psychic functions are relevant to psychosocial adaptation, and each has accumulated a literature of cross-cultural replication in recent years. In accordance with the principles stated in the Introduction, however, I have favored works dealing with dispositions that cut across such specific aspects of psychic functioning as cognition and emotion, and represent organizations of functions for social adaptation and intrapsychic homeostasis. I have also favored those works whose implications for the cross-cultural study of personality variations—as manifested in emotional display, sex role behavior, and reactions to parenthood, infancy, death, and aging—are fairly direct and clear. Last and hardly least, I have chosen works whose topics are returned to in later sections and that can serve as suitable background for those subsequent readings.

The reader may find it useful to note the continuities between the chapters in this section and those appearing later in the book, particularly in Part II. D'Andrade's chapter (2) on sex differences is closely related to the analysis of sex differences in child behavior by Beatrice Whiting and Carolyn Edwards (Chapter 9). Kaufman's chapter (3) on the biology of parenthood provides relevant background for Obeyesekere's study of Sinhalese pregnancy (Chapter 10). The brief selection (Chapter 4) from Mary Ainsworth's important monograph on 28 Uganda infants and their mothers (which I recommend to the reader for a full presentation of the data on which her phase descriptions are based) is relevant to Chapter 7, the study of Japanese sleeping arrangements by Caudill and Plath, as well as to Chapter 18 by Munroe and Munroe, who reanalyze some of her data. Pollock's conceptualization of mourning (Chapter 5) forms a background for Matchett's clinical study of Hopi mourning (Chapter 11). Finally, Gutmann presents, in Chapter 6, universals of the aging process that are complemented by his own culture-specific treatment of the Druze in Chapter 12.

To summarize, the groups of related chapters are presented below, with the chapter on universals located on the left:

$$
\begin{aligned}
\text{Chapters}\quad &2{:}9 \\
&3{:}10 \\
&4{:}7,\ 18 \\
&5{:}11 \\
&6{:}12
\end{aligned}
$$

1. UNIVERSAL FACIAL EXPRESSIONS OF EMOTION

PAUL EKMAN

Paul Ekman is Professor of Psychology and Director of the Laboratory for the Study of Human Interaction and Conflict at the University of California, San Francisco. Reprinted with permission from *California Mental Health Research Digest* (1970) 8(4). Copyright © 1970 by California Department of Mental Hygiene.

PROLONGED AND AT times heated controversy has failed to settle the question of whether there are any facial behaviors associated with emotion which are universal for man. Darwin (1872) proposed universal facial expressions of emotion on the basis of his evolutionary theory. Floyd Allport (1924), Asch (1952) and Tomkins (1962, 1963) also postulated universal emotional facial behavior, although each writer offered a different theoretical basis for his expectation. These theorists also recognized that there would be cultural differences in facial behavior as well, and each made a partial attempt to explain these cultural variations in facial behavior.

The culture specific view, that facial behaviors are associated with emotion through culturally variable learning, received support from Klineberg's (1938) descriptions of how the facial behaviors described in Chinese literature differed from the facial behaviors associated with emotions in the Western world. Klineberg has recently said that the axiom "what shows on the face is written there by culture" is not a fair picture of his view, and that there are certain types of expressive behavior which are common to all human societies. LaBarre (1947) has taken a more extreme view, "there is no 'natural' language of emotion gesture." But this quote emphasizes LaBarre's failure to distinguish facial gestures from facial expressions of emotion. While there is overlap in that some emotional expressions of the face can be used as intentional gestures to state explicitly a message to another person (for example, the smile), there are many facial gestures which are independent of facial expressions of emotion (for example, head shake no, raising one brow, winking, and so forth), and these gestures may well be culturally variable.

Perhaps the most influential writer arguing for the culture specific view of facial expressions of emotion is Birdwhistell. In describing the history of his own work, Birdwhistell said, "When I first became interested in studying body motion . . . I anticipated a research strategy which could first isolate universal signs of feeling that were species specific. . . . As research proceeded, and even before the development of kinesics, it became clear that this search for universals was culture bound. . . . there are probably no universal symbols of emotional state . . ." (1963:126).

Thus there has been a long history of argument about the existence of any universal facial expressions of emotion. Neither side in the dispute has had systematically gathered quantitative data to support their view. I will describe our two lines of systematic inquiry on this topic, which I believe have firmly established pan-cultural elements in facial expressions of emotion. But first, I will describe a theoretical framework which reconciles the two opposite sides of this controversy by distinguishing between those elements of facial behavior that are universal and those that are culture specific.

THEORETICAL FRAMEWORK

Ekman and Friesen (1967, 1969a) have hypothesized that the universals are to be found in the relationship between distinctive movements of the facial muscles and particular emotions (such as happiness, sadness, anger, fear, surprise, disgust, interest). They suggested that cultural differences in facial behavior would be seen because some of the stimuli which through learning become established as elicitors of particular emotions will vary across cultures, because the rules for controlling facial behavior in particular social settings will vary across cultures, and because many of the consequences of emotional arousal will also vary with culture.

While there may well be certain *evoking stimuli* which universally are associated with particular emotions, many of the stimuli which elicit emotion are learned; they are the products of and will vary with culture. A common pitfall in cross-cultural research on facial expressions of emotion is to infer a common emotional state simply because the same event was compared in two cultures. In actuality the event may evoke a different affect in each culture, and the differences in facial behavior may reflect those differences rather than differences in the facial muscles associated with affect in each culture. For example, culture X might show up-turned lips, nasalabial folds, and almost closed eyelids at funerals, while culture Y might show down-turned lip, partially closed eyelids, and nostril dilations at funerals. Before concluding that the facial display of sadness varies across cultures, it would be necessary to verify that the stimulus "funeral" normatively evokes the same affect in the two cultures, rather than being a stimulus for joy in one culture and for sadness in another.

Display rules are socially learned techniques acquired early in life for the management and control of facial appearance. Four management techniques can be distinguished. One technique is to de-intensify the appearance clues to a given emotion; for example, when one is extremely fearful, he must attempt to look only moderately or slightly fearful. A second management technique is to over-intensify the felt emotion. A third management technique is to look affectless or neutral. A fourth management technique is to mask the felt emotion as completely as possible by simulating another covering emotion; for example, when one is fearful, he must attempt to look happy. The display rule specifies which of these management techniques should be applied to which facial behavior and under what circumstances. The display rule dictates the occasion for the applicability of a particular management technique in terms of (a) static characteristics of the persons within the situation (that is, age, sex, physical body size), (b) static characteristic of the setting (that is, ecological factors, and social definition of the situation, such as funeral, wedding, job interview, waiting for a bus), (c) transient characteristics of the persons (that is, role, attitude), and (d) transient regularities during the course of the social interaction (that is, entrances, exits, transition points, periods in conversation, listening, and so forth). Display rules should govern facial behavior on a habitual basis, such that they are more noticeable when violated than when followed. The face appears to be the most skilled nonverbal communicator and perhaps for that reason the best "nonverbal liar", capable not only of withholding information but of simulating the facial behavior associated with a feeling which the person in no way is experiencing. In cross-cultural comparisons of facial expressions, it is important not to interpret evidence as showing a basic difference in the muscles involved in facial expression when the difference was due to the application of display rules differently in the cultures being compared. Returning to our example of a funeral, let us suppose that we are comparing two cultures where this event has the same evoking characteristic of sadness; it is still possible that in one culture the display rule will be to over-intensify the affect, while in the other the display rule will be to mask it with a pleasant demeanor. Without high-speed photography and slow motion inspection of the films to see the initial sad movements in the one culture, the observer may gain the impression that sadness produces different facial muscle movements in the two cultures.

A last variable to be considered is the *behavioral consequence* of a facial expression of emotion. The behavioral consequence can be most readily determined from the body posture and movements, although the face may show the affect associated with a given behavioral consequence. We interpret the movements and postures of the body which coincide with and follow a facial expression of emotion as coping with the facially shown affect.

Such movements often do not differentiate one facial affect from another; for example, the behavioral consequence of flight may occur as a coping procedure for anger, fear, or even disgust in particular social contexts. The fact that people show very different body movements after showing the same facial affect should not be interpreted as meaning that the facial affect is meaningless, or inconsequential.

We agree with Darwin and Tomkins that there are distinctive movements of the facial muscles for each of a number of primary affect states, and these are universal to mankind. While what may elicit an emotion may vary from one culture to another, and the display rules for the management of facial appearance may vary, and the consequences may vary with culture, the particular muscles of the face which would move will be the same. For example, lowering and drawing together of the brows, with the tightened lower lid and the firmly pressed together lips is one of the distinctive muscular patterns for anger, and it is such facial patterns which we claim are universal. What makes one person angry may be different from what makes another person angry, but they will both show the same muscular movement on the face if they are not applying different display rules to manage or modify their facial appearance. Obviously if a person in one culture is applying the display rule to mask with happiness and a person in another culture is applying the display rule to intensify the anger, then they will appear quite different.

We have been arguing that the movements of the facial muscles are the basic building blocks of facial expressions of emotion, and that these are the pan-cultural elements of affect.

Yet, such movements are embedded in a context; they may be elicited by different stimuli, be operated upon by different display rules, and be followed by different behavioral consequences. We do not mean to belittle these factors; in actuality we want to focus attention on these factors as the major sources of cultural differences in facial expressions of emotion. But our argument has been to emphasize the difficulty in uncovering the pancultural elements, and to caution against the danger that they may be obscured by a failure to isolate each of the variables listed in our figure.

RESEARCH EVIDENCE

I will now describe two different research approaches which we have undertaken to demonstrate the existence of universal facial expressions. In the first line of investigation, we utilized a research method for studying the face first employed by Charles Darwin. Darwin showed photographs of the face to observers to determine if they could agree about the emotion. We conducted similar experiments in which we showed still photographs of faces to people from different cultures in order to determine whether the same facial behavior would be judged as the same emotion regardless of the observer's culture. The faces were selected on the basis of their representing the distinctive facial muscular patterns described in Ekman, Friesen, and Tomkins' (1971) Facial Affect Scoring Technique. College educated students in Brazil, the United States, Argentina, Chile, and Japan were found to identify the same faces with the same emotion words, (parts of these results were reported in Ekman, Sorenson, and Friesen 1969). For 29 of the 30 facial expressions used in the experiments, the majority of the observers in every culture chose the same emotion for each face. Izard (1971), working independently with his own set of faces, obtained comparable results across seven other culture-language groups.

While we wanted to interpret these results as evidence of universal facial expressions, this interpretation was open to argument; because all the cultures which had been compared had also been exposed to some of the same mass media portrayals of facial behavior, members of those cultures might have learned to recognize the same set of conventions, or become familiar with each others' different facial behavior. To overcome this difficulty in interpretation, it was necessary to demonstrate that cultures which have had minimal visual contact with literate cultures show similarity to these cultures in their interpretation of facial behavior.

Members of the Fore linguistic-cultural group of the Southeast Highlands of New Guinea were studied (Ekman and Friesen 1971). Until 12 years ago, this was an isolated, Neolithic, material culture. While many of these people now have had extensive contact with missionaries, government workers, traders, and United States scientists, some have had little such contact. Only subjects who met criteria established to screen out all but those who had minimal opportunity to learn to imitate or recognize uniquely Western facial behaviors were recruited for this experiment. These criteria made it quite unlikely that subjects could have so completely learned some foreign set of facial expressions of emotion that their judgments would be no different from those of members of literate cultures. Those selected had seen no movies, neither spoke nor understood English or Pidgin, had not lived in any of the Western settlement or government towns, and had never worked for a Caucasian. One hundred and eighty-nine adults and 130 children, male and female, met these criteria. This sample comprises about three percent of the members of this culture.

A different task had to be devised to work with these people, in order to circumvent language difficulties, and problems encountered in utilizing a list of emotion words. Instead of showing the faces one at a time and asking the observers to pick an emotion from a list of six or seven words, as was done with the observers in the literate cultures, the procedure was reversed. The observer was shown three photographs, was told a story about a particular emotion, and was asked to pick the picture which fit with the story. The results were very clear, supporting our hypothesis that there is a pan-cultural element in facial expressions of emotion. With but one exception, the faces judged in literate cultures as showing particular emotions were comparably judged by people from this preliterate culture who had minimal opportunity to have learned to recognize any uniquely Western facial expressions. The only exception was in regard to fear, which the New Guineans discriminated from sadness, anger, disgust, and happy faces, but not from surprise faces.

In the last experiment within this first set of studies, we asked the New Guineans to themselves pose emotion. Videotapes of these posed emotions by New Guineans were then shown to college students in the United States who were able to accurately judge the emotion the New Guineans had been depicting.

The second line of research we have pursued used a very different approach to establish evidence of universal facial expressions of emotion. In this study (Ekman, Lazarus, Opton, Friesen, Averill, and Malmstrom 1970), we have taken videotape of subjects' facial expressions, without their knowledge, while they sat in a laboratory and watched a film which showed both neutral material and stress-inducing films of body mutilation. Such videotapes of the facial response to stress and neutral stimuli were obtained on 25 Japanese college students in Tokyo, and on a similar number of college students in the United States. We have applied a new measurement procedure for isolating and quantifying the movements of the facial muscles (the Facial Affect Scoring Technique) to these records. Our analysis, which is almost complete, shows the same facial responses to stress by members of these two presumably quite different cultures. The correlation between Japanese and American subjects in the frequency that they showed anger, fear, disgust, surprise, sadness, and happiness was .88. The cultural differences in facial behavior were seen later in this experiment when a fellow countryman entered the laboratory and discussed the stress film with the subject. Now that the situation became a social encounter, display rules were operative, and the facial behavior of the Japanese and Americans was quite different. The Japanese masked negative affect with polite smiles while the Americans replayed and showed the negative affect they had experienced.

CONCLUSIONS AND APPLICATIONS

These findings provide conclusive evidence that there is a pan-cultural element in facial expressions of emotion. This element must be the particular associations between movements of specific facial muscles and emotions, since the results obtained in the judgment experiments required that in every culture some of the same facial behaviors be recognized and interpreted as the same emotion. There may well be such a pan-cultural element for more than the six emotions we have studied—happiness, sadness, anger, fear, surprise, and disgust. It should be noted, however, that these emotions are not simply a random choice of possible emotion words but include most of the emotion concepts which have been most consistently found by investigators who have studied facial expression of emotion *within* any one culture (Ekman, Friesen, and Ellsworth 1971).

The conclusion that there are such constants across cultures in emotional facial behavior is further supported by Eibl-Eibesfeldt's research (1970) in which illustrative films have been gathered which depict similar facial expressions across various cultures. Evidence of universal facial expressions of emotion is also consistent with early studies which showed many similarities between the facial behavior of blind and sighted children (Fulcher 1942; Goodenough 1932; Thompson 1941). Universals in facial expression of emotion can be explained from a number of nonexclusive viewpoints as being due to evolution, innate neural programs, or learning experiences common to human development re-

gardless of culture (for example, those of F. Allport 1924; S. Asch 1952; Darwin 1872; Ekman and Friesen 1969a; Huber 1931; Izard 1971; Peiper 1963; Tomkins 1962, 1963). To evaluate these different viewpoints will require further research, particularly on early development.

Let me now explain some of the applications of our findings on universal facial expressions. The evidence of universal facial expressions led to our development of the Facial Affect Scoring Technique, a procedure which delineates the particular muscular movements relevant to the measurement of each of the emotions. We are applying this measurement procedure to a study of how facial expressions of emotion differ with the changes in psychopathology which occur from the time a patient is admitted to the time of discharge from a mental hospital. A second application of our findings is utilizing the Facial Affect Scoring Technique to study the difference between felt and simulated emotion in a situation where normal individuals are engaged in deceptive and honest interactions. We are testing some of our theories (Ekman and Friesen 1969b) about the specific facial behaviors which provide leakage (the betrayal of an emotion the person is attempting to conceal) and deception clues (behaviors which do not provide leakage but are informative that deception is in progress). This research was initiated, in part, because of a clinical interest in being able to determine whether the patient who says he is no longer contemplating suicide is actually telling the truth or deceiving in order to be free of hospital restraints so as to commit suicide. A third application of our findings on universal expressions of emotion is a test procedure which we have devised to measure an individual's sensitivity and blocks in recognizing particular emotions. Utilizing still photographs of different facial behaviors, presented at very brief speeds in a tachistoscope, we have found differences between de-pressive and schizophrenics, and among normal individuals in relation to mood. These differences are *not* in terms of ability to recognize emotions, but instead are in terms of their inability to recognize specific emotions.

REFERENCES

Allport, F. H.
  1924   *Social Psychology*. Boston: Houghton Mifflin.
Asch, Solomon E.
  1952   *Social Psychology*. Englewood Cliffs, NJ: Prentice Hall.
Birdwhistell, Ray L.
  1963   The kinesic level in the investigation of the emotions. *In* Peter H. Knapp, MD, (ed.), *Expression of the Emotions in Man*. New York: International Universities Press.
Darwin, Charles
  1872   *The Expression of the Emotions in Man and Animals*. London: Murray.
Eibl-Eibesfeldt, Irenaus
  1970   *Ethology*. New York: Holt, Rinehart and Winston.
Ekman, P., and W. V. Friesen
  1967   Origin, usage and coding: The basis for five categories of nonverbal behavior. Paper given at the Symposium on Communication Theory and Linguistic Models, Buenos Aires.
  1969a The repertoire of nonverbal behavior—categories, origins, usage and coding. *Semiotica* 1(1): 49-98.
  1969b Nonverbal leakage and clues to deception. *Psychiatry* 32(1): 88-105.
  1971   Constants across cultures in the face and emotion. *Journal of Personality and Social Psychology* 17(2): 124-129.
Ekman, P., W. F. Friesen, and P. Ellsworth
  1971   *The Face and Emotion*. New York: Pergamon.
Ekman, P., W. V. Friesen, and S. S. Tomkins
  1971   Facial affect scoring technique (FAST): A first validity study. Semiotica.
Ekman, P., R. S. Lazarus, E. T. Opton, W. V. Friesen, J. R. Averill, and E. J. Malmstrom
  1970   *Facial Behavior and Stress in Two Cultures*. Ms.
Ekman, P., E. R. Sorenson, and W. V. Friesen
  1969   Pan-cultural elements in facial displays of emotions. *Science* 164 (3875): 86-88.
Fulcher, J. S.
  1942   "Voluntary" facial expression in blind and seeing children. *Archives of Psychology* 38(272).
Goodenough, Florence L.
  1932-33 Expression of the emotions in a blind-deaf child. *Journal of Abnormal and Social Psychology* 27: 328-333.
Huber, E.
  1931   *Evolution of Facial Musculature and Facial Expression*. Baltimore: John Hopkins Press.
Izard, C. E.
  1971   The emotions and emotion constructs in personality and culture research. *In* R. B. Cattell (ed.), *Handbook of Modern Personality Theory*. Chicago: Aldine.
Klineberg, O.
  1938   Emotional expression in Chinese literature. *Journal of Abnormal and Social Psychology* 33: 517-520.

LaBarre, W.
  1947 The cultural basis of emotions and gestures. *Journal of Personality* 16: 49-68.
Peiper, A.
  1963 *Cerebral Function in Infancy and Childhood.* New York: Consultants Bureau.
Thompson, Jane
  1941 Development of facial expression of emotion in blind and seeing children. *Archives of Psychology* 37(264).
Tomkins, S. S.
  1962 *Affect, Imagery, Consciousness,* Volume 1, *The Positive Affects.* New York: Springer.
  1963 *Affect, Imagery, Consciousness,* Volume 2, *The Negative Affects.* New York: Springer.

2. SEX DIFFERENCES AND CULTURAL INSTITUTIONS

ROY G. D'ANDRADE

Roy G. D'Andrade is Professor of Anthropology, University of California, San Diego. Reprinted from *The Development of Sex Differences,* edited by Eleanor E. Maccoby with the permission of the publishers, Stanford University Press and (in England) Tavistock Publications, Ltd. © 1966 by the Board of Trustees of the Leland Stanford Junior University.

PSYCHOLOGY TENDS to consider sex differences as differences in personal characteristics. Anthropology, on the other hand, generally conceives of sex differences as social and cultural institutions. From this point of view sex differences are not simply characteristics of individuals; they are also culturally transmitted patterns of behavior determined in part by the functioning of society. Some of the ways in which sex differences have been culturally institutionalized will be reviewed in this chapter. Cross-cultural trends for male-female differences in the performance of daily activities, in the ascription of social statuses, in interpersonal behavior, in gender identity, and in fantasy productions will be presented. Also an attempt will be made to explain some of these empirically observed behavorial sex differences.

Anthropology, like astronomy, is a natural science in which experimentation is rarely possible. Unfortunately, under such conditions good descriptions are easier to construct than good explanations. At present there is even considerable disagreement within anthropology about what constitutes a proper or possible explanation of cultural phenomena. The four major types of explanation currently in use are: the *historical* (a particular custom exists because it was invented at some

previous time, and then transmitted from generation to generation, or from society to society, to its present location in time and space); the *structural* (a particular custom exists as an expression of some more basic or underlying cultural or social condition, and can only be understood as a manifestation of this more basic condition); the *functional* (a particular custom exists because it maintains or integrates social life in some beneficial way); and the *reductionistic* (a particular custom exists because of the operation of some psychological or physiological mechanism). While all of these types of explanation carry some information and can be used predictively, in this review the primary emphasis will be on reductionistic explanations.

PHYSICAL DIFFERENCES

A comprehensive review of cross-cultural findings about physical sex differences will not be attempted here. However, some of these physical differences should be mentioned since they are basic to many of the explanations of behavioral sex differences. In all known human populations, males and females differ in primary sex characteristics and in many secondary

16

characteristics as well. These secondary characteristics include, for the male, greater height, a higher muscle-to-fat ratio, a more massive skeleton, more body hair, etc. However, most of these differences in secondary sex characteristics are not absolute; they hold true only for a particular population. Furthermore, the average differences between the sexes vary from population to population. In height, for example, the mean difference between males and females is less than two inches for the Klamath, approximately six inches for the Nootka (both American Indian groups from the Northwest coast), and almost eight inches for the Shilluk (an African Negro group from the Eastern Sudan). As a result of the variance in population means, it is generally impossible to sex-type accurately on the basis of secondary sex characteristics alone unless population parameters are known. (Very probably this holds true not only for sex-linked physical characteristics, but also for behavioral characteristics as well.)

Secondary sex characteristics are not completely under genetic control, and can be affected by cultural and environmental factors. For example, cultural heightening of genetic secondary sex characteristics occurs frequently with regard to physical strength. The genetically determined greater size and more muscular body composition of the male results in a fairly large difference in physical strength between the sexes. This difference is often increased, however, by the tendency for males in most societies to perform those activities requiring rapid and extreme exertion. In Bali, where males do little heavy lifting work, preferring instead light, steady, many-handed labor, both males and females have slender somatypes. However,

Balinese men who work as dock coolies under European supervision develop the heavy musculature more typical of males (Mead 1949).

Generally biological differences in primary and secondary sex characteristics are considered major factors in explaining universal cultural patterning of sex-typed roles. The family has been said to be "a biological phenomenon, . . . as rooted in organic and physiological structures as insect societies" (LaBarre 1954, p. 104). Thus LaBarre argues that the human mother-child relationship is based on the mutual gratifications involved in long term breast feeding, and the husband-wife relationship on the permanent sexuality of the female. However, most anthropological explanations of regularities in sex differences are not based on biological differences alone, but on the complex interactions of biological differences with environmental and technological factors.

THE DIVISION OF LABOR

One well documented finding about behavioral sex differences is that men and women not only tend to perform different activities in every culture, but that men tend to perform particular types of activities and women to perform others. This division of labor is especially sharp for subsistence and other economic activities. The following table, adapted from one of Murdock's early cross-cultural studies, presents the frequencies with which 224 societies have a sex-based division of labor with respect to activities dealing mainly with food production and collection (Murdock 1935).

The sex differences in Table 2.1 are quite strong for all activities except dairy operation, soil preparation, fowl

TABLE 2.1

CROSS-CULTURAL DATA FROM 224 SOCIETIES ON SUBSISTENCE
ACTIVITIES AND DIVISION OF LABOR BY SEX

Activity	Number of Societies in Which Activity is Performed by				
	Men always	Men usually	Either sex	Women usually	Women always
Pursuit of sea mammals	34	1	0	0	0
Hunting	166	13	0	0	0
Trapping small animals	128	13	4	1	2
Herding	38	8	4	0	5
Fishing	98	34	19	3	4
Clearing land for agriculture	73	22	17	5	13
Dairy operations	17	4	3	1	13
Preparing and planting soil	31	23	33	20	37
Erecting and dismantling shelter	14	2	5	6	22
Tending fowl and small animals	21	4	8	1	39
Tending and harvesting crops	10	15	35	39	44
Gathering shellfish	9	4	8	7	25
Making and tending fires	18	6	25	22	62
Bearing burdens	12	6	35	20	57
Preparing drinks and narcotics	20	1	13	8	57
Gathering fruits, berries, nuts	12	3	15	13	63
Gathering fuel	22	1	10	19	89
Preservation of meat and fish	8	2	10	14	74
Gathering herbs, roots, seeds	8	1	11	7	74
Cooking	5	1	9	28	158
Carrying water	7	0	5	7	119
Grinding Grain	2	4	5	13	114

tending, and shelter erection. Generally the male activities appear to involve behavior which is strenuous, cooperative, and which may require long periods of travel. The female activities, on the other hand, are more likely to involve the physically easier, more solitary, and less mobile activities. These differences appear to be more or less the direct result of physical male-female differences.

However, not all sex-specialized activities can be explained by physical differences. Most of the results in Table 2.2, which presents data on sex differences in the manufacture of objects, cannot be so explained. Weapon making, for example, is predominantly a male activity, even though it does not necessarily require more physical

strength than the manufacture and repair of clothing. One possible explanation for the sex differences found in the manufacture of objects is that the objects being made are intended for use in activities that are directly related to physical differences. Thus weapon making is anticipatory to activities that do involve physically strenuous and mobile behavior. Murdock (1949, p. 7) states:

It is unnecessary to invoke innate psychological differences to account for the division of labor by sex; the indisputable differences in reproductive functions suffice to lay out the broad lines of cleavage. New tasks as they arise are assigned to one sphere of activities or the other in accordance with convenience and precedent. Habituation to different occupations in adulthood and early sex typing in childhood may well explain the observable differences in sex temperament instead of *vice versa.*

The thesis here, to be considered in more detail below, is that the division of labor by sex comes about as a result of generalization from activities directly related to physical sex differences to activities only indirectly related to these differences; that is, from behaviors which are differentially reinforced as a result of physical differences to behaviors which are anticipatory or similar to such directly conditioned activities. Perhaps the complexity and strength of the factors that bring about and maintain the division of labor by sex can be illustrated by the following excerpt from M. E. Spiro's (1956, pp. 221-230) study of an Israeli Kibbutz.

The social structure of the Kibbutz is responsible for a problem of . . . serious proportions—"the problem of the woman. . . ." With the exception of politics, nothing occupies so much attention in the Kibbutz. . . . It is no exaggeration to say that if Kiryat Yedidim should ever disintegrate, the "problem of the woman" will be one of the main contributing factors.

In a society in which the equality of the sexes is a fundamental premise, and in which the emancipation of women is a major goal, the fact that there is a "problem of the woman" requires analysis. . . . The Youth Movement from which many Kibbutz values are derived was strongly femininist in orientation. The woman in bourgeois society, it is believed, was subjected to the male and tied to her home and family. This "biological tragedy of woman" forced her into menial roles, such as house cleaning, cooking, and other domestic duties, and prevented her from taking her place be-

TABLE 2.2
CROSS-CULTURAL DATA ON THE MANUFACTURE OF OBJECTS AND DIVISION OF LABOR BY SEX

Activity	Number of Societies in Which Activity is Performed by				
	Men always	Men usually	Either sex	Women usually	Women always
Metalworking	78	0	0	0	0
Weapon making	121	1	0	0	0
Boat building	91	4	4	0	1
Manufacture of musical instruments	45	2	0	0	1
Work in wood and bark	113	9	5	1	1
Work in stone	68	3	2	0	2
Work in bone, horn, shell	67	4	3	0	3
Manufacture of ceremonial objects	37	1	13	0	1
House building	86	32	25	3	14
Net making	44	6	4	2	11
Manufacture of ornaments	24	3	40	6	18
Manufacture of leather products	29	3	9	3	32
Hide preparation	31	2	4	4	49
Manufacture of nontextile fabrics	14	0	9	2	32
Manufacture of thread and cordage	23	2	11	10	73
Basket making	25	3	10	6	82
Mat making	16	2	6	4	61
Weaving	19	2	2	6	67
Pottery making	13	2	6	8	77
Manufacture and repair of clothing	12	3	8	9	95

side the man in the fields, the workshop, the laboratory, and the lecture hall.

In the new society all this was to be changed. The woman would be relieved of her domestic burdens by means of the various institutions of collective living, and she could then take her place as man's equal in all the activities of life. The communal dining room would free her from the burden of cooking; the communal nurseries, from the responsibilities of raising children; the small rooms, from the job of cleaning.

In a formal sense, the Kibbutz has been successful in this task. . . . In spite of "emancipation" which they have experienced in the Kibbutz, there is considerable sentiment among the women . . . that they would prefer not to have been "emancipated." Almost every couple who has left the Kibbutz has done so because of the unhappiness of the woman. . . . At a town meeting devoted to the "problem of the woman," one of the most respected women in Kiryat Yedidim —the wife of a leader of the Kibbutz movement—publicly proclaimed that the Kibbutz women had not achieved what they had originally hoped for; as for herself, after thirty years in Kiryat Yedidim she could pronounce her life a disappointment.

One source of the woman's poor morale is that many women are dissatisfied with their economic roles. . . . When the vattikim [original settlers] first settled on the land, there was no sexual division of labor. Women, like men, worked in the fields and drove tractors; men, like women, worked in the kitchen and in the laundry. Men and women, it was assumed, were equal and could perform their jobs equally well. It was soon discovered, however, that men and women were not equal. For obvious biological reasons, women could not undertake many of the physical tasks of which men were capable; tractor driving, harvesting, and other heavy labor proved too difficult for them. Moreover, women were compelled at times to take temporary leave from that physical labor of which they were capable. A pregnant woman, for example, could not work too long, even in the vegetable garden, and a nursing mother had to work near the Infants House in order to be able to feed her child. Hence, as the Kibbutz grew older and the birth rate increased, more and more women were forced to leave the "productive" branches of the economy and enter its "service" branches. But as they left the "productive" branches, it was necessary that their places be filled, and they were filled by men. The result was that the women found themselves in the same jobs from which they were supposed to have been emancipated—*cooking, cleaning, laundering, teaching, caring for children, etc.*

. . . What has been substituted for the traditional routine of housekeeping . . . is more housekeeping—and a restricted and narrow kind of housekeeping at that. Instead of cooking and sewing and baking and cleaning and laundering and caring for children, the woman in Kiryat Yedidim cooks *or* sews *or* launders *or* takes care of children for eight hours a day. . . . This new housekeeping is more boring and less rewarding than the traditional type. It is small wonder, then, given this combination of low prestige, difficult working conditions, and monotony, that the chavera [female member of the Kibbutz] has found little happiness in her economic activities.

The outcome of this attempt to alter radically the sexual basis of the division of labor appears to have been a tragedy. Margaret Mead (1949, p. 77) has pointed out that "envy of the male role can come as much from an undervaluation of the role of wife and mother as from an overvaluation of the public aspects of achievement that have been reserved for men." Apparently a cultural undervaluation of women cannot be corrected by abolishing the female role.

It is of interest that the Kibbutz had to alter the organization of the family in order to free women to perform previously male activities, especially in light of the anthropologist's argument that the formation of the family depends not only on biological differences and sexual alliance, but on the division of labor as well. Washburn and DeVore (1961, pp. 97-100) state:

The origin of the human family presents three problems: (1) the evolution of a helpless, slow-growing human infant, (2) the loss of oestrus, and (3) the male's role as an economic provider. . . . The male's role as an economic provider had certainly appeared by the Middle Pleistocene, when men were killing large animals. Hunting large animals was probably based on cooperation, and the band must have shared in the eating.

It cannot be proved, of course, that incest prohibitions and exogamous matings arose in the Middle Pleistocene, but it can be shown that the conditions which made such regulation advantageous arose at that time. All data suggest that the killing of large animals is a task for adult men and that, once hunting became important to the group, children had to depend on adults for many years. Both by increasing the importance of the male as provider, and by making control of a hunting area essential, large scale hunting activity created conditions that favored exogamous mating. The offspring of *Australopithecus* may have been just as independent as those of a chimpanzee, but the children of Ternifine or Peking man depended on the hunting of adult males, and their survival depended upon the relations between the young and the hunters. It is impossible to date the beginning of the human family or of the incest tabu, but the conditions that made these institutions advantageous in the evolution of the species are concomitant with the hunting of large animals.

SEX DISTINCTIONS IN SOCIAL STRUCTURE

The speculative historical sequence proposed by Washburn and DeVore contains a series of causal links that relate physical sex differences, subsistence activities, and forms of social organization. While the hypothesis about the origins of the family is not directly testable, the more general notion that forms of social organization are related to sex differences in subsistence activities can be partially investigated by an examination of the cross-cultural data.

First, with respect to the variety of forms of social organization found cross-culturally, it should be pointed out that the distinction of gender is basic to understanding many of these forms. That is, the distinction of gender is used not only as a basis for assigning activities, as in the division of labor, but also as a basis for transmitting rights and duties in the proper allocation of social statuses. Thus in the marital rules of residence, in the permitted forms of multiple marriage, in the criteria for membership in descent groups, and in kinship terminology, gender is used to decide who will live where, who can marry whom, who will belong to which group, and so on.

Furthermore, there tends to be a general cross-cultural bias concerning the use of gender as social criteria. The majority of societies organize their social institutions around males rather than females. For example, certain types of rules of residence group together spatially a core of kin-related males, while other rules of residence group together a core of kin-related females. In Murdock's World Ethnographic Sample (1957) of 565 societies, 376 societies are labeled as predominantly patrilocal (i.e., sons after marriage reside with or near their parental family), while only 84 are rated predominantly matrilocal (i.e., daughters after marriage tend to live with or near their parental family). With respect to descent groups, the ratio is roughly four to one in favor of membership being transmitted patrilineally through a line of males rather than matrilineally through females. For forms of multiple marriage the sex ratio is even more biased. Of the 431 societies that permit polygamous marriage, 427 permit men to have more than one wife, but only four permit women to have more than one husband.

TABLE 2.3

CROSS-CULTURAL DATA ON THE ASSOCIATION BETWEEN RULES OF
RESIDENCE AND DESCENT GROUP FOR 428 SOCIETIES

Rules of Residence	Descent Group				
	Patri-lineal	Matri-lineal	Mat. & Pat.	None	Total
Patrilocal	**177**	**9**	**17**	**78**	281
Matrilocal	0	**32**	2	**30**	64
Avunculocal	0	**15**	1	1	17
Bilocal	3	1	1	**33**	38
Neolocal	1	1	0	**26**	28
TOTAL	181	58	21	168	428

NOTE: Boldface indicates social organizations listed in typology presented below.

Returning to the relation between subsistence activities and forms of social organization, it is possible, using only the categories of residence and descent group, to construct a simple typology of nine types of social organization that will account for over 95 percent of the societies in Murdock's World Ethnographic Sample (see Table 2.3). These nine types of social organization are:

1. No descent group—neolocal residence.
2. No descent group—bilocal residence.
3. No descent group—patrilocal residence.
4. No descent group—matrilocal residence.
5. Matrilineal descent group—matrilocal residence.
6. Matrilineal descent group—avunculocal residence.
7. Matrilineal descent group—patrilocal residence.
8. Patrilineal descent group—patrilocal residence.
9. Both matrilineal and patrilineal descent group—patrilocal residence.

Both the dominant form of subsistence activity and the degree of sex difference in the division of labor appear to affect which of these nine types of social organization will occur. Table 2.4 presents these data taken from a subsample of Murdock's World Ethnographic Sample (1957).

The results indicate that there is a complete network of relationships between division of labor by sex, subsistence activities, and types of social organization. Generally those subsistence activities which require predominantly male effort and which involve the use of economic capital, such as animal husbandry and agriculture with cattle, are likely to be both patrilineal and patrilocal. There are a large number of neolocal societies without descent groups that have agriculture with cattle subsistence economies, but this is perhaps because most of these societies belong to the Western European tradition in which industrial manufacture rather than agriculture is actually the predominant form of economic activity.

In contrast to agriculture with cattle and animal husbandry, agriculture without cattle, which frequently involves both slash-and-burn techniques of farming and root crops rather than cereal grains, is more likely to depend on a greater proportion of female labor, and to occur with matrilineal

TABLE 2.4

CROSS-CULTURAL DATA ON SEX DIVISION OF LABOR (BY SUBSISTENCE ACTIVITY) AND TYPE OF SOCIAL ORGANIZATION (BY DESCENT GROUP AND RESIDENCE)

Sex Division of Labor	No Descent Group				Matrilineal			Patrilineal	Mat. & Pat.	Total
	Neo-local	Bi-local	Patri-local	Matri-local	Matri-local	Avuncu-local	Patri-local	Patri-local	Patri-local	
Agriculture with cattle										
Men do most	11	6	6	1	1	0	1	34	1	61
Both do	6	2	9	3	4	1	0	40	2	67
Women do most	0	0	0	1	0	0	1	12	2	16
TOTAL	17	8	15	5	5	1	2	86	5	144
Animal husbandry										
Men do most	0	0	2	0	0	0	1	14	0	17
Both do	1	0	2	0	0	1	0	10	1	15
Women do most	0	0	0	0	0	0	0	0	0	0
TOTAL	1	0	4	0	0	1	1	24	1	32
Agriculture without cattle										
Men do most	3	5	13	2	6	0	1	5	0	35
Both do	0	2	0	4	5	10	1	27	2	51
Women do most	2	4	9	4	5	2	1	14	2	43
TOTAL	5	11	22	10	16	12	3	46	4	129
Fishing										
Men do most	1	4	11	0	2	0	1	3	1	23
Both do	0	1	0	2	0	0	1	2	0	6
Women do most	1	0	1	0	0	0	0	0	0	1
TOTAL	1	5	12	2	2	0	2	5	1	30
Hunting and gathering										
Men do most	0	1	7	3	0	0	0	2	0	13
Both do	1	8	10	6	1	0	1	6	6	39
Women do most	0	0	0	0	0	0	0	0	0	0
TOTAL	1	9	17	9	1	0	1	8	6	52
TOTAL	25	33	70	26	24	14	9	169	17	387

descent groupings and matrilocal or avunculocal residence. Avunculocal residence, in which a man moves with his wife at marriage to live with his mother's brother or a classificatory equivalent, groups together a core of males who are matrilineally related. Such a rule of residence is thought to be a result of factors that operate to produce patrilocal residence acting on a previously matrilineal-matrilocal system (Murdock 1949). It is interesting that avunculocal residence most often occurs in societies that have a fairly balanced division of labor by sex. Aberle (1961), using Murdock's sample, found that avunculocal residence is also more likely to occur in societies with a hereditary aristocracy.

Hunting and gathering and fishing apparently only rarely create the kind of capital that is utilized in corporate descent groups; both sets of subsistence activities have few matrilineal or patrilineal groups, despite the fact that fishing and hunting are predominantly male activities with a high frequency of patrilocal residence.

The overall results suggest that both economic capital and sex bias in the use and control of this capital are important in forming corporate descent groups and in determining rules of residence. Although sex differences in who does the work appear to help determine which sex controls the economic capital, the evidence does not indicate that sex bias in the division of labor by itself can determine the type of residence or the formation of kinship groups.

INTERPERSONAL BEHAVIOR

Present interest in sex differences appears to emphasize the degree to which different kinds of interpersonal behaviors are innately sex-linked or are learned. Most anthropologists, having experienced the sense of discontinuity that comes from living in another culture, take the tremendous impact of learning on shaping sex-specific behaviors for granted. As Mead concluded in her 1935, pp. 190-191) study of sex and temperament among three New Guinea tribes:

We have now considered in detail the approved personalities of each sex among three primitive peoples. We found the Arapesh—both men and women—displaying a personality that, out of our historically limited preoccupations, we would call maternal in its parental aspects, and feminine in its sexual aspects. We found men, as well as women, trained to be cooperative, unaggressive, responsive to the needs and demands of others. We found no idea that sex was a powerful driving force either for men or for women. In marked contrast to these attitudes, we found among the Mundugumor that both men and women developed as ruthless, aggressive, positively sexed individuals, with the maternal cherishing aspects of personality at a minimum. Both men and women approximated to a personality type that we in our culture would find only in an undisciplined and very violent male. Neither the Arapesh nor the Mundugumor profit by a contrast between the sexes: the Arapesh ideal is the mild, responsive man married to the mild, responsive woman; the Mundugumor ideal is the violent aggressive man married to the violent aggressive woman. In the third tribe, the Tchambuli, we found a genuine reversal of the sex-attitudes of our own culture, with the woman the dominant, impersonal, managing partner, the man the less responsible and the emotionally dependent person. These three situations suggest, then, a very definite conclusion. If those temperamental attitudes which we have traditionally regarded as feminine—such as passivity, responsiveness, and a willingness to cherish children—can so easily be set up as the masculine pattern in one tribe, and in another to be outlawed for the majority of men, we no longer have any basis for regarding such aspects of behavior as sex-linked.

We are forced to conclude that human nature is almost unbelievably malleable, responding accurately and contrastingly to contrasting cultural conditions. . . . Standardized personality differences between the sexes are of this order, cultural creations to which each generation, male or female, is trained to conform. There remains, however, the problem of the origin of these socially standardized differences.

How did these socially standardized differences in interpersonal behavior develop? Once we acknowledge the plasticity of human behavior, we must make some attempt to account for both the cross-cultural model tendencies in behavior and the variation from these modes. For each of the kinds of interpersonal behavior discussed below, an estimate of the modal cross-cultural arrangement with respect to sex differences is presented, and then an attempt to find explanatory correlates of these behaviors is made.

SEXUAL BEHAVIOR

In an extensive survey of sexual behavior, Ford and Beach (1951) report a number of male-female differences that occur in most, if not all, of the 200 societies in their sample.

According to the rules of etiquette in our society the initiative in sexual advances should always be taken by the man. As in the sex act proper, the male is expected to assume the more active role. The majority of other societies for whom this information is available also believe that only men should take the initiative in seeking and arranging a sexual affair. (p. 110.)

Viewed in cross-cultural perspective, the practice of concealing the woman's genital region with some type of clothing is far more common than is covering the masculine sex organs. There are a number of societies in which the woman customarily covers her pubic region with some form of clothing, whereas the man does not conceal his genitals. Although there are a few societies in which both sexes are usually nude, there are no peoples who insist upon the man covering his genitals and at the same time permit the woman to expose her genital region. (p. 103).

Sixty-one percent of the 139 societies in our sample for whom evidence is available forbid a mated woman to engage in extra-mateship liaisons. In some societies the mated man is similarly restricted, although the great majority of these peoples are much more concerned with the behavior of the mated woman than with the mated man. (p. 123.)

The development of love magic has been particularly widespread in human societies. In nearly every society love potions or medicines, magical charms, or ritual acts are available for the man or woman who seeks the affection of a particular partner. . . . In cross-cultural perspective, generally speaking, love charms are much more often employed by men than by women. (pp. 108-9.)

In 49 (64 percent) of the 76 societies other than our own for which information is available, homosexual activities of one sort or another are considered normal and acceptable for certain members of the community. The most common form of institutionalized homosexuality is that of the berdache or transvestite. The berdache is a male who dresses like a woman, performs woman's tasks, and adopts some aspects of the feminine role in sexual behavior with male partners. Less frequently a woman dresses like a man and seeks to adopt the male sex role. (p. 137.)

. . . It appears highly likely that human females are less likely than males to engage in homosexual relations. At any rate, in most other societies, as in our own, feminine homosexuality is accorded much less attention than is comparable behavior among males. In fact, specific information concerning homosexual women is available for only 17 of the peoples included in our sample. (p. 140.) . . . In all human societies for which there is adequate information males are more likely than females to stimulate their own sexual organs. (p. 248.) In our own and many other societies it is generally believed that the majority of women need more protracted stimulation than men if they are to experience sexual climax. . . . Attitudes of people in other cultures toward this problem are of interest. But references to orgasm in the female in societies other than our own are relatively rare. This problem reflects a failure on the part of investigators to obtain such information, since no statements could be found which indicate that the women of any society fail to experience a sexual climax. (pp. 43-44.)

As far as actual sexual behavior is concerned, it develops somewhat more rapidly in certain societies than others. Some cultures fully approve of a variety of sexual practices among young boys and girls and between adolescents of both sexes. When there is any difference in treatment, the behavior of girls is more carefully controlled than is that of boys. (p. 204.)

In general, then, males appear to be more sexually active, females more sexually restricted. The evidence also suggests not only that sexual restrictions are more typically applied to females, but that females tend to be more inhibited by sexual restrictions than males (mutuality in sexual activity appears only in societies that are permissive rather than restrictive). The result of both these factors—greater sexual restrictiveness applied to women and greater ease of inhibiting female sexuality—would tend to create greater sex differences in the amount and kind of sexual activity in those societies that have more severe sex restrictions, with the males being much more active than the females and the females much less responsive than the males.

At present, two major social correlates of sexual restrictiveness have been found in cross-cultural research. One of these correlates, discussed by William Stephens (1963), involves the effect, of "civilization" and the "autocratic political state" on sexual activity. Stephens presents data taken from ethnographies and interviews with ethnographers which indicate that culturally permitted premarital and ex-

tramarital liaisons occur more frequently in noncivilized communities (24 out of 31 cases), and less frequently in civilized communities (2 out of 18 cases). Civilized communities, which are defined as communities belonging to "a society that embraces cities," are thought to have less sexual freedom because of their association with the autocratic state.

Why are civilized communities relatively strict about the regulation of sex and primitive societies rather liberal? . . . I think the answer ultimately lies in the development of the state. Until 200 years ago, almost all civilized communities were parts of kingdoms, that is, autocratic agrarian states. . . . The development of the kingdom seems to bring with it certain basic changes in the family. Among these are an elaboration of deference customs between family members and a tightening of sex restrictions. When the kingdom, the autocratic agrarian state, evolves into a democratic state, these family customs seem to gradually liberalize. (Stephens 1963, pp. 256-58.)

A second social correlate that has been found to be related to sexual restrictiveness is the form of family organization. For example, of the nine societies surveyed by Ford and Beach in which females but not males are sexually restricted in childhood and adolescence, eight are strongly polygynous. Of the 26 sexually permissive societies for which information is available, only nine are strongly polygynous. Sexual restrictiveness, as measured by the Whiting and Child rating of the severity of socialization of sexual behavior, has also been found to be significantly related to polygyny (Whiting and Child 1953, Whiting 1961).

The reason for the relationship between polygyny and sexual restrictiveness (especially toward the female) is not obvious. Perhaps restrictiveness is needed because strong female sexuality on the part of adult women poses too great a threat for the husband of many wives; strong female sexuality may also pose a threat to the polygynously married mother who must control the sexual behavior of her male children with only diluted support from her husband. Or perhaps because both polygyny and autocratic states create or rely on unequal distributions of authority and deference, mutuality in sexual behavior, which tends to establish intimacy and equality, is discouraged.

AUTHORITY AND DEFERENCE

A second dimension of interpersonal behavior that has been investigated cross-culturally with respect to sex differences involves authority and respect relationships. Stephens, in a systematic study of authority and deference between husband and wife, finds that in 21 of the 31 societies in his sample there is clear evidence that the husband exercises "considerable" authority over his wife; in six societies the husbands are "mildly" dominant over wives, and in five societies there is fairly equal sharing of authority. In six other cases there appear to be separate spheres of authority for husband and wife. In only four societies from this sample does it appear that women may have more de facto authority in the family than males: the people of Modjokuta, Java, the Tchambuli of New Guinea, the Jivaro of South America, and the Berbers of North Africa. However, if power over groups larger than the family is considered, it is very likely all societies would be found to be male controlled (Stephens 1963).

In deference between husband and wife, Stephens finds a similar male bias. By deference, Stephens means the ritualistic acknowledgment of power, measured by the presence or absence of such behaviors as bowing or kneeling before another, having special speech etiquette, not joking, not contradicting, not being positionally higher than the other person, and so on. In only one society out of four is the wife not required to observe some of these customs with respect to her husband. Very rarely does the husband make any kind of deference to his wife —with the exception of the chivalrous males of Western European cultures, for whom this order is reversed.

Stephens finds the degree of deference between husband and wife to be strongly correlated with the degree of deference between father and son. Deference within the family, like sexual restrictiveness, correlates with an autocratic political state rather than a "tribal" political system.

One thing we see here is another patterning regularity, a parallel between family relationships and the larger social hierarchy. Autocratic societies, that is, autocratic agrarian societies—kingdoms —have autocratic families. As the king rules his subjects and the nobles subjugate and exploit the commoners, so does husband tend to lord it over wife, father rule over son, and . . . Ego defer to grandfather, uncle, and elder brother. The family, in such societies, looks like a sort of kingdom in microcosm. As Ego defers to father and grandfather, so do the commoners defer to the nobles; and the deference customs are quite similar. Sometimes the *same* deference custom is given both to one's father and to the local lord. (Stephens 1963, p. 335.)

Another variable that appears to affect the distribution of authority and deference between the sexes is the degree to which men rather than women control and mediate property; and this in turn, it has been argued above, is affected by the division of labor and the cultural capacity to create capital.

Support for this hypothesis is found in Gouldner and Peterson's correlation and factor-analytic study of cross-cultural data (Gouldner and Peterson 1962). The actual data were collected by Leo Simmons (1945), who scored 71 primarily nonliterate societies on 99 culture traits by means of a four-point scale of importance-unimportance. Fifty-nine of these traits were subjected to a factor analysis by Gouldner and Peterson. Table 2.5 presents the correlation coefficients for culture traits that are significantly related to patripotestal family authority and the subjection or inferiority of women. Generally we find that societies in which inheritance, succession, and descent-group membership are through males rather than females are more likely to concentrate power and respect in the hands of men. However, these structural variables do not always tell us which sex actually controls scarce resources and holds authority. Murdock presents the example of the Lovedu, one of the Bantu-speaking tribes of South Africa, as a culture which, despite its patrilineal, patrilocal, and polygynous structure, has granted a relatively high status to women (Murdock 1959). Among the Lovedu, polygynous women form strong coalitions against their husbands, forcing them to treat each wife with strict fairness. The Lovedu women's high status is partly the result of a matrilateral cross-cousin marriage system—a system in which a man marries his mother's brother's daughter or some woman from his mother's patrilineage. In such a system a woman holds an advantage in negotiating marriages; the Lovedu women, for example, have gained control of the bride prices, which involve considerable amounts of cattle.

It is interesting that the Tchambuli (the New Guinea tribe studied by Margaret Mead) also have a patrilineal system with matrilateral (mother's brother's daughter) cross-cousin marriage and female control of important property. Women appear to be the actual holders of power and to have the more practical and instrumental type of temperament. Marriage conditions parallel those of the Lovedu; the application of the matrilateral cross-cousin marriage rule results in a polygynously married Tchambuli man having wives who are clan sisters and who typically form strong coalitions against him (Mead 1935).

Similar in many ways to the authority dimension of interpersonal be-

TABLE 2.5
CORRELATES OF FAMILY AUTHORITY AND THE POSITION OF WOMEN

	Subjection or Inferiority of Women	Patripotestal Family Authority
Patrilineal inheritance	.58	.65
Patrilineal succession	.51	.57
Patrilineal descent	.44	.66
Patrilocal residence	.25	.38
Herding	.21	.26
Matrilineal residence	−.24	−.23
Matrilineal descent	−.34	−.39
Matrilineal inheritance	−.41	−.63
Subjection or inferiority of women	—	.41

havior is the instrumental-expressive dimension of role behavior. Zelditch (1955) found consistent cross-cultural regularities among almost all societies having the husband-father role described as more instrumental, and the wife-mother role as more expressive. Whether this differentiation is based on factors external to the nuclear family or on the universal requirements of the family as a social system is not clear, although both kinds of factors may be involved.

AGGRESSION, CONFLICT, AND RESPONSIBILITY

A detailed and systematic cross-cultural study of sex differences in interpersonal behavior has been carried out by the Six Culture Socialization Project, directed by J. Whiting, I. Child, W. Lambert, and B. Whiting. (See B. Whiting 1963 for ethnographic descriptions of these cultures.) In this study 24 children (aged three to ten) from each of the six cultures were observed by trained fieldworkers for 20 five-minute periods. Each child's behavior was then systematically recorded and coded. The initial results indicate that boys are more likely than girls to engage in physical aggression in all six cultures, while girls are more likely to act affectionately and responsibly. In five of the six cultures, girls are more likely to act sociably and succorantly; but in one cultural group, a Mixtecan Indian barrio in Oaxaca, Mexico, boys are significantly more sociable and succorant than girls (J. Whiting, personal communication).

Although the differences recorded above may be due to differential child-training practices rather than to innate sex-linked behavioral tendencies, the fact that the largest sex differences occur in the younger (three to six) rather than in the older (seven to ten) group gives less weight to the training hypothesis, which would predict the opposite result.

A second systematic investigation of the interpersonal behavior of children has been made by Melford Spiro in his study of children reared in an Israeli Kibbutz. These children were reared in peer groups primarily by female nurses in a culture in which sex differences are deliberately played down in accordance with the norms of Kibbutz ideology. Thus the effects on the child's behavior of different-sex socializers and cultural sex stereotypes are to some extent absent in this study. The children in the sample range in age from one to five years. Twenty-four boys and twenty-three girls were observed. In the area of interpersonal behavior, Spiro compares the frequencies of child-to-child interaction for the categories of integrative behavior, conflict behavior, and aggressive behavior by sex of initiator and sex of object. He summarizes his findings as follows:

In all (age) groups girls are more integrative (give aid, share, act affectionate, cooperate, etc.) than boys, and boys more disintegrative. In all groups boys engage in more acts of conflict (seizure of another child's possessions) than girls, and in all but one group the boys engage in more acts of aggression (disobedience, hitting, insulting, etc.) than the girls. Boys, moreover, are the recipients of the girls' excess integrations—boys are integrated more than the girls—but the girls are recipients of only part of the boys' excess disintegration. For though girls are the more frequent victims of conflict, boys are the more frequent victims of aggression.

Though more integrative than boys, girls also display more frequent symptoms of regression than boys. In all groups but one, for example, girls have a higher incidence of thumbsucking, and in the two groups for which there are data, girls exhibit more regressive play than do boys. (Spiro 1958, pp. 247-48.)

For each observed sex difference, Spiro speculates on whether the difference is due to innate causes or to the child's attempts to model sex-linked adult behaviors. In many cases, both these factors seem to be present. However, it is Spiro's general conclusion that in this particular culture many of the sex differences observed are most reasonably accounted for by the innate sex-linked behavior hypothesis. Also, insofar as Spiro's categories of aggression and integration are similar to the Whitings' categories of physical aggression and responsibility, the sex differences in the Kibbutz study are in the same direction as in the six-culture study.

Even though some sex differences in interpersonal behavior may be biologically influenced, there is considerable evidence that the interpersonal behaviors of boys and girls are socialized quite differently. Barry, Bacon, and Child, in a cross-cultural survey based on ethnographic reports for 110 societies, found very consistent sex differences in the socialization of children age four or older. In general they found that boys are trained to be self-reliant and to achieve, while girls are trained to be nurturant, responsible,

and obedient. Table 2.6 summarizes these findings.

Concerning the validity of these findings, Barry et al. considered and discounted two possible sources of bias: the ethnographers and the raters. Ethnographers are trained, insofar as possible, not to translate their own cultural expectations to other cultures. And it is highly unlikely that the raters were the source of bias; if they had been, there would have been more of a tendency for the ambiguously recorded data to be interpreted in terms of the raters' own cultural conceptions of sex differences. However, the more ambiguous cases (in which only one of the two judges was able to make a rating) do not show an increase in sex differences. Therefore Barry et al. hypothesize that these sex differences are due to:

. . . Universal tendencies in the differentiation of the adult sex role. In the economic sphere, men are more frequently allotted tasks that involve leaving home and engaging in activities where a high level of skill yields important returns; hunting is a prime example. Emphasis on training in self-reliance and achievement for boys would function as preparation for such an economic role. Women, on the other hand, are more frequently allotted tasks at or near home that minister most immediately to the needs of others (such as cooking and water carry-

TABLE 2.6

CROSS-CULTURAL RATINGS FOR SEX DIFFERENCES ON FIVE VARIABLES OF
CHILDHOOD SOCIALIZATION PRESSURE
(FROM BARRY, BACON, AND CHILD 1957)

Variable	Number of Cultures with Ratable Information	Percentage of Cultures with Evidence of Sex Difference in Direction of		
		Boys	Neither	Girls
Nurturance	33	0	18	82
Responsibility	84	11	28	61
Obedience	69	3	62	35
Achievement	31	87	10	3
Self-reliance	82	85	15	0

ing); and in their pursuit a responsible carrying out of established routines is likely to be more important than the development of an especially high order of skill. Thus training in nurturance, responsibility, and less clearly, obedience, may contribute to preparation for this economic role. (Barry, Bacon, and Child 1957, p. 329.)

The argument presented here is similar to the one presented above in the discussion of the division of labor: that sex specialization occurs as a result of generalization from activities more directly conditioned by physical sex differences to activities anticipatory or similar to the directly conditioned activities. The strongest evidence for this hypothesis is the extent to which sex differences in socialization are associated with types of subsistence activities. Using Murdock's World Ethnographic Sample, Barry et al. tested the relationship between the extent of sex differences in socialization and other cultural variables such as residence rules, forms of marriage, and degree of political integration. Out of 40 comparisons, six significant associations were found. These were: (1) grain rather than root crops grown, (2) large or milk-producing animals rather than small animals kept, (3) nomadic rather than sedentary residence, (4) large animals hunted, (5) fishing unimportant or absent, (6) polygyny rather than monogamy.

Of these six variables, four deal directly with subsistence activities, and another, nomadism, is closely related to subsistence activities. Barry, Bacon, and Child conclude from these results that large sex differences will occur in "an economy that places a high premium on the superior strength and superior development of motor skills requiring strength, which characterize the male" (1957, p. 330). The correlation between large sex differ-

ences in socialization and polygyny, however, is thought to be due to the effect of larger family units, which permit sharper sex differentiation than an isolated nuclear family in which the illness, death, or absence of one parent forces the other to take over some of the missing parent's activities. Romney, in a re-analysis of these data, suggests that the correlation between the types of subsistence activity that involve food accumulation and a child-training emphasis on compliance rather than assertion may be confounded with type of family organization. Thus, societies that rely primarily on food accumulation are also very likely to have father-absent families. If the sex of the socializing parent affects the way the child is socialized, the correlation between types of economy and child-rearing might then be the result of their relationship to type of family organization (Romney 1965).

IDENTITY

In the beginning of this review, it was emphasized that in all cultures biological sex differences are recognized as distinct social statuses for men and women. On the individual level these social statuses become psychological identities involving evaluative discriminations about one's own self and behavior. A male or female identity can be a product both of direct tuition (the child is taught to call and perceive himself as male or female) and of indirect tuition (the child is responded to or taught to behave in sex-specific ways, and so comes to respond to himself as others respond to him). Kohlberg (1966) discusses the hypothesis that children first learn their sex identities, and then attempt to acquire and master sex-appropriate activities.

Thus almost everyone in every society learns his sex status and the role behaviors appropriate to it (Linton 1942). Even the biological hermaphrodite can apparently learn one or the other of its possible sex statuses without great difficulty if one status is firmly assigned and not switched (Hampson 1965). Nevertheless, not everyone wishes to occupy only his or her actual sex status. Burton and Whiting (1961, p. 86) distinguish three different kinds of status or identity:

We would like to define a person's position or positions in the status systems of this society as his identity. Furthermore, we would like to distinguish three kinds of identity: attributed, subjective, and optative. *Attributed identity* consists of the statuses assigned to a person by other members of his society. *Subjective identity* consists of the statuses a person sees himself as occupying. And finally, *optative identity* consists of those statuses a person wishes he could occupy. . . . It is our thesis that the aim of socialization in any society is to produce an adult whose attributed, subjective, and optative identities are isomorphic: "I see myself as others see me, and I am what I want to be."

One of the ways in which a culture can institutionalize the potential discrepancy between assigned and optative identities is to permit certain persons to take on many of the role behaviors of the opposite sex, as, for example, in the institution of the berdache. Such transvestism often, but not always, involves homosexual behavior. Unlike transvestism, which is an open and overt expression of the wish to assume a feminine status, institutions such as the couvade and male initiation rites are thought to express a disguised and less conscious cross-sex optative identity. The couvade is a set of customs in which a husband participates ritually in the birth of his child by adopting some of the behavior and taboos of his wife, sometimes actually experiencing labor pains and post-partum fatigue.

Initiation ceremonies also appear to express an envy of the female role. For example, the initiation is often culturally perceived as a rebirth ritual in which men take a child and bring about his birth as a man by magical techniques stolen long ago from women. These techniques would lose their magical efficacy if women were ever to observe them. The need for the initiate to prove his manhood by bearing extreme fatigue and pain without complaint appears to indicate some uncertainty in sex identity.

What then are the cultural arrangements that might make men envy the opposite sex? Mead, in discussing societies known to her personally, observes:

What we find within these seven societies is that in [those societies] which have emphasized sucking [in nursing], the most complementary relationship of all bodily learning experience, there is the greatest symbolic preoccupation with the differentials between men and women, the greatest envy, over-compensation, ritual mimicry of the opposite sex, and so on. . . . When in addition male separateness from women has been developed into a strong institution, with a men's house and male initiation ceremonies, then the whole system becomes an endlessly reinforcing one, in which each generation of little boys grows up among women, identified with women, envying women, and then, to assert the endangered certainty of their manhood, isolate themselves from women. (Mead 1949, pp. 73-74.)

Working with cross-cultural data, Whiting and his associates have come to similar conclusions concerning the role of status envy and cross-sex identification in the functioning of initiation rites and in the couvade. Whiting distinguishes two sets of conditions: the first pertains to the persons who surround the infant and young child, those persons who presumably create the child's "primary" optative identity; the second pertains to the child's experiences in later childhood and adolescence, which create a "secondary," and sometimes conflicting, optative identity. The first set of conditions appears to involve mainly the presence versus the absence of the father in the household, with the expectation that "in the exclusive mother-infant case the mother should be seen as all powerful, all important, and insofar as she sometimes withholds resources, the person to be envied; and we predict the infant will covertly practice her role, and his optative identity will be female." (Burton and Whiting 1961, p. 88.)

In fact, this hypothesis has empirical support; societies that have exclusive mother-infant sleeping arrangements (in which the father sleeps in either a different hut or different bed while the mother and infant sleep together) are significantly more likely to have male initiation rites and couvade than societies without such exclusive arrangements (Whiting 1961).

Whether the males who form a primary cross-sex optative identity express their envy of, and identification with, females in couvade or male initiation rites appears to be determined by a second set of conditions. Thus male initiation rites occur more frequently in patrilocal societies, while couvade is more likely to be practiced in matrilocal societies. It appears that in societies with exclusive mother-infant arrangements, later patrilocal residence, in which kin-related males are grouped together, creates a conflicting secondary optative identity for the

young boy. This conflict in primary and secondary identities appears to be resolved in part by initiation rites, which symbolically remove the young boy's clinging femininity and reward masculine behavior. In matrilocal societies, on the other hand, no such conflict is created, so that the male envy of women is more directly acted out in an imitation of female child-bearing. (See Young 1962, for a contrary view of the functions of male initiation ceremonies.)

In order to test some of these hypotheses more directly, Whiting and his students have begun research in specific cultures that present internal contrasts relevant to identification theories. These studies have found the composition of the family in which the infant and young child is reared to be related to a number of variables, including math-verbal differences (Carlsmith 1964), individual participation in the ritual of couvade (Munroe 1964), interpersonal behavior (Longabaugh 1962), and psychological tests of sex identity (D'Andrade 1962). Generally the results of these studies are congruent with the hypothesis that optative identity and related behaviors are influenced by identification with significant others, and that the person with whom the child identifies is strongly influenced by the physical presence or absence of family members.

SEX DIFFERENCES IN FANTASY AND COGNITION

Perhaps the most complete cross-cultural investigation of sex difference in fantasy is Colby's study of dreams. From a collection of 1,853 reported dreams from 75 "tribal" societies, Colby selected one dream from each subject (366 males and 183 females), and coded each dream for the presence or absence of nineteen "qualities." For example, the quality "wife" was scored as present if the dream contained either the words "my wife" or "his wife" or "brother's wife" or "Felicia" when it was known that Felicia was the dreamer's wife. Table 2.7 presents the results of this study.

Colby's initial hypothesis, based on work with American subjects, was that males would dream more about qualities associated with "female mating choice" and "intensified penetration of space," while females would dream more about "male mating choice objects." Generally, cross-cultural results support this hypothesis, although some modification in the definition of these categories was necessary.

One question with respect to these findings is whether these male-female differences in visual images are due to the expression of "body imagery" or to the fact that these visual images are reinforced in the daily performance of sex-typed activities. In other words, as a result of the division of labor, are males more likely to have higher frequencies of rewarding activities relating to such objects as dead animals, weapons, or wives, and females more likely to have rewarding activities relating to clothes, husbands, children, and the like? The fact that male-female differences in dreams correspond roughly to these differences in daily activities could then be the result of simple contiguity. However, to the extent that physiological sex differences affect the reinforcement values of external events, sex differences in fantasy (or any other behavior) would be found despite identical external environmental conditions. This double confounding of stimulus conditions, in which males and females inhabit somewhat different internal *and* external environments, makes ambiguous the interpretation of many sex differences in fantasy productions.

Turning to the Rorschach data and other projective-test materials on sex

TABLE 2.7

SEX DIFFERENCES IN FANTASY: DREAM QUALITIES REPORTED BY
SUBJECTS FROM 75 TRIBAL SOCIETIES
(FROM COLBY 1963)

Male Preferred Qualities			Female Preferred Qualities		
Quality	Total no. of dreams	M F ratio	Quality	Total no. of dreams	F M ratio
grass	11	5.0*	husband	25	10.5
coitus	23	3.3	clothes	21	2.7
wife	37	2.6	mother	37	1.9
weapon	60	2.0	father	40	1.7
animal	179	1.6	child	61	1.6
death	121	1.5	home	52	1.6
red	16	1.5	female figure	198	1.3
vehicle	83	1.4	cry	29	1.1
hit	70	1.4	male figure	317	1.01
ineffectual attempt	14	1.2			

* That is, the quality "grass" appeared in five times as many men's dreams as women's. Since there were twice as many men as women in the sample, we had to double the number of women's dreams to obtain true ratios.

differences in fantasy, a somewhat surprising picture of sex differences emerges. In general, females appear to have a better psychological adjustment than males. The following quotes from Lindzey's (1961) review of cross-cultural applications of projective tests may be taken as indicative:

The natives of Montserrat (Abel and Metraux 1959) as a whole are characterized by strong unconscious dependency needs, a lack of repression, free expression of affect, a practical non-abstract orientation toward the outer world, and little understanding of inner psychological processes. When the females are compared with males, they share unconscious dependency needs but show more of a tendency to "accept and cling to objects" and are more imaginative and creative in their inner life. Adolescents seem generally to have more anxiety than adults, but the female adolescent seems better able to cope with this anxiety than the male. (p. 225.)
A comparison of the two profiles (male and female Menomini Rorschach responses) displayed a number of differences and supported the conclusion that there is a "picture of disturbance, tension, and diffuse anxiety, and decrease in emotional controls among modal males that is not represented among the females." (p. 237; Lindzey is quoting here from Spindler and Spindler 1958, pp. 223-24.)
When male and female subjects born in China are compared (on Rorschach profiles, Abel and Hsu 1949), the females display greater flexibility, somewhat more freedom in expression of affect, and superior imaginative powers. . . . Of the American born (Chinese) subjects, the females appear to deal with their adjustment problems more directly and make less use of repressive mechanisms than the males. (p. 240.)
This point (projective tests provide hypothesis) is elaborated in a separate paper (Gladwin, 1953) discussing sex differences among the Trukese. Gladwin makes clear that after four years of contact with these people he returned home convinced that men were dominant and generally more secure than women, who appeared ". . . subservient, insecure, and afraid to express themselves in the pres-

ence of their lords and masters." (p. 306, Gladwin 1953). Much to his surprise, the analysis of the projective-test protocols suggested to Sarason that men were more anxious than women and less competent to deal with ambiguous or conflict situations. Prodded by this finding, Gladwin took a second look at the ethnographic data and found, again to his surprise, a considerable amount of information (incidence of suicide attempts, successful resistance to parental pressure in regard to marriage, male and female roles in adulterous relations, treatment of brother and sister at puberty separated by cultural decree, and so on) which supported Sarason's interpretation and forced a new formulation. (p. 273.)

Similar results appear in the Rorschach data from Tepoztlan, Mexico (Abel and Calabresi 1951) and also in the Ojibwa protocols (Hallowell 1955). One might speculate, then, that if these Rorschach results have some validity, the typical masculine prerogatives of deference, power, and sexual initiative may have some psychic cost. A number of investigators of sex differences have commented that men seem to have greater difficulty adjusting to their roles. The more frequent cultural institutionalization of male homosexuality, and the greater severity of male initiation rites (Brown 1963) would seem to support this notion.

Another factor that may be related to the greater anxiety found for males on the Rorschach involves the effects of acculturation on men. That is, since men typically occupy the public, political, and instrumental roles in a society, rapid social change, especially when externally imposed, would seem more likely to disturb the adjustment of men than women (Hallowell 1955). L. S. Spindler (1962), in a study of Menomini women, concludes that male-female differences on the Rorschach can be related directly to differences in role adjustment produced by acculturation. Most of the males had been forced to conform to "white" values and standards, while only the "elite" group of Indian women had to face such pressures. However, the degree to which acculturation is responsible for the greater male anxiety among the other societies mentioned above cannot be estimated from present information.

SUMMARY AND IMPLICATIONS

In all known human populations males differ from females not only in primary sex characteristics, but also in secondary characteristics, males tending, on the average, to have greater height, more massive skeletons, a higher ratio of muscle to fat, more body hair, etc. However, these differences hold only within particular populations; sex typing on the basis of secondary characteristics from unknown populations is extremely unreliable.

The division of labor by sex involved in subsistence and other activities is strongly influenced by primary and secondary sex characteristics: generally males tend to perform those activities that are physically strenuous, dangerous, involve long periods of travel, and demand a high level of cooperation.

Specialization by sex in activities generalizes from those activities that are differentially conditioned by physical differences to activities which are anticipatory or similar to the more directly conditioned activities. These sex differences can be seen in the division of labor, in the manufacture of various objects, in sex differences in socialization, and perhaps even in fantasy.

Sex bias in forms of social organization, such as rules of residence and types of descent groups, is related to subsistence activities and the division of labor by sex; the sex which performs or initiates the basic subsistence activities is more likely to control the property that is involved in these activities, and more likely to reside together and to form a descent group.

The cross-cultural mode is that males are more sexually active, more dominant, more deferred to, more aggressive, less responsible, less nurturant, and less emotionally expressive than females. The extent of these differences varies by culture. And in some cultures some of these differences do not exist (and occasionally the trend is actually reversed). These differences are related to and presumably influenced by which sex controls economic capital, the extent and kind of division of labor by sex, the degree of political "authoritarianism," and family composition.

Maleness and femaleness are institutionalized as statuses in all cultures. Such statuses become psychological identities for most individuals. Usually individuals learn to want to occupy the sex status they are assigned; however, special cultural conditions can affect the degree to which one sex envies the status of the other. Male envy of female status appears to be increased by paternal absence, and is culturally institutionalized in rites such as the couvade and male initiation ceremonies or in special transvestite statuses.

In fantasy dreams male and female differences can be seen as expressions of body imagery or as reflections of culturally institutionalized differences in activities and their reinforcement contingencies.

In projective tests (such as the Rorschach) males from a number of cultures have been found to be more insecure and anxious than females. This, if true, might be due to the greater stress and danger involved in male roles, or to the effects of acculturation, which appears to disrupt the cultural adjustment of males more than females.

In this chapter we have considered some of the very complex mechanisms that play a part in the development of sex differences in all human societies. To understand these mechanisms, it might be helpful to imagine an experiment in which two groups of randomly selected male albino rats are subjected to conditions in which the activities, reinforcement contingencies, and classes of discriminative stimuli are made as different for each group as possible. Would not any operant response measure, such as amount of exploratory behavior, resistance to temptation, or horizontal eye movements during dreaming, be likely to show group differences? These differences would not always be large, but they would probably always be consistent. Finding out exactly which set of experimental conditions was responsible for creating these differences might often be both complex and tedious.

This hypothetical laboratory world differs from the human cultural environment in three major respects. First, the activities, reinforcement contingencies, discriminative stimuli, etc., of the woman's world are not as different as possible from those of the man's world; there is considerable overlap. Second, because of the genetic biological differences between human males and females, some of the differences on various response measures will be innately determined rather than learned. (Indeed, the very fact that some of the present biological sex differences exist may be due to selective factors operating as a result of cultural universals in the division of labor.) Third, in human societies, these differences compound into complex causal chains, resulting in sets of institutional structures that "act back" on the conditions that created them in the first place, sometimes amplifying the original conditions, sometimes elaborating them in a variety of ways. This chapter has attempted to describe some of these phenomena, emphasizing the cultural and social factors that seem to have contributed to the institutionalization of sex differences.

REFERENCES

Abel, Theodora M., and R. A. Calabrese
  1951 The people [Tepoztecans] from their Rorschach tests. *In* O. Lewis (ed.), *Life in a Mexican Village: Tepoztlan Restudied.* Urbana: University of Illinois Press.

Abel, Theodora M., and F. L. K. Hsu
  1949 Some aspects of personality of Chinese as revealed by the Rorschach test. *Rorschach Research Exchange* 13: 285-301.

Abel, Theodora M., and Rhoda Metraux
  1959 Sex differences in a Negro peasant community, Montserrat, B. W. I. *Journal of Projective Techniques and Personality Assessment* 23: 127-33.

Aberle, D. F.
  1961 Matrilineal descent in cross-cutting perspective. *In* Schneider and Gough (eds.), *Matrilineal Kinship.* Berkeley: University of California Press.

Barry, H. III, Margaret K. Bacon, and I. I. Child
  1957 A cross-cultural survey of some sex differences in socialization. *Journal of Social and Abnormal Psychology* 55: 327-32.

Brown, Judith K.
1963   A cross-cultural study of female initiation rites. *American Anthropologist* 65: 837-53.

Burton, R. V., and J. W. M. Whiting
1961   The absent father and cross-sex identity. *Merrill-Palmer Quarterly* 7(2): 85-95.

Carlsmith, Lyn
1964   Effect of early father absence on scholastic aptitude. *Harvard Educational Review* 34: 3-21.

Colby, K. M.
1963   Sex differences in dreams of primitive tribes. *American Anthropologist* 65: 1116-21.

D'Andrade, R. G.
1962   Paternal absence and cross-sex identification. Ph.D. dissertation, Harvard University.

Ford, C. S., and F. Beach
1951   *Patterns of Sexual Behavior.* New York: Harper and Bros.

Gladwin, T.
1953   The role of man and woman on Truk: A problem in personality and culture. *Transactions of the New York Academy of Science,* Ser. II, 15: 305-09.

Gouldner, A. W., and R. A. Peterson
1962   Notes on Technology and the Moral Order. Indianapolis: Bobbs-Merrill.

Hampson, J. L.
1965   Determinants of psychosexual orientation. *In* F. Beach (ed.), *Sex and Behavior.* New York: John Wiley.

Hallowell, A. I.
1955   *Culture and Experience.* Philadelphia: University of Pennsylvania Press.

Kohlberg, Lawrence
1966   A cognitive-developmental analysis of children's sex-role concepts and attitudes. *In* E. E. Maccoby (ed.), *The Development of Sex Differences.* Stanford: Stanford University Press.

LaBarre, W.
1954   *The Human Animal.* Chicago: University of Chicago Press.

Lindzey, G.
1961   *Projective Techniques and Cross-Cultural Research.* New York: Appleton-Century-Crofts.

Linton, R.
1942   Age and sex categories. *American Sociological Review* 7: 589-603.

Longabaugh, R. H. W.
1962   The description of mother-child interaction. Ed.D. thesis, Harvard University.

Mead, Margaret
1935   *Sex and Temperament.* New York: William Morrow, and Mentor.
1949   *Male and Female.* New York: William Morrow.

Munroe, R. L.
1964   Couvade practices of the Black Carib: a psychological study. Ph.D. thesis, Harvard University.

Murdock, G. P.
1935   Comparative data on the division of labor by sex. *Social Forces* 15: 551-53.
1949   *Social Structure.* New York: Macmillan.
1957   World ethnographic sample. *American Anthropologist* 59: 664-87.
1959   *Africa: Its Peoples and Their Culture History.* New York: McGraw-Hill.

Romney, A. K.
1965   Variations in household structure as determinants of sex-typed behavior. *In* F. Beach (ed.), *Sex and Behavior.* New York: John Wiley.

Simmons, Leo W.
1945   *The Role of the Aged in Primitive Society.* New Haven: Yale University Press.

Spindler, Louise S.
  1962 Menomini women and cultural change. Memoir 91. *American Anthropologist* 64 (pt. 2).
Spindler, Louise S., and George D. Spindler
  1958 Male and female adaptations in culture change. *American Anthropologist* 60: 217-33. (Study revised for B. Kaplan (ed.), *Studying Personality Cross-Culturally.)*
Spiro, M. E.
  1956 *Kibbutz: Venture in Utopia.* Cambridge: Harvard University Press.
  1958 *Children of the Kibbutz.* Cambridge: Harvard University Press.
Stephens, W. N.
  1963 *The Family in Cross-Cultural Perspective.* New York: Holt, Rinehart and Winston.
Washburn, S. L., and I. DeVore
  1961 Social behavior of baboons and early man. *In* S. L. Washburn (ed.), *Social Life of Early Man.* Chicago: Aldine.
Whiting, Beatrice B. (ed.)
  1963 *Six Cultures: Studies of Child Rearing.* New York and London: John Wiley.
Whiting, J. W. M.
  1961 Socialization process and personality. *In* F. L. K. Hsu (ed.), *Psychological Anthropology.* Homewood, IL: Dorsey Press.
Whiting, J. W. M., and I. L. Child
  1953 *Child Training and Personality Development.* New Haven: Yale University Press.
Young, F. W.
  1962 The function of male initiation ceremonies. *American Journal of Sociology* 67: 379-96.
Zelditch, M., Jr.
  1955 Role differentiation in the nuclear family: A comparative study. *In* T. Parsons and R. F. Bales (eds.), *Family, Socialization and Interaction Process.* Glencoe, IL: The Free Press.

3. BIOLOGIC CONSIDERATIONS OF PARENTHOOD

I. CHARLES KAUFMAN

I. Charles Kaufman, M.D., is Professor of Psychiatry, University of Colorado School of Medicine, Denver. Reprinted with permission from *Parenthood: Its Psychology and Psychopathology,* E. James Anthony and Therese Benedek, editors, Little, Brown and Company, 1970.

IN ONE SENSE parenthood is as old as life itself, since so far as we know all cells issue directly from other (parent) cells. Each organism is thus dependent upon others for at least part of its life history. This dependence is the ultimate basis of all evolved systems of parental behavior and indeed of all social existence. However, there is an obvious and enormous difference between the parental nature of a cell which gives rise by fission to daughter cells and that of a human mother or father. Yet, evolutionary theory provides a basis for examining the relationships among the various forms of life, both morphologically and behaviorally.

Even after sexual reproduction had evolved in the seas, the relationship between parents in many species was limited to a single interaction in the breeding season, consisting of courtship behavior and spawning. In the stickleback, for example, males leave the school in the breeding season to take up territories. Females leave the school when ready to spawn; each goes through a complicated courtship with a male in the male's own territory, spawns, and then rejoins the school. The male fertilizes the eggs, takes over their care, and later cares for the fry. This system of external fertilization is wasteful since large numbers of gametes must be produced in order that relatively few zygotes may successfully become mature animals. Any arrangement that raises the chances that ova will be fertilized by sperm and that zygotes will grow to maturity is clearly advantageous to the species.

Internal fertilization by copulation had this advantage, and when it evolved, early reptiles became land animals, no longer dependent on water for external fertilization. Another evolutionary advance to favor the survival of a zygote that benefited the reptiles was the development of an amniote egg, with a shell and membranes to protect it and to enclose an aqueous environment on dry land. Zygotes growing inside shells must develop until they are large enough and fully formed enough to break out and fend for themselves; meanwhile they live on food supply, yolk, produced in the female reproductive tract just prior to the secretion of the shell. To insure a certain number of offspring, these reptiles still produced many eggs which were hidden and left to hatch alone. The young animals on their own were easy prey to carnivores. In many species of fish, reptiles, and certainly birds, however, parents protect eggs which are laid in special nests. As birds are warm-blooded, their eggs must be kept warm, which is accomplished by incubation, a task often shared by the parents. After hatching, many birds are naked and require brooding by the parents, as well as feeding. Also, in many species parents protect young birds against predators.

A major evolutionary advance was the development of the placenta, an elaboration of the uterus by means of which materials are exchanged between the blood of the mother and that of the developing embryo. Viviparity—keeping the fertilized egg and its nourishment within the mother until considerable growth has occurred —is a particular feature of the mammals, who thereby improved their reproductive economy, that is reduced the loss of eggs and young. The close association of mother and fetus in placental mammals provides great protection and a continuous supply of food and oxygen. The hemoglobin of mammalian embryos is even adjusted to this stage with an oxygen dissociation curve that differs from the mother's in such a way as to favor transfer of oxygen from mother to embryo across the membrane. In the higher primates, including man, a hemochorial placenta was evolved, in which only fetal tissue separates the fetal and maternal blood streams, with fetal vessels actually penetrating the endometrial vessels. This provides the optimum conditions for the embryo, an improved supply of oxygen and food, a better system for removing waste products, and improved transmission of antibodies.

Of at least equal significance, mammals also evolved a behavioral program of reproductive economy, namely, a higher order of parental care of the young after birth, without the consequence of which it is impossible to visualize the development of man. Care of the very young was already evolved in fish, reptiles, and especially birds, but what made possible the tremendous advance in mammals was the system of feeding the infant, through special glands, a substance, milk, which contains everything needed for growth and development. The improved feeding arrangement keeps the young physically close to the mother and thus safer from harm. The progressive reduction in mortality is reflected in a reduction in the number of eggs fertilized each year from millions in fishes to dozens in reptiles to one in the higher primates. Finally, and very importantly, the close physical relationship and the shared personal experience provided to the infant and mother by the feeding from her body constitute a degree of contact and intimacy which creates a new kind of bond, with durable characteristics, one major effect of which is to allow the infant a slower rate of growth.[1]

This bond, with its affective potential, loomed large in the further evolution of parental behavior and, in fact, of social behavior generally. Darwin (1871) said: "The feeling of pleasure from society is probably an extension of the parental or filial affections, since the social instinct seems to be developed by the young remaining for a long time with their parents; and this extension may be attributed in part to habit, but chiefly to natural selection." The wisdom of this statement has been confirmed by various studies which show that, in organisms with advanced development of the central nervous system, repeated interactions (i.e., reciprocal stimulation) lead to the development of affective relationships (Cairns 1966; Tobach and Schneirla 1969) that such affective relationships may be generalized or transferred (Freud 1921), that the affective components reinforce the experiences they accompany and possess motivational status, and that affective relationships and societal living have been selected as biologic adaptations (Hamburg 1963; McBride 1966).

Another significant step in the evolution of parental care occurred in the higher primates (anthropoidea), probably as an adaptation to an arboreal existence, namely, the birth of a single offspring (Washburn and Lancaster 1968). A basic aspect of the evolutionary process is competition, which is usually more marked within a species than between species, because members of one species require the same habitat and food, whereas members of another species generally do not. Intraspecific competition is found in infants and embryos too, so that in animals that produce several young at one birth the intrauterine competition for a limited supply of nourishment and space is considerable. The production of a single fetus is thus of great advantage, eliminating the competition for survival and allowing for a slowing down of development. The longer the single offspring is preserved in the uterus the more unhurried its development may be, and the more likely that it will be preserved for the species. Even so the general slowing of development means that at birth the anthropoid infant is relatively helpless, which provides for a longer period of dependence upon the mother[2] and new kinds of social organization.

SOCIAL STRUCTURE AND BIOLOGIC ADAPTATION

In the higher primates, social organization has reached much higher levels while clearly serving biologic adaptation (Hamburg 1969; Washburn and DeVore 1961b). Group living has functioned to provide mutual defense, a territory large enough to supply food for all its members, and an internal stability, largely derived from the dominance hierarchy, which serves to facilitate reproduction, as well as the education and socialization of the young in ways appropriate to their given environment. There is a pooled experience in a group which necessarily exceeds that of an individual mother or father. The social facilitation of learning was undoubtedly of major significance in the evolution of higher intelligence as well as culture.

Since the parent-young relationship is inextricably embedded in the social structure of the higher primates, we must examine this structure. It is highly variable. It used to be thought that there is no breeding season in monkeys and apes, and that the persistence throughout the year of social organization was due to continuous sexual attraction (Zuckerman 1932). It is now clear that many species do in fact have a breeding season and a birth peak, a time of year at which births tend to be concentrated (Lancaster and Lee 1965). "This is highly adaptive for widely distributed species, for it allows the majority of births to occur at the optimum time for each locality while maintaining a widely variable basic pattern," according to Washburn et al. (1965).

There is also considerable variation among species in frequency of copulation and in the number of sexual partners. Social patterning is variable as well. However, Hallowell (1961) has pointed out that the basis of most primate societies is a group consisting of X males, X females, X infants, and X juveniles. This is generally true, although there are exceptions such as groups with only males or only mothers and offspring.

The most stable groups are those in which there are dominance hierarchies headed by males who lead the group and provide protection. Hierarchical structure is based on the emergence of three evolutionary developments: (1) intraspecific aggressiveness, (2) the capacity for individual recognition, and (3) patterns of submission which do not ordinarily involve flight, and in fact make flight unnecessary (McBride 1969). The submissive behavior has the function of controlling or preventing aggressiveness. There are also integrative behaviors in a hierarchy that tend to maintain affiliations. These allow the distance between neighbors to be reduced while actually decreasing the level of aggression. This process is aided by recognition, which implies also the ability to distinguish strangers against whom aggression may be increased. Ordinarily, contact behaviors tend to reinforce affiliations (see note 6), and in many nonhuman primates mutual grooming is a major form of bond-servicing between individuals. (In human beings we frequently speak of keeping in touch when we do not mean physical contact, and small talk often seems to serve the same function that grooming does in other primates.)

By inhibiting aggression and fostering affiliations the dominance hierarchy provides order and stability. It also largely controls population growth. There are a variety of factors which control population density. Included among the key factors are fertility, disease and accidents, stress, migration, food supply, and war (Harcourt and Leroux 1967). In most species dramatic fluctuations do not occur very often, and population control is generally maintained through the dominance hierarchy. In some instances fertility may be limited to the more dominant animals (Conaway and Ko-

ford 1964; Koford 1963a; Washburn and DeVore 1961a), but this is not the only mechanism at work. The dominant animals are the more advantaged in every way. They are usually bigger, stronger, and have the greatest freedom of action and the greatest access to food. Subordinate animals have a rather different existence. They are very often peripheral in a group and have less access to everything. If anything occurs to increase aggressive interactions within a group, for example, an increase in density or a shortage of food, the aggression will be directed down the hierarchy. If the stress continues, it will often ultimately be relieved by the adaptation of dispersal. Invariably it is the subordinates who must disperse. If there are physical or social limitations on dispersal, it has been shown in a number of species that the stressed animals undergo a series of physiologic changes, primarily associated with an increase in size and activity of the adrenal glands, which in the short term are adaptive but in the long term have serious effects (Christian and Davis 1964; McBride 1968; Myers 1966; Thiessen 1964). Resistance is impaired to a wide range of stresses, including starvation, parasites, virus infections, and bacterial diseases. There may be suppression of growth and reproduction. Sexual maturity is delayed and at higher population densities totally inhibited. In mature females estrous cycles are prolonged, while ovulation and implantation decrease. Intrauterine mortality increases, and there are upsets in normal maternal behavior. These effects are themselves adaptive since they lower the reproductive performance of these particular animals and thus the density of the group. In this way the culls are eliminated, while the selected reproduce. The advantage of dominance is clear.

In primates dominance depends at least in part upon the hierarchical status of the parents, acting through both genetic and ontogenetic factors. In addition to the selective factor the social status of the mother is in many species conferred upon the offspring (Kawai 1958; Kawamura 1958; Koford 1963b; Sade 1967). This comes about in several ways. First, in various species mothers and infants occupy a special location in the center of the group with the dominant males (Imanishi 1960; Washburn and DeVore 1961a). As juveniles, most of the males are forced to the periphery where they become subordinate or subdominant. Exceptions are the male offspring of the dominant females, who remain in the center where they have privileged relations to the dominant males, with greater opportunity to learn from them, to identify with them, according to Imanishi, and then themselves to achieve top status (Imanishi 1963). Second, dominant mothers intercede on behalf of their offspring in encounters with other animals, so that the offspring have greater freedom of movement, and thus greater familiarity with the surround, and a greater repertoire of behaviors and coping techniques (Kaufman and Rosenblum 1967; Koford 1963b). Like the other aspects of primate society we have considered, the character of the dominance hierarchy also varies, in some species being very constant and rigid (S. Altmann 1962; Hall and DeVore 1965; Jay 1965), and in others being very flexible or at times seemingly nonexistent (Goodall 1965; Schaller 1965).

MATERNAL BEHAVIOR

There is one feature of primate social organization, however, that is constant—the enduring tie and economic responsibility of the mother for her offspring. Whatever the grouping may be in each species, young infants are invariably found with or near their mothers, who nurse them, raise them, and in various ways teach them that which their species needs to know in order to thrive in that environment (Hamburg 1969). The interest of other members of the group in infants is considerable but varies greatly among primate species, whereas the interest of the mother is constant. She generally cleans the neonate, usually eats the placenta, and often helps the infant cling during locomotion until it can hang on through its own strength. Ordinarily, primate mothers effectively nurse, groom, protect, and transport their young.

There are differences in maternal care, of course, both between and within species (Mason 1965). Langur mothers, for example, allow other females to handle and carry their newborn (Jay 1965); bonnet macaque mothers immediately rejoin friendly huddles after parturition (Kaufman and Rosenblum 1969b); whereas pigtail and rhesus macaques (Kaufman and Rosenblum 1969b; Southwick et al. 1965) tend to jealousy, holding their infants close and away from others. Within a species there are differences in efficiency. The experienced multipara tend to be the most efficient handlers of the young. They are more confident and expend less effort in keeping the newborn quiet (Jay 1962). Young inexperienced mothers are more cautious in handling their infants, and yet their motions are sometimes quick and startle them. According to Jay (1963a), "Females range from the very capable, through those which constantly readjust the infant's position, to a few extremely inept ones which hold the newborn infant too tightly, in awkward upside-down positions, or constantly away from their bodies."

DeVore (1963) found that the baboon mother's status influences the infant very greatly. "There seemed to be a high correlation between the amount of frustration and 'insecurity' displayed by an infant and its mother's position in the female dominance hierarchy." He found infants to be very sensitive to the mother's emotional state so that when she was upset, as by a fight, the infant was very upset too and would run to her. Subordinate mothers who take a lot of punishment from dominant females he found to be short-tempered and less responsive to their infants. Jay (1963a) found that the temperament and personality of langur mothers, most particularly their patience and calmness, affect their aptitude in handling their infants. "A tense, nervous, and easily irritated female frequently startles the infant with quick or unpredictable motions; a calm, relaxed female makes few sudden movements."

Jay also found (1963b) that langur mothers threaten, chase, or even slap males who accidentally frighten their infants. Other adult females nearby may join in chasing the male away. Similar behavior has been reported for other species, including nonprimates.[3]

Mothers of various primate species have been known to tend to dead babies for days, to retrieve them, protect them, and carry them until only skin and skeleton remain (Carpenter 1942). After finally abandoning dead infants, chimpanzee mothers are reported to look intently at other infants for several days (Goodall 1967).

Recent studies of both monkeys and apes have shown clearly that the relationship between mother and offspring is a very intense one with considerable durability. Chimpanzees have been known to return periodically to their mothers until they are 12 years old and fully mature (Goodall 1965). In several macaque species it has been demonstrated that all the offspring of a female, even when they are fully grown themselves, maintain a special relationship both to her and to their siblings, a clan relationship (Kaufman and Rosenblum 1963; Sade 1965). It seems clear that the bond which develops between the mother and infant is the basis for much of subsequent social behavior. Grooming of the fur and skin is probably the most common social activity and serves not only to keep the skin clean and free of parasites but also to build up and maintain affectional bonds. Mothers groom young infants a great deal. At times it is clear, as the infant is growing older, that the grooming by the mother serves to keep the infant close to her at a time when he is on the verge of leaving (Kaufman and Rosenblum 1963). Grooming is also seen to inhibit rising aggressiveness (Sade 1965). Members of a clan groom each other more than they do other animals in their troop. Maternal behavior and the mother-infant relationship are thus very literally the matrix of primate society. The bond between mother and infant generates the positive affect which ordinarily characterizes much of the behavior within primate groups.[4] Sexual relations between mother and son are said not to occur. In some instances this appears to be a consequence of inhibition by more dominant males, but in my laboratory it has also seemed clear that where there is a continuity of relationship[5] between mother and son that relationship retains certain special qualities, including dominance by the mother, which effectively inhibit sexual relationship between them.

Part of the socialization process in all species involves a progression from maximal dependence by the infant toward more independent functioning. Two factors have been cited as playing a significant role in this emancipation of the primate child from the mother. Some studies appear to show that the prime determinant of filial independence is maternal rejection, of which weaning is the most obvious aspect. Weaning appears very traumatic in some species such as the langur, with early mild rejection ultimately replaced by severely punitive behavior and total physical rejection, which sometimes leads to tantrums in the year-old infants (Jay 1963a). If the mother has resumed estrus, the rejection during weaning is even more intense (DeVore 1963). In response to the rejection the infant is thought to turn to peers and play, and thus develop greater independence (Hansen 1966; Jensen and Bobbitt 1967).

However, the various studies which indicate an enduring relationship to mother and clan in monkey and ape societies would tend to question this conclusion. Instead, the studies by J. H. Kaufmann of rhesus infants (1966) indicate: "Rejection of the infant seemed insignificant compared to the infant's interest in other monkeys, especially other infants." Also, in chimpanzees Goodall (1965) found little rejection by the mother, but a rather consistent initiative by the infant with respect to exploration and interactions with peers and older juveniles. Studies in my laboratory tend also to favor the second thesis, namely, that the growing infant and juvenile primate has a very considerable exploratory tendency which is largely responsible for his growing independence. Rejection by the mother tends to increase dependent behavior by the infant rather than decrease it (Kaufman and Rosenblum 1969a). Also, as will be made clear in a comparison of bonnet and pigtail monkeys, the bonnet infants who were rejected less seemed to be both the more secure and the more independent. Finally, the drive toward independence of the young has been noted in the human (Spock 1963) and stressed by Mahler and McDevitt (1968) in her studies of separation-individuation.

PATERNAL BEHAVIOR

The role of the father in primate society is variable. Paternal behavior by males shows little in the way of a distinct evolutionary course. Of course in some fashion or another the male must fertilize the eggs externally or internally. This may or may not be preceded by courtship or followed by further close contact with the female or the young. Among mammals there are several species in which the males are strongly parental and normally participate in the care of the young. This is particularly true within the order Rodentia where the male may wash the young, rebuild the nest if destroyed, help the female move it if necessary, retrieve and clean young, or adopt foster young (Beach 1967). It has also been demonstrated that male (and virgin female) rats which have been repeatedly exposed to newborn young will care for infants of their own species.

Beach has pointed out that such behavior would likely be most highly developed in those species whose reproductive pattern includes formation of a pair bond and extended post-parturitional association between the partners. Also, if the mother carries out her reproductive function within a well-structured group it is more likely that individuals other than the mother will be involved in care of the young. Beach (1967) states: "This feature characterizes the behavior of several species of primates, canids, and cetaceans."

Primate males vary greatly in parental behavior. The South American monkey male usually carries the infant virtually all the time except when it is being nursed (Mason 1966). Barbary macaque dominant males have been reported to take active roles in infant care, although mothers provide the major care (Lahiri and Southwick 1966). The dominant males handle the infants, groom them, and carry them around somewhat from the first day on. Usually the male first has to placate the mother, with lip-smacking or grooming, for example, before he can get the infant away from her.

In the Japanese macaque Itani (1963) has reported parental behavior by males of high rank that takes place at that time of year when females let their infants go so they may deliver new babies. Among one-year-old infants protected by the males there are equal numbers of each sex, but among the two-year-olds there are mostly females—by this time most of the males have formed into a juvenile group and been peripheralized, while the females stay in the central part of the troop. Itani makes it clear that there is no evidence of a blood relationship between the adult males and the infants they protect.

Male langurs apparently lack interest in young infants and associate only with older male infants (Jay 1962). A report by Sugiyama (1965) on Hanuman langurs describes how a previous bachelor male who was part of an all-male group, through a series of attacks by the group upon a troop with females and infants under a dominant male, became the new leader of the troop. He then proceeded to bite to death all the infants who were fairly quickly abandoned by their mothers. The mothers soon thereafter showed signs of estrus and then engaged in copulatory behavior with the new leader. This led to a distinct change in the troop, with replacement of the previous offspring by offspring of the new dominant male.

The relationship of adult male baboons to offspring tends to be close. In the chacma baboon, mothers with infants move to the center of the troop near the oldest, most dominant males, who protect them closely (Washburn and DeVore 1961a). Juvenile and young adult males are not much interested in infants, but the older males are, and frequently come and touch the babies. They are very straightforward, and the mother cringes when a male fondles her infant. The males frequently accompany their approach with conciliatory lip-smacking. They may carry infants on their bellies, and they respond to distress cries immediately. DeVore (1963) says:

It is scarcely possible to overemphasize the significance of the newborn baboon for the other troop members. Of the many behavior patterns which bind the members of a baboon troop together, the presence of young infants is of foremost importance. Grooming is the most frequent and obvious expression of "friendliness" and well-being, and the grooming clusters in a baboon troop are almost always formed around the mothers with the youngest infants. The protective presence of the adult males and the attraction of the infants combine to draw the other troop members toward the center of the troop.

As infants grow older their own mothers and other females become less tolerant of them, but the adult males remain tolerant and play with them, which facilitates attachment of the older infants to the adult males. DeVore (1963) says: "The evidence from baboons and Japanese macaques suggests that social bonds between adult males and infants are very strong in these terrestrial species, in striking contrast to the weak bonds between infants and adult males in more arboreal species." This would go along with the increased sexual dimorphism of terrestrial species, notably the bigger bodies and larger canine teeth of the males. In monkeys it is clear that dimorphism is based primarily on the adaptation of the male for defense and fighting. Such differences do not appear as often in arboreal species, where escape is much easier and predators fewer. Campbell (1966, p. 261) says, in accord with Darwin (1871): "Sexual dimorphism has evolved with the male animal's role as defender of the primate troop as well as a result of sexual selection resulting from dominance." He says dimorphism has been reduced in man because man does not rely on physical strength and teeth, and the development of the family led to a reduction in intermale rivalry. McBride (1969) points out that dimorphism is related not so much to sex and reproduction, but rather to a division of labor in social functions. Each caste makes a different contribution to the functioning of society and accordingly has specialized adaptations for different social functions that can be either behavioral or morphologic.

In my laboratory we have seen striking differences in two species of macaques in the behavior of the adult males with respect to the young. The adult male pigtail macaque is rather disinterested in the young and does not provide them with care, even if their mothers are removed (Kaufman and Rosenblum 1967). In contrast, the male bonnet macaque will play with older infants, and if the mother is removed he may hold and carry the infant, as well as protect him (Kaufman and Rosenblum 1969b).

It is difficult, then, to make a simple statement about paternal behavior in nonhuman primates. Adult males may be very attentive to infants or extremely indifferent, but they tend not to be overtly hostile; they may play with infants or juveniles. In species where protection of the group against predators is a major function of the males there is a greater likelihood of close interaction with infants, but even this is variable. At times, in certain species, under certain conditions, males will show maternal behaviors toward infants, perhaps when the mother is ill, occupied, or absent. More generally it seems that adult males play a role with older offspring, especially males, as they enter later stages of development in which gender identities become finalized. At such a point socialization by adult males becomes more critical.

In none of these instances is the parental behavior necessarily directed at the male's own offspring. In fact, in most primate groups there is no way even to know. Two exceptions are of interest. Among gibbons a single male and female pair and raise offspring. There is very little closeness, however, between the adult male and the offspring. He tolerates them until they are about two and a half years old but then he becomes increasingly antagonistic and protective of his own food supply; finally he appears to chase out the juveniles (Ellefson 1967). The other type of one-male group is exemplified by the hamadryas baboon of Ethiopia. Baboons generally sleep in tree tops, but in this barren region there are not very many trees; these baboons are found to sleep on rocky cliffs in groups of many hundreds. In the morning these very large groups break up into much smaller groups of perhaps 50 animals, which then further divide into family-sized one-male groups (Kummer 1968; Kummer and Kurt 1963). The one-male groups, which contain one or several females and their young, remain stable over long periods of time. They maintain their identity as they gather at night with each other to form larger groups whose constituents are far more variable. The one-male groups come about by the male collecting juvenile females, one at a time, to form a small harem. He mates only with his own females and protects only his own and their offspring. This small grouping appears to be an adaptation to food scarcity; the savannah (or chacma) baboon at times of great food shortages has also been reported to break down into one-male units (Hall 1963b). The same has been reported for the langur (Sugiyama 1965), the gelada (Crook 1967), and the patas (Hall 1965). As we shall see later this may be homologous to a similar adaptation by man when he came down out of the trees.

SEXUAL BEHAVIOR

One aspect of monkey and ape parental behavior is disruptive to parental function. Female monkeys and apes have estrous cycles recurring monthly, at least throughout the breeding season. In many species the female has very evident external signs of estrus, particularly in the so-called sex skin which becomes engorged and very prominent. In other species it is not so evident visually, but there is very good evidence that the information is broadcast in odors (Michael 1968). In any case, the female in estrus shows a much greater interest in males, and they in turn show very great interest in her. During the time that estrus lasts, the female and associated males are very much preoccupied with sexual activity. Ordinarily there is, following birth and during lactation, a period of months in which estrus does not return. However, it does return long before the infants are fully grown or even juveniles. The sexual mania during estrus interrupts normal social behavior and interferes with the care of infants. Accordingly the loss of estrus in the human was a very significant change with respect to the development of family life. Behavior relating to estrus sheds some light on one role of sexuality in sociality.[6] The female in estrus becomes of greater interest to the male, has greater privilege with him than at other times, and is less apt to receive aggressive behavior from him at other times. In the monkey this privilege usually lasts only as long as estrus, but the mechanism may be of significance in the evolution of permanent relationships and the human family (Etkin 1962). The sexual object is precious and privileged.

The loss of estrus in humans, that is, the escape from endocrinologic domination of sexual behavior, made it possible for sexual behavior to be better controlled, for the female to have a longer period for rearing each child without the loss of sexual activity or reproductive capability, and for relatively permanent male-female relationships to develop in a less competitive sexual atmosphere. It thus seems to have played a great role in the formation of family life in the human.

THE EMERGENCE OF MAN

When the ape-man (Australopithecus) came down to the ground out of the trees, the evidence is that he was already largely bipedal and erect, capable of using primitive tools, but with a brain not much larger than the ape's and still largely a vegetarian. It seems likely that the scarcity of food in the open plains then led to the formation of one-male groups.[7]

Washburn (1960) has succinctly described the emergence of early man:

Some very limited bipedalism left the hands sufficiently free from locomotor function so that stones or sticks could be carried, played with and used. The advantage that these objects gave to their users led both to more bipedalism and to more efficient tool use. English lacks any neat expression for this sort of situation, forcing us to speak of cause and effects as if they were separated, whereas in natural selection cause and effect are interrelated. Selection is based on successful behavior, and in the man-apes the beginnings of the human way of life depended on both inherited locomotor capacity and on the learned skills of tool-using. The success of the new way of life based on the use of tools changed the selection pressures on many parts of the body, notably the teeth, hands and brain, as well as on the pelvis. . . . The emergence of man's large brain occasioned a profound change in the plan of human reproduction. The human mother-child relationship is unique among the primates. . . . In all the apes and monkeys the baby clings to the mother; to be able to do so, the baby must be born with its central nervous system in an advanced state of development. But the brain of the fetus must be small enough so that birth may take place. In man adaptation to bipedal locomotion decreased the size of the bony birth canal at the same time that the exigencies of tool use selected for larger brains. This obstetrical dilemma was solved by delivery of the fetus at a much earlier stage of development. But this was possible only because the mother, already bipedal and with hands free of locomotor necessities, could hold the helpless, immature infant. . . . Bipedalism, tool use and selection for large brains thus slowed human development and invoked far greater maternal responsibility. The slow-moving mother, carrying the baby, could not hunt, and the combination of the woman's obligation to care for slow-developing babies and the man's occupation of hunting imposed a fundamental pattern on the social organization of the human species.*

The great disadvantage in the helplessness of the newborn, including his poorly developed homeostatic mechanisms, was overcome by the evolution of diligent parental care.

With his bipedalism, increasing tool use, and brain capacity, man became a hunter. His ability to procure mammal meat through hunting opened up a whole new source of food supply and led to very great changes in social organization. In order to track and catch larger animals, men banded together in small groups. With the development of cooperative hunting in the Middle Pleistocene Age, females became finally and fully dependent on males for meat, and the one-male group became bonded together more closely, with a division of labor and economic dependence. The woman would gather food and rear the children, and in return she and the children would receive protection and meat.

With the need for cooperation among the males some form of marriage contract between each man and woman arose as part of the political bond between descent groups. This was necessary for social stability, since man could survive only through the social hunt and other social institutions. Thus was the social group enlarged, not as a promiscuous troop but as a broad political structure which united descent groups through intermarriage. Exogamy, which requires the incest barrier, appears to have been the key to this type of social structure. Also the appearance of exogamy and the resultant increase in genetic mixture and variability may have played a great role in the further rapid evolution of the Hominidae, in contrast to the inbreeding monkeys who have not changed in millions of years.

The family became an integrated structure with a clear division of roles throughout; Campbell (1966, pp. 321-322) says these underlie the process of individualization.

The fact that particular males and females are interdependent means that one individual is ultimately important to another, if only at an economic level. With the appearance of one-male groups the interdependence became sexual and it expanded still further with the evolution of the family.[8] The wife and husband recognize each other as economic and social sexual partners. The frontal position in coitus enhances this recognition; role names, such as wife, husband, father, mother appeared and reflected the division of labor within the family.

We can see the human family as having arisen as an adaptation to economic and political needs, as well as through permanent sexual relations. It is a unique group in that there are young of differing ages who have to remain with the parents for a very long time in order to reach maturity. This is possible not only because of the evolution of parents who care a great deal but also because various cultural institutions have evolved based on man's enormous biologic adaptability and capacity for learning.

THE ADAPTIVE ASPECTS OF SLOW GROWTH AND DEVELOPMENT

A major factor accounting for man's vast cultural development was the evolution of a very slow rate of growth,[9] that is, growth and development continue for a very long time. Every period of development is lengthened compared to other primates—gestation, the infantile period to the eruption of the first permanent teeth, the juvenile period to the eruption of the last permanent teeth, the adult period to the end of life, and the various stages of reproductive life. Also as mentioned before, man is born at an early stage[10] of development to overcome the limitation imposed by the size of the mother's pelvis. The brain at birth is only about one quarter of it final size. It grows rapidly for several years, reaches 90 percent of final weight by six years of age, but continues to grow until about age 20.

The human infant at birth is far more helpless than other primates, whose brains are at least half-grown at birth, and who have a much more developed motor apparatus and the ability to cling to the mother. The problem this creates, and the solution, are clear. Lidz (1963) has pointed out that the prolonged helplessness of the human infant dictates that he be reared in a family whose members are attached to him and care about his needs.

The period of infant dependency, which is a matter of months in most mammals, a year in monkeys, and several years in apes, becomes six to eight years in humans. Beyond this, of course, there is the long period of cultural dependency. The close relationship between generations which follows upon suckling and caring for the young makes it possible to transmit learned behavior in a variety of ways, instead of depending solely upon learning through direct experience, as happens in many lower species. The experience of generations can thus be assimilated during a long period of training and instruction. Prolonged dependency and the presence of experienced adults have clearly been major factors in the evolution of human society.

Our focus is on parental rather than infant behavior, but a few comments about the learning process during the long period of growth are in order. Lidz (1963) has suggested a modification of Hartmann's statement that the infant is born adapted to survive in an average expectable environment. He proposes rather that within each society institutions arise that take into account the essential needs of the young. At the same time that parents provide physical care, they also communicate to the child the mores and instrumental techniques evolved by the society to deal with the environment. Parents provide the basic education in affective behavior and in techniques of communicating, relating, and living with others in social groups. In so doing, they and their ways become part of the child through identification.

Many similar processes are to be found in other species. Mead (1958) says:

There is one kind of transmitted experience in which—if we ignore for a moment the presence of language—there is no break between the kind of learning described for red deer or prairie dogs and that which occurs in human society, that is, learning which can occur only when the behaving, individual model is present, because the learning is unverbalized, inarticulate, recorded in no artifact, and represented in no symbolic form. Posture and gesture systems and the unsymbolized parts of a language—stress, cadence, and accent—all belong to this category. As the senior female red deer or the old ewes lead the herd or flock so older members of human groups guide the behavior of the younger members through the experience of a mass of patterned behaviors, specific to a given ecological setting and characteristic of a given society, with much of this never becoming conscious teaching or conscious learning.

Young monkeys and apes learn a great deal by observation and imitation, so that the behavior of the mother is very important to the education of the young. Furthermore, as Hall (1963a) points out, "Early learning goes on in intimate relationship with positive emotional attitudes . . . in the affective context provided by the mother and others." Many emotional reactions seem to be learned from observation or kinesthetically derived from the mother's reaction. Learning what is dangerous seems to be in this category. There is evidence that young monkeys showed no fear of snakes if they were raised in such a way as not to have the opportunity to see older monkeys react to snakes with fear.

Practice, as in play, is a major technique for primate learning. For example, male juvenile monkeys observe sexual behavior and then practice mounting with peers. Finally, estrous females help them learn to mount. Washburn (1968) says: "Play is the educational system for the nonhuman primate. The acts that will be important in adult life and learned in social situations are practiced in play." However, they rarely play with objects and are "tool dumb" (Washburn and Lancaster 1968).

This shows, say Washburn et al. (1965), that learning "is not a generalized ability; animals are able to learn some things with great ease and other things only with the greatest difficulty. Learning is part of the adaptive pattern of the species and can be understood only when it is seen as the process of acquiring skills and attitudes that are of evolutionary significance to a species when living in the environment to which it is adapted." Washburn and Hamburg (1965) state: "Learning can profitably be viewed in the adaptive context of evolutionary biology. The biology of a species expresses itself through behavior, and limits what can be learned. Evolution, through selection, has built the biological base so that many behaviors are easily, almost inevitably learned." Finally, Washburn (1968) says: "In the field studies we see the power of play, social learning, and identification creating adults whose biology and learning have both fitted them for their adult roles. The patas male is built to flee and he has learned when this behavior is appropriate. The baboon male is built to fight, and he has learned the behavior of his troop. Biology and experience make possible the appropriate behaviors of the species."

The slow rate of growth as an opportunity for learning is seen in still other ways. Whereas in most primate species females enter upon reproductive life with the achievement of nubility, males usually experience a further lag. In chacma baboons, for example, young adult males are allowed to copulate, but usually only with females at the beginning of estrus, whereas older more dominant males take over later in estrus when ovulation takes place, so that it is the older dominant males who are fathering the young (Washburn and DeVore 1961a). Thus the young male satisfies his sex drives but does not contribute much to the gene pool until he gets older. A similar situation is found in polygamous people even today, where the young men have to wait many years to take wives while the older men are taking their third and fourth (Campbell 1966). The long apprenticeship provides maximum opportunity for weeding out the unhealthy and less intelligent males while allowing the selected to gain further experience. In human society reproduction is thus delayed until the male is in a position to provide economically for his family.

Among females a delay in childbearing after nubility occurs only in the human, and is clearly cultural. This delay is curiously at variance with a gradual change in the age of menarche in Western Europe over the last hundred years from 15 to 16 to around 13 years of age (Tanner 1962). This is rather remarkable in that it is completely opposite from the overall direction of human evolution toward a slower growth rate. The earlier age of menarche is thought to be due to changed ecologic conditions, bringing about an increase in growth rate in the female. Yet reproduction remains delayed since culturally the assumption of parenthood at nubility seems inappropriate. This delay provides an opportunity for the young adult female to assimilate cultural traditions more fully before having to pass them on to her children. This seems to be a more recent development than the situation in males, where activity for the benefit of the society in many species has usually preceded a full reproductive role.

In connection with the above, it is of interest that among monkeys and apes, fairly early in development, a behavioral dimorphism becomes quite evident in most species. Juvenile and even infant males show in their play much more active and aggressive behaviors than do females; these behaviors then develop into the more adult types of aggressive behavior which characterize dominance encounters or group protective fighting (Jensen et al. 1967; Rosenblum 1961). Young females, on the other hand, who do not show this kind of behavior, do show a great deal of interest in infants that is not shown by the young males. Female juveniles watch and then participate in the handling of young infants. There is also evidence, from several species, of maternal behavior by adult females without offspring, the so-called aunts (Bowden et al. 1967; Rowell et al. 1964). This practice would seem to serve the juveniles and aunts in good stead later when they become mothers. Supporting the importance of experience in the development of motherhood is the experimental work of Harlow et al. (1966) with rhesus females raised on dummy mothers in isolation. They never received mothering, nor did they have an opportunity to observe or practice. They were totally inadequate mothers themselves when they had first infants. They were indifferent or abusive to them, and they did not feed them, so that the infants would have starved if they had not been artificially fed. Yet even these females became more adequate mothers with second offspring.

In the nonhuman primates we can see how the early sexual differences interact with the social milieu to provide the experience relevant to the development of adult parental function. The same is true in the human to an even greater degree. The human family provides a much longer opportunity for observation, practice, and further acculturation even beyond nubility before reproduction takes place. In this learning of **sexual behavior**, gender role, and parental function we see neatly illustrated the relationship between biology and learning.[11]

Another aspect of the slow rate of growth is the greater length of life and the remarkable extent to which humans live beyond their reproductive years, especially women. This is an uncommon situation in other species. In trying to understand how this might have been selected in evolution we have to consider first the fact that, due to the slow growth of children, parents are needed for at least 15 to 20 years after birth, which in itself would take many mothers beyond the menopause. Secondly, the cultural contribution of the postreproductive individual appears to be great. The evolution of culture emphasized the importance of learning and the value to the breeding population of the learned individual. Campbell (1966, p. 271) says:

The wise old man will be greatly valued in a social group for his knowledge of hunting, tool-making, and other masculine activities, and in particular for his experience of rare and occasional events, such as flood, drought, locust infestation, and so on. Similarly, the old woman will be valued for her knowledge and experience in childbirth, child-rearing, food-gathering and preparation, and other household odds. The old make a unique contribution to the survival of the cultural animal, for they are the storehouse of knowledge and wisdom.

NOTES

1. This character of slow development reaches its greatest extent and importance in human evolution, and will be discussed at considerable length later in this chapter.

2. The relation between slow development and dependence is not a simple causal one. See Washburn's comments (1960) on the interrelation between cause and effect in natural selection.

3. M. Altmann (1963) has reported that a moose cow in the beginning of the rutting season will not tolerate the courtship of a bull moose unless he is friendly toward her calf. She also reports that a moose cow has been known to beat up a bear which carries off her calf. "The maternal state obviously endows the moose cow with an aggressive spirit comparable to that of the broody hen defending her chicks."

4. On the other hand, Carpenter (1942) described how under conditions of stress rhesus females may chase their infants away from food or even kill them over food, as when they were being brought from India to Puerto Rico by boat and were frustrated by confinement and a limited food supply.

5. We have seen a five-year-old pigtail copulate with his mother when placed with her after three years of separation.

6. Marler (1968) has recently noted that many behaviors which reduce distance or maintain proximity between primates are forms of contact which often involve the genitalia and/or mouth. In addition he has noted the frequency with which embraces and other greeting gestures by males are accompanied by penile erections or involve mounting. The recurrence of sexual elements in situations that are obviously not copulatory suggests to him that they have an "alternate social role," that is, to effect closeness. His proposal, based on studies of monkeys and apes, is remarkably like Freud's theoretical constructions on the broad social role of libido. Presumably, the tactile, olfactory, and visual stimuli from conspecifics may produce a pleasurable state, akin to sexual arousal, which serves to promote recognition and reinforce social interaction. I have proposed (1960): "The basis of the continuity and ultimate unity of libidinal drive [in humans] must be sought . . . in some characteristic physiological mechanism underlying sexual excitation."

7. See earlier comments on the hamadryas baboon.

8. The permanent bond between male and female brought the male into the mother-child relationship (Campbell 1966, p. 260).

9. It is of interest that among mammals the amount of protein in the milk is closely correlated with the early growth of the infant; the more protein in the milk the sooner is the birth weight doubled (Silversten 1941). The human has the least.

10. This is so in still another way, in that human evolution is believed to have been subject to neoteny, a process in which there is a retention of the fetal or juvenile plasticity of ancestral forms in the later postnatal stages of development (Montagu 1962). Man retains many features that are fetal but not adult characteristics of apes, for example, the cranial flexure and the absence of brow ridges and cranial crests. The idea is that an essential feature of human evolution has been the avoidance of the specializations of ancestral primates and the preservation into adulthood of the fetal and infantile characteristics of growth. The birth of only one offspring made possible the establishment of mutations favoring neoteny and slow development, there no longer being selective advantage in rapid development.

11. The roles of hormones and the central nervous system are critical in this regard. Studies in recent years have demonstrated fairly conclusively that sex hormones have a double-action effect on the brain (Harris 1964). During fetal and neonatal life they act on the undifferentiated brain as they do on the undifferentiated genital tract, in an inductive way to organize brain circuits in male or female patterns. In the adult they act on the nervous system in either an excitatory or an inhibitory way, affecting the neural regulation of sex hormone secretion and the expression of overt patterns of sexual behavior. In experiments pregnant monkeys

have been given androgen injections, and as a consequence they have borne female pseudohermaphrodites who behave like male infants, especially in the increased amount of aggressive play, although they are clearly females (Young et al. 1964). In interpreting this, Hamburg and Lunde (1966) say: "Perhaps the influence of androgen during a critical period in brain development on the circuits destined later to mediate aggressive behavior would have central nervous system-differentiating effects that would facilitate the ease of learning aggressive patterns and increased readiness to learn such patterns . . . [The] threshold of response to certain agonistic stimuli might be lowered, with the result that the simuli might take on distinctly arousing properties. Or, certain patterns of action might become more rewarding as a result of early hormone action on the central nervous system; e.g., the large muscle movements so critical in agonistic encounters might be experienced as highly gratifying and therefore be frequently repeated." This would suggest that the early action of sex hormones on the central nervous system produces a dimorphic predisposition—males to aggressive behavior and females to maternal behavior—which is then developed through social learning, and ultimately put to adaptively significant use. This is clearer in the monkeys and apes but may have some relevance to man as well.

REFERENCES

Altmann, M.
    1963   Naturalistic studies of maternal care in moose and elk. *In* H. L. Rheingold (ed.), *Maternal Behavior in Mammals*. New York: Wiley.
Altmann, S. A.
    1962   A field study of the sociobiology of rhesus monkeys, *Macaca mulatta*. *Annals of the New York Academy of Science* 102: 338-435.
Beach, F. A.
    1967   Maternal behavior in males of various species (letter to the editor). *Science* 157: 1591.
Bowden, D., P. Winter, and D. Ploog
    1967   Pregnancy and delivery behavior in the squirrel monkey *(Saimuri scuireus)* and other primates. *Folia Primatologica* (Basel) 5: 1-42.
Cairns, R. B.
    1966   Attachment behavior of mammals. *Psychological Review* 73: 409-426.
Campbell, B.
    1966   *Human Evolution*. Chicago: Aldine.
Carpenter, C. R.
    1942   Societies of monkeys and apes. *Biological Symposia* 8: 177-204.
Christian, J. J., and D. E. Davis
    1964   Endocrines, behavior and population. *Science* 146: 1550-1560.
Conaway, C. H., and C. B. Koford
    1964   Estrous cycles and mating behavior in a free-ranging band of rhesus monkeys. *Journal of Mammalogy* 45: 577-588.
Crook, J. H.
    1967   Evolutionary change in primate societies. *Science Journal* 3: 66-72.
Darwin, C.
    1871   *The Descent of Man*. London: Murray.
DeVore, I.
    1963   Mother-infant relations in free-ranging baboons. *In* H. L. Rheingold (ed.), *Maternal Behavior in Mammals*. New York: Wiley.
Ellefson, J. O.
    1967   A natural history of gibbons *(Hylobates lar)* in the Malay Peninsula. Ph.D. thesis, University of California, Berkeley.
Etkin, W.
    1962   Social behavior and the evolution of man's mental faculties. *In* M. F. A. Montagu (ed.), *Culture and the Evolution of Man*. New York: Oxford University Press.

Freud, S.
1921   Group psychology and the analysis of the ego. *In* J. Strachey (ed.), *The Standard Edition of the Complete Psychological Works of Sigmund Freud,* Vol. 18. London: Hogarth, 1955.

Goodall, J. Van Lawick
1965   Chimpanzees of the Gombe Stream Reserve. *In* I. DeVore (ed.), *Primate Behavior.* New York: Holt, Rinehart and Winston.
1967   Mother-offspring relationships in free-ranging chimpanzees. *In* D. Morris (ed.), *Primate Ethology.* Chicago: Aldine.

Hall, K. R. L.
1963a   Observational learning in monkeys and apes. *British Journal of Psychology* 54: 201-226.
1963b   Variations in the ecology of the chacma baboon, *Papio ursinus. Symposia of the Zoological Society of London* 10: 1-28.
1965   Behaviour and ecology of wild patas monkeys, *Erythrocebus patas,* in Uganda. *Journal of the Zoological Society of London* 148: 15-87.

Hall, K. R. L., and I. DeVore
1965   Baboon social behavior. *In* I. DeVore (ed.), *Primate Behavior.* New York: Holt, Rinehart and Winston.

Hallowell, A. I.
1961   The procultural foundations of human adaptation. *In* S. L. Washburn (ed.), *Social Life of Early Man.* Chicago: Aldine.

Hamburg, D. A.
1963   Emotions in the perspective of human evolution. *In* P. H. Knapp (ed.), *Expression of the Emotions in Man.* New York: International Universities Press.
1969   Mother-infant interaction in primate field studies. *In* B. Foss (ed.), *Determinants of Infant Behaviour,* Vol. IV. London: Methuen.

Hamburg, D. A., and D. T. Lunde
1966   Sex hormones in the development of sex differences in human behavior. *In* E. E. Maccoby (ed.), *The Development of Sex Differences.* Stanford: Stanford University Press.

Hansen, E. W.
1966   The development of maternal and infant behavior in the rhesus monkey. *Behaviour* 27: 107-149.

Harcourt, D. G., and E. J. Leroux
1967   Population regulation in insects and man. *American Scientist* 55: 400-415.

Harlow, H. F.
1959   Love in infant monkeys. *Scientific American* 200: 68-74.

Harlow, H. F., M. K. Harlow, R. D. Dodsworth, and G. L. Arling
1966   Maternal behavior of rhesus monkeys deprived of mothering and peer associations in infancy. *Proceedings of the American Philosophical Society* 110: 58-66.

Harris, G.
1964   Sex hormones, brain development, and brain function. *Endocrinology* 175: 627-648.

Imanishi, K.
1960   Social organization of subhuman primates in their natural habitat. *Current Anthropology* 1: 393-407.
1963   Social behavior in Japanese monkeys, *Macaca fuscata. In* C. H. Southwick (ed.), *Primate Social Behavior.* Princeton: Van Nostrand.

Itani, J.
1963   Parental care in the wild Japanese monkey, *Macaca fuscata. In* C. H. Southwick (ed.), *Primate Social Behavior.* Princeton: Van Nostrand.

Jay, P. C.
1962   Aspects of maternal behavior among langurs. *Annals of the New York Academy of Science* 102: 468-476.
1963a   Mother-infant relations in langurs. *In* H. L. Rheingold (ed.), *Maternal Behavior in Mammals.* New York: Wiley.

1963b The Indian langur monkey *(Presbytis entellus). In* C. H. Southwick (ed.), *Primate Social Behavior.* Princeton: Van Nostrand.
1965 The common langur of North India. *In* I. DeVore (ed.), *Primate Behavior.* New York: Holt, Rinehart and Winston.

Jensen, G. D., and R. A. Bobbitt
1967 Implications of primate research for understanding infant development. *In* J. Helmuth (ed.), *Exceptional Infant.* Vol. I, *The Normal Infant.* Seattle: Special Child Publications of the Seattle Seguin School.

Jensen, G. D., R. A. Bobbitt, and B. N. Gordon
1967 Sex differences in mother-infant interaction. *In* J. Wortis (ed.), *Recent Advances in Biological Psychiatry,* Vol. 8. New York: Plenum.

Kaufman, I. C., and L. A. Rosenblum
1963 Unpublished data.
1967 The reaction to separation in infant monkeys: Anaclitic depression and conservation-withdrawal. *Psychosomatic Medicine* 29: 648-675.
1969a The waning of the mother-infant bond in two species of macaque. *In* B. Foss (ed.), *Determinants of Infant Behaviour,* Vol. IV. London: Methuen.
1969b Effects of separation from mother on the emotional behavior of infant monkeys. *Annals of the New York Academy of Science* 159: 681-695.

Kaufmann, J. H.
1966 Behavior of infant rhesus monkeys and their mothers in a free-ranging band. *Zoologica* 51: 17-28.

Kawai, M.
1958 On the rank system in a natural group of Japanese monkeys: I. The basic and dependent rank. *Primates* 1: 111-132.

Kawamura, S.
1958 The matriarchal social order in the Minoo-B group: A study on the rank system of Japanese macaque. *Primates* 1: 149-153.

Koford, C. B.
1963a Group relations in an island colony of rhesus monkeys. *In* C. H. Southwick (ed.), *Primate Social Behavior.* Princeton: Van Nostrand.
1963b Rank of mothers and sons in bands of rhesus monkeys. *Science* 141: 356-357.

Kummer, H.
1968 *Social Organization of Hamadryas Baboons: A Field Study.* Chicago: University of Chicago Press.

Kummer, H., and F. Kurt
1963 Social units of a free-living population of hamadryas baboons. *Folia Primatologica* (Basel) 1: 4-19.

Lahiri, R. K., and C. H. Southwick
1966 Parental care in *Macaca sylvana. Folia Primatologica* (Basel) 4: 257-264.

Lancaster, J. B., and R. B. Lee
1965 The annual reproductive cycle in monkeys and apes. *In* I. DeVore (ed.), *Primate Behavior.* New York: Holt, Rinehart and Winston.

Lidz, T.
1963 *The Family and Human Adaptation.* New York: International Universities Press.

Mahler, M. S., and J. B. McDevitt
1968 Observations on adaptation and defense in statu nascendi. *Psychoanalytic Quarterly* 37: 1-21.

Marler, P.
1968 Aggregation and dispersal: Two functions in primate communication. *In* P. Jay (ed.), *Primates: Studies in Adaptation and Variability.* New York: Holt, Rinehart and Winston.

Mason, W. A.
1965 The social development of monkeys and apes. *In* I. DeVore (ed.), *Primate Behavior.* New York: Holt, Rinehart and Winston.
1966 Social organization of the South American monkey *Callicebus moloch:* A preliminary report. *Tulane Studies in Zoology* 13: 23-28.

McBride, G.
1966 Society evolution. *Proceedings of the Ecological Society of Australia* 1: 1-13.
1968 Behavioral measurement of social stress. *In* E. S. E. Hafex (ed.), *Adaptation of Domestic Animals*. Philadelphia: Lea and Febiger.
1969 Personal communication.
Mead, M.
1958 Cultural determinants of behavior. *In* A. Roe and G. G. Simpson (eds.), *Behavior and Evolution*. New Haven: Yale University Press.
Michael, R. P.
1968 Unpublished data.
Montagu, M. F. A.
1962 Time, morphology, and neoteny in the evolution of man. *In* M. F. A. Montagu (ed.), *Culture and the Evolution of Man*. New York: Oxford University Press.
Myers, K.
1966 The effects of density on sociality and health in mammals. *Proceedings of the Ecological Society of Australia* 1: 40-64.
Rosenblum, L. A.
1961 The development of social behavior in the rhesus monkey. Ph.D. thesis, University of Wisconsin.
Rowell, T. E., R. A. Hinde, and Y. Spencer-Booth
1964 "Aunt"-infant interaction in captive rhesus monkeys. *Animal Behavior* 12: 219-226.
Sade, D. S.
1965 Some aspects of parent-offspring and sibling relations in a group of rhesus monkeys, with a discussion of grooming. *American Journal of Physical Anthropology* 23: 1-18.
1967 Determinants of dominance in a group of free-ranging rhesus monkeys. *In* S. A. Altmann (ed.), *Social Communication among Primates*. Chicago: University of Chicago Press.
Schaller, G. B.
1965 Behavioral comparisons of the apes. *In* I. DeVore (ed.), *Primate Behavior*. New York: Holt, Rinehart and Winston.
Silversten, E.
1941 On the biology of the harp seal. *Hvalradets Skrifter* 26: 1-166.
Southwick, C. H., M. A. Beg, and M. R. Siddiqi
1965 Rhesus monkeys in North India. *In* I. DeVore (ed.), *Primate Behavior*. New York: Holt, Rinehart and Winston.
Spock, B.
1963 The striving for autonomy and regressive object relationships. *Psychoanalytic Study of the Child* 18: 361-366.
Sugiyama, Y.
1965 On the social change of Hanuman langurs *(Presbytis entellus)* in their natural condition. *Primates* 6: 381-418.
Tanner, J. M.
1962 *Growth at Adolescence* (2nd ed.). Oxford, England: Blackwell.
Thiessen, D. D.
1964 Population density and behavior: A review of theoretical and physiological contributions. *Texas Reports on Biology and Medicine* 22: 266-313.
Tobach, E., and T. C. Schneirla
1969 The biopsychology of social behavior in animals. *In* R. E. Cooke (ed.), *The Biologic Basis of Pediatric Practice*. New York: McGraw-Hill.
Washburn, S. L.
1960 Tools and human evolution. *Scientific American* 203: 63-75.
1968 Speculations on the problem of man coming to the ground. *In* B. Rothblatt (ed.), *Changing Perspectives on Man*. Chicago: University of Chicago Press.
Washburn, S. L., and I. DeVore
1961a The social life of baboons. *Scientific American* 204: 62-71.

1961b   Social behavior of baboons and early man. *In* S. L. Washburn (ed.), *Social Life of Early Man*. Chicago: Aldine.

Washburn, S. L., and D. A. Hamburg
1965   The implications of primate research. *In* I. DeVore (ed.), *Primate Behavior*. New York: Holt, Rinehart and Winston.

Washburn, S. L., P. C. Jay, and J. B. Lancaster
1965   Field studies of old world monkeys and apes. *Science* 150: 1541-1547.

Washburn, S. L., and J. Lancaster
1968   Human evolution. *In* D. L. Sills (ed.), *International Encyclopedia of the Social Sciences*. New York: Macmillan.

Young, W. C., R. Goy, and C. Phoenix
1964   Hormones and sexual behavior. *Science* 143: 212-218.

Zuckerman, S.
1932   *The Social Life of Monkeys and Apes*. London: Routledge and Kegan Paul.

4. PHASES OF THE DEVELOPMENT OF INFANT-MOTHER ATTACHMENT

MARY AINSWORTH

Mary Ainsworth is Professor of Psychology, Johns Hopkins University, Baltimore. Reprinted with permission from *Infancy in Uganda,* by Mary Ainsworth. Copyright © 1967 by The Johns Hopkins University Press, Baltimore, Maryland 21218.

[Editor's note: This selection represents some of the conclusions of Professor Ainsworth's detailed study of 28 children of the Ganda people in Uganda, East Africa. Following the model of naturalistic observation used by ethological students of animal behavior, she observed each infant repeatedly during the first and second year of life (though not all during the same period) and recorded the behavior of mother and infant. Later, having replicated the study with American mothers and infants, she formulated the sequence of phases in the development of infant-mother attachment that is presented here. It should be seen as a hypothesis concerning a universal pattern of social development in the earliest segment of the human life.]

ALTHOUGH THE FOUR quarters of the first year may be distinguished one from the other in regard to attachment behavior, nevertheless, the quarterly divisions to some extent cut across functional divisions. Let us turn now to a distinction between phases of attachment, where less emphasis is placed on chronological age.

PHASE I: THE UNDISCRIMINATING PHASE

The first phase is characterized by the lack of discrimination between people. Even here one could distinguish two periods, although perhaps not in this particular Ganda sample. Nevertheless, both from my more intensive work with an American sample and from an examination of the findings of other investigations I would propose that this undiscriminating phase has a first, neonatal period in which the baby is unresponsive to social advances, except that he makes a general postural adjustment when held and a specific reflex adjustment to the feeding situation. The second period in the undiscriminating phase is characterized by undiscriminating social responsiveness. The baby smiles when presented with adequate stimulation, especially when presented with the human face in a face-to-face confrontation, and most especially if this is accompanied with head-wagging and vocalization. But at this time it does not matter whose face it is; the baby responds to a stranger just as readily as to his mother, given the same close confrontation.

In this study of Ganda babies, observations began at the very end of the undiscriminating phase; hence, there is nothing that our observations can add to what is already known.

PHASE II: THE PHASE OF DIFFERENTIAL RESPONSIVENESS

The baby begins to discriminate be-

61

tween his mother and other people and to behave differentially. The chief ways in which he can express this differentiation are differential crying, differential smiling, differential vocalization, and a differential postural adjustment. In this sample the only response that was systematically explored was differential crying. The baby cried when held by someone else but stopped when taken by the mother. When crying the baby could be comforted more readily by the mother than by anyone else. Perhaps another manifestation of differential crying was that the baby cried when put down by the mother, but did not protest being put down by someone else—although this was not explored in the present sample. In this sample the earliest instance of differential crying was observed at nine weeks and the latest at eleven weeks—but the cases were so few that no generalization can be validly made.

As I have mentioned before, we did not set out to observe any other kind of differential response. Nevertheless, I am sure that discrimination may be shown by differential smiling —by smiling more frequently, more readily, and more fully to the mother than to anyone else—and that in some societies differential smiling might well precede differential crying. In all societies differential vocalization is likely to be later than either differential crying or differential smiling, if only because non-crying vocalization is sparse at the beginning. Nevertheless, future studies of the development of attachment should attend to this differential response, especially because studies of maternal deprivation have shown that the amount of vocalization differentiates significantly between deprived and non-deprived babies.

After having completed a study, researchers sometimes suffer from re-grets regarding the significant behavior that they did not adequately observe, behavior that was relevant to their problem and which should have been observed. I feel this way about postural adjustment. I now believe that the baby's postural adjustment when held is the first response that becomes differential, perhaps excepting sucking and rooting and the whole complex of responses associated with feeding. It is now known that babies who are bottle-fed by more than one parent figure learn very early to adjust differentially if they are held in different feeding positions by different figures. Discrimination between different modes of being held was shown by three of the six Ganda babies observed in the first quarter; they indicated their appreciation of the difference by protesting being held by a stranger and quieting when taken by their mothers. These protests began to be noticed in the range of from nine to eleven weeks.

In this Ganda sample the second phase of discriminating behavior seems to last from nine weeks of age at the earliest to 25 weeks at the latest.

PHASE III: THE PHASE OF DIFFERENTIAL RESPONSIVENESS AT A DISTANCE

In this phase discrimination is manifested through distance receptors and perhaps especially through vision. This is shown when the child cries when his mother leaves the room—as early as 15 weeks of age in one child but more characteristically between 20 and 24 weeks. At about the same time, babies began to greet their mothers across a distance. And they began to indicate recognition of the strangeness of strangers at some distance by staring at the newcomers.

PHASE IV: THE PHASE OF ACTIVE INITIATIVE

The fourth phase is characterized by active initiative in making, sustaining, and renewing contact and interaction. Following the mother when she leaves the room is a criterion of active initiative and so is approaching. Although both of these behavior patterns depend upon the emergence of locomotion, active greeting by lifting the arms or clapping the hands does not. Scrambling and burying the face are other active patterns, and so, of course, is clinging. One child, Petero, clearly manifested these active patterns before the onset of locomotion, but in this sample they were, in general, observed at the same time as, or after, the onset of following and locomotion. The earliest age at which active initiative was manifested in this sample was 20 weeks, and in several babies it seemed to succeed Phase III very rapidly. The last child to reach this phase was Maryamu, sometime between 38 and 41 weeks.

The active initiative manifests itself also in behavior which is directed away from the mother. At the same time that babies show themselves so active in seeking contact, they also begin to use the mother as a secure base from which to explore the world, leaving her and returning to her or at least checking on her whereabouts. Furthermore, active initiative in seeking interaction with other familiar figures also emerges, and it is not merely a response to familiarity because there is a high degree of specificity shown by some babies in their preferences. Finally, during this phase of development the typical response to strangers is one of some reserve—reluctance to approach strangers and constraint or tension when held by a stranger, but with no marked stranger anxiety and usually with some willingness to warm up to a stranger after the period of reserve.

PHASE V: THE PHASE OF STRANGER ANXIETY

The chief developments in this phase are stranger anxiety on the one hand and marked clinging to the mother (or other object of attachment) on the other. Babies to whom we were not total strangers tended to show a more marked constraint or avoidance than they had in Phase IV, and babies to whom we were quite new manifested intense anxiety. It was the intense anxiety in response to strangers which seemed to evoke the clear-cut clinging response—clasping tightly and actively resisting any diminution of contact, not merely the fussy clinging of the baby who is insecure, hungry, tired, or ill. In our sample it was the mother to whom the child clung in most instances, but another person to whom the child was attached could serve as a haven of safety if the mother was absent. In this sample the earliest panic to strangers was observed at 37 weeks, but generally Phase V seemed to coincide fairly well with the last quarter of the first year of life.

In what phase of development can the baby first be described as attached? If the criterion is separation anxiety, then it is Phase III, when the baby cries at seeing his mother leave the room, although previously he had been content to be at some distance from her. If the criterion is stranger anxiety, then it is Phase V. But if we apply Piaget's (1954) stringent criterion of object permanence to attachment, requiring that the child demonstrate that he conceives of his mother as having an identity and a permanence independent of his own subjective experience, then attachment probably is not fully consolidated until the middle of the second year of life. My own inclination is to believe that attachment begins to be consolidated in Phase IV, after the first indications of separation anxiety and before full-blown stranger anxiety. This inclination has been reflected in Ainsworth (1967, Chaps. 20-22). But it is obviously a question of which objectively observable patterns of behavior can be taken as criteria for attachment because attachment itself must consist of some inner representation or structuring that cannot be observed directly and that can only be inferred from behavior.

Even though this study of Ganda babies does not enable us to answer some of the most crucial questions about attachment, it has highlighted several very significant points: attachment develops in an orderly way; a number of patterns of behavior have been identified as attachment behavior and emerge in orderly sequence over time; separation anxiety and stranger anxiety also undergo a developmental sequence, and although interlocked with the development of attachment, neither seems to be an adequate sole criterion for attachment; attachment to familiar figures other than the mother can emerge very soon after attachment to the mother (if not simultaneously), and this is perhaps particularly noteworthy in a society in which there is an especially close and intimate infant-mother relationship. Furthermore, it is believed that infant-care practices influence the development of attachment, facilitating it or delaying it and shaping the quality of the attachment relationship. This is implicit in some of the discussion in this chapter which contrasts Ganda practices with American practices. But even among the babies in this Ganda sample, differences emerge which are related to infant-care practices.

NOTE

1. In my earlier accounts (Ainsworth 1967) of the phases of development of attachment behavior I did not distinguish Phase III from Phase II.

REFERENCES

Ainsworth, Mary
  1967 *Infancy in Uganda.* Baltimore: Johns Hopkins University Press.
Piaget, J.
  1954 *The Construction of Reality in the Child.* New York: Basic Books.

5. MOURNING AND ADAPTATION

GEORGE H. POLLOCK

George H. Pollock, M.D., is Director of the Chicago Institute for Psychoanalysis and Professor of Psychiatry, Northwestern University. Reprinted with permission from *International Journal of Psycho-Analysis* (1961) 42: 341-361.

ADAPTATION

CLAUDE BERNARD (1813-1878), the French physiologist, was the first to advance the concept that animals exist in two environments: an external milieu in which the organism is actually situated, and an internal milieu in which the tissue elements are present. Although Bernard (1865) was concerned mainly with the physiological and biochemical aspects of the organism, he concluded that the "primary condition for freedom and independence of existence" was the constancy and stability of the internal milieu and the mechanisms that allowed this state to continue. Bernard felt that the organism had to be "so perfect that it can continually compensate for and counterbalance external variations." The equilibrium had to be constantly maintained and all vital mechanisms had "only one object: that of preserving constant the conditions of life in the milieu intérieur."

I am taking the liberty of extending Bernard's ideas to the psychological environment. Here too we find an external and an internal milieu. In both we find definite regulatory devices designed to deal with various alterations that may occur. Freud extensively studied the internal psychological milieu and advanced various theoretical constructs which allowed a conceptual framework to be formulated. As early as 1892, Freud alone and with Breuer proposed the idea of the constancy of

excitation. When the nervous system had difficulty in dealing with increases in excitation through associative thinking or motor discharge, Freud and Breuer suggested that a "psychical trauma" occurred. In 1911, Freud advanced his understanding of psychological processes with his "Formulations on the Two Principles of Mental Functioning." Here he introduced two modes of constancy adaptations—the immediate energetic discharge or avoidance of the pleasure-pain principle, and the capacity, oriented to external reality, for discharge delay of the reality principle. This later type of adaptation used mechanisms involving consciousness, attention, notation, and memory storage as well as decision-making with action to alter external reality and thought, as means of coping with new and potentially disrupting situations. In *Beyond the Pleasure Principle*, Freud once more emphasized the principle of constancy and its relationship to the mental apparatus. We can see that Freud's idea of the psychological constancy of the internal milieu paralleled Bernard's model of the physico-biochemical stability. In both the internal milieu was optimally maintained within a certain range. Less variation could occur here in contrast to the external milieu, and various defense mechanisms were necessary to maintain this constancy of the inside.

Walter Cannon (1871-1945) extended and elaborated this concept of stability by his principle of homeostasis, which emphasized the various biological processes tending to re-establish steady states of equilibrium and constancy when disturbing elements upset the state of balance. As biologists have continued their investigations, various optimal ranges for particular body processes have been discovered. With disease interferences, these ranges vary in accordance with the degree of impairment imposed upon the organism, as well as with the restitutive capacity operative within the organism.

Cannon (1939) envisioned the extension of his homeostasis idea to include "some general principles for the establishment, regulation, and control of steady states" which could be applicable to social and industrial organizations. He wrote that "perhaps a comparative study would show that every complex organization must have more or less effective self-righting adjustments in order to prevent a check on its functions or a rapid disintegration of its parts when it is subjected to stress."

Although Freud was aware of defensive maneuvers utilized in psychological adaptation early in his work, it was in 1923 that he first presented us with the structural organization of the mental apparatus in *The Ego and the Id*. The ego's integrative role was elaborated and its relationship to the external milieu (reality) as well as to the psychic internal milieu explained. In 1936, Anna Freud (1936) developed in further detail the protective and sustaining aspects of the ego's function. In 1937, Hartmann's classic essay on *Ego Psychology and the Problem of Adaptation* first appeared. These last two contributions focused the direction of later psychoanalytic developments and investigations upon ego activities.

It was Cannon who noted that "the perfection of the process of holding a stable state in spite of extensive shifts of outer circumstance is not a special gift bestowed upon the highest organisms but is the consequence of a gradual evolution."

Charles Darwin (1809-1882), in *The Origin of Species,* suggested that, by a process of natural selection, less well adapted forms of life would have on the average a heavier death-rate and a lower multiplication-rate. Again dealing with physical characteristics, he postulated his idea of the "survival of the fittest." Undoubtedly the homeostatic stabilizing mechanisms came into being through a process of gradual evolution and natural selection. These included both psychological and physiological processes for reintegrating and re-establishing the self-regulating internal equilibrium. It was Bernard who wrote that "the phenomena of living beings must be considered as a harmonious whole."

We can thus see that a fundamental property of every living organism, at every stage of its existence, is the capacity for adaptive response to its external environment which allows for a state of balance in its internal milieu. Natural selection seems to have favored those individuals and species that possess the greatest power of responsive plasticity of the individual within the optimal range of adaptation. Both the theory of evolution and that of the dynamic steady state or homeostatic adaptation are necessary to the understanding of human responses to psychological and physiological stresses both external and internal. We must have adaptation to the environment now, and the capacity for it in future, if smooth functioning is to be secured.

Adaptation involves a series of processes that are goal-directed and designed to facilitate the establishment of a state of equilibrium between the organism and its environment. In some instances the optimal level of equilibrium is fixed and various mechanisms attempt to adjust to this constancy. In other situations, devices are utilized to allow for a state as close to the optimal as possible. In any event the adaptational process is a dynamic one, having its roots in the biological structure and constantly attempting to balance intersystemic and intrasystemic tensions by way of the ego (Hartmann 1939).

Phylogenetic evolution has been directed toward allowing the organism increased independence of its environment, but this freedom is operative only within a certain range. As biological evolution has proceeded there has been a concomitant internalization of vital structures and functions. This applies to essential physiological, anatomical, and psychological process and structures. We may view the appearance of intra-psychic structures along this continuum of evolving internalization. The simplest unicellular organism operates on the uncomplicated stimulus-response level. Man also may in some instances do this, but he can perceive many stimuli which can be internally understood and stored without any immediate external response. Hartmann suggests that animals may have some kind of ego, though it is not comparable to that which we think is present in man. He feels that in lower animals reality relationships provide the patterns for the aims and means of pleasure-gain to a greater extent than they do in adult man. In view of Freud's "Formulations on the Two Principles of Mental Functioning," this statement can be elaborated to indicate that certain infra-human species, as well as the egos of very young children, operate primarily on the basis of the pleasure principle,

whereas more mature and integrated human egos function in accordance with the reality principle and utilize secondary process thinking which includes intra-psychic representations of external objects and memory. Pleasure-principle operations view the object mainly in terms of the function it performs for the individual being, namely that of the reduction of tension. Only with greater maturation and development does the object become differentiated as an individual entity with distinct personal characteristics of its own in addition to those that are overtly functional. We see that psychological adaptation may occur at levels which have phylogenetic significance as well as ontogenetic importance.

Hartmann differentiates the state of adaptedness from the adaptive process which brings this state about. In this adaptive process, various defensive techniques are utilized. But "adaptation achievements may turn into adaptation disturbances," when reality situations are altered. Thus when an object relationship is interrupted by the death of one of the significant participants, a new ego-adaptive process has to be instituted in order to deal with the altered internal-external psychological situation. Where there is a possibility of substitution with little difficulty, the adaptive task may be easily accomplished, as is the case with certain animals and very young infants. But when the lost object has taken on psychic significance in addition to functional fulfillment, the adaptive process involves in part an undoing of the previous adaptational equilibrium established with that object, and the gradual re-establishment of new relationships with reality-present figures. The complex adaptive process instituted in such a situation is called mourning.

A process may come about in one of two ways. There may be the stepwise series of consecutively followed specific stages, or the situation where many stages exist simultaneously and concomitantly. Even in this latter type of process, where varying intermediate phases are present at the same time, there are quantitative differences between the varying stages, but definite starting and end points may be ascertained. In the intermediate phases of the process, reactions and interactions may have inhibitory, facilitatory, or neutralizing effects.

It is only by carefully studying each component part that we can gain an approximate appreciation of the complex relationship of the entire process. For the sake of simplicity, this second type of process may be described as if it occurred in seemingly isolated consecutive steps, although this may not be so in fact.

The mourning process consists of a series of operations and stages whose appearance seems to follow a sequential pattern. In line with the above, however, it is necessary to indicate that although certain aspects of the process are more apparent at particular times, the succession of one stage by another does not necessarily indicate that a former stage may not be present later in time, or that a later one was not in evidence earlier.

THE MOURNING PROCESS IN MAN

Psychological lesions result when there is a disruption of the state of equilibrium that is established to allow for optimal functioning. As indicated above, reactions evoked by the upset in adaptation give rise to a process designed to re-establish an intra-psy-chic homeostatic steady state. Characteristically, mourning refers to the response following the deaths of a meaningful figure. As will be postulated below, this mourning reaction is an ego-adaptive process which includes the reaction to the loss of the object, as well as the readjustment to an external environment wherein this object no longer exists in reality. The mourning process is not species-specific, and is obviously intrapsychic, as the external loss cannot be undone. Usually we assume that mourning and the reaction to permanent loss without death are equivalent. This equation, though not rejected, requires further demonstration. Differences may be present which allow for more precise description.

The ante-mortem nature of the relationship between the bereaved and the deceased will be an important factor in the resultant mourning process. The type of ego development, maturation, and the level of integration and organization, however, will be the crucial variables in determining the course and extent of the mourning process. Thus an ego that has developed to the point where reality is correctly perceived, and objects distinctly and uniquely differentiated, will mourn differently from an ego that is poorly integrated and immature.

HISTORICAL CONSIDERATIONS

In a discussion attached to the case history of Fraulein Elisabeth von R, which appeared in the *Studies on Hysteria* (1893), Freud described

a highly-gifted lady who suffers from slight nervous states and whose whole character bears evidence of hysteria, though she has never had to seek medical help or been unable to carry on her duties. She has already nursed to the end three of four of those whom she loved.

Each time she reached a state of complete exhaustion; but she did not fall ill after these tragic efforts. Shortly after her patient's death, however, there would begin in her a work of reproduction which once more brought up before her eyes the scents of the illness and death. Every day she would go through each impression once more, would weep over it and console herself—at her leisure, one might say. This process of dealing with her impressions was dovetailed into her everyday tasks without the two activities interfering with each other. The whole thing would pass through her mind in chronological sequence. I cannot say whether the work of recollection corresponded day by day with the past.

An editorial comment in the Standard Edition at this point indicates that this account of the "work of recollection" anticipated Freud's later concept of the "work of mourning."

Freud goes on to say that "In addition to these outbursts of weeping with which she made up arrears and which followed close upon the fatal termination of the illness, this lady celebrated annual festivals of remembrance at the period of her various catastrophes, and on these occasions her vivid visual reproduction and expressions of feeling kept to the date precisely." Freud gives a specific instance of this woman crying actively on the occasion of her husband's death which had occurred three years earlier.

This careful clinical description not only presented Freud's precursory ideas referable to the mourning work, but also was the first conceptualization of what we now call anniversary reactions. This type of reaction, more currently rediscovered and elaborated upon, is clearly a variation and an incomplete form of the mourning process. In the patient described by Freud, these observations are made only in passing, but in retrospect they already

predict some of his later significant contributions.

In 1895 in Draft G, on Melancholia, Freud related depression and melancholia to mourning and grief. He spoke of a "longing for something that is lost," and "a loss in the subject's instinctual life." Again anticipating his later formulations, he also commented that "the uncoupling of associations is always painful." In Draft N, written on 31 May 1897, Freud not only gave us the first hint of the oedipus complex, but also connected mourning with melancholia. This comparison he further commented on in his 1910 discussion of suicide, where he referred to the "affect of mourning."

Freud described mourning as a normal emotional process in his *Five Lectures on Psycho-Analysis* (1909), and in the same year in his "Notes Upon A Case of Obsessional Neurosis," he states that "I told him, a normal period of mourning would last from one to two years." The essays on *Totem and Taboo* (1912-13) further develop Freud's ideas on the mourning process. He writes that "Mourning has a quite specific psychical task to perform: its function is to detach the survivors' memories and hopes from the dead. When this has been achieved, the pain grows less and with it the remorse and self-reproach." (p. 65). In the same work Freud points out that after a death both affection and hostility to the deceased exist. The mourning relates to the positive feelings, while satisfaction is the reaction of triumph related to the hostile feelings. The hostility, however, is repressed and becomes unconscious, because the mourning process which derives from an intensification of the loving feelings does not allow of any satisfaction. But this hostility may be dealt with by projection onto the dead object, and this gives rise to the fear of the dead. This phenomenon also is related to the feelings of anger which will be discussed below.

In January 1914, Freud spoke to Jones about his paper on mourning and melancholia, and in December of that year he presented his ideas to the Vienna Psychoanalytical Society. He wrote his first draft in February 1915, and the manuscript was finished in May 1915. In March and April 1915, Freud wrote his paper "Thoughts for the Times on War and Death." In November 1915, Freud's "On Transience" was written, and published the following year.

In attempting a correlation of events in Freud's life (Jones 1953-1957) with the appearance of these papers, we note that Freud's father died on 23 October 1896. In July 1897 Freud began his self-analysis, and on 15 October 1897 in a letter to Fliess announced his discovery of the Oedipus complex. Draft N, it seems, was written at a time when Freud himself was in the midst of working out his own mourning for his dead father. In 1910 the difficulties with Adler were increasing, and in 1911 the break with him actually occurred. In 1913 the dissension with Jung was very painful to Freud, and in 1914 came Jung's resignation from psychoanalytic associations. The distress these oppositions caused to Freud is well known. Although it is speculative, his more formal conceptualization of mourning may have been related to his grief over the loss of Jung and what Jung represented to him. The 1913 Congress was an unpleasant experience for Freud, and in 1914 Jung's formal separation occurred. In November 1914, Freud's beloved brother Emmanuel died in a railway accident. Jones states "he was

eighty-one years old, the same as their father when he died." About this same time, "there was also the loss of the famous raider, the *Emden*, to be mourned; Freud said he had got quite attached to her." In December 1914, "Freud's spirits were very low, and he begged Abraham to come and cheer him up." It was in the same month that Freud spoke to the Vienna Society on mourning and melancholia in a discussion of a paper by Tausk on melancholia.

In 1915 Freud's two sons were actively involved in the war and he was quite concerned over them. Jones (1957-1957) notes that "Freud had several dreams about calamities to his sons, which he interpreted as envy of their youth." Many of his close associates (Abraham, Ferenczi, Rank, Sachs) were also on army service during this period. It was in 1915 that the three major works above referred to were written. We may infer that the losses, disappointments, and threats undoubtedly influenced Freud, so that his introspective activities yielded insights on mourning that were reflected in his papers on this theme.

In his essay "On Transience," Freud notes that individuals "recoil from anything that is painful," and so there is "a revolt in their minds against mourning." Thus thoughts about the transience of an object involve "a foretaste of mourning over its decease" with resultant avoidance of thoughts on this theme. Until recent months surprisingly few investigations have been made of the mourning process *per se* by psychoanalysts and others involved in psychological research. Perhaps Freud's statements quoted above are in part an explanation of the apparent lack of study of this normal and omnipresent phenomenon.

In "Mourning and Melancholia" Freud states that "mourning is regularly the reaction to the loss of a loved person, or to the loss of some abstraction which has taken the place of one, such as fatherland, liberty, an ideal, and so on." He indicates that a mourning process as such can occur after varying losses. The loss of the abstraction, however, is reacted to as if it were the intra-psychic object that is lost. In this investigation, the loss following the death of a significant figure will be the major source of clinical data, and the major definition of the mourning process. In the various clinical and theoretical reports appearing on this subject some terminological differences seem to confuse aspects of the mourning process. Thus grief is an affect that may follow on a multitude of situations. It is seen in the mourning process, but grief as such may be seen in situations where there is no such process. Transitory object loss in time and in space may give rise to various reactions that are components of the mourning process, but this again must be differentiated from the permanent loss in time and space of a significant object.

In *The Ego and The Id*, Freud states that the "character of the ego is a precipitate of abandoned object-cathexes" as well as the recording of "past object-choices." Thus all prior frustrations and renunciations were seemingly followed by mourning processes. When viewed in this broad way, the mourning process becomes very significant, as it is apparently one of the more universal forms of adaptation and growth through structuralization available to man. Not all aspects of this process necessarily occur with every loss. In studying the response to the death of meaningful figures, various facets not usually seen in other types of frustration and loss may be described and delineated. Mourning may result when there is rejection by an object not by death, but the important focus here is on the resulting process and not necessarily on the precipitating event. We mourn something that is lost but previously had been strongly cathected, and through this process the ego is built.

Klein has commented on the close connection between the testing of reality in normal mourning and the early mental processes. It is her contention that the early mourning characteristic of the child's reactions to frustrations is revived and re-experienced whenever grief occurs in later life. Just as Freud has stressed the importance of reality testing as the most important part of the adult mourning work, so Klein emphasizes this ego activity in overcoming a mourning-like process seen in young children where in external reality no death has occurred.

In this paper an attempt will be made mainly to delineate and discuss more specifically the various stages of the mourning process as it customarily occurs in man after the death of an object. These findings will then in the last section be related to observations made on infra-human responses to death. More deviant types of mourning reactions will be briefly mentioned, to be more fully elaborated in a later paper.

STAGES OF THE MOURNING PROCESS

Approximately five years ago, while intimately involved in a mourning adaptation of his own, the author had occasion to experience and observe more closely the changing aspects of the mourning process in himself and also in family members of various ages and developmental levels. As the mourning continued it became apparent that different aspects of the process could be distinguished. These stages consisted of a series of reactions occurring in a temporal sequence, having distinct degrees of acuteness and chronicity, and seemingly divided into component parts. Stimulated by these observations, a more systematic study of the mourning process was undertaken, and the following conclusions were arrived at.

When a death occurs, the first response is that of shock. This results from the sudden upset in ego equilibrium, and is related to the initial awareness that the object no longer exists in space, time, or person. The particular emotional orientation to this being is disrupted, and initially there is excessive stimulation due to this initial awareness that cannot be integrated. The overwhelming task may unsuccessfully be dealt with and result in a panic response, which includes shrieking, wailing, or moaning, or may be manifested by a complete collapse with paralysis and motor retardation. The behavior in this shock stage indicates acute regression to a much earlier ego-organizational level. The narcissistic loss, related to the resulting shock, is connected with the suddenness of the event. The phenomenon of narcissistic mortification is applicable to this shock state. There is "a sudden loss of control over external or internal reality, or both, by virtue of which the emotion of terror is produced, along with the damming up of narcissistic libido or destrudo" (Eidelberg 1959). The shock phase results when the ego is narcissistically immobilized by the suddenness and massiveness of the task that confronts it.

The response noted in this initial stage varies in intensity according to the suddenness of the death and the degree of preparation the ego underwent prior to the death. Thus death following chronic and prolonged serious illness is reacted to differently from the acute unexpected demise of a close object. Nonetheless, a shock response will be present in both situations, although the intensity will vary. Previous shocks of a similar kind may suddenly be catapulted into this most recent one and can result in a total regressive immobilization. In susceptible individuals this shock can be of such magnitude as to precipitate a serious somatic dysfunction such as thyrotoxicosis (Alexander, Ham, and Carmichael 1951). In instances where death is anticipated as a result of a long-standing debilitation, acute mourning reactions may occur prior to the actual death. In several patients, whose parents were dying of malignant conditions, the shock response came when the patients first heard of the hopeless malignant diagnosis, and only very slightly when the actual death occurred. In these persons, the ego was able to react to the upset in present reality more gradually, so that when death supervened much preparation had already been done.

It is the sudden impingement of reality on the unprepared ego that results in an overwhelming of the stimulus barrier and the integrative capacity of the organism. Massive regression with panic can ensue until further restitutive activities take over. The duration of this shock phase is usually short, although the immobilization may persist owing to faulty later reparative reactions. It may be that the degree of shock ranges through a spectrum of responses depending upon the type of ego stimuli barriers that have previously been integrated.

The second stage in the mourning process, very closely following the shock response, is the grief reaction. Darwin describes the physical aspects of this response in his *Expression of the Emotions in Man and Animals* (1872). He indicates that early grief is characterized by much muscular hyperactivity such as hand wringing, aimless wild walking, hair and clothes pulling. Darwin interprets this behavior as indicative of the impotence the bereaved feels to undo the death that has just occurred. This frantic movement changes when it is realized that nothing can be done. Then deep despair and sorrow take over and the sufferer becomes very quiet, sits motionless or gently rocks to and fro, sighs deeply, and becomes muscularly flaccid. All the facial features are lengthened and the characteristic grief appearance results. Darwin specially calls attention to the grief muscles, whose innervation results in the typical obliquity of the eyebrow and the depression of the corners of the mouth. As grief lessens, the change may be detected in muscular alterations even before feelings are altered. Lindemann (1944) has described the feelings of fatigue, exhaustion, and anorexia seen in this acute grief phase. The energy impoverishment seen in grief has been related to the mourning process by Freud in his *Inhibitions, Symptoms and Anxiety*.

As the shock stage merges into the grief phase a subjective feeling of intense psychic pain is felt. The suffering ache is initially of much greater intensity than what subsequently follows in the later chronic grief phase. Accompanying this psychic pain may be the sudden screaming, yelling, and other non-verbal but vocal manifestations of this grief reaction. This acute initial response later becomes the more characteristic depression. The spasmodic crying changes to tearful lamentations, and gradually verbal communications become more frequent, though still accompanied by much sobbing.

What explanations can we seek for the phenomena described in this phase? Initially we must consider the "Formulations on the Two Principles of Mental Functioning" of Freud. The pleasure ego, operating under the pleasure-pain principle, strives for the release of tension and excitement. In the very young child this is completely related to the external object. Thus when there is an increase in excitation without release because the object is absent, pain results. With the death of the object, there is temporary ego disruption with regression to an ego state where the pleasure-pain principle is the chief axis of mental functioning. Since reality principle functioning is temporarily abrogated, the capacity to wait for discharge and the ability to seek alternative ways of handling the increase in tension is very much diminished.

Thus the external reality loss so overwhelms the ego that immobilization and shock occur with regression to the earlier pleasure-pain principle operation. This pain may result from the heightened non-discharged energic cathexis due to the absence of the object. As greater ego integration occurs, reality-principle functioning and secondary process thinking return with the resulting amelioration of the psychic pain. Freud has noted the feeling of pain that occurs in mourning in his "Mourning and Melancholia." In this paper, however, Freud initially refers to the pain as *Schmerz* and not *Unlust*, the "mental antithesis of pleasure," also translated as pain. Later he calls the pain that is present *Schmerz-Unlust*. It is my contention that this pain is both *Schmerz* and

Unlust, and represents the regression to the earlier phase of mental functioning. The idea that the lost object can no longer hopefully fulfill the needs of the mourner seems to be the key point. This reality awareness, however, is more characteristic of the later chronic mourning process. This early intense pain is seemingly more closely tied to the reaction to frustration at not having the object there.

In his paper "On Narcissism," Freud notes that as libidinal interest and investment is withdrawn from a love object into the ego, there is a damming-up of libido in the ego. With this increase in tension, pain is experienced. This conceptualization allows us to view this aspect of the mourning process as analogous to the model of the actual neuroses. When the libido is discharged, the pain diminishes.

The pain phenomenon may alternatively be approached from the point of view of Federn. Thus the object is gone and temporarily libido may be avulsed along with it. This can result in an ego impoverishment and an inability to bind stimuli so that withdrawal is the emergency adaptation to conserve libido by avoiding stimuli that additionally tax the ego. Regression to an earlier ego state requires less expenditure of ego cathexis. Utilizing this concept of ego depletion in mourning may assist in differentiating the reaction after the death of an object from that on the loss of an object not through death but through growth. Thus in analysis mourning-like reactions occur when childhood objects are given up. The grief involved in losing all retained relationships revived in the transference neurosis is not due to impoverishment. This latter is a living process leading to a particular goal of detachment.

This process is different from the mourning following the actual death of a significant being. I cannot say whether the avulsion hypothesis or the "swelling" hypothesis causes the pain. Either phenomenon can result in this reaction, and further study is necessary to find specifically which is more significant.

Convergent evidence for the presence of pain is to be found in understanding the rather "animal-like" crying seen in the earlier phase of mourning. The cry is an alarm signal that is vocalized very early in life. In addition it expresses unpleasurable feelings and emotions. The cry is not only a proclamation of pain or some other nonpleasurable state, but is also the earliest form of vocal communication and command. It seems to announce that something undesired is present, and it usually arouses the simple and appropriate response on the part of those who hear it. Thus as pain occurs, it is accompanied initially by the primitive crying that is indicative of this pain. As the local communications become more verbal, the crying also seems to be less primitive and less wail-like, and the needs are expressed in more advanced ways.

With separation we get crying. This is commonly seen when a young child is spatially and temporally removed from its mother. It is also seen in adults on various occasions of parting. French (personal communication) has postulated that underlying the crying is the wish for reconciliation. In certain of the anthropoids this seems to be the case; initially, however, it is the cry of distress that accompanies separation from the mother. When the child becomes aware of the mother's response to the crying, it may then become the signal for reconciliation in addition to its earlier significance.

In "Mourning and Melancholia," Freud states that mourning work involves the testing of reality that shows that the loved object no longer exists and requires that all the libido shall be withdrawn from its attachment to this object." Thus when reality-principle operation takes over, there is a consciousness of the external world without the departed object. This absence is not only perceived but is confirmed by repeated confrontations with the external world, and is finally noted and remembered. There may be a partial repression of the pain involved in the loss. This pain will be re-experienced periodically throughout the mourning process and the experience integrated in the later stage of mourning work. As the ego passes judgment on the truth and permanence of the loss, action and thought processes are utilized to facilitate appropriate alterations of reality with subsequent adaptation.

Fantasy-making and day-dreaming, however, not being dependent upon real objects and reality testing, still remain subordinated to the pleasure-principle alone, and so repression remains as the all-powerful defense. Thus fantasies and day-dreams concerning the deceased object can interfere with the mourning work, and in instances where the death of the object is not realistically appreciated, the object may continue to exist as an unassimilated introject with whom internal conversations can be carried on. This phenomenon has been observed in several patients who lost their parents in childhood. The use of fantasy defensively in ignoring reality is commonly seen in various clinical pictures. But the fantasied monologue and interior dialogue are quite frequently found in this phase of the mourning process.

In the "Formulation on the Two Principles of Mental Functioning," Freud relates a repetitive dream of a man whose father died after a long illness, the dream occurring months after the death. In it the father was alive again and the patient talked to him as of old. "But as he did so he felt it exceedingly painful that his father was nevertheless dead, only not aware of the fact." Freud in 1911, involved in working out problems of id psychology, related the pain to the dreamer's death wishes towards the father when he was alive. This pain, however, may have resulted from the awareness of the death as it has been described above, and in the dream we can see how the reality of the father's death is avoided by portraying him as alive, and yet the dreamer is simultaneously aware of the fact that he is dead. In other words, this dream represents the mourning work involved in partially accepting the father's death, yet at the same time avoiding this recognition.

In his paper on "Fetishism" (1927), Freud discusses two male analysands who lost their fathers at the age of two and ten respectively. He mentions that each patient had refused to acknowledge his father's death, yet neither of them had developed a psychosis. On further investigation, Freud found that "only one current of their mental processes" had not accepted the father's death. "There was another which was fully aware of the fact; the one which was consistent with reality stood alongside the one which accorded with a wish." One of these cases was a severe obsessional and "in every situation in life he oscillated between two assumptions—on the one his father was still alive and hindered him from action, on the other his father was dead and he had a right to regard himself as his successor." We can infer here that the patient's mourning process was such that he still could not accept the reality of the father's death. Freud (1938) points out that in certain states of conflict the synthetic function of the ego is abrogated and both reality and instinct may be satisfied at great cost. This type of non-synthetic ego functioning related to isolation may be the adaptive technique utilized by this patient.

In the chronic mourning stage, pain may continue to be felt. It is however less intense, less generalized, and less continuous, related to specific recollections or perceptions, and gradually extinguished. In the acute mourning phase the pain does not have these buffering characteristics.

In instances of chronic illness, these painful grief responses may antedate the actual death, as we have said above for the shock responses. The reaction here is that the loved person is already lost in the internal milieu, even though death has not yet occurred in reality. An individual speaking of a close relative who had recently been diagnosed as having a fatal illness, referred to the ill person in the past tense throughout the conversation. Spontaneously the speaker remarked, "You know he is dead for me already." This indicated that the internal loss and mourning process was already in motion. Mourning work is still required, however, after the actual death has occurred. If there is no evidence of it, it may represent a defensive short-circuiting of the process to avoid pain, and hence does not allow for full resolution and integration.

To be sure, any previous ambivalent feelings, conflicts, or hostilities with death wishes can play an important part in the mourning process. The magical belief in the causality of the death with great guilt may be the major contributor to subsequent serious psycho-pathology. Freud discussed this point in his paper on "Dostoevsky and Parricide" (1928). There he clearly related the pre-death wish for the object's demise to the actual death of the object followed by a transient period of triumph and joy. This, however, quickly gave rise to guilt, and the self-punishing attitude persisted. In his biography (1953-1957), Jones mentions that when Freud was 19 months old, his next younger sibling, a brother, died aged eight months. "In a letter to Fliess (1897) he [Freud] admits the evil wishes he had against his rival and adds that their fulfilment in his death had aroused self-reproaches, a tendency to which had remained ever since." These self-reproaches can in susceptible persons result in abnormal mourning reactions, which may include melancholia and psychosis. In this paper, these pathological conditions, though considered, are not specifically focused upon.

The third phase of the acute mourning process is that of the separation reaction. This may manifest itself in various ways, and will be more intense in individuals with earlier unresolved conflicts in this sphere. The reality of the loss intensifies this reaction, and initially recognition of the traumatic event may be avoided. Thus the absence of grief described by Deutsch (1937) may be involved in this inability to recognize that the object's absence is not temporary but permanent, and that the object is dead.

A patient talking of her inability to face the idea of her mother's death reported in an analytic session that to face it was "too difficult." Not only had she become aware of her grief and pain, but she was attempting to defend herself against what she described as feelings of "nothingness and emptiness." She gradually recognized that to mourn was to acknowledge the nothingness of her mother, and this meant emptiness inside her. Defensively she kept her mother alive in heaven and used religion as an aid to her ego in avoiding the "total nothingness of death."

The ego-adaptive task in this aspect of the mourning process requires a reorientation in the perceptual sphere involving both self and object. In order to master that part of the early anxiety experience related to separation, a total internalization is required, or a greater dependence on previously internalized and integrated relationships in the ego of object representations. Anna Freud (1936) has described this as object constancy. Where internal object representations are not well integrated, where tensions exist in the form of ambivalences unsolved and with non-neutralized aggression, the energy balance is seriously disturbed. The integrative task becomes greater at reconciling external reality with internal structures where the prior developmental pattern was defective or distorted.

The representation of the lost object is recathected because the instinctual energies that would have been discharged in actual relationship to the object, being now undischarged, recathect the internalized object image. Where there is poor differentation between self and not-self, where there is poor ego integration, the hypercathected internal object may be projected and hallucinated as an external figure. The hallucinatory process in this instance is a manifestation of what happens when instinctual tension is not discharged because the real object is lost, and we have a primitive type of ego organization. Separation is not accepted and the lost object is hallucinatively retained.

Introjection and identification in terms of psychic structural formation relate to this point. Both, however, are internalization operations. If we view introjection as a process, mode, or technique, and identification as the end-result of the process in which introjection is initially present, the confusion between these two terms may be clarified and may shed light on subsequent mourning processes.

In a healthy object relationship, where there has been total assimilation or identification, the mourning process is comparatively short-lived, and comes to a spontaneous end. It may reflect whatever unresolved components of incorporation without identification are still present, but a comparatively healthy ego integration allows reality to be perceived, accepted, and dealt with appropriately without lasting ego immobilization. Grief is present, but is of such intensity and duration that it is not considered pathological. When an object has been introjected without identification, it exists as an encapsulated image in the ego as the result of the lack of assimilation. This introjected object retains characteristics of the original object, in many ways intensified as a result of the ambivalent feelings connected with the object. When the external object dies, an abnormal mourning process ensues. This may be reflected in the inability to accept the actual death of the object, and the retention of the introjected image with responses indicative of the fact that this introjected object still exists. Because of the lack of completeness of identification and ego integration, the ambivalences directed towards this object enhance the mourning process, if it occurs, with the formation of severe symptoms of melancholia or self-destruction, or both. When the actual death of the external object is totally denied with the absence of grief, what is found is a retention of the introjected object as an entity of the relationship, and this object is perpetuated externally by means of secret internal communications with this object. An example of this phenomenon has been observed in three adult patients, one of whom has been briefly discussed above.

In all the cases a parent had died prior to the patient's sixth birthday. Throughout the years there had been a retention of the deceased parent in the form of a fantasied figure who was in heaven; to whom the patient could talk and tell whatever he or she wished; who never verbally or actively responded to the patient; and who was always all-seeing and omnipresent. The fantasies about these retained figures came out with great caution and difficulty lest the patients be shamed for retaining these images. In all three instances the patients denied ever visiting the cemetery where the deceased parent was buried, and there was a period of amnesia that extended from the moment when the patient was told of the parent's death until many months later.

In one of these cases, the man's father died when he was a very young child, and his mother died when he was an adult. The process described above was observed in connection with his father's decease. In the case of his mother, however, he was able to accept her death, but continued to visit her grave regularly and to speak to her. He still envisoned her as alive, but not able to answer him.

This retention of the object as a figure that can be spoken to and envisioned, and the denial of its demise, interferes with mourning. When there has been incomplete identification, that is, when the identification process has not come about or has been arrested at a preliminary stage owing to immaturity or arrest of development, there is either a melancholic depressive response, or a denial of the death of the deceased with ego arrestation, distortion, or defect.

Patients report that following particular analytic hours they continue to talk to the analyst even though they have left his office. In these reports the analyst rarely answers, and as the analytic process proceeds, this "talking to the analyst as analyst" gradually diminishes and finally ceases with the integrated assumption of a "communication with self." It is maintained that in these instances a process occurs similar to that mentioned above, namely initial introjection of the analyst as an object with later identification and assimilation. He is retained in a somewhat encapsulated form with whom internal communication proceeds. When identification is complete, the introject is assimilated and the presence of the separate imago disappears.

In "Group Psychology and the Analysis of the Ego," Freud discusses the relationship of identifications to object cathexes and object relations. Object cathexis implies an object that is outside and energized. Identification is the process and end result wherein changes occur in the ego and actions take place without reference to the assimilated object. "Identification with an object that is renounced or lost as a substitute for that object" occurs through the "introjection of it into the ego." We assume that "identification is the earliest and original form of emotional tie with an object." Thus "in a regressive way it becomes a substitute for a libidinal object-tie" by introjection. In identification with an object, the result is being like the object; in choosing the person as an object, the result is having the object. Identification may appear regressively and defensively in lieu of "object-choice." In mourning this defensive wholesale identification with the lost object can be used to avoid the painful resolution of mourning work.

In Freud's monumental *Inhibitions, Symptoms and Anxiety,* (1926), the last seven pages are directed to a discussion of anxiety, pain, and mourning. In this section, Freud differentiates mourning from anxiety, in that the former results from the loss of an object, while the latter is "a reaction to the danger of losing the object." In both responses there is pain, although it may be more clearly identified in the mourning reaction of the adult. Freud, citing the infant's response to the loss of the mother, even on a temporary basis, states that "the first determinant of anxiety which the ego itself introduces is loss of perception of the object (which is equated with loss of the object itself)." This antedates the fear of loss of love which has not as yet appeared. It is regression to this early stage of separation and its defenses that characterizes this phase of the mourning process.

The response to recognizing the separation and its permanence gives rise to anxiety and also to anger. Both these affects are experienced in the acute mourning stage. Defenses to deal with these threatening affects may quickly come into existence. Freud states that pain is "the actual reaction to the loss of the object, and anxiety is the reaction to the danger which that loss entails, and in its further displacement a reaction to the danger of the loss of the object itself." This differentiation, though valid, need not be mutually exclusive. The object is dead and is no longer externally present. This results in pain, but also in anxiety. The ego cannot completely accept the reality and finality of the separation in time and space, and so anxiety about the loss is experienced. That part of the ego which regresses to pleasure-principle operation does feel the pain owing to the absence of the object. The later chronic mourning work is not characterized by excessive anxiety, as the object is more and more accepted as permanently gone. Instead pain continues "in view of the high degree and insatiable nature of the cathexis of longing which is concentrated on the object by the bereaved person during the reproduction of the situations in which he must undo the ties that attach him to it."

The anger at being left and frustrated is also characteristically part of the acute separation reaction. Typically it comes out in an undisguised fashion in children. They are frustrated and enraged. In adults, however, this anger may be displaced onto others, as hostility to the dead is not easily tolerated by the mourning ego. Thus physicians, hospital personnel, undertakers, become the focus of displaced hostility. There may be accusations against close relatives, or even self-accusations about what the mourner could or should have done. This anger is usually unrealistic and unwarranted, and in the adult may not be present in identifiable form. It may fuse with the grief, and in the chronic mourning work be indicated by feelings of depression or through various guilt-expiating rituals.

When there is anger about the loss, it is indicative that the separation is recognized and acknowledged. In this sense anger is restitutive, as cathexis can be discharged through the affective experience of anger. Thus the anger is in the service of mastery of the shock, panic, and grief. As to the reasons for the anger, we must recognize that the range is a narcissistic rage. It is as if the child is screaming "It happens to me and I have no control over it. It is the parents' fault and they should have prevented it." When the rage is discharged diffusely, frustration at being left is avoided, as is the feeling of helplessness.

Clinically the frustration consequent on the death of a parent or spouse is due not only to the factors mentioned above, but also to the increased demand made upon the bereaved by the other survivors. Thus the child who loses a parent and is expected to fulfill the needs of the bereaved surviving parent suffers a double loss and is angry at this. The handling of the bereavement by the various mourners as well as by the social mores and religious customs can aid or reinforce various expressive and inhibitory activities involved in the mourning process. This latter point will be discussed elsewhere.

Separation anxiety may manifest itself in various ways. There may be a reluctance to be separated from the corpse. Thus one may look longingly and fixedly at it, at the coffin, or at the grave. There may be the false perception that the dead is still breathing or moving. Afterwards there may be an inability to accept that the lost object is permanently gone. Thus Queen Victoria ordered that her husband's study must not be disturbed in a single detail after his death. It almost seemed as though the reality of permanent separation could be avoided by keeping the room ready for occupation. Variations of this denial of separation may be manifested by displacement of cathexis from the object onto auxiliaries which are reminders of the departed. Thus old letters, keepsakes, portraits, eyeglasses, bits of hair, clothing, and other intimate possessions are treated as if they have to be constant reminders of the existence of the object. In some instances this reflects the inability to let the object die, be buried and let life go on. In "Mourning and Melancholia," Freud notes that the struggle involved in abandoning a libido position previously occupied by a loved object could be so intense that "a turning away from reality" can result and the object "clung to through the medium of an hallucinatory wish-psychosis." Eventually, however, in the normal individual reality gains the day.

In mourning, libido detachment or object decathexis occurs topographically in the system Unconscious. The process then proceeds through the Preconscious into the Conscious. It is here that reality perception can occur. When this path is blocked owing to ambivalence, as Freud pointed out in "Mourning and Melancholia," repression continues to operate and pathological mourning results.

The task of mourning consist of internal object decathexis with the freeing of energy for later recathectic activities. As Freud pointed out, this process may be stopped at the level of a hallucinatory wish-psychosis which denies the death of the object, or it may go on to completion wherein the ego becomes free and uninhibited when the mourning work is finished.

The mourning process end result may stop at various intermediate steps short of completion. Thus one may get total or partial undifferentiated identification with the object, as was seen in the clinical data cited above. or on the side of completion of mourning, partially unneutralized cathexis that is only moderately changed though still bound and ego-inhibiting.

To recapitulate briefly, the acute stage of the mourning process refers to the immediate phases following the loss of the object. These phases consist of the shock, grief, pain, reaction to separation, and the beginning internal object decathexis with the recognition of the loss. The reaction to separation brings with it anxiety as the perception of the loss in time and space is integrated, as well as the anger reaction.

As the acute stage of the mourning process progresses, the chronic stage gradually takes over. Here we find various manifestations of adaptive mechanisms attempting to integrate the experience of the loss with reality so that life activities can go on. Adaptation in the chronic stage of mourning involves the further integration of newer reality demands which include newer functional need gratifications and demands. The ego is able to withstand the more immediate effects of the loss of the object, and to begin the reparative aspect of the more lasting adaptation. Freud has described this chronic stage of the mourning process as the mourning work. This work is a continuation of the process that began more acutely immediately following the loss.

The sequential dreams occurring during the mourning process are indicators of this work of the ego. Changes occurring in the perception of the lost object in the dream reveal the gradual withdrawal of cathexis from the object and its associations. Thus in one instance, initial dreams of the departed object immediately after the death still keep the object alive, functioning and communicating. Gradually the object disappeared from the dreams per se, and in late phases of the chronic mourning process, a dream was reported wherein an individual spoke of a funeral and burial that had occurred several months previously. Associations to the dream dealt with "finally accepting" that the figure was dead, buried although still remembered. Here the acceptance of the reality of the loss came about, and secondary process reality-principle-oriented behavior utilizing memory was in evidence.

Another patient reported that as he accepted the reality of the death of his father. his dreams began to lose color. Grey was the predominant shade, until one day a grey dream was reported as having a "sprig of green" in it. His associations dealt with "something coming to life again." It was as though the freed energy heralded "the arrival of spring, when things began to grow again after a long cold grey winter."

In analysis the mourning work can be followed by noting the varying restitutive ego activities. One of the patients mentioned above was unable to mourn, as it was indicative of the acceptance of the death. If the death was not accepted, then mourning was not going to occur. This patient at times even wondered if she had ever had a real mother. As the analysis proceeded, her great guilt towards her mother came out. The mother had died when the patient was four and a half. The multi-ambivalences overwhelmed the patient with excessive guilt and anxiety. This was strongly reinforced by the strong oedipal feelings towards the father. As the analysis continued, the mourning process gradually began and proceeded in the fashion described above. The transference neurosis provided this woman with objects that rekindled her repressed conflicts. Various shades of her mixed feelings emerged, and her dreams began to deal with meaningful figures. In a similar way to the dreams mentioned above, her early dreams dealt with the deceased object as being alive. This woman actually retained her mother in heaven as a live figure. Each night she spoke to her, and the patient "knew that mother" heard her. As the analyst was cathected, he became the replacement for the mother, and thus it was with him that conversations took place by night. With the energizing of the introject of the analyst, the mother was allowed to die, and the patient began to grieve, feel anxious, cry, and dream of meaningful figures who had died. This long and interesting analysis clearly indicated that the degree of ambivalence towards the dead object before the death occurred was related to the stage of psychic development achieved at the time of the loss. This ego distortion in part determined the length of the mourning work as well as the type of mourning reaction. In instances where melancholia or absent mourning occurs, we must look for the pathological interferences with the mourning process. It is not within the scope of this paper to discuss the effect of therapy on the mourning process. This problem has been dealt with by Fleming and Altschul (1959), and also by the present author elsewhere.

Any death in childhood, especially that of a parent, interferes with the growth and developmental processes of the gradual detachment of libido from infantile images of the object. These parental internalizations are important in the integration and structuralization of the ego and superego.

In considering the mourning process, it is important to note that similarities can be observed in all such adaptational activities. But there are significant differences also. Firstly, the type of loss suffered must be considered. A permanent loss through death may be quite different from a temporary separation that is time-limited and not absolute. A sudden unexpected death results in a more acute response than a chronic loss due to institutionalization or even death. Secondly, we must recognize the significance of who or what is lost. The death of a parent in childhood differs from the death of a parent in adulthood. The death of the mother during the oedipal stage of a girl may have a different effect from what it has for an oedipal boy. The death of a sibling in childhood differs from the death of one's own child. The death of a spouse may be more significant than the loss of a political election in which there may be great involvement. It is difficult to generalize in this field, but further precision and delineation are necessary in our study of different types of losses and of the different objects that can be lost.

We must also recognize that the degree of maturity of the psychic apparatus of the mourner will be another important variable to investigate in the mourning process. Ego defects, distortions, or arrests cannot result in healthy mourning processes. The function of the lost object to the mourner is closely related to object replacement after the mourning process has ended.

In all probability the purest form of the mourning process occurs in mature adults. Even here, however, the loss of a child can never be fully integrated and totally accepted by the mother or the father. In an exchange of letters with Ludwig Binswanger (1957), Freud wrote on the anniversary of his dead daughter's thirty-sixth birthday, "We know that the acute grief we feel after a loss will come to an end, but that we will remain inconsolable, and will never find a substitute. Everything that comes to take the place of the lost object, even if it fills it completely, nevertheless remains something different." In a later note, Freud recalls that he cannot forget the younger child of his deceased daughter, who also had died several years earlier. About this child Freud wrote, "to me this child had taken the place of all of my children and other grandchildren, and since then, since Heinele's death, I don't care for my grandchildren any more, but find no joy in life either. This is also the secret of my indifference—it was called courage—towards the danger to my own life."

Freud touches on the possible different mourning reactions that may occur in later life and senescence. Energies may not be so freely available as internal objects may not be so easily decathected. What one can do with these liberated energies in older age differs from what may result earlier in life. Personal observations made on this point reveal that external objects may not be invested with the decathected libido, if it is available, by older people. More frequently, economic investments of less object-directed activities are made, and more narcissistic withdrawal occurs. Where there is an inability to make such shifts, too much ego depletion results and death may occur. It is not infrequently observed that shortly after the death of a long-standing marital partner, the survivor also succumbs.

In these instances adaptation to life without the object is not possible.

The acute mourning reactions gradually become less intense and more distanced. As the ego is able to perceive reality correctly, various discharge techniques become more apparent. Little episodes that are suddenly recalled may serve as poignant reminders of the past. They may rekindle the dying fire of grief and tears for a short time. The response, however, is short-lived. There may be gradual acceptance of the fact that someone is not in a particular place at a specific time. Slips in conversation may indicate that the death of the object is still partially unaccepted. With the disposal of the dead figure's possessions, and having to deal with the alterations in practical reality, the ego begins to cathect new activities. True, the need to give up a house, a social group, or the like as a result of the separation may serve to institute new mourning processes and increase the integrative task of the ego, but these also are gradually worked through.

As personal possessions are dispersed, living arrangements altered, decisions made without reference to the lost object, the ego recognizes that narcissistic supply can be had elsewhere. Newer external objects become the focus of "give and take." These newer objects are seen not as exact substitutes for the lost objects, but as figures which permit reality relations that are mutually satisfactory. The loss of the dead object is assimilated, accepted, and the bereavement can come to an end.

Intra-psychically the object that is lost becomes part of the ego through identification. This may be manifested by activity such as a woman showed after the death and mourning for her husband. When confronted with a problem one day she said, "I deliberately looked at this in a way that my husband might have done had he been alive. I was surprised that I could honestly face it and deal with it in a way I never could have previously." This identification with facets of the lost object is frequently seen after the death of a close relative. In part it may be due to an increased cathexis of the internalized object to overcome the effects of the external loss, and thus take over some of the functional activities that the dead object previously provided.

Identification with the analyst after the termination of analysis allows the process of self-analysis to continue. The observing ego of the patient becomes sufficiently expanded and integrated for observation, interpretation, and experiencing to occur autonomously and non-volitionally. This healthy development is the end product following termination of a successful analysis. The mechanism is similar to though not the same as that following the successful completion of a mourning process. The ego is enriched and different, and can take over functions that were previously handled by the strongly cathected external object.

In the essay on "Transience," Freud notes that mourning comes to a spontaneous end "when it has renounced everything that has been lost, then it has consumed itself, and one's libido is once more free (in so far as we are still young and active) to replace the lost objects by fresh ones equally or still more previous." The lost object is not forgotten, nor is the new object identical with the lost if the mourner's ego is capable of differentiation. The end of mourning occurs with a re-

sultant identification in the form of a consciously decathected memory trace.

Sporadic episodes of mourning may still occur in connection with specific events or items, but these become fewer and less time-concentrated. New mourning experiences can serve to revive past mourning reactions that may still have bits of unresolved work present. In the instance of the loss of a very significant object, the total mourning process may never be completed.

Various religious rituals, when divested of their theological implications, emphasize the cultural evolution of mores and folkways which can defensively assist the ego in the adaptation involved in the mourning process. These will be discussed in another paper.

Mourning as a process of adaptation to a significant loss occurs in the attempt to maintain the constancy of the internal psychic equilibrium. The process consists of an acute and chronic stage. Various phases of these stages as well as their characteristic defensive operations have been presented. The ego's ability to perceive the reality of the loss; to appreciate the temporal and spatial permanence of the loss; to acknowledge the significance of the loss; to be able to deal with the acute sudden disruption following the loss with attendant fears of weakness, helplessness, frustration, rage, pain, and anger; to be able effectively to reinvest new objects or ideals with energy, and so re-establish different but satisfactory relationships, are the key factors in this process. The process has certain phenomena, utilizes certain mechanisms, and has a definite end-point. Pathological interferences with it result in maladaptations with resultant psychopathology.

INFRA-HUMAN RESPONSES TO DEATH

As mentioned in the first section of this presentation, the evolution of adaptive mechanisms and processes is related to survival of the species. When attempting to find information dealing with the phylogenetic roots of the mourning process, we quickly realize that little has been reported about the response of infra-human animals to death. When accounts have appeared, they have usually been either anecdotal or detailed observational reports and inferences by field workers. Systematic investigations of this problem have not been made. In the examples cited below, the reported data will be presented and comparisons will be made to note any similarities with various component phases of the human mourning process.

Death is a universal biological phenomenon from which no individual animal other than certain protozoa escapes. Although a biological event, with the evolution of familial organization, and psychological internalizations and structuralizations, it has taken on psycho-social significance. Involved in this is the need to differentiate the mourning response for a meaningful deceased object from the significance of death as an event that may involve the survivor himself. It is not my intention here to deal with the latter area except as it relates to the mourning response. Nature has seemingly evolved a homeostatic process to cope with the event of separation through death in the form of the mourning process in man. Investigating the responses of certain animals to the death of meaningful figures, I feel that the mourning process is an adaptation that has evolved phylogenetically. Although we cannot equate the responses observed in infra-human animals to the events of the mourning process as it is characteristically seen in man, the strikingly parallel reactions in non-human animals to certain phases of the mourning process in man seem to indicate phylogenetic evolutionary anlage for the human mourning process.

Systematic observations and investigations of animals' responses to the death of a previously meaningful object have not been carried out. Reports of such events are found with great difficulty, and these are mainly behavioristic observations. Dr. Schneirla, of the American Museum of Natural History, informed the author that behavior described as depression, occurring after the removal of a meaningful figure, has been observed in certain mammals and birds, but not in reptiles, amphibians, or fish. This would seemingly set a phylogenetic base for the development of this adaptational process. In this paper, only the mammalian references will be cited.

It is common knowledge that dogs attached to their owners go through various grief and mourning responses when separations occur. A recent description of such an event, quoted from the newspaper account, stated that:

Corky, a small, forlorn fox terrier, ran away three times to sit in front of Our Lady of the Angels School, waiting for his mistress, Angelene. Angelene, 14, had died in the fire-scarred building. But Corky could not comprehend this. Three times the runaway dog was brought home to Angelene's mother, Mrs. Julia Lechnik. Finally, she locked Corky inside the house. Mournfully the dog wandered to Angelene's room and crawled under her bed. Corky did not come out for four days. He neither ate nor slept.

Towards Christmas, Corky at last began to perk up. "He'd still go to the front door in the afternoon, looking for Angie," Mrs. Lechnik said, "but at least he began eating again."

Another report concerned a Japanese dog named Hachi:

Born on 20 November, 1923, Hachi was sold a month later to a professor at Tokyo University. Hachi soon formed the habit of going to the railroad station with his master each morning, and waiting there until he returned from the university on the afternoon train.

When the professor died in 1925, his family moved to another part of Tokyo. Hachi, however, returned to the railroad station each day to await the master who would never return. He set out for the station in the morning and remained there until evening. Hachi made his daily trip to the station for ten years, until he died on 8 March, 1935.

Interestingly a statue of Hachi was erected in front of the Tokyo railroad station with the inscription "The Faithful Dog, Hachi." In 1953, Japan issued a stamp in his honor.

Lorenz (1952, 1954), has also reported his own experiences of the faithful devotion shown him by his lupus-derived dogs. His pet, Stasi, refused to return to her young puppies when it interfered with her being with Lorenz. Lorenz has noted that a lupus dog (wolf-derived) who has once sworn his allegiance to a certain man, is forever a one-man dog. No stranger can take the master's place, and if the master leaves, the animal becomes "literally unbalanced," obeying no one and acting like "an ownerless cur." Lorenz has observed that lupus bitches seem to have a monagamous type of fidelity to a particular dog, and in chows especially the oath of fidelity is seemingly irrevocable. Lorenz has advanced a theory that explains the difference in this fixed type of object relationship characteristic of wolf-derived dogs as contrasted with other canine varieties. It would carry us far afield to elaborate his hypothetical premises here. Instead it is interesting to note that the behavior described as grief, denial, and time-limited anorexia following the death of Angelene seems similar to what we see in man during acute phases of the mourning process. Corky seems to have been able eventually to accept his mistress's absence, but Hachi (wolf-derived no doubt) presumably could not adapt to the change in his life.

J. L. Jones (1958) has described the behavior of a ewe when her lamb has died. The ewe does not wish to leave her dead lamb, and if she loses sight of it she "will race around and bleat in demented searching." In order to effect the adoption of another lamb by the bereaved ewe, the farmer quickly ties a length of twine to the lamb's neck and then, when the ewe is near, gives it a little tug. The ewe sees movement, fancies her lamb is alive, and makes to follow. The lamb is kept moving with little tugs of the string until the ewe is following it into the barn, where it is quickly whisked out of sight round the corner and as rapidly as possible a live lamb is presented to the questing mother.

We can infer from this report that the anxiety attendant on the separation of the dead lamb from its mother is short-lived when a viable substitute is carefully introduced as a new object. Movement as an indicator of life is quite important in sheep. When a viable moving lamb could be substituted for the dead one, the ewe presumably did not know the difference provided no delay occurred. The primitiveness of this response is one that is akin to the functional substitution that is possible for the human neonate in the early months of life. The association of life with bodily movement is also not limited to sheep. We know it is frequently used as evidence of life or death by man as well. Dr. Schneirla (personal communication) described the behavior of a cat, reared with a rat, when the two were separated. The cat yowled, cried, ate very little, and lost weight. Similar accounts for various birds have been recorded by Lorenz and others. The reports of the dogs, unlike that of the ewe, seem to indicate a reaction that includes greater specificity and differentiation of the object.

Spitz (1946) writes that substitution of the mother or absence from the mother prior to the sixth month does not give rise to anaclitic depression. If the mother was a "good" object, removal after the sixth month for an unbroken period of three months gave rise to anaclitic depression, whereas if the mother had been a "bad" one, the incidence of depression was markedly reduced, as was its severity when it occurred. Spitz relates these findings to the ego organization in the second half of the first year. The ego then can coordinate elementary perception and apperception, can coordinate elementary volitional motility, and has "a capacity for elementary differentiation of affect as is involved in the capacity to produce distinctly discernible positive or negative affective reactions on appropriate stimulation." Before six months, the infant has achieved no locomotion and so is quite passive in its social demands from the environment. The adult initiates all activity. In the sheep, the response seemingly is that of the young child before the sixth month of age. In both, substitution and equivalence are possible without difficulty.

The reports of simian responses to death are more impressive in connection with an evolutionary concept of the mourning process. Professor Washburn has sent me the following direct account of his observations of baboons:

I witnessed one case of the relations of a mother to a dead baby baboon. One day I heard a tremendous scream of a kind I had not heard before. When I located the troop of baboons (a troop which I had seen repeatedly and knew well) I saw that one of the larger babies was dead. A baby of this size jumps on its mother's back when the troop moves and takes care of itself pretty well. The mother walked away from the baby, but the largest male of the troop refused to leave it and set up a terrific noise of screaming and barking until the mother came back. She then picked up the baby and carried it while walking on three legs. This process was repeated at least four or five times until the troop finally reached their sleeping trees.

I believe this case is unique in that it was the leader of the troop who urged the mother back to the baby after she had left it. Small babies who die are carried by the mother without the urging of other baboons. I never saw this, but it has been observed many times.

The need to deny death and effect separation is inferred from this first-hand report. Zuckerman (1932) also in studying baboons has found similar behavior indicative of the denial of death. Thus young animals would cling to the carcasses of their dead mothers, or mothers would cling to their dead young, and in the London Zoological Gardens baboons as well as apes tried to prevent the removal of a dead animal as if it were the abduction of a live one. Even in the sexual sphere, "When a female baboon dies in a 'sexual fight' on Monkey Hill, the males continue to quarrel over her dead body, which they also use as a sexual object until it is forcibly removed by the keepers." This retention of the dead and attempt to treat it as sill living is characteristic only for the higher anthropoids and man. Other species may show some response to the death of the object, but deal with the actual dead body as dead and having no functional appeal. Zuckerman concludes that "monkeys and apes . . . react to their dead companions as if the latter are alive but passive." This may be the manifestation of the primitive denial of death mechanisms relating to separation anxiety that is seen in early stages of mourning in man. Eissler (1955), however, feels that only the human species knows of death and that the apes are ignorant of it. This may be so; animals, however, can discern things that are not alive, so that responding to non-living animals as if they were alive seems rather to involve a denial-like mechanism.

Chimpanzees seem to show even more dramatic responses to death. Brown in his paper "Grief in the Chimpanzee" (1879), writing about the behavior of the surviving chimpanzee after his partner died, states:

With the chimpanzee, the evidences of a certain degree of genuine grief were well marked. The two animals had lived together for many months, and were much attached to each other; they were seldom apart and generally had their arms about each other's neck; they never quarrelled, even over a pretended display of partiality by their keeper in feeding them, and if occasion required one to be handled with any degree of force, the other was always prepared to do battle in its behalf on the first cry of fright. After the death of the female, which took place early in the morning, the remaining one made many attempts to rouse her, and when he found this to be impossible his rage and grief were painful to witness. Tearing the hair, or rather snatching at the short hair on his head, was always one of his common expressions of extreme anger, and was now largely indulged in, but the ordinary yell of rage which he set up at first, finally changed to a cry which the keeper of the animals assures me he had never heard before, and which would be most nearly represented by hah-ah-ah-ah-ah, uttered somewhat under the breath, and with a plaintive sound like a moan. With this he made repeated efforts to arouse her, lifting up her head and hands, pushing her violently and rolling her over. After her body was removed from the cage—a proceeding which he violently opposed—he became more quiet, and remained so as long as his keeper was with him, but catching sight of the body once when the door was opened and again when it was carried past the front of the cage, he became violent, and cried for the rest of the day. The day following, he sat still most of the time and moaned continuously—this gradually passed away, however, and from that time he has only manifested a sense of a change in his surroundings by a more devoted attachment to his keeper, and a longer fit of anger when he leaves him. On these occasions it is curious to observe that the plaintive cry first heard when the female died is frequently, though not always, made use of, and when present, is heard towards the close of the fit of anger. It may well be that this sound having been specialized as a note of grief, and in this case never having been previously called into use by the occurrence of its proper emotion, now finds expression on the return of even the lesser degree of the same feeling given rise to by the absence of his keeper, and follows the first outbreak of rage in the same manner as the sobbing of a child in the natural sequence of a passionate fit of crying. It may be noted too, that as his attachment to his keeper is evidently stronger than when there was another to divide with him the attention which they received, the grief now caused by the man's absence would naturally be much stronger and a more exact representation of the gestures of grief would be made.

Notwithstanding the intensity of his sorrow at first, it seems sufficiently evident that now a vivid recollection of the nature of the past association is not present. To test this a mirror was placed before him, with the expectation that on seeing a figure so exactly like his lost mate, some of the customary signs of recognition would take place, but even by caressing and pretending to feed the figure in the glass, not a trace of the expected feeling could be excited. In fact, the only visible indication of a change of circumstances is that while the two of them were accustomed to sleep at night in each other's arms on a blanket on the floor, which they moved from place to place to suit their convenience, since the death of the one, the other has invariably slept on a cross-beam at the top of the cage, returning to inherited habit and showing, probably, that the apprehension of unseen dangers has been heightened by his sense of loneliness.

On looking over the field of animal emotion it seems evident that any high degree of permanence in grief of this nature belongs only to man; slight indications of its persistence in memory are visible in some of the higher animals and domesticated races, but in most of them the feeling appears to be excited only by the failure of the inanimate body, while present to the sight, to perform the accustomed actions.

The foundation of the sentiment of grief is probably in a perception of loss sustained in being deprived of services which had been of use. An unrestrained indulgence in an emotion so powerful as this has become in its higher forms, would undoubtedly prevent due attention to the bodily necessities of the animal subjected to it; in man, its prostrating effects are mainly counteracted by an intelligent recognition of the desirability of repairing the injury suffered, and in him, therefore, the feeling may exist without serious detriment to his welfare, but among the lower animals it would seem probable that any tendency to its development would be checked by its own destructive effects—the feeling, for instance, would most frequently occur on the death of a mate—a deep and lasting grief would then tend to prevent a new association of like nature and would thus impede the performance of the first function of an animal in its relation to its kind—that of reproduction.

We can see illustrated here the shock, grief, and separation anxiety stages characteristic of the acute mourning responses of man. The sustained mourning work seemed, however, to be absent. This phase of the mourning process seems to be uniquely human. Brown suggests this is because of memory differences. The difference in type of object relationships with intra-psychic representation of specific objects and structuralizations would be the more precise explanation. The apparent anger of the chimpanzee at his inability to rouse his dead companion is seemingly connected with the impotent grief activity described above for man. To be sure, we might postulate that this could be reflective of anger at being left or frustrated, but this would be only a speculative interpretation of these data. In our patients this anger response is often found, though concealed by the depression that is present.

Garner (1900) has also reported extensively on the history and observations made on a particular chimpanzee, Aaron, which he studied extensively from his capture in the jungle until his death in captivity. I shall quote parts of his report, as they pertain to our present interest.

At the time of his capture his mother was killed in the act of defending him from the cruel hunters. When she fell to the earth, mortally wounded, this brave little fellow stood by her trembling body defending it against her slayers, until he was overcome by superior force, seized by his captors, bound with strips of bark, and carried away into captivity.

After he was captured, Aaron was placed with another chimpanzee, Moses. In time Moses fell ill, and the following reaction was reported:

At night, when they were put to rest, they lay cuddled up in each other's arms, and in the morning they were always found in the same close embrace.

But on the morning Moses died the conduct of Aaron was unlike anything I had observed before. When I approached their snug little house and drew aside the curtain, I found him sitting in one corner of the cage. His face wore a look of concern, as if he were aware that something awful had occurred. When I opened the door he neither moved nor uttered any sound. I do not know whether or not apes have any name for death, but they surely know what it is.

Moses was dead. His cold body lay in its usual place; but it was entirely covered over with the piece of canvas kept in the cage for bed-clothing. I do not know whether or not Aaron had covered him up, but he seemed to realize the situation. I took him by the hand and lifted him out of the cage, but he was reluctant. I had the body removed and placed on a bench about thirty feet away, in order to dissect it and prepare the skin and the skeleton for preservation. When I proceeded to do this, I had Aaron confined to the cage, lest he should annoy and hinder me at the work; but he cried and fretted until he was re-released. It is not meant that he shed tears over the loss of his companion, for the lachrymal glands and ducts are not developed in these apes; but they manifest concern and regret, which are motives of the passion of sorrow. But being left alone was the cause of Aaron's sorrow. When released he came and took his seat near the dead body, where he sat the whole day long and watched the operation.

After this Aaron was never quiet for a moment if he could see or hear me, until I secured another of his kind as companion for him; then his interest in me abated in a measure, but his affection for me remained intact. . . .

The new companion, Elisheba, a female, became ill, and once more the opportunity to observe Aaron's reactions presented itself. Hour after hour Aaron sat holding her locked in his arms. He was not posing for a picture, nor was he aware how deeply his manners touched the human heart. Even the brawny men who work about the place paused to watch him in his tender offices to her, and his staid keeper was moved to pity by his kindness and his patience. For days she lingered on the verge of death. She became too feeble to sit up; but as she lay on her bed of straw, he sat by her side, resting his folded arms upon her and refusing to allow any one to touch her. His look of deep concern showed that he felt the gravity of her case in a degree that bordered on grief. He was grave and silent, as if he foresaw the sad end that was near at hand. My frequent visits were a source of comfort to him, and he evinced a pleasure in my coming.

On the morning of her decease I found him sitting by her as usual. At my approach he quietly rose to his feet and advanced to the front of the cage. Opening the door, I put my arm in and caressed him. He looked into my face and then at the prostrate form of his mate. The last dim sparks of life were not yet gone out, as the slight motion of the breast betrayed; but the limbs were cold and limp. While I leaned over to examine more closely, he crouched down by her side and watched with deep concern to see the result. I laid my hand upon her heart to ascertain if the last hope was gone; he looked at me, and then placed his own hand by the side of mine, and held it there as if he knew the purport of the act.

At length the breast grew still, and the feeble beating of the heart ceased. The lips were parted, and the dim eyes were half-way closed; but he sat by as if she were asleep. The sturdy keeper came to remove the body from the cage; but Aaron clung to it and refused to allow him to touch it. I took the little mourner in my arms, but he watched the keeper jealously and did not want him to remove or disturb the body. It was laid on a bunch of straw in front of the cage, and he was returned to his place; but he clung to me so firmly that it was difficult to release his hold. He cried in a piteous tone and fretted and worried, as if he fully realized the worst. The body was then removed from view, but poor little Aaron was not consoled.

After this he grew more attached to me than ever. When I went to visit him he was happy and cheerful in my presence; but the keeper said that while I was away he was often gloomy and morose. As long as he could see me or hear my voice, he would fret and cry for me to come to him. When I had left him, he would scream as long as he had any hope of inducing me to return.

A few days after the death of Elisheba the keeper put a young monkey in the cage with him, for company. This gave him some relief from the monotony of his own society, but never quite filled the place of the lost one. With this little friend, however, he amused himself in many ways. He nursed it so zealously and hugged it so tightly that the poor little monkey was often glad to escape from him in order to have a rest. But the task of catching it again afforded him almost as much pleasure as he found in nursing it.

Shortly after Elisheba's death, Aaron himself died. Not having been present during his short illness or at the time of his death, I cannot relate any of the scenes accompanying them; but the kind old keeper who attended him declares that he never became reconciled to the death of Elisheba, and that his loneliness preyed upon him almost as much as the disease.

The description of Aaron's reaction, though colored by the sentimental terms used by Garner, could seemingly be a behavioristic account of the acute mourning phase in man. Again we have no evidence of mourning work per se, but we have ample evidence of grief-like reactions following what seems to have been some form of meaningful object relationship. The possible utilization of Garner as a new object after Moses' death bears some similarity to the recathectic phase following the completion of the mourning work.

Yerkes (1925) has described the screaming responses of survivors in gorillas and monkeys, as well as in chimpanzees. In other reports (1929), surviving animals insisted on following the body of the deceased companion when it was removed, and on being prevented from doing this, cried for a while, and then became listless and spiritless for several days. They further state "that depression, grief, and sorrow are occasionally manifested by the chimpanzee is beyond dispute. Definitely established also is the fact that weeping in the human sense does not occur. The typical approach to it is whining, moaning, or crying in the manner of a person in distress. Tears we have never observed."

This tearless moan has been reported to the author by two patients. In one instance when the patient first saw the corpse of his mother, he cried and screamed in what was described as "an inhuman howl." He had no tears. In the second case, the patient on hearing of the death of her mother screamed and shrieked "like an animal" but without tears. In both instances the tears occurred after the shock period passed and the grief phase came into focus. This crying response, unlike the tears accompanying grief and depression, is very rarely recovered in any but the original stimulating situation. It is transitory, but undoubtedly is a most primitive means of communication of the unpleasant affect accompanying the first awareness of the death of the object. This initial human reaction, though infrequently reported in man, seems to be common in anthropoids.

The cry heard in the howling monkeys when there is an acute separation from the mother has been described by Carpenter (1934). It serves initially to indicate distress in the young animal and can signal retrieving activity. Concomitantly, the mother wails and groans until recovery of the infant occurs. The cries of the infant serves as cues which localize it for the other animals that might retrieve it, while the mother's wails not only express her distress, but focus the activities of the clan on recovery of the infant, while also producing stimulation to which the infant may orient and move. Carpenter has been able to distinguish and categorize these cries so that they can be identified.

Carpenter (1940, 1942), studying gibbons, has also identified the separation cry of the infant. In gibbons, the family groupings are monogamous, and are inferred to be relatively stable. Thus the tie between infant and mother may more clearly approximate to that of the human infant. Carpenter has reported an interesting observation on the mother-dead child interaction. He states "I have observed two rhesus mothers which carried dead babies until only the skin and skeletons remained. They guarded these remains persistently for over three days and seemed confused by the lack of normal responses on the part of the dead infants." He reported no crying on the part of the mothers, but Garner (1900) has noted that monkeys do not talk when alone, so perhaps the auditory signals between the mothers were sufficient stimuli and this more distressed response was not evoked.

On the basis of the above data and discussion, the hypothesis is advanced that infra-human mammals do show responses to the death of significant figures in their environment. The anthropoids and chimpanzees particularly seem to react in a fashion similar to those of the acute mourning stages as seen in man. No data or evidence exist that true mourning work occurs after the acute reactions. The level of ego functioning in these animals would be comparable to that of a very young pleasure-seeking child. Further investigations of mourning responses in children of various developmental levels of integration are needed to complete our ontogenetic picture of this process of adaptation. It is to be hoped that anthropologists and psychologists may also assist in providing us with additional facts that can confirm or refute the propositions presented in this section.

SUMMARY

The mourning process as an adaptational adjustment of the internal psychic milieu to an altered external milieu has been discussed. This process involves the series of responses to the loss of the object as well as the later reparative aspects of the process. Adaptation must include the capacity to adjust to the failure of a prior adaptation, as well as the capacity to make the initial adaptation. One example of this situation is seen in the response to the death of a significant object. In man, the object relationships that existed prior to death can become anti-adaptational after that object is no longer existent. In order to re-establish ego equilibrium, a mourning process begins. This process consists of an acute and a chronic stage. The first stage may seemingly be seen in mammals and birds, especially in chimpanzees and baboons. The chronic mourning stage, consisting mainly of the mourning work of object decathexis, is predicted on a qualitatively different type of psychic organization characteristic of the more mature human ego (intra-psychic differentiation and object representation, memory, reality-principle secondary process thinking). Apparently phylogenetic evolution has allowed, through natural selection, for additional adaptation with new object ties after reality has interfered with a prior object relationship. In man object replacement after death depends upon the instinctual needs of the mourner, the degree of energy liberation or replenishment resulting from the mourning process, and the maturity of the ego and the superego. The cathexis of new objects is not part of the mourning process per se, but an indicator of its degree of resolution. The objects newly chosen may be substitutes or replacements, but are rarely exact equivalents for the lost object.

REFERENCES

The individual papers and works of Sigmund Freud are referred to specifically in the body of the paper. Wherever possible the *Standard Edition* has been utilized, in other instances the *Collected Papers* is cited. These latter references are specifically noted below.

Alexander, F., G. Ham, and H. Carmichael
1951 A psychosomatic theory of thyrotoxicosis. *Psychosomatic Medicine* 13: 18-35.

Bernard, C.
1865 *An Introduction to the Study of Experimental Medicine.* New York: Dover, 1957.

Binswanger, L.
1957 *Sigmund Freud: Reminiscences of a Friendship.* New York: Grune and Stratton.

Brown, A. E.
1879 Grief in the chimpanzee. *American Naturalist* 13: 173-175.

Cannon, W. B.
1939 *The Wisdom of the Body.* New York: Norton.

Carpenter, C. R.
1934 A field study of the behavior and social relations of howling monkeys. *Comparative Psychology Monographs* 10: 1-168.
1940 A field study in Siam of the behaviour and social relations of the gibbon. *Comparative Psychology Monographs* 16: 1-212.
1942 Societies of monkeys and apes. *Biological Symposia* 8: 177-204.

Darwin, C.
1859 *The Origin of Species by Means of Natural Selection,* and 1871 *The Decent of Man and Selection in Relation to Sex.* New York: Modern Library.
1872 *The Expression of the Emotions in Man and Animals.* London: Murray.

Deutsch, H.
1937 Absence of grief. *Psychoanalytic Quarterly* 6: 12-22.

Eidelberg, L.
1959 The concept of narcissistic mortification. *International Journal of Psycho-Analysis* 40: 164-68.

Eissler, K. R.
1955 *The Psychiatrist and the Dying Patient.* New York: International Universities Press.

Federn, P.
1952 *Ego Psychology and the Psychoses.* New York: Basic Books.

Fleming, J., and S. Altschul
1959 Activation of mourning and growth by psychoanalysis. *Bulletin of the Philadelphia Association for Psychoanalysis* 9: 37-38.

Freud, A.
1936 *The Ego and the Mechanisms of Defence.* London: Hogarth.

Freud, S.
1892 Letter to Joseph Breuer, June 29. *Collected Papers* 5: 25-26.
1938 Splitting of the ego in the defensive process. *Collected Papers* 5: 372-375.
1954 *The Origins of Psycho-Analysis: Letters, Drafts and Notes: 1887-1902.* New York: Basic Books.

Freud, S., and J. Breuer
1892 On the theory of hysterical attacks. *Collected Papers* 5: 27-30.

Garner, R. L.
1900 *Apes and Monkeys: Their Life and Language.* Boston: Ginn.

Hartmann, H.
1939 *Ego Psychology and the Problem of Adaptation.* New York: International Universities Press, 1958.

Jones, E.
1953-7 *Sigmund Freud: Life and Work*. London: Hogarth.
Jones, J. L.
1958 Animal psychology on the farm. *Country Life:* 1512-1513.
Klein, M.
1938 Mourning and its relation to manic-depressive states. *In Contributions to Psychoanalysis*. London: Hogarth, 1948.
Lindemann, E.
1944 Symptomatology and management of acute grief. *American Journal of Psychiatry* 101: 141-49.
Lorenz, K.
1952 *King Solomon's Ring*. London: Methuen.
1954 *Man Meets Dog*. London: Methuen.
Spitz, R. A.
1946 Anaclitic depression. *The Psychoanalytic Study of the Child* 2: 313-42.
Yerkes, R. M.
1925 *Almost Human*. New York: Century.
Yerkes, R. M., and A. W. Yerkes
1929 *The Great Apes*. New Haven: Yale University Press.
Zuckerman, S.
1932 *The Social Life of Monkeys and Apes*. London: Kegan Paul.

6. THE COUNTRY OF OLD MEN: CROSS-CULTURAL STUDIES IN THE PSYCHOLOGY OF LATER LIFE

DAVID L. GUTMANN

David L. Gutmann is Professor of Psychology, University of Michigan. Reprinted with permission from the Occasional Papers in Gerontology Series, April, 1969. Institute of Gerontology, University of Michigan—Wayne State University.

THIS CHAPTER OUTLINES some results thus far obtained from an on-going program of research on the psychological characteristics of older men undertaken in a variety of mainly preliterate societies.[1] The contention of this study, first developed from urban United States data, has been that certain modes of relating, of experiencing, and of knowing distribute more predictably by age than they do by culture. Put in another way, the contention of this study has been that men age psychologically according to an intrinsic schedule of ego mastery stages that follow a sequence of some fixity, some predictability, across a panel of diverse cultures. In this paper we will describe the mastery stages, as well as the recurrent ways in which they register themselves in the content of fantasy and in the forms of thought, across cultures which themselves maintain differing conventions about these matters.

A MASTERY TYPOLOGY

The studies which led to initial formulation of the typology were undertaken as part of the Kansas City Studies of Adult Life, of the Committee on Human Development, University of Chicago. The research, described in greater detail elsewhere (Neugarten and Gutmann 1958; Gutmann 1964) involved a sample of 145 mentally and physically fit White males, 40 to 70 years in age, all residents of the Kansas City area. The data consisted of Thematic Apperception Test (TAT) stories given in response to selected stimulus cards. Three major types and six component subtypes emerged from the TAT analysis, each presumably representing a special form of relatedness toward the world, and each representing a distinct solution to the ego's task of maintaining internal and external mastery.

As shown in Table 6.1, younger Kansas City men (aged 40-54) tend significantly towards Active Mastery, while older Kansas City men (aged 55-71) favor Passive or Magical Mastery. Thus, the types significantly discriminate age groups, suggesting the possibility that the mastery typology defines a continuum of ego states through which men move as they age. Before the cross-cultural tests of this "developmental" hypothesis are reported, each mastery type will be briefly discussed in terms of the salient motives, relational modes, and coping styles that it embodies.

ACTIVE MASTERY

The Active (or Alloplastic) Mastery style seems to have as its motivational

TABLE 6.1
DISTRIBUTION OF THE KANSAS CITY MALE SAMPLE BY MAJOR AGE PERIODS, AND BY MASTERY ORIENTATIONS

		40-49	50-59	60-71	
ACTIVE MASTERY	Promethean-Competitive	7* } 17	8 } 26	3 } 12	
	Productive-Autonomous	10	18	9	
PASSIVE MASTERY	Emphasized Receptivity	8 } 8	20 } 26	12 } 23	
	Anxious Constriction	0	6	11	
MAGICAL MASTERY		4	15	14	
		29	67	49	145

* This distribution of the mastery cell subtotals is significant at the .02 level ($x^2 = 17.417$; DF = 8).

foundation strivings towards autonomy, competence, and control. The Active Mastery individual works within or collaborates with external action systems in order to maximize his effect on them, in order to bring some part of them under his control. He is wary of having his actions and choices limited by others, and he is therefore mistrustful of any dependent wishes in himself that would lead him to trade compliance for security.

Generally speaking, the Active Mastery individual is not much interested in any nuances of feeling, whether tender or otherwise, either in himself or in others. His sensitivity is turned outwards to the kinds of behavior that can be measured, predicted, and counteracted; and he is not much concerned with the ideational or emotional counterparts of such behavior. Consistent with this externalizing tendency, such men also tend to refer potentially troubling inner conflicts to the outer world. Active Mastery men do not ruminate much over inner problems identified as such;

rather they look for outer agents which represent—or can be held responsible for—what they dislike and fear in themselves. They legislate their inner problems into collective enterprises, for example, realistic fights against political abuse, intruding enemies, or some refractory segment of external nature.

The various dispositions cumulate to what might be called an "active-productive" orientation. Like all men, the Active Mastery individual desires emotional and physical security, but he is happiest when he can supply these needs through his own capacities, and when he is a source of security to others. He is most comfortable with resources—be they a business, a flock, or a cornfield—that he has generated for himself and for his dependents out of his own competence, boldness, and disciplined effort.

The Active Mastery orientation includes "Promethean-competitive" and "productive-autonomous" subtypes. These may be found together within some Active Mastery individuals or they may in other cases discriminate between men of this general orientation. The first subtype emphasizes combat and competition; strength and prestige are trophies won from an enemy. The second subtype emphasizes self-reliance and autonomy, enacted through vigorous and productive efforts. In productive autonomy there is less emphasis on external enemies and challenges, more emphasis on living up to high internal standards. One competes, in effect, against oneself.

PASSIVE MASTERY

The Passive (autoplastic) Mastery individual also needs to control the sources of his pleasure and security. But the Passive Mastery individual does not feel effective enough to create, by himself, his own emotional and physical logistic base. From his standpoint, strong, independent, and capricious external agents control what he needs. The Passive Mastery individual can only influence the powers-that-be indirectly, through what he does to himself. He shapes himself to fit their expectations; he demonstrates mildness rather than challenge; and he tries to expunge those tendencies that might lead him into dangerous conflict. He does not, in the Promethean fashion of the Active Mastery men, try to *wrest* power from the gods; rather he participates passively in external power by identifying with and complying with those who control it. Humility and accommodation are the keynotes of this stage.

The world of the Passive Mastery individual tends to be closed, bounded by prohibitions that he cannot revoke and by dangers that he cannot survive. Fantasy and rumination precede action and substitute for action; in this world one moves mainly to discover the limitations on movement and to justify staying put. The passive individuals, therefore, retrench. They draw back into those familiar, limited terrains that reflect their schedule, that are still responsive to their will. This is the "tend your own garden" style, and the passive person convinces himself that little value exists beyond the precincts of his garden. This is the style of internal rather than external engineering: the productive style moves inward, toward the cultivation, in a redundant world, of pleasant thoughts, pleasant sensations, and predictable experiences.

This orientation includes anxious/constricted and emphasized receptivity subtypes. Again, these may be found together within some Passive Mastery individuals, while they differentiate between others. In anxiety/constriction, passivity is the consequence of fearful inhibition. In emphasized receptivity, the focus is on nurturance to the self and from the self. One passively accepts what others give; and one passively puts oneself at the disposal of others to meet their requirements. Both positions involve overt gentleness and avoidance of strife.

MAGICAL MASTERY

The preceding orientations are mainly centered around aggressive motives which are to be expressed (as in Active Mastery) or controlled (as in Passive Mastery). But for Magical Mastery individuals the receptive motives dominate, (as is the case in syntonic receptivity). However, Magical Mastery individuals do not have the capacity to delay gratification or to identify with the pleasure of others that is part of the syntonic receptivity state. Furthermore, in

Active and Passive Mastery, instrumental actions and realistic cognitions intervene between impulse and gratification. But in this state, rather primitive defense mechanisms substitute for instrumental action either against the world or against the self. Denial replaces instrumental action against outer troubles; threatening agents are arbitrarily seen as benign; projection substitutes for reformative action against the ego; troublesome wishes and impulses are conveniently located in others rather than in the self. Thus, in the magical ego state (particularly at times of stress and arousal), wish, cognition, and action are mingled such that the wish guarantees its own fulfillment. Reality is altered through perceptual changes, and external agents are seen to play out roles in a personal psychodrama.

Thus, for Magical Mastery men, the world is seen in simplistic and extreme terms; the world is full of potential providers (who can never provide enough) and potential predators. Vulnerability is the keynote of their relationship to the world.

THE MASTERY TYPES AND
OTHER MEASURES

These ego states are not mutually exclusive. The same individual can display them all in different contexts, or at different times within the same context. They are here presented as exclusive states for heuristic purposes in order to highlight real inter-type differences. Moreover, the typology does have an empirical basis: men sorted into these types on the basis of their TAT performance were also discriminated by interviewers' ratings of overt behavior and affect; by performance on the "Draw-A-Person" test; by the "Life Satisfaction" rating

—a validated scale devised by Neugarten and associates (1961); and by other independent measures derived from interview and observational data provided by these same subjects (see Gutmann 1964, pp. 137-142; see also Williams and Wirths 1965, pp. 209-210). In general, the prediction was that the Active Mastery men would achieve high ratings on these measures of energy, affective liveliness, and life satisfaction, and that the Passive and especially the Magical Mastery men would receive lower ratings. In the main, at a statistically significant level, these predictions were confirmed.

Accordingly, while they may coexist within persons, each mastery orientation seemingly refers to a distinct psychic system that coordinates across persons, a fairly standard panel of motives, attitudes, and behaviors. But the finding that the types are distinct does not shed light on their meaning and origin. The question remains: Are these types developmental in nature, corresponding to stages of the individual life cycle; or, are they extrinsic in nature, having to do with specific psychological and cultural differences between the generations in United States society? The major part of this report deals with the steps thus far taken to investigate this problem.

THE CROSS-CULTURAL STUDY OF THE MASTERY TYPOLOGY

Thus far, the hypothesis considered here—that men age psychologically along a continuum delineated by the Active, the Passive, and the Magical Mastery orientations—has received some support from the findings of other students of aging psychology in American populations. Thus, Schaw and Henry (1956), Rosen and Neugarten (1960), Shukin and Neugarten (1964), and Hays (1952) tend to report findings similar to those cited here.

Working with another urban United States sample, Clark (1967, pp. 62) found that the self-conceptions of normal San Francisco subjects, aged 60 and over, were consistent with Passive Mastery criteria, as predicted for this age group.

Confirmatory clinical observations have also been made by psychiatrists (Meerloo 1955; Zinberg and Kaufman 1963; and Berezin 1963). All the above stress the aging American's withdrawal from active engagement with the world in favor of more cerebral, introversive, and self-centered positions.

However, while these independent observations support mine, they do not in themselves support the *developmental* conclusions that I would draw from the finding of age-graded psychological differences in a population of adult United States men. Socio-cultural influences may still account for the observed generational differences. The developmental implications of the United States findings have been tested in four groups of preliterate agriculturalists: the Lowland and Highland Maya of Mexico, the Western Navajo of Arizona, and the Druze tribesmen of Israel. In this design, we make intergenerational comparisons across a variety of cultural settings. If the same psychological variables continue to discriminate the generations across this range of diverse societies, socio-cultural explanations cannot account for the predicted uniformities, and intrinsic or developmental explanations become more powerful.

The following considerations have governed the choice of study sites: (1)

Subject societies should be significantly different from each other in terms of child-rearing practices, important value orientations, and age-grading systems.

(2) It is important to control for those extrinsic, socio-cultural factors that might independently bring about the age differences in ego orientation that are predicted by the developmental theory being tested. Accordingly, the subject societies should have maintained, for some generations, a stable consensus as to what is good and bad, real and unreal, possible and impossible. That is, the subject societies should be tradition-directed; and the means for communicating the tradition should also have remained fairly stable across some generations.

(3) The theory being tested proposes mandatory age-graded regression in ego functions, towards Magical Mastery. In order to further rule out extrinsic contributions to this decline, the theory is most rigorously tested in societies which provide ample ego supports to older men. These are societies where older men are respected, where they have an advisory role towards the young, and where with increasing age they tend to amass political and/or ceremonial power less available to younger men.

Regarding criterion (1), the Lowland Maya, Highland Maya, Navajo and Druze societies differ from each other (and from Kansas City) in major economic, cultural, and ecological respects. Thus, both Mayan groups are composed of subsistence level, village-dwelling corn farmers who nonetheless show greatly contrasting cultural and personal styles. The Lowland Maya represent the "Protestant Ethic" of thrift, industry, and moderation, while the Highland Maya, a more oppressed and unruly people, rely on external authorities to control the unmodulated rage and envy that they sense in themselves and fear openly in their neighbors.

The traditional Navajo, migratory herdsmen, are notably different from both the Highland and Lowland aspects of the Maya. They turn away from White influences; they do not live in organized villages; and they mingle extremes of suspicion and humor, vulnerability and toughness, pragmatism and superstition.

The Druze tribesmen of the Galilean highland are village-dwelling herdsmen and agriculturalists, accounted heretics in Islam, who have nevertheless maintained their cultural continuity in the Levant for over 800 years, though in the face of much persecution. As might be expected, core features of individual Druze character are stubbornness, piety, and reserve.[2]

Regarding criterion (2), these four groups—although they differ from each other—tend to be generationally homogeneous within themselves. Young men can see in their elders something of what they will become, and older men see in the younger men something of what they themselves have been.

Finally, as regards criterion (3), in each setting the older men are respected and at least formally deferred to. Thus, among the Lowland Maya, old men lack secular power but are indulged and supported out of a mixture of love and respect. In contrast, the Highland Maya and Druze patriarchs have much political, economic, and religious power. Similarly, older traditional Navajo often remain economically productive, and they also perform, through the medicine man role, important healing and ceremonial functions. Generally speaking, the socio-emotional situation of older men

at all the study sites appears to be better than that of their relatively isolated, working-class age-peers of urban America.

For each of the subject cultures, the prediction has been that the age distribution of mastery orientations, as registered in TAT and other data, would replicate the age distribution of these orientations in the Kansas City sample to repeat mastery orientations that distribute more predictably by age than by culture and can be regarded as developmental bench-marks, attributes of the human life cycle, and not as cultural styles that differentiate the generations within societies.

DATA COLLECTION

The approach to data collection tended to vary with local conditions,[3] and as field competence increased we tended to generate more extensive and intensive data. However, despite such variations, across the four subject societies relatively equivalent sets of TAT data have been gathered under roughly similar field conditions. Prior to TAT administration, subjects were first invited to ask questions of the investigator. Once their curiosity and suspicion had been dealt with, they were intensively interviewed concerning past and present life issues, childhood memories, sources of contentment, causes of discontent, favored remedies for discontent, and dreams. These topics were not necessarily covered in any fixed order but were brought up as they meshed with the respondent's subjective priorities. Interviews were gathered by myself and by students trained in this "naturalistic" interviewing approach.

Following the interview, subjects were shown a battery of approximately twelve TAT cards, which had as its regular basis four Murray TAT cards, and two cards originally designed for an Amerindian population. These six "core" cards presented ambiguous situations that had no particular cultural referents; and they were used in their unmodified form at all sites. The remaining six cards presented standard species human situations, (e.g., family life, cross-generational interaction, etc.,) and were altered in detail (through hopefully, not in import) to correspond to the local versions of these events.[4]

While subjects were routinely asked to tell a story about the card, this instruction was often confusing to literal minded, concretely oriented Indian subjects. They could not see the card as an occasion for an imaginative exercise, recognized as such, but automatically assumed that the card presented some specific drama, intrinsic to it, that they were to discover. Accordingly, whenever we encountered this concrete attitude, we shift our instructions to, "Tell me what is happening there." Probes around introduced content were used to elicit the final "story."

DATA ANALYSIS

The original, orienting conceptions of this study came from the TAT, and we have thus far been mainly studying the pools of presumably comparable TAT data generated by cards—such as the rope climber of the Murray set —that were presented without modification to all appropriate subjects at all study sites. As with the Kansas City data, the approach to the cross-cultural data has been exploratory and inductive. The basic analytic units have been the data generated from one respondent, by one card. The goal of

the analytic procedures has been to make themes and trends which are (1) implicit in data, and (2) relevant to the ego mastery conceptions, explicit and comparable. This has involved the standard application of interpretive procedures and guidelines, based on mastery typology criteria, to the data generated by each card in each culture.

Thus, for any card and for any culture, Active Mastery stories were those in which card issues were recognized by the respondent, active stances were proposed in regard to the issue, and vigorous action led to good consequences. Passive Mastery stories were those in which hero figures were seen as ineffectual, overwhelmed by external force, or in a receptive position vis a vis some external provider. Magical Mastery stories were those in which major stimulus features, particularly those suggestive of conflict and trouble, were either grossly distorted or ignored. Again, for each card thus analyzed, the prediction has been that the age by mastery type distributions would discriminate older from younger men, at any site, along the lines first noted in the Kansas City data.[5]

CARD ANALYSIS

Results of comparisons thus far undertaken have been encouraging. In those cases where a particular card has been used at all sites, the age by mastery position distributions from most or all Indian groups have roughly corresponded to the original Kansas City distributions for the same card. Then, too, while some findings have proved equivocal in terms of the predictions advanced, *none* of the data from other cultures has been grossly discrepant with the original hypotheses of this study.

The analytic methods and some typical findings are illustrated in the following discussion which deals with the data developed by four cards, two of which were used in their original, unmodified form at all sites (including Kansas City) and two of which were used at all Indian sites (though not at Kansas City). Some of the most representative findings emerged from the data of the rope climber card, which has been used at all sites and is discussed below.

The Rope Climber Card. This card suggests to many respondents—in any culture—a vigorous, muscular, and possibly nude figure who could be going up or down a rope. Because the card suggests nudity and strength, and because it does not depict any social agents besides the protagonist, the stimulus might be regarded as a representation of the impulsive, instinctual aspects of life. Hence, the latent card issue is presumably "impulsive vigor" and the card presumably asks the respondent, "What is *your* conception of strength, of impulse and where do you locate these qualities?" Accordingly, respondents' estimates of the qualities, goals, and activities of this figure were regarded as metaphors of their personal relationship to their own impulse life. The various phrasings of this relationship were expressed in a set of thematic categories which are presented below, grouped according to their respective mastery orientations.

Active Mastery
A. Promethean
1. Challenge and competition: The hero demonstrates his strength, usually in successful competion. However, the rope may break at the moment of triumph; and the respondent himself may deride the hero as a show-off.

B. Productive-Autonomous
2. Productive effort: The hero strives vigorously, sometimes zestfully, towards a self-determined productive goal. He does not compete against others, nor flaunt his strength.

Passive Mastery
A. Anxious Constriction
3. Externalized inhibition: The hero is immobilized by environmental agents which do not collaborate with his action, or which block it, the rope is slack; the cliff is slippery.
4. Threat from internal or external aggression: The hero is threatened by destructive external forces; alternatively, the hero's aggression is turned against himself (suicide) or is out of control and constitutes a threat to others (the hero is homicidal).
5. Role dominated: The hero climbs, though without much involvement, for conventional purposes. Or, the respondent conforms to his role as subject by giving a minimal though accurate description of the card.
B. Syntonic passivity
6. Somaticized passivity: The hero lacks force to match his purpose; he is tired or ill.
7. Sensual receptivity: The hero has hedonic or security-seeking (rather than productive) purposes, he plays on the rope; he dives into water; he climbs to see something, to get a morsel of food, or to find his home.

Magical Mastery
8. The hero is not erect; or the rope is not a rope (the hero is lying down; the hero is wounded; the rope is a snake, etc.)

The Rope Climber: Age Trends. Table 6.2 presents the distribution of responses by the above card categories, by age, and by culture. Though

TABLE 6.2

THE ROPE CLIMBER CARD: DISTRIBUTION OF STORIES
BY AGE, CULTURE, AND THEME

		35-49	50-59	60+
ACTIVE MASTERY				
A. Promethean	Kansas City	21	33	10
1. Competitive	Trad. Navajo	5 } 31*	1 } 36	6 } 19
	Lowland Maya	3	2	2
	Highland Maya	2	0	1
B. Autonomous	Kansas City	4	10	7
2. Productive	Trad. Navajo	6 } 15	6 } 19	10 } 20
	Lowland Maya	3	2	2
	Highland Maya	2	1	1
PASSIVE MASTERY				
A. Anxious Constriction	Kansas City	—	3	—
3. External inhibition	Trad. Navajo	— } 7+	1 } 4	— } 0
	Lowland Maya	6	—	—
	Highland Maya	1	—	—
4. External aggression	Kansas City	3	7	12
	Trad. Navajo	3 } 8	— } 8	7 } 21
	Lowland Maya	2	1	1
	Highland Maya	—	—	—
5. Constriction	Kansas City	1	11	5
	Trad. Navajo	1 } 8	5 } 23	9 } 26
	Lowland Maya	1	5	7
	Highland Maya	5	2	5
B. Syntonic Passivity	Kansas City	—	1	—
6. Somatic passivity	Trad. Navajo	— } 0+	1 } 2	2 } 2
	Lowland Maya	—	—	—
	Highland Maya	—	—	—
7. Sensual receptivity	Kansas City	2	2	7
	Trad. Navajo	3 } 12	3 } 17	10 } 38
	Lowland Maya	3	5	14
	Highland Maya	4	7	7
MAGICAL MASTERY				
8. Magical mastery	Kansas City	—	2	2
	Trad. Navajo	— } 1	— } 4	3 } 8
	Lowland Maya	—	1	2
	Highland Maya	1	1	1
		82	113	134

Kansas City   N = 144
Trad. Navajo   N = 81
Lowland Maya   N = 62
Highland Maya   N = 42
TOTAL   N = 329

* Chi Square (of cell totals) = 42.558, DF = 12, P < .001
+ These cell totals have been combined with those of next lower category for computational purposes.

societies vary in overall degree of activity and passivity that they ascribe to the rope climber, the intergenerational comparisons within cultures and across cultures indicate that younger men generally favor the more active, productive possibilities, while older men generally favor the more hedonic, inert, less instrumental possibilities. This point is dramatized by Table 6.6, which allows us to compare age cohorts across cultures, for each card. For example, in regard to Active Mastery, Table 6.6 shows that this orientation, as estimated by the rope climber card, is always lower, across cultures, for the 60-year-olds than it is for the 40-year-olds. Conversely, Passive Mastery is always higher for the 60-year-olds than it is for the 40-year-olds; and, except for the Highland Maya, the same is true for Magical Mastery. Despite intercultural differences in mastery preferences, there is a clear and independent age effect in these terms.

Thus, each culture shows age variation in its interpretations, but most of the variation occurs within a thematic band that is characteristic of the culture. For example, younger American respondents mainly propose that the rope climber competes against other athletes, that he demonstrates his strength to an admiring audience, or that he escapes from prison. Many also propose that successful striving has its dangers: at the moment of victory or freedom the rope will break, or the prisoner will be recaptured. Generally, younger United States subjects see a Promethean who strives against dangers that he has, by his own daring, created for himself. But older Americans to a significant degree locate energy and menace outside of this figure: for them the rope climber escapes from a fire or from

some similar external threat. The card asks where they locate strength; the older Americans reply: Force is an external menace, and my job is to keep out of trouble. Thus, as a group the majority of Kansas City men, whether young or old, are more preoccupied than are the Indian respondents with the aggression variable; it is the location of aggression—from inside to outside the self—that is seen to shift with age.

Unlike the younger Americans, the younger Mexican and American Indians do not often regard the rope climber as a Promethean, competing figure. Instead, younger Indian men emphasize a more temperate version of striving. They propose that the rope climber more or less adequately fills an already defined productive role, and they do not suggest that he strives with others. But the older Indians are more blatantly passive. In these three societies, the tendencies to see the rope climber as inert (asleep, dead), as playful ("fooling around"), or as receptive to sensual inputs ("he wants to see"), most clearly discriminate the older from the younger men. Thus, the younger Mexican and American Indians appear more passive than their urban American age peers; but, as in the American case, their versions of the rope climber's activities are consistently less inert and less hedonic than is the case for the older men of their own Mayan or Navajo societies.[6]

The trend away from active productivity and towards greater receptivity is especially sharp when we consider all responses to the rope climber card wherein the hero is portrayed as looking or being looked at. Table 6.3 shows that younger Americans most often propose that the hero is the center of some audience's admiring attention: "He's showing off his strength," or "The audience gets a thrill out of seeing him." A confident, "look at me!" self-conception is projected through such responses. By contrast, older Americans are more likely to propose that the rope climber looks towards the audience for response and for direction: the *audience* tells him if he is doing a good job. Here the shift from confident, assertive inner-direction to cautious other-direction is clear.

Similarly, younger Mexican and American Indians usually suggest that the rope climber's visual activity is instrumental; the hero checks progress towards some goal. But for older Indians, looking *is in itself the goal* of the activity; the hero climbs to see something, to get a better view. (In this regard, a few older—and no younger—Kansas City men see the rope climber as a sexual voyeur.)

The Heterosexual Conflict Card. The heterosexual conflict card of the Murray TAT depicts a young man turned away from a young woman who reaches towards him. Like the rope climber, this card has been shown to male respondents at all sites. In the typical drama, conflict is proposed between an angry, sometimes rejecting

TABLE 6.3
DISTRIBUTION BY AGE, THEMATIC CATEGORY, AND CULTURE OF WATCHFULNESS RESPONSES (ROPE CLIMBER CARD)

		30-54		55-95	
1. Hero watched (attentively or admiringly).	Kansas City	17		10	
	Navajo	4	25*	6	20
	Lowland Maya	—		—	
	Highland Maya	4		4	
2. Hero is watchful for productive, task-centered reasons	Kansas City	5		2	
	Navajo	6	15	11	18
	Lowland Maya	—		4	
	Highland Maya	4		1	
3. Hero is watchful of audience response to his performance	Kansas City	3		8	
	Navajo	—	4	—	8
	Lowland Maya	—		—	
	Highland Maya	1		—	
4. Climbing and un-motivated watchfulness are hero's only activity.	United States	6		1	
	Navajo	—	13	2	7
	Lowland Maya	3		1	
	Highland Maya	4		3	
5. Emphasized (erotized) watchfulness: increased visual input is hero's chief goal.	United States	1		5	
	Navajo	2	7	7	26
	Lowland Maya	4		11	
	Highland Maya	—		3	
TOTAL		64		79	143

$X^2 = 13.473$ (for cell totals)
DF = 4, P < .01

Kansas City	N = 58
Navajo	N = 38
Lowland Maya	N = 23
Highland Maya	N = 24

man and a solicitous and/or retentive woman. Thus, the card issue concerns the collision between potentially dangerous male energy, and more nutritive, less directly intrusive female qualities.

Accordingly, in deriving the mastery orientation of particular stories, particularly when the respondents are men, we consider such content issues as the deployment and consequences of male energy; the locus of forces, internal or external, inhibiting such energy; and the qualities and powers ascribed to the young woman figure. Thus, Active Mastery stories portray a vigorous young man who is intrinsically impelled towards productive, amorous, or combative exploits, and who is relatively impervious to either the tenderness or the fear expressed by the young woman. Passive Mastery stories are those in which significant power is located outside of the young man. A domineering, retentive woman restricts the outward movement of a still assertive young man; or a young man, defeated in or menaced by the outer world, moves back to the comfort and security offered by the young woman. Magical Mastery stories are those in which the usually noted conflict possibilities are overlooked, and the emphasis is instead on some peaceful, though undifferentiated, relationship between the young man and young woman.

Grouped under their respective mastery orientations, the specific categories that accommodated all card data, from all cultures, are these:

Active Mastery
A. Promethean
1. Male aggressive initiatives: Young man's intrinsic sex, aggression, and autonomy needs constitute a problem for a gentle nurturant young woman, and potential danger for himself.
B. Autonomous
2. Male autonomy needs: Young man forcefully rejects the young woman's nurturance. In some cases, he turns away from the consolation of the young woman to the impersonal consolation of liquor, which also sponsors his aggression.

Passive Mastery
A. Externalized Aggression
3. Female initiatives and dominance: Young man's anger is not intrinsic to him, but is in reaction to the young woman's dominance and/or rejection of him; she is a nagging or a cheating wife.
B. Syntonic Passivity
4. Rationalized male succorance: Menaced by external forces, or defeated in his outer-world striving, the young man looks for or accepts female nurturance and control.

Magical Mastery
5. Untroubled affiliation (or syntonic dependency): Mild, untroubled affiliation between relatively undifferentiated young man and woman.

The Heterosexual Card: Age Trends. Table 6.4 indicates the age-theme-culture distributions to this card. Again the intergenerational, intercultural comparisons tend to conform to predictions; a later life shift towards the passive and magical end of the psychological spectrum was observed in the data from three out of the four societies studied.

Table 6.4 indicates more clearly that in all but the Highland Maya case,[7] Active Mastery declines steadily across age groups; Passive Mastery rises steadily across age groups, and if Magical Mastery appears at all, it is always higher among the 60-year-olds than among the 40-year-olds.[8]

Otto Fenichel, the psychoanalytic theorist, explicitly links scoptophilia with oral eroticism: "The eye may represent pregenital erogenous zones symbolically. As a sense organ it may express oral-incorporative and oral-sadistic longings in particular." (Fenichel 1945, p. 227). Accordingly, the striking emphasis among older men in a variety of cultures on "looking" for its own sake is indirect evidence of the hypothesized motivational shift in later life away from assertive productivity and towards pregenital versions of receptivity. The visual zone comes under the dominance of the oral-incorporative modality: the visual inputs of older men no longer

TABLE 6.4
THE HETEROSEXUAL CARD: DISTRIBUTION OF STORIES BY AGE, CULTURE, AND THEME

		35-49		50-59		60+	
ACTIVE MASTERY							
A. Promethean	Kansas City	21		12		10	
1. Male aggressive	Navajo	9	36*	7	20	9	21
initiative	Lowland Maya	4		1		2	
	Highland Maya	2		—		—	
B. Autonomous	Kansas City	1		3		—	
2. Male autonomy	Navajo	4	12	4	14	4	12
needs	Lowland Maya	7		5		7	
	Highland Maya	—		2		1	
PASSIVE MASTERY							
A. Externalized	Kansas City	6		5		6	
Aggression	Navajo	—	9	3	9	9	19
3. Female dominance	Lowland Maya	—		—		2	
	Highland Maya	3		1		2	
B. Syntonic Passivity	Kansas City	—		1		4	
4. Rationalized male	Navajo	—	1	1	3	12	20
succorance	Lowland Maya	—		1		2	
	Highland Maya	1		—		2	
MAGICAL MASTERY							
5. Untroubled	Kansas City	—		—		—	
affiliation	Navajo	1	12	6	16	6	26
	Lowland Maya	3		7		12	
	Highland Maya	8		3		3	
	N =	70		62		98	

* Chi Square (of cell totals) = 24.643, DF = 8, P < .005

Kansas City	N = 69
Navajo	N = 75
Lowland Maya	N = 53
Highland Maya	N = 33
TOTAL	N = 230

serve ego executive functions primarily, but are valued for themselves as sensual supplies. The world is "eaten" through the eyes.

Cultural anthropologists have tended to insist that all organized mental contents are products of prior cultural indoctrination. But the striking similarity in the age distributions, across cultures, of specific imagery with high visual content, suggest that intrinsic, untrained psychosexual modalities may be ubiquitous, and that they can be registered in predictable ways and without prior cultural sponsorship in the content of thought, imagery, and behavior.

In the main, then, in regard to the heterosexual card the between-age cohorts across cultures comparisons tend to replicate the results from equivalent rope climber comparisons, and provide further evidence of the shift away from exuberant and outward-directed male aggression towards more security-seeking, receptive stances. Thus, younger men propose that the male hero brushes aside a beseeching woman and pushes into a dangerous but exciting world of combat, carouse, and mistresses. To the same stimulus, older men propose more anergic, constricted, or pregenital themes. In their version, the young woman tends to domineer; or the male protagonist retreats back to her consolation, and away from a world in which he has known danger and defeat. In either case, initatives and strength have migrated away from the young man toward the young woman or toward vaguely defined external agents which threaten the young man or the young couple. Finally, for many older men, the male protagonist does not reject the nurturance offered by the young woman, but instead dwells with her in happy, seamless harmony.

Potential trouble comes from outside, not within, the dyad, and menaces the young man and woman equally.

The Heterosexual Card: Cultural Differences. Regarding the between cultures comparisons, the culture-by-theme distributions for the heterosexual card also replicate those refracted by the rope climber card. Again, both younger and older United States men are notable for their common concern with the young man's aggression. While passive definitions of the young male figure increase in later life, they do not, even for the 60-year-old Kansas City group, supersede Active Mastery as the dominant orientation elicited by this card. Younger Kansas City men tend to be more concerned with the outer world, presumably masculine, reactions to their aggression, while older men are more concerned with the domestic reactions (perhaps from their wives). Most Kansas City men, young or old, are concerned with the deployment of their aggression. The primary orientation stays fairly constant; it is the theater of action that changes with age. It is significant that older Kansas City men never move to the Magical Mastery, nonconflict view of this card. They never propose the unrealistic, total harmony solution.

By contrast to Kansas City respondents of all ages, and by contrast to the younger Indian men, the older Indian men—as with the rope climber card—cluster significantly at the magical end of this card's thematic spectrum. These older Navajo and Mayan men to a striking extent agree that the card mainly depicts harmonious male-female interaction. Thus, as in the case of the rope climber, American respondents of any age are more concerned with the expression, the consequences, and the control of aggression; Indian respondents are generally more attuned to the hedonic and affiliative card implications.[9]

The Rope Climber and Heterosexual Cards: Common Age Trends. To summarize, both cards that raise for respondents the issue of the nature and deployment of masculine energies outline an age-graded, transcultural consensus around these matters. That is, young men define strength as an ambivalently valued internal resource: the strong, competitive man also stirs up trouble for himself (the rope climber can fall at the moment of triumph; the young man rejects a woman and gets into fights with men.) The old men also retain this ambivalent relationship towards strength—it can help them or hurt them—but they see it as lodged outside of themselves, in relatively capricious agencies, institutions, or authorities. Both cards also agree on the age shift to more openly needful and incorporative positions, towards immediate affectional, oral, and ocular supplies. In their apparent need to legislate the world into a secure storehouse of consumable supplies, older men will determinedly overlook potential conflicts and troubles that are clear to younger men. Thus, the older men, as predicted, rely on defensive denial, rather than on action, to remove the sense of threat. Instead of "taking arms against a sea of troubles," they may revise their perception, and claim that the world holds neither troubles nor arms.

The Desert Scene. The data from the rope climber and heterosexual conflict cards indicate that men relate to the world in different ways, depending on their age-status. Younger men look for challenge, opportunity, and assertion; older men look for oral, visual, and affectional supplies. In each case, the relational modalities correspond to the central themes of the mastery orientations which presumably characterize these age cohorts. These relational shifts also have consequences for the defensive aspect of ego function. The data from the desert scene card illustrate the predicted age trend towards reliance on the ego defense of denial, which is pivotal to the Magical Mastery ego state. This card shown only to Indian respondents, portrays a desert scene, gullied in the foreground, empty of people, but transected by a trail and by barb-wire fences.

The majority of Indian respondents visualized in this card one or another version of aridity, and they were judged to be responding to the card issue of "innurturant environment." Category criteria took account of the degree to which respondents recognized this aridity, proposed reasonable human efforts to counteract it, or tried to deny it. Thus, Active Mastery categories grouped those stories in which the reality of a hostile environment was admitted, without palliation and also those stories which proposed restitutive human effort. Passive Mastery categories grouped those stories in which it was proposed that restorative rain or water would appear through some natural agency, but under human control. Magical Mastery categories grouped those stories in which key elements of the scene were misperceived, and it was proposed that water already covered the ground, or that helpful supernatural agents were concretely present on the scene. The particular categories, grouped by mastery orientations, are as follows:

Active Mastery
A. Coping
1. Human agency: Emphasis on human effort in the face of a hostile environment; or on those human systems and structures that might oppose the ravages of nature (fenced fields, road systems, etc.).
B. Realism
2. Innurturance: Emphasis on an arid environment, hostile to life and to human effort.

Passive Mastery
A. Anxious Constriction
3. Perceptual restriction: Emphasis on a few accurately perceived details, but avoidance of total, integrated scene.
B. Syntonic Passivity
4. Fantasied relief from innurturance: Description of arid desert, and suggestion that background clouds might bring rain.
5. Integrated denial of innurturance: Rain actually falls from distant clouds; or the foreground gully forms the banks of a body of water.

Magical Mastery
A. Denial
6. Gross perceptual denial: Arbitrary introduction of helpful, fertile or nurturant agents—angels, churches, flowers, money, sheets of water.
B. Projection
7. Uncontrolled natural forces: Floods, marine volcanoes, sea battles, sinking ships, drowning or dangerous animals.

Desert Scene: Age Trends. Table 6.5 shows a clear age progression in the data, defined especially by categories 1, 2, 4, 5, and 6, away from recognition of card issues, and towards various perceptual metaphors of denial. 48 percent of responses given by all men in the youngest group cluster in categories 1 and 2, indicating the relative readiness of this group to look squarely at unpleasant issues. By contrast, 62 percent of responses given by 50-year-olds are found in 5 and 6, the two perceptual denial categories, as are 75 percent of the responses from men aged 60 and over.

Regarding the intergenerational, intercultural comparison of the mastery distributions, Table 6.5 indicates that across cultures, Active Mastery follows the predicted course, always declining with age from its starting point. Passive Mastery does not, however, always conform to prediction, and sometimes falls or stays constant with increasing age. However, we also see that in those cases where, contrary to prediction Passive Mastery drops off in later life, Magical Mastery rises; and in general, across cultures, Magical Mastery always shows the predicted age graded increase. Thus, as regards this card, Passive Mastery in some instances follows the age career that was predicted for Active Mastery; and Magical Mastery follows the course that was predicted for Passive Mastery. That is, the desert scene card, by contrast to other cards, seems to shift all age groups in all the subject cultures, towards the more passive and regressive end of the mastery spectrum, while maintaining the relative distinctions as to mastery preferences between them. Possibly, this card, which depicts the natural rather than the personal world, registers in these three Indian societies the preliterate world view towards nature. One can be effective among one's own people, but nature is refractory, and one is either stoic about this, or hopes for the best.[10] And with advanced age it appears that the boundary between wish and reality may break down, such

TABLE 6.5
THE DESERT SCENE: DISTRIBUTION OF STORIES
BY AGE, CULTURE, AND THEME

		35-49	50-59	60+
ACTIVE MASTERY				
A. Coping	Navajo	5	3	2
1. Human agency	Lowland Maya	5 } 13*	1 } 5	— } 2
	Highland Maya	3	1	—
B. Realism	Navajo	7	1	1
2. Innurturance	Lowland Maya	— } 9	1 } 3	— } 1
	Highland Maya	2	1	—
PASSIVE MASTERY				
A. Anxious Constriction	Navajo	4	5	10
3. Constriction	Lowland Maya	— } 6	1 } 7	1 } 13
	Highland Maya	2	1	2
B. Syntonic Passivity	Navajo	5	7	9
4. Fantasied relief	Lowland Maya	2 } 7	— } 8	— } 9
from innurturance	Highland Maya	—	1	—
5. Integrated denial	Navajo	5	8	5
of innurturance	Lowland Maya	3 } 10	2 } 10	1 } 6
	Highland Maya	2	—	—
MAGICAL MASTERY				
A. Denial	Navajo	1	2	11
6. Gross perceptual	Lowland Maya	— } 7	9 } 16	14 } 31
denial	Highland Maya	6	5	6
B. Projection	Navajo	1	2	6
7. Uncontrolled	Lowland Maya	6 } 8	1 } 3	6 } 12
natural forces	Highland Maya	1	—	—
		60	52	74

* Chi Square = 38.297,
DF = 12, P < .001

Navajo N = 100
Lowland Maya N = 53
Highland Maya N = 33

TOTAL N = 186

that one's wishes regarding nature are legislated into a consoling picture of it. The way things "ought to be" becomes in later life a design for "the way things are."

SUMMARY OF TAT FINDINGS

To sum up, thus far the results of the TAT analysis lead to various inter-card, intercultural, and intergenerational comparisons, most of which support the conclusion that the thematic criteria for the various mastery orientations give rise to categories which discriminate age groups in standard fashion across cards within cultures, and across cultures within cards (see Table 6.6). While the relative rankings among the mastery

TABLE 6.6
DISTRIBUTION OF MASTERY BY CARD, BY CULTURE, AND BY AGE

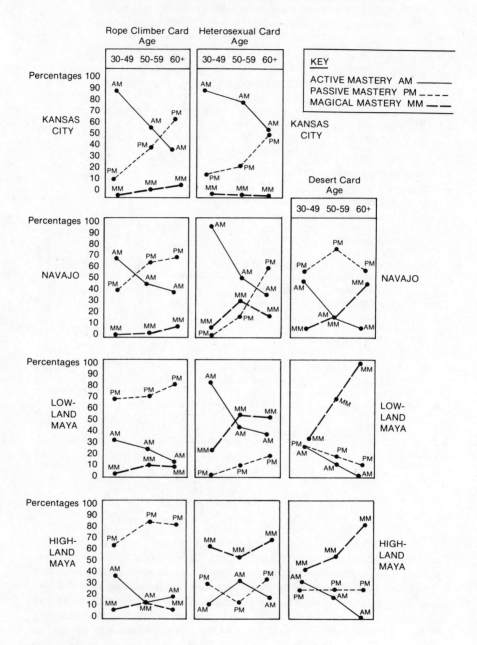

orientations can vary by card and by culture, these card and culture effects tend to be constant, and there is an age effect which appears to be independent both of cards and of cultures. As predicted, and with few exceptions, Active Mastery declines with age, while the percentage of Passive and Magical Mastery stories increases with age, according to the sequence, Active→Passive or Magical Mastery.

This consistency in the age distributions and in the cultural distributions of standardized data—where the original stories were different as to manifest content and card stimulus —suggest that the mastery orientations have transcultural distribution; and that while cultural influences can amplify or retard particular mastery orientations, these decline or unfold according to an intrinsic schedule that is consistent with a developmental theory of aging. These results also suggest that the individual card judgments are reliable, that they measure what they purport to measure, and that the criteria upon which such judgments are based can be standardly applied across different cards and across different cultures.

ANALYSIS OF INTERVIEW DATA

We have thus far reviewed some age changes, across cultures, in the subjective postures of the ego, of the sort that are consistent with the hypothesized age-staging of mastery orientations. Thus, the TAT data map out some of the predicted relational and defensive shifts that were found in the Kansas City population and that in their American version gave rise to the developmental theory of mastery stages. We also touched on

some serendipitous findings concerning the later life emergence of a visual-sensual modality which is consistent with the theory, though not specifically predicted by it. Furthermore, the analysis of interview data suggests that the subjective shifts from Active towards Passive and Magical Mastery, as revealed in TAT stories, have implications for more overt attitudes and behavior.

SOURCES OF CONTENTMENT, DISCONTENTMENT, AND REMEDY

In the course of the interviewing that preceded projective testing, Navajo and Highland Maya men were routinely asked, "What makes you happy?", "What makes you unhappy?", and, "When you are unhappy, how do you make yourself contented again?" Again, categories were devised which integrated the thematic emphases of the actual responses with mastery typology criteria. Tables 6.7, 6.8, and 6.9 indicate various category criteria and the response distributions: by these categories, by age, and by culture. Starting with responses to the question, "What makes you happy?" Table 6.7 indicates that both the younger Highland Maya and the younger Navajo equate pleasure with productive work. They are happy when they acquire livestock, when they bring new cornfields under cultivation, or when they find lucrative wage work. But older men are most likely to define happiness in passive-receptive terms. They are made happy by visits from relatives, by their accustomed food, by pleasant music, by the sight of a flourishing vegetable garden, or by a pretty view. The younger men take pleasure in that which they make or gain and in the

TABLE 6.7

AGE AND THEMATIC DISTRIBUTION: TRADITIONAL NAVAJO AND HIGHLAND MAYA RESPONSES TO QUESTION, "WHAT MAKES YOU HAPPY?"

Age:		Productive Work		Maintaining Status Quo		Passive-Receptivity	
30-49	Highland Maya	9	} 13*	0	} 3	4	} 5
	Navajo	4		3		1	
50-90†	Highland Maya	6	} 10	6	} 16	9	} 22
	Navajo	4		10		13	

* $X^2 = 11.168$
  DF = 2, P < .005

† 6 Navajo, 2 Highland Maya S's aged 80 and over.

Highland Maya N = 34
Navajo N = 35
TOTAL N = 69

TABLE 6.8

AGE AND THEMATIC DISTRIBUTION: TRADITIONAL NAVAJO AND HIGHLAND MAYA RESPONSES TO QUESTION, "WHAT MAKES YOU UNHAPPY?"

Age		Interruptions of Production; Enmity of Competitors		Illness		Anaclitic Concerns; Objects Loss, etc.	
30-49	Highland Maya	10	} 17*	1	} 2	0	} 4
	Navajo	7		1		4	
50-96†	Highland Maya	2	} 10	7	} 9	8	} 22
	Navajo	8		2		14	

* X^2 (of cell totals) = 14.843
  DF = 2, P < .001

† 6 Navajo, 2 Highland Maya S's aged 60 and over

Highland Maya N = 28
Navajo N = 36
TOTAL N = 64

activities associated with production, but the older men are made happy by the pleasant sights, sounds, tastes, and friendly sentiments that come to them as earned or unearned gratuities from the outside.

Similarly, as seen from Tables 6.8 and 6.9, younger Navajo and Highland Maya men are mainly made unhappy by work stoppages and their major remedy for any trouble is to get back to work. Older Navajo and Maya are mainly troubled by losses of family, friends, and providers, and they look for remedy to powerful allies (village authorities, saints, doctors) or, again, to suppliers of food, drink, and friendly attention. The older men of both societies clearly visualize themselves in Passive Mastery terms, that is, as receptors; and the younger men clearly visualize themselves in Active Mastery terms, that is, as centers of action and influence.

MASTERY ORIENTATIONS AND EARLY MEMORIES

Other interview data suggest that the individual's current ego orientation not only directs behavior and attitude in the present, but also has implication for the reconstruction, in memory, of the past. Given their predominately Passive Mastery orientation, it was predicted that older men, as they recalled their past, would give most attention to the material figures associated with the earliest satisfactions (or frustrations) of succorant demands. By contrast, the more Active Mastery, production oriented younger men were expected to give greater prominence to memories of the paternal figures who had provided their first models of a manly competence. As predicted, the percentage of maternal memories spontaneously put forth by traditional

TABLE 6.9

AGE AND THEMATIC DISTRIBUTION: TRADITIONAL NAVAJO AND HIGHLAND MAYA RESPONSES TO QUESTION, "HOW DO YOU RESTORE CONTENTMENT?"

Age:		Reliance on Instrumental Action		Reliance on "Omnipotent" Figures		Reliance on Oral (and other) Supplies	
30-49	Highland Maya	8	} 13*	2	} 3	1	} 3
	Navajo	5		1		2	
50-96†	Highland Maya	5	} 11	5	} 15	7	} 19
	Navajo	6		10		12	

* X^2 (of cell totals) = 11.066
  DF = 2, P < .005

† 6 Navajo, 2 Highland Maya
S's aged 80 and over;
2 Highland Maya under 35

Highland Maya   N = 28
Navajo   N = 36
TOTAL   N = 64

Navajo interviewees increases markedly with age, while spontaneous memories of paternal figures decrease at a corresponding rate (See Table 6.10).[11]

MASTERY ORIENTATIONS AND ORALITY

The hypothesized association between Passive Mastery, Magical Mastery, and receptivity in later life was further tested through studies of the orality variable. The prediction was that specifically oral interests would increase in later life in conformity with the general increase in Passive and Magical Mastery orientations. To this end, the Navajo interview and projective data were coded

TABLE 6.10

TRADITIONAL NAVAJO AGE GROUP COMPARISONS: PERCENTAGES OF
MEMORY MATERIALS RELATING TO MOTHERS AND FATHERS*

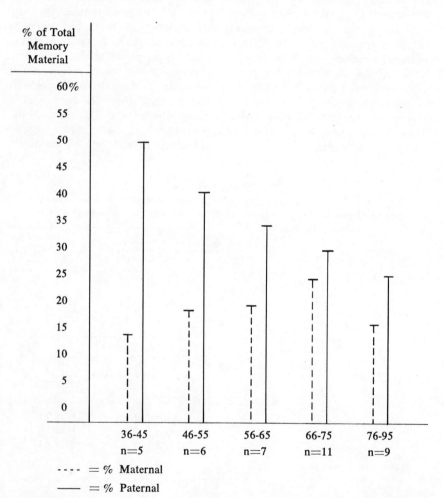

---- = % Maternal

——— = % Paternal

* For this chart and the work that it represents I gratefully acknowledged the efforts of Jeffrey Urist.

for the orality variable. All mentions of eating, food preparation, purchase, or production were assigned weights which reflected the intensity of oral need that they presumably expressed. The orality scores are presently being checked for reliability, but the first assessments differentiate older from younger Navajo and in the predicted direction. More interesting are the findings that the highest proportion of young men's scores derive from mentions of food production, while the highest roportion of old men's scores derive from mentions of eating and pleasure in food. Thus far then, the age variations in the Navajo orality scores tend to be consistent with the age variation in the mastery orientations.

Another, unexpected, finding concerns the within-protocols age shifts: as shown in Table 6.11, younger men displayed oral yearnings mainly through externalized, projective forms of fantasy. They dream about people who eat, and they can vividly describe the hunger and nutriment of people

TABLE 6.11

AGE GROUP COMPARISONS: MODE OF EXPRESSING ORAL INTERESTS
AMONG THE WESTERN NAVAJO

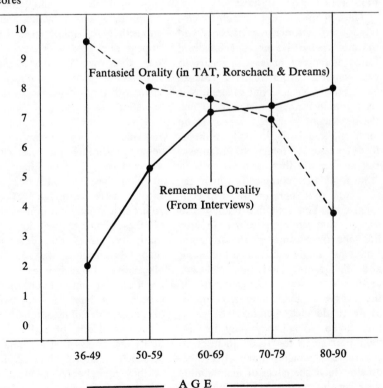

depicted in the TAT, but they are not likely to talk of their own lives, past or present, in these terms. By contrast, older men are much less likely to ascribe hunger or eating to TAT stimulus figures, but such oral content suffuses interview accounts of their activities and concerns, and is particularly pervasive in their reminiscences of early life. Where younger men remember the fathers who trained them for competence, older men dwell with greater frequency on the mothers who fed them, and on the food that these mothers prepared. A common theme in older men's interviews is that of the "lost oral paradise." "When I was a boy there was more green grass and good grazing. Berries and pinon nuts for eating grew all over the ground. Now we have to buy all our food from the trading post."

Thus, there seems to be an inverse relationship between reminiscence and the more projective or depersonalized forms of fantasy, at least in regard to oral content: as oral material leaches out of the TAT and out of dreams it reappears in the early memories. Thus, the dependent yearnings appear to be problematic in early life and are therefore repressed, or managed, in fantasy. But in later life there appears to be a "return of the repressed," which restores the oral representations to consciousness. This tentative finding also suggests that reminiscence may in later life take over some of the dynamic functions usually ascribed to dreaming and other fantasy activities. We have observed that our older subjects in the course of their interviews move easily to detailed memories of early life. In so doing, they may rework their past so as to "feed" themselves experiences which—much like the dream—have the effect of maintaining their present psychic equilibrium.

CONCLUSION

A mixed bag of evidence, derived from work still in progress and not from completed analytic programs, has been presented. The fragmentary picture thus far developed supports the contention that changes in the psychosexual, relational, ego defensive, and cognitive aspects of personality proceed in a variety of preliterate Indian cultures along continua whose outlines were first discerned in data derived from middle-aged and older urban American men. Men from these societies move—with different pacing and different priorities—through successive Active, Passive, and Magical Mastery ego stages, toward oral definitions of pleasure and pain, toward simplistic defensive tactics, and toward subjectivity of thinking. It begins to appear that aged men across cultures have their own "country of old men", a dominion that they do not share even with their own sons, in their own societies.

However, while it now appears that individuals so move in predictable sequence through the mastery stages, we cannot yet claim that this progression has an intrinsic, developmental basis. Although we can now rule out a strictly cultural explanation of these findings, we do not automatically prove the developmental theory by refuting the socio-cultural alternative. There are existential necessities that impinge on most men, especially in later life—the exigencies of illness, of failing strength, of approaching death, of reduced opportunity and hope—that are independent of specific cultural circumstances just as they may be independent of any prior psychological or developmental events. These existential imperatives may be the independent variables, the independent engines of psychological change in later life, which set in motion, as dependent events, the universal passage across the mastery continuum that we have described.

Thus, there are those who propose that human beings are not in the end *driven* towards Magical Mastery, but that they *choose* it. These critics would see in the final psychic postures of life not a compelled developmental outcome, but an ego directed response to the imminence of death. In this view, the common reality that unites older men is the universal recognition of death, and not some somatic program outside of human awareness. The seeming regression of the ego towards Magical Mastery does not in this view represent ego debility; it represents an executive act, performed by the ego upon itself, in defiance of approaching death. Passive and especially Magical Mastery have much in them of early ego states. Therefore, faced

with its own ending, and lacking any rational, instrumental means for avoiding that end, the ego may regress in its own service, and revive the appetitive, relational, and cognitive climate of its beginning.

Our present data do not allow us to make final choice between the developmental and the more cognitive or "ego executive" explanations of the findings developed by the cross-cultural work. At this time, I believe that there is an interaction, such that developmental variables may regulate the individual's sensitivity to the existential imperatives that we have described, with different consequences for different stages of life. The young man may view the imposed necessity of illness as an arbitrary interruption of his life work; an older man may secretely welcome the same illness because it rationalizes an emergent passivity.[12]

But at this point we only glimpse the interesting questions. More field work may provide the answers, or suggest better questions.

Notes

1. The overall program of cross-cultural research has been supported by Career Development Award no. 5-K3-HD-6043-04, from the National Institutes of Child Health and Human Development. Field expenses for Indian studies in Mexico and America were covered by Faculty Research Grants nos. 1344 and 1412 from the Rackham School of Graduate Studies, The University of Michigan; and by grant no. MH 13031-01 from the National Institutes of Mental Health. Field work expenses among the Israeli Druze were covered by grant no. M66-345 from the Foundation's Fund for Research in Psychiatry.

2. The traditional Druze enclaves have been studied; but the Six Day's War and the resultant Israeli mobilization interfered with the transcription of our data tapes, so that the analysis of individual Druze protocols has not yet begun. No formal findings will be reported from this group.

3. Given the realities of field work in remote areas, one cannot be obsessive about meeting criteria for random and representative samples. The particular subjects demanded by a sampling design often turn out to be sick, in trouble with the police, drunk, or working away from the community.

In any event, working in a small village, or in a sparsely settled region, one eventually contacts all those potential subjects who are willing or able to talk to a foreign investigator. Thus, the study sample tends to be coextensive with the local set of possible subjects, and thereby meets the criteria for representativeness, if not for randomness.

We generally recruited subjects by first making ourselves known to men of reasonable reputation, without important disability, in the age range 35-75. In larger villages, where we did not expect to study all possible subjects, we tried to reduce the sampling bias inherent in the use of a single sponsor by patronizing several principal men, hopefully from different village clans or factions. Interpreters of good local reputation were relied on at all sites; these also helped to recruit subjects and further legitimized our presence in the village or on the reservation.

4. The desert scene TAT card is part of a set of American Indian TAT pictures originally designed for research on Indian education. This study was sponsored by the United States Office of Indian Affairs and the Committee on Human Development, Univerity of Chicago. Robert J. Havighurst was primarily responsible for the design of the American Indian pictures. They were first used by William E. Henry (1947).

5. Positive results would validate the original judgments concerning the degree of activity, passivity, of "magical" arbitrariness registered in particular response themes. Also supported is the a priori assumption often contested by anthropologists — that data from other cultures can be analyzed from a conceptual framework not indigenous to those cultures.

6. Note also that the rope climber card not only distinguishes between the Kansas City and the Indian respondents, but that it also distinguishes between the Indian societies in terms of the mastery orientations along lines predictable from their socio-cultural makeup. Table 6.6 shows that the individualistic Navajo, who live in small bands rather than organized villages, who value mobility, and who still remember their Apachean warrior tradition, maintain a higher level of Active Mastery at any age than either of the two village-dwelling, sedentary Mayan groups. And for both Mayan groups, Passive Mastery is always higher than Active Mastery for any age cohort (though this lead increases with age).

7. Both the younger and older Highland Maya men depicted the young man figure as relatively mild and inert relative to the outer world or the young woman figure. But men of this group are very inhibited and fearful concerning sexual matters, and their anxiety may have been reflected in their particularly constricted definitions of the young man figure. Thus, the data generated by this card from this group may not be comparable to data from the other societies where sex is far less problematic.

8. Along the same lines, older respondents again emphasize visual content: 11 Indian men over 50 (and only two men younger than 50) propose that the young couple *look out* toward some undefined external presence. Again, older men substitute visual intensity in place of the aggression and sexuality stressed by younger men. Findings of this sort, from TAT data, suggest that the visual interests of the aged are scoptophilic in nature—pregenital versions of sexuality.

9. The heterosexual card data not only distinguish the Kansas City from the Indian distributions as a whole, but also replicate the rankings *between* the Indian groups first developed by the rope climber card. Thus we see from Table 6.6 that Active Mastery is usually much higher among the Navajo than it is for either of the Mayan groups, and that Passive Mastery is the dominant Navajo later life orientation, while Magical Mastery dominates among the Mayan elders. Indeed, Magical Mastery is lower at any age for the Navajo than it is for the two Mayan groups. Thus, despite the independent, predicted age effects, we find consistent inter-societal differences where, in terms of Active Mastery, Kansas City > Navajo > Maya (Highland and Lowland); and in terms of Magical Mastery (which can vary independently of Active Mastery), Maya (Highland and Lowland) > Navajo > Kansas City.

10. Though the desert card portrays the familiar arid terrain of the Navajo, we see from Table 6.5 that this card, like the rope climber and heterosexual cards, continues to rank the Navajo higher in terms of Active Mastery, and lower in terms of Magical Mastery, than either of the two Mayan groups. Where Magical Mastery is the major Mayan orientation to the desert card for any age group, Passive Mastery has priority among the Navajo, and Magical Mastery only begins to compete with Passive Mastery for dominance among the 60-year-old Navajo.

11. Note that for the 76-95-year-old-group, paternal memories again lead over maternal memories, whereas in the preceding age groups the two phrasings of parental memory had gradually but consistently moved toward equality. This irregular pattern may indicate the unreliability of the measure, but it also should be remembered that any remote-dwelling Navajo who survive into their seventies are unusually hardy men by anybody's standards. Accordingly, the data from this group are not comparable with that from the more typical younger Navajo. If these longevous Navajo show an unexpected dominance, reminiscent of younger men, of paternal over maternal memories, it may be because of some association between longevity and the independent, productive (hence father-oriented) stance.

12. Thus, among the Navajo, we found a very high incidence of diagnosed psychosomatic incapacity among the "Rice Christians," the passive dispirited Navajo who live near the Indian Agency towns, and near the provident missionaries. These men are, by all psychological measures, a highly succorant group. In their early forties they quit work, live on handouts, on welfare, and on their wives' rug-weaving earnings. Their typical rationale is that they fell off a horse, that they are dizzy and ache all over, and thus can no longer work. The remote-living non-Christian Navajo emerge in the same measures as a counter-dependent group, and their older men will minimize real illnesses, and continue to strive despite them. Obviously, the former group amplifies illness in order to justify dependency. Dependency precedes illness, and not vice versa.

REFERENCES

Berezin, M. A.
    1963   Some intra-psychic aspects of aging. *In* N. Zinberg (ed.), *The Normal Psychology of the Aging Process.* New York: International Universities Press.
Clark, M.
    1967   The anthropology of aging: A new area for studies of culture and personality. *The Gerontologist* 7: 55-64.
Fenichel, O.
    1945   *Psychoanalytic Theory of Neurosis.* New York: Norton.
Gutmann, D.
    1964   An exploration of ego configurations in middle and later life. *In* B. Neugarten (ed.), *Personality in Middle and Later Life.* New York: Atherton.
Hays, W.
    1952   Age and sex differences in the Rorschach experience balance. *Journal of Abnormal and Social Psychology* 47 sup.: 390-393.
Henry, W. E.
    1947   The thematic apperception technique in the study of culture-personality relations. *Genetic Psychology Monographs* 35: 3-135.
Meerloo, J.
    1955   Transference and resistance in geriatric psychotherapy. *Psychoanalytic Review* 42: 72-82.
Neugarten, B., and D. Gutmann
    1958   Age-sex role and personality in middle age: A thematic apperception study. *Psychological Monographs* 72 (17) Whole No. 470.
Neugarten, B., R. Havighurst, and S. Tobin
    1961   The measurement of life satisfaction. *Journal of Gerontology* 16: 134-143.
Rosen, J., and B. Neugarten
    1960   Ego functions in the middle and later years. *Journal of Gerontology* 15: 62-67.
Schaw, L., and W. E. Henry
    1956   A method for the comparison of groups: A study in thematic apperception. *Genetic Psychology Monographs* 50: 207-253.

Shukin, A., and B. Neugarten
   1964   Personality and social interaction. *In* B. Neugarten (ed.), *Personality in Middle and Later Life*. New York: Atherton.
Williams, R., and C. Wirths
   1965   *Lives Through the Years*. New York: Atherton.
Zinberg, N., and I. Kaufman
   1963   Cultural and personality factors associated with aging: An introduction. *In* N. Zinberg (ed.), *The Normal Psychology of the Aging Process*. New York: International Universities Press.

II. CULTURAL VARIATIONS IN THE LIFE CYCLE

EVER SINCE MARGARET MEAD went in 1926 to Samoa in search of adolescent turmoil, anthropologists have been collecting psychologically relevant data about the life cycle in diverse cultures. There is an enormous body of evidence to show that populations vary widely in cultural definitions of the stages of life and their attributes and in the cultural beliefs and values available to them for managing life events and processes from birth to death. The psychological effects of these variations, at any point in the course of life, have been a major focus of inquiry in culture and personality research. There are three distinct questions in this area that investigators such as those represented in the readings have pursued:

1. Do cultural beliefs and values about a particular segment of the life cycle actually structure the environment of the individual in a way that differs from one culture to another and that should have a psychological impact according to one or more theories of development? For example, do parents in different populations use the distinctive beliefs and values of their environments as normative guides to child care in ways we have reason to believe might influence child development?

2. Do culturally differing ways of managing parts of the life cycle make a discernible difference in the behavior and experience of individuals undergoing them? In other words, if infants in two cultures are handled differently, does it alter their behavior in infancy and early childhood? If the aged are given more respect than the middle-aged, does it make a difference in how they feel about becoming elderly? If boys are given

different tasks than girls, does it affect their respective patterns of social behavior and their views of sex roles while they are children?

3. Do cultural variations in environment, experience, and behavior at one point or phase of the life cycle have long range effects on the individual's behavior and experience at later points? This is the cross-cultural form of the question, so prominent in developmental psychology, about the impact of early experience.

The readings in this section give attention to all three of these questions, in the context of one or more cultures. I have chosen works offering evidence that bears directly on questions 1 and 2 and indirectly on question 3. The evidence is not yet conclusive, but culture and personality research, represented in the chapters that follow, has made substantial progress in dealing with these large and difficult problems.

REFERENCE

Mead, Margaret
1928 *Coming of Age in Samoa.* New York: William Morrow.

7. WHO SLEEPS BY WHOM? PARENT-CHILD INVOLVEMENT IN URBAN JAPANESE FAMILIES

WILLIAM CAUDILL and DAVID W. PLATH

The late William Caudill was Chief of the Section on Personality and Environment, Laboratory of Socio-Environmental Studies, National Institute of Mental Health. David W. Plath is Professor of Anthropology, University of Illinois, Urbana. Reprinted with permission from *Psychiatry* (1966) 29: 344-366.

IF A THIRD OF LIFE is passed in bed, with whom this time is spent is not a trivial matter. As ethnologists, we expect co-sleeping customs to be consonant with major interpersonal and emotional patterns of family life in a culture, and at the same time to reflect cross-cultural differences (see Whiting et al. 1958; Burton and Whiting 1961). Westerners viewing Japanese sleeping arrangements usually sense a high degree of "overcrowding," which they say results from lack of space in "densely populated" Japan. We argue that this apparent "overcrowding" in the bedroom is only in part a function of lack of space: it derives more directly from the strength of family bonds. We argue further that the frequency with which children co-sleep with parents expresses a strong cultural emphasis upon the nurturant aspects of family life and a correlative deemphasis of its sexual aspects. We support our arguments by asking, of data from urban families, who sleeps by whom?

SELECTION AND CHARACTERISTICS OF THE SAMPLE

Co-sleeping in Japan usually occurs behind closed shutters and is not open to easy observation. Participant observation has its limits and an ethnographer who asked to sleep all around town probably would not be welcomed. But both of us found that Japanese would willingly sketch their dwelling spaces and indicate where each person slept. We happened upon this independently and for different purposes, but have combined our data in a joint report.

The sketches were drawn in the course of individual interviews. The interviews in Caudill's research were conducted in 1962 at three hospitals, two of them in Tokyo and one in Kyoto. At each hospital information was obtained from the first 100 mothers coming to the well-baby clinic who had, at the time of interview, a three- to four-month-old infant.[1] The interviews in Plath's research were conducted in 1960 in Matsumoto City, and information was obtained from fathers or mothers in 30 households in two neighborhoods.[2]

Discarding seven cases with inadequate data, we have a total sample of 323 households—198 in Tokyo, 99 in Kyoto, and 26 in Matsumoto. Each household consists of at least an unmarried child and both of his parents; and in many cases there are additional children, extended kin, and unrelated persons (maids, roomers, and employees in the family business). We examined household sleeping arrangements in terms of city of residence, size of household, number of generations living together, style of life, social class, and density. Statistically, density proved to be the most important single variable. Several of the other variables, however, were of minor importance in influencing co-sleeping patterns, and these results will be given at the appropriate points in the analysis. The meaning we assign to these variables is discussed in the following paragraphs, and the distribution of the sample in terms of them is given in Table 7.1.

In designing the research, our aim was to clarify parent-child co-sleeping patterns, and we chose our sample of households accordingly. We wished to obtain a sufficient number and spread of households on each variable to permit comparative analysis rather than trying to collect a sample that would be statistically representative of the general population. Thus, in con- trast to the general population, our sample contains no one-person or two-person households, a greater proportion of three-generation households, more households whose main income is from a family business, and more upper middle-class and lower middle-class households.[3]

CITY OF RESIDENCE

Japanese tend to think of life in Tokyo as being more modern than that in other parts of Japan, and to think of life in Kyoto as being especially traditional. The image of life in Matsumoto falls between the two, and carries an aura of provincialism. From city to city there are minor variations in sleeping arrangements— notably in central Kyoto, with its older and larger houses, where families are somewhat more spread out in their sleeping arrangements than in Tokyo or Matsumoto. But if the data by city are controlled by any other variable, these differences vanish.

TABLE 7.1

DISTRIBUTION OF HOUSEHOLDS IN THE SAMPLE BY NUMBER OF GENERATIONS, STYLE OF LIFE, SOCIAL CLASS, AND DENSITY

Category	Tokyo (N = 198)	Kyoto (N = 99)	Matsumoto (N = 26)	Total Households (N = 323)
Number of generations in household				
Two	128	60	23	211
Three	70	39	3	112*
Style of life: main source of income				
Salary and wages	104	71	11	186
Family business	94	28	15	137
Social class				
Upper middle	65	60	6	131
Lower middle	71	29	8	108
Working	62	10	12	84
Density				
High	155	43	17	215
Low	43	56	9	108

* Includes 4 four-generation households.

HOUSEHOLD SIZE

The total sample has an average of 4.8 persons per household, and city-to-city differences are minor—5.0 for Tokyo, 4.6 for Kyoto, and 4.5 for Matsumoto. In this regard the sample is close to the 1960 census, which found (for households of like composition) an average of 4.8 persons per household for all urban areas, 4.9 for Tokyo, and 4.8 for Kyoto. Census figures for Matsumoto are not available to us.[4] As will be seen, size of household does prove to be a useful variable in certain respects.

NUMBER OF GENERATIONS

In line with the patrilineal emphasis in Japanese culture, 79 percent of the three-generation households in the sample include one or both of the husband's parents, while only 21 percent include one or both of the wife's parents. No household contains grandparents from both paternal and maternal sides.

STYLE OF LIFE

The distinction concerning the main source of income for a household is related more to a style of life than to economic matters. Following World War II, the role of the "salaryman" has become more important and desirable, and is seen as a modern way of life free from some of the traditional constraints associated with working in a small family business. It should be noted that style of life is conceptually separate from social class.[5] And, as will be seen, style of life does play a minor role as a meaningful variable in sleeping arrangements.

SOCIAL CLASS

To determine social class we first separated our households into five logical groups based on the occupation and education of the head of the household. Because there were so few cases in groups one and five, we combined the first two groups into an "upper middle class," we retained the third group and labeled it "lower middle class," and we combined the last two groups under the heading of "working class." We did not, however, find any important differences by social class in sleeping arrangements.[6]

DENSITY

We define density as the ratio between the number of rooms available to a household for sleeping purposes, and the number of persons residing in the household. When there are fewer available sleeping rooms than persons, we call this *high density;* when there are as many or more sleeping rooms than persons, we call it *low density.*

It should be noted that we define density in terms of space available, not space actually used. In tabulating rooms available for sleeping, we excluded kitchens, baths, toilets, halls, porches, storage areas, and rooms used predominately for business purposes (that is, the "shop"). We counted all other rooms as available for sleeping, including a room that a household might reserve for visitors during the daytime. Because of the ordinary construction of the Japanese dwelling, almost all of the rooms counted as available are mat-floored (*tatami*) rooms; people sleep in such rooms on quilts (*futon*) which are spread out each evening and taken up during the day. Ninety percent of the adults in the sample sleep in this manner, while ten percent use Western-style beds. We shall return later to this question of bedding.[7]

As can be seen in Table 7.1, density varies by city, being highest in Tokyo. In this regard, the sample seems to reflect the fact that Tokyo's population has been increasing two to three times faster than that of Kyoto or Matsumoto; in addition, both of these latter cities have a large proportion of old multiple-room houses because they were not bombed during World War II, whereas Tokyo was gutted by fire-bomb raids in 1945. Japan, in general, continues to suffer from a shortage of housing. Conditions probably have improved since 1955, the latest year for which we have reliable figures, but at that times in cities over 200,000 population the average dwelling space per person was still ten percent below what it had been in 1941 (see Gleason 1964). And the average Japanese urban household in 1955 had nearly twice as many persons per room as did its American counterpart—1.22 persons in Japan to 0.67 persons in the United States (Gleason 1964, p. 28).

But if there is need for more living space in general in Japan, the need for more sleeping space in particular is less apparent.

AVAILABILITY AND USE OF SLEEPING SPACE

Our first question is: How much available sleeping space do the households in the sample have, and how much of it do they regularly use? Table 7.2 shows the distribution of the 323 households in the sample by number of persons in a household and number of rooms it has available for sleeping. The households to the left of the step-line have less than one sleeping room available per person, and these 215 households (67 percent) have a high density. The households to the right of the step-line have one or more rooms available per person, and these 108 households (33 percent) have a low density. These latter households could provide a separate room for each member if they chose to do so.

In contrast, Table 7.3 shows the

TABLE 7.2

NUMBER OF PERSONS IN HOUSEHOLD BY NUMBER OF ROOMS AVAILABLE FOR SLEEPING

Number of Persons in Household	Number of Rooms Available for Sleeping										Total Households
	1	2	3	4	5	6	7	8	9	10+	
3	31	45	17	8	10	3			1	2	117
4	6	20	15	17	3	2	2	1			66
5		8	4	13	9	4	3			1	42
6	1	1	3	7	7	8		2	1	2	32
7		1	1	7	6	2	3		1	2	23
8				7	4	2	4	4		1	22
9			1	3	3		1				8
10				1		1	1			1	4
11+				2		2	1		1	3	9
Total Households	38	75	41	65	42	24	15	7	4	12	323

TABLE 7.3
NUMBER OF PERSONS IN HOUSEHOLD BY NUMBER OF
ROOMS USED FOR SLEEPING

Number of Persons in Household	Number of Rooms Used for Sleeping										Total Households
	1	2	3	4	5	6	7	8	9	10+	
3	102	14	1								117
4	23	41	2								66
5	5	25	11	1							42
6	1	8	17	6							32
7		2	11	10							23
8			8	11	3						22
9			3	3	2						8
10			1	3							4
11+				2	5		2				9
Total Households	131	90	54	36	10		2				323

distribution of all households by number of persons and number of rooms actually used for sleeping. There is a dramatic shift to the left of the step-line, and of the 108 households in Table 7.2 that could provide each member with a separate room, only one remains to the right of the line in Table 7.3.

A more detailed comparison of Tables 7.2 and 7.3 will show that three-person households in our sample prefer to sleep in one room, whereas four-person households are more likely to divide into two rooms. Given the household composition of our sample, this is perhaps not so surprising, but if one continues to look in Table 7.3 for the modal frequency in terms of size of household relative to number of rooms used for sleeping, the idea begins to dawn that Japanese prefer to sleep in clusters of two or three persons, and prefer not to sleep alone.

We do not, of course, expect every person in a household, even if this were possible, to sleep in a separate room. It would be highly unusual even among privacy-minded American households. Each of the households

in the sample contains at least one married couple, and most of them also contain an infant. Presumably most of the married couples, and some of the mothers and infants, will co-sleep. This in itself makes it unlikely that many households will exhaust their available sleeping rooms.

But if some amount of co-sleeping seems likely a priori, the next question we ask is: To what extent does the amount of available space influence the degree of co-sleeping? If, for example, Japanese parents and children co-sleep simply because they lack space, then they should tend to disperse as more rooms become available. We can begin to test this as follows.

First, we exclude 38 households that have only one sleeping room available.[8] We assume that they have no opportunity to disperse, save that of bedding down members in kitchens or hallways. The remaining 285 households, however, have some freedom of choice in sleeping arrangements, since each of them has at least two sleeping rooms available.

Next, for each of these 285 households we compute two indexes. The first we call *use density*. To obtain this we divide the number of persons in a household by the number of rooms they now use for sleeping. For example, a four-person household sleeping in two rooms has a use density of two persons per room. The second index we call *available-space density*. To obtain this we divide the number of persons in a household by the number of available rooms, up to the point where the ratio equals one. For example, a four-person household with four available rooms has an available-space density of one person per room. A household with more available rooms than members would have a theoretical available-space density of less than one person per room, but we have set a lower limit of one for this index because it seems a bit unrealistic to expect a person regularly to use more than one sleeping room.

Finally, we examine the correlation (by the Pearson r method) between use density and available-space density for each group of households having the same number of members. There are nine such groups, ranging from three-person to eleven-or-more-person households (see Tables 7.2 and 7.3). The results of this analysis are: (1) the correlation is not significant ($r = -.05$) for three-person households; (2) the correlations are significant ($r = .25$, n.s.; $r = .29$ to .89, $p < .05$) for seven of the eight groups of households having four to eleven or more members; and (3) the correlation is significant ($r = .47$, $p < .01$) when all households having four or more members are considered together.

These results mean that three-person households do not tend to disperse for sleep even when rooms are available, but larger households do tend to disperse to some extent. For the larger households, the correlation tells us that

the availability of space accounts for 22 percent (r^2) of the variance in the actual use of space. In other words, lack of space does make a difference in co-sleeping arrangements in our urban Japanese households having more than three members, but space alone tells only about one-fifth of the story. To fill out the story, we must ask, Who sleeps by whom?

SLEEP AND SOCIAL STRUCTURE

Our question now becomes: Which kinship roles are most likely to co-sleep, and which to disperse? Once again we exclude the 38 households having only one sleeping room available; and, for the households having at least two sleeping rooms, we consider separately the 86 three-person households and the 199 four-or-more-person households.

Each of the three-person households consists of a child with both parents and in 79 of the cases the child is an infant of three to four months. Thus it is perhaps not too unusual that all members sleep together in one room in 71 (86 percent) of the households. Another 14 (16 percent) use two rooms; in nine of these cases it is the child who is alone, but in five cases it is the father. In one household the three members each sleep alone.

Given the high number of infants in these three-person households, one might argue that the instrumental need to look after the infant at night would favor keeping him in the parental bedroom. But if convenience were the only consideration, the infant would probably be excluded from the room a few months to a year after birth. This tends to happen in American households but is much less true for Japanese households,[9] as will be seen in detail at a later point.

The next question we must ask is: What happens when a household becomes larger? We turn now to 199 four-or-more-person households in which density does make a difference. Remember that each of these households contains a father, mother, and child, plus some combination of additional children, extended kin, and unrelated persons. Table 7.4 presents data on sleeping arrangements by kinship category for all persons in these households. The table should be read horizontally: for example, of the 132 fathers in high density households, three percent sleep alone; 97 percent sleep in nuclear family groupings, of two (15 percent), three (44 percent), and four or more (38 percent) persons; and one percent sleep with an extended kinsman. Complex-mixed sleeping groups are composed of three or more persons with at least one representative from each of the three categories—nuclear family, extended kin, and nonrelated persons.

The first point to be made from Table 7.4 concerns the effect of household social structure on who sleeps by whom. As indicated by the percentages within the heavy lines, to a striking extent nuclear kin co-sleep with nuclear kin, extended kin with extended kin, and nonrelated persons with nonrelated persons. For the father, mother, and infant, the exceptions to this generalization are trivial; and for the child, extended kin, and nonrelated persons, the exceptions occur somewhat more often in high density households. We did not fully anticipate this result, and it shows a highly regular sorting by social roles within the general tendency to cluster into co-sleeping groups.[10]

The second point to be made from

Table 7.4 concerns the size of co-sleeping groups. Within the nuclear family, regardless of density, the three-person group is most common for the father, mother, and infant. This pattern is particularly apparent in low density households, whereas high density households have a substantial percentage of four-or-more-person groups. A child is found most often in a four-or-more-person group in high density households, but in a two- or three-person-group in low density households. If anyone sleeps alone in the nuclear family, it is most likely to be an infant in a low density household.

Among extended kin, regardless of density, the most frequent pattern is to co-sleep in a two-person group, and the next most frequent is to sleep alone. Nonrelated persons are most frequently found alone, and this is especially true in low density households.

The manner in which data are presented in Table 7.4 obscures two dimensions that require examination. First, the table does not fully indicate which persons are co-sleeping in terms of social roles. For example, it tells us that about one father in five co-sleeps with some one other person; it does not tell us who that other person may be. American common sense might suggest that it is his wife—but here American common sense is not the best predictor. Second, the table combines information from families that are at different stages in their life cycle. Let us re-sort the data with these points in mind.

CO-SLEEPING AND THE LIFE CYCLE OF THE NUCLEAR FAMILY

From the point of view of the

TABLE 7.4

PERCENTAGE DISTRIBUTION OF PARTICIPATION IN VARIOUS TYPES OF CO-SLEEPING GROUPS BY KINSHIP CATEGORY AND DENSITY OF HOUSEHOLD FOR ALL PERSONS IN 199 HOUSEHOLDS HAVING FOUR OR MORE MEMBERS

Types of Co-Sleeping Groups by Number of Persons Co-Sleeping

Kinship Category	Density	Sleeping Alone	Nuclear Family 2	3	4+	Extended Kin 2	3	4+	Nonrelated 2	3	4+	Complex-Mixed 3	4+	Total Per-cent*	Total Persons
Father	High	3	15	44	38	1								101	132
	Low	9	19	64	8									100	67
Mother	High		15	47	37							1	1	101	132
	Low		23	70	8									101	67
Infant	High	3	10	50	36							1	1	101	125
	Low	14	10	68	8									100	55
Child	High	2	19	13	53	6	4						3	100	120
	Low	8	40	30	17	6								101	34
Extended kin	High	22	3	*	*	44	18	3	2	*	*	5	1	98	231
	Low	35	2			52	6	4		*				99	92
Nonrelated persons	High	28				4		4	21	27	12	2	3	101	112
	Low	63				7			20	10				100	30

* Totals do not add to 100 percent because of rounding; an asterisk indicates less than .5 of a percent.

parents, the life cycle of a nuclear family begins at marriage; it continues through the birth, rearing, and subsequent marriage of the children, until toward the end only the spouses remain; they are separated by the death of one; and finally the family ceases to exist upon the death of the other. We shall focus upon the intermediate stages of this cycle, since our data are inadequate for generalizations about the beginning and ending stages.[11]

Once again we exclude the 38 households with only one sleeping room. The remaining 285 households all contain a primary nuclear family that is in almost all cases a younger family in one of the early stages of the cycle. In addition, 110 households contain a secondary nuclear family, or the remnants thereof, which is in almost all cases in the later stages of the cycle. These older nuclear families make up the great bulk of the extended kin in Table 7.4[12] Since we have already shown that there is little co-sleeping between extended kin and other groupings, let us also in a sense stand the sample on its head and look at sleeping arrangements from the point of view of these older nuclear families, being careful to note those situations in which older nuclears occur in the sleeping ranks of younger nuclears, and vice versa.

We have, then, 285 primary and 110 secondary nuclear families to consider across the stages of the nuclear family cycle. The sample can be divided readily into seven stages, of which the first three occur among younger nuclear families and the last four among older ones. These stages are: (1) both parents and an infant, (2) both parents and an infant plus one or more young children, (3) both parents and one or more older children, (4) both parents and one or more adult children, (5) both parents only, (6) one parent and one or more adult children, and (7) one parent only.

These stages are logically exclusive except for the line to be drawn between older children and adult children in stages 3 and 4. We decided this empirically by looking at sleeping arrangements in terms of the age of the child among the total 535 children in the 285 primary and 110 secondary nuclear families.

As can be seen in Table 7.5, the sharpest break in sleeping arrangements comes between the children who are 11 to 15 years old and those who are 16 to 20 years old. The former have a 50 percent chance of co-sleeping in a two-generation group (with a parent or extended kin member), whereas the latter have only a 17 percent chance of so doing. Moreover, although the numbers involved are smaller, the break clearly seems to fall between children who are 13 to 15 years old and children who are 16 to 18 years old. The implication here is rather strong that puberty for the boy and the onset of menstruation for the girl set the stage for a withdrawal from co-sleeping with parents or extended kin. For these reasons we draw the line between stages 3 and 4 at 15 years of age. That is, we place a nuclear family in stage 3 if they have at least one child who is 15 years or younger. And we place a family in stage 4 if all of their children are 16 years or older.

Looking across thet early years of life in a more general sense, it is apparent in Table 7.5 that from the point of view of a child he can expect to co-sleep with an adult until he is ten years old. The period from 11 to 15 years is one of transition, with the greatest increase being in the co-

TABLE 7.5

PERCENTAGE DISTRIBUTION OF SLEEPING ARRANGEMENTS BY AGE FOR 535 CHILDREN FROM PRIMARY AND SECONDARY NUCLEAR FAMILIES

Sleeping Arrangements	Age of Child						
	3-4 Months (N = 259)	1-5 Years (N = 103)	6-10 Years (N = 28)	11-15 Years (N = 28)	16-20 Years (N = 46)	21-25 Years (N = 38)	26+ Years (N = 33)
Two-Generations	90	91	79	50	17	24	18
With parent(s)	90	79	68	46	15	24	15
With extended kin	—	12	11	4	2	—	3
One-Generation	2	7	11	36	46	40	33
With sibling(s)	2	7	11	36	46	37	21
With nonrelated person(s)	—	—	—	—	—	3	12
Alone	8	2	11	14	37	37	49
Total Percent*	100	100	101	100	100	101	100

* Totals do not add to 100 percent because of rounding.

TABLE 7.6

SOURCE OF DATA ON NUCLEAR FAMILIES ACROSS THE STAGES OF THE NUCLEAR FAMILY CYCLE

| | Younger Nuclear Families | | | | Older Nuclear Families | | | |
	1 Both Parents, Infant Only	2 Both Parents, Infant, Child(ren)	3 Both Parents, Older Child(ren)	4 Both Parents, Adult Child(ren)	5 Both Parents Only	6 One Parent, Adult Child(ren)	7 One Parent Only	Total Families
Source of Data								
Primary Nuclear Families								
From 86 three-person households	79	—	5	2	—	—	—	86
From 199 four-or-more-person households	92	88	16	3	—	—	—	199
Secondary Nuclear Families								
From 199 four-or-more-person households	—	—	10	36	32	13	19	110
Total Families	171	88	31	41	32	13	19	395
Median Age:								
Mother	26	29	40	56	58	55	63	
Father	29	33	45	61	63	66	68	
Child	3-4 mos.	3-4 mos., 3	13	24	—	22	—	

sleeping with a sibling. After the age of 16, a child is more likely to co-sleep with a sibling or to be alone, but there always remains a fair chance (at about the 20 percent level) that he will co-sleep with a parent. As for sex differences, which are not shown in Table 7.5, there are none until after the 11 to 15 years old period. From 16 years on, there is a tendency for daughters more than sons to co-sleep with a parent. In these later periods both daughters and sons are about equally likely to co-sleep with a sibling, but sons are more likely to sleep alone than are daughters.[13]

Having established a reasonable cutting point between stages 3 and 4 in the nuclear family cycle, we show, in Table 7.6, the frequency distribution of the families across the seven stages. The table also gives the median ages of the parents and children at each stage. In these stages, where data are drawn from several sources (that is, stages 1, 3, and 4), we first checked to see if the pattern of sleeping arrangements differed significantly according to the source. There were no differences, so we combined the cases to obtain the total families indicated in each stage.

The importance of the median ages given in the table will be explained more fully later. For now, we point out only that the median ages of the mother (26 years) and father (29 years) in stage 1 are in close agreement with findings in other studies. Since the infants in these families are three to four months old, it is likely that he parents were married one to two years earlier, on the average. At that time, the wife would have been about 24 or 25, and the husband about 27 or 28. In a study conducted in 1959, Blood (1967) found the median age of marriage to be 24 for wives and 28 for husbands among 444 young married couples living in three government apartment houses in Tokyo; and Taeuber cities data for 1935 on Japan as a whole giving an average age of first marriage of 24 for women and 28 for men. It is also apparent from the 1960 census in Japan that the average age of marriage is increasing, particularly in densely populated urban areas (see Taeuber 1958; Bureau of Statistics 1962a, pp. 72-73).

PARENTAL SLEEPING ARRANGEMENTS
IN THE EARLY STAGES

Table 7.7 presents the data for sleeping arrangements from the point of view of the parents in stages 1 through 3. Four broad categories of sleeping arrangements are used, and these need a word of explanation. In the first category, *Two Generations: Together,* both parents and at least one child are co-sleeping. This category is subdivided into those families in which all nuclear members are literally together, in that both parents and all children share a sleeping room; and those families which are more symbolically together, in that at least one of the children co-sleeps with both parents. In the second category, *Two Generations: Consanguineous,* the parents separate in order to provide parental co-sleeping partners for the children. This category is also subdivided into those situations where each parent takes one or more children as a co-sleeping partner, and those situations where the father sleeps alone while the mother co-sleeps with one or more children. The third category, *One Generation: Conjugal,* is the usual American pattern where the parents are co-sleeping as a couple, and the children are elsewhere. Finally, in the

TABLE 7.7

PERCENTAGE DISTRIBUTION OF PARENTAL SLEEPING ARRANGEMENTS BY STAGE
IN FAMILY CYCLE FOR YOUNGER NUCLEAR FAMILIES

	Stages in Family Cycle		
Parental Sleeping Arrangements	*1* Both Parents, Infant Only (3-4 mos.)* (N = 171 families)	*2* Both Parents, Infant, Child(ren) (3-4 mos. and 3 yrs.)* (N = 88 families)	*3* Both Parents, Older Child(ren) (13 yrs.)* (N = 31 families)
Two Generations: Together	86	73	52
Both parents and all children	86	53	29
Both parents and child(ren)—another child elsewhere	n.a. †	19	23
Two Generations: Consanguineous	4	22	10
Separation of parents, each with child(ren)	n.a.	15	3
Exclusion of father, mother with child(ren)	4	7	7
One Generation: Conjugal	10	6	35
Parents together, all children elsewhere			
One Generation: Separate	—	—	3
Parents sleep separately, and children sleep separately from parents			
Total Percent ‡	100	101	100

* Median ages for infants and children.
† n.a. = not applicable.
‡ Totals do not add to 100 percent because of rounding.

fourth category, *One Generation: Separate,* the parents separate, each sleeping alone, and the children are elsewhere.

In stage 1 the overwhelming proportion (86 percent) of parents co-sleep with their infant. In ten percent of the cases, the parents sleep conjugally, but we found no variable that distinguishes this group. And in a few cases, the father sleeps alone.

In stage 2 the most important change is the substantial increase (to 22 percent) in the *Two Generation: Consanguineous* pattern, even though the *Two-Generation: Together* pattern remains high (73 percent). Remember

that in stage 2 each family has two or more children—an infant and at least one young child whose median age is three years. The amount of two-generation co-sleeping actually increases from stage 1 to stage 2 if the first two categories are added together (from 90 percent to 95 percent). It is as if the Japanese parents, wanting to provide a parental sleeping partner for all children at this stage and faced with the issue of sleeping four or more to a room, which they dislike (possibly because of the size of the room, as indicated in note 7), have, in about one-fifth of the cases, decided to separate in order to meet the problem.

We have some evidence that spouses are not likely to separate if they have an alternative. And the preferred alternative is to send one or more children to co-sleep with a kinswoman. Of the 88 families in stage 2, 40 households include extended kin and 48 do not. Parents in the latter households are significantly more likely to separate than those in the former. This tendency can be seen even more sharply when we focus on the 30 families in stage 2 that are included in the sleeping patterns of both parents and one or more children (19 percent, or 17 families), and separation of parents (15 percent, or 13 families). Among the 17 families where both parents are together, 13 households contain extended kin, and four do not; on the other hand, among the 13 families where the parents are separated, only one household contains extended kin, and 12 do not (chi square = 13.6, 1 df, $p < .001$). Clearly, in households where there are extended kin, the parents have decided to remain together; when there are no extended kin available, the parents have decided to sleep separately.

We can explore this question further by asking where the "other" child sleeps among the 17 families in which both parents are together with one or more children. Four of these households do not include extended kin, and in all four the "other" child sleeps alone. But, in the 13 households that include extended kin, the "other" child co-sleeps with a kinswoman in 11 instances, and is alone only in two. Two points stand out here. First, it is always a child who goes to sleep with extended kin; the infant (and sometimes other children) remains with the parents. Second, it is usually an older kinswoman who takes the child (the husband's mother in six cases, the wife's mother in two, the husband's unmarried sister in three). In short, if an older kinswoman is present during stage 2, she is likely to become a mother surrogate for co-sleeping.

Among the 13 families in which the parents are separated, the one household containing extended kin includes a husband's father who sleeps alone. Since in this pattern each parent is co-sleeping with one or more children, it is of interest to know how the children are distributed. The fathers in these families always co-sleep with a child and never with an infant, and the sex of the child apparently does not matter—in eight cases it is a son, and in five cases it is a daughter. The mothers always co-sleep with the infant, who is joined by a child in four cases (the additional child being a son in three cases and a daughter in one case).

In stage 2, the remaining sleeping patterns are not proportionately very important, but when the father sleeps separately (7 percent), he is most often alone, and the mother is with all of the children. Finally, in the few families in which the parents sleep conjugally (6 percent), the infant and a sibling usually share another room.

In stage 3, in which there are only older children and no infants, the total proportion of two-generation co-sleeping declines but remains high (62 percent). The decrease occurs primarily in the categories of parents co-sleeping with all children, and of parents sleeping separately, each with one or more children. The proportion of parents sleeping conjugally, however, rises nearly sixfold, although at 35 percent this still seems well below American norms.

In stage 3, if the nuclear family is

not co-sleeping all together (29 percent), the parents usually keep the youngest child with them (23 percent). There are seven families in this latter pattern, and although there is no difference by density, it is informative to look at the three low-density families (which could provide, if they chose to do so, a separate room for each member). In the first case, the parents share a room with a 15-year-old son, while a 23-year-old daughter and a 19-year-old son share another room. In the second case, the parents co-sleep with a 10-year-old daughter, and two older daughters (15 and 13 years of age) share another room. And in the third case, the parents are with a 14-year-old daughter, and a 20-year-old daughter is alone.

In the consanguineous patterns (ten percent) there are only three cases. In two of these the father sleeps alone while the mother co-sleeps with all of the children, and in one case the father co-sleeps with a ten-year-old daughter and the mother with two other daughters (thirteen and nine years of age).

Where the parents sleep conjugally (35 percent), most often the children also all share another room—about half of the time with a sibling of the opposite sex. Most of these cases are high density families and are crowded for space as, for example, the family in which the parents share one room and the other room is occupied by four children (two sons, 23 and 16 years of age, and two daughters, 20 and 14 years of age). Still, the one low density family arranges itself with the parents in one room and the two children (an eight-year-old daughter and a fourteen-year-old son) in another.

Finally, there is one individualistic family with three members, each of whom sleeps alone (father, mother, and 14-year-old daughter).

PARENT'S SLEEPING ARRANGEMENTS IN THE LATER STAGES

The data for parental sleeping arrangements in the later stages of the nuclear family cycle are given in Table 7.8. Remember that each of these 105 older families is living in the same household with a married child. This is a common—and preferred—situation in Japan. For example, a national survey on aged persons (65 years and over) conducted by the Ministry of Health and Welfare in 1960 found that in Japan's six largest cities, 51 percent of the households containing aged persons also contained a married child; in smaller cities the proportion rose to 64 percent.[14] It seems probable, therefore, that our findings should be valid for about half of the older nuclear families in urban areas.

In stage 4, in which the adult children have a median age of 24, for the first time the proportion of parents sleeping conjugally rises above the proportion of two-generation co-sleeping. There would seem to be three types of parents at this stage. The most numerous are those who have decided to sleep conjugally (68 percent), now that their children have become adults. A second group continues two-generation sleeping habits, either with an adult child or a grandchild (22 percent). And third, a small proportion separate and sleep alone (ten percent).

More in detail, among the 28 cases (68 percent) in which the parents sleep conjugally, the children sleep alone in 20 cases, with siblings of the same sex in four cases, and with cross-sex siblings in three cases; in one case

TABLE 7.8

PERCENTAGE DISTRIBUTION OF PARENTAL SLEEPING ARRANGEMENTS BY STAGE IN FAMILY CYCLE FOR OLDER NUCLEAR FAMILIES

Parental Sleeping Arrangements	Stages in Family Cycle			
	4 *Both Parents, Adult Child(ren) (24 years)* (N = 41 families)*	*5* *Both Parents Only (N = 32 families)*	*6* *One Parent, Adult Child(ren) (22 years)* (N = 13 families)*	*7* *One Parent Only (N = 19 families)*
Two Generations:				
Together	15	16	n.a.	n.a.
Both parents and child(ren)	10	n.a.	n.a.	n.a.
Both parents and grandchild(ren)	5	16	n.a.	n.a.
Two Generations:				
Consanguineous	7	3	62	32
Separation of parents, each with child(ren) or grandchild(ren)	—	—	n.a.	n.a.
Exclusion of father, mother with child(ren) or grandchild(ren)	7	3	n.a.	n.a.
Widowed parent with child(ren) or grandchild(ren)	n.a. †	n.a.	62	32
One Generation: Conjugal Parents together, child(ren) or grandchild(ren) elsewhere	68	75	n.a.	n.a.
One Generation: Separate Parents, or widowed parent, sleep separately and alone	10	6	39	68
Total Percent ‡	100	100	101	100

* Median age for children.
† **n.a.** = not applicable.
‡ Totals do not add to 100 percent because of rounding.

a son co-sleeps with a male employee. Among the nine cases (22 percent) in which the parents sleep in some two-generation combination, seven cases involve children and two cases involve grandchildren. For example, the parents in a low-density family choose to co-sleep with a 24-year-old son; and the mother in a low density family co-sleeps with her unmarried 35-year-old eldest son while the father sleeps alone (a younger son is married, and his family forms the younger nuclear family in this household). Finally, among the four cases (ten percent) in which the parents sleep separately, in one case three sons share a room together, and there are three rather peculiar cases in which not only the mother and father but also each of the children sleeps alone.

In stages 5 both older parents remain, but there are no unmarried adult children. In this stage, conjugal sleeping reaches its highest proportion (75 percent), followed by two-generation co-sleeping with a grandchild (19 percent), and with a small proportion sleeping separately and alone (six percent). It would seem that there are always about one-fifth of the grandparents in this kind of household who volunteer, or who are pressed into service, to care for the needs of a grandchild at night.

Stages 6 and 7 represent the fragmented remains of the nuclear family at the end of its cycle. The situations in these two stages appear to be reciprocal: in stage 6, where there is an unmarried child, the widowed parent tends to co-sleep with the child or with a grandchild (62 percent of the time); in stage 7, where there is no unmarried child, the widowed parent tends to sleep, at the end, alone (68 percent of the time) unless a grandchild is available.

In support of the above generalization, the 13 cases in stage 6 are made up of ten widowed mothers and three widowed fathers who do have an unmarried child living in the household. Among the ten mothers, six co-sleep with a child (four with daughters and two with sons), one co-sleeps in a cluster with three grandchildren, and three sleep alone. Among the three fathers, one co-sleeps with a daughter, and the other two sleep alone.

The 19 cases in stage 7 are made up of 16 widowed mothers and three widowed fathers who do not, of course, have an unmarried child living in the household, and must co-sleep with a grandchild if they are not to sleep alone. Among the 16 mothers, five co-sleep with a grandchild, and among the three fathers, one co-sleeps with a grandchild.

There is a further point of interest. If we combine the cases in stages 4 and 6, and the cases in stages 5 and 7, we have two types of older nuclear families—those that contain older parents and adult unmarried children (54 cases), and those that contain only older parents (51 cases). Here style of family life does make a difference. Households with a "small family business" style of life contain more older nuclear families having parents and adult unmarried children, whereas households with a "salaryman" style of life contain more older nuclear families having only parents.[15] It would seem that young married salarymen are willing to assume responsibility for their parents, but are less willing to have their adult unmarried siblings living with them. In contrast, adult unmarried siblings seem to be more welcome in small business households where they may more directly contribute to the work of the family.

CO-SLEEPING AND THE LIFE CYCLE OF THE INDIVIDUAL

So far we have considered co-sleeping mostly in terms of the life cycle of the nuclear family. What about the co-sleeping career of an individual from birth to death? What are his co-sleeping "chances" at different ages? We have already seen (Table 7.5) that until the age of 15 a child has about a 50 percent chance of sleeping with one or both parents. From birth to age 15, a child's chances of co-sleeping with a sibling gradually increases; and before age 15 only a few children are likely to sleep alone.

In these early years of life, co-sleeping bears importantly upon questions of socialization and identity (Whiting et al. 1958; Burton and Whiting 1961). We have shown that, in general, when a family has more than one child, the parents may separate and each co-sleep with a child, or sometimes a child may be sent to co-sleep with an older kinswoman. On the whole we would expect that the older a child, the more likely he is to be removed from the parental bedroom. One way to test this is to contrast the treatment of infants and young children. Of the 88 families in stage 2, 73 have exactly two children—in each case an infant of three to four months, and a child with a median age of three years (see Table 7.7). We constructed a five-point scale of physical closeness to a parent in sleeping arrangements, and then asked of the data for each family: Who is closer, the infant or the child? The results are given in Table 7.9.

In each family, the infant and child are assigned a position on the five-point scale, and a tie occurs where both occupy the same position. The scale is as follows: (1) *Alone* means sleeping in a room by oneself. (2) *Other Person's Room* means co-sleeping in a room with a person other than a parent. This can occur when the infant and child are sharing a room (in which case it is a tie), or it can occur when the infant or the child is co-sleeping with an adult (usually a grandmother). (3) *Parent's Room in Own Bed* means that the infant or child is sleeping in his own Western-style bed or crib in the same room with both parents, or with either the mother or father separately. (4) *Parent's Room in Own Futon* means that the infant or child is sleeping in his own individual *futon* (quilts spread on the floor) with both parents, or with either the mother or father separately. (5) *In Parent's Bedding* means that the infant is sleeping in the same bedding (either in a Western-style bed or in Japanese *futon*) with both parents, or with either the mother or father separately.

We consider sleeping in one's own *futon* to be closer in access to a parent than sleeping in one's own bed or crib for this reason: the Japanese quilts of the several co-sleepers are usually laid out next to each other with the edges almost touching. This means that a parent need only reach over to care for an infant or child, without the necessity of getting up. In contrast, a bed or crib is a more distinctly separate "container," and a parent needs to get up in order to care for an infant or child. In fact, cribs are mainly used only during the first year of life; after this the crib is put away, and the young child is given his own *futon*. Even during the first year, the crib may be used only as a daytime container, and the infant will be brought down on the mats to sleep in *futon* during the night. Therefore, we scored beds and *futon* differently, but these points on the scale may be collapsed into a single category of "In a Parent's Room in Own Bedding." We will give the results in both ways.[16]

In Table 7.9, cases falling on the diagonal represent ties between infant and child in closeness of access to a parent. Cases above the diagonal represent situations in which the infant is closer, and cases below the diagonal represent situations in which the child is closer.

Using the full five-point scale, it is clear that the child is closer to a parent than is the infant. There are 20 ties; the infant is closer in 16 cases; and the child is closer in 37 cases (chi square = 10.0, 2 *df*, *p* < .01). There is no significant difference in this pattern by density, social class, or style

of life. There is a difference, however, by whether or not there are extended kin living in the household—a result which we have previously seen in the more general analysis of the data for stage 2.

In the data in Table 7.9 there are 33 families in which extended kin are present, and 40 families in which they are not. In the extended kin families, the infant and child are equal in access to a parent (nine ties, 12 infant closer, and 12 child closer) because the child is frequently provided with a "substitute mother" and is sleeping in another person's room while the infant is with the mother (or with both parents). In the families with only nuclear members, the child is closer to a parent (11 ties, four infant closer,

TABLE 7.9

COMPARISON OF CLOSENESS OF ACCESS TO PARENTS IN SLEEPING ARRANGEMENTS
FOR INFANT AND CHILD IN 73 FAMILIES HAVING ONE INFANT AND ONE CHILD

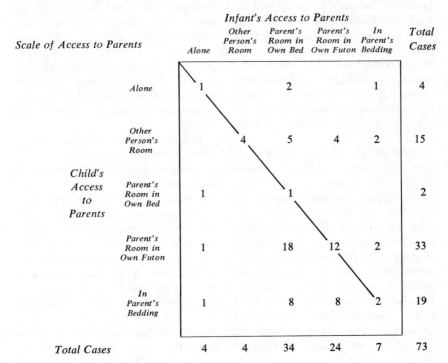

Scale of Access to Parents		Infant's Access to Parents					Total Cases
		Alone	Other Person's Room	Parent's Room in Own Bed	Parent's Room in Own Futon	In Parent's Bedding	
	Alone	1		2		1	4
	Other Person's Room		4	5	4	2	15
Child's Access to Parents	Parent's Room in Own Bed	1		1			2
	Parent's Room in Own Futon	1		18	12	2	33
	In Parent's Bedding	1		8	8	2	19
Total Cases		4	4	34	24	7	73

and 25 child closer). The comparison of closeness to a parent in these two types of families is significant (chi square = 8.2, 2 df, $p < .02$).

If the distinction between sleeping in own bed and in own *futon* is collapsed into a broader category of sleeping in own bedding, then the infant and child become equidistant in access to a parent (38 ties, 16 infant closer, and 19 child closer).

We conclude that, at the very least, there is little change in access to a parent in sleeping arrangements during the transition from infancy to childhood. In contrast, there is a sharp physical separation from the parents during this transition in the urban American family, if indeed such a separation had not already been made in infancy.[17] The relative conception of the path to be followed in the socialization of the young child would seem to be different in the two cultures. In Japan, the path seems to lead toward increasing interdependence with other persons, whereas in America the path seems to lead toward increasing independence from others. As we have shown, even in stage 3, at a time when the median age of the child is 13 years, the proportion of two-generation co-sleeping remains very high (see Table 7.7).

From the age of 16 to 26 or more (see Table 7.5), roughly 20 percent of the children continue to co-sleep in a two-generation group, mainly with a parent; and about 40 percent co-sleep in a one-generation group, mostly with a sibling. At this older age sleeping alone rises significantly, to 37 percent from age 16 to 25, and to 40 percent by age 26 or more. If our data included children living away from home,[18] then the total proportion of children sleeping alone between the ages of 16 and 26 and older would probably be over 50 percent.

As we have seen, however, daughters tend to marry in urban Japan around the age of 24 to 26, and sons a few years later around the age of 27 to 30. Presumably, after marriage the young couple sleeps conjugally for a year or two until the birth of their first child. But, from that point on, for at least the following 15 years the parents will usually co-sleep in a two-generation group containing one or more of their children. This repeats, of course, their own childhood experience, as can be seen in Table 7.10, which summarizes the data on sleeping arrangements across our seven stages in the nuclear family cycle.

Somewhere between stages 3 and 4, when the mother is in her middle to late forties and the father is in his late forties to early fifties, the balance shifts for the parents in favor of conjugal sleeping. This pattern persists through stage 5 and until one of the parents dies. Then, if there is an unmarried child available, the widowed parent tends to revert to the earlier pattern of co-sleeping with a child in stage 6. Finally, in stage 7, when there is only the widowed parent, the proportion of sleeping alone rises steeply.

In summary, then, an individual in urban Japan can expect to co-sleep in a two-generation group, first as a child and then as a parent, over approximately half of his life. This starts at birth and continues until puberty; it resumes after the birth of the first child and continues until about the time of menopause for the mother; and it reoccurs for a few years in old age. In the interim years the individual can expect to co-sleep in a one-generation group with a sibling after puberty, with a spouse for a few years after marriage, and

TABLE 7.10

SUMMARY PERCENTAGE DISTRIBUTION OF PARENTAL SLEEPING ARRANGEMENTS ACROSS STAGES IN THE NUCLEAR FAMILY CYCLE

	\		Stages in Family Cycle				
Parental Sleeping Arrangements	1 Both Parents, Infant Only (N = 171 families)	2 Both Parents, Infant, Child(ren) (N = 88 families)	3 Both Parents, Older Child(ren) (N = 31 families)	4 Both Parents, Adult Child(ren) (N = 41 families)	5 Both Parents Only (N = 32 families)	6 One Parent, Adult Child(ren) (N = 13 families)	7 One Parent Only (N = 19 families)
Two Generations: Together	86	73	52	15	16	n.a.*	n.a.
Two Generations: Consanguineous	4	22	10	7	3	62	32
One Generation: Conjugal	10	6	35	68	75	n.a.	n.a.
One Generation: Separate	—	—	3	10	6	39	68
Total Percent †	100	101	100	100	100	101	100
Median Age of Parents:							
Mother	26	29	40	56	58	55	63
Father	29	33	45	61	63	66	68

* n.a. = not applicable.
† Totals do not add to 100 percent because of rounding.

again with a spouse in late middle age. Sleeping alone appears to be an alternative most commonly found in the years between puberty and marriage, and to be a reluctantly accepted necessity for the widowed parent toward the end.

We wish to make one broad generalization, and one speculation. The generalization is that sleeping arrangements in Japanese families tend to blur the distinctions between generations and between the sexes, to emphasize the interdependence more than the separateness of individuals, and to underplay (or largely ignore) the potentiality for the growth of conjugal intimacy between husband and wife in sexual and other matters in favor of a more general familial cohesion.[19]

The speculation concerns the coincidence of those age periods when sleeping alone is most likely to occur, with the age periods when suicide is most likely to occur in Japan. The rates for both types of behavior are highest in adolescence and young adulthood, and again in old age.[20] It might be that sleeping alone in these two periods contributes to a sense of isolation and alienation for an individual who, throughout the rest of his life cycle, seems to derive a significant part of his sense of being a meaningful person from his sleeping physically close by other family members. We are not suggesting that sleeping alone causes suicide, but rather that this type of separation is an added increment in the unusually difficult problems that Japanese young people seem to have in making the transition from youth to early adulthood as they shift from high school to college, enter the occupational world, and get married. Such transitions do involve the establishment of an identity more separate from one's natal family, and

this is made harder by the long period of very close involvement in family life. Similarly, in old age, after a second long period of close familial investment, to come finally to sleep alone probably carries with it a greater sense of separation than it does in the West.

CULTURE AND CO-SLEEPING

Others before us have hinted in a general way at the importance of co-sleeping in Japanese family life. But we believe that our work documents this with a degree of precision not achieved before, and at the same time demonstrates the wider relevance of what might otherwise appear to be only an offbeat sort of sociometry.

Dore, for example, writes of life in a Tokyo ward as follows: "Beyond the limits of actual cramped discomfort, crowded sleeping seems to be considered to be more pleasant than isolation in separate rooms. The individual gains a comforting security, and it is a sign that a spirit of happy intimacy pervades the family" (1958, p. 49). The co-sleeping-as-intimacy theme also occurs frequently in Japanese fiction and biography. For example, the twentieth-century social reformer, Toyohiko Kagawa, as a child prized—and later vividly remembered—opportunities to sleep by his elder brother. As a seminarian he was deeply impressed when a missionary offered to share his bed even though Kagawa was tubercular. When he recovered, Kagawa in turn shared his bed in the Kobe slums with criminals, alcoholics, the ill, and the destitute. And throughout his adult life he enjoyed praying in bed but was embarrassed because he feared the

Almighty might take this as a sign of disrespectful familiarity (see Axling 1932; Bradshaw 1952; Topping 1935).

Evidence of a negative sort comes from collective societies that attempt to weaken parent-child bonds by requiring children to sleep away from the home. The Israeli kibbutzim are usually cited in this regard; two Japanese collectives tried this method but abandoned it after a period. For example, the Yamagishi community in Mie prefecture once had all children sleep in a dormitory from the age of three months, but now the children move to the dormitory in the third year of primary school (at about age 8). Also at the Yamagishi community, co-sleeping among adults is self-consciously used as a means of weakening interpersonal barriers. During training sessions for prospective members, they live together in one room and are expected to sleep in same sex pairs. Trainers are told that co-sleeping will help reduce the strength of selfish desires (see Plath 0000).

In another collective, Shinkyō village in Nara prefecture, a children's sleeping room was also tried, but at present children generally co-sleep with their parents. The following comment by one member is revealing:

During the first stages of collective living, our plan to give the same love to every child led us at times to deliberately separate bawling children from their parents and make them sleep with other parents, and at times we had all the children sleep together. But lately we have not been particularly concerned about it either way; we are letting matters take their natural course. That is, a younger child sleeps with its parents, an older child sleeps with some other adult. Thus, there are couples who sleep by themselves even though they have children, and there are childless couples who sleep with other peoples' children. . . . Since we are all part of one family, these things can be arranged according to **need.** . . . Adults and children share their joys and sorrows alike, whatever their ages; so it is simply unthinkable that the emotional foundations of our collective **life** could shake over whether adults **and** children sleep together or not. (Sugihara 1962, pp. 214-215)

Vogel's work is perhaps closest to our own, and we have earlier cited his data on sleeping arrangements for infants and young children. (Vogel 1963). He goes on to note: "When a second child is born, and the mother must sleep with the baby, the eldest child ordinarily stops sleeping with the mother and begins sleeping with the father or a grandparent. While elementary-school-age children often sleep in a separate room, . . . it is not unusual for grown children to sleep next to their parents" (1963, p. 231). These observations are in general in line with the results of our analysis, although we believe we have defined the alternative patterns of sleeping arrangements more clearly, and shown that the separation of parents, each with a child, is an important variant pattern at the stage when there is an infant and one or more young children in the family.

Vogel stresses the mutual dependency of mother and child and relates it to what he feels is the basic alignment in the family: "mother and children versus father" (1963, p. 211). This alignment is not usually hostile, but refers to a real psychological and behavioral division within the family despite (or in some senses because of) the predominance of all-together sleeping arrangements. The relative lack of husband-wife intimacy in sexual and other matters is related to this division, as is the elaborate world of pleasure for males outside the home. This world of bars, restaurants, and clubs is, however, a great deal less sexual than Americans like to imagine. True, sex is available if a man has the money and time, and the motivation and energy, to invest in the relationship; but for the most part this world is a play-acting one which is entered for a few hours after work and then left for the long ride home to family and to bed.

Thus, our analysis of sleeping arrangements has ramifications beyond the confines of the family, and is related to the patterning of values and emotions in Japan in general. Japanese place great emphasis on collaterality (group inter-relatedness) not only in the family but in many spheres of activity. They also find much of their enjoyment in the simple physical pleasures of bathing, eating, and sleeping in the company of others. Given these emphases in values and emotions, it is not surprising that individual assertiveness and the open indication of sexual feelings have negative connotations (see Caudill and Scarr 1962; Caudill 1962; Caudill and Doi 1963).

A certain proportion of Japanese, however, as would be true among people in any society, have difficulty in behaving, thinking, and feeling according to the norm. Such variant persons may have good or poor adjustments to life. Among the latter, it is interesting that schizophrenic patients in Japan show more sleep disturbance and greater physical assaultiveness (especially toward their mothers) than do comparable American patients in the year prior to hospitalization (Schooler and Caudill 1964). There may, therefore, be something mildly ironic in the fact that it is usual to provide patients in small private psychiatric hospitals (which make up the bulk of psychiatric hospitals in Japan) with a personal female attendant who as a matter of routine care is with the patient throughout the day and sleeps in the room with him at night (Caudill 1961).

In Western eyes, Japanese co-sleeping patterns may appear pathogenic, or at least to be taken as a denial of maturation and individuation. And yet, there is no evidence that on the whole people are not as happy and productive in Japan as in America, and there does not seem to be more grief in one country than in the other. It is true that the rhythm of life across the years is different in the two countries, and we have shown this particularly for sleeping arrangements. But two cautions are necessary here. First, we have little information about sleeping arrangements in America, but what we do have suggests more variation than might be supposed.[21] Because a child in middle-class America is given a separate room in which to sleep does not mean that he stays in it throughout the night; how do the parents handle his situation? Secondly, the comparison of Japan with America results in sharp differences, but if the comparison were made between Japan and other Eastern or even European countries, the differences might be minor.

Finally, it seems that at least for the first few years of life, the tendency for mother and child to co-sleep is a natural one that human beings share in a general way with other mammals. Only recently has Western society tried to interfere. As Peiper (1963, p. 611) notes:

As late as in the eighteenth century the child slept with his mother. . . . The custom was so widespread—especially because it had such ancient origins—and the conditions so bad that legislators many times had to take measures against it. For example, as late as 1817 the general law for the Prussian States decreed, under threat of imprisonment or physical punishment: "Mothers and wet nurses are not allowed to take children under two years of age into their beds at night or to let them sleep with them or others."

If the pattern of sleeping together was so common in the West as late as the eighteenth century (see also Ariès 1962), then we need more information about these matters over the years up to the present. Social change has been rapid in both Japan and America in recent decades, but it is likely that such changes have been greater in technological and occupational sectors than in patterns of family life.

In both cultures, in the flow of events across days and nights and years, as evening descends and the focus of the family turns from contact with the outside to the ordering of life within the house, who sleeps by whom is an issue with serious implications that warrant further study.

NOTES

1. The three hospitals used were St. Luke's International Hospital and Tsukiji Metropolitan Maternity Hospital in Tokyo, and Kyoto Metropolitan Medical School Hospital in Kyoto. In addition to having a three- to four-month-old infant, a mother selected for interview could, and frequently did, have other children as well. The several hospitals were picked so as to insure a good spread of cases by social class and style of life. The reason for focusing on mothers with infants was to provide background on various aspects of family life, not only sleeping arrangements, from a fairly large sample of such cases in order to supplement Caudill's intensive study in the homes of 30 Japanese and 30 American infants and their mothers. On this, see Caudill and Weinstein (1968).

2. Matsumoto City, and life in it, is described in Plath (1964); see Chapter 2 in particular. Concerning sleeping arrangements in the Matsumoto area, Plath read a preliminary report, including 20 rural cases omitted here, at the 1964 annual meeting of the American Anthropological Association in Detroit.

3. The proportion of two-generation to three-generation households is roughly 2 to 1 in our sample, whereas it is roughly 4 to 1 in comparable households (census household types 4, 5, and 11, 12) for all urban areas (that is, "densely inhabited districts of all *shi*") in Japan. The proportion of salary and wage households to family business households is 1.4 to 1 in our sample, whereas it is 3.0 to 1 for all urban areas in Japan. There is no easy way to estimate accurately the distribution of households by social class from census data, but we are certain that our sample has more households in higher social classes than is true in the general population. See Bureau of Statistics (1962b, pp. 139 and 428).

4. The 1960 census data were recomputed, omitting households of two persons or less, so as to be in line with the household composition of our sample. See Bureau of Statistics (1962b, pp. 20-21).

5. A person may be at the top of the social system working in a family business or an individual enterprise—for example, a well-known physician in private practice —or he may be at the bottom as the owner of a cigarette stand. Similarly, he may work for salary or wages as an executive, or as a janitor in a large company. In research in Japan, a useful operational break can be made between these two ways of life by classifying businesses having less than 30 employees as "small independent businesses," and by considering owners or employees of such businesses as participating in a way of life that is meaningfully different, in occupational and familial terms, from that of owners or employees in "large businesses." Such a cut-off point is, of course, arbitrary to a degree, and the distinction is more readily apparent between businesses having less than 10 employees and those having more than 100

employees—and this latter classification would still cover the great bulk of cases. We have followed this sort of reasoning in our classification in this research, although our data on occupation of the head of the household are not sufficient for such precise placement. More generally, concerning the meaning of these two styles of life, see Plath (1964); Caudill and Weinstein (1968); and particularly Vogel (1963).

6. In devising these procedures for estimating social-class position, we made use of the work of Hollingshead on American populations, and modified it to approximate the Japanese situation along lines suggested by the work of Odaka. See Hollingshead and Redlich (1958, esp. pp. 387-397). See also Research Committee of the Japan Sociological Society (1958); Odaka and Nishihira (1965); Odaka (1964, 1965); Inkeles and Rossi (1956); Ramsey and Smith (1960).

Our final three social-class groups may be described as follows. The upper middle class consists mainly of heads of households who are college graduates, and who are in professional or supervisory positions or are owners of substantial businesses. The lower middle class consists mainly of heads of households who are high-school graduates, and who are white-collar workers or owners of small businesses with paid employees. The working class is equally divided between heads of households who are high school graduates and those who have less than a high school education, and who are technicians, skilled or unskilled workers, paid employees of small businesses, or owners of small family shops with no paid employees.

7. Mat-floored rooms in Japanese dwellings lack the specificity of purpose usually assigned to rooms in Western dwellings. Thus, the ordinary Japanese house is not sharply divided into living rooms, bedrooms, dining rooms, recreation rooms, and so on. In part this reflects the relative sparsity of furniture in the Japanese house. Nevertheless, household members do tend to divide the space among themselves and to assign the use of a particular room to one or several persons. In addition, a household with multiple rooms is likely to set aside one of them as a living room or guest room. The size of a room is usually given in terms of the number of mats it contains. One mat is roughly six by three feet in size and two inches in thickness, and it is made of packed rice straw covered with a finely woven rush. The edges of better quality mats are bound in cloth. The most common sizes for rooms in Japan are six mats (roughly 9 by 12 feet) and four and one-half mats (roughly 9 by 9 feet). On these matters of use and construction of rooms see Dore, (1958); Beardsley, Hall, and Ward (1959); Taut (1958).

8. Two of these households include extended kin; the other 36 are composed of nuclear kin only.

9. For example, in the observational study of 60 three-to-four-month-old infants by Caudill and Weinstein (1968), 17 of the 30 American infants slept alone, and the parents of the remaining 13 infants planned to move to a larger apartment by the end of the first year so as to provide a separate bedroom for the baby. All of the 30 Japanese infants co-slept with their parents, to whom the idea of moving to provide more space for the baby never occurred. In other reports, Pease found that in one Tokyo suburb a child co-sleeps with his mother for an average of 92 months; and Vogel found that the interval varies from 35 months among Tokyo shopkeeping families to 130 months in a deep-sea fishing village in Miyagi prefecture. See Pease (1961); Vogel (1963, pp. 229-230).

In contrast, the only fairly large-scale study for the United States that we have found reports data on sleeping arrangements for children in Baltimore who were patients at a psychiatric outpatient clinic, and for a control group, in answer to the question: "Did your child ever sleep in the same room with you and his/her father?" This question assumes that co-sleeping may be an unusual and infrequent event (as at times of sickness), and thus the answers are not strictly comparable with our Japanese data, which are reported in terms of habitual sleeping arrangements. The Baltimore study found no differences between children who were patients and those who were controls. Of the total group of 370 children, 61 percent either had never co-slept with parents (39 percent) or had stopped by the end of the first year (22 percent). Of the remainder, 21 percent had stopped by the end of the fourth year, and 17 percent had continued beyond the end of the fourth year. These results are from unpublished data supplied by Martha S. Oleinick, Office of

Biometry, National Institute of Mental Health. See also Oleinick, Bahn, Eisenberg, and Lilienfeld (n.d.).

10. Discussions of Japanese family life often stress the role played by the grandparents when they are present in the household—particularly the grandmother—in the rearing of children. Table 7.4 shows that 13 percent of the children in high density families and 6 percent in low density families co-sleep in some combination with an extended kin member who is, in fact, most often a grandmother. These percentages do not seem to represent a "considerable influence" in this regard on the lives of our group of children, but we defer discussion of this issue until the next section of the paper. It is also not unusual to find reference to the importance of the role of a family servant in the rearing of children. And yet, in our data, no nonrelated person co-sleeps exclusively with a nuclear family member; and the likelihood of a nonrelated person co-sleeping at all with a nuclear family member is at most five percent in complex-mixed groups in high density households.

11. We are indebted to Koyama for pointing out the necessity to consider the various stages in the family life cycle when analyzing social characteristics of the Japanese family. We have not made use of all of his stages here, and have made finer subdivisions in others. See Takashi Koyama (1962).

12. Within the 199 households represented in Table 7.4, there are 323 entended kin members (231 in high density and 92 in low density households). These members live in 123 households. Of these, 13 households contain only adult unmarried brothers or sisters of the husband or wife in the younger nuclear family. These unmarried brothers or sisters sleep alone, or co-sleep in same-sex groups of two. Our concern here is with the remaining 110 households that contain at least one parent of the husband or wife in the younger nuclear family, and may contain the other parent plus the parents' grown unmarried children.

13. In considering these data for children who are 16 years of age or more, remember that these show the sleeping arrangements of older children who are *living at home*. If they have left the home, and are living in company dormitories, rooming houses, apartments, and so on, their sleeping arrangements most likely show higher proportions of co-sleeping with nonrelated persons, or alone. A survey conducted in October, 1965, by the Economic Planning Agency concerning the patterns of life of 2,500 young unmarried workers between 15 and 29 years of age in large companies in Tokyo and Osaka, found that 76 percent of the young women, and 44 percent of the young men, were living with their parents. See Japan Information Service (1966).

14. Percentages for other types of households that include aged persons are: (1) In the six largest cities an additional 25 percent of the aged lived with adult unmarried children, and 18 percent lived with a spouse only or alone; (2) in the smaller cities an additional 17 percent lived with adult unmarried children, and 13 percent lived with a spouse or alone. The remaining percentages for the two kinds of cities include miscellaneous types of households in which the aged lived with grandchildren, with other aged persons, in institutions, and so on. All of these data are cited by Watanabe (1963).

15. The data are as follows: Small business households contain 34 cases of parents and adult unmarried children, and 20 cases of only parents; salaryman households contain 20 cases of parents and adult unmarried children, and 31 cases of only parents. This fourfold comparison is significant (chi square = 5.9, 1 *df, p* < .02).

16. The main reason given by Japanese mothers for the use of cribs during the first year is that they are easier to clean than *futon* if the infant should soil his bedding. A secondary reason is the fear of rolling on the infant while asleep, although this applies mostly to the situation where the infant is sleeping in a parent's *futon* rather than in his own *futon*. The types of bedding used by individuals in our sample present some interesting contrasts. Restricting the analysis to the 259 households which include an infant and have two or more sleeping rooms, the following results are found. Among the 259 infants, 172 use cribs and 87 use *futon;* whereas among the 105 children in these households, only 10 use beds and 95 use *futon*. Thus, only 34 percent of the infants use *futon,* but 91 percent of the children do so. Among infants, the use of cribs is linked to higher social class (*p* < .001), to a salaryman style of life (*p* < .01), and to residence in Tokyo (*p*

< .05). There are, of course, 518 parents of the infants in the 259 households, and the overwhelming proportion, 85 percent, of these parents sleep in *futon* (439 *futon* to 79 beds). Variations in parental use of beds or *futon* are influenced by several variable. First of all, beds are found in Tokyo more than Kyoto ($p < .05$), in low density households ($p < .01$), among salarymen rather than small businessmen ($p < .001$), and are concentrated at upper social levels ($p < .001$). Secondly, double beds, in contrast to single beds, are used in high density households ($p < .001$); and, equally, double *futon*, in contrast to single *futon*, are used in high density households ($p < .02$). So it would seem that when things are crowded people adjust by using a container in which they can double up, whether they choose a bed or a *futon*.

17. See footnote 9.

18. See footnote 13.

19. To be sure, sexual relations between parents take place, but in what is reported as a brief and "businesslike" manner (for example, see Beardsley, Hall, and Ward 1959, p. 333). Vogel, citing his own data and that of Shinozaki in a larger study, indicates that, compared to American couples, Japanese couples have intercourse less frequently, and have less foreplay and afterplay (1963, pp. 220-222). As might be presumed from the sleeping arrangements shown in our data, sexual intercourse in Japan frequently takes place in the presence of sleeping children. The most usual answer given by the 30 Japanese mothers in an intensive case study of mother-child relations (see Caudill and Weinstein 1968) was that the parents wait until they think the child is sound asleep and then have intercourse. In addition, as Table 7.4 shows, the parents are usually the only adults in the bedroom, at least until they are in late middle age, and hence have a certain degree of privacy. In more traditional Japan, however, it was not too unusual for a young married couple to co-sleep with the husband's parents even though other rooms were available. In his regard, the famous Meiji reformer Fukuzawa urged that young married couples have a room apart from the husband's parents. Apparently Fukuzawa was not concerned about sex so much as he was with providing the young wife with at least a nocturnal sanctuary away from her carping mother-in-law. However, Fukuzawa did not practice his own precepts. See Blacker (1964, pp. 88, 157-158).

20. In our data, as indicated, sleeping alone is most likely during the ages of 16-26 and after approximately age 65. Suicide in Japan, as DeVos and others have pointed out, is of special interest because of its sex and age distribution. The ratio of women to men is higher than in any other country, and the concentration of suicide in early life (15-24 years) and old age (60 years and over) is unique in having this U-shaped pattern. Moreover, these phenomena have occurred yearly as far back as reliable Japanese statistics have been kept. For example, in terms of the rates in Japan per 100,000 population for 1952-1954: For ages 15-19 the rate among males is 26.1, and among females is 18.7; for ages 20-24 the rate among males is 60.0, and among females is 35.5. In the United States, the comparable rates are: for ages 15-19, males 1.7 and females 1.6; and for ages 20-24, males 7.8 and females 2.8. In old age in Japan the rates for ages 60-69 are 58.1 for males and 34.6 for females; whereas in the United States the rates are 42.4 for males and 8.9 for females. See George A. DeVos (1966, 1962).

21. See footnote 9.

REFERENCES

Aries, Philippe
1962 *Centuries of Childhood*. New York: Knopf.
Axling, William
1932 *Kagawa*. London: Student Christian Movement Press.
Beardsley, Richard K., J. W. Hall, and R. E. Ward
1959 *Village Japan*. Chicago: University of Chicago Press.

Blacker, Carmen
 1964 *The Japanese Enlightenment.* Cambridge: University of Cambridge Oriental Publications, N. 10.
Blood, Robert O., Jr.
 1967 *Love-Match and Arranged Marriage.* New York: Free Press.
Bradshaw, Emerson O.
 1952 *Unconquerable Kagawa.* St. Paul: Macalester Park.
Bureau of Statistics
 1962a *1960 Population Census of Japan, Vol. 2: One Percent Tabulation, Part 1: Age, Marital Status, Legal Nationality, Education and Fertility.* Tokyo: Office of the Prime Minister.
 1962b *1960 Population Census of Japan, Vol. 2: One Percent Tabulation, Part 5: Household.* Tokyo: Office of the Prime Minister.
Burton, Roger V., and John W. M. Whiting
 1961 The absent father and cross-sex identity. Merrill-Palmer Quarterly 7: 85-95.
Caudill, William
 1961 Around the clock patient care in Japanese psychiatric hospitals: The role of the *Tsukisoi. American Sociological Review* 26: 204-214.
 1962 Patterns of emotion in modern Japan. *In* R. J. Smith and R. K. Beardsley (eds.), *Japanese Culture: Its Development and Characteristics.* Chicago: Aldine.
Caudill, William, and L. Takeo Doi
 1963 Interrelations of psychiatry, culture and emotion in Japan. *In* I. Galdston (ed.), *Man's Image in Medicine and Anthropology.* New York: International Universities Press.
Caudill, William, and Harry A. Scarr
 1962 Japanese value orientations and culture change. *Ethnology* 1: 53-91.
Caudill, William, and Helen Weinstein
 1968 Maternal care and infant behavior in Japanese and American urban middle class families. *In* R. Konig and R. Hill (eds.), *Yearbook of the International Sociological Association, 1966.*
DeVos, George A.
 1962 Deviancy and social change: A psychocultural evaluation of trends in Japanese delinquency and suicide. *In* R. J. Smith and R. K. Beardsley (eds.), *Japanese Culture: Its Development and Characteristics.* Chicago: Aldine.
 1966 Role narcissism and the etiology of Japanese suicide. *Transcultural Psychiatric Research* 3: 13-17.
Dore, Ronald
 1958 *City Life in Japan.* London: Routledge and Kegan Paul.
Gleason, Alan H.
 1964 Postwar housing in Japan and the United States, a case in international comparison. *In* Occasional Papers, N. 8, *Studies on Economic Life in Japan.* University of Michigan, Center for Japanese Studies.
Hollingshead, August B., and Fredrick C. Redlich
 1958 *Social Class and Mental Illness.* New York: Wiley.
Inkeles, Alex, and Peter H. Rossi
 1956 National comparisons of occupational prestige, *American Journal of Sociology* 61: 329-339.
Japan Information Service
 1966 Survey taken on finances of young Japanese workers. *Japan Report* 12 (8, April 30): 5-7.
Koyama, Takashi
 1962 Changing family structure in Japan. *In* R. J. Smith and R. K. Beardsley (eds.), *Japanese Culture: Its Development and Characteristics.* Chicago: Aldine.
Odaka, Kunio
 1964-65 The middle classes in Japan. *Contemporary Japan* 28: 10-32, 268-296.
Odaka, Kunio, and Shigeki Nishihira
 1965 Social mobility in Japan: A report on the 1955 survey of social stratification and social mobility in Japan. *East Asian Cultural Studies* 4 (1-4): 83-126.
Oleinick, M. S., A. K. Bahn, L. Eisenberg, and A. M. Lilienfeld
 n.d. A retrospective study of the early socialization experiences and intrafamilial

environment of psychiatric out-patient clinic children and control group children. Manuscript.

Pease, Demaris
    1961   Some child rearing practices in Japanese families. *Marriage and Family Living* 23: 179-181.

Peiper, Albrecht
    1963   *Cerebral Function in Infancy and Childhood.* New York: Consultants Bureau.

Plath, David W.
    1964   *The After Hours: Modern Japan and the Search for Enjoyment.* Berkeley: University of California Press.
    1967   Utopian rhetoric: Conversion and conversation in a Japanese cult. In *The Visual and Verbal Arts: Proceedings of the 1966 Annual Spring Meeting of the American Ethnological Society.*

Ramsey, Charles E., and Robert J. Smith
    1960   Japanese and American perceptions of occupations. *American Journal of Sociology* 65: 475-82.

Research Committee of the Japan Sociological Society *(Nihon Shakai Gakkai Chōsa Jinkai Hen)* (ed.)
    1958   *The Class Structure of Japanese Society. (Nihon Shakai no Kaisōteki Kōzo).* Tokyo: Yuhikaku.

Schooler, Carmi, and William Caudill
    1964   Symptomatology in Japanese and American schizophrenics. *Ethnology* 3: 172-78.

Sugihara, Yoshie
    1962   *Shinkyō Buraku* (The Shinkyō Community). Tokyo: Shunjusha.

Taeuber, Irene B.
    1958   *The Population of Japan.* Princeton: Princeton University Press.

Taut, Bruno
    1958   *Houses and People of Japan.* Tokyo: Sanseido.

Topping, Helen F.
    1935   *Introducing Kagawa.* Chicago: Willett, Clark.

Vogel, Ezra F.
    1963   *Japan's New Middle Class.* Berkeley: University of California Press.

Watanabe, Sadamu
    1963   *Old People in Transitional Japan.* Tokyo: The Gerontological Association of Japan.

Whiting, J. W. M., R. Kluckhohn, and Albert Anthony
    1958   The function of male initiation ceremonies at puberty. *In* E. E. Maccoby, T. M. Newcomb, and E. L. Hartley (eds.), *Readings in Social Psychology.* New York: Holt.

8. THE LEARNING OF VALUES

JOHN W. M. WHITING,
ELEANOR HOLLENBERG CHASDI,
HELEN FAIGIN ANTONOVSKY,
and BARBARA CHARTIER AYRES

John W. M. Whiting is Professor of Social Anthropology, Harvard University. Eleanor Hollenberg Chasdi is Chairman, Department of Psychology, Wheelock College, Boston, Massachusetts. Helen Faigin Antonovsky is Research Associate, Israel Institute of Applied Social Research. Barbara Chartier Ayres is Associate Professor of Anthropology, University of Massachusetts, Boston. Reprinted by permission of the publishers from Evon Z. Vogt and Ethel M. Albert, editors, *People of Rimrock: A Study of Values in Five Cultures,* Cambridge, Mass.: Harvard University Press, Copyright ©, 1966, by the President and Fellows of Harvard College.

CERTAIN DOMINANT VALUES of a culture influence the way in which a parent responds to his or her child. If love and warmth are an important positive value for social interaction, this may govern a mother's behavior toward her child, even though at the same time she may believe she is spoiling him. In those societies where parents believe that their own actions, rather than fate or heredity, have some effect upon the moral development of their children, the value system of the culture will be an important part of what is consciously and intentionally transmitted to the child. Certain aspects of the child-rearing process seem to have the effect of, if not creating, at least strengthening values far beyond the conscious intent of the agents of socialization.

In the summers of 1950 and 1951, research teams[1] from the Laboratory of Human Development of the Harvard Graduate School of Education carried out a research project focusing on socialization in three of the groups under consideration in this volume—the Texans, the Mormons, and the Zuni. The field work consisted of ethnographic and standardized interviews, participant observation, and various pencil and paper tests given to a sample of children in each society. The sample, consisting of all the

children in the third through the sixth grades in the Mormon and Texan communities, and from the fourth, fifth, and sixth grades of the Zuni Country Day School, is described in Table 8.1.

All the mothers of the children tested in the two Anglo groups were interviewed on their child-rearing practices. Since several mothers had two or more children in school, there were fewer interviews with mothers than children tested—fifteen Mormons and sixteen Texans. Since it was not feasible to interview all the Zuni mothers of the child sample, fifteen were chosen, on the basis of their knowledge of English and their willingness to cooperate, approximately the number in the other two groups. The sample of Zuni mothers is thus somewhat biased toward acculturation. Although their children were in no way strikingly different in their responses to the tests from the remaining Zuni children tested, this bias should be kept in mind.

The interviews were standard only in that the same topics were covered, and generally, but not invariably, in the same order. Questions were not asked in standard form, nor were standard probes employed. Although a few Mormon interviews were electrically recorded and transcribed verbatim, most were dictated from notes

TABLE 8.1
SAMPLE OF CHILDREN TESTED IN THE SUMMER OF 1950

Group	Number of boys	Number of girls	Age range (years)	Mean age
Mormon	8	15	8-14	10.5
Texan	13	12	9-13	10.8
Zuni	32	43	10-14	12.4

directly after the interview and consisted of from eight to twelve pages of single-spaced typescript.

The tests used, all of the paper and pencil variety, were administered to the children in groups. This was done in the school at Zuni, but since school was not in session in the two Anglo communities, the children had to be brought together especially for the purpose. The details of those tests will be described when their results are reported.

THE SETTING

Since socialization takes place in the context of the total society, it is necessary to review certain elements of the cultural setting which have particular relevance to child-rearing: the size and type of dwelling; the membership and authority structure of the household; the economic responsibilities of each parent; and the place where each carries on his or her tasks.

The flat-roofed Zuni houses vary considerably both in size and in number of rooms. We have no information on the number of rooms for the houses of our Zuni sample but they are similar to the three dwellings described by Roberts which had three, six, and eight rooms respectively, occupied by six, ten, and twenty regular household members and three, five, and three associate members (J. M. Roberts 1965). The Mormon houses

vary in size from two to six rooms, the modal size being four. The average number of members of the nuclear Mormon household is between four and five. The typical Texan house consists of three rooms, and the size of their nuclear household also approximates five members. The modal number of persons per room is one for the Mormons, two for the Texans, and three for the Zuni. The Texans are considerably more crowded than the Mormons, but less so than the Zuni. All but one of the Texan mothers living in a three room house volunteered the information that they were planning to add a room since they desired more privacy.

The Zuni house is occupied during the day not only by all adult female members and by children not attending school but also by the majority of the men. Where sheepherding is a major economic pursuit, the adult males take turns, two at a time, in tending their combined flocks (Roberts 1965). Most Zuni men are therefore free to remain at home all but a few months of the year to work on silver and jewelry, which is done in the house. It is rare, however, that one would find either a Texan or a Mormon man in the house during a weekday, except at mealtime, and for the Texans, when the bean crop must be attended to, the whole family may be in the fields.

In each group as many rooms as possible and set aside exclusively for sleeping. However, this is not always possible. A living-room-bedroom combination is frequently resorted to by the Texans. In no instance in the Anglo groups is space used for sleeping also used for cooking and eating, although this may be done in Zuni households. This functional division of rooms leads to unusually crowded sleeping arrangements. Although one Mormon mentioned with pride that each of her children had his or her own bedroom, this is the exception rather than the rule for any of the groups. In both Anglo groups there is a tendency for the parents and the younger children to sleep in one room and the older children, separated according to sex if possible, to occupy the other bedroom or bedrooms. Among the Zuni, the pattern is for each nuclear family in a house to have a sleeping room of its own. Thus, the grandparents, with perhaps some of the younger grandchildren, occupy one bedroom, and each married daughter with her husband and children, if possible, has her own room. The youngest married daughter is the last to get a room of her own and may share a bedroom with her parents.

The three groups differ in the authority patterns within the household. The Mormon father is ideally the patriarch, and in most of the households of our sample, he is considered the final authority in all family matters. The Texan husband and wife are supposed to discuss and come to common agreement on matters of policy; although either may be dominant, in the majority of the families studied, authority is shared. Among the Zuni, the authority pattern is much more complex. Usually neither of the parents of young children is in a position of final authority. Decisions regarding household matters are made by the matrilineal grandparents, particularly the mother's mother who is the owner of the house. Before making any major decision, however, she would generally consult her husband and, more particularly, her brother who, although he does not live in the house, is an important associate member and frequent visitor. The typical Zuni household, therefore, would have a hierarchy somewhat as follows: (1) the grandmother, (2) her brother, (3) the grandfather, (4) the mother, (5) the mother's brother, (6) the father, and (7) the child.

The mothers of our sample were asked whether they or their husbands had primary responsibility for policy decisions with respect to child-rearing. Their answers are summarized in Table 8.2. Unfortunately, the Zuni informants were not asked about the authority of grandparents which would have been a more pertinent question. Their answers nevertheless indicate the relatively high responsibility of Zuni mothers in contrast to the other two societies.

TABLE 8.2
RESPONSIBILITY (IN PERCENTAGES) FOR CHILD-REARING POLICY
AS REPORTED BY MOTHERS

Responsibility assigned to	Mormons	Texans	Zuni
Primarily mother	11	11	42
Both parents	22	67	50
Primarily father	67	22	8
N =	15	16	15

There are also clear differences in the economic systems of the three groups. The Mormon and Zuni economic system may be described as bureaucratic, whereas the Texans' is entrepreneurial. The Mormon Land and Development Company and the Zuni Sheep Camp groups bring together the heads of households in joint economic enterprise involving the differentiation of authority, whereas each adult Texan male is his own boss, and works his own land, sharing his profits only with his wife and children.

In sum, children in the three societies are born into contrasting physical and social settings. The world of the Zuni child consists of a medium-sized house, whose occupants, in addition to his own parents and siblings, are his matrilineally related aunts, uncles, and grandparents. Final authority in this group is jointly held by his grandmother and her brother, the latter being an associate member of the household generally living elsewhere. The Mormon child is born into a partriarchal, nuclear family household living in a moderate-sized house. The Texan child is born in a small, crowded house whose members consist of the nuclear family with authority shared between mother and father. Mormon and Zuni fathers work with other men in joint economic enterprises; the Texan father works on his own.

INFANCY

Mormon and Texan infants generally sleep in the same bed with their parents as long as they are nursing. The reasons given for this, however, are quite different in the two societies. Mormon informants explain that they do this to keep their babies warm.

As one mother whose infant slept in the parental bed for eighteen months put it: "It's very cold out here and we were in a cold house and he couldn't keep warm sleeping alone, so he slept with me. And you know, every time I'd touch the baby he'd wake up and want to nurse, and sometimes I'd go off to sleep and he'd nurse for two or three hours." None of the Texan informants mentioned the cold, and their rationalizations were more varied. Two said that they were afraid that the infant would roll off the bed if he were alone, and one of them claimed that it was easier to nurse the infant if he were sleeping with her. Crowded living conditions, however, seem in fact to be the reason. All Texan families living in houses with three rooms or less took their infants into the parental bed, whereas three of the four families who had four rooms or more did not do so. From this, and from the fact that several Texans complained of the lack of privacy, it appears that their ideal would be for the infant to sleep alone, even though this was not possible for the majority of families. By contrast, the Mormon ideal seemed to be for the infant to share the parental bed. Even though their houses are larger, only one Mormon informant clearly indicated that an infant should sleep in his own crib. Zuni infants usually sleep bound in a cradleboard which at night is placed next to the parental bed. Thus, although, as in the other two groups, the Zuni infant sleeps near its parents and may be nursed during the night with ease, he is not in physical contact with the mother as is the Mormon and Texan infant.

With rare exceptions, in all three groups the infant shares the bed with or is close to not only the mother but also the father. Of course, the Zuni father is sometimes away for several months at a time performing his sheep-herding duties and may from time to time stay at his sister's place. In at least one Texan family, the husband had an out-of-town job which kept him away during the week. In this instance, the mother slept with her two-year-old son while he was away, and the father slept with him during the weekends, when the mother shared a bed with her ten-year-old daughter. In another Texan family each parent slept with one of the children, the mother with her nine-year-old daughter and the father with a four-year-old son.

During the day, Zuni infants have the most constant attention from a wide variety of caretakers. This is well illustrated in Roberts' observations of the activities of a Zuni household (1965, pp. 45-53). From 7:00 A.M. until 8:30 A.M. a Zuni boy of eighteen months was held, carried, played with, and walked by the following members of the household: grandmother (age fifty-one), grandfather (age fifty-eight), aunt (age nineteen), aunt's husband (age twenty-seven), aunt (age fourteen), aunt (age forty), uncle (age eight), and cousin (age three). During all but five minutes of this period he was either held or closely attended by someone. During this time the mother finished her breakfast, cleared the table, washed the dishes, and started on her silver work. At 8:30, the infant began to fuss and cry, whereupon the mother got up from the bench, came and took the baby, strapped him in a cradleboard, nursed him, changed his diapers, and rocked him to sleep.

The daily life of the Texan infant is quite different. Although we do not have the detailed observational record to make exact comparison with the Zuni, there are a number of obvious differences. Early in the morning the father usually leaves for work and, except in the summer, the older children go off to school, and the mother is left alone to do the house-work and care for her infant and younger children. In addition, most Texan mothers feel that they have to aid in the economic support of the family, and therefore, assume responsi-bility for a home garden. It is usually near the house, so that as soon as the mother has finished the housework she can go outside to work in it, leaving the infant inside but able to hear if he sounds disturbed. During planting and harvesting she may also help her husband in the bean fields, in which case she may either leave the infant in the care of an older daughter or take him with her and leave him bedded in the truck. Although older daughters of the family help the mothers with housekeeping and baby-tending whenever they are not in school or working in the fields, the Texan nuclear household cannot approach the manpower for infant care found in the Zuni extended household. Of necessity, the Texan infant learns to be alone and to fend for himself at a very early age.

The nuclear household of the Mormons is in many respects similar to that of the Texans. Here again, the father generally leaves for work in the morning, and the mother must do the housework. Two factors, however, make the Mormon situation quite different from the Texan. In the Mormon value system baby care ranks first as a woman's duty. Furthermore, according to Mormon ideals and church doctrine, a Mormon mother is not expected to do outside work. A pamphlet, *Parent and Child*, put out by the Church describing the ideal role of a mother begins with the following statement: "A good wife and mother is not expected to do any grand works outside her home. Her province lies in gentleness, contented housewifery, and management of her children." The Mormon mother is encouraged to and does devote considerably more time and attention to the care of her infants. Every Mormon mother in our sample who had children under two and a half years of age held her child in her lap during most of the interview. In contrast only one of the Texan mothers with small children did so, most of them leaving their infants in charge of an older sibling, or letting them play by themselves. A typical comment of a Texan mother when a small child called for attention during the interview was: "Don't bother me. Can't you see I'm talking with Miss Z?"—a comment never made by a Mormon mother.

Texan fathers are more likely to take responsibilities for the care of infants than fathers in the other two groups. Of eleven cases, three fathers helped a great deal, four helped some, and four assumed no responsibility for infant care. Only one Mormon mother reported that her husband helped appreciably in infant care, and no Zuni mothers did so. It should not be inferred from this that fathers who did not feel responsible for feeding or changing the diapers of infants ignored them. The typical father in all three groups would hold infants and play with them from time to time, but except among the Texans, the responsibility for infant care was felt to be exclusively woman's work.

Breast feeding is practiced by the majority of mothers in all three societies. Two Mormon and two Zuni mothers of our sample did not breast feed one of their children for medical reasons. They did, however, breast feed all the others. This was also true of three of the Texan mothers, but in addition there were two Texan mothers with three and four children who bottle fed all of their children, apparently from preference. Table 8.3 indicates the frequency with which four methods of infant feeding were practiced by mothers in the three societies: breast feeding followed by weaning to the cup, breast feeding followed by bottle feeding before weaning to the cup, breast feeding supplemented by concurrent feeding with the bottle before weaning to the cup, and bottle feeding only before weaning to the cup. Eighty-six percent of the Zuni children were entirely breast fed, as were 68 percent of the Mormons and 44 percent of the Texans.

Texan and Mormon mothers who breast fed their children gave different reasons for doing so. Some Texan mothers commented that it was cheaper or more convenient than bottle feeding, but most of them claimed that it was more natural and healthy for the child. A number of Mormon mothers expressed similar sentiments. The typical

TABLE 8.3
FREQUENCY OF VARIOUS METHODS OF INFANT FEEDING*

Method	Mormon	Texan	Zuni
Breast to cup	34	27	62
Breast and bottle to cup	4	12	7
Breast to bottle to cup	10	12	1
Bottle to cup	2	10	2

* Figures indicate the number of infants reported to have been fed in the manner listed. Many of these children are members of the same families.

Mormon response, however, which was not made by any of the Texan mothers is illustrated by the following quotation: "Oh, yes, it's much better to breast feed your children. Then you're closer to them, you have to hold them and love them up and show them a lot of affection. With the bottle you can just lay them down and give them the bottle—you don't have the closeness, the feeling of warmth and affection that you do when you breast feed them. It's very important to be close and warm to your children."

Half of our Texan mothers reported having fed their infants on a fairly strict schedule as compared with two of nineteen Mormon mothers and no Zuni mothers. One of the Texan mothers apologized for feeding her children on a self-demand schedule by saying, "I know it's thought best nowadays to follow a strict schedule, but that just isn't my temperament." Several mothers mentioned either that the doctor recommended a schedule or that they had read it was best.

The Texans wean their children earlier than Zuni or Mormon mothers. The median age of weaning for those Texan mothers who breast fed their children was nine months, with a range of six to 13 months. For the Mormons the median age was eleven months, with a range of from eight to 17 months. The median age of weaning for the Zuni was two years, although there was an essentially bi-modal distribution, with nearly 40 percent of the sample stating that they had weaned their children at the age of twelve months. A few Zuni mothers reported having nursed at least one of their children for considerably longer than the median age, the extremes being four years reported by one mother and five by another. One of these mothers claimed that nursing was necessary

because she could not afford to buy milk.

Bottle fed Texan children were weaned somewhat later than their breast fed peers, the median age being twelve months as against nine months. This was true also for the Mormon girls, but not for the boys. The median age of beginning weaning from the bottle for the Mormon girls was eighteen months, in contrast to twelve months for their breast fed peers. Some informants from both the Texan and Mormon groups reported using the bottle as a pacifier until the child was two years old or more. One five-year-old Mormon girl still was taking the bottle to bed with her.

Most Texan parents reported that they had little difficulty weaning their children, but many Mormon and Zuni parents reported that their children were quite disturbed by the process. This confirms the finding of previous studies that weaning between the ages of one and two years is more disturbing to children than either earlier or later (Whiting 1954; Sears et al 1957). Texan and Mormon children who were weaned before twelve months and Zuni children who were weaned after two years caused less trouble than children in any of the groups weaned between twelve months and two years.

The pattern for toilet training is similar to that for weaning. The Texans begin earliest (the median age is nine months) and complete the training earliest (with median age between twelve and fifteen months). The Mormons begin when the child is a year old, and complete the process between 18 months and two years. The Zuni start last, typically at 18 months, and complete training when the child is between two and three years old. Twelve of 18 Texan mothers and nine of 14 Mormon mothers reported that they had considerable difficulty in training their children and had to resort to punitive measures, most frequently shaming the children by telling them they were dirty. Only three of 16 Zuni mothers reported any difficulty in training and they used scolding, spanking, and not letting the offenders go out to play as punitive techniques.

During infancy, then, Zuni child-rearing is characterized by diffused and constant care and late training, the Texan by the least caretaking and the earliest training, and the Mormon by emphasis upon the warmth of the relationship between mother and infant, the timing of socialization falling between that of the other two groups.

EARLY CHILDHOOD

From the time children are weaned until they go to school, roughly between the ages of two and six, the main pressure upon them in each of the societies is to learn to take care of themselves, amuse themselves, and not expect the kind of attention they received as babies. Much of their time is spent playing with siblings in the house or close by in the yard. Mothers keep an eye on their children during this period and tend not to let them out of their sight or hearing unless they are in he care of an older person, generally an older sibling.

The transition from the almost complete dependence upon caretakers which has characterized infancy to the self-reliance and responsibility expected in later childhood is often difficult for the child, and is managed differently in each of the three societies. For the Zuni child the shift is the most dramatic. Whereas before wean-

ing someone always responded to him, now the same people ignore him unless they consider that he really needs help. One Zuni informant put it as follows: "By the time a child is two or three years old, he should know better than to be spoiled. You have to teach them differently then. They can't come around and want to climb in your lap. If you let them do that, they'll get in the habit of wanting attention all the time. That isn't good because when you're busy working they'll always be next to you, wanting something or other. You have to stop paying attention to them. Just send them outside to play or have one of the older children take them out of the house. Maybe you have to scold them a lot, but they have to learn." There is no such sharp break in caretaking for either of the Anglo groups. The transition to independence is characterized rather by a gradual reduction in the amount of attention paid them by their mothers. In absolute terms, the Mormon toddler probably gets the most attention. His mother will often still take him on her lap or lie down with him at nap time. The busy Texan mother has less time to do this, but several informants commented that they would like more time to cuddle and play with their children.

Although toddlers are kept track of by older siblings, parents, or relatives in all three groups, Mormon mothers were most protective in this regard and several parents reported that they had punished children of this age for running away or wandering off without telling them where they were going. None of the informants of the other two societies showed such concern.

Early childhood is a time for play, and playfellows become important to toddlers. Children of this age get along fairly well, although minor tiffs and squabbles are not unusual. Young children like to play with older children, but this is often not reciprocated unless the older child is willing to assume a caretaking role or the game being played permits a wide discrepancy in skills. In the extended Zuni households, the probability of having a cousin or two of approximately the same age to play with is high. In one of the households observed by Roberts there were six children between the ages of two and six who spent much of the day of observation playing with one another in various groupings (1965, pp. 45ff.). A child in a nuclear household is not so lucky. Only two of eleven children of this age grade among the Texans, and three of eleven young Mormon children had siblings in their own age grade. Mormon mothers make up for this to some extent by having the children of neighbors or relatives in or permitting their own children to visit next door. For the isolated Texan households, however, this is not possible. Except for an occasional Sunday picnic, Texan families cannot afford either the time or the gasoline to arrange to have playmates for their young children, and, especially when the older siblings are at school, the young Texan child is left pretty much to his own devices.

Toys, all bought from the same commercial sources, do not differ much among the three groups. Dolls, doll houses, and toy dishes are the favorites of the girls, and toy trucks, tractors, and automobiles are preferred by the boys. Texan children are also likely to make pets out of the farm animals—dogs, cats, calves, and chickens making up for their lack of playmates.

When children of this age do play together it is generally not long before a squabble starts and the first lessons in the control of aggression occur. Although Texan parents often allow fighting and quarreling with playmates in children of this age, they keep them under reasonable control and will separate and sometimes punish the children if things go too far. As one informant put it, "they are not old enough to know any better." Mormon parents are nearly as tolerant but they are more apt to step in earlier and more likely to use distractions or reasoning to stop the fighting. The following incident illustrates the reaction of a Mormon mother to fighting among siblings.

During the interview, Jane (age five) and Mary (age two) were at first playing outside. Mary came in after a while and crawled up in her mother's lap for a few minutes, then went out again. Shortly both girls came in and Mary started playing with a doll house. Jane came up to Mary and pushed her aside, whereupon she started to cry and then to hit her older sister fairly hard five to six times on the arm. Jane retaliated with some not very well aimed blows. Both girls by this time were crying and screaming at each other. The mother then got up with a big smile on her face, laughed and said, "Now, Jane, you know that Mary was there first, so you'll have to let her play." This made Jane very angry and she started to prance around crying. She was soon distracted, however, and then stopped. The mother resumed the interview.

Zuni parents consider fighting a serious matter and believe that children should be taught to control their tempers at an early age. Reasoning is the technique usually employed. This is well-exemplified by the following statement from a Zuni informant.

My husband tells them not to fight. He tells them that fighting between brothers and sisters is not a good thing. He says that if brothers and sisters fight and are mean to each other, they'll be the same way when they grow up. They'll be mean to each other. Then if one brother or sister wants help from the others when he is in trouble, the others won't help them. All of us tell the children that. I tell it to them and so does my mother. Another thing I tell them is, "how would you like it if your grandfather and father started to fight? Would you like that? Then there would be trouble in the family. Nothing would work right. You might not even have a father or a grandfather because one of them would get mad and maybe leave the house for good." Then I show them by example. I tell them about their uncle. He likes to drink. He often gets caught when he drinks and gets fined. Then he comes to his brothers and sisters and asks for help, for some money. Well, they help him out. I tell the children if the family didn't get along well with each other, no one would help the uncle when he needed it. We try to teach them that way. We tell them it is a good thing when all the family get along well.

If such reasoning is unsuccessful, some families resort to spanking, others to bringing in the "scare Kachina," a masked impersonator of a god carrying a stone knife. One informant who used the latter device explained it as follows: "Once when my son and daughter were younger they used to fight and quarrel and would not stop, so one day my brother called out one of the dancers and he told them not to fight any more and be good children, that a brother should love his sister and the sister her brother. The children were very scared and the girl started to cry. Before he left, the dancer said that if they didn't mind and stop fighting he would come back and cut their ears off. I guess the children were pretty scared. After that there was no fighting." Only two of the 14 Zuni informants admitted having called in a scare Kachina. Six reported spanking, six claimed reasoning was enough, and one reported that she tied the children

in chairs facing one another until they promised not to fight again.

Lest the above description of Zuni methods for teaching aggression control give an exaggerated impression, it should be noted that Roberts (1965, p. 61) reported three different squabbles among children of this age. Two of them were ignored and in the case of the third, which involved a little girl of three who threw an apple at her 18-month-old baby cousin and then slapped him, the mother scolded her daughter. When she started to cry her grandfather took her on his knee and talked to her. One informant expressed this more permissive attitude as follows: "Many parents around town, when their children fight each other get mad and stay mad. That's all wrong. Children will fight together one minute and play together the next. They never hold any grudges or stay mad at each other the way adults do." Despite this evidence, the Zuni are more concerned than either of the other groups about the expression of aggression in young children.

The children of each group during this age get some training in modesty. The Zuni parents are the most casual; children up to the age of four or five are often permitted to run about both indoors and out without clothes on. The Mormon parents are the most modest, believing that even young children should not expose their bodies, and parents should certainly not be seen naked by their children. The Texans vary. Some mothers reported that they went to considerable pains, even in the crowded quarters in which they lived, to maintain standards of modesty, whereas others treated the matter quite casually. None of them, however, permitted children of this age to be seen nude in public.

Since each group was living in close contact with sheep and cattle, all young children acquire a practical knowledge of the reproductive process. Although a few parents attempted to promote the stork story or its equivalent, few of them made any attempt to discuss theories of human reproduction with their children.

Finally, it is at this age that children learn to dress themselves, wash their faces and hands, and comb their hair, and, in the Anglo groups but not in Zuni, to perform such household chores as bringing in chips for the fire, feeding the chickens, gathering the eggs, and helping to wash and dry the dishes. In Mormon households, these tasks are defined as "helping," and the mother and child do them together. Texan children, by contrast, are urged to do these little tasks by themselves, and are praised when they succeed. One mother reported with pride that her son started working in the fields at the age of three, as soon as he could hold a pitchfork. Although young Zuni children sometimes help with housework, they are not urged or expected to do so. With them it is a matter of play rather than of duty or achievement.

LATE CHILDHOOD

Going to school, which occurs when the child is about six years old, marks a dramatic change in the life of children in each group. Zuni and Mormon children walk to school, but most Texan children have to take a long bus ride. For the Zuni child, this is the greatest change from his previous life, for he has to learn a strange language and his teacher is a member of a different society.

Although the children of each of the three societies have been given some knowledge of the religious beliefs and practices of their parents in early childhood, serious formal training does not begin until the child is five or six years old. Zuni children have already overheard their parents discussing witchcraft, and some have been visited by the Kachina impersonators; the young Mormons have heard their parents discuss church affairs and have participated in prayers with their families; children of the more religious Texan families may have been to Sunday School.

Formal religious training for the Zuni boys, and, in rare cases, girls, is focused on their initiation into one of the religious fraternities. The initiation comes at the end of a long and elaborate ceremony that generally takes place once every four years, in the spring. The ceremony emphasizes the relation of men to the gods and is meant to insure the fertility of the seeds to be planted. At one point in the ceremony, the boys, riding on the shoulders of a "godfather," are whipped with yucca branches by adult males dressed to impersonate the same Kachina gods who may have disciplined the boys during early childhood. The ritual beating is said to prevent bad luck. Despite the explanation that it is "for their own good," according to most reports, the boys are terrified by the experience. Following the whipping, each boy is given an eagle feather to wear and some kernels of corn to plant. For four days following the whipping the initiates are not permitted to eat meat. At the end of this period they exchange bowls of stew with their ceremonial parents and the ceremony is at an end.

From the age of four Mormon

children are expected to go to Church School twice a week. There they are taught the tenets and values of Mormon religion, and the importance of the Church as an organization is transmitted to them. Although in any one session, only about half of the children attend, most children go to Church School at least once a week. Some school-age Texan children attend Sunday School, but attendance is small and the meetings are held only once a week. By comparison with both the Zuni and Mormons, there is much less emphasis on sacred subjects or concepts. The Sunday School teacher tells the children simplified versions of Bible stories, and, although there is some attempt to draw moral lessons from these stories and from Biblical quotations, the teacher is generally more concerned that the children behave and enjoy themselves.

In all three societies, the routines of housework and farmwork are learned during this period of late childhood by both observation and participation. Girls learn to wash dishes, to make beds, to clean and to sweep, to cook, and to sew. Boys learn to milk and herd cattle or sheep, care for chickens, drive tractors and cars, operate farm machinery, and do carpentry. Before they reach their teens, most children have mastered all the routine skills required of adults. Texan families exert the strongest pressure on their children to perform these tasks early. One mother reported proudly that her daughter was milking two or three cows a day at the age of six; another that her six-year-old son had as a regular daily duty the feeding and watering of the chickens and seeing to it that the light in the incubator was turned on every night. Another mother "admitted" that her six-year-old son,

although he helped with the chores, had no responsibilities of his own as yet. Believing that seven or eight was early enough, she criticized her neighbors for starting to give responsibilities too young. The Texan ideal was expressed by the mother who said, "I want each child to feel he has to pull his own weight in the world. I gave them responsibilities as soon as they could understand the word."

Whereas individual responsibility is emphasized among the Texans, helpfulness and obedience is stressed among the Mormons. Mormon girls "help" their mothers with the housework, and the boys "help" their fathers with the farmwork. Regular tasks were not allotted to them until a much later age than the Texan average. A Mormon mother with girls of thirteen and eight said: "We haven't given them definite responsibilities yet. Lots of times the girls will do different things around the house like watching the fire, making the beds. One of them will help with the dishes in the morning and the other with the dishes at night . . . As they grow older I think they should have definite responsibilities each day so that they'll have something to do and something to look forward to each day." Another mother considered her eight-year-old daughter too young to be given too much responsibility: "After all, she's only eight." The attitude toward work is perhaps best summarized by the following statement: "I think when they learn together for the common good there's more of a spirit of cooperation."

Zuni children are not expected to do as much during this age period as those in either Anglo group. There are many hands to do the housework in the extended family household. Framework and herding are generally carried out by matrilineally related kin groups involving several nuclear families so that here, too, there are many hands. Thus, girls do not make a serious contribution to housework until they are in their teens, nor do boys help materially with the herding until this age. The youngest boys who actually helped with the herding in Robert's observation of the sheep camp were 12, 13, and 14. An idealized but somewhat deviant statement was made by one Zuni informant on training boys to herd sheep:

"I'm going to tell you how we train our boys. It is better to train our own boys while they are just about seven years old, because the older they get, they won't want to be trained I guess. They may start something else instead of getting to be a good sheepherder . . . That is why we keep our boys here with us, and so we can always put them in different work so that they can do different work and see different ways of handling sheep in the bunches . . . So we always train our boys out here. It is a good place to train them . . . We could instruct them like the White man does with the books, but they still wouldn't learn too well—it would be better to take them out to where the sheep are so we could show them just what they should know and just what they should do if they want to be good sheepmen . . . You might say that you think all Zuni boys would know how to handle the sheep, but then it is not the way. Very few Zunis are good sheepherders, and the rest are just ordinary Indians." (Roberts 1965, p. 93)

Many Mormon mothers reported that trying to keep their children from quarreling was their worst problem. One said: "I can't stand to have children fight. I just put a stop to it. If that doesn't work, I tie their hands behind their back and make them sit down." Another mother: "Quarreling among children annoys me most. It happens in most families. You can't expect children to be sweet and pleasant to one another all the time, but it sure does upset me when

the children argue. I try to get them interested in something else at a time like this." Another: "The two older girls, twelve and nine, fight most of the time but I get after them with a strap." Still another of her two girls, twelve and eight: "Oh, no, they don't fight, they just love each other! They just try to kill each other . . . I don't know what's wrong with them. Last night they made me so mad I had to end up by pulling the younger one's hair." Only two Mormon mothers reported they had no trouble, and one of them had children spaced ten years apart.

Although most Texan mothers also considered fighting and quarreling a problem, they seemed less concerned about it than the Mormons. The opinion was often expressed that if children were quarreling they should "fight it out," or "settle it themselves," or "get it out of their systems." As one mother put it: "If I feel angry, I express myself. If the children are angry, let them express themselves. When I'm mad I want to be left alone. I assume it is the same way with the children, so I ignore them and it passes." Even these more permissive parents, however, would "step in" if things got too rough or if a smaller child was being picked on unjustly. One family used an extreme form of fighting-it-out pattern in a distinctive way. When two of the daughters were fighting the father gave each of them a strap and forced them to hit each other until they were quite upset. Then he told them that the next time they wanted to fight, to come to him and he'd show them how. One group of Texan mothers who were upset by quarreling admitted that they "didn't know what they could do about it." They reported that they would shout and threaten but that it seldom did any good and they seldom carried out their threats. Only a few families were strict about fighting and stopped it effectively by separating the children, taking away their privileges, or strapping them.

Only two Zuni mothers reported problems with aggression in their children. Since by contrast eleven Mormon and thirteen Texan mothers did so, it might seem that Zuni culture was indifferent to the expression of aggression in children of this age. This, however, was far from the case. Rather, most Zuni children had, by this age, learned not to be "mean." Furthermore, to prevent possible backsliding, moral lectures on the subject were given by both parents and uncles. The initiation rite described above further emphasized the importance of controlling aggression. The Kachina gods that played a central part in this ceremony were the same gods that came to the houses of many of the children to warn them against aggression when they were little.

When the mothers of the three societies were rated on a scale measuring intolerance of aggression among peers, 77 percent (N = 17) of the Zuni and 69 percent (N = 19) of the Mormon mothers scored above the median for the three groups, whereas only six percent (N = 17) of the Texan mothers scored as high. The difference between the Texans and the other two groups is highly significant statistically (P < 0.001). There was a tendency for each society to be more intolerant of aggression in girls than in boys. This difference was slight and not statistically significant among the Texans and Zuni, but it was marked and significant (P = 0.047) among the Mormons.

Attitudes relative to aggression toward parents in the form of disrespect, "sassing," or defiance show much the same pattern as those towards peer quarreling. Most Zuni and Mormon families do not permit and severely punish such behavior, whereas in Texan families a considerable amount is tolerated. Whereas the Zuni stress the control of aggression between siblings, particularly between brother and sister, the Mormons stress respect for parents, and particularly the father, as the following quotation from a Mormon tract indicates: "The first form of authority before the child is that of the parent, and to the parent he has to be subject. The child is bound to obey his parent without hesitation or reply. There must be respect for age and experience, and a sense of the great sacrifices a parent has made for his children's welfare." Most Mormon and Texan mothers reported that their children were more obedient and respectful of their fathers than of them. Although one Texan father required his children to call him "Sir," most fathers in this group were casual in demanding such signs of respect from their children, compared to the typical Mormon father.

ADOLESCENCE

At adolescence pressure to assume responsibility for adult roles in society is important for most children. For girls, this consists of thinking about and preparing for marriage, and for boys, starting to make money, first for self-support and then for the support of a family. Only a few Texan and Mormon children thought of higher education, and few of them progressed beyond high school. Most of the boys, therefore, either sought outside jobs or took their places as serious contributors to the economic endeavors of their fathers. The girls had already become responsible helpers to their mothers in the home. Although some tried to earn money, there were few paying jobs available for them, and their main preoccupation was getting a husband. The average age of marriage for girls in each group was lower than the average for the United States as a whole. Of the 65 children of the mothers of our Mormon sample, there were seven girls over 17. All but one of them were married, and most of them already had children of their own. All but three of the nine girls over 18 in our Texan sample were also married. Of the six girls of the middle generation (between 18 and 30) in the three Zuni households described by Roberts, all were married or had been married, and all of them had children. Dating and courtship, therefore, are a major preoccupation among the adolescents in the three groups, but the rules governing these forms of behavior vary.

The Mormons keep the most rigid control over courtship. The following quotation from a Mormon tract states some of the values by which Mormon parents attempt to govern their adolescent girls during this period:

The dominant evil of the world and one of the gravest dangers to human welfare are [sic] lawless sex gratification. We believe . . . that sexual sin is second only to the shedding of innocent blood in the category of personal crimes; and that the adulterer shall have no part in the exaltation of the blessed.

Love does not spring from lust. Virtue is youth's dearest possession; and chastity is the strongest bulwark against the many temptations of life. Of all earthly possessions, virtue should be cherished most . . . one must enter the married state with an unstained, unviolated body.

Young women should help young men keep pure. By their actions they may restrain their male friends from improper suggestions and behavior.

It is far more wise that our girls of immature growth should be escorted where necessary to and from evening sociables by their fathers and brothers than that they should be attended only by boyfriends.

Parties exclusively for boys or for girls may be commended as postponing the coming of that day which will arrive all too soon, despite all we can do as parents to retard its coming, when our children will seek companionship among those of the opposite sex in the possible jeopardy of their morals and in the certain lessening of their efficiency in schoolwork and in other necessary employments.

Many religious people regard dancing as one of the most pernicious practices that can be indulged in. The Latter-Day Saints, on the other hand, have defended this amusement when carried on under proper conditions as innocent and promotive of culture. Dancing is an ancient art, and practically a universal one.

There is a crying demand that mothers know more about the amusements of their daughters. An honorable man will find out before he begins inviting a girl to dances, theaters, or other amusements, that his attentions are agreeable to her parents. He will also be ready to have her mother or some other lady friend accompany them. *(Parent and Child)*

Although the ideals stated above by no means represent actual practice, there is a strong attempt by the Mormon Church to organize the social life of adolescents so as to keep firm control over children until they are married. This is not to say that these affairs are joyless. Dancing is favored and even kissing games are sponsored by adults, but there is a strong feeling that all cross-sex interaction among adolescents should occur in the presence of the parental generation. In actuality there is some unchaperoned dating. As one informant put it: "Girls start dating when they are about 14 or 15 years old. This usually involves riding around for a short while after a dance or going to the movies in town with a boy-friend. They may ride around a bit after the movies. Almost always they go out two couples at a time. Once in a while kids go into Railtown on dates. This doesn't happen until the girls are about 16. A couple never goes in alone. They usually have some of their friends along. I guess this is the form of chaperonage out here."

The Texans disapprove of premarital sexual behavior, particularly in girls, but nevertheless keep much less close control over their adolescent children than the Mormons. Although explicitly disapproved, it was tacitly assumed that the boys would "sow their wild oats," but the Texan informants agreed that it was an exceptional girl who was not a virgin when she was married. Dancing and dating were less carefully chaperoned by the Texans. Drinking was not uncommon, particularly among the older boys, an indulgence strictly taboo for the Mormons.

Trysting is an accepted Zuni pattern, and premarital sexual intercourse is expected as a part of the culture. Courtship is often initiated by the girl and premarital affairs take place in her home. According to one male Zuni informant: "If a girl asks you to her house, you just sleep with her, and you leave before morning several times. Then one day you stay later and you're seen, and then everyone knows you're married." In the old days, boys and girls of different clans would carry on preliminary courtship and make arrangements at the well where the girls went to get water. Nowadays the school provides an opportunity for young people of different clans to get to know one another.

Comparatively speaking, the Mormons are more severe than the other two groups in their control of adolescent sexual behavior. A rating on the severity of sex training taken from interviews with mothers showed 57 percent (N=19) of the Mormon mothers to be above the pooled median

on this scale, in contrast to 35 percent (N=14) for the Texans and 33 percent (N=9) for the Zuni. In each of the three societies, boys marry later than girls, and there is a general feeling, especially in the two Anglo groups, that a boy should not get married until he is able to support a wife. In Zuni also, a boy should give promise of being a good provider before he is accepted by a girl and her parents.

SUMMARY OF CHILD-REARING PRACTICES

The main emphases on child rearing for each of the three societies may be summarized as follows: (1) The Zuni infant is indulgently treated by many caretakers. This indulgence comes to an abrupt end at about the age of two or three, at which time he is taught to keep his temper and not to fight. Little is expected of him in the way of performing economic tasks until he approaches adolescence. (2) The Texan infant receives much less care from his busy mother who weans him and starts his socialization at an early age. During childhood, the emphasis is on assuming individual responsibility for the performance of tasks. Relatively little pressure is exerted against fighting. (3) The Mormon infant is indulged nearly as much as the Zuni, but differs from the Zuni infant in that the mother is mainly responsible for caretaking. Mormon children are weaned later than the Texan, but earlier than the Zuni children, and the Mormon mother continues to be more nurturant and protective of her child for a longer period than in either of the other two societies. Dependency weaning is late and gradual. Mormon children are expected to perform tasks very similar to those expected of a Texan child, but these tasks are defined as helping the mother or the father, who remains responsible for them rather than as the individual responsibility of the child. Obedience and helpfulness are stressed rather than individual achievement and responsibility. The main pressure against emotional expressiveness is in the area of sex, which is considered by the Mormons as one of the worst sins.

RESULTS OF TESTS

MAGIC MAN TEST

To determine some of the effects of the differences in child-rearing methods described above, tests were given to samples of children in each of the three societies. The *Magic Man* test was intended to obtain an estimate of a child's motives, conflicts, and preferences. This test consisted of three questions; the instructions stated that there were no wrong answers:

1. Once upon a time a magic man met a child and said, "I'm going to change you into something else. You can be any kind of person you like." If you were this child, what kind of person would you want to be? Write down what this person would be like.
2. Suppose that you could be changed into a father or a mother or a sister or a brother. Which would you want to be? Put a line under the one you would want to be.
3. If the magic man could make you just as old or as young as you wanted to be, how old would you want to be.

A method of scoring this test for achievement has been validated by Mischel (1964). He showed in a study of Trinidadian Negro children that responses to the question that involve the choice of an occupation (nurse, schoolteacher, farmer, or rancher) or of a personal quality clearly indicating achievement (a successful man, a wealthy woman) were significantly related to achievement scores derived from TAT, using the procedure developed by McClelland and his associates (1953). Using the same scoring procedure, we found that 57 percent of the Texan children gave scores indicating achievement, whereas only 38 percent of the Mormon children and 20 percent of the Zuni children responded with this type of imagery. Although the difference between Texans and Mormons was not statistically significant, that between Texans and Zuni was (P=0.001).

This Texan preoccupation with success and achievement is strikingly shown by the answers of the Texan children to the first question of the test. One Texan boy stated that he wanted to be "a great doctor in the Mayo Clinic in Minneapolis, Minnesota, who had done many things toward man's health;" another stated, "I want to be a rancher and raise beef cattle so I can get some money;" another that he wanted to be "a great Yankee baseball player; I will be the pitcher." By contrast, the most popular choices for the Mormons were to be good, kind, or happy as exemplified by the following: "good, honest, and kind to everyone I meet," or, I would "fish, run around on the hills, and go swimming." The most popular Zuni choice was to be a man or a woman, without specific qualification, or, simply, to be a Zuni.

Although they did not occur frequently, when cross-sex choices on this part of the test did occur they gave insight into the relative status of men and women in the three cultures. The egalitarian Texans made no cross-sex choices, whereas ten percent of the Zuni boys chose to be females, and 23 percent of the Mormon girls chose to be males. No Mormon boys or Zuni girls made cross-sex choices. These responses reflect the relatively high status of women in Zuni and of men among the Mormons. Three Zuni girls said that they would like to be White; one Mormon boy expressed the wish to be changed into an Indian; another Mormon boy and a Mormon girl chose to be animals. Perhaps the cross-sex, cross-race, and cross-species choices indicate a need to escape from a culturally defined status that is felt to be unsatisfactory.

The intent of the next Magic Man question was to obtain the preference for roles within the family. The results of this part of the tests are shown in Table 8.4. As can be seen, the majority of boys in all three groups prefer the role nearest their sex and age. The girls show considerably more diversity. Only the Zuni girls show a pattern similar to the boys in the popularity of the status nearest their sex and age (sister). Both the Texan and Mormon girls reflect the values of their culture in their votes. That seven of nine Texan girls thought it best to be a mother rather than a sister is consonant with the Texan emphasis on achievement and growing up. The three Mormon girls who chose to be brothers indicate the patriarchal emphasis in their culture.

The third Magic Man question was designed to measure status preference in terms of age alone. Answers reflect the importance of both sex and culture as determinants. The mean age desired by the girls was 19.4 for the Texans, 15.8 for the Mormons, and 12.3 for the Zuni. Remembering that the median age of these girls was eleven years, these choices seem to reflect the relative emphasis on achievement and success in the three societies, the Texan girls showing the greatest wish to grow up, and the Zuni girls the strongest satisfaction with the status quo. They are consonant with the results of the previous Magic Man question. The results for the boys on this question, however, were somewhat unexpected. Zuni boys, like their sisters, are satisfied with the status quo, their mean desired age being 11.9. The Mormon and Texan boys, however, show a reversal, the former having a mean desired age of 19.7, the latter, 15.7. This may reflect the relatively high status of Mormon men as compared with Texan men as overriding a simple wish to grow up.

To summarize, the results of the Magic Man questions are for the most part consonant with our knowledge of the social structure and socialization practices of the three groups. They reflect the high status of Mormon men and of Zuni women and the relative equality of the statuses of the sexes among the Texans. They indicate the

TABLE 8.4

CHOICES OF FAMILY ROLES IN THE MAGIC MAN TEST

Role	Boys			Girls		
	Mormon	Texan	Zuni	Mormon	Texan	Zuni
Father	2	4	6	0	0	0
Brother	6	9	24	3	1	5
Mother	0	0	0	3	7	3
Sister	0	0	0	5	1	35

Texan value for success, achievement, and growing up, and Zuni satisfaction with the status quo. The Mormon emphasis on virtue and control is reflected only by inference in the frequency of the choice of the children of this culture for carefree freedom.

CONFLICT AND ANXIETY TEST

In order to estimate the major source of conflict and anxiety in each society, the children were asked what they felt was the worst thing that could happen to them. Answers to this question can be scored in two ways, by the nature of the injury or by its agent or source. The responses classified by type of injury are presented in Table 8.5. The most common fear for both the Mormon and Texan boys

and for the Texan girls is death or injury, but, within this category, dismemberment—breaking an arm or a leg, or getting it cut off—is the most frequent response by the Mormon boys. In the light of Mormon emphasis on the control of sexual behavior, this may well indicate the presence of castration anxiety as an underlying fear of these four boys. The Texans seem more preoccupied with death or with some accident whose consequences are unspecified.

The most common fear of Mormon girls and of Zuni children of both sexes is punishment. For the Zuni it is most commonly spanking, whereas for the Mormons it is to be put in jail, scolded, or denied privileges. The relatively high frequency among the Zuni, particularly the boys, of the response

TABLE 8.5

INJURIES DESCRIBED BY CHILDREN IN ANSWER TO THE QUESTION
"WHAT IS THE WORST THING THAT COULD HAPPEN TO YOU?"

Worst thing	Mormons		Texans		Zuni	
	Boys	Girls	Boys	Girls	Boys	Girls
Death or injury:						
Death	1	2	3	1	3	2
Accident	2	0	4	2	4	8
Dismemberment	4	2	0	1	2	1
Total	7	4	7	4	9	11
Punishment:						
Physical	1	1	1	2	7	15
Other	1	4	0	0	3	6
Total	2	5	1	2	10	21
Separation:						
Ostracism	2	4	0	2	1	0
Death of family	0	0	2	1	0	0
Total	2	4	2	3	1	0
Wrongdoing:						
Fighting	0	0	0	0	9	3
"Go to Devil"	0	0	0	1	0	0
Total	0	0	0	1	9	3

that fighting is the worst thing that could happen is consonant with the strong taboo on aggression in this society. The relative frequency of fear of separation from the family is striking for the Mormons, particularly the girls, and this is consistent with the culture's emphasis on the importance of the family.

An analysis of the agent of injury is presented in Table 8.6. To construct this table the responses were coded as follows: if the response indicated that the subject was responsible for the injury, such as "if I fell down and broke my arm," or "if I die," it was scored under the "I" category, whereas responses such as "They will spank me," or "to be put in jail," were scored as belonging in the "they" category. When the agent was an animal or something impersonal, such as a car or a tractor, the agent was scored as "it."

The modal response for both Mormon and Texan boys and for the Mormon girls is "I." This is consonant with the emphasis on individual responsibility in the Anglo groups. The modal response for the remaining groups is "they." The most striking is the great preponderance of the "they" category for Zuni children of both sexes. This is consonant with the hypothesis that severe punishment for aggression of Zuni children leads to its projection and a consequent paranoid fear of others. Since in all three

societies girls were more severely punished for aggression than were boys, it is interesting to note that among the two Anglo groups, nearly twice as many girls as boys fear others.

There are at least two possible explanations for the popularity of the "it" category for the Texans. It may be a consequence of their lack of nurturance during infancy: the relation of this factor to the fear of the supernatural has been established (Whiting 1959). Or, the isolated conditions of living in a scattered land settlement pattern and the earliness with which children are forced to cope with their environment may make it seem dangerous so that they would be more apt to have a fear of being eaten by bears or tipping over on a tractor than of "I" or "they" agents of harm.

AFFIRMATIVE VALUES TEST

The final question asked that is relevant to the content of values was: "What is the nicest thing that could happen to you?" The responses, shown in Table 8.7, were scored according to four categories. The first, "goods," included money, candy, toys, clothes, and so on. "Status" included being rich, famous, or powerful. "Fun" included playing, going on trips, and being happy. The "security" category included not being sick, not being punished, and not being separated from the family.

TABLE 8.6
CHILDREN'S IDENTIFICATION OF AGENTS OF INJURY

Agent	Mormons		Texans		Zuni*	
	Boys	Girls	Boys	Girls	Boys	Girls
I	7	7	4	2	7	9
It	1	0	3	4	2	7
They	3	6	3	5	22	22

* Responses from three Zuni boys and one Zuni girl were unscorable.

TABLE 8.7
CHILDREN'S RESPONSES TO THE QUESTION "WHAT IS THE NICEST THING
THAT COULD HAPPEN TO YOU?"

Nicest thing	Mormons		Texans		Zuni	
	Boys	Girls	Boys	Girls	Boys	Girls
Goods	2	1	1	2	19	24
Status	4	2	7	5	2	2
Fun	1	5	1	3	6	7
Security	2	5	1	0	2	4

It can be seen from the table that Zuni children are predominantly concerned with consumable goods: candy, clothes, or money to buy something from the store occurred in protocol after protocol. The Texan children, particularly the boys, were most concerned with status gain. Status gain was also the modal response for the Mormon boys, although not to so marked a degree. Mormon girls desired either fun or security, again reflecting the tight family organization considered by some girls to be an asset and by others as something from which to escape.

SOCIAL STRUCTURE, CHILD-REARING, AND VALUES

Although there are many similarities, some striking differences are apparent in the child-rearing practices of these three groups and in the responses of the children to the tests given them. By way of illustration, and frankly oversimplifying the problem, we shall select one aspect of socialization for each of the three societies that seem to contrast most strongly with the other two, and which also is most discrepant from the mean for socialization practices the world over. We would like to speculate as to why each society came to adopt such extreme practices, what effect they have upon the personalities and conflicts of the people living in the Rimrock area, and what cultural adjustments each society has made to reduce or relieve these conflicts. For the Zuni we have chosen the rigid training for the control of aggression as the child-rearing variable, and harmony as the relevant value; for the Texans we have chosen early weaning and early and strong pressure on self reliance and individual achievement as the child-rearing variables and success as the value; for the Mormons we have chosen the warm and seductive relationship between mother and infant followed by the severe control of sexual impulses and behavior in later childhood and adolescence as the child-rearing variables, and virtue as the dominant value.

Because each of these groups lives in the Rimrock area under comparable ecological conditions, neither the child-rearing practices nor the adult values produced by them can be explained in terms of adjustment to the current environment, and we shall seek an answer in the historical past of each society. Inasmuch as little is known about the details of socialization of these societies in the past, and, since it would be inappropriate to the scope of this chapter to search for or document in detail whatever may be available as to past values, we intend to be selective and interpretative in piecing together information that seems to be relevant and to lend some plausibility to our hypothesis.

Since the Zuni were the earliest inhabitants of the area, we will begin with them. Before A.D. 1000 the Rimrock area was inhabited by farming peoples who lived in scattered villages and dwelt in small single family pit houses. As Chang (1958, p. 319) puts it: "On the whole, the household is the basic social unit throughout, and domestically self-sufficient and independent. This is evident in Basket Maker II and Pueblo I periods when each house was separate and had its own living quarters; workshop, fire pit and storage bins and granaries. This isolation disappeared superficially with the conjunction of houses which began in Pueblo II. Nevertheless, domestic self-sufficiency is still indicated by the partitions between neighboring houses, the functional self-sufficiency of each house is shown by its material content and the arrangements of doors." About this time archaeological evidence indicates that a dramatic change occurred in household structure and by A.D. 1300 the small isolated households had been replaced by the great pueblos. This change in settlement pattern was dictated by the need for defense and must have been the consequence of some military crisis. Whether it was the result of internal strife, arising from a rapid rise in population, or of invasion of Apache bands from the north has not been definitely determined, but a drastic shift from nuclear to extended households and from isolated homesteads to compact pueblos occurred in a relatively short period of time. Many of these multiple-dwelling pueblos failed and were abandoned, but the Zuni pueblo was one of the few which were successful.

It is our hypothesis that this shift had a profound effect upon both values and child-rearing practices. Specifically, we presume that crowded living conditions required an emphasis on harmony and strict control of aggression. We believe this to be a consequence, not so much of the sheer number of people living under one roof, as of the requirement that several women share in the running of the household. To check the reasonableness of this interpretation, we have made a cross-cultural test. We have taken a world-wide sample of societies which have been scored in Whiting and Child (1953) on the severity with which children are punished for aggression and which have been typed as to household by Murdock (1957). We have grouped Murdock's categories of stem, lineal, and extended families under the single heading of extended families. The association between punishment for aggression and household type is presented in Table 8.8.

Twenty-five of 30 cases, approximately 80 percent, confirm our expectation. The two-sided 99 percent confidence limits of this association vary from 65 to 97 percent (Hald 1952). Perhaps a more striking way of putting the relationship is that 92 percent of the extended families are above the median in the severity with which children's aggression is punished, whereas but 22 percent of the societies with nuclear family households are equally severe. The Zuni are in the list of societies above the median in the severity with which they punish aggression.

How long after they moved into the extended family pueblos it took the ancestors of the modern Zuni to discover that aggression must be controlled is, of course, impossible to say. It is our thesis that this adaptation occurred very rapidly, and that a sig-

TABLE 8.8
RELATION BETWEEN THE SEVERITY WITH WHICH CHILDREN ARE PUNISHED FOR AGGRESSION AND CONTRASTING HOUSEHOLD STRUCTURES IN THIRTY SOCIETIES*

Severity of aggression training	Households			
	Nuclear		Extended	
High			Hopi	18
			Jivaro	17
			Kwakiutl	16
			Lepcha	17
			Maori	14
			Papago	15
			Samoans	14
	Alorese	16	Sanpoil	14
	Chamorro	18	Tenino	13
	Dobuans	15	Yakut	13
	Kutenai	14	Zuni	15
Low	Abipone	7	Ontong Java	12
	Andamanese	9		
	Balinese	11		
	Chenchu	9		
	Copper Eskimo	9		
	Ifugao	12		
	Lakher	12		
	Lamba	12		
	Manus	7		
	Marshallese	9		
	Navaho	11		
	Pukapukans	12		
	Tikopia	10		
	Trobrianders	8		

* Numbers indicate rating on severity of aggression training. Relationship between household structure and severity of aggression training: $p = < 0.001$ (Fisher exact test).
Source: Whiting and Child, *Child Training and Personality*, 1953.

nificant change in child-rearing came as a consequence. The value system of the pre-crisis Zuni is lost in the past, but we presume that the emphasis of the modern Zuni on harmony as one of their essential values was developed as part of a pattern which included severe control of aggression and the extended family.

Since we have a long tradition of written history for the two Anglo cultures we do not have to rest our case on an interpretation of archaeological remains to gain historical perspective. For the most part, the forebears of both the Texans and the Mormons were British, and we can obtain information about their common culture in the British Isles before and during the early days of migration to America. Here again, we find a dramatic change in family and household structure similar to that which occurred in the Zuni society, but in the opposite direction. British culture was characterized by a patrilocal extended family living in an extended household. This type of family brought to America by the early colonists is described by Bailyn (1960, pp. 15-16):

The family familiar to the early colonists was a patrilineal group of extended kinship gathered into a single household. By modern standards it was large. Besides children, who often remained in the home well into maturity, it included a wide range of other dependents: nieces, nephews, cousins, and except for families at the lowest rung of society, servants in filial discipline. In the Elizabethan family the conjugal unit was only the nucleus of a broad kinship community whose outer edges merged almost imperceptibly into the society at large.

The organization of this group reflected and reinforced the general structure of social authority. Control rested with the male head to whom all others were subordinate. His sanctions were powerful; they were rooted deep in the cultural soil. They rested upon tradition that went back beyond the memory of man; on the instinctive sense of order as hierarchy, whether in the cosmic chain of being or in human society; on the process of law that reduced the female to perpetual dependency and calibrated a detailed scale of male subordination and servitude; and, above all, on the restrictions of the economy, which made the establishment of independent households a difficult enterprise.

A recent study by Alice Ryerson of books written in English from 1550 to 1900 giving advice to mothers shows striking uniformity during the first two centuries. As long as the "Elizabethan family" was the cultural ideal, doctors advised relatively late weaning (two years), self-demand schedules, swaddling, and the use of cradles. The practice of singing and rocking the child to sleep was condoned. Dependence was more valued than independence, and obedience was strictly demanded. The child was believed to be born evil and therefore potentially aggressive, and it was the duty of the parents to control this by stern discipline (Ryerson 1959).

The Elizabethan family fell upon hard times soon after the arrival in America of the colonists. The family heads did not know how to cope with the new and strange environment any better than their children. Furthermore, patriarchs often engaged in the menial labor necessary for survival, with the result that their authority was sharply challenged. For a time, the society attempted to maintain the familiar social structure by legal force. As Bailyn (1960, p. 23) puts it:

There is no more poignant, dramatic reading than the seventeenth century laws and admonitions relating to family life. Those of Massachusetts are deservedly best known: they are most profuse and charged with Old Testament passion. But they are not different in kind from the others. Within a decade of their founding all the colonies passed laws demanding obedience from children and specifying penalties for contempt and abuse. Nothing less than capital punishment, it was ruled in Connecticut and Massachusetts, was the fitting punishment for filial disobedience.

Not only was patriarchal authority challenged, but the availability of land and the possibility of westward migration soon made the extended family household nonfunctional and impossible to maintain. This was true particularly for those who, like the ancestors of the Texans, moved westward in nuclear units. The family pattern became more independent, isolated, and nuclear with each step.

By the middle of the eighteenth century the classic lineaments of the American family as modern sociologists described them—the "isolation of the conjugal unit," the "maximum of dispersion of the lines of descent," partible inheritance and multilineal growth—had appeared. The consequences can hardly be exaggerated. Fundamental aspects of social life were affected. In the reduced, nuclear family, thrown back upon itself, traditional gradations in status tended to fall to the level of necessity. Relationships tended more toward achievement than ascription. The status of women rose; marriage, even in the eyes of the law, tended to become a contract between equals. Above all, the development of the child was affected. (Bailyn 1960, pp. 24-25)

Coincident with these changes in family structure were changes in the literature giving advice and counsel to mothers (Ryerson 1959). After 1750, they were told that they should begin to wean their children between nine months and one year, that they should feed them on schedule, and that they should not swaddle their infants but should permit them to exercise freely so that they might develop more rapidly. Cradles were frowned upon, and mothers were told that singing and rocking the child to sleep was a bad practice. Independence supplanted obedience as a goal of socialization. At this same time there was a dramatic change with respect to ideas about the nature of the child: it was now believed that he was born good, and aggression was considered a normal component of his individualism and independence. The child-rearing practices of modern Texans conform strikingly to this advice: they wean early, value individualism and early independence, and are permissive with respect to aggression.

As shown above, one of the strong contrasts between the extended and nuclear households is that the former are severe in the control of aggression. The contrast between the Elizabethan and the modern Texan homesteader family is an example of this difference. The Texan family has relaxed its pressure on the control of aggression and on the requirement of obedience, and it has substituted an exaggerated and early demand for independence. Whereas Elizabethan parents may have feared that their children would be aggressive and disobedient the major concern of the Texan parent is that

the child might be excessively dependent.

To discover whether the difference between the Elizabethan and Texan families is unique or general, let us turn again to our cross-cultural sample. A recent study of child-rearing practices by Barry, Bacon, and Child (1957) provides an estimate of the age at which independence training is begun, as judged by the time when there is reduced contact between mother and child. When these scores are correlated with Murdock's judgments of household structure, the median age for the nuclear household is 18 months, in sharp contract to the median age of 30 months for all other household structures. Furthermore, cross-cultural evidence indicates that the pressure for independence in the nuclear household in contrast to all others is not only strikingly earlier, but also more severe, as indicated in Table 8.9. This table correlates the Murdock household scores with the Barry, Bacon, and Child scores of transition anxiety (the anxiety generated in the child during the shift of status from infancy to childhood).

The shift from the historical Elizabethan extended family to the independent nuclear family and household that characterizes the modern Texans is apparently not a unique event but a change in social structure that has general consequences for patterns of child-rearing. What are the consequences of these changes with respect to values? Obviously, we can presume a shift from obedience to independence and from group responsibility to individualism, but we are concerned here with another value which has been shown to follow from the child-rearing practices associated with independent nuclear households —the value of success. Assuming that

TABLE 8.9
RELATION BETWEEN HOUSEHOLD STRUCTURE AND TRANSITION ANXIETY IN THIRTY SOCIETIES*

Transition anxiety	Households			
	Nuclear		Extended	
High	Rocky Roaders	14		
	Aymara	13		
	Chamorro	13		
	Wolcans	12		
	Balinese	12		
	Lamba	12		
	Kaska	11		
	Chenchu	11	Yakut	12
	Pukapukans	10	Winnebago	11
	Navaho	10	Maori	10
	Alorese	10	Hopi	10
Low	Trobrianders	7	Truk	9
	Manus	6	Zuni	9
	Lakher	5	Lepcha	8
			Klamath	7
			Tenetehara	7
			Wichita	7
			Auracanians	6
			Papago	6
			Ontong Java	5
			Samoa	5
			Cuna	2
			Tupinamba	2

* Numbers indicate ratings on severity of transition anxiety. Relationship between household structure and transition anxiety: $p = 0.007$ (Fisher exact test).
Source: Barry, Bacon, Child, "Sex Differences in Socialization"; Murdock, "World Ethnographic Sample."

this value is measured by achievement imagery in folk tales, a cross-cultural study by McClelland and Friedman (1952) shows that such imagery is significantly greater in societies with early and severe independence training than in societies which are late and lax in these matters.

Further evidence for a change in values during the eighteenth century is supplied by a study of the relation between "need achievement" and economic development by McClelland. The achievement imagery in drama, accounts of sea voyages, and street ballads in England from 1400 to 1830 was used as an index of need achieve-ment. A striking change in the number of achievement images per one hundred lines occurred in the eighteenth century: the average was 2.99 in 1700, 4.23 in 1750, and 6.00 in 1800. McClelland (1961) interprets this change as a consequence of the Protestant revival. We would rather interpret it as a consequence of the change in family and household structure to which we have alluded. Although his data refer to Great Britain rather than to colonial America, if our hypothesis is correct, the Elizabethan family was becoming nucleated in England too. Two types of evidence suggest that this was true.

First, just as the son of a colonial family could move west from the eastern seaboard, so could the British sons emigrate to America. The population increase in America of 750,000 during the period from 1690 to 1745 can largely be accounted for by immigrants from Great Britain. The correlative loss should have put a strain on the Elizabethan family in England similar to that upon its counterpart on the east coast of America. Second, the abrupt change in advice and counsel to mothers was parallel, both in time and content, in England and in America. This change was consonant with the change in family structure that we have posited.

That the Texans are extreme with respect to child-rearing practices that promote a strong drive for success is indicated by the age at which they wean their children, assuming this is the first step in training for independence. Of fifty-two societies reported in Whiting and Child (1953), the onset of weaning was rated as under a year in but two, the Chamorro and the Marquesans. The average age that our Texan mothers began to wean their children was under nine months. Thus, the ancestors of the Texans, like the ancestors of the Zuni, underwent a crisis which resulted in a change in their family structure, which in turn altered both their child-rearing practices and their value system, but in opposite directions.

The Mormon case is especially interesting. During the last two hundred years, they have undergone major crises that have affected their social structure and value system. The first crisis, migration from England to the rigors of frontier life was identical with that faced by the ancestors of the Texans. The families which later became Mormons, however, were those who refused to accept the independent nuclear household as a solution to the crisis. By 1840, they finally had succumbed to the pressure for change and evolved a modification of the Elizabethan family that was quite different from the one adopted by the ancestors of the Texans.[2] Modeling themselves on the example of the Old Testament, the Latter-Day Saints, led by Joseph Smith, made a valiant and successful attempt to retain some of the essential structure of their ancestral extended family. The Elizabethan pattern of patriarchal authority, subjugated status of women, and complete filial obedience characterized the ideals of the Mormon family from the beginning.

There was, however, one modification of the Elizabethan pattern of great importance—the adoption of polygyny and the concomitant establishment of the mother-child household in contrast to the extended family household. The causes for this change in structure are difficult to determine, and a number of hypotheses have been advanced. One factor which no doubt played a part was the personality of Joseph Smith. From contemporary accounts, he was quite a ladies' man and had liaisons with at least twenty women before polygyny was officially adopted by the Mormon Church. Since other leaders of the Church quickly followed in his footsteps, it is doubtful that the adoption of polygyny can be entirely attributed to Smith's charismatic leadership. Another factor which undoubtedly was responsible was the success with which early Mormon missionaries made female converts in Great Britain, where the lot of women was a hard one and the land of promise alluring. It seems to us, however, that perhaps one of the most important reasons was that the Elizabethan family was breaking up—its sacred and traditional status had been challenged, thus permitting innovations.

Certain features of Mormon polygyny are of particular importance in this chapter. First, it took the form of the mother-child rather than the polygynous household. A Mormon man would build a house for each of his wives and establish her in it as soon as he could afford to do so. Rarely would the wives live under the same roof, and, when this did occur, each wife generally had her own apartment with separate cooking facilities (Young 1954). Second, although a polygynous husband would carefully rotate among his wives, the routine was interrupted if any wife had a nursing infant, since there was, as a matter of church doctrine, a prohibition against sexual intercourse during this time. The practice of the so-called postpartum sex taboo is closely correlated with polygyny the world over and rarely occurs with monogamy. Although we do not have definite evidence, it is probable that the Mormons adopted at this time another feature very closely associated with the polygynous mother-child household, exclusive mother-infant sleeping arrangements. The present-day Rimrock Mormon infant generally sleeps in the parental bed. It is very likely, therefore, that he did so during the period of polygyny.

Several recent studies have suggested that the polygynous mother-child household and exclusive mother-infant sleeping arrangements lead to the unconscious seduction of the male infant by the mother during the time when the mother is deprived of adult sexual satisfaction and the son has exclusive possession of her. They suggest that the control of incest and of sex is the focal problem in societies with such family and household arrangements (Stephens 1962; Whiting, Kluckhohn and Anthony 1958; Whiting 1959). Thus, it would be expected that the control of sexual impulses during childhood and adolescence would be a major problem. Since the validity of this assumption is important for our interpretation of the Mormon case, it was decided to test the hypothesis cross-culturally. Table 8.10 correlates the severity of sex-training scores with sleeping arrangements (Whiting and Child 1953; Whiting and D'Andrade 1959). In the ten cases where the mother and infant share a bed and the father sleeps elsewhere, eight are above the median in the severity with which sex is punished in later childhood, whereas in the eight cases where the father and mother sleep together and the infant sleeps elsewhere, only two are severe in sex training.

As has been shown earlier in this chapter the greatest emphasis of Mormon child-rearing practices was placed upon the control of sex. However, the strong Mormon value statement concerning sex that was cited came from a Mormon tract, not from one of our informants. It therefore represents church doctrine, which was evolved during the period of polygyny. It has persisted as a statement of Mormon ideals even though, as we shall show, it is no longer consonant with their social structure.

The next crisis which the Mormons underwent occurred in 1890 when the United States Government outlawed polygyny. Although many Mormons tried to retain their family and household arrangements—some migrating to Mexico, some maintaining illicit wives secretly, and so on—by the time of our study, none of the Mormon

TABLE 8.10
RELATION BETWEEN MOTHER-INFANT SLEEPING ARRANGEMENTS AND THE SEVERITY OF SEX TRAINING IN EIGHTEEN SOCIETIES*

Severity of sex training	Nonexclusive		Exclusive	
High			Alorese	13
			Arapesh	16
			Chiricahua	17
			Kurtachi	18
			Kwoma	15
			Samoa	13
	Manus	16	Tanala	13
	Navaho	14	Wogeo	16
Low	Baiga	8	Siriono	5
	Hopi	12	Trobriands	9
	Lepcha	6		
	Maori	8		
	Papago	9		
	Pukapuka	5		

* Numbers indicate score on severity of sex training. Relationship between type of sleeping arrangements and severity of sex training: $p = 0.03$ (Fisher exact test).
Source: Whiting and Child, *Child Training and Personality;* Whiting and D'Andrade, "Sleeping Arrangements."

families was polygynous, nor were there any mother-child households. The standard American independent family and nuclear household had been universally adopted in Rimrock village. Along with this change in social structure should go a shift from virtue to success as a dominant value and, along with this, more emphasis on independence and less concern with the control of sex. There is considerable evidence that the Rimrock Mormons in 1950 were moving rapidly in this direction. Approximately one-third of our sample were indistinguishable from the Texans in their child-rearing practices. They weaned their children as early, were lenient with respect to sex, and were egalitarian- and success-oriented. Furthermore, 38 percent of the Mormon children gave responses indicating achievement imagery on the Magic Man test. Therefore, we see the Mormons in a state of transition from

their polygynous phase to the general American pattern, and we predict that in another generation, the Mormon and Texan family structure and value system will be indistinguishable. A comparison of Mormon child-rearing practices with those of societies where there is polygyny and a mother-child household suggests that they have already moved a long way toward the dominant American pattern exemplified by the Texans.

Thus, each of the three societies[3] under consideration apparently enjoyed a period, of indeterminate duration, when its culture was relatively stable, before experiencing a sudden dramatic change that gave rise to present child-rearing emphases and their associated dominant values. For the Zuni, the crisis was the invasion of the Apache and Navaho, which led to a shift in household structure from isolated nuclear arrangements to the extended family households and a consequent severe control of the expression of aggression and the emphasis on harmony as a value. For the Texans, the crisis was the break-up of the Elizabethan extended family, due to many factors but particularly to migration to the new world. The result of these events was the adoption of the independent nuclear family household and a consequent shift to exceedingly early socialization, a pressure toward individualism and independence, and an emphasis upon success as a crucial value. For the Mormons, the crisis is assumed also to have been thet break-up of the Elizabethan family. It was met with a different solution. They retained the patriarchal features of the Elizabethan family, but adopted polygyny and the mother-child household. This led to a shift in child-rearing practices, exclusive mother-infant sleeping arrangements, and the adoption of the postpartum sex taboo, which in turn led to a strengthening of incestuous feelings between mother and son, countered by strong control of sex in later childhood and adolescence.

Each of the three cultures was characterized by a period of stability in family structure, interrupted by a period of rapid change, followed by another period of stability. This parallels the modern view of biological change as operating in a nonmonotonic manner and suggests that cultural change may often operate in this manner, rather than, as many have presumed, in a steady monotonic drift.

What are the consequences of these child-rearing emphases and the exaggeration of a dominant value when the period of crisis is over? Today, the Zuni need not protect themselves against predatory neighbors, yet they continue to live in extended family households, punish their children severely for fighting, and insist on harmony as a value. The Texans do not have to rely on individual success and isolated nuclearity of their families, but could join a union, get a job in a factory, and adjust to bureaucracy. If they should do this, as Miller and Swanson (1958) have shown, early socialization and stress on independence and success would be notably diminished. With the outlawing of polygyny, the Mormons faced a new crisis, and they have not yet reached a stable equilibrium of value system, social structure, and child-rearing practices.

We would like to present the hypothesis here that, when a culture meets a crisis by changing its social structure, child-rearing, and value system, this is done at some psychological cost to the individual members of the society and leads to the development of cultural defenses against the conflicts engendered by the crisis adjustment. Specifically, the Zuni had to defend themselves against feelings of aggression and hostility; the Texans must protect themselves against failure; and the Mormons had to protect themselves against strong incestuous feelings.

One of the functions of any culture is to provide its members with a ready-made and culturally acceptable set of defenses, rather than permitting each individual to develop and choose his own idiosyncratic defenses against the crisis-engendered conflict. Certain aspects of the culture of each of the three societies may be so interpreted. The culturally acceptable defensive system for the Zuni consists of the denial and projection of aggression. The Zuni see themselves as peaceful and harmonious, although, as Smith and Roberts have shown, their murder rate is unusually high and they are notorious for their bitter factionalism and malicious gossip. Cultural blinders permit the Zuni to believe that these events are not truly a part of their culture, but that they come from some outside, non-Zuni source, such as foreigners, or sorcerers, or bad Zuni who have been trained by an external evil force. Here is the classical paranoid defense consisting of the denial of one's own aggression and the projection of one's own hostile feelings onto others, which then permits the expression of justifiable anger. Sorcerers in Zuni are executed with culturally sanctioned sadistic relish (Smith and Roberts 1954).

Texan culture also provides a ready-made defense against failure which employs denial and projection. The principal economic activity—growing pinto beans in this semi-arid area—is not likely to satisfy anyone with a strong need to suceed, and failure is in fact the common lot. Texan culture, however, provides its members with two modes of escape. It permits them to boast of their "metropolis" as "Homestead—Pinto Bean Capital of the World," and it permits them to attribute failure to some external source, such as the weather or bad luck. If the rules of the culture required each individual to admit to himself and to others that failure was due to his own bad judgment, lack of skill, or laziness, life would be intolerable.

The Mormons developed elaborate defenses against the strong incestuous feelings that we have posited to be a consequence of their child-rearing practices and their need to remain virtuous. One of these is sending the adolescent boys away on a "mission," which breaks up, by spatial separation, the warm and intimate relation between mother and son that charac-

terizes the Mormon family during infancy and early childhood. Sending adolescent boys out of the home is a common cultural adjustment as shown by a recent cross-cultural study (Whiting and D'Andrade 1959).

Another way in which Mormon culture protected the virtue of its members was by strong taboos against drinking and smoking, rationalized as pathways to sin. According to our interpretation, these taboos are a means of maintaining their sexual inhibitions and of keeping incestuous feelings under control. Finally, the emphasis of Mormon culture on proselytizing may be interpreted as another method of protecting the virtue of its members. As in the other two societies the conflict is projected outside the group. Proselytizing implies that the Gentiles, not the Mormons, have sinful sexual feelings. If all the world were converted to Mormonism and were virtuous, there would be no dangerous temptations.

In conclusion, to summarize the above thesis, it is hypothesized that certain crises may require a society to modify its social structure, particularly its living arrangements and family organization. These, in turn, may require the extraordinary control of certain impulses such as aggression, dependence, or sex. This leads to the development of child-rearing practices which will insure that these impulses be controlled and the acceptance and elaboration of dominant values—in the present instance, harmony, success, and virtue—to stand against these dangerous impulses. Finally, these child-rearing and value emphases require the development of culturally accepted defenses which enable the individual members of the society to tolerate the conflicts produced by the culture.

NOTES

1. In 1950 the team consisted of Eleanor Hollenberg Chasdi, Helen Faigin Antonovsky, and Margaret Sperry Lawrence. In 1951 Barbara Chartier Ayres replaced Margaret Sperry Lawrence on the team. Although the senior author had some responsibility for the research design, much of it was worked out in detail by the field teams, particularly Eleanor Hollenberg Chasdi and Helen Faigin Antonovsky, for whom this research was the basis of doctoral theses in the Department of Social Relations. They and Dr. Ayres were also responsible for the major part of the organization and analysis of the materials, such as coding the interviews, developing scales, and rating both the mothers and children on certain dimensions.

2. During the same period, a large number of Utopian movements (such as the Shakers, Owenites, and Fourients) appeared, most of them advocating a modification in the family household and structure.

3. In the following discussion, the Mormons will be considered as though they were still in their classical polygynous phase.

REFERENCES

Bailyn, Bernard
    1960   *Education in the Forming of American Society*. Chapel Hill: University of North Carolina Press.
Barry, H. A., M. K. Bacon, and I. L. Child
    1957   A cross-cultural survey of some sex differences in socialization. *Journal of Abnormal and Social Psychology* 55: 327-332.
Chang, Kwang-Chih
    1958   Study of the Neolithic social grouping: Examples from the New World. *American Anthropologist* 60: 298-334.
Hald, A.
    1952   *Statistical Tables and Formulas*. New York: Wiley.
McClelland, David C.
    1961   *The Achieving Society*. Princeton: Van Nostrand.
McClelland, David C., et al.
    1953   *The Achievement Motive*. New York: Appleton-Century-Crofts.
McClelland, David C., and G. A. Friedman
    1952   A cross-cultural study of the relationship between child-training practices and achievement motivation appearing in folk tales. *In* G. E. Swanson, T. M. Newcomb, and E. L. Hartley (eds.), *Readings in Social Psychology*. New York: Holt.
Miller, Daniel R., and Guy E. Swanson
    1958   *The Changing American Parent*. New York: Wiley.
Mischel, Walter
    1964   Delay of gratification, need for achievement, and acquiescence in another culture. *Journal of Abnormal and Social Psychology* 62: 543-552.
Murdock, George P.
    1957   World Ethnographic Sample. *American Anthropologist* 59: 664-687.
Roberts, John M.
    1965   *Zuni Daily Life*. Behavior Science Reprint. New Haven: Human Relations Area Files.
Ryerson, Alice
    1959   Medical advice on child rearing, 1550-1900. Ph.D. dissertation, Harvard University.
Sears, R. R., E. E. Maccoby, and H. Levin
    1957   *Patterns of Child Rearing*. Evanston, IL: Row, Peterson.

Smith, W., and J. M. Roberts
1954 *Zuni Law, a Field of Values.* Cambridge, Mass.: Papers of the Peabody Museum of American Archaeology and Ethnology, Vol. 43, No. 1.
Stephens, William N.
1962 *The Oedipus Complex: Cross-Cultural Evidence.* Glencoe, IL: Free Press.
Whiting, John W. M.
1954 The cross-cultural method. *In* G. Lindzey (ed.), *Handbook of Social Psychology.* Boston: Addison-Wesley.
1959 Sorcery, sin and the superego: A cross-cultural study of some mechanisms of social control. In *Symposium on Motivation.* Lincoln: University of Nebraska Press.
Whiting, J. W. M., and I. L. Child
1953 *Child Training and Personality: A Cross-Cultural Study.* New Haven: Yale University Press.
Whiting, J. W. M., and R. G. D'Andrade
1959 Sleeping arrangements and social structure: A cross-cultural study. Presented at American Anthropological Association Annual Meetings, Mexico City, December, 1959.
Whiting, J. W. M., R. Kluckhohn, and A. S. Anthony
1958 The function of male initiation ceremonies at puberty. *In* E. E. Maccoby, T. M. Newcomb, and E. L. Hartley (eds.) *Readings in Social Psychology.* New York: Holt.
Young, Kimball
1954 *Isn't One Wife Enough?* New York: Holt.

9. A CROSS-CULTURAL ANALYSIS OF SEX DIFFERENCES IN THE BEHAVIOR OF CHILDREN AGED THREE THROUGH ELEVEN

BEATRICE WHITING and CAROLYN P. EDWARDS

Beatrice Whiting is a Professor in the Graduate School of Education, Harvard University. Carolyn P. Edwards is research assistant and doctoral candidate at the Graduate School of Education, Harvard University. Reprinted with permission from *The Journal of Social Psychology* (1973) 91.

THIS PAPER INVESTIGATES the validity of the stereotypes of sex differences as evidenced by behavior of children between the ages of three and eleven, observed in natural settings in seven different parts of the world.[1]

Females are frequently characterized as more dependent, passive, compliant, nurturant, responsible, and sociable than males, who in turn are characterized as more dominant, aggressive, and active. Assuming that these statements imply observable behaviors, the authors have attempted to define the stereotypes in such a way as to relate them to the categories of interactions which have been used in a series of observational studies of children in natural settings.

There are two major research issues: are there observable differences in male and female behavior, and if so, are these differences biological and genetically determined or the result of learning a society's definition of appropriate sex role behavior? To begin to answer these questions one can proceed by asking first, whether or not the behaviors said to characterize the male and the female are present in all societies, and second, assuming they are found in societies with a variety of cultures, are there associ-

ated universal sex role requirements and associated sex typed socialization pressures?

It is our assumption that sex differences reported for the United States or another Western-type culture may reflect only an idiosyncratic type of socialization. If, however, the same differences appear in societies with divergent cultures and life styles, the assumption of universality gains credence. To determine whether sex differences in behavior are biologically determined or the result of universal sex role requirements is far more difficult. Since our study does not include observations of neonates and young infants, it cannot speak to the possible influence and interaction of biological and social variables. It is possible, however, to note age changes during the three to eleven year age span and the presence of associated socialization pressures, and to consider the consistency of sex differences across samples of children.

METHOD

Six of the samples are the children of the Six Culture Study (Minturn and Lambert 1964; B. B. Whiting

1963) observed in 1954-56 by field teams who lived in communities located in Nyansongo in Kenya, Taira in Okinawa, Khalapur in India, Tarong in the Philippines, Juxtlahuaca in Mexico, and Orchard Town in New England.[2] The societies were selected by the field teams on the basis of interest. They vary in complexity as reflected in occupational specialization, political structure and settlement pattern, and in social structure. Three societies favor patrilineal extended families, the other three nuclear families. In three societies children sleep and eat with their mother, father, and siblings; in three they share intimate space with other kin. (For detailed analysis of the cultures see Whiting and Whiting, in press)

The children were all three to eleven years of age, with 12 girls and 12 boys in four of the societies, 11 girls and 11 boys in Juxtlahuaca, and 8 girls and 8 boys in Nyansongo. The children were observed in natural settings, most frequently in their house or yard, on an average of 17 different times for five minute periods over a period of six to fourteen months. The observations were focused on one child at a time by one of the members of the field team plus a bilingual assistant. The social interaction recorded in these paragraphs was subsequently coded at the Laboratory of Human Development at Harvard University. The code was designed to identify the instigator and instigation, if any, to the child's act and the action immediately following his act. The analysis of the 8,500 interactions was done on a computer. Of the more than 70 original types of interactions coded, 12 summary types were selected for analysis. For detailed description of methodology, see Imamura (1965, pp. 3-18), B. Whiting (1963), and Whiting and Whiting (in press, ch. 3). The 12 behaviors are:

Offering help: offering food, toys, tools, or general help.

Offering support: offering emotional support and comfort.

Seeking help and comfort: seeking instrumental help or emotional support.

Seeking attention and approval: seeking approval of either positive or negative attention.

Acting sociably: greeting, initiating friendly interaction, or engaging in friendly interaction.

Dominating: attempting to change the ongoing behavior of another to meet one's own egoistic desires.

Suggesting responsibly or prosocial dominance: suggesting that another change his behavior in such a way as to meet the rules of the family or other group, or serve the welfare of the group.

Reprimanding: criticizing another's behavior after the fact.

Seeking or offering physical contact: nonaggressive touching or holding.

Engaging in rough and tumble play: playing which includes physical contact, wrestling, and playful aggression.

Insulting: verbally derogating another.

Assaulting: attempting to injure another.

In 1968-70 a sample of 70 children between the ages of two and ten were observed in Ngecha, a village situated twenty miles north of Nairobi in Kenya. The children were observed by students for periods of 30 minutes over the course of two years, and their behavior was recorded in running paragraphs and then coded by the observers. The code used was a revised version of the six culture code. The children between three and ten years of age have been selected for the analysis in this paper, there were 21 girls and 18 boys aged 3-6 years, and nine girls and nine boys aged 7-10.

In order to relate the stereotypes of female and male behavior to the behavior we have observed and coded in our studies, we have attempted to define the stereotypes operationally and then selected from our codes those categories which seem to best represent the definitions. To measure the sex differences in these behaviors, we have used the proportion scores of each child for each of the relevant types of observed behavior, and computed a set of group means from those individual proportion scores. The children have been divided into groups on the basis of sex, age (3-6 years old versus 7-11 years old), and cultural sample.

Comparisons between girls and boys in each culture are based on the differences between the mean proportion scores for the behavior types. Significance levels are based on t-tests between the means of the sex age groups. The comparisons for the pooled samples are based on scores standardized by culture. Nyansongo and Juxtlahuaca, because of the smaller number of children (16 and 22 respectively), are slightly underrepresented when the standardized scores are pooled.

RESULTS

DEPENDENCE
STEREOTYPE: GIRLS ARE MORE
DEPENDENT THAN BOYS

There are three types of behavior which have been traditionally classi-fied under this heading: (1) seeking help, (2) seeking attention, (3) seeking physical contact. In the six culture study, seeking for help included both asking for instrumental help—that is, requesting help in reaching a goal, asking for an object needed to reach a goal, or requesting food—and asking for comfort or reassurance. Seeking attention included bids for approval and attempts to call attention to oneself by boasting or by performing either praiseworthy or blameworthy acts with the intent of becoming the focus of another person's attention. The category of seeking or offering physcial contact included behavior in which the child sought proximity to another, or touched, held, or clung to another.

Table 9.1 presents the comparisons. It can be seen that in five of the six societies girls aged 3-6 were observed to seek help more frequently than did the boys aged 3-6, and that the difference between the pooled groups of younger girls and boys is significant at the .05 level. In the 7-11 year old comparison, however, there is an equal split; in three societies girls were observed to seek help more than boys and in three the reverse was true.

Seeking attention is more characteristic of boys than girls. In four of the samples boys 3-6 seek attention more frequently than do girls, but for the pooled sample of six societies there is no significant difference. Among 7-11 year olds in the four societies where there are differences, boys seek attention more frequently and the difference is significant at the .05 level.

Girls were observed to seek or offer physical contact more frequently than boys. For the young group as a whole there is a marked sex difference, girls seeking or offering physcial contact

TABLE 9.1
DIFFERENCE BETWEEN THE MEAN PROPORTION SCORES
OF BOYS AND GIRLS IN THE SIX CULTURE STUDY

		Nyan-songo	Juxtla-huaca	Tarong	Taira	Khalapur	Orchard Town	All
Dependency								
1. Seeks help	3-6	+	+	+	+	+*	—	+*
	7-11	—	—	+	+	—**	+	—
2. Seeks attention	3-6	+	—	—	—	—	+	—
	7-11	—	—**	—	=	=	—	—*
3. Physical contact	3-6	+	+	—	+	+	+	+**
	7-11	+	+	+	—	+	+	+
4. *Sociability*	3-6	+	—	—	+	+	+	+
	7-11	+	—	+	+	+*	—	+
Passivity								
5. Withdrawal from aggressive insti-gations	3-6	+	—	+	+	—	+	+
	7-11	—	+	+	—	+	—	+
6. Counter agression in response to an aggres-sive instigation	3-6	—	—	+	+	+	—	—
	7-11	—	+	—	—*	—	—*	—**
7. Compliance to domi-nant instigation (pro-social egoistic)	3-6	—	—	+	+	+	—	+
	7-11	+	+	+	=	—	—	+
8. Initiative (% of acts which are self-instigated)	3-6	—	—	+	—	+	—	—
	7-11	+	—	—	—*	—	+	—
Nurturance								
9. Offers help	3-6	—	+	+	+	+	—	+
	7-11	+	+	+**	—	+	+	+**
10. Gives support	3-6	—	+	+	+*	—	+	+
	7-11	+	+*	+	+	+	+	+***
11. *Suggests Responsibly*	3-6	+	+	+	+	+	+	+*
	7-11	—	+	—	+	—*	+	—
12. *Dominance*	3-6	—	—	+	—	—	—	—*
	7-11	—	+	—	—	—	—	—
Aggression								
13. Rough and tumble play	3-6	+	—	—	—	—	+	—*
	7-11	+	—	—	—	—	—	—*
14. Insults	3-6	—	—	—	—**	—	—	—**
	7-11	—	—	—	—**	—	+	—*
15. Assaults	3-6	—	—	—	—	—	+	—
	7-11	+	—	—	—	+	—	—

A (+) indicates that the girls' score was higher than the boys'.
A (—) indicates that the boys' score was higher than the girls'.
* P < .05; ** P < .01; *** P < .001

more frequently than boys (p < .01).

In sum, the stereotype of female dependency holds for two of the types of behavior—seeking help and seeking or offering physical contact—but it is mainly true of the younger age groups, there being no significant difference in these behaviors in the 7-11 year olds. Seeking attention, on the other hand, is a male form of "dependency," is clearly present in the 7-11 year old group, and is the only type of "dependent" behavior in which there are significant differences in the older age group.

SOCIABILITY
STEREOTYPE: GIRLS ARE MORE SOCIABLE THAN BOYS

"Sociability," which includes greeting behavior and all acts judged to have the primary intent of seeking or offering friendly interaction, is correlated with "dependent" behavior. As can be seen in Table 9.1, row 4, there is a slight tendency for girls to be more sociable than boys but the differences are not significant.

PASSIVITY
STEREOTYPE: GIRLS ARE PASSIVE

"Passivity" is frequently associated with dependency in the stereotypes of female behavior. This concept is more difficult to operationalize, and we have accepted the definitions of Kagan and Moss (1962). They list among other behavioral indices of passivity in the preschool child (a) retreat when dominated by a sibling; (b) no reaction when goal object is lost; (c) withdrawal when blocked from goal by environmental obstacle; and (d) withdrawal from mildly noxious or potentially dangerous situations. During the school years, their passivity measures included: (a) withdrawal

from attack or social rejection; and (b) withdrawal from difficult and frustrating situations.

The six culture code included instigational situations described as encountering difficulty, being blocked, having property taken away, being challenged to competition; being insulted or physically attacked, and being dominated. In these situations, if we accept the above definition of "passivity," girls should, according to the stereotype, respond by withdrawal. Two types of instigations occur with sufficient frequency to make analysis possible: (1) aggressive instigations, including being insulted, roughed up in a playful fashion, and being physically attacked by peers; and (2) dominant instigations. We have analyzed the proportion of responses which are compliant and the proportion of those which are counter-aggressive. Table 9.1 presents the findings. "Withdrawal" includes behavior coded as complies, hides, avoids, breaks interaction, deprecates self, and acts shy. "Counter-aggression" includes playful aggression or rough and tumble play, insulting behavior, and assaulting with the judged intent of injuring another.

It can be seen (Table 9.1, row 5) that there is no consistent trend in the six samples in relation to withdrawal from aggressive instigations of peers, although there is an overall tendency for girls to withdraw more frequently than boys. If one contrasts the proportion of counter-aggressive responses when attacked by peers, the findings are more consistent. There is no significant difference between girls and boys in the 3-6 age group but by 7-11 boys react proportionately and significantly more frequently with counter-aggression than do the girls (Table 1, row 6).

Sex differences in compliance to prosocial and egoistically dominant instigations (Table 1, row 7) are only slightly in the direction the stereotype would predict. There is one type of compliance which is significantly different for girls and boys, namely obedience to the mother. In the 7-11 age group girls are significantly more compliant to their mothers' commands and suggestions (p $<$ .05). However, this kind of compliance seems a much better operational measure of a variable that might be called "cooperativeness" than it is of passivity. One might interpret that the 7-11 year old girls have identified with their mothers and their mothers' goals and are therefore willing to cooperate when their mothers assign tasks.

In sum, older boys respond more aggressively than girls to aggressive instigations and there is a trend for boys to be less compliant than girls to the wishes of others. However, these differences are not as great as the literature would imply (Bardwick 1971).

There is another dimension of behavior which might be considered the obverse of "passivity," namely "initiative." As operationalized here, initiative is measured by a proportion score, the proportion of the child's acts which were judged to be self-instigated, rather than responses to the instigations of others. Table 1, row 8, presents the comparison. It can be seen that in the younger group the proportion of self-instigated acts is similar for boys and girls. In the older age groups boys were judged to initiate interaction proportionately more frequently than were girls, but the difference between the two groups does not reach an acceptable level of significance. What accounts for this slight difference? It could be either that girls initiate fewer acts than boys

or that they receive proportionately more instigations than do boys. Girls initiate social interaction somewhat more frequently than do boys as judged by rate scores. However, girls receive proportionately more *mands* from others than do boys. That is, other individuals interrupt and try to change the ongoing behavior of girls more than that of boys. It is this higher rate of interruptions or instigations received which makes the older girls have a slightly lower proportion of self-instigated acts than have the boys. Perhaps this higher rate of attempts to change girls' behavior is related to the Western stereotype of feminine "sensitivity" or "responsiveness" and to the reports that girls have greater awareness of their immediate environment than do boys (Witkin et al. 1962).

NURTURANCE
STEREOTYPE: GIRLS ARE MORE
NURTURANT THAN BOYS

Table 9.1, rows 9 and 10, presents the difference between boys and girls on two components of this behavior system. It can be seen that in the 3-6 year old period there are not consistent trends across the six societies and no significant differences. By 7-11, however, girls are observed to offer help and support significantly more than boys (p $<$ .01 and $<$ .001 respectively). That there are no sex differences in the early age group, but rather marked increases with age, does not fit the innate differences hypothesis.

RESPONSIBILITY
STEREOTYPE: GIRLS ARE MORE
RESPONSIBLE THAN BOYS

In the six culture study any attempt to change the behavior of others with the judged intent of seeing to the welfare of the group and the maintenance of socially approved behavior has been coded as "suggests responsibly" (prosocial dominance) and distinguished from "dominance," which was defined as attempts to change the behavior of another to meet the egoistic desires of the actor. As can be seen in Table 9.1, row 11, in the 3-6 year old group girls offered responsible suggestions more frequently than boys in all six samples, the difference significant at the .05 level of confidence. By 7-11 however there is no difference, the boys having increased markedly.

DOMINANCE

STEREOTYPE: BOYS ARE MORE DOMINANT THAN GIRLS

Egoistic dominance (Table 9.1, row 12), on the other hand, as the stereotype would have it, was observed more frequently in boys. The level of significance is .05 for the young group and not significant in the 7-11 sample.

AGGRESSION

STEREOTYPE: BOYS ARE MORE PHYSICALLY AGGRESSIVE THAN GIRLS; GIRLS ARE MORE VERBALLY AGGRESSIVE

We have coded three types of aggression: (1) rough and tumble play, aggression which has a strong sociable component; (2) verbal aggression, primarily verbal communications judged to be motivated by the desire to derogate and insult; and (3) assaulting, physical aggression judged to be motivated by the desire to cause pain and injury. As can be seen (Table 9.1, row 13), boys were observed in rough and tumble play significantly more frequently than girls in both age groups. They were also,

contrary to the stereotype, significantly more insulting than girls—the level of significance reaching .01 for the young and .05 for the older group (Table 9.1, row 14). Assaulting with the intent to injure (Table 9.1, row 15) was not observed with great enough frequency to make any definitive statement. In five of the samples, the 3-6 year old boys assaulted more; by 7-11 the frequency of the behavior is roughly similar in four samples. The reader is referred back to the findings concerning responses to aggressive instigations. In sum, on all measures of aggression, boys score higher than girls but the differences are significant only in rough and tumble play and verbal aggression, and in the older group in counter-aggression when attacked by peers.

DISCUSSION

Insulting, rough and tumble play, and dominating egoistically are the most clearly "masculine" types of behavior in the 3-6 year old age group, and seeking or offering physical contact, seeking help, and suggesting responsibly or prosocial dominance the most clearly "feminine." The fact that body contact is involved in both rough and tumble play and touching behavior suggests that they are alternative modes of establishing cutaneous contact. One may also dichotomize two types of dominance— straight commanding (dominates), the male mode, and dominance justified by rules of appropriate behavior (suggesting responsibly), the female mode. In the older age group nurturance becomes a clearly "feminine" characteristic, and the measures of aggression distinguish the boys. Seeking attention appears to be both a "masculine" form of dependency and, in its self-arrogating aspects, a measure of competitiveness.

Although it is obviously impossible to do more than speculate about biophysical determinants of these behaviors, the sex differences which are greatest in the younger group might be considered the best candidates for sex-linked characteristics. The age trends in the behavioral systems are presented in Table 9.2. Seeking and offering of physical contact, a behavior that differentiates the sexes clearly in the 3-6 year old group, decreases significantly with age. One might interpret this as a decrease in the desire for physical contact, contact which may have served as a pain and anxiety reducer at the younger age and now is less frequently needed. The significant increase of nurturance and responsibility with age suggests that these are behaviors which increase with socialization pressure. Nurturance increases significantly in girls, responsibility of prosocial dominance increases in both girls and boys, at the .06 level of significance for girls and the .001 level for boys. Since by 7-11

TABLE 9.2

SHOWING SIGNIFICANT CHANGES IN THE MEAN OF THE PROPORTION SCORES OF THE BEHAVIOR OF GIRLS AND BOYS FROM AGES 3-6 to 7-11

	Girls	Boys
Offers help	$+$ **	
Offers support	$+$ *	
Suggests responsibility		$+$ ***
Seeks or offers physical contact		$-$ ***
Proportion of self-instigated acts		$+$ *

* P $<$ .05; ** P $<$ .01; *** P $<$ .001

A ($+$) indicates an increase with age, a ($-$) indicates a decrease

years of age there is no significant sex difference in the proportion of responsible suggestions, the significant increase for the boys may indicate that pressure for responsibility begins at an earlier age for girls.[3] The proportionate increase of self-instigated acts of boys may reflect the fact that girls are assigned tasks which keep them closer to the house and adults, tasks and settings which are associated with more requests and demands from others.

There is evidence in our data of differential pressure on girls and boys to be nurturant. Older girls in our sample took care of children under 18 months of age more frequently than did boys (p $<$ .05), and infant care is undoubtedly one of the variables contributing to the significant increase in the proportion of offering help and support. There is also evidence that more girls than boys in the younger age group are assigned responsible tasks. By the older age group, however, boys are engaged in animal husbandry, and both girls and boys are beginning to help in agricultural work. Boys feed and pasture animals significantly more frequently than girls (p $<$ .001); girls do significantly more domestic chores (cleaning p $<$ .001, food preparation, cooking, and grinding p $<$ .001) and care for siblings more frequently. The number of tasks assigned to both boys and girls increases significantly with age (Minturn and Lambert 1964).

These sex differences in assigned work are associated with the different frequency with which boys and girls interact with various categories of people, that is, with adults, infants, and peers. Caring for infants and performing domestic chores require that girls stay in the vicinity of the house and yard and hence remain more frequently in the company of adult females. Both young and older girls interact with female adults more frequently than do boys (p < .05 and < .01 respectively) and older girls interact with infants significantly more than do boys (p < .01). Herding and other animal husbandry chores take the boy away from the house, and therefore, boys interact less frequently with adults and infants and proportionately and significantly more with peers (3-4 years p < .05, 7-10 p < .01), especially male peers.

What can be said about the consequences of this difference in type of dyadic interaction? To answer this question we analyzed the types of behavior which children direct most frequently to adults, to infants, and to child peers. These three age grades of people seem to draw different types of behavior from children, and the behavior which children direct to a given category is remarkably similar across cultures (Whiting and Whiting in press). The acts most frequently directed toward adults are (1) seeking help, (2) seeking or offering physical contact, (3) seeking attention, and (4) seeking friendly interaction, or "sociability"—the first two of these being "feminine" type behavior (see Table 9.1). When interacting with infants, children most frequently offer help, support, and sociability—the first two again "feminine" type behaviors. In contrast, when interacting with peers, sociability, rough and tumble play, and derogatory and insulting interchanges are most frequent, the last two of these "masculine" type behaviors.

Two studies in Kenya and research in progress in Guatemala confirm our deduction that girls are at home more frequently than are boys (Munroe and Munroe 1971; Nerlove et al. 1971; Nerlove, private communication). In Kenya, Sara Nerlove working in Nyansongo and Robert and Ruth Munroe working in Vihiga made observational studies of same aged pairs of girls and boys. At the same time each day they sought out the children's whereabouts and measured their distance from home. The girls were found to be nearer to home significantly more often than the boys. Although these findings may be interpreted to indicate that girls are innately more timid than boys, it seems more parsimonious to assume that they reflect socialization pressure and differential task assignment, girls being kept home to perform infant tending and domestic chores.

The question then becomes why girls are assigned domestic chores and the care of infants significantly more frequently than are boys. Is it because girls are innately better suited to such tasks or does it simply reflect a universal sex typing and preparation of young girls for their adult roles? In all the societies we have studied women have the major responsibility for the care of infants and for domestic chores. This is in accord with the findings of cross-cultural studies on the division of labor (D'Andrade 1966). Assigning these chores to girls rather than boys may simply reflect the early training of girls for the expected female role.

This differential socialization pressure on girls is in accord with the findings of Barry, Bacon, and Child (1957) in their cross-cultural study of sex differences in socialization based on ratings made from published ethnographic reports of societies distributed around the world. They found that girls received more pressure to be nurturant, obedient, and responsible, boys more pressure to achieve and be self-reliant. In our sample the greater frequency in the proportion of nurturant behavior, its increase with age, and the greater compliance of girls to mothers are as one would predict from the Barry, Bacon and Child findings. As noted above the greater amount of time spent caring for infants can be interpreted as greater pressure toward nurturance. Pressure toward obedience as reported by the mothers of the six cultures is greatest in those societies which assign infant care and consequently is exerted more on girls than on boys (Whiting and Whiting 1971, in press). It is also greater in those societies in which children are engaged in animal husbandry. Responsible behavior, as we have measured it, does not show significant sex differences in the six culture samples but does in recent observational studies in Kenya (see note 3). However, since there is a high correlation between the Barry, Bacon, and Child ratings on pressure toward responsibility and the number of chores assigned to girls and boys as reported in the ethnographic monographs, the significant difference in the number of chores assigned to girls and boys in the 3-6 year old age group is in accord with their findings. In the older group there is great variation from one society to another. The crucial variable seems to be economic: in societies with animal husbandry or agricultural work that can be assigned to boys, there are no sex differences in amount of work required of girls and boys after 7-8 years of age.

Our measures of achievement-oriented and self-reliant behavior are less direct but are also in accord with the sex differences in socialization reported by Barry, Bacon, and Child. Seeking attention as we have coded it includes self-arrogation and boasting. In the older age group, as reported above, boys are proportionately significantly higher than girls in this type of behavior. If we assume that these behaviors are motivated by achievement needs, the findings are as predicted. The proportion of self-instigated acts might be considered a measure of self-reliance. There is a trend, as reported above, for boys 7-11 to be proportionately higher in acts which were not judged to be clearly instigated by the actions of others. It should be noted again here, however, that this measure may simply reflect the fact that boys are interrupted less frequently by the mands of others than are girls. The ethnographic sources make it difficult to distinguish between self-reliance and being allowed to do what one wishes unsupervised by others.[4]

In sum, our evidence suggests that the nature of the tasks assigned to girls is the best predictor of four of the five primary types of "feminine" behavior (see Table 9.1) since (1) the tasks require more frequent interaction with infants and adults, and (2) the nature of the tasks themselves involves care of others—offering help and comfort to infants, preparing and offering food to the entire family—all work focused on the needs of others and the welfare of the family. These tasks clearly require a child to be compliant, and to be willing to service the requests of others and to obey task-related instructions. Furthermore, all of these tasks require the girl to be tolerant of interruptions and demands for succorance, and require her to be constantly alert to the motivational states of others—behaviors possibly related to field dependence, a quality commonly attributed to women (Witkin et al. 1962).

It is interesting to note here societal differences in "femininity" scores. Orchard Town girls, for example, score low in offering help and support and do significantly less infant care than girls in other societies.

Further insight into the possible consequences of task assignment can be gained by looking at the "masculine" and "feminine" profiles of boys who are assigned domestic chores and the care of infants. There are many societies in which young boys are required to do such work. Among these are East African societies in which women are the agriculturalists, men traditionally and pastoralists and warriors. In these societies young boys are classified with women and girls until they approach pubescence, at which time they are frequently initiated into manhood in formal *rites de passage*. Nyansongo, one of the six cultures, is an example of such a society. The women, who work four or five hours a day in the gardens, assign the care of infants to a designated older sibling and the tending of the cooking fire and the washing of utensils to the same or some other child of the family. Although mothers prefer girl nurses, it is not considered inappropriate to delegate the responsibility to a boy if there is no female of the proper age—in this case under ten years of age—since older girls are either in school or helping in agricultural work.

Our evidence suggests that requiring boys to tend babies and perform domestic chores reduces sex differences in the mean proportion scores of "masculine" and "feminine" behavior in two of these East African societies. In Nyansongo half of the boys aged five and over took care of infants and half helped with domestic chores. When one contrasts the mean proportion scores of the boys and girls, the magnitude of the sex differences is smaller than in any of the six societies with the exception of Orchard Town, which will be discussed later. Nyan-

songo boys score higher than would be predicted on offering help and offering support, young boys scoring higher than young girls on both types of behavior. Nyansongo girls are aberrantly high in rough and tumble play, younger girls in assaulting, and boys retreat from aggressive attacks from peers as frequently as do girls. The comparisons are similar in Ngecha, our other East African sample. In the Ngecha sample, the older boys offer help and support somewhat more frequently than do the girls (p < .22), the younger boys seek sociability significantly more than do the girls (p < .05), the older girls seek attention slightly more frequently than do the boys (p < .23), and the girls of both ages were observed in rough and tumble play as frequently as the boys.

A more detailed analysis of the effect of assigning "feminine" tasks to boys has been presented by Carol Ember (1973). In 1968 when she was working in Oyugis in Western Kenya, by a fluke of sex ratios there were an unusually large number of households in which there was no girl of the appropriate age to care for an infant sibling. Hence there was quite a large sample of boys who were acting as nurses and doing domestic chores. Using this unusual opportunity Ember undertook an observational study of these boys. She compared them to a matched sample of boys who were not responsible for "feminine" chores as well as to a sample of girls. She used a code similar to that used in the six culture study. Her observations were made when the children were not working.

Her findings based on a linear regression of the means for the three groups—boys who did little child tending or domestic chores which kept them inside the homestead, boys who did many such tasks, and girls—show significant differences between the three samples. Boys high on feminine work had behavior profiles which were more "feminine" than boys who did not perform such work. They were more responsible (prosocially dominant), less aggressive (including assaulting and insulting), less dependent (including seeking help, support, attention, information, and material goods),[5] and less egoistically dominant (including dominating, reprimanding, and prohibiting action egoistically). All differences were significant at the .01 level. The differences were not great, however, when Ember compared boys who were and who were not assigned "feminine" chores which took them *outside* the homestead, that is, carrying water, fetching wood, digging root crops, picking vegetables, and going to the market to mill flour. Her data do not show the predicted differences in nurturant behavior.

In sum, in societies where boys take care of infants, cook, and perform other domestic chores, there are fewer sex differences between boys and girls, and this decrease is due primarily to the decrease in "masculine" behavior in boys; boys are less egoistically dominant, score proportionately lower in some forms of aggression, seek attention proportionately less frequently, and score higher on suggesting responsibily. On the other hand, the 3-6 year old girls in these societies are high on assaulting and miscellaneous aggression and both younger and older girls score low on sociability (Whiting and Whiting n.d.).

Although there are no samples of girls in any of the six cultures who do "masculine" type tasks, the girls of Orchard Town, New England, as mentioned above, do very little infant care. Since most New England families consist of two children averaging around two years apart in age and

since there are no courtyard cousins, young nieces, nephews, or half-siblings as in extended and polygynous families, there is little opportunity for Orchard Town girls to care for infants except as paid baby sitters. In general, however, Orchard Town mothers do not hire baby sitters under eleven years of age. Orchard Town girls are also more strongly committed to education and may aspire to jobs which are considered appropriate to both sexes. Their work in school is practically identical with that of boys. It is interesting, therefore, to see how this sample of United States girls fits the predicted patterns on the behaviors which we have found to be significantly different between boys and girls in the pooled samples. As in Nyansongo, the magnitude of the differences is small. The direction of the insignificant differences are as expected with one exception, the young girls scoring higher than the boys in the proportion of attention seeking, a "masculine" type behavior. They also score higher than any other sample of girls on this type of behavior, behavior which in general is higher among the children of the more complex societies (Orchard Town, Khalapur, and Taira) where schooling and achievement are more highly valued (Whiting and Whiting in press). It is a type of behavior which, when directed toward adults, is frequently motivated by a desire for approval and, as discussed above, when directed toward peers may have affiliation or self-arrogation as its goal. It is a frequent behavior in New England classrooms.

As noted above, the Orchard Town girls score the lowest of the samples of girls on offering help and support, "feminine" traits, and have one of the lowest percentages of interaction with infants.

In sum, in both the East African

societies where "feminine" work is assigned to boys and in Orchard Town, New England, where less "feminine" work is assigned to girls and where there is less difference in the daily routine of boys and girls, the behavior of girls and boys does not show as great differences as in other societies.

SUMMARY

Our story suggests that: (a) there are universal sex differences in the behavior of children 3-11 years of age, but the differences are not consistent nor as great as the studies of American and Western European children would suggest; (b) socialization pressure in the form of task assignment and the associated frequency of interaction with different categories of individuals (infants, adults, and peers) may well explain many of these differences; (c) aggression, perhaps especially rough and tumble play, and touching behavior seem the best candidates for biophysical genesis; (d) all of the behaviors which are characteristic of males and females seem remarkably malleable under the impact of socialization pressures, which seem to be remarkably consistent from one society to another; and (e) the differences in many of the types of behavior seems to be one of style rather than intent, for example, seeking help ("feminine") rather than attention ("masculine"), and justifying dominance by appealing to the rules ("feminine") rather than straight egoistic dominance ("masculine").

Although our findings do not speak for adolescent and adult male and female behavior, they should caution the social scientists and animal ethologists who are interested in possible evolutionary and survival theories not to underestimate the effect of learning environments. These learning environments may well be responsible for the behavior frequently attributed to the innate characteristic of male and female primates as inherited by their human descendents.

NOTES

1. This study is based on the field work of the six culture study, financed by the Behavioral Science Division of the Ford Foundation, and on field work in Kenya by the Child Development Research Unit, financed by the Carnegie Corporation. The analysis of the data has been made possible by a United Public Health Grant, MH-0196.

2. Observations were gathered by Robert A. LeVine and Barbara LeVine, Thomas and Hatsumi Maretzki, Leigh Minturn, William and Corrine Nydegger, A. Kimball and Romaine Romney, and John and Ann Fischer.

3. In Ember's study in Western Kenya and in the ongoing research in Kenya there are significant sex differences in prosocial dominance, girls scoring significantly higher than boys in the 7-11 year age groups.

4. For discussion of the problem, and data on achievment and self-reliance among the !Kung Bushmen of the Kalahari, see Patricia L. Draper (1971).

5. It is unfortunate that dependency as operationally defined by Ember included both the masculine and feminine modes.

REFERENCES

Bardwick, J. M.
1971 *Psychology of Women: A Study of Bio-Cultural Conflicts.* New York: Harper and Row.

Barry, H. III, M. K. Bacon, and I. L. Child
1957 A cross-cultural survey of some sex differences in socialization. *Journal of Abnormal and Social Psychology* 55: 327-332.

D'Andrade, R. G.
1966 Sex differences and cultural institutions. *In* E. E. Maccoby (Ed.), *The Development of Sex Differences.* Stanford: Stanford University Press.

Draper, P. L.
1971 !Kung bushman childhood: A review of the Barry, Child and Bacon hypothesis regarding the relation of child training practices to subsistence economy. Paper presented at the annual meetings of the American Anthropological Association, New York.

Ember, Carol R.
1973 The effect of feminine task assignment on the social behavior of boys. *Ethos,* in press.

Imamura, S.
1965 Mother and blind child: The influence of child rearing practices on the behavior of preschool blind children. New York: American Foundation for the Blind.

Kagan, J., and H. A. Moss
1962 *Birth to Maturity.* New York: Wiley.

Minturn, L., and W. W. Lambert
1964 *Mothers of Six Cultures: Antecedents of Child Rearing.* New York: Wiley.

Munroe, R. L., and R. H. Munroe
1971 Effect of environmental experience on spatial ability in an East African society. *Journal of Social Psychology* 83: 15-22.

Nerlove, S. B., R. H. Munroe and R. L. Munroe
1971 Effect of environmental experience on spatial ability: A replication. *Journal of Social Psychology* 84: 3-10.

Whiting, B. B. (Ed.)
1963 *Six Cultures: Studies of Child Rearing. New York: Wiley.*

Whiting, B. B., and J. W. M. Whiting
1971 Task assignment and personality: A consideration of the effect of herding on boys. *In* W. W. Lambert and R. Weisbrod (Eds.), *Comparative Perspectives on Social Psychology.* Boston: Little, Brown.

Whiting, J. W. M., and B. B. Whiting, in collaboration with R. Longabaugh
in press Children of Six Cultures. Cambridge, Mass.: Harvard University Press.

Witkin, H. A., R. B. Dyk, H. R. Faterson, D. R. Goodenough, and S. A. Karp
1962 *Psychological Differentiation.* New York: Wiley.

10. PREGNANCY CRAVINGS (DOLA-DUKA) IN RELATION TO SOCIAL STRUCTURE AND PERSONALITY IN A SINHALESE VILLAGE

GANANATH OBEYESEKERE

Gananath Obeyesekere is Professor of Anthropology, University of California, San Diego. Reproduced by permission of the American Anthropological Association from the *American Anthropologist* 65 (2), 1963.

THE PRESENT PAPER[1] is concerned with an anthropological analysis of a cultural complex associated with the early months of pregnancy in women and well known in India as *dola-duka*. In contemporary village life in Ceylon dola-duka is a widely spread and well known phenomenon, but, as far as I know, no socio-cultural analysis of the institution exists in social science literature. The following analysis is an attempt to understand the dola-duka complex as it is institutionalized in Rambadeniya, an isolated jungle village in the Pattu (district) of Laggala, which lies to the northeast of Matale in the Central Province of Ceylon. In this village dola-duka is a well defined and clearly marked out cultural complex, importantly related to the social structure of the village and the female personality problems it fosters.

Even in Ceylon, most people equate dola-duka with the "perverse appetite" of women commencing from the second month of pregnancy and lasting generally for a period of three months. But dola-duka is something more. It refers also to the "suffering" or *duka* the woman experiences during this period, that is, her nausea, vomiting, bodily weakness, and the desire for certain objects, which is painful to

the individual till satisfied. However, the most conspicuous aspect of dola-duka is the perverse appetite, or *dola* that women have during this period. The word "dola" could best be translated as "craving," a compulsion to eat or possess a certain object (often food). Demons, for example, are said to have dola for specific types of foods, and these foods must be provided during propitiatory rites for them. Dola therefore is something more than wishes, fancies or desires that people ordinarily experience: it it a craving that *has* to be satisfied at any cost. For example, a woman in Laggala may ordinarily *desire* a sweet, banana, or cookie, and may buy one from the village boutique and eat it. But if she does not satisfy her desire it would not make much difference to her. A craving is of a different order entirely: she would feel an absolute compulsion to eat a sweet or cookie, and would feel considerable anxiety and suffering till her craving was satisfied. Moreover, craving cannot be equated with hunger, for often the woman may not feel hungry at all, but may nevertheless crave for foods. Hence the quantity of food consumed is not what matters but the consumption of a specific kind of food, often eaten more like a sacramental than an ordinary meal. In this respect, it is analogous to the craving or dola of demons: demons are propitiated with only a few scraps of food, but this is said to satisfy their craving. In other words, it is not the quantity of food, but the fact of possessing or obtaining the craved food that satisfies the woman. Though usually the craving is for food—both classically and in Laggala—it could also refer to other objects, as for example, craving for arrack, cigars, or cloth by women in Laggala, or the craving such as Vihara Maha Devi, the Sinhalese Queen of the 3rd century B.C. had for the blood of an Indian Tamil General (Geiger 1937, pp. 194-159).

The manner of satisfying the craving is also stereotyped in Laggala (and classically). The objects or behaviors craved for are often, though not always, considered unusual and shameful, so that it is not generally confided in people except those one can trust such as husbands and parents. Hence it was difficult to get a woman to talk about the specific cravings she experienced, though anyone in a village could inform us what women *in general* would crave during this period. In order to ensure that the women would get the objects she craves, threats are held before the husband, confidant, or relation who helps to satisfy her cravings. To deny a women her cravings is considered a sin (*pav*), which may seriously damage one's rebirth chances. More immediately, it is held that the ears of the fetus will rot if the woman's cravings are not satisfied.

THE PSYCHOLOGICAL BASIS OF DOLA-DUKA

Dola-duka, as it is understood in Indo-Ceylon cultures, is in some respects an intensification of analogous normal states reported for Western women during the first trimester of pregnancy. These states are characterized according to psychoanalytic writers, as a regression to an oral phase, with oral expulsive and incorporative traits such as nausea, vomiting and craving for certain foods. The psychobiological determinants of these have been well described by Deutsch (1945) and Benedek (1959). Benedek says that at this time "passive-dependent needs revived, the pregnant woman thrives on the solicitude of her environment" (1959, pp. 739). Says Deutsch:

Each woman brings into pregnancy certain emotional factors and conflict situations, which come into relation with her condition as a whole, and with the organic manifestations characteristic of pregnancy. On the other hand various typical groups of organic pregnancy processes also mobilize definite emotional attitudes that now emerge openly, exposing the entire dynamic background associated with them, even though this latter is not directly concerned with pregnancy. For example, the organically determined nausea can bring to the fore all the feelings of disgust that have been preserved in the unconscious for years without manifesting themselves. Inversely, feelings of disgust that have become associated with definite ideas of pregnancy often strongly reinforce the organic provocation of nausea and may then lead to pathologic vomiting. . . . In pregnancy a normally preformed somatic phenomenon becomes the immediate expression of definite psychic contents. (Deutsch 1945, pp. 127)

According to psychoanalytic opinion, it is apparent there is a strong biologic base for regression and the expression of unconscious or semi-conscious psychological problems during pregnancy. Nausea which women experience in Western society and in the Sinhalese dola-duka has a physiological base but "the psychogenic intensification of the oral pregnancy symptom of vomiting takes place only when the oral expulsive tendencies are accompanied by unconscious and sometimes even manifest (or about to become manifest) emotions of hostility to pregnancy or to the foetus" (Deutsch 1945, pp. 128). Similarly the "perverse appetite" of the woman during pregnancy is "provoked" by biological factors. "It is as though a somatic signal form the modified secretory processes have received a latent compulsion" (Deutsch 1945, pp. 130). However the *compulsion* to eat certain foods is an expression of oral tendencies manifest during this time. The cravings are neatly dichotomized by Deutsch into two categories—those expressive of *in-corporation* (acceptance) and those expressive of *destruction* (hostility): "Very often those cravings express an obsession to consume foods that are familiar to psychoanalysis and folklore as symbols of fecundation, a symbolic affirmation followed by an opposite tendency, cannibalistic destruction. Often the new symbolic fecundation is revealed as an obsessive undoing of an unconscious tendency to destroy the child" (Deutsch 1945, pp. 129).

The present writer does not quarrel with the psychoanalytic position; on the contrary, he is greatly indebted to psychoanalytic theory for the interpretation of his data. However, the interpretation of the pregnancy symptoms of Western women by these writers does not satisfactorily explain the Indian complex of dola-duka as manifested in the isolated jungle village in Ceylon. While accepting the physiological bases of these compulsions and the overlay of psychological factors, dola-duka, as seen in Laggala, is a culturally constituted structure, built on the psychobiological base described by these writers. In a final analysis dola-duka should be treated as a cultural complex, and not as a simple psychobiological constellation of symptoms, as it may be in Western society. Such a position is of course entirely consonant with anthropological thinking: most social institutions have some psychobiological base on which they are erected, but in their final existing form they are cultural or social structures to be understood and analyzed as such.

The four components just described —regression, nausea, vomiting (and spitting in Ceylon), and food cravings —are the clearly connected parts that go to form the cultural complex of dola-duka. In so far as these symptoms are exaggerated and intensified, we would agree with Deutsch that these cravings are influenced importantly by, and are the influence of, psychological problems such as hostility to the fetus. But the food cravings in dola-duka are quite different in both motive and function from those described by Deutsch. In the first place, in dola-duka there is a great variety of foods desired by the woman. Many of these foods are not chosen arbitrarily by the woman but are culturally recognized as the "normal" foods eaten by women during this period. The appetite of the woman may be perverse but the foods selected are often culturally determined. Secondly, these foods cannot be dichotomized into incorporating ones symbolic of fecundity and those symbolic of ravenous destruction. While admitting the symbolic nature of the foods, we find that in dola-duka the symbolism is more complex and cannot be covered by this over simple dichotomy. Thirdly, the psychological problems expressed through the complex of dola-duka are mostly (though not entirely) culturally and socially created. In other words dola-duka will be viewed as a symbol system, related very importantly to the psychological needs of the women of this village.

THE CULTURAL BACKGROUND OF DOLA-DUKA

In Laggala a distinct cultural preference for males is shown, typical of most social structures of the Indian culture area. The male, particularly the father-husband, is associated with dominance and authority in the family, and the wife with subservience and submissiveness. Division of labor is consonant with these ideal patterns. Women are considered physically and mentally weak (though actual facts belie these prejudices), and are supposed to engage in domestic activity, cook, draw water, bring firewood, look after the welfare of the children and husband, while the husband-father is the provider, one who supplies the household with food and other amenities by his superior physical and mental abilities. The ideal wife according to a village moralist is one who is devoted, faithful, a person who does not question her husband, but merely obeys him. The good wife should not even look her husband in the face, but look aside when addressing him. She should not trample the mat he sleeps on. She must look after the interests of the husband and children, and see that the latter are fed and clothed. She should regularly and faithfully cook the family meals, never take offense at the husband even if he is idling, and never hurt him by word or deed.

Laggala moralists say that ideal wives are rare, and certainly not found in Laggala. What they mean is that Laggala women are unfaithful to their husbands, abuse them sometimes, and often have to be coerced to perform their socially recognized roles. This is because women are inherently inferior and incapable of idealism and fidelity. Men in Laggala view their women as possessed of certain inherent weaknesses: *Seductiveness*— women are viewed as sexually easily excitable, inducing the male to adultery, and thus a threat to the integrity of the family; *Untrustworthiness*—no woman can be trusted, neither one's wife nor even one's own mother, say the villagers with practical unanimity. Women are also *jara* (unclean), manifested most clearly in their inevitable menstrual periodicity. A woman is a creeper trailing where it listeth, feeding on filth, excrement or dung. She has neither the strength nor the intelligence of the male, nor can she provide for herself, work at arduous tasks or go about alone; she has to suffer the pangs of childbirth and has to be under the domination of the husband for her whole life. Here is essentially a low birth (*pahatjati*), unlike the noble (*utum*) *jati* of the man. Her birth as female is a result of bad karma (sin), but once born as a female it is very difficult to achieve malehood in subsequent births.

Even before the birth of the infant, cultural symbols are at work expressing cultural prejudices and preferences regarding the unborn baby. Certain prognostications in dreams predict the sex of the infant (according to the village belief). If, for instance, the mother were to dream during pregnancy of bags of money, treasures, the moon, gold, precious jewelry and other valuable things, she would have a baby boy; if she were to dream of objects made of iron and one-cent pieces, silver jewelry and other common objects, she would give birth to a baby girl. The cultural preference for the valued male sex is seen in this symbolism of dreams. Considerable anxiety is displayed by mothers as to the sex of the future offspring, particularly by those women who are having their first pregnancy or those without male children. The cultural ideal is that the two eldest children should be males, and the husband feels considerable disappointment if his first born is a female. If by chance the son is the only male child in the family, he is pampered and doted on by parents and siblings.

In the first few years of life little distinction is made between boy and girl; both are given considerable care and affection by both parents. It is a common sight in Laggala to see a father playing with his infant girl fondly and affectionately. In fact, young children are often addressed by their parents as "son" (*puta*), irrespective of their sexual differences. When children cry, anything is done to hush them—sometimes threats of the dreaded bogey-man, very often by distraction and promises of sweets from the local boutique. I cannot give details of socialization of the child in Laggala here except to make the following points:

(a) As the child grows up, the father acts as disciplinarian to male children and the mother to females. In the case of girls the father does not show overt signs of affection to them after the age of six or seven, though it would be wrong to characterize this as a withdrawal of affection. What really happens is that after the age of about six or seven, girls are expected to help the mother in her domestic work, particularly in looking after younger siblings. The boys are expected to assist the father in the fields.

(b) Prepubertal girls have a relatively carefree time with plenty of leisure for fun and games. In a purely physical sense they are unconstricted, not tied like their mothers to a life of domestic responsibility. One thing that impresses the visitor to Laggala is the shouts and laughter of children at play.

(c) By the time girls have neared puberty they have become increasingly involved as help to their parents in both domestic work and agricultural activities. They have learned to cook, sew, weave, and work in the fields. But they are by no means psychologically prepared for the responsibility of adult roles—the social roles of wife and mother—which follow soon after puberty. At marriage they are in some sense immature girls who have not left their carefree girlhoods of meadow and playground behind.

Menarche, with the onset of the sacred menstrual flow, ritually marks the change of status from girlhood to adulthood. It is this occurrence that makes the girls aware of the fact that they are women now and have to behave as women, and soon after as wives and mothers. More important, the cultural attitudes regarding women are dramatically impressed on the women through the ritual significance of menstrual blood. The social attitudes regarding prepubertal girls are quite different from those towards postpubertal women: the latter are unclean (*apirisidu*), *jara* (dirty) because of their association with menstrual blood which causes ritual impurity (*kili*). *Kili* alters the ritual status of the person, making her unfavorably sacred, and owing to its contagious character, affecting the status of those who come into contact with her. Through the blood of her first menstruation, and thereafter through all her periods, the woman is made aware symbolically of her inferior social status as adult woman. However, though puberty ritually marks out the transition from girlhood to adult status, there is no real *psychological* transition. In many societies there are puberty rites for females, which have the function of not merely transferring the woman from one status to another, but, as A. I. Richards has convincingly shown for the Bemba of East Africa, to prepare the girls psychologically for the responsibilities they have to face as adult women in the society in which they live, so that at the conclusion of these rites, a veritable psychological metamorphosis has been effected (Richards 1956, pp. 120-134). By contrast, puberty rites for Sinhalese girls are very brief. A girl is secluded for a period of ten days, during which period she is afflicted with kili, and at the conclusion of this period she is bathed by the washerwoman in order to banish her ritual impurity. In no sense do Sinhalese puberty rites prepare the woman for psychological or social maturity. By and large the unmarried postpubertal girl is still rooted in the ethos of her childhood, among friends and kin known to her from birth, and upon whom she could depend; yet, at the same time, she is also confronted with the fact of her womanhood and the accompanying new roles and statuses, and the new social attitudes concerning her. She is faced at puberty with a fundamental problem of adjustment.

The cultural ideal is that marriage should occur soon after puberty and indeed a great majority of Laggala marriages come close to this prescription. The women who marry late (i.e., say, at 20 years) would have lived at least under the knowledge that they would have to marry soon after puberty. The residence rule is virilocal, with a few cases of uxorilocality. The marriages are arranged by the girl's parents, the most important criterion being the husband's economic position —caste and other social status factors being equal. These rules have various implications for the woman. At marriage she leaves the security of her own family of orientation to live with her husband in another village. The fact that her husband and his kin may have been related to her even before marriage does not materially detract from the psychological picture: the security and intimacy of her own village cannot be duplicated or even approached. In the case of the few uxorilocal marriages the woman is better off, as she does not have to leave her natal village; however, she lives in her own nuclear household with a husband who has superordinate status as a male. In the case of marriages within the village, the husband is in a very dominant position, though the woman also has the social support of close kinsmen. But such support often is not much use, because the privileges of the husband are clearly defined so that the woman's kin would think twice about supporting wife against husband, particularly since the latter is also a known kinsman. For example, Mutu Menika, who is married to Somadasa from the next hamlet, Gangahenwela, was once badly treated by Somadasa, but Mutu Menika's brother and mother felt they had no right to interfere since the husband has a right to beat his wife.

Whatever the rule of residence, the woman has to live the rest of her life in a society where a married woman has a very subordinate status. Once married, her freedom becomes dramatically restricted. The contrast with the girlhood she has left behind is striking. She lives with the knowledge that once every year she is potentially capable of producing a baby. In some societies (say, the Arapesh of New Guinea) a post-partum taboo on sexual intercourse lasting for a long period, sometimes a year or two, has the function of spacing children, thus giving the woman of the society considerable leisure and freedom. In Ceylon no taboo exists. Furthermore, since techniques of birth control are not known, the potentiality for childbearing of each woman is fully tapped. The continued production of babies until the commencement of the menopause has literally the function of tying the woman to a life of domesticity and of restricting her freedom. She has to look after her children and though elder children may help, the responsibility and all real care of the children are in her hands. In societies with extended families, as in neighboring South India, there could very well be adult kinsfolk to help the mother with her domestic chores, but in this society where the elementary family is the nuclear unit, such help is not readily available. Even the help of the elder children is not available to her in the first seven or eight years of married life. In this respect older married women are better off since they usually do have older daughters capable of assisting them with the domestic chores.

The one eternal complaint of the women of Laggala concerns their lack of leisure: our investigations reveal that this complaint is well founded, most of their time being taken up in looking after children, cooking, and helping in agricultural work. Any spare time—generally in the early afternoon—is spent in gossip. Gossip is the most significant employment of leisure; dancing is taboo as unwomanly, and games are meant only for unmarried girls. Real diversion from the monotony of everyday activity is provided on certain rare occasions:

(a) Visits to kinsmen in neighboring villages and visits from kinsmen. These occur once a year, particularly after the Sinhalese New Year (in April). On these trips certain foods are given—oil cakes (*kavun*), *imbulkiri bat,* and other kinds of sweetmeats.

(b) Pilgrimages. Annual pilgrimages are made to important places of worship, the most important of them being Mahiyangana, 35 miles away. When going on pilgrimage or on similar trips one carries a *batmula*—rice wrapped in a leaf (*kolapota*) in picnic bags, the leaf wrapping adding a special flavor to the rice. Women enjoy these trips, spending money in the fairs, singing songs on the road.

(c) Feasts, and rituals for placating demons. These occasions too provide considerable diversion for the women. Here, too, oil cakes and other festival foods are eaten. As a gathering of near kinsmen, these are also opportunities for renewing old acquaintanceships and meaningful ties. Of the feasts two are particularly significant—the New Year (April 14th) and *Wesak* (Full Moon in May, birthday of the Buddha) celebrations. The former is essentially a secular festival, where one cooks *kavun* and entertains kinsmen; the latter is a religious festival, but is also an occasion for witnessing dances and shows in one's own village or in neighboring villages and townships. It must be remembered that these occasions are rare and are highly valued as opportunities for diversion, fun, and the recapitulation of the lost freedoms of girlhood.

The inferior social and ritual status of the women is validated and defined through the concept of kili or impurity. Kili is associated with the ritual impurity of women, as stated earlier, and the ritual impurity of death. Thus the pollution of death is associated with the pollution attendant on certain points in the life cycle of a postpubertal woman. In other words, men can be polluting only when they are no longer social beings; when they have moved for good out of the social structure. Women are polluting while they occupy certain definite positions in the social structure, between two events in their life cycle—puberty and menopause. Thus, at puberty the women's new status is initially ritually legitimated through kili. This is subsequently reaffirmed every month at her periods: she is made symbolically aware, as is her society, particularly members of her domestic group, of her status as potential and, later actual, wife. When she conceives, her menstrual flow stops, and for a period of about eight months there is a suspension of this symbolic affirmation of her status. With childbirth the woman's status has changed again; she is now not only a wife, but also a mother. As a result, her status is once again ritually redefined: kili at childbirth is even more dangerous and polluting than at puberty. This revised position is reaffirmed at the following menstrual periods and subsequent childbirths. No wonder, then, that when questioned whether a woman's life is happy or contented, women would often say: "How can it be so? Look at us with our monthly periods." To a Laggala woman the monthly period is something more than

menstruation: it is a mechanism which ritually defines and affirms her status, and validates the cultural prejudices regarding women believed in by the society. It is also not surprising that in such a situation dysmenorrhoea is a frequent ailment of Laggala women.

As actual, potential, or past kili bearers, women are debarred from the communal rites of intensification of the group—the *adukku*—performed biannually after the two harvests. It is at the adukku that the ancestral gods of the group, particularly Bandara Deiyo, a provident father figure, are propitiated. The adukku with its rule excluding women fosters the solidarity of the male group in the village irrespective of caste, for men of all castes can participate in the adukku. There are, however, no equivalent institutions for women—no rites of intensification which could ensure the solidarity of the female group and enhance their self-esteem. In many societies where the division between the sexes is clearly marked, each sex often has its own communal rites which permit the group to meet and assert its solidarity, strength and self-esteem. Women in Laggala have perforce to be content with the secondary cult activity of the group— rites performed to placate demons who may have caused sickness to a member of the domestic group to which the woman belongs. Of late this village has been learning more of orthodox Buddhism than it had ever known in its history. According to Buddhism kili is no bar to worship, and any woman, including those menstruating, could participate in the Buddhist rites. Buddhism therefore has a distinct appeal to the women of the village. The most important religious activity in this great tradition is meditation and prayer (*sil*) on holy (*poya*) days. But all women who observe *sil* in this village are past child-bearing; and others, according to them, are so busy with their domestic chores that they cannot spare one whole day of leisure required for *sil*, and are not in the proper frame of mind for meditation.

The social situation fosters antagonism between the sexes. Various manifestations, covert and overt, of such antagonism could be observed in the social structure. Such antagonisms are not ritualized as they are in some societies, but receive expression in culturally uncanalized directions. The most obvious manifestation of inter-sex antagonism is overt hostility, in the form of physical violence on the part of the male, and vituperation on the part of the female. Our field notes show that all men beat their wives or, in the case of elder men with grown-up children, have beaten them when they were younger. Most of the physical assaults are on wives who are capable of bearing children (those addressed as *kella*, girl) and not on the older wives who are past the menopause (addressed as *pavula*) and have grown children. The younger the wife the greater the physical punishment she receives at the hands of her husband. Husbands often tell the anthropologist that the younger wives are beaten so often because they talk back to their husbands; they are so cocky and full of spirit that they have to be tamed in the first few years of marriage (not at all a surprising fact). These physical assaults are sometimes quite serious, often causing bodily injury to the wife. Some cases called for hospitalization. The typical provocations for wifebeating seems to be (a) abuse by the wife; (b) failure to obey the husband or look to his needs,

such as preparing his food at the right time; (c) suspicion of infidelity. The wife, incidentally, is no passive recipient of assaults—she often abuses her husband, particularly for idleness, and when she is beaten, out rushes a spate of filth and obscenity.

The antagonism between the sexes is manifest in less obvious ways. For example, a pervasive feeling of distrust and suspicion exists between the sexes. There is a universal pattern of adultery in the village; all women except one have committed adultery at various times in secret. According to the moral code of the village, adultery is very heinous if the women commit it, rather than the men. It is also likely that one of the motivations driving women to adultery is an attempt to violate the code, as an expression of resentment and revenge against their husbands. In the case of the man, distrust and hatred of women is manifested in fantasies of violence to the vagina. This is clearly seen in certain words of abuse sometimes used by men to scold women:

mirisganava—I shall rub chili powder (on your vagina).
sutugula arinava—I shall thrust the branding iron used for castrating bulls (into your vagina).
moraul arinava—I shall thrust pointed 'mora' stakes (into your vagina).

Similar fantasies are expressed in folk song:

While going to eat *katuvala* (thorny yam), friend,
A katuvala thorn got stuck in the vagina;
What medicine for this complaint, friend?
Pour milk of one coconut into your vagina.
Pour some ground *kocci* (chili-pepper) into your vagina.
If it starts to burn, what, my friend?
Thrust your father's penis in your vagina. . . .

These fantasies are sometimes translated into serious threats; we have at least one case of this. The village Headman suspected his wife of adultery with his elder brother who was staying in his house for a few days. After the brother left, he forced his wife to grind some chilies on the flat stone grinder. Fortunately, she ran out of the house and sought the help of neighbors before he could actually rub the dreaded spice on her genitals.

The socio-cultural background sketched above creates certain pressing psychological problems for the women of the village, in the opinion of the present writer. These problems, for purposes of convenience, can be classified as follows: (a) the problem of adjustment; (b) ambivalence toward children; and (c) male envy. Dola-duka is an institutionalized non-idiosyncratic defense provided by the culture itself for coping with these problems. Regarding the first, enough has already been said: a fundamental cleavage exists as far as the woman is concerned between two life phases, childhood and adulthood, ritually demarcated by the onset of the menstrual flow. Dola-duka, as will be shown presently, gives the woman an opportunity to escape from her adult roles into the emotionally gratifying phase of childhood. The second conclusion is less easy to illustrate. Ambivalence probably characterizes any normal relationship between parents and children, but such feelings would build up mostly during the postnatal interaction between parent and child, specifically in a context of socialization. The ambivalence felt by Laggala women is more fundamental; ambivalence to children is also a function of not wishing to have children. The problem could be better seen in the light of what Deutsch says about the

pregnancy period in women. According to Deutsch, certain women, owing to problems private and personal to them (problems which could be understood only in terms of the individual's life history), have unconscious desires not to have children. These desires seek expression during the oral-regressive condition of early pregnancy, and influence the *meaning* of pregnancy for the women (Deutsch 1945, Chaps. 5, 6). Our contention is that there are socio-cultural factors in Laggala which influence the meaning that pregnancy has for the women of this village. Children, for example, are associated with the social roles of wife and mother, determining women's inferior status and the cultural prejudices directed toward them. Moreover, the continual birth of babies, as we have seen, literally circumscribes the freedom of the woman and ties her to a life of domesticity. And in the case of the younger of the women, there is considerable anxiety regarding the sex of the future offspring. According to the value system of the village, children are desired; but my conclusion is that, in spite of this, the wish not to have children is very strong, owing to the conditions mentioned earlier. If this conclusion is right, it appears that these women would be eager to accept techniques of birth control. All the women questioned on this subject by a female interviewer evinced a remarkably spontaneous interest in the subject, which surprised even the anthropologists. Some of the spontaneous replies given are very illuminating:

Mutu Menika: "Oh, lady, if there is some medicine that could rid me of this (referring to her fetus), I shall take it immediately."

Ukku Amma: "I will worship your

feet if you give me something to check birth."

Some women were even willing to be sterilized for life, even after the implications of sterilization were explained to them. In this context dola-duka is very significant: it gives an opportunity for the women to express their hostility to the fetus in a culturally acceptable form, as we shall soon show.

Our third conclusion is that the social situation in Laggala, with its antagonism between the sexes, the inferior or subordinate social status of the female, and the dominance of the male is conductive to the formation of what should be conceptualized as *male envy*. We prefer this term to the wider Freudian concept of the biologically derived *penis envy*, leading to the formation of the Oedipus complex in women. Our concept has a more limited reference. Male envy is defined here as an "envy for male roles by the female as a result of the socially inferior statuses and roles of the latter." The culture with its heavy premium on male greatness and superordination provides very few mechanisms for the expression of psychological states like male envy. The social life of the village strongly disapproves of women in any way attempting to behave like men, though there are few cases of masculine type women. Tabooed and socially disapproved though expressions of masculinity may be in the culture, women nevertheless seek expression in many contexts:

(a) *In obscenity:* One of the favorite swear words of women in the village is "penis" (*pittambaya*). Sentences are spiced with the word. "I don't want that penis," referring to some object she does not like. "Penis!" (simple exclamation) "will someone look after the children?"

"Penis" (in the sense of *nuisance*), "I can't draw water from the river now." The frequent use of this swear word is an indication of the wish, not simply to possess the organ as the official psychoanalytic position may postulate, but to take male roles.

(b) *In exclusive female groups:* When women are in their own company, out of the sight of the men—particularly when they are in the jungle gathering firewood—they often emulate male roles. For example, it is considered wrong for a woman to urinate in a standing position—this is essentially a male posture. But out alone in the jungle, women often urinate in the disapproved position. Again, it is considered unseemly for women to climb trees, but when they are alone, they do not hesitate to do so.

(c) *In Buddhism:* This could be done in two ways. First, by fulfilling faithfully the ideal role of subservience, humility, fidelity, and implicit loyalty to her husband and then obtaining his permission (*varan*) and blessing in order to be born as a man in some other birth. The other alternative was more common and less difficult, though not considered as efficacious as the former. This is through *pratna* or wish attached to a specific act of Buddhist piety. After performing an act of piety—say, worshipping in the temple, women often made a wish that they be reborn as men in their next birth.

The mechanism of dola-duka, we will show, gives a woman an opportunity to emulate male roles and thus give expression to male envy in a culturally approved manner.

DOLA-DUKA: TECHNIQUE OF INTERPRETATION

The unique feature about dola-duka

is the craving by the woman for certain objects. In Laggala, these are mostly foods. These foods, we believe, cannot be significantly related to nutritional needs. The hypothesis is a psychological one: these foods which uniquely constitute the symptomatology of dola-duka are symbolic. The dynamics involved here are analogous to symptom-formation in the psychoneuroses to some extent. Any psychoneurotic symptom (e.g., a phobia) is (a) symbolic of an inner psychic state, (b) is an attempt made by the personality to control or give expression to that psychic state. However, there is one important difference —a psychoneurotic symptom is an unsuccessful attempt to cope with a personality problem, and is *basically dysfunctional*. Secondly, it is a purely idiosyncratic solution to an individual problem. In the case of dola-duka, which is a culturally constituted structure, the majority of symbols are culturally defined, and symptomatic of psychological problems common to most female members of the society. Moreover, these symbols actually promote the personal adjustment of these members of the group and are therefore functional. The symbolism in dola-duka has a wish-fulfilling character which makes it closer to the symbolism of dreams: dreams, while symbolizing unconscious wishes, also give expression and ventilation to these wishes. The symbolism of dreams occurs in the regressive state of sleep; the symbols of dola-duka occur in an analogously regressive state. There are some important differences, however: (a) dreams are symbolic techniques of wish fulfillment common to the species, whereas dola-duka is a culturally constituted structure found in some societies. (b) Dreams have a greater fantasy element, dola-duka has

a greater reality element. These foods, however symbolic they may be, are concrete, highly cathected, tangible objects that are eaten. In dola-duka the wishes are, as in dreams, vicariously realized, but the introjective and incorporative techniques adopted in dola-duka make it a more satisfying fulfillment of wishes.

The technique of interpretation of symbolic foods is basically the same as that employed by Freud in the analysis of dreams (Freud 1950). However, dola-duka analysis is much less complicated. As in dream analysis, we are not very concerned with the manifest content of the symbol but only with its latent meaning. In dream analysis, the latent meaning is elicited through the evocation of the patient's *associations* clustering around the symbol: it requires a thorough knowledge of the individual case history of the patient. In dola-duka analysis, the cultural associations centering on the symbol and a knowledge of the culturally created psychological problems are needed (though, of course, each case has also a few unique symbols, as we shall see). Finally, the difficulties and distortions produced by censorship are not encountered, since the symbol system is largely culturally constituted and designed to prevent such distortions.

PHYSICAL AND PSYCHOLOGICAL CONDITION OF THE WOMEN DURING DOLA-DUKA

The women of Laggala are physically weak, their bodies "cold" during the three months of dola-duka. This weakness may be partly natural, the result of the "normal" condition of pregnancy, but partly also due to the fact that women reject food during this period. In other words, physical weakness is partly due to the culturally important fact that women are *expected* to be weak. Together with this weakness is the attendant nausea and vomiting. In Western societies this is characterized as "morning sickness," but as far as Laggala is concerned this description is inappropriate, since nausea and vomiting, when it is experienced, can occur at any time of the day, without any particular virulence in the morning. Moreover, not all women experience this; nausea is quite rare, though vomiting is more common. Spitting, however, is universal—women spit out all the time during the period of dola-duka. Psychoanalysts have interpreted nausea and vomiting as symbolic of disgust or as attempts to symbolically throw out the fetus, owing to the strong ambivalence felt by the mother to her future offspring. If in Western societies the typical symbols of rejection and disgust are nausea and vomiting, in Sinhalese society the symbol is spitting. Spitting, both within and outside the context of dola-duka, is the typical Sinhalese expression of disgust. For example, if a Sinhalese person sees some feces lying somewhere, his first reaction would be to spit out. If he were to hear something unpleasant, say something unpleasant, witness something unpleasant, or do something unpleasant, his behavior would be accompanied by spitting. If one does not actually spit out, the word "thu" would be used by him to onomatopoetically connote the act of spitting. This symbol transferred to dola-duka has the same meanings that nausea and vomiting have typically for the woman in Western society.

The regressive character of dola-duka is seen in the more obvious aspects of the behavior of the woman during this period. She lies on a mat for a good part of the day for anything up to a period of three months. She is petulant, easily irritated, "behaves like a child," as one informant put it. Her perverse wishes have to be satisfied. She lays off work more or less completely, cutting down to a minimum those employments which characterize the work program of a Laggala housewife—cooking, pounding rice, drawing water, gathering firewood, looking after her children. In this she is assisted by her female kinsfold, neighbors, and elder daughters, if any. There is nothing unusual in such kinship assistance. Such assistance is given and received even in the normal life of the woman. The difference in assistance during this period is one of degree, not of kind, *except in respect to the assistance received from her husband.* During dola-duka the domestic situation is such that the husband is forced to draw water, bring firewood, look after the children and even cook on occasion. In normal living women are expected to obey and serve their husbands; but here the roles are inverted and the husband is compelled by custom to serve the wife. He has to yield unto her "perverse" demands, often walking long miles and incurring great expenditures and inconvenience in order to bring her the required foods. In normal life it would be utterly demeaning for the husband to act in this fashion, but in dola-duka the otherwise adhered to division of labor between the sexes is reversed. The woman, for a certain period, not only suspends, partially or completely, her traditional roles, but compels the *hated* husband to adopt these *hated* roles. The "female husband" is compelled to serve, as we shall soon see, the "male wife."

In her ordinary workaday life, the woman has to attend to the needs of her husband and children; during dola-duka the overworked and culturally despised woman is the object of attention, concern, and solicitude. It is considered great sin or *pay* to ill-treat or neglect the woman during this period. Husbands who are normally irascible and ill-tempered show the customary concern. Women are rarely beaten, an exception being Piyadasa, who once beat his wife during dola-duka but felt ashamed of it later. By and large, it would be true to say that women are not treated with sympathy and consideration. Dola-duka gives the Laggala woman a much-needed "holiday from life."

FOOD REJECTION—
PRECONDITION TO CRAVING

As a precondition to the acceptance of foods listed in the following categories, women reject certain symbolic foods. The rejected foods are those normally eaten by them in their daily lives, strongly associated with their social roles of wife and mother. These foods are typically those following:

Rice: Rice is strongly associated with the social role of women. It is the staple Sinhalese food; the woman helps her husband in the fields to make it grow, and to reap it. Long hours are spent in drying it in the sun and arduously pounding it in a primitive mortar. The wife cooks rice once or twice a day and if by chance it is not properly cooked, or if she fails to cook it at the right time, she is invariably abused and sometimes beaten. The pots and pans have to be washed and cleaned.

No wonder then that women reject rice, and cannot stand the smell of rice being cooked.[2] By contrast, they like cold rice and rice in picnic bags, which have different symbolical associations.

Kurakkan roti (tortilla from millet): Also an important food, and a substitute for rice. It is probably cooked as often as rice, especially by the lower income groups. Some women like kurakkan as a porridge, since this is a rarer and tastier dish.

Everyday curries: The curries that are usually eaten are also largely held in revulsion, especially *dhall* (a lentil) and dried fish, that constitute the typical Laggala curries. Some women also detest coconut milk, essential for cooking curries, but prefer the more expensive coconut oil.

Jaggery: Most women hate the crystallized treacle (*jaggery*) always eaten in Laggala as a substitute for the expensive cane sugar. However, they eat the same food in disguised form in sweetmeats.

Cold water: Two cases evinced a repulsion for cold water. They refused to drink it or bathe in it. One explanation for this may be that in their physically weak condition, cold water is rejected by the body. However, we should note that the water in the nearby stream is coolly refreshing, and never "cold" except during the rainy month of December. A villager's proud boast is that his water is the best in the whole Laggala area. Therefore it may well be that among pregnant women other motives are at work. Water is strongly associated with the social role of women—one of their major tasks is to bring water from the river in pots for domestic purposes. Bathing, too, is a part of the daily workaday activity. These activities are symbolically rejected. Furthermore, the refusal to bathe is indicative of the regressive nature of dola-duka: the woman is behaving like a child. Whatever the motives, the rejection of these foods has the function of focusing attention on the woman, for the husband has now to boil water, or brew tea for the "sick" woman to drink. Our conclusion is that by rejecting the foods strongly associated with their social roles, women in Laggala symbolically reject these roles.

FOOD CRAVINGS

For the purposes of analysis I have picked out from the case histories at my disposal certain foods which I feel are not simply personal or idiosyncratic choices, but cultural choices. These are selected on the basis of widest acceptance by the women. Cultural choices are recognized as such by the women themselves. They would say that such and such are the foods that *women in general* desire during this period. These foods have been classified in certain categories by the author, on the basis of the symbolic meaning of the foods. By and large, any woman in Laggala would have picked out one or more foods from each category to the satisfaction of their cravings.

FOOD CATEGORY NO. 1: SWEETS, COOKIES, LOZENGES (CHILDHOOD FOODS).

Most women crave these trifles. It is a craving that is easily satisfied because lollies and sweets are found in plenty at Pallegama town, five miles away, and cookies are always available in the village boutique. But why crave that which is easily available? What are the motives that are satisfied by the consumption of these dainties? An examination of the associations clustering round these objects will give us the answer, that is, in what cultural contexts other than dola-duka are these foods eaten? Anyone, whether male or female, adult or child, in Laggala will eat sweets if given *gratis,* but typically they are eaten by children in the following contexts: (a) When children cry they are often promised sweets or cookies; children constantly remind the adults of these promises, and the adults placate them with sweets. If the child has to be placated immediately, the adult buys a cookie from the village boutique and gives it to him; otherwise he may, particularly in the case of older children, bring lozenges from his periodic visits to town. (b) One of the most pleasurable events in the life of a child is the return of the father from the visit to town. He inevitably brings with him something nice for the children.

The consumption of these heavily charged foods facilitates regression, in a culturally acceptable form, into something approaching the security of childhood. As we saw earlier, the stage is all set for regression; the woman has laid off work and sleeps a good part of the time. Furthermore, we have to note that it is the father, who as provider to the family, most often brought her the trifles, particularly during the first few years of childhood (approximately to the age of six). After this, fathers are expected to be more formal towards their female children. The discipline and training of female children is the mother's task. The consumption of these dainties also enables the woman to recapitulate vicariously a satisfying experience with the father.

FOOD CATEGORY NO. 2: SOUR FOODS.

This category of foods is also related to the first, but is treated separately because it has a pan-Sinhalese applicability. Sinhalese women of all classes and castes crave this type of food for dola-duka, almost without exception. In Laggala these include tamarind, various kinds of citrus fruits, and pickles. Women sometimes explain these preferences by saying that their bite and strong flavor appeal to their weary palates. My hypothesis regarding the motives for eating these foods is quite different. The only other significant context in which these foods are desired is in childhood. If there is one thing that children all over Ceylon love it is sour things and pickles. Often these are eaten secretly, for parents disapprove of their consumption. When children suffer from stomach aches, blame is attributed to their consumption of these foods. Of course, the very fact that they are disapproved makes them doubly attractive to the children. The craving to eat these foods is motivated once again by the wish to regress into the comfort and security of childhood.

FOOD CATEGORY NO. 3: FESTIVAL FOODS.

The women of Laggala demand foods which are associated with feasts and festive occasions. These are *kavun*, *aggala*, and other sweetmeats. These foods are mostly eaten at weddings and New Year celebrations. They help the woman to recapitulate moments of fun and relaxation.

Imbulkiribat (made of rice and jaggery) is the typical food taken by Laggala folk on visits to kinsmen. Children are especially fond of this and eagerly await visits from kinsmen. The craving for this food helps the woman to recapitulate visits she herself paid, or received from kinsfolk, and probably relive childhood experiences of fun and security among kinsfolk in her natal village. *Batmula* (picnic rice) is probably the most significant food in this category. As mentioned earlier, women reject warm rice, but accept eagerly rice in a batmula. All women demand and get this. In fact, neighbors anticipate these desires and send gifts of batmula to the afflicted woman. The batmula typically represents the life of outdoor activity and relaxation which the women of Laggala rarely enjoy. A batmula is taken by villagers on visits to relations and, typically, in pilgrimages. On these trips, particularly in the latter, everyone has a good time. A major part of the village goes on these trips, the women singing religious songs on the way. For the women these trips are also shopping sprees, occasions for showing off their best clothes, and opportunities for shedding their domestic cares. And when one is tired one rests on a river bank and eats the batmula one has brought (the anthropologist who has himself shared the experience knows how wonderful it can be). The batmula then represents, together with the other foods in this category, occasions of fun, relaxation, leisure, so rare in the women's normal workaday life. These foods permit the women to relive such experiences vicariously. They are also wish-fulfillment symbols expressing what the woman would most wish to do but cannot, owing to her station in life. In this respect they are again analogous to dreams, but in so far as they are introjected they have greater reality than dreams.

FOOD CATEGORY NO. 4: EXPENSIVE
AND RARE FOODS.

Some of the foods demanded by
the woman during dola-duka are considered by the culture to be expensive
and rare. These foods typically are
the following: ginger beer, sambhur
meat, canned fish, dried fish from
the Maldive Islands, grapes—all items
considered to be expensive middle-
class foods. Grapes in particular are
very expensive in Ceylon and are
generally given as gifts to invalids.
For the village, in addition to their
expense, they are hard to obtain. In
order to get grapes, the husband has
to walk five miles to the bus terminal,
give the bus driver the money, and
cool his heels for half a day until the
precious cargo arrives from the town
of Matale, eighteen miles away. For
sambhur meat the husband spends one
whole day in the hunt. By demanding
these foods the woman forces her
husband to pay her compulsory attention and solicitude; she transfers
her role of subservience to her
husband and compels him to recognize
her as an individual.

FOOD CATEGORY NO. 5: FOODS
EXPRESSING HOSTILITY.

This category of foods expresses the
hostile feelings of the mother in respect to the fetus: the wish that the
fetus be destroyed and that she return
to "normal health" again.

Pineapple: All Sinhalese people sub-
scribe to the view that pineapples are
bad for the pregnant mother and may
do damage to the fetus. For example,
unripe pineapple is eaten by women
in all Sinhalese villages who wish to
effect a miscarriage. People in Laggala

hold the same views, women included.
Nevertheless, all women desire to eat
pineapple during this period. Most
husbands are compelled by custom to
accede to these wishes, even though
they know that it is "bad." But then
the husband is placed in a very unen-
viable position—if he gives pineapple
to the woman, the fetus may be destroyed; if he does not, the ears of
the unborn child may rot. Some
husbands, however, refuse to accede to
the women's requests for pineapples.

Wild Boar Meat: This meat again
may cause miscarriage according to
the village opinion, particularly in the
first few months (i.e., the period of
dola-duka), yet it is a greatly desired
food. The craving for these foods, in
spite of the cultural injunctions regarding their danger, gives expression
to unconscious wishes of the mother
that the fetus be destroyed. Note the
fact that these wishes are actually
carried out in miniature, symbolically.

Bees Honey: This is a food classically desired by women in Indian
literature. It is also a typical craving
of Laggala women. According to Sinhalese idiom, honey is a symbol for
the menstrual flow, the honeycomb
referring to the vagina. For instance,
if a young man is seen out alone late
in the evening someone may ask him
"Why? Are you going to pick a honeycomb?" Similarly, the period of
menstruation is referred to as *pani
berana kale,* (honey-dripping period).
Further analogies are recognized.
Honey, like menstruation, obtains only
periodically. Laggala women recognize
that honey is a symbol for the
menstrual flow. Therefore, when a
woman tells her husband, "I want
some honey to satisfy my pregnancy
cravings," psychodynamically, in the
context of the sociocultural background presented earlier, she means,

"I want my menstrual flow back," expressive once again of the rejection of the child in her womb.

FOOD CATEGORY NO. 6: MALE FOODS.

Some of the foods craved by the women are generally consumed by males, and normally taboo to females. The desire for such foods must specifically be related to the problem of *male envy* in this village.

Kiroti (milk pancake): All women without exception demand kiroti for their dola-duka. Now, kiroti is the ritual food eaten by men in the exclusively male cult of the *adukku*. This craving expresses an envy for the male role, a desire to participate in the envied male activity.

Cigars, Cigarettes, Arrack: A majority of the women interviewed had craved some or all of these items. Smoking and drinking in Laggala, and Sinhalese society in general, is strictly taboo to women—they are exclusively and essentially masculine habits, strongly associated with maleness. It would be unthinkable for a woman to indulge in these habits: she would be the victim of ridicule, vituperation, or assault. These desires are an indication of the strength of the motives to emulate male roles, for in spite of the shamefulness of the act women are eager to smoke, and drink arrack.

FOOD CATEGORY NO. 7: PENIS SYMBOLS.

The seventh category of foods are even more vividly related to male envy.

Dandulena (lumpy squirrel, a large squirrel found in Ceylon jungles): A number of women interviewed expressed a desire to eat the flesh of a dandulena. Now dandulena, in the euphemistic parlance of the village, also means penis. A woman's desire for a dandulena, when translated psychodynamically simply means "I want a penis," or "I wish I were a man."

Bananas: Probably represents the same wish. Bananas are eaten outside the context of dola-duka often, and are not considered a rarity at all, unlike dandulena flesh which is difficult to obtain. I would be reluctant to interpret bananas in the same terms as dandulena, except for the fact that women *crave* them during the dola-duka period. It is an urgent need that has to be satisfied—quite unlike the situation in normal living when a woman may buy a banana from a boutique and eat it. In the latter instance, there is no compulsion; in the former, the woman feels anxiety or tension. It is in the context of a woman's craving that I would equate bananas with a wish for a penis, and not in a normal context. Incidentally the banana, in Sinhalese ritual contexts, is used as a penis symbol.

FOOD CATEGORY NO. 8: IDIOSYNCRATIC FOODS.

Some of the foods demanded by the women during dola-duka are without the cultural associations mentioned earlier, but are unique to the particular case. Analysis of the symbolism becomes difficult, for one has to elicit the personal significance of the symbol through a knowledge of the individual's life history. It is also likely that some of the motives involved may be personal to the individual. For example we have no idea why one woman, Dingiri Menika, pregnant for the first time, wanted a green cloth as a pregnancy craving. Very often, then, idiosyncratic foods are selected because they have a great deal of personal meaning for the individual, and are more effective than the cultural choice for the expression of the chooser's needs. One case will illustrate this. Dingiri Amma craved for mangoes and *kurumba* (drinking coconut), tapicoa and sweet potatoes. In most Sinhalese villages there are easily available, and for a moment even the anthropologist was tempted to disregard their significance. But soon it struck us that none of these foods are available in Rambadeniya itself, and that all of these were available in Dingiri Amma's natal village and the village of her foster-father. Moreover, she *had* to have these from these two villages. It was obvious that these foods had considerable meaning in the personal life history of Dingiri Amma, strongly associated with a period of premarital security. Furthermore, the manner in which these foods were obtained is noteworthy. She not only demanded these foods but saw that they came from her near kinsmen (mother and brother); they brought these foods to her, or she sent her husband to obtain them directly from them. Through these foods she established sentimental links with her close kin from whom she had been separated, reviving vicariously old associations of security. Thus many of these "non-prescribed" foods often at first glance seem meaningless but assume significance in the personal life of the individual.

CONCLUSION

The cultural and social structure of Laggala creates certain psychological problems—needs, motives or tensions —which, owing to their pressing nature, have to be coped with or solved in some way or other. Various alternatives are open: one, a direct solution of these problems through the use of the mechanisms of defense, for example, repression. But this may result in increased psychological strain and in symptom formation and may eventuate in the breakdown of the personality. The solution could take the form of socially disapproved behavior, for example, transvestism (male envy), direct expression of hostility to children (ambivalence), or any socially disapproved form of regression (adjustment). Dola-duka provides a much more effective solution. It is a defense provided by the culture itself, an opportunity for the expression of pressing needs in a socially approved manner. For obvious methodological reasons I have treated dola-duka in Laggala as if it represented a unique case, but dola-duka as a "culturally constituted defense" is found in the Indian civilizational area and has existed there from very ancient times, as the classical literature suggests. It is also my belief that the kind of analysis conducted here will help elucidate the less structured counterparts of dola-duka in other societies.

NOTES

1. My thanks are due to the Asia Foundation in Ceylon for a generous grant given to carry out field work in Laggala in 1958-60. Thanks are due also to my students in the Department of Sociology, University of Ceylon, P. A. S. Saram, Sarath Amunugama, J. C. de S. Jayaingha, M. Cooray, who assisted me in my field work; to Miss Sumana Saparamadu of the Associated Newspapers of Ceylon,

whose ability to make friends with Laggala women resulted in valuable information; to the women of Laggala who patiently suffered meticulous inquiry into their private lives; and to my *guru,* Melford E. Spiro, for the intellectual stimulation to undertake this kind of analysis, and the use of two important concepts, "culturally constituted defense," and "male envy." Charles Valentine kindly read an originally overlong paper and suggested emendations. For any theoretical loopholes in the essay and matter of style and presentation I am entirely responsible.

This paper was first read at the annual sessions of the Ceylon Association for the Advancement of Science (Section F) in November, 1960.

2. This is not the only instance of the distortion of olfactory perception. We have two cases of women who got a "bad smell" when the husband and/or children were about. The reasons were obvious.

REFERENCES

BENEDEK, THERESE F.
  1959   Sexual function of women and their disturbance. *In American Handbook of Psychiatry* I, Part V. New York: Basic Books.
DEUTSCH, HELENE
  1945   *The Psychology of Women.* Vol. II. New York: Grune and Stratton.
FREUD, SIGMUND
  1950   *Interpretation of Dreams.* Translated by A. A. Brill. New York: The Modern Library.
GEIGER, W.
  1934   *Mahavamsa, Pali Text Society.* Oxford University Press.
RICHARDS, AUDREY I.
  1956   *Chisungu.* New York: Grove Press.

11. REPEATED HALLUCINATORY EXPERIENCES AS A PART OF THE MOURNING PROCESS AMONG HOPI INDIAN WOMEN

WILLIAM FOSTER MATCHETT

William Foster Matchett, M.D., is Assistant Professor of Psychiatry, Yale University. Reprinted by special permission of The William Alanson White Psychiatric Foundation, Inc., from *Psychiatry* (1972) 35: 185-194. Copyright © The William Alanson White Psychiatric Foundation.

THERE ARE MANY ways in which a person can go about dealing emotionally with the death of a loved one. One of the most frequently used techniques seems to be a variety of mental mechanism which makes it possible for the bereaved to feel, if only briefly, that the dead person is still present in his life. Much "bringing back the dead" goes on in fantasy, rumination, dream, and even formal seance as a reasonably well-accepted part of many cultures, and there is reason to suspect that it occurred much more openly in our own cultural past. Among the Hopi Indians of Arizona, the experience to be described is neither truly seance nor truly dream, but appears to represent a mental state with some similarities to both. The apparition is real enough to the beholder to be conversed with, to be described in great visual detail, and even at times to be struggled with physically. However, it is clear to the beholder, even during the experience, that this presence with which he argues and struggles as if it were real occurs somewhere outside the usual definition of reality. The phenomenon appears to the beholder only in a darkened room and when outside stimuli are limited sufficiently to eliminate distractions. Most subjects seem to feel that the experience is not a dream and that they are not asleep when it occurs, although some disagree on this point. The degree of volition involved in bringing about a visitation from the apparition appears to vary from subject to subject. In my psychiatric contacts with the Hopi I have heard of the phenomenon frequently enough to think that its occurrence is rather common during a period of loss, but I cannot document this statistically. All cases in which I have seen it are women. I do not know whether this is because only women are subject to the experience or because only women would be willing to tell an Anglo psychiatrist about it. It is clear that among American Indians the phenomenon is not limited to the Hopi, as I have heard casual reports of it from members of other tribes. Literary references—and I shall later cite a few from the Bible, Shakespeare, and Dickens—testify that something very similar must be a part of our own cultural past. I report it among the Hopi not because there is something uniquely Hopi about it, but because it still seems to be a sufficiently active and accepted part of the Hopi experience that it does not yet suffer in full measure those distortions accrued by a phenomenon when outside pressures force it completely underground.

The Hopi Indians are a numerically

small tribe living on a reservation in northeastern Arizona. A few statements about them may be of value if recognized as gross generalizations. Their ancestry and cultural background is of the Pueblo Indian type. They live for the most part in small, compact villages atop several mesas of their reservation, and have traditionally subsisted on dry farming. Almost always, the edge of town on at least one side of village (and in some cases on two or three sides) is defined by a precipitous cliff several hundred feet in height, marking the edge of the mesa. The villages themselves are isolated and crowded, and yet from every part of them one looks down upon immense expanses of dry, unpeopled plains below. No physical barrier is ever placed along the edge of the cliff which rings the village, so that even small children must learn to control themselves to avoid blundering over the edge of the ever present precipice. Perhaps in part because of the physical setting of Hopi villages, healthy Hopi character tends in a rather obsessive, ruminative direction (again, this is a generalization and is not incompatible with sudden "hysterical" outpourings of the habitually pent-up emotions). Physical gestures are small and inhibited, conformity is valued, and individual self-expression is often in large part limited to a verbal sphere. A further fact of life important to Hopi character is their seeing themselves as a relatively small group of people, different from and surrounded by a sea of more "primitive" and unpredictably hostile peoples. By a quirk of history, the Hopi reservation now lies at the very center of the Navajo reservation, surrounded on all sides by the Navajo people, who vastly outnumber the Hopi, who differ enormously from them culturally, and whom the Hopi constantly fear will inundate their already diminished tribal lands. Uncomfortable as this situation may be for the Hopi, it does not seem to be anything particularly new to them. For the better part of a thousand years their legends and their objective history show them living a ghettolike existence in small, very dense population groups where freedom of action outside the ghetto was limited by the unpredictability of the outside population. One may well wonder whether this ghettolike existence, if continued for enough generations, can, as Malkin suggests,[1] contribute to a people's turning away from aggressive action in the outside world and developing fascination with and sophistication about intrapersonal processes. Be that as it may, one encounters among the Hopi an extraordinarily complex and sophisticated level of interest in their own intrapsychic lives, and an unusual articulateness in expressing it. Two further cultural notes are important to the material covered here: Among the Hopi there is a very high level of fluency in English, and the level of formal education is roughly comparable to that of the general population in the United States. Despite their fluency in English, most patients have told me that they speak Hopi or Tewa at home. Finally, Hopi tradition permits talking freely about a deceased person and mourning him in a relatively open, genuine way, so long as public outpourings of raw affect are kept carefully in check.[2]

EXAMPLES OF THE HALLUCINATORY EXPERIENCES[3]

EXAMPLE 1

Mrs. C. B., age 58, was referred to

me by the homemaker service because she was meddlesome, irritable, and difficult for their homemaker to work with. She is diabetic and has been on insulin for the past 14 years, but has never had to be hospitalized for an episode of acidosis. However, in the past year, she has had serious diabetic vascular problems, which are now under relatively good control. Her first husband, by whom she had three sons, was a prominent citizen of the tribe; she was divorced from him 14 years ago, reportedly because she had been meddlesome and irritable toward him too. Her second husband died six years ago from a metastatic carcinoma, having spent his last few years surviving one highly mutilative surgical procedure after another. She claims that any feelings she had over his dying were dissipated by his lengthy and inevitable downhill course. Three years ago, two of her three sons died. The first was found lying dead in a desolate area several miles from her home. She had suspected that he had been murdered, but the autopsy indicated that he had frozen to death, and she seems satisfied now that he was not murdered. The second son died several months later in an accident while intoxicated, and at that time Mrs. C. B. took his daughter, who was then seven, to live with her. The third son is away at school. Of her sons' deaths, she says:

I miss my sons so much I just want to cry when I think about them. . . . I feel angry with them for leaving me; I know it's not their fault they died, but sometimes I think maybe they did it on purpose. I just can't help feeling mad at them for going away and leaving me. . . . I'm just mad at my sons, but I feel like I'm mad at everyone, so that's why I act that way even though I'm really not mad at other people.

It is important to point out that this was her interpretation of the situation, not mine, and that I did little but listen.

Her hallucinatory experiences were as follows. For a period of time soon after her sons' deaths she began to see at a particular window the son who froze to death. Her visions are all of this son, who seems to have been her favorite. She nailed a piece of cloth over the window and he no longer appeared to her there. This sequence in itself seems to be common, almost ritualistic occurrence among the Hopi. Subsequently, nocturnal visitations began. She would be in bed with the lights off, in a state of readiness for sleep. Suddenly, she would see her son standing in the room—not appearing transparent or ghostlike but looking much as he did just before he died ("not black, the way he was when they found him in the desert"). Her son would not talk to her, but she would berate him angrily, saying such things as, "Why did you leave me? You did it on purpose. Who will care for me now?" The experience would always end by her getting up to turn on the light.

When she reported this to me during the interview, I asked, "Why did you do that? Were you frightened?" She replied, "No, I wanted to see if he was really there." "Was he?" "No, there was just myself, and I could see my granddaughter still in the other bed there, sleeping."

I saw Mrs. C. B. several times for brief appointments after the initial interview. She was assigned a new homemaker, and there was every indication that she was at least making an effort to avoid driving this one away. Her son was still appearing to her from time to time, but the continuation of the "visits" did not seem to be greatly upsetting her life. Indeed, they may have been of some comfort to her. There was never any indication that she was psychotic.

EXAMPLE 2

Mrs. L. D. apparently actually experienced the hallucinatory phenomenon during my interview with her, making the interview at times seem something like a seance. She was a 69-year-old widow whom the general medical officer referred to me because she was depressed, she was having visions which were increasingly frightening to her, and she had not responded to the course of an antidepressant, amitriptyline, which he had been giving her for some weeks prior to this interview. At this point she had to be hospitalized, so terrifying were her hallucinatory experiences when she was at home alone.

For lack of any other private place to see her, I interviewed her in the scrub room of the abandoned surgical suite of the hospital. The room, used partially for storage, had no functioning light of its own, and was semidark, with only a small amount of sunlight coming through the doors of the two adjoining unused operating rooms. Present during the interview were the referring physician, a mental health technician, the patient, and myself. Only the patient and I spoke.

She began by talking very freely and appropriately about herself, and in general came across as intelligent; she was entirely coherent and had an excellent command of the English language. She appeared depressed, but by no means psychotic. She chose to focus on her husband's death as the issue she seemed to feel was most closely related to the way she felt now, telling us that her husband had died two years ago in an automobile accident on the way to work. She said she had not wanted him to go that day because she feared he would be killed, and that she knew he had been killed when she saw people coming to tell her about it. She also talked about her present life situation: She had formerly lived in a village with her husband, but now lived in a very isolated house outside the village with her son's family. She occupied a room at the end of the house, and its only door opened to the outside, not into the rest of the house. She spent much of her time there, alone.

Suddenly, during a sequence in which she was telling about the circumstances surrounding her husband's death, she gave a start, gasped, burst into tears, and then began to stare at something in front of her. I had the impression that she had entered a self-hypnotic state at this point. I asked her what was making her cry, and she said that she was seeing her husband at that moment. She told us that he said not to bring him back any more—"He always says that."

She seemed to remain in a trance-like state throughout the remainder of the interview, and she began to talk about the other occasions on which this had happened to her. She described how she would sit alone in her room in the evening and draw all the shades, and then, almost nightly, a vision of her deceased husband would appear before her chair. He would say little to her. At first she found this experience a very comforting one, and looked forward to his presence. Later, he began quite persistently to say things like, "I'm gone now; don't bring me back any more; I don't want to come back." In the last month before her hospitalization, the apparition stood in front of her chair, caressed her hair, then softly touched her cheek. She could distinctly feel his fingers move gently from her cheek to her neck; then suddenly he began to strangle her. She sprang to her feet in terror, "struggled free," threw on the light, and "he was gone."

Gradually, the apparition began to show signs of physical decay. She reported that the flesh on his hands and arms was turning to "skin and bones" and that his clothing was deteriorating. Just before the hospitalization, when "he came to [her]" and stood in front of her chair, at first she did not look up to his face, but she knew it was he "because he had on the same red and black lumber jacket he was wearing on the day he was killed." Gradually, she looked up at his face, then shrieked in terror. "That face was like a skull, but the hair was still on." He said to her, "Remember me as I was. See how I am now. Don't bring me back any more."

It appeared to me that she was still in a state of self-induced hypnosis at this point in the interview, and I thought that an intervention in the manner of a posthypnotic suggestion might perhaps be helpful to her. I told her that I thought her husband's wishes were clear and that she should obey them. He did not wish to be brought back, and she must therefore stop bringing him back. She agreed, the trance seemed to lift, she wiped away her tears, all four of us began to talk at once, and the session was over.

The following day she was discharged. She was lax about keeping her follow-up appointments with the general medical officer upon whom she had formerly been so demanding, but according to family reports, she appeared to be doing well. No one knew whether the "visitations" from her husband continued.

EXAMPLE 3

Mrs. C.Z. is a 68-year-old widow whom I saw in consultation because she was reportedly depressed and had not responded to an antidepressant, amitriptyline, that had been administered for a month under the supervision of a general medical officer. When I first saw her, she was indeed clinically depressed: she had little energy, felt very sad most of the time, and wept a great deal both when alone and during the interview. However, she showed no self-deprecating trends in her thinking, did not reveal any tendency toward somatization of her feelings, and did not (other than her hallucinatory experiences) show any evidence of psychosis. Five years previously her husband had died from cancer. The couple had been childless but had raised two nieces from infancy, and the nieces had continued to live with Mrs. C.Z. in the immediate period after her husband's death. A year and a half ago, Mrs. C.Z.'s house had been destroyed by fire, and her two "children," much to her consternation, had moved to another village to live with their biological parents. Mrs. C.Z. then found a house for herself, and later her first cousin, an elderly man, moved in with her as a sort of boarder. He worked in the trading post, kept her company, and would bring her small items from the trading post to supplement their meager purchasing power. A few months ago, the cousin died, apparently from cancer. This left Mrs. C.Z. totally alone again, and forced her to attempt to subsist on about $65 a month in Social Security payments. As she finds it impossible to survive on this, she is taking lessons in basket weaving, hoping eventually to become proficient enough to begin selling baskets to tourists.

Shortly after her cousin's death, Mrs. C.Z.'s "dreams" began to interfere with her sleep. She was quite insistent in identifying the phenomena she described as dreams, despite their resemblance to many aspects of the phenomena I have described in the other two women, who preferred to distinguish them from dreams. She reported to me: "Almost every night he came to me. I go to bed and shut out the lights. Then I begin to dream." He appears to enter the room, seizes her, and shakes her "awake." She tells him to go away, and says that she knows he is "gone" and that this is only a dream. He argues with her, saying, "Look, I am alive; I am here with you. You can see that you are wrong; you can see that I am not dead. This is no dream." He also offers her gifts—small items from the trading post. She has been warned by an older woman not to accept the gifts. I asked her, "Why shouldn't you accept them?" "Because if I did I would be dead." The visitations frighten her, "because they are just a dream." After a long argument with the apparition about whether he is real, she leaps up, turns on the light, and finds herself alone again. This goes on nightly, and his presence is very real to her, despite her insistence to the "ghost" that he is only a dream.

The short-term outcome in this case was relatively good. I saw Mrs. C.Z. several times for brief follow-up visits, as did the general medical officer who had been following her previously. She felt less sad, wept much less, and made a significant increase in her level of activity. She remained on the antidepressant medication. On the basis of what she told me directly and what I can surmise, the "visitations" became far less of a problem to her, but I would guess that they did not cease entirely.

DISCUSSION

The experience these three women went through is obviously extraordinarily rich in implications and could fruitfully be followed in a great variety of directions. I shall limit myself to commenting on the phenomenon of the hallucinatory experience itself, on the comparative aspects of this as a cultural phenomenon, and on the psychodynamic function of the phenomenon. These areas, of course, are not mutually exclusive.

The three examples I gave were not identical, but seemed to share a certain core of experience which was approached from different angles. (I use the term "examples" here because I feel uncomfortable with the label "patients" or "cases," as that tends to overemphasize the pathological aspects of the situation.) All three examples involve older women (although the phenomenon does occur with diminished frequency in younger women) who had experienced a series of meaningful object losses and who were clinically depressed. None were clinically psychotic and none had any previously recorded history of psychiatric treatment. All were experiencing "visitations" from someone whom they identified as being a recently deceased family member. They chose to explain the experience differently, but all were convinced that the vision appearing to them did not fit the usual definition of reality. In attempting to label the phenomenon, one is tempted to describe it in terms of what it was not. It shared something of the seance, of the dream, or of a self-hypnosis, but was identical to none of these. It would be incorrect simply to categorize it as a "hallucinosis" or a "hypnagogic phenomenon," although of course it was in some part both of these. Like a seance, these things seemed to occur only when the person was in an environment and a state of mind contributory to shutting out external stimuli and concentrating on the phenomenon itself. In some, as in Example 2, there seemed to be a very definite volition to "bring back" the deceased and perhaps a self-induced hypnotic state to help make it possible. Unlike the standard Anglo seance, however, this experience was usually solitary, no props or gimmicks were necessary, and there seemed to be no standard messages returned (i.e., predictions about the future, or messages such as "I'm all right here; I love you," from an ambivalently loved deceased spouse). The hallucinatory experience described here seemed to be relatively well attached to reality. It also seemed relatively direct in the expression of true affect. For example, in the first illustration, Mrs. C.B. found that the presence of the apparition gave her an opportunity to berate her son for leaving her by dying, and in the second illustration, the ambivalent relationship between Mrs. L. D. and her husband was symbolically acted out, but rather clearly expressed. The reality-testing aspect of the experience is one of its most interesting characteristics, as the phenomenon appears to have occurred, as it were, at the junction between faulty and intact reality testing. The visitor appeared to the beholder as someone very real and alive, who could be talked to, but then much of the conversation with him concerned the fact that he was dead and gone—so much so that in Example 2 the apparition even under-

went a gradual and appropriate process of physical decay. Here too there were arguments in which the beholder debated with the apparition, just as if he were very real; but paradoxically the content of the argument was the beholder's firm conviction that the being with whom he was so earnestly debating about reality was not real at all.

Our own cultural history is rich in examples of phenomena which sound akin to this kind of hallucinatory experience. One would not expect and does not find complete congruence, but there seems to be a common thread to human experience running through the stories of Jacob and his struggle with an apparition which seemed to him very real and solid; of Job tormented by visions after suffering his devastating series of losses; or of Christ's "reappearance" to his disciples after his death in a form solid enough to satisfy even those who wished to touch him. Often, the unbeliever writes off this sort of tale either as poetic license or as psychosis, pure and simple, when in fact it might represent another type of mental mechanism neither truly poetic nor truly psychotic.

Although most of Shakespeare's ghosts and visions do not resemble this phenomenon, one very well-known example does: Brutus sits alone in his tent, having recently helped to kill Caesar, whom he loved and respected. Night has fallen, and his servants have left him or have fallen asleep. He is attempting to read by the dim light. Caesar's Ghost enters, and Brutus says:

How ill this taper burns! Ha! Who comes
  here?
I think it is the weakness of mine eyes
That shapes this monstrous apparition.
. . . Art thou anything?

Art thou some god, some angel, or some
 devil,
That mak'st my blood cold and my hair
 to stare?
Speak to me what thou art.[4]

One wonders whether Shakespeare
was banking on a belief in ghosts
among his countrymen at the time, or
whether he was talking about a more
commonly shared and very "real"
experience which his countrymen
could understand and probably identify with, having perhaps suffered
through the same experience themselves.

The tale most similar to my examples is probably the most familiar:
Ebenezer Scrooge and his encounter
with the ghost of Jacob Marley.
Scrooge was elderly, solitary, and
deeply deprived emotionally. One
night, when returning to his room,
painfully aware of his solitude, he
sat alone in the dim light of his
chamber and was visited by an apparition. Remember here in particular his debate with the apparition in
which he discoursed with it as if it
were entirely real, and yet the content
of his discourse was to the effect that
it was not real at all, that it was
nothing but ". . . a blot of mustard,
a crumb of cheese, a fragment of an
underdone potato."[5] Remember also
the skillful way in which Dickens
introduces the confusion in Scrooge's
mind as to whether these things
happen to him in a sleeping or
walking state. As with Shakespeare,
one wonders whether Dickens was
writing of something which was entirely a product of his own fertile
imagination, or whether instead he
was alluding to a phenomenon which
was quite familiar to the people of
his day.

Freud's lifetime, of course, spanned
the gap between Dickens' time and our

own. He clearly had the opportunity
to see this sort of psychic process and
others like it spelled out in dramatic,
visible style, and had the fortunate
genius (as did Dickens and Shakespeare before him) for making sense
out of such colorful activity in terms
of what it meant in a more universal
way about the workings of the individual mind. It is unfortunate that
often in dealing with transcultural
phenomena, one tends (in attempting
to go beyond the naivete of labeling
as illness all psychic phenomena which
are different from those of one's own
culture) to become fixated at the level
of fascination with differences between
cultures. Along with this goes an unfortunate implication that one can
understand the individual human
beings within a given culture simply
by understanding thoroughly the differences between cultures. While I firmly
believe that an understanding of the
individuals within a culture cannot
take place without an understanding
of the cultural context, I think there
is a step beyond this which can and
must be made. The next level, as it
were, is where one recognizes that
very common universal human needs
and universal psychic mechanisms can
often be expressed in idiosyncratic
ways in different cultures; but in
most cases the inner need can be rediscovered by tracing back from the
colorful and idiosyncratic external
manifestation which society has imposed upon it to the underlying inner
feeling, which is familiar to us all. It
is in this frame of mind that I would
approach the dramatic hallucinatory
experiences of the Hopi.

Finally, the place of this hallucinatory phenomenon in the individual psychic economy of those who experience
it should be mentioned. It is apparently
one facet of the varied responses a

person has available to him in attempting to bear a period of intense grief. For some, it seems effective in mitigating the psychic pain. For others, as can happen in the most effective of mental mechanisms, the mechanism itself has gotten out of hand and has added another burden of crippling fear. When it does work, however, the repeated vivid hallucination of the lost object accomplishes a number of tasks. It offers first of all restitution of an otherwise intolerable loss, without necessitating any global loss of basic reality testing. One experiences comfort from the lost object's presence, or, failing comfort, one finds an arena in which old conflicts and old relationships can be re-experienced and perhaps mastered—all of this taking place without the need for transference of the old attitudes and interactions onto a new object. Notable is the explicitness of the wish fulfillment, which differs somewhat from what happens in a genuine dream. Conventional dramas are sometimes interpreted as expressing the kind of thoughts and wishes that are expressed in these hallucinatory phenomena, but dreams usually (not always) couch their statement in a more covert form. In the true dream, wish and reality battle one another and obscure parts of one another within the very substance of the dream before the material contained therein is ever allowed to enter conscious awareness. In these hallucinatory phenomena a wish is expressed in a relatively raw and explicit form, and the correction for reality is battled out and brought about within the realm of conscious awareness some time after the undistorted expression of the wish. (This is not to say, of course, that in hallucinating all of the wishes get expressed in an undistorted form all of the time.)

My data permit me to make only a rather general summarization of how Hopi society comes into play to induce, maintain, or abate this specific psychic phenomenon in any individual. At this point in Hopi history, apparently the phenomenon is widely recognized to exist but is talked about with little enthusiasm among Hopis themselves; they are even more reluctant to discuss it with strangers. It is apparently tolerated or even accepted, but not only encouraged. In wondering why so prevalent a phenomenon should be relegated to a somewhat sub-rosa existence, one should keep in mind that Hopi society as a whole, particularly through its many dances and rituals, perceives itself as providing adequate outlets or receptacles for the psychological energies of a normal person. At time of extreme stress it does not do so, but there is considerable investment in maintaining the idea that it does, for the sake of maintaining society. Thus, necessary mechanisms such as these hallucinatory phenomena, which do not fit in with the society's self-perception, are tolerated, but are expected to remain sub-rosa. There is obviously nothing in the least bit peculiar to the Hopi about this approach. Finally, and most important, Hopi society discourages open expression of strong affect by the individual, not unlike what might be expected in the same emotional context in segments of the English population. For all patients who began to talk with me about their hallucinatory experiences, the mere description of the experience led relatively quickly to a flood of anger, pain, desolation, and grief, which I suspect would have shamed them greatly had they been asked to account for themselves in the face of their better-controlled peers.

I can only speculate as to why these women chose to talk to someone outside their own culture about such intimate occurrences, and why they generally seemed to show considerable improvement after doing so. Many factors may be at work here, but one would suppose that their own decision to get well is of critical importance. It is possible that they were using the interview with me (regardless of what I may have thought I was doing) as a sort of ritual in which they were given permission to shed the symptom complex. It would be interesting to know what sort of transference role is assigned to the psychiatrist in this situation.

Notes

1. Personal communication, Michael Malkin, Service Unit Director, Keams Canyon Indian Hospital.
2. This statement is based upon my own observation. I recognize that there is some difference of opinion on this point.
3. A few nonrelevant details have been altered in these histories to maintain anonymity.
4. *The Tragedy of Julius Caesar;* Act IV, Scene iii, Lines 274-280.
5. Charles Dickens, *A Christmas Carol;* Walter J. Black, 1932; p. 16.

12. ALTERNATIVES TO DISEN-GAGEMENT: THE OLD MEN OF THE HIGHLAND DRUZE

DAVID L. GUTMANN

David L. Gutmann is Professor of Psychology, University of Michigan. Reprinted with permission from *Later Life: Readings in the Sociology of Aging Situations and Roles,* Jaber F. Gubrium, editor, Charles C. Thomas, Publisher, Springfield, Illinois.

THIS PAPER REPORTS some recent results, based on data from the middle aged and older men of the Druze sect resident in highland villages of the Golan, Galilee and Carmel regions of Syria and Israel. The overall aim of the research of which this study is a part has been to establish, through application of the comparative method, some basis for a developmental psychology of aging. Generally, the research program has involved intensive interviewing and projective testing of younger (aged 35-54) and older (aged 55+) men of traditional and usually preliterate societies—the Lowland and Highland Maya of Mexico, the traditional or Western Navajo, and the Druze of Israel (including the Golan Heights).[1] These societies differ from each other in language, ethnic composition, the content of culture, and physical environment. They are alike in that they are composed of marginal agriculturalists, dwelling in relatively remote communities, who hold to their traditional life ways. Given their traditional orientation, these societies tend to be culturally homogeneous across the generations, and the pace of social change is fairly slow. Accordingly, if the data analysis turns up standard differences in psychological functioning between the younger and older men of such societies, the variation can be imputed

to intrinsic and developmental, rather than extrinsic social influences. The guiding hypothesis of this research program was originally developed from findings in an urban United States sample. Briefly stated, it holds that important psychological orientations, based around passivity and aggressivity, dependence and autonomy would discriminate age groups within culturally homogeneous societies—in effect, that these orientations would distribute more reliably by age than by culture. Accordingly, it was proposed that younger men across cultures would reveal motives, attitudes, and images characteristic of an active, production centered, and competitive stance, while older men were expected to show the converse pattern. They would give priority to community over agency, to receptivity over productivity, to mildness and humility over competition. The predicted age shift then is from the mode of *Active Mastery* in younger men, to the mode of *Passive Mastery* in older men. It was further expected that the oldest men of the various samples, those aged 65 and over, would protect their retreat from action, and maintain their tenuous sense of security in the face of oncoming death through a reliance on *Magical Mastery*, a conformation based on the primitive, reality-distorting defenses of denial and projection. Thus far, the hypothesis has been borne out, by both cross-sectional and longitudinal data from the United States, Mexican, and Middle Eastern study sites (see Gutmann 1964, 1966, 1967, 1969; Krohn and Gutmann 1971; Goldstine and Gutmann 1972). Though the societies surveyed vary in the degree to which they emphasize or sponsor Active, Passive or Magical Mastery as a dominant mode, there is in all cases an age shift away from Active Mastery and towards the Passive and/or Magical orientations. Thus, despite profound cultural differences in our samples, age accounts for a greater part of the variance in the personality measures than does the variable of culture; and this independent age effect points to the contribution of intrinsic, or *developmental* influences to the psychology of aging men.

NATURE AND NURTURE: THEIR IMPACT IN LATER LIFE

But the finding of intrinsic age related influences does not rule out the socio-cultural influence over the psychic life. Men who are partly shaped by intrinsic processes must still find the setting for their development in socially organized worlds; and they are continually influenced by the age norms set by society over their behaviors and attitudes. Covert, universal influences do not make men *less* sensitive to overt social influences, but only direct that sensitivity to particular subsets of the available social norms, usages, understandings. Thus, younger men might recognize the existence of a religious tradition in their society, and be knowledgeable about its precepts, but their subjective relation to that tradition would differ

from their father's. The younger men could report—as anthropological informants, for example—on the rules of the religious tradition, but they would not always refer to them for regulation of their behavior. By the same token, the aging fathers of these young men, would know a good deal about the social usages that governed the productive life in their society, but would find these less personally relevant than those which organized the religious life, and the relationship to God. Thus, owing to the influence of emerging developmental dispositions, older men would give personal reality to social norms and conventions which had far less impact for them when they were younger.

The nature versus nurture issue is perhaps the central question in the behavioral sciences, and cannot be put to rest by a single study. Nevertheless, the case of the Highland Druze of the Middle East suggests an integrating model: it suggests the ways in which age-graded role requirements and developmental potentials can coexist, as reciprocals and metaphors of each other, in the traditional community. This discussion begins with a necessarily brief description of Druze history, culture, and modal personality.[2]

THE HIGHLAND DRUZE

The villages of the Druze, sited for defense, are scattered through the highland regions of Lebanon, Syria, and Galilean Israel. The Druze people are mainly agriculturalists, involved in the cultivation of fruits, olives, wheat, and tobacco. However, throughout their history, individual Druze have been prominent in the political and particularly in the military affairs of the Middle East. The Druze are a people who chose a minority status, on religious grounds, within the larger Arab world. They speak Arabic, and their life style is in most respects similar to that of the patriarchal Muslim villagers of the Levant. However, the Druze broke with the Muslim religion on doctrinal points, and thereby let themselves in for the difficulties that go with self-elected minority status. Over the past 800 years the Druze have suffered many episodes of religious persecution at the hands of the Muslim majority; and they have managed to develop the personal and cultural traits that generally characterize a minority that survives in the face of odds. Since they could not take the goodwill of the majority for granted, they have learned as a group to mainly trust themselves—the courage, strength, and wit of the Druze people. Each individual Druze tends to reproduce in his personality the general stance of the culture. Thus, individual Druze are fiercely self-reliant, and will only allow themselves to depend on their own strengths, or on resources that they themselves have cultivated—the produce of their fields, or the strength of their sons. In effect, they trust very little that comes from outside of themselves as gift or gratuity, and this mistrust of that which is not under self-control extends even to their mental life. Thus, the Druze are extremely stubborn and refractory as individuals, not only against coercion from other's will, but against coercion from their *own* willfulness, their own spontaneous emotions. They do not allow themselves to become excited; even illiterate Druze peasants give priority to rationality over emotionality. In effect, they value the mental resource that they have created for themselves over the emotions that have been "foisted" on them. As part of their self-reliance, they must deny any needfulness, and must hold themselves in the position of the giver, rather than the receiver. Thus, they are unfailingly and sometimes even aggressively hospitable.

A major political problem for the Druze is the coordination of their own community life, centered as it is around their religion, with the requirements and demands of the non-Druze majority, which has frequently been hostile to their faith. Over the centuries they have learned to blend flexibility and accommodation with firmness and traditional rigidity. In effect, they change and compromise in minor ways which do not touch on the core of their religious tradition, in order to maintain that same core inviolate and unchanged. Thus, they typically raise their sons to be career soldiers and policemen for the majority government—in effect, they trade their sons for political security —and they are usually meticulously loyal to the letter of the secular law. But they will not tolerate any violation, by the non-Druze majority, of the core of their religion or their tradition. They will not for example tolerate any attack on the honor of their women or of their priests. If compliance does not succeed in starving off dishonor and sacrilege, then the Druze will, almost to the last man, go to war. Though their villages have always been scattered over different countries, the Druze say to themselves that they are like a large brass plate: "strike one corner, then the whole will vibrate." True to this motto, the Druze led the post-World War I revolution against the French which gave rise to the establishment of modern Syria. They are famous throughout the Middle East for their ardor in battle.

DRUZE AGE ROLES

Since the Druze people form a religious sect, their religion is central to the workings of their society and to the sense of Druze identity. Yet it is kept a secret, not only from the outside world, but also from Druze women and from the younger men of the community. Thus, the schedules which govern admission to the inner circles of the Druze religion also determine the age-grade systems, the social norms and shared understandings which partially order the latter half of the life cycle for the typical Druze male. The Druze have learned to treat their heretic religion as a kind of conspiracy within the body of Islam; therefore, the younger Druze—who might rashly reveal their identity to non-Druze neighbors—are not instructed in the religion or even told that they are Druze until they reach the age of discretion. This tradition of keeping the religion secret from the younger members of the community has survived even until these more liberal times. Thus, younger Druze men, those not yet initiated to the secret books, are known as *Jahil,* the "unknowing" ones. The older men, those who have been accepted into the religious society, and who have received their copy of the secret text, are known as *Aqil,* literally, those who "know." In the more traditional villages some men might become *Aqil* in early middle age, after they have established their family of procreation, and there are even a few *Aqil* youths, seminary-trained sons of famous religious leaders. But for the most part, men are not invited to become *Aqil* until late middle age, after they have led an exemplary life. As noted earlier, Druze men of any age are generally formal and punctilious, but this manner is intensified after a man becomes *Aqil.* He shaves his head, he adopts special garb, and there is a notable behavior shift toward even greater propriety. Furthermore, he gives up alcohol and tobacco, he devotes much time to prayers, and he is expected to appear at all important social functions. Even the inner life of the *Aqil* is regulated: he is expected to devote himself to good and pious thoughts and to forget the errors and stupidities of his life before he was introduced to true knowledge. It is therefore very difficult to interview an old *Aqil* concerning his childhood experiences. He becomes remote or evasive, and at times angry: "Why do you ask me about the time when I was ignorant, before I became close to God? I was like an animal then, I did not think of God, and it is a shame to remember such things!"

In sum, the old *Aqil* purge themselves, consciously at least, of the appetites—and even the memories of the appetites—which do not fit the prescriptions of the religious life. In effect, as the typical Druze man passes into late middle life and old age he appears to shunt into the behavioral and attitudinal tracks that have been prepared for him by the age-grade system of Druze society. His life appears to be almost completely governed by parochial requirements of the sort that have meaning only to the religious Druze.

UNIVERSAL TRENDS IN DRUZE AGING

However, the projective data from

these same Druze men suggests that their inner, subjective life changes in later years in accord with universal developments as well as with extrinsic, parochial constraints. These data indicate a pattern of psychological changes that is in conformity with those observed in their age peers from radically different cultures, where older men do *not* necessarily enter a rigorous religious subculture. The comparative analysis of the Druze projective materials, between age cohorts and across cultures, supports the hypothesis of universal psychological patterns in aging, developments which are mandatory regardless of the requirements set by particular cultures.

Thus, if we inspect Table 12.1, and compare the age *x* theme distribution of Druze responses to the rope climber card of the TAT[3]—a card used in its original form at all sites—we find that this distribution replicates that developed by the same card among the younger and older men of the Mayan (both Highland and Lowland), the Navajo and the United States cultures. The younger men, whether urban American, Navajo, Mayan or Druze tend to interpret this stimulus in those ways—listed in categories 1 and 2—which reflect the various components (competitive, rebellious and productive) of the Active Mastery orientation. For them, the rope climber competes against other climbers, trains for future contests or escapes from prison (category 1); if the hero is seen to be in danger, it is a risk that he has incurred for himself, by virtue of his own initiative, or boldness. While substantial numbers of older men continue to see the climber in active ways, he is no longer seen by them as an aggressive figure. For them—as the category 2 age totals indicate—the hero might struggle

against physical nature, or against his own weakness, but he does not struggle against society, or against other men. The shift from aggressive interpretations of the rope climber among older men is matched by their notably greater tendency to see in him the expressions of Passive Mastery. Thus, he is relaxed and pleasure-seeking (category 3); or, he is menaced—either by his own fatigue and weakness, or by the superior strength of some external agent, such as a human enemy, beast, or fire (category 4). In addition, older men, including older Druze, far outweigh younger men in their use of Magical Mastery—represented by images of the rope climber as dead, asleep or penetrated by a spear (category 5).

Equivalent age differences in the distribution of Active, Passive and Magical perceptions are developed by the heterosexual-conflict card of the standard TAT. The card depicts a young woman reaching towards a young man who is turned away from her. Again, as shown in Table 12.2, younger Druze, like the younger men of other societies, see in the male figure a representation of Active Mastery. For them, he is impelled out of the picture by his own intrinsic energy, on some *macho* mission: he is fighting a man who has insulted his woman; he is going to work; he has a more desirable woman (category 1). For the younger men, sex roles are sharply distinguished. If there is concern about the possibly dangerous consequences of the young man's assertive behavior, then that concern is lodged in the timorous woman; the young man is all restlessness and fire. But the older Druze, like other old men, shape their perceptions of these figures in keeping with Passive Mastery principles. For them, the

TABLE 12.1

DISTRIBUTION OF RESPONSES TO THE ROPE CLIMBER CARD,
BY AGE, CULTURE AND THEME

		35-49		50-59		60+	
1. The climber demonstrates his strength, often in the face of competition. However, triumph has its price: the rope may break at the moment of victory.	Kansas City	21		35		10	
	Navajo	5		1		6	
	Lowland Maya	3	42*	2	43	2	25
	Highland Maya	2		0		1	
	Druze	11		5		6	
2. The climber acts in the service of relatively limited but productive goals: he searches for a short-cut, for food, or for herds. He trains for future competition. If he is thwarted, it is by the physical environment, and not by other men, or by his own weakness.	Kansas City	4		13		7	
	Navajo	6		7		10	
	Lowland Maya	9	43	2	42	2	43
	Highland Maya	3		1		1	
	Druze	21		19		23	
3. The climber indulges his physical weakness, or his wish for pleasure: he rests, he enjoys the view, he dives into water, he plays on the rope.	Kansas City	2		3		7	
	Navajo	3		4		12	
	Lowland Maya	3	13	5	20	14	41
	Highland Maya	4		7		7	
	Druze	1		1		1	
4. The climber is menaced by external forces, or by his own weakness: he flees from enemy, beast or fire; he is too tired to climb, and clings to the rope; he is on a rope, but not in motion.	Kansas City	4		18		17	
	Navajo	4		5		16	
	Lowland Maya	3	24	6	35	8	59
	Highland Maya	5		2		6	
	Druze	8		4		12	
5. Either the rope or the climber is grossly misperceived: the climber is lying down, or dead; the rope is a snake, etc.	Kansas City	—		—		2	
	Navajo	—		—		3	
	Lowland Maya	—	3	1	2	2	22
	Highland Maya	1		1		1	
	Druze	2		—		14	
		125		142		190	

Kansas City	N = 143	Highland Maya	N = 42
Navajo	N = 82	Druze**	N = 128
Lowland Maya	N = 62	Total	N = 457

* Chi Square (of cell totals) = 48.712
 DF = 8, P < .001
** Druze Group includes Golan, (Syrian) Galilean and Carmel (Israeli) subjects.

TABLE 12.2
THE HETEROSEXUAL-CONFLICT CARD: DISTRIBUTION OF STORIES BY AGE, CULTURE AND THEME

		35-49		50-59		60+	
1. Male initiative and dominance: Young man's intrinsic sex, aggression and autonomy needs constitute a problem for a gentle, nurturant young woman, and potential danger for himself.	Kansas City	21		12		10	
	Navajo	9		7		9	
	Lowland Maya	4	56*	1	33	2	28
	Highland Maya	2		—		—	
	Druze	20		13		7	
2. Domestic problems: Problem centered around young man's aggression; but direction, scope, nature of cause, or outcome of this aggression is unclear.	Kansas City	1		3		—	
	Navajo	4		4		4	
	Lowland Maya	7	20	5	22	7	20
	Highland Maya	—		2		1	
	Druze	8		8		8	
3. Female initiatives and dominance: Young man's anger is reactive to young woman's rejection of him, or dominance over him.	Kansas City	6		5		6	
	Navajo	—		3		9	
	Lowland Maya	—	14	—	13	2	27
	Highland Maya	3		1		2	
	Druze	5		4		8	
4. Rationalized male succorance: Menaced by external forces, or defeated in his outer-world achievement strivings, the young man looks for or accepts female nurturance and control.	Kansas City	—		1		4	
	Navajo	—		1		12	
	Lowland Maya	—	19	1	8	2	42
	Highland Maya	1		—		2	
	Druze	18		5		22	
5. Untroubled Affiliation (or Syntonic Dependency): mild, untroubled affiliation between relatively undifferentiated young man and woman.	Kansas City	—		—		—	
	Navajo	1		6		6	
	Lowland Maya	3	23	7	25	12	53
	Highland Maya	8		3		3	
	Druze	11		9		32	
	N =	132		101		170	

Kansas City	N = 69	Highland Maya	N = 28
Navajo	N = 75	Druze**	N = 178
Lowland Maya	N = 53	Total	N = 403

* Chi Square (of cell totals) = 42.165, DF = 8, p < .001
** Druze group includes Golan, (Syrian) Galilean and Carmel (Israeli) Druze.

younger woman becomes the dominant, initiating figure (category 3); or, impelled by sickness or fear the young man woves back "into" the picture, to find comfort in the young woman's arms; or, the man and woman look out, with equal apprehension toward some menacing agent not visible in the picture (category 4). Finally, the oldest men tend to deny the aspect of conflict, either between the man and woman, or between the couple and the world, and depict instead a mildly affectionate unisex couple, alike as to their qualities and feelings for each other (category 5). Again, as with the rope climber card,

younger men locate energy and assertion within the figure, older men locate it in the environment, and the oldest men overlook or deny it altogether.

The transcultural age trends elicited by the rope-climber and heterosexual-conflict cards hold for the majority of TAT cards used at all sites. However, despite the relative thematic unanimity among age-peers of different societies, the criticism has been raised that such age differences in card interpretation reflect cohort differences between generations, rather than intra-individual, developmental shifts. However, longitudinal studies

TABLE 12.3

LONGITUDINAL CHANGES IN TAT IMAGERY OF NAVAJO AND DRUZE SUBJECTS, ELICITED BY THE ROPE CLIMBER CARD

	No. of passive images discarded in favor of more active imagery after Time 1*			No. of passive images appearing only at Time 2		
	Navajo	Druze	total	Navajo	Druze	total
Climber's activity is discredited; he does some evil or crazy thing.	2	2	4	6	3	9
Climber descends on the rope.	8	1	9	13	3	16
Climber flees from beast, fire, flood, or enemy	1	1	2	9	4	13
Tired climber, unable to ascend, clutches the rope	2	1	3	3	4	7
Menaced by external threats, or by his own weariness, the climber looks for help	3	2	5	6	4	10
The climber is dead, sick or crippled	—	1	1	4	—	4
The climber seeks pleasure: he looks at pleasant scenes, or plays on the rope.	4	1	5	7	4	11
	Total no. of passive images discarded by Time 2 29			Total no. of new passive images by Time 2 ....70**		

* Time 1 — Time 2 interval is four years in the Navajo case, and five years in the Druze case. The Galilean and Carmel Druze, but not the Golan Druze, were re-interviewed for the Time 2 study.

** *Note:* These are not independent entries: A single story may be entered under more than one heading.

undertaken with both Navajo and Druze subjects indicate that variations over five year intervals in card perceptions *within* individuals replicate those already found between age cohorts in both these societies. Thus, when we contrast the time 1 and time 2 perceptions of the same individuals to the same cards (see Tables 12.3 and 12.4) we find the predicted appearance of more passive or magical imagery at time 2 in a significant percentage of all subjects. Navajo or Druze men who saw the rope climber as moving vigorously for some productive purpose at time 1 may see him clinging anxiously to that same rope at time 2, or as fleeing from some wild beast. By the same token, subjects who saw the young man of the heterosexual-conflict card in some active role at time 1 have in many cases by time 2 come to see him as more subdued, as dominated by his wife, or as gravely ill. Clearly, the statistically significant age differences that we have been picking up across cultures appear to be the artifacts of developmental change in later life, rather than socially induced differences between generations.

TABLE 12.4

LONGITUDINAL CHANGES IN TAT IMAGERY OF NAVAJO AND DRUZE SUBJECTS ELICITED BY THE HETEROSEXUAL-CONFLICT CARD

	No. of passive images discarded in favor of more active imagery after Time 1**			No. of passive images appearing only at Time 2		
	Navajo	Druze	total	Navajo	Druze	total
Male aggression is in reaction to female dominance	3	1	4	8	3	11
Man is inactive; woman is active and/or dominant	2	2	4	4	7	11
Man and woman both look at troubling or pleasant scene	3	2	5	5	7	12
Man is sick; woman is his nurse, or is concerned about him	1	3	4	6	4	10
Man is tired, or old (woman may be his daughter)	1	2	3	2	5	7
Man and woman like or love each other. No conflict or role distinctions	1	9**	10	8	4	12

Total no. of passive images discarded by Time 2 ...30   Total no. of new passive images by Time 2 ..63***

* Time 1 — Time 2 interval is four years in the Navajo case, and five years in the Druze case. The Galilean and Carmel Druze, but not the Golan Druze, were reinterviewed for the Time 2 study.
** ⅔ of the Druze reversals in this category towards more "active" imagery occur among men younger than age 65; ¾ of the new perceptions of an affiliative and un-differentiated couple occur in men aged 65 and over.
*** *Note:* These are not independent entries. A single story may be entered under more than one heading.

THE SOCIAL AND THE PERSONAL IN DRUZE RELIGIOUS LIFE

If the passive leanings that emerge openly in the TAT protocols of elderly Druze are universal in scope, we can argue that they should also be powerful; they should have a peremptory effect on behavior. Yet, as noted earlier, at least the public behavior of the older *Aqil* seems to be completely ordered by his local culture, and not by some species-wide undertow towards passivity. When we look at the conventional behavior of the religious man, we find him going busily from place to place, from one ceremonial visit to another; praying, or receiving guests with elaborate hospitality. In his social relations he is not submissive, but even dogmatic and dictatorial, laying down the law to his younger relations. Within the framework of the religious life the older *Aqil* seems to behave in an active rather than a passive fashion.

When we ask the *Aqil* what he *does* as a religious man, he describes an energetic life. However, when we ask him about the *meaning* that the religious life holds for him, when we ask about his *subjective* relation to the religious life, and to God, we get a different picture. It is at this level that the passive yearnings inferred from the TAT seem to make their appearance, and it is at this point that the *Aqil* resembles his overtly passive age-peers in other societies, and not only his Druze coreligionists. When they talk about their relationship to Allah, fierce, patriarchal old Druze, who dominate their grown sons will adopt completely the posture and the tone of the passive, self-effacing supplicant: "Allah is all and I am nothing; I live only in his will, and by his will . . I do not question his will . . I do not complain about my illness, because this is from God; and to complain about my illness is to question God . ." . . . These older men are *not* playing back the prescription for conventional religious behavior: when we ask young *Aqil* about the meaning of the religious life, they tell us that their task is to seek out sinners, to correct their ways, and through this action to make the village acceptable in the eyes of God. In effect, the younger *Aqil* are social workers for God; their relationship to Allah is mediated by their *action* in his service.

It is only among the old *Aqil* that we get the sense of a direct and personal relation to Allah, mediated not by work, but by supplication and prayer. Allah is for them an intensely felt and loving presence: as they talk of God their eyes shine, and the voices of these old patriarchs tremble with emotion. They become not unlike the stereotype of a submissive woman speaking fearfully and yearningly of her master. There are no rules in Druze society that tell young *Aqil* to have a relation to Allah that is centered on their own action, and for older men to have a relationship that is centered on the power and actions of that same Allah. Clearly, there is a range of permissible postures towards Allah available to the Druze, regardless of age, but each age-cohort finds certain stances within this range more congenial than others. The younger *Aqil* define a relationship to Allah that is in conformity with the principles of Active Mastery, while older *Aqil* enact the themes of Passive Mastery, and these age preferences reflect intrinsic rather than social coercion. Evidently then, the religious role allows the passive strivings noted in the older man's TAT to find their dramatic expression, and their outlet.

This example illustrates the relatively seamless fit that often exists between particular roles and psychic potentials that are developmental in nature in the traditional community. As we have seen, the older Druze shares with his age peers in other societies the tendency toward what might be called the normal bisexuality of later life. However, in his case he does not need to make some final and conflictful choice between active and passive, "masculine" and "feminine" relational styles. The traditional religious sector of society provides a particular psychosocial niche in which he can live out passive and even "feminine" strivings, while he continues to domineer his sons. Thus, the religious role requires and gives definition to those psychic potentials which are released by the older man's withdrawal from the active tasks of parenthood and production. The yearnings that men in secular societies might experience in the form of neurotic symptoms, the old traditional Druze experiences as his worshipful linkage to God.

THE SOCIAL UTILITY OF PASSIVE MASTERY

While the religious role fits the special needs of older men, their tendencies towards mildness and accommodation are particularly fitted to the requirements of the religious role. In the preliterate mind, life-sustaining vitality or power does not originate in the mundane, everyday world. Life-sustaining power has its ultimate origin in supernatural, extracommunal sources—in the spirits of ancestral dead, in totemic animals, in enemy, and particularly in the Gods. The particular source of power varies by cultural prescription, but the idea that the prosaic world is kept real and vital by power imported from the supernaturals is general across the preliterate world. Wherever this world view is institutionalized specially anointed figures are required to live on the interface between the mundane and supernatural worlds, so as to "attract" the benevolent aspect of supernatural power, to contain it, and to make it available to the life forms of the community and its ecosystem. Roheim (1930) has cited a large body of data from preliterate societies to document the point that this "transformer" or "power-Bringer" role is enacted through submissive and even masochistic behavior: across cultures the Gods mainly give power to those who approach them humbly and sometimes even in the guise of women. Thus, in the religious community it is the older men, the potential reservoir of humility and receptivity, and not the Promethean, competitive young men who can draw good influences from the gods, for the benefit of the community, and without offending the divinity. In this case the office does not create the worshipful old man; he —in common with old men of less traditional, less prayerful societies— has ego potentials that are reciprocal to the prayerful role; and so the office seeks him.

In sum, in the traditional society as exemplified by the Druze, the potentially destructive passivity of the older man is reformed, through the religious role, into a vehicle of social power. The old man's emerging humility and submissiveness fits him to live on the dangerous interface between the gods and the mundane community, and, through his prayers, to bring life-sustaining forces into the community, so as to maintain and increase children, flocks, and crops. The passivity that could lead to vulnerability, depression, and psychosomatic illness in other settings becomes in the traditional society the very core and pivot of the older man's social prestige and personal identity.[4]

DISENGAGEMENT OR ROLE TRANSITION?

The theory of later life disengagement put forward by Cuming and Henry (1961) is perhaps the most important conception in the social psychology of aging. In essence, it proposes a mutual disengagement whereby the agencies of society withdraw their attention from the aged, and the aged withdraw from society's normative restraints, to become more idiosyncratic, but also more "liberated." Though the theory was developed exclusively from United States urban studies, and was not tested cross-culturally, the authors claim that disengagement is both mandatory, and universal.[5] As such, disengagement is a developmental event; the older person who sets himself to oppose this dictate of nature is fighting a losing battle, and may even do so at his peril.

Cumming and Henry partly justify the case for a developmental (hence universal) underpinning to disengagement by relating this process to another presumably developmental event —the later-life emergence of passive ego states. Thus, various associates of Cumming and Henry (the present author among them) scored the TAT protocols from their United States subjects on various indicators of the passive state, and found that older subjects scored consistently higher on these: they were more likely than younger subjects to introduce Passive Mastery themes into their stories, they were less likely to infuse stimulus figures with assertive energy or emotional intensity, and they were less likely to introduce outside figures or conflict possibilities (1961, Chap. 6). Since the age trend towards TAT metaphors of passivity matched the age trend on other social barometers towards disengagement in the study population, Cumming and Henry concluded that the two trends were linked into one developmental event, such that he increased passivity of later life represented the inner, subjective correlate of the total disengagement process.

However, the case of the Druze *Aqil* indicates that disengagement need not be compulsory, and it particularly demonstrates that passivity is not inextricably tied to disengagement. Quite the contrary: in the Druze case—and probably in the case of other traditional folk societies with a strong religious orientation—the so-called passivity of the older man can be the central, *necessary* component of his engagement with age appropriate social roles, traditions, and associated normative controls. Clearly, the older Druze *Aqil* switches his allegiance from the norms that govern the productive and secular-productive life to those which govern the traditional and moral life, but in this transition he does not stray from the influence of normative controls as such. If anything, they gain increased influence over him. The older Druze may detach his interest and allegiance from those social codes which are no longer congenial to his passive needs, but he certainly does not detach himself from society per se. Rather, he links himself subjectively to the religious dimension of his society, and in so doing plays out the theme of Passive Mastery— the need to be in personal touch with a powerful, benevolent, and productive agent. He relinquishes his own productivity, but not productivity per se. Instead of being the center of enterprise, he is now the bridge between the community and the productive, life sustaining potencies of Allah. The old *Aqil* now carries forward the moral rather than the material work of the community. Thus, guided by needs and sensibilities which reflect his emerging passivity, the older Druze transits from one normative order to another *within* society; in that transition he becomes, quite completely, the instrument and the representation of the traditional moral order that he has adopted and that has adopted him.

Incidentally, what is true for the Druze is also in general true for the men of other tradition oriented societies. As Simmons (1945) reports in the *Role of the Aged in Primitive Society* the traditional elders of pre-literate groups do not usually disengage from the social order and its normative prescriptions; on the contrary, they often become the interpreters and administrators of the *moral* sector of society. They become the norm bearers. Thus, the disengagement that Cumming and Henry found in our society does not generalize all versions of the human condition; it is the exception rather than the rule. The disengagement that Cumming and Henry found is only the first step in a total process of *transition,* a process that can reach its natural terminus in a traditional society, but that is interrupted or aborted in a secular society. Thus, it may well be that disengagement is only an artifact of secular society, which does not offer the old man a moral order, based on tradition, to relate to once he has decoupled from those social norms which regulate the parental and productive life periods.

In sum, it is the movement towards Passive and Magical Mastery that appears to be universal, and not the movement towards disengagement. The inner, subjective shift appears now to be transcultural: but it does not necessarily lead to disengagement. The Druze case shows that the inexorable psychic developments of later life are not necessarily a prelude to social withdrawal and physical death; given a society which recognizes the emerging dispositions, values them, and gives them role articulation, the so-called passivity of later life can provide the ground for a later life revival, for a kind of social rebirth.

NOTES

1. The overall program of cross-cultural research has been supported by Career Development Award No. 5-K3-Hd-6043 from the National Institutes of Child Health and Human Development. Field expenses for Indian studies in Mexico and America were covered by Faculty Research Grants Nos. 1344 and 1412 from the Rackham School of Graduate Studies, the University of Michigan, and by Grant No. MH 13031-01 from the National Institutes of Mental Health. Field work expenses among the Druze were covered by Grant No. M66-345 from the Foundation's Fund for Research in Psychiatry.
2. The Druze study reported here would have been impossible were it not for the friendship and dedicated help of Mr. Kassem Y. Kassem, a Druze social worker,

and resident of the Galilean village of Rami, who worked closely with me during three field trips among his people. The entire Kassem family extended me their help and hospitality on these occasions, and this too is most gratefully acknowledged.

3. The Rope Climber card, card 17BM of the standard Murray Thematic Apperception Test, shows a muscular man, possibly clad in tight-fitting gymnast's clothing, in the position of one who either climbs or descends a rope—the card is ambiguous as to the direction of movement.

4. We should not be surprised by this finding in the Druze community, namely, that the emergent propensities of later life mortise, in the traditional society, into those age specific roles that both require them, and that sponsor their further development, as identity resources. By far the longest period of human species existence was passed in isolate, preliterate, traditionally oriented communities. These were the species specific settings in which human characteristics—particularly, those ego executive capacities that organize personal-communal relationships— evolved. Thus, the personal-social integrations that we find among older traditionals are not accidental, and they were, in human prehistory, the rule rather than the exception. They may register a process of interlocking evolution that over the millenia selected for viable human traits and for viabl institutions—for roles and conventions that lifted crude human potentials to the level of communication and social utility. Thus, the study of the old traditionals may constitute a kind of social archaeology: they may reveal to us the close, almost umbilical articulation between man and the folk community that was once the general human condition.

5. The authors state: "This theory is intended to apply to the aging process in all societies, although the initiation of the process may vary from culture to culture, as may the pattern of the process itself. For example, in those traditional cultures in which the old are valued for their wisdom, it may well be that the aging person openly initiates the process; in primitive, and especially in impoverished cultures, he may resist the process until it is forced upon him" (1961, p. 17).

REFERENCES

Cumming, E., and W. E. Henry
   1961   *Growing Old: The Process of Disengagement.* New York: Basic Books.
Goldstine, T., and D. Gutmann
   1972   A TAT study of Navajo aging. *Psychiatry* 35: 373-384.
Gutmann, D.
   1964   An exploration of ego configurations in middle and later life. *In* B. Neugarten (ed.), *Personality in Middle and Later Life.* New York: Atherton.
   1966   Mayan aging—A comparative TAT study. *Psychiatry* 29: 246-259.
   1967   Aging among the Highland Maya: A comparative study. *Journal of Personality and Social Psychology* (1, pt. 1): 28-35.
   1969   The country of old men: Cross-cultural studies in the psychology of later life. *In* W. Donahue (ed.), *Occasional Papers in Gerontology,* Ann Arbor, Institute of Gerontology, University of Michigan.
Krohn, A., and D. Gutmann
   1971   Changes in mastery style with age: A study of Navajo dreams. *Psychiatry* 34: 289-300.
Róheim, G.
   1930   *Animism, Magic and the Divine King.* London: Kegan Paul.
Simmons, L. W.
   1945   *The Role of the Aged in Primitive Society.* New Haven: Yale University Press.

III. CULTURAL INFLUENCE IN INDIVIDUAL EXPERIENCE: EMIC VIEWS OF NORMAL AND ABNORMAL BEHAVIOR

TWENTIETH CENTURY SOCIAL anthropology is profoundly relativistic in theory and method. It assumes that different cultures represent radically divergent views of what is true, good, and beautiful, and its ethnographic procedures require the investigator to adopt the point of view of those whose culture is being studied in order to understand it and attempt a description. Nothing is more characteristic of anthropological field work than this effort at taking the insider's viewpoint, understanding his culture as he understands it. Recent decades have seen many attempts at systematizing this procedure, most notably in formal semantic analysis and other linguistically based methods designed to develop a cultural phenomenology that reduces the subjective content of culture to objective, or at least translatable, data.

Out of the controversies over these cultural phenomenologies have come several lasting effects for the study of culture and personality. One is the sensitivity to the distinction between *emic* approaches that use the insider's cultural categories for description of belief and behavior, and *etic* approaches that use a single, presumably universal, set of categories for describing belief and behavior everywhere regardless of culture. In the past, psychological comparisons of culturally differing populations were often naively etic, ignoring the differential effects of cultural meaning contexts on response to psychological tests or assessments of psychopathology. It is now recognized, however—in cross-cultural psychology as well as culture and personality research—that if etic categories are to be

247

used they must be shown to have roughly equivalent meanings in the cultures being compared. Another consequence of the interest in systematizing cultural phenomenology is the development of *ethnopsychology* and *ethnopsychiatry* as topics of semantic exploration parallel to other domains of ethnoscience (the study of folk nomenclature, belief, and conceptualization in areas of knowledge for which Western science has developed concepts). Ethnopsychology refers to folk categories and beliefs about individual behavior and mental processes; ethnopsychiatry means folk systems of diagnosis and treatment of mental disorder. They are not clearly differentiated from each other, nor—in many cultural contexts— from cultural systems of religion and medicine, but since they are significantly involved in how individuals think about their own behavior and experience, they have a special importance in the comparative study of personality.

The readings in this section represent the special importance of an emic perspective on understanding psychological functioning in differing cultures. These works are derived not from formal semantic analysis or ethnoscience but from the psycho-cultural relativism characterizing the culture and personality field from its beginning; their sensitivity to cultural categories in the processing of individual experience nevertheless approximates that of ethnopsychology and ethnopsychiatry. They show by illustration how cultural categories penetrate the innermost thoughts and feelings of the individual, giving cognitive organization to his subjective experience of affects and altered states of consciousness, involving themselves in his response to stress, and providing cognitive material for the defensive system of ideas by which he maintains his sense of well-being.

These selections address themselves in a distinctively anthropological manner to a central issue in culture and personality: to what extent does culture, which is a set of institutionalized ideas and rules, dominate intrapsychic function and malfunction in the individual organism? Each of the authors is convinced that, beginning in early life, individuals make their culture's categories part of their own system of inner regulations, adopting the language of the cultural system for their private fantasies, motives, and ideals. In normal and abnormal functioning, they are seen to be products of their enculturation.

13. THE VOCABULARY OF EMOTION: A STUDY OF JAVANESE SOCIALIZATION PROCESSES

HILDRED GEERTZ

Hildred Geertz is Associate Professor of Anthropology, Princeton University. Reprinted by special permission of The William Alanson White Psychiatric Foundation, Inc., from *Psychiatry* (1959) 22: 225-237. Copyright © The William Alanson White Psychiatric Foundation.

EVERY CULTURAL SYSTEM includes patterned ideas regarding certain interpersonal relationships and certain affective states, which represent a selection from the entire potential range of interpersonal and emotional experiences. The child, growing up within the culture and gradually internalizing these premises, undergoes a process of socially guided emotional specialization. He learns, in a sense, a special vocabulary of emotion. This paper will examine a set of Javanese ideas regarding those interpersonal relationships which involve status differences and the emotional states considered appropriate to them.

Discussions of the processes of socialization often stress that the significant element in the child's experience is not the actual child-training procedures themselves, so much as the *meaning* that the adults in the child's world give to these procedures. What is important is the message that is transmitted to the child by means of these nonverbal and verbal communicative actions (see, for example, Erikson 1950, p. 121; Hartmann et al. 1951, p. 26; Benedict 1949; Mead 1949). This formulation of the socialization process as communication suggests that a phenomenological approach to the learning of feeling-states or emotions in a particular culture could throw considerable light on the whole process by which a merely human infant becomes transformed into an adult of a specific culture. Such an examination of the symbolic meaning of the acts of adults toward the child should be supplemented with an analysis of the steps by which the child gains comprehension and internalization of this message, steps which are governed, in their timing and also their significance, by the stages of psychophysical maturation through which he passes.

The range and quality of emotional experience is potentially the same for all human beings: such terms as anxiety or hostility, insofar as they are operationally defined in terms of a scientific theory of personality, refer to basically human—that is, universal—emotions. In the course of the growth of a given person, this potential range of emotional experience becomes narrowed, and out of it certain qualitative aspects are socially selected, elaborated, and emphasized. In the process of interaction with a group of bearers of a particular culture, the child builds up a specific view of himself and of his feelings toward himself and others. The adults around him provide not only the situation for his learning about himself and his world, but also definitions and interpretations of this situation, and conceptualizations of their feelings and his feelings within it. This aspect of the child's learning, this progressive narrowing of perceptions of situation, self, and feeling-states, can be a key to the understanding of personality differences found between members of different cultures.

While the subject for analysis in this paper is specifically the Javanese cultural premises regarding status and respect, a comparable analysis might be made of any of the other premises of the culture. Status is, however, one of the central elements in the patterning of Javanese culture, and hence a significant aspect of the growing child's experience and of the Javanese adult's interpretation of the meaning of that experience. For a Javanese nearly every social relationship involves an element of status difference, which is qualitatively similar whether the relationship is between king and subject, village headman and villager, teacher and student, or father and son. Further, a Javanese perceives such status situations in terms of special, accepted definitions of the "respect" called for and the kinds of feeling-states thought to be appropriate.

The process of socialization of the Javanese child—or perhaps more accurately here, his "Javanization"—can be seen in terms of the ways in which these particular ideas are communicated to the child, the timing, social context, and method of transmission of these premises. An examination of the sequence of experiences of the Javanese in learning these ideas suggests that they are not only significant aspects of Javanese culture but also internalized elements in the personalities of the Javanese people.

JAVANESE CHARACTER

Validation of the hypothesis just stated awaits the systematic study in depth of the personalities of a sample of Javanese individuals. In the absence of such a study the following impressionistic sketch of some characteristics patterns of emotional response of the Javanese is presented as a point of orientation. It is an impression built up in the course of two years of intensive work with the Javanese, interviewing them on a variety of subjects, working with them, and living with them.[1] It is purposely not phrased in psychological concepts because it is not a scientific description of their "modal personality."

The Javanese give a basic impression of quiet security, self-control, and formality. There is a pervasive orderliness in their lives; their persons and property are always clean and well kept. Their bodily movements have the perfect grace and control of a fine dancer's, the kind of "effortless" poise which is based not on an absence of effort, but on complete mastery of the body. Their quietness and calmness give an appearance of passivity, which is, however, illusory. Their poise and control are not relaxed, but vigilant; they seem to be always on their guard, protecting themselves against any sudden shock which might disturb their delicate equilibrium. They have a word, bingung, which describes a feeling of mental confusion, of being mixed up, upset, lost. In its most specific meaning, bingung refers to losing one's sense of direction or one's control of one's whereabouts, "not knowing which way is north." And they have another word, kagèt, which means to be suddenly startled or shocked by something that happens outside of one, so that one becomes disoriented, or bingung. Both of these words are constantly on their lips, and the feelings which the words describe are apparently extremely threatening. It is interesting that although alcoholic drinks are available and there is little social stigma attached to drinking, few of the Javanese drink, for they find the effects of even one drink very disturbing and unpleasant.

They dislike any strong expression of emotion and have few genuine friendship or love relationships. Javanese women are less quiet and subdued than the men; they are much more expressive and keep up a steady stream of conversation and joking most of the day. But this stream of chatter seems to perform the same function as reserve does for the men; it keeps people at a proper distance. The Javanese rarely quarrel openly, rarely raise their voices in anger or their hands against one another. There are just as many quarrels in a Javanese village as elsewhere—between husbands and wives, neighbors, siblings, in-laws, and so on—but the arguments are kept in a low key, carried on by hints, slights, and allusions rather than by direct accusation and attack; and if a quarrel threatens to erupt into an uncontrollable fight, the opponents forestall it by cutting off relationships with one another.

The Javanese withdraw into themselves at times, close off their contact with the world and turn their attention inward, finding the events of the inner world more engrossing than those in the outside world. Yet they hate to be alone, and are constantly seeking out companionship and new experiences. Actually, it is when they are in a crowd that they seem most withdrawn. They like to sit whiling away the hours in a large group of their acquaintances, talking, and occasionally quietly musing to themselves. They seem to feel the need of a constant supply of low level stimulation, finding both absence of excitement and too much excitement unpleasant. They believe, however, that for genuine accomplishment one should be able to cut oneself off from these pleasant distractions and pursue one's goal with single-minded concentration and self-control; but most of them feel that this is an almost superhuman ability, and beyond their own capacities.

In their relations with other people they are constantly concerned with giving and receiving, and with calculating how much they can get from the other person or keep the other from getting. They appear to have a very low capacity to bear frustration of their desires, for, once they have made a request, they deeply resent a refusal. They have a word, *iklas,* which describes a desirable state of mind in which one gives up something without caring, and in which one is simply resigned to one's fate. Here again the concern for control is present: one controls one's desires, or one dulls one's emotions of frustration or resentment to the point that they never affect one.

Generally, the Javanese appear to be successful in their pursuit of order and control in their personal lives; they usually accomplish whatever goals they set for themselves. They have a genuine esthetic talent, especially in the nonvisual and kinesthetic arts, such as music, dance, drama, and poetry. Many of the men are serious thinkers, working over abstract philosophical problems in their leisure. Incidentally, I would predict that if the social sciences ever become a major concern in Javanese thought, some of the Javanese will make an important contribution in the field of psychology, for the direction of their thought is markedly introspective.[3]

GENERAL ASPECTS OF JAVANESE SOCIETY

The island of Java, in the Republic of Indonesia, is one of the most densely populated areas in the world. Ninety three percent of this population consists of peasants, growing rice primarily, and also cassava, corn, soybeans, and—although this was more extensive before the war—commercial export crops such as sugar, coffee, and tea. The other seven percent of the people live in town and cities which are scattered throughout the island. (For a good description and analysis of present day Indonesian society, see Wertheim 1956.)

The towns, despite their comparatively small population, are exceedingly important in Javanese social structure. No peasant village is located far from a town, and the towns serve many purposes for village society: they are junctures in a vigorous network of trade; they are points of contact with the central bureaucracy; they are symbols of both the refinement and elegance of the finest in Javanese civilization, and of its coarseness and temptations; and they are the centers of diffusion of cultural influences from the outside, from other parts of Asia, and from Europe. In performing this last function, the towns and cities of Java have, in the course of the last two thousand years, funneled to the peasants a series of waves of foreign ideas and goods, selected and interpreted to become integral parts of Javanese culture.

The first of these waves came from southern India during the first thousand years A.D., bringing Hinduism and Buddhism and their complex patterns of religious and political thought and organization, including a belief in a god-king and his court as a supreme symbol of the welfare of the entire country. While Hinduism and Buddhism as such are no longer found in Java, they made significant contributions to the present day world-view of the Javanese. The next wave of influence came from western and northern India and the Near East, starting around 1200 A.D., and bringing international trade and Islam. Soon after this came the next wave: European—primarily Dutch—colonialism, with its ideas of commerce, modern technology, industrial organization of agriculture, and ultimately nationalism. The most recent major change in the social organization and culture of Indonesia came from within —the overthrow of the Dutch government and the establishment of the independent Republic of Indonesia.

The religious beliefs of the Javanese, while nominally Islamic, are a complex blend of Hindu-Buddhism, Islam, and an indigenous animism (Geertz 1959). This blend is not uniform throughout the society: some of the peasants and many of the town-dwelling laborers stress the animistic element over the others; some other peasants and the bulk of the trading class emphasize the Islamic components; and the members of the bureaucracy find the Hindu-Buddhistic mystic aspects most compelling. In spite of this diversity, there is a basic Javanese world-view, which all the members of the society share, of which the attitudes toward prestige and status discussed in this paper form a part. While the caste system usually associated with Hinduism was never adopted by the Javanese, one of the main premises of Hinduism became a central pattern in Javanese culture. This is the idea that higher status derives not from worldly power and influence—economic or political—but from inner spiritual worth. This inner spiritual worth may be either inherited from one's parents or reached through concentrated spiritual exercise. It is on the basis of this premise that the members of the various sultans' courts, and, by extension, the members of the central government bureaucracy, are granted the highest prestige and deference. But even within the peasant village, where status differences are much less, higher status persons are granted the same sort of diffuse respect.

The kinship system is bilateral, generational, and with a variant type of Hawaiian cousin terminology. There are no extended corporate groupings of kinsmen. The nuclear family is the basic kinship unit in Javanese society; it is a close in-group, set off physically and socially from the rest of the kinsmen. It is the nuclear family which effectively owns and utilizes the land, and it is this unit which as a group enters into economic relationships of all kinds. It is also a religious unit: the main ritual of the Javanese—particularly of the peasants—is one in which each male head of the household, usually the father, representing his household, meets with other men from the neighborhood for a brief sharing of food and prayers at the home of one of them, after which the leftovers of the little dinner are brought back by each man to his own family. Adult children are expected to provide for their parents if they are in need, but they have no strong obligations to any other relatives. Usually at marriage the young couple sets up a household of its own, which is often in the same village or town as the parents of the bride or the groom. In one village census 75 percent of the households consisted only of a nuclear family that included no other relatives (Jay 1969).

There is an extremely high divorce rate; for every two marriages there is one divorce, in some areas. Many people have been married five or six times, most people twice. One of the major causes for the high divorce rate is that the courtship period is extremely abbreviated, and in many cases completely omitted. Parents arrange marriages for their adolescent children, and these marriages rarely work out. After the first marriage, the person is free to choose his own spouse, but the choice is rarely made with much thought: a Javanese couple has the wedding first, and then they see whether or not they will get along together. Another factor conducive to the high divorce rate is the absence of any institutionalized inhibiting elements, such as repayment of brideprice, religious prohibition, or legal barriers. There is no scandal about divorce, which, like marriage, is easy and cheap to obtain.

When the unity and solidarity of the nuclear family is modified—as it frequently is by divorce—any doubling up of households is likely to occur on the female side. There is a general, informal, unverbalized avoidance between the grown men of a family—between father and son, and between brothers—so that a household rarely includes more than one able bodied man. On the other hand, the tie between mother and daughter and between sisters is a close one. Thus, for instance, if there is a divorce in a family in which there are children, the wife and the children—whose strongest tie is always with their mother rather than their father—may go to her mother's home to live; but the husband, instead of returning to his parental home, usually looks for another wife. In other circumstances, too, female relatives may double up together; and if a male relative—an aged father, for instance—is dependent, he will usually live in his daughter's home, rather than in his son's.

Thus Javanese households are woman-centered, with one or two women and their children as core, and the men on the periphery. Strengthening this pattern even further is the fact that it is the wife who makes all of the minor, and most of the major, decisions about household affairs; she holds the purse strings, and she keeps her husband in a position of either equality or actual dependency. Javanese women may do almost any kind of work that a man can do, and have almost all the same kinds of legal rights that men have. This gives the woman a very strong position within the household.

Another important characteristic of Javanese family structure is the pattern of respect among family members. The same patterns of exaggerated formal behavior toward one's superiors which are practiced in the external world are carried over within the family. The father has the highest status position, and he is always spoken to with great circumlocution by both his wife and children. In many families he eats alone, being served the best food first while the others wait. Children are supposed to be quiet in his presence, and one of the stated reasons why a grown son rarely sits in the same room with his father is out of respect for him. The children are expected to show some respect toward their mother, but not to the same degree as toward their father. The same pattern of respectful behavior toward elders from younger people and toward males from females is extended to other kinsmen—except

that a grandchild may often, throughout his life, be impudent and free with a favored grandparent.

SOCIALIZATION PROCESSES

Three phases in a Javanese child's growth can be schematically distinguished: (1) infancy—from birth to weaning and walking, (2) early childhood—to about the fifth year, (3) childhood—to the onset of puberty. The first period is dominated by the mother-child tie; the second is the only period in which the father is close to the child, and ends as the father begins to draw aloof again; and the third period is marked by gradually widening relationships with peers and adults outside the family. Between each of these phases—which are not sharply cut off from each other, either in the view of the Javanese or in actual fact—there are long transition periods, the first when the child is being weaned and learning adequate walking, and the second when he is beginning to learn to relate to people outside his family, to give up the earlier freedom and warmth of permissiveness and to learn responsibility and self-control.

A child, especially in the first two phases, is said to be *durung djawa,* which literally means "not yet Javaneses." The same phrase is applied to mentally unbalanced persons and to adults who are not properly respectful toward their elders, for instance, a daughter-in-law who is rude to her parents-in-law. This term implies that the person is not yet civilized, not yet able to control emotions in an adult manner, not yet able to speak with the proper respectful circumlocutions appropriate to different social occasions. Such a person is also said to be *du-*

rung ngerti, "does not yet understand," and therefore it is thought that there is no point in forcing him to be what he is not or punishing him for faults which are incomprehensible to him. These two related notions, of being *djawa* and *ngerti,* sum up for the Javanese their ideas of maturity and adult interpersonal relationships, and are the key to the whole complex of such ideas that are communicated to the growing child. But in the first phase of his life and for most of the second phase, these criteria for judging behavior are held in abeyance.

The infant is thought to be extremely vulnerable to emotional upset. Should anything exceedingly unpleasant, such as sudden noises, rough handling, strong tastes, physical discomfort, occur to the child, he might become *kagèt,* "shocked and upset." Should this happen, he then has no psychological defenses against the onslaught of the evil-spirits who are constantly around the mother and new baby, and who cause sickness and death. All of the customs of infant care can be seen as attempts to ward off this danger.

The baby is handled in a relaxed, completely supportive, gentle, unemotional manner. He is constantly in his mother's arms and lap when awake; if he is sound asleep and the mother must move around, she places him on a cushion of clean cloths on a sleeping bench, with pillows surrounding him so that he will not roll off. At the first cry, actually at the first sign of awakening, he is taken up and cleaned, if necessary, and nursed. A crying baby is rarely heard, mainly because no Javanese can bear to hear the sound without trying to do something about it, no matter whose baby it is. Many babies are placed in a soft cocoon of cloths wound around their bodies. This swaddling is firm but not tight, and if the child squirms or kicks it readily comes off. An active baby may dislike the wrapping; if so, it is dispensed with. At night the swaddling is removed, and the baby sleeps next to his mother, where he will sleep for the greater part of his childhood. Swaddling usually is stopped after the first month, although it may be resumed sporadically, especially if the child is weak or sick.

The second phase of the child's life is formally opened at his seventh-month birthday by a ceremony celebrating his first setting foot on the earth. Although in actuality this phase is not really underway for another five or ten months, when the child actually begins to walk, the Javanese feel that after the seventh month he is psychologically stronger, and can now be expected to begin to grow up. When he is about 14 months old—or sometimes much later, if no younger sibling has intervened—the mother weans the child. Almost from the beginning of his life he has been given supplementary feeding, in the form of banana mush, rice, and other bland foods, so that there is usually little trauma associated with weaning. It is interesting, however, that the mothers are much afraid of upsetting the child by a too abrupt or severe weaning, and try to make it as gradual as possible. They even have a little ritual for easing the transition, which instructs the baby to "forget your mother and go to your grandmother for food." Sometimes a mother's timidity and ambivalence about weaning are such that the child goes through a long period of inconsistent treatment, being weaned and then returned to the breast, and then weaned again. That weaning is seen by the Javanese as a significant transition is shown by the fact that they call a child in this second phase the *sapi-han,* "the weaned one."

Walking is another significant trans-sition, one which is given a peculiarly Javanese flavor, for until the child's muscles are developed enough for him to actually support himself erect, he is not permitted to move about alone. A Javanese baby misses the crawling stage entirely. All during his infancy he is carried about by his mother in a sling-like shawl on her hip. He passively hangs there, close to the breast where he may suckle at will, and is given constant attention by his mother. Sometimes an older sibling carries him in this way. His every wish is anticipated and he is expected to have no initiative of his own. As his muscles develop, he is dandled on the mother's or father's lap a good deal, and given a chance to try to stand. But only when he can actually stand and squat and totter along by himself is he permitted any freedom. This aspect of the child's experience is exceedingly important, in view of the extent to which adult Javanese are concerned with bodily equilibrium and spatial orientation. The long period of being supported on the mother's hip must be related to the adult's tendency toward passive spectatorship rather than active participation in the world around him.

Wtih the accomplishment of weaning and walking, the main characteristic of the second phase is that the child now can move independently of the mother, and some sort of social rather than merely physical control of his actions is needed. The most common techniques used in this early period are first, detailed, unemotional instructions to the child, unaccompanied by threats of punishment from the parents; but, second, threats of horrible fates at the hands of out-siders or spirits if the child is bad. Actual punishment by the family members themselves is rare, and threats of withdrawal of love are never employed. No demands are made on the child until he is considered old enough to comprehend verbal instructions. These are delivered in a calm, steady stream by the adults: "Go around back of the house to urinate . . . Fix your dress . . . Don't run so fast . . . Say good-bye." The assumption seems to be that the child is completely without resources of his own with which to face these little everyday problems. If the child does not obey these instructions—and usually the Javanese child learns early that evasion is more effective than direct disobedience—the adult does not show anger, but merely waits for another opportunity to teach the child. There is no attempt or desire to let the child develop initiative or independence. Toilet training and the teaching of bodily modesty are dealt with in the same gradual, unemotional way.

During the period of weaning and learning to walk, the father begins to take an interest in the child. There are many moments of warmth, affection, and fondling between the father and child during this second phase, which are given heightened meaning by the fact that the father is frequently away from the house, or, if at home, pre-occupied with his own thoughts or entertaining friends, and the further fact that the relationship changes radically after the child is about five. While mothers are described as "loving" (*trisna*) their children, fathers are expected only to "take pleasure" (*seneng*) in them. The relationship with the mother remains as strong and secure as before, as it does throughout the person's life. She is seen as a bulwark of strength and love to whom one can always turn, in contrast to the father, who is distant and must always be treated respectfully. It is the mother who instructs the child in social forms, who makes countless decisions for him, and who performs most punishments. The father is usually only a court of last appeal and a model for imitation. He is expected to be, above all, patient and dignified (*sabar*) with his wife and children: he should lead them with a gentle, though firm, hand, not interfering with their petty quarrels, but being always available to give solemn sanction to his wife's punishments of disobedient children. Only from around the end of the child's first year to about his fifth does he feel close to his father; the time then comes when he can no longer play next to his father or trail along with him on visits, but must respectfully stay away from him and speak circumspectly and softly to him. At about this same time the child's behavior in general seems to undergo a change; once spontaneous and laughing, he now adopts the docile, restrained, formal, controlled demeanor of his elders. The two events are somehow related.

The shift in the father's role from one of affection and warmth to one of distance and reserve is only one of a whole series of events through which the child learns the specific Javanese concepts of self-control and respect. It is probably the most significant event, both because of the crucial place of the father in the child's emotional life, and because this transition occurs presumably during a period of Oedipal crisis. But it would not have the impact it has, if it had not been presaged and followed up by certain other events in the child's life, or, perhaps more important, if it were not set in a meaningful context of Javanese ideas.

THE CONCEPT OF "RESPECT"

The central concept of "respect" (*urmat, adji*) is a notion so peculiarly Javanese that it cannot be easily translated. Unlike the Western word, it does not necessarily refer to an attitude toward a person superior in power: in the family the mother holds the real power in the family, while the father receives the respect. And, secondly, it is not the personal characteristics of the man himself that call forth this patterned behavior, but his status, as father, headman, educated government official, or the like. A further difference from Western ideas is that it does not matter whether the person who grants him respect actually "feels" respectful "inside" or merely acts as if he does. This is a significant aspect of all Javanese social relationships: the important thing is not the sincerity of the action, but the successful cover-up of all dissonant elements in the relationship.

This does not mean that there is no emotional aspect to respectful behavior; on the contrary, sometimes there can be a very acutely felt accompaniment. This emotional component of respect is signified by the three Javanese words, *wedi*, *isin*, and *sungkan*, which denote three kinds of feeling states felt to be appropriate to situations demanding respectful behavior. The three words form a sort of continuum of intensity and specificity, ranging from *wedi* which is most intense and diffuse, to *sungkan* which is least intense and most specific.

Wedi means "afraid" in both the physical sense and the social sense of apprehension of unpleasant consequences of an action. Sometimes children when approached by me, a strange White woman, would tremble on the verge of nervous tears, and the mother would say, *"Adja wedi, ora ana, apa-apa."* (Don't be afraid; it is nothing.) Informants, when asked to give examples of the meaning of *wedi,* would say, for instance: "If I have to go out to the toilet at night, I am *wedi* of spirits." "A child who is punished by his father is *wedi* to be naughty after that." "My grandmother tells me all children should be *wedi* of their elders; if they don't obey them, they are not *wedi* of them." "If I borrow some rice from a neighbor and can't pay it back, I feel *wedi* of that neighbor."

Isin may be translated as "shame, shyness, embarrassment, guilt." As a child grows, he is thought to begin to *ngerti isin*—that is, to know *isin*— and this is considered the first step toward maturity. This first experience of the feeling usually comes in relation to outsiders: when a guest comes to the house, the child withdraws into himself with an intensely felt sense of shyness and becomes completely unresponsive, and the parents say, "He is *isin.*" One informant described his own feelings as a child: "For instance, you are taken visiting with your grandmother and they ask you to sit down, and you say, 'I don't want to,' and they say, 'Go and play with the other children,' and you say, 'I don't want to.' You just want to be left alone." The child just stands there or buries his head in his mother's skirts, paralyzed with shame. Other illustrations of the meaning of *isin* are: "If you are seen through the doorway without any clothes on, you feel *isin.*" "If you sleep with another man and your husband finds out, you feel *isin.*" "If you borrow some money and can't pay

it back, you feel *isin* and hide from your creditor when he goes by." "If you ask to borrow something from someone and he refuses to lend it to you, you feel *isin.*" "For instance, there is a club, and if I have a position in the club lower than anyone else, I feel *isin.*" "If a village woman comes calling at her child's teacher's house, she feels *isin* and doesn't say much or accept anything to eat."

As can be seen by a comparison of the examples of the two words, *wedi* and *isin,* there is an appreciable overlap. *Wedi* is a fear reaction, especially to strange things; *isin* is a complex anxiety reaction, involving not only fear but also lowered self-esteem, and concerns only social anxieties, usually those having to do with social distance, including distance self-imposed through social transgression. While *wedi* may be a reaction to threats arising from the same kinds of social situations, it can also refer to simple physical threats.

Wedi and *isin,* although complex, are close enough to American ideas to be translated "fear" and "shame or guilt," but *sungkan,* the third feeling state associated with respect, is something peculiarly Javanese. Roughly speaking, *sungkan* refers to a feeling of respectful politeness before a superior or an unfamiliar equal, an attitude of constraint, a repression of one's own impulses and desires, so as not to disturb the emotional equanimity of one who may be spiritually higher. "*Sungkan* is like *isin* only lighter." "*Sungkan* is like *isin* only without the feeling of doing something wrong." "If a delegation of official visitors comes to my house and they sit at my table, I sit off in a chair in the corner; that's *sungkan.*" "If a guest comes to my house and I give him dinner, I say, '*sampun sungkan-sung-*

kan' [don't be *sungkan*], and I mean, 'Don't stand on ceremony, eat a lot as if you were in your home.'" The respectful thing to do is to eat only one or two mouthfuls. Some village people in Java do not, however, make the distinction between *isin* and *sungkan*, considering the latter simply a more refined synonym. They associate the word with the world of aristocratic townsmen and its ranks and values, where the ritual of politeness is practiced with subtlety and sensitivity. To know *isin* is simply to know the basic social properties of self-control and avoidance of disapproval, whereas to know *sungkan* is to be able to perform the social minuet with grace.

An analytic distinction should be clearly drawn between assuming that these Javanese words are *descriptions of actual emotional response patterns of the Javanese* (for which no acceptable evidence is available), and interpreting them as *categories within Javanese thought about emotional states* —that is, their *ideas* of what emotional states human beings have or ought to have.

It is only in the second, cultural sense that these terms are being discussed here, and the hypothesis is advanced for future study that these cultural concepts may become internalized partly as moral prescriptions and partly as motivational elements in the personalities of Javanese individuals. Javanese children are *taught* how and when to be *wedi* and *isin;* they are praised for being *wedi* to their elders and *isin* to their betters. They learn *wedi* first, before they are capable of the differentiated internal response that self-esteem implies or of the differentiated cognition of social differences. As they grow older *isin* is taught them, first by a mobilization of the already established *wedi* reac-

tions, later by playing on the developing self-esteem by deliberate shaming. The last and most specific idea in the series, *sungkan*, is then taught them on the basis of this foundation.

Thus the nature of discipline and the canons of obedience change as the child grows. When he is just learning to walk and talk and has not yet learned the meaning of *wedi, isin,* and *sungkan,* the adults do not attempt to persuade him to follow other than his own impulses, and try to structure affairs so as to minimize the emergence of impulses disruptive of social life. Keeping the child fed, clean, and amused is the main task during these first years; the main technique of controlling his behavior is distraction of his attention, and the only technique utilizing anxiety as a lever is the threat of fearful outside retribution. This is *wedi* in the simplest physical sense.

From his earliest years, the child is taught that there is an inner group of people—his mother and his immediate family—whom he may completely trust, and that the rest of the world, made up of strangers and evil spirits, can be expected only to do him harm, especially if he is bad. These are the people toward whom he is first expected to be *wedi*, for, his mother tells him, they might punish him, hurt him, or even destroy him, if he does wrong. The outsider as a result is not neutrally viewed, but acutely feared. As the child grows older and enters the third phase of relative independence, the feeling of fear toward outsiders recedes, leaving simply a wariness.

In about the middle of the second phase of the child's socialization, he begins to find that the people around him are not responding as they used to, that his weeping goes ignored, and that, if he does not obey the wishes of his parents, they punish him, instead of letting it pass as they used to. Punishment ranges from a threatening look, a sharp remark, a tiny painful pinch, or a quick slap, to actual beating, although this last is extremely rare. In this way the second meaning of *wedi*, respect due to the parent because of her capacity to punish, is taught. It should be noted, however, that the child is seldom actually punished. He has from the first been accustomed to a minimum of thinking for himself and to passive adjustment of tensions; this, combined with the fact that the parents are now consistent in their demands, has the result that he rarely directly disobeys them.

The outsider, who was earlier used as a symbol of fantasied physical punishment, now is used as a symbol of fantasied social disapproval to induce a feeling of shame or *isin*. The threat, "If you are not quiet, the stranger over there will bite you," changes to, "Aren't you ashamed to be noisy in front of that strange man?" The feeling of *isin* before strangers, at first disproportionately and paralyzingly great, gradually becomes more appropriate in intensity, and the child becomes more and more able to cope with a variety of nonfamily social situations, culminating in his mastery of *sungkan* and its associated behavior patterns of etiquette.

How does the child learn this last, culminating, ultra-Javanese kind of respect? He has already learned an acute awareness of other people's moods and opinions, an attitude of tuning in on the desires of the other person, through his education in *isin*. And toward the end of the second phase he has begun to learn self-renunciation and impulse control, for now he is likely to have a younger sibling to care for, one who, like himself as an infant,

may not be permitted to be frustrated or upset. And now his father, formerly warm and affectionate, like an "insider," begins to act like an "outsider" toward him, and to expect him to behave in his presence according to the social forms appropriate to outsiders. The child finds himself now feeling *isin* in front of his father, and being told, moreover, to be *sungkan* in his presence.

This change in the father's role occurs some time around the fifth year, and marks the transition into what psychologically is probably the latency period. Now, too, the child is permitted to roam away from the house and to join playgroups of his peers, which are usually only of one sex. Girls are now given more responsibility around the home, taking care of their younger siblings, marketing, cooking, and so on, while the boys are permitted a much longer period of irresponsible play. Both boys and girls go to school now, and, with their teachers, get a further opportunity to practice their newly learned attitudes of respect.

As a further reinforcement of the socialization process, the child is often sent away from his home to live with a relative for several years, usually his mother's sister, because of the emotional closeness between sisters. This lending of children takes place because every couple wants to have a child in the house, but, because of the high infant mortality, the high divorce rate, and the frequency of parental deaths, there is always a maldistribution of children. A family with many children is often beseiged by relatives with requests for the children, and a divorced or widowed woman has no trouble finding a kinsman to take a child off her hands. Sometimes sending children to another household is thought of as an educational technique: the children are said to learn obedience and good manners when they are separated from their too-permissive mothers. This is indeed the result, for the Javanese child never feels unrestricted or relaxed in any other house than his own, and further, he is expected to be appropriately *isin* and *sungkan* while living with these outsiders.

To the Javanese, *isin* and *sungkan* represent civilized, mature inner states; a person who "knows" (and by this they mean something like "has internalized") these attitudes, and "knows" when and where they are appropriate, can be said to be *djawa*, "Javanese." They are, however, attitudes which are not appropriate to one's relationship with one's mother, or with anyone with whom one has close primary ties —with the single remarkable exception of the father. Javanese say one could never feel *isin* toward one's mother, because she loves one—a feeling which, to them, excludes the possibility of shame—and although one should obey one's mother and treat her with consideration, the idea of being *sungkan* to her is incredible. These are feelings that belong to the outside world, the world of adults, and it is through the shift in the role of the father, which gives the child an opportunity to play a role appropriate to adults, that the Javanese child has his first extended and meaningful chance to make the leap to maturity, to a Javanese kind of maturity.

CONCLUSION

Three orders of data are necessary for a complete analysis of the intricate relationship between social forms, cultural patterns, and personality types:

(1) Systematically gathered data on the personalities of adults in a particular society, arranged to show alternative and deviant modes of response as well as the statistically most frequent types. (2) A full picture of the structure and functioning of the society, organized in terms of its impact on its members, including such elements as the explicitly or implicitly expected motivations and behaviors, the sources of psychological strain, and the areas of freedom and permissible tension release. (3) An account of the childhood experience of the members of the society, the processes by which the developing individual first learns the rewards and frustrations of coping with his social world.

The last of these three kinds of data is actually only a special case of the second, which is given particular attention because of the overwhelming importance of the earliest social experience in forming the durable response patterns which are called personality. During this period the cultural expectations and demands concerning the child's behavior, the repetition of forms of interpersonal relationships in which he takes part, the strains and inconsistencies in these patterns, the areas of activity in which he is permitted free expression of his impulses to offset frustrations in other areas, all have a lasting effect on the organization and functioning of his personality.

The present essay is an exploration of a neglected aspect of this socialization process: the kinds of expectations and demands by the adults—not so much regarding the child's behavior, the usual focus of socialization studies, but regarding his emotions in themselves. The actual child-training procedures—the ways in which the adults handle the child and what significance they give to the bodily maturational transitions through which he passes—are very important, but they are not the only point of articulation between culture and personality.

The assumptions held by the members of a society regarding the nature of inner emotional life are another important aspect of the growing child's social and cultural environment. Which aspects of the universally potential emotional experience are emphasized, which are de-emphasized, and which are grouped by a particular society should make a considerable difference in the kind of personality produced by that society, as compared with another society.[3] The failure of the Javanese to distinguish shame from guilt, and their association of both of these with fear on the one hand (*wedi*), and with respectful constriction of the impulses (*sungkan*) on the other, must have significant repercussions on the actual personality organization of the Javanese.[4]

Other clusters of Javanese concepts of feeling-states could with equal profit be analyzed in the same manner that I have analyzed respect—for instance, the cluster of ideas surrounding giving and receiving, and the cluster around maintaining intensity of effort and concentration of attention on work of any sort. Both of these sets of ideas are highly patterned in Javanese culture, and both also play a significant part in the socialization of Javanese individuals.

To take the matter previously mentioned of giving and receiving as an example, Javanese culture emphasizes not the feelings of "generosity" and "gratitude," as does American culture, but rather two other kinds of feeling states. When giving something away, a Javanese wants or expects to feel a sort of stoic forbearance, a feeling of "not caring" (*iklas*); he considers it important to give his present with no residue of regret or resentment. And on the other hand, on receipt of a gift, the institutionalized pattern is not "gratitude"—although of course it may be felt—but rather one of being content or satisfied with whatever one receives, controlling one's wishes so that one does not expect more, summed up in the word, *trima*. It is interesting that the pair of American words refer to an attitude toward the other person, while the two Javanese words are concerned with one's own inner states. Again, just as *wedi, isin,* and *sungkan* were shown to be related to the techniques of social control of the child, and to the Oedipal crisis and the father's role in it, so also the learning of the set of premises about one's feelings in giving and receiving can be given a temporal and maturational dimension. Its beginnings can be traced to the time of the child's weaning, particularly in those cases in which the mother was ambivalent about the act, and its further development traced to the situation surrounding the birth of a younger sibling and the renunciation of other gratifications which this entails.

Thus the cultural system plays a part in the process of socialization of the child in several ways: It structures the situation of the child's learning about himself and his world by regulating to a large extent the actions of the adults around him, so that they may either emphasize or play down the various transitions through which he must pass, transitions brought about both by the maturational sequence of his body, and by the progressive enlargement of his social sphere of action. At the same time the cultural system does more: It provides a series of interpretations of the meanings of these transition points, and recipes for the child's reactions to them. The culture presents not only a set of suggested answers on *how to behave* in these situations, but also clues to *how to feel* about his actions. And, since his education in the emotional lexicon of his society begins so early and is coincident with so many other significant events in his life, the child in each society learns his lesson well, a lesson which as he grows older provides meaning, form, and apparent predictability to his inner experience.

NOTES

1. The data for this paper were gathered during a fifteen-month field study of a town in central Java, conducted during the period from May, 1953 through September 1954. This was a group project of five anthropologists and a sociologist, carried out under the auspices of the Center for International Studies at Massachusetts Institute of Technology, and financed by the Ford Foundation. I am indebted to all the members of the group, and most particularly to Robert Jay and Clifford Geertz for critical reading of the paper. Further acknowledgements are due to Arnold Green and Peggy Golde, and also to Alfred Stanton and the Staff Seminar at McLean Hospital for comments and criticisms. A more detailed description of the socialization processes and the kinship system of the Javanese is presented in H. Geertz (1961).

2. See Bateson and Mead (1942) and Belo (1956) for a description of Balinese character, which is markedly similar to the Javanese. A systematic comparison of personality formation in these two historically related societies would be highly profitable. In view of this similarity, it is interesting to note that the pattern of parental teasing of the child almost to an emotional climax, and refusing to allow him to fully reach it—considered by Bateson and Mead as an important element in Balinese character formation—is absent from the Javanese treatment of children.

3. An early paper by Jules Henry (1936) uses a technique of analysis similar to that employed here.

4. The distinction between *shame* and *guilt* which anthropologists have attempted to employ for characterization of personality differences observed in different societies, with no notable clarity or success, may be a similar kind of "folk-psychological" concept, peculiar to Western culture in the same way that the *wedi, isin, sungkan* distinction is peculiar to Javanese culture. The shame-guilt distinction may have little to contribute to a scientific typology of personality, and, because of its cultural specificity, be actually a hindrance to genuine understanding. The use of shame and guilt as labels for whole cultures would be about as defensible as an attempt to classify all cultures or personalities according to primacy of *wedi, isin,* or *sungkan*. See Piers and Singer (1953) for an excellent discussion of the problem.

REFERENCES

Bateson, Gregory, and Margaret Mead
    1942 *Balinese Character: A Photographic Analysis.* New York: New York Academy of Sciences.
Belo, Jane
    1956 The Balinese temper. *In* D. G. Haring (ed.), *Personal Character and Cultural Milieu.* Syracuse, NY: Syracuse University Press.
Benedict, Ruth
    1949 Child rearing in certain European countries. *American Journal of Orthopsychiatry* 19: 342-48.
Erikson, Erik H.
    1950 *Childhood and Society.* New York: Norton.

Geertz, Clifford
  1959   *The Religion of Java.* Glencoe, IL: The Free Press.
Geertz, Hildred
  1961   *The Javanese Family.* Glencoe, IL: The Free Press.
Hartmann, Heinz, Ernst Kris, and R. M. Loewenstein
  1951   Some psychoanalytic comments on "culture and personality." *In* G. B. Wilbur and W. Muensterberger (eds.), *Psychoanalysis and Culture.* New York: International Universities Press.
Henry, Jules
  1936   The linguistic expression of emotion. *American Anthropologist* 38: 250-56.
Jay, Robert R.
  1969   *Javanese Villagers: Social Relations in Rural Modjokuto.* Cambridge: MIT Press.
Mead, Margaret
  1949   Discussion. *American Journal of Orthopsychiatry* 19: 349-50.
Piers, Gerhart, and Milton B. Singer
  1953   *Shame and Guilt.* Springfield, IL: Thomas.
Wertheim, W. F.
  1956   *Indonesian Society in Transition.* The Hague: W. van Hoeve.

14. HOPI DREAMS IN CULTURAL PERSPECTIVE

DOROTHY EGGAN

The late Dorothy Eggan was a psychological anthropologist who resided in Chicago. Reprinted from *The Dream and Human Societies*, G. E. Von Grunebaum and Roger Caillois, editors, 1966. Originally published by the University of California Press; reprinted by permission of The Regents of the University of California.

THIS STUDY[1] IS CONCERNED with the Hopi Indians, a small sedentary, agricultural pueblo tribe in the southwestern desert plateau of the United States. It must be emphasized that "Hopi" in this or other papers by the writer refers to those individuals who had attained maturity and full tribal responsibility before 1939, when my research among them began. Much of it would apply less strongly to their children and grandchildren, who, particularly since World War II, have been subjected more positively to White pressures. It discusses certain religious beliefs and ceremonies, particularly those that feature Palulukon, the Water Serpent, and a number of Hopi dreams related to them. We shall see that Hopi culture not only stressed the importance of dreams, but that their religious ceremonies provided a rich source of imagery, which was present from infancy to death, and which served both the purposes of the dreamer and the interests of the society. We suggest that dreams may be thought of as a triangular production involving (1) the latent content that is said to appear in universal symbols, and represents material not accessible to consciousness; (2) the dreamer's personality organization, and his personal situation at the time of the dream; and (3) the *relation of the dreams to cultural provision*, with

which this paper is directly concerned.

In order to understand the vitality of Hopi social structure and religion, and its impact on the individuals who maintained it, one should first examine the educational system through which it was instilled, and consider also the harsh physical environment into which successive generations of this farming people have been born. For they, or groups ancestral to them, have occupied for more than a thousand years villages on or near the three arid mesas of sand and rock on which they now live. Surrounded by nomadic enemies, at the mercy of the always fickle and frequently destructive elements, strongly conditioned interdependence was their only hope for survival. A relentless environment thus became the ultimate axis around which an all-inclusive, thoroughly interconnected social and religious structure was built. In fact, these united into a system of thought and action which, as we shall see below, was so demanding, that it was in a sense as coercive as the environment itself.

It was, however, more rewarding. A strongly functioning maternal household, with extended matrilocal residence, surrounded the individual and gave him support against those outside the clan; and a dramatic, colorful kaleidoscope of religious ceremonies built on Hopi mythology wove the

265

beauty of extraordinary theater through all of the years of a Hopi life span. From the moment an infant's eyes could follow moving objects, beautiful masked gods—Kachinas—danced into and out of his awareness as he lay comfortably in his mother's lap. The color, the singing, and the drums that accompanied the dance, the graceful rhythm and intense concentration of the dancers, all combined into a superb artistry that is a hypnotic and impressive form of prayer. And as soon as an infant could sense moods in those around him, he must have been aware of the at once happy and absorbed attitude that pervaded the entire group on dance days. As the child grew, his participation increased, and understanding became inextricably interwoven with affect, each constantly reinforcing the other, as need patterns became organized through social process around specific ways of satisfying them.

For the purposes of this discussion, then, we are interested in those aspects of integrated perception which are *learned,* and which are thus modified and eventually canalized through socially defined experiences (for the following discussion, see Murphy 1947, Chaps. 8, 9, 11, 12, 14; Asch 1952). All facets of these experiences among the Hopi were consistent, and this consistency, plus affect in teaching, was combined with the fact that their language made exchange of ideas with other groups difficult, so that the whole created a situation in which psychological anchorage occurred in a much less diffuse field than in our society. The resulting reaction patterns became deeply ingrained and resistant to change, and the individual then responded to incoming stimuli with selective attention depending partly upon whether they aroused confusion or antagonism, or whether they were congenial enough to the perceptual structure so that motivation was aroused to try to integrate them with what had gone before. With ourselves the learning process calls to mind the ever widening waves produced by a pebble into still water; but the Hopi speak of their social and religious organization as "concentric walls." Thus their learning process is not so much wide as deep.

Elsewhere we have discussed the role of the Hopi educational system in the continuity of their culture (Eggan 1956), but we must briefly describe it here in order to provide a framework into which the dream action can be placed. The instruction through which a Hopi acquired the personality organization that made him so consistently and determinedly Hopi was deliberate and systematic. The early and continued conditioning of the individual in the Hopi maternal extended family was, on every level, an inculcation of interdependence as contrasted with our striving for independence. At the same time, and never separated from it, there was an emphasis on religious observance and beliefs, also stressing interdependence, a constant preoccupation with the ceremonial cycle, and frequent reference to myth and dreams, for storytelling and dreams played an important role in the Hopi world.

If we examine the pattern of integration through which the Hopi erected a communal wall around their children, we find that their maternal kinship system, with matrilocal residence and an extended household, was the foundation of it. From birth the young of the household were attended by a wide variety of relatives in addition to the mother. These attentions came both from household members and from visitors in it. In no way was a baby ever as dependent upon his physical mother as are children in our culture. Weaning, of course, when discussed in personality contexts, means more than a transition from milk to solid food. It is also a gradual process of achieving independence from the comfort of a mother's body and care, of transferring affections to other persons, and of finding satisfactions within oneself and in the outside world. Most people learn to eat solid food; many of us are never weaned, which has unfortunate consequences in a society where individual effort and competitive independence are stressed. The Hopi child, on the other hand, from the day of his birth was being weaned from his biological mother. Many arms gave him comfort, many faces smiled or frowned at him, and from a very early age he was given bits of food which were chewed by various members of the family and placed in his mouth. So, for a Hopi, the outside world in which he needed to find satisfaction was never far away. He was not put in a room by himself and told to go to sleep; every room was crowded with sleepers of all ages, and he normally slept with a mother, a grandmother, or another adult. He was in no way forced to find satisfaction with himself; rather, in infancy these were provided for him, if possible, by his household and clan group. His weaning, then, was from the breast only, and as he was being weaned from his biological mother, he was at the same time in a situation that increased his emotional orientation toward the intimate in-group of the extended family, which was consistent with the interests of Hopi social structure. Thus, considering weaning in its wider implications, a Hopi was never weaned; it was not intended that he should be.

For, as *self* emerged for the Hopi, he was at the same time being taught to deny it, rather than to exercise it; he was taught that this emerging entity was an important part of the *group-self*, past, present and future (on the positive role anxiety may play in a society, and on theories of self, cf. Hallowell 1955, Chap. 4; see also Murphy 1947, p. 855; Asch 1952, pp. 334-335, 605ff.) In other words, he was taught to achieve self-fulfillment only in group-fulfillment, in contrast to our creed of reveling in selfhood, of exercising it, and striving to reach self-fulfillment through competitive independence. He was not merely told that Hopi beliefs were right or wise; he lived them as he grew, and in his total environment (as contrasted with our separation of teaching at home, in school, and in Sunday school), until these responses on the overt behavior level became largely automatic. Within these concentric walls of "Hopiness" then, each individual was first a learner and then a teacher, in an atmosphere conducive to conviction rather than doubt.

We can now examine the hypotheses that are central to this discussion: (*a*) that the conceptual universe of the Hopi (described in the section on concepts and values) was not delimited, as ours is, by notions of time and space which made of dreams an experience apart from reality; and (*b*) that much of the learning process among the Hopi, especially with reference to religion, involved perception through *imagery derived from dramatic rituals* enacted over and over again before learners, and that this imagery later, according to individual need patterns, could easily be, and frequently was, translated directly into dreams.

For as memory, thought, and even perception can be trained by repetitive response to needs through consistent opportunities to satisfy the needs by specific responses, it would seem that, as Murphy suggests (1947, p. 397), the richness and form of imagery available to a dreamer would depend in part "upon the specific way in which training and broader cultural emphasis have enriched, intensified, or inhibited the imaginal processes of the individual." We have suggested that a tightly structured society such as the Hopi tends to yield a uniform continuity of needs, and a consistent satisfaction of these needs, from birth to death; and that experience is limited in Hopi culture, both because of an isolated environment and because the society deliberately channeled experience in patterned ways for all members of it.

It would thus seem to follow that when such a society conveys much religious and recreational experience through dramatic and richly satisfying images, as Hopi society does, the self-world of individuals would be richly endowed with images, particularly since these images were consistently presented long before conscious thought began to catalogue the world of experience, and continued to be presented throughout one's lifetime. This cataloguing is obviously always done largely below the level of awareness, and experimental evidence seems to indicate that much of what has been registered on the edge of consciousness, or just below it, is a particularly rich source of imagery (Murphy 1947, Chap. 16; Tauber and Green 1959; cf. Fisher and Paul 1959). But, in any event, it is evident that not only imaginative experience but logical thought draws upon this inner source, since no form of mentation could function without it. Logical thought, however, also depends upon the *outer* world's verbalized definitions of experience, and a Hopi, like the rest of us, soon learns that one's subjective experience, and another's definition of it, may be radically different.

No matter how tightly the society is structured, nor how thoroughly individuals in it are integrated with the society, there is always an insistent whisper from self, a point beyond which an entity that the Hopi call *hikwsi*—the Spirit of the Breath or Breath Body—resists what they sometimes call *himu,*[2] the Mighty Something, which may be thought of not as a god, but rather as their composite concept of divinity. But when Hopi *hikwsi* resists *himu,* self-awareness in this interdependent household and society then becomes far more of a threat than it does among ourselves. Here a confused, unhappy, or guilty Hopi self searches for familiar anchors in the field of his inner world, so that often for a time dream fantasy carries the burden of self. And the Hopi, with a wisdom often shown by nonliterate groups,[3] acknowledges the dream as a type of thought-action in which *hikwsi* explores the world within and the world without, often bringing the two into closer alignment, through images and experiences provided by Hopi religion. In fact, the importance attached to a dream is indicated by the Hopi term for it, *dimoki,* which one Hopi "philosopher" translated in the following way: "It means a bundle of the dead body prepared for burial; it means a bundle of corn [corn being literally the staff of life for the Hopi] ready to carry on your back; and it means dream—maybe you could think of it as a bundle of thought. But anyway, all three have a *deep meaning.*"

A bad dream, in fact, was considered so important that one must immediately arouse a sleeping partner and report it, after which one must go outside and spit four times, in order to complete the elimination of bad thoughts. A good dream, however, had to be "held in the heart" and not told until after it had been fulfilled.

SELECTED DREAMS

We now present brief versions of several Hopi dreams, and subsequently consider the religious background to which they are related before we examine them further.

The first dream is prefaced by a long discussion in which the dreamer relates what his father has told him: that people with good hearts have nothing to fear from Palulukon, the Water Serpent, and that if one is brave enough to take prayer objects to this serpent, the reward will be sufficient water for good crops.

DREAM 1

In the dream, the dreamer has crossed a sacred cornmeal path laid down by the Hopi Snake Society, whose members are out gathering snakes for the famous Hopi Snake Dance. [This is a relatively small society which is said to have no direct connection with Palulukon.][4] Having thus trespassed upon the Society, he knows he can be forcibly initiated into it. He remembers that he would then have to dance with live snakes in his mouth and is afraid he would get bitten and die. But the Snake Priests give him a choice between joining the Society and taking sacred prayer objects to Palulukon, the Water Serpent, in a sacred spring. [The Snake Priests may either initiate a male trespasser or impose a heavy fine unless the offender can join a woman or women before he is caught. The Priests may not approach women during the ceremony.] After much self-

doubt, and much advice from the Snake Priests, he goes to the spring where the Water Serpent emerges. The dreamer finds that the Serpent is indeed beautiful, as the old people have said, colored like a rainbow. Although frightened, he gives the prayer objects to Palulukon and says: "The serpent's eyes are so bright, kind of yellowish red and he look very colored and nice—he look like a tame serpent and I wish I could catch him for a pet." After a long prayer, the dreamer deposits his sacred gifts and says, "I'm afraid to turn around; that powerful snake may catch hold of my legs and hold me tight. But I look on myself and found I'm a middle-age man and have to put all those childish thoughts away and act like a man."

After the dreamer leaves the spring, he looks back and finds the snake gone and: "I make my lively steps away from there." A terrific storm comes up. The lightning flashes, there is roaring thunder, and the dreamer is knocked down by the lightning which strikes the edge of the mesa. "I hear a wall of the mesa fall down to the bottom and this scare me and I woke up suddenly, so I didn't get back to tell the Priests I had seen the snake."

Having been sent on legitimate business, even though in penalty for wrongdoing, the dreamer proves his bravery and says it was a good dream, although he felt frightened after he woke up.

In a second dream, this same dreamer is less fortunate.

DREAM 2

He finds a hole like the *sipapu* [the hole through which the Hopi emerged from the Lowerworld] in which yellowish water is boiling up and coming toward the top. He is afraid that the Water Serpent may rise up, and he is shaking with fear. The creature does appear, and is described typically as brightly colored, red and green, with white belly and with a head like a cat, and fur along its body. The dreamer says: "What shall I do to get away from that terrible Serpent? But I thought of my Grandfather's story. He say a brave person can pull fur from the Serpent's body to make prayer sticks for the Cloud People and that Serpent will not harm him."

The dreamer looks guiltily around to see if anyone is near and says "I don't want to be seen." The Serpent then commands the dreamer to put his arms around its neck: no one is watching so the dreamer then breathes his prayer on his sacred cornmeal and goes to the Serpent. "I was kinda scared but the Serpent told me to obey. Down into the water we go. I woke up with a scream, finding myself in bed and I tell my dream out right away."

This whole dream is charged with guilt. The dreamer is *not* on sacred tribal business, but he is snooping around a sacred spot where he should not be. At the time of the dream he had been discharged from a sacred office where a large part of his duties was the making of prayer sticks in a traditional way—not with fur from the Water Serpent's body. In other dreams he has been praised for his refusal to learn special magic from an uncle.

At another time, when he was in great conflict with his people, he records a third dream about Palulukon.

DREAM 3

"I come toward my home village. People are frightened. Children run toward where I am and tell me there is a big Water Serpent in the pond [where there is in fact no pond] standing out of it four feet high, making an awful noise." When the dreamer nears the pond the Water Serpent is looking at him "sharply . . . as if he is thinking he has seen me before. It look like one I have seen before. The people are all frighten . . . and ask me what can be done to make the Serpent go away." The dreamer reminds his neighbors that they all dislike him and deride him, and that they cannot expect help from him. By the time he reaches his house the village is shaking in an earthquake. He is hungry but his wife begs him to prevent destruction

of the village. The dreamer eats, then makes prayer sticks, and takes these with sacred cornmeal to the water. People cry and beg him to save them. The Serpent now stands eight feet high and is shining like a star.

The dreamer [who cannot swim] strips, swims to Palulukon, and tells the serpent to go back where he belongs. The Serpent lowers his head and is given the sacred objects while the dreamer breathes a prayer.

The creature disappears, and the dreamer lectures his neighbors about their bad habits (particularly gossip about the dreamer), and returns home.

Soon a station wagon arrives bringing the writer and her husband [who have never arrived in one], and then he sees Greyhound Buses coming toward his village, bringing more White friends. He wakes in surprise "feeling good."

This dreamer is very unpopular in his village, and prominent among the many causes of his difficulties is his work with Whites. He is also said to be a coward. He desires companionship with White people, but shows guilt over his desire. He also shows constant need in his dreams to identify with his culture's heroes and to prove himself brave and of good heart, both necessary qualifications if one is to approach Palulukon.

Here is a fourth dream by this man.

DREAM 4

He is carried in his bed toward the west [west being the direction of the land of the dead] by five men who are wearing Kachina masks. They have tried to put a mask on him but he has said that he could not wear a mask because he has been incontinent. The men throw him in a pond. He has felt numb with fear, but regains his strength, climbs out, and throws all five men in the water. They sink, and as he looks back he sees five Water Serpents standing out of the water, beautifully colored.

He tries to go home and is lost in a narrow canyon. His strength is gone. The Sun is coming up out of the west;

he sees a river running east where there is no river. He wakes sweating, and calls it a bad dream.

This dreamer dreams frequently of incontinence in connection with Kachina dancing, often being assured by people who want him to dance that "it is all right anyway." The dreamer lost all five of his babies, and one of these was said to have died because he was incontinent before taking part in a Kachina dance. In his life history he mentions only four children, and when asked about this he said he forgot the fifth. In discussing another dream he "remembered" the accusations of incontinence connected with the death of one of them.

A second dreamer from a different village, who takes life much less seriously, records the following dream of trespass.

DREAM 5

He is taking a walk and his attention is diverted by a car accident in which a small White girl is killed. He finds that he and his companion have trespassed across the sacred cornmeal path of the snake-gatherers before a Snake Dance. They run away from the Snake Priests and take refuge with some women, and he then finds himself in the peculiar situation of helping them with their washing; but as long as he is with women he is safe from the Snake Priests. There is a heavy rain and the dreamer finds shelter in bed with two women, both of whom are holding him "tight around the waist and neck." He awakens and comments regretfully that "this sure didn't seem like a dream but it was anyway."

Awake or dreaming, this solution to the problem of trespass upon Snake Priests is more pleasantly typical for the Hopi male than the one recorded in the preceding dream. In fact this form of protection becomes a game,

and many humorous stories are told about it.

This is a second dream recorded by the same man.

DREAM 6

Some men and girls are swimming nude in a government dam near a sheep corral. Someone pushed the dreamer in and he came up with a bleeding nose "looking like a Mud Head." [This Kachina often acts as a drummer in Palulukon ceremonies.] He then asks a girl to go away with him (romance in mind) and they become aware that the others are all running, clothes in hand, looking back at "something in the water." The girl screams for help, saying "There is something looking at us from the water." The dreamer puts her on his back; they run, he with one leg in his trousers, leaving the rest of his clothes behind. They laugh at their predicament, find a deserted house, and try again, but are again interrupted. The girl jumps from a ledge and lands in the dreamer's arms with her legs "tight around my hips." But he wakes up, and says it was a bad time to wake up.

The dreamer awoke laughing after both of these dreams, and when asked what it was in the water which frightened the swimmers, he said he was in too much of a hurry to look, but "it must have been the Water Serpent because we were behaving that way." At the time this dream was recorded nudity was said to be a rare favor bestowed on few lovers. Both of these dreams and the dreamer's comments on them have a humorous quality that is characteristic of his waking behavior, and he usually manages to find an audience that includes his hapless companions in his dreams.

The following dream concerns a spring in which a famous Palulukon lives, and is from a male dreamer who was under much family pressure to become Christian.

DREAM 7

"I was walking toward the spring in the old village. I have been told that evening that the village is going to be flooded because of some kind of mistake the people have made. In this dream an earthquake started, and it have already made large cracks in the earth so I couldn't turn back. Everywhere the water is flowing and great streams of water were coming down from the mesas on all sides. People were drowning one after another when they fall into cracks trying to run some place. I was trying to run but I couldn't run far. Then I saw something in the water. It was all white. Its feet are not in the water. As it came closer I recognized Jesus Christ. I was waiting to see what He would do or say to the people around there when I woke up before he got to the village. Awful dream!"

This dream plainly states the confusion between two ways of life which plagues this dreamer in waking life, but punishment—a flood—still comes from Palulukon.

A woman dreams the following.

DREAM 8

The woman and her husband's deceased mother are cleaning sand from a spring. Two Water Serpents are standing out from the spring. The dreamer is afraid but the older woman says these are good serpents and will not harm the workers, so they keep at their task. There is only a narrow passage with little steps leading out from the spring, and the dreamer wonders how they are going to get out of it, but the older woman assures her that they can do so. And, "the passage sure gets larger as we are going out so that we come out all right. Then on the way home I see my old uncle asleep in another spring, and there are two Water Serpents sticking out of it and they might harm him. But when I wake him up he say that the Serpent won't harm him but they might harm the ladies. I didn't get home when I wake up but I didn't feel scared when I wake up."

We shall find later that women do, indeed have more to fear from Palulukon than do men, and the dreamer's dead mother-in-law and dead uncle are not reassuring companions in a dream. This is particularly true when one remembers that among the Hopi discipline is in the hands of one's uncles, and that *this* uncle reminds his niece—who at the time was involved in several affairs—that Palulukon can harm women of careless virtue.

The next dream was recorded from a younger woman who was a recent and seemingly ardent convert to Christianity. Her mother and grandmother had also been "converted," but in conversation and in dreams they expressed as much respect for the old Hopi gods as they had had before their conversion.

DREAM 9

In this dream the young woman and a companion go to the village spring for water. Her grandmother has told her about seeing a snake in agitated water in the spring and has said that now no one wants to go there for water. But the dreamer and her companion ignore the warning and when they arrive at the spring, a little girls tells them that the water won't get still, but just keeps going round and round. They then see a black and white Water Serpent and it is bigger than a horse. They start running away, but the water catches up with them, and even though they were holding on to each other in order to stand up, they kept slipping on something. They finally realize that they are slipping on the snake, although it is now much smaller, and they don't know what to do. "I woke up half crying, my heart just jumping so hard I was glad I was only dreaming this awful dream."

Here a recent report by the dreamer's grandmother of a water serpent in a specific spring, plus the dreamer's guilt over a current disgraceful affair with a clan relative—a brother of her companion in this dream—combined to produce a dream of sheer terror in which the snake is unquestionably a sexual symbol.

This is a second dream recorded from this woman.

DREAM 10

The dreamer is wandering around an ancient deserted village populated with spirit people. She went into the house of an aunt long dead who recognized her. Numb with fright, the dreamer tried to leave. She found a snake in her shoe. She killed it and threw it over the cliff. It had been raining but had cleared. Looking down the dreamer suddenly sees a great flood and people are trying to climb up the cliff to get away from their flooded homes. The dreamer sits crying and hoping that her family will be among those who come, but they are not. She awakens in fright.

It was through the pressure from her family that this woman joined a Christian church. One does not kill a snake carelessly among the Hopi, and the violence implied in killing one and throwing it over the cliff is a very un-Hopi-like gesture. Although Palulukon is not specifically mentioned in the dream, the connection (see no. 9) between an earthly snake and the mythical one is plainly indicated by a great flood that destroys the people, including the dreamer's family.

HOPI CONCEPTS AND VALUES

The symbolism in these dreams is in one sense too obvious to require comment, particularly since the maleness of Palulukon is consciously verbalized in Hopi tales. But if we consider the symbolism only, we neglect many aspects of the personal situation drawn sharply in the dreams, and we would also lose the richness of an added dimension of the dream triangle: that of the relation of these dreams to what may be thought of as a culturally conditioned and very consistent "tribal Super-Ego,"[5] which was internalized by these older Hopi to a very remarkable degree, for each dream given calls attention to personal infringement of the tribal code through the use of imagery drawn from the dramatization of an important figure in it. In contrast, the average person in Western society does not make recognizable contact with a God in a dream, possibly because our religion is not taught as intensely, nor pictured and dramatized so vividly, nor absorbed into our lives with the same conviction. Instead, our symbolism of authority in dreams—whether snake or another—is usually uniquely tailored to our own personal experiences with it and symbolized ambiguously.

And, since we cannot divide ourselves between two worlds and expect to find each equally intelligible, if we are to understand the deep conviction that stemmed from the religious mosaic built into the concentric walls of "Hopi-ness" mentioned above, and its relation to imagery in their dreams, we shall have to attempt to cross a bridge of language and live for a time in the Hopi Indian universe where reality does not dwell exclusively in propositions that can be examined through mathematical equations and scientific experiment, as it does in our intellectual world. In doing so we shall frequently find that this bridge of language affords at best a precarious passage, and that if we do leave behind much of the intellectual luggage we have acquired in our own world we cannot cross it at all. For we, no less than the Hopi, have a perceptual structure engineered by language (cf.

Boss 1958; Tauber and Green 1959; Whorf 1956). The requirements of communication thus direct those aspects of perception which can be verbally symbolized into concepts provided by language, and by the time one has acquired the verbal system of his culture, he has also, without being aware of the process, created a situation that serves as a context in which subsequent stimuli are interpreted.

Much in human experience, however, defies verbal projection in any microcosm. Experience more convincing than any mathematical equation forces upon intellectual man, as upon nonliterate man, an awareness of something that our language calls "psyche" and the Hopi call *hikwsi*. Certain nondiscursive aspects of existence are thus conceptually objectivized, and in order to further examine this objectivized psyche we abstract layers of it so as to deal more intellectually with it. But most of our intellectual world does not accept "being" in any but its physical aspects. We thus study psyche—a nonknowable phenomenon—in a manifestation that many investigators are convinced is a concept rather than a reality, and we do so through techniques designed only for *knowing*. The Hopi rightly say that intellectual man stands embarrassed on the threshold of a mystery which he carries within himself, and which is therefore thrust upon him; that this mystery does not fit intelligibly into the web of scientific propositions from which he has created a surrealistic God of geometric space and time, held together by a tension system so tightly anchored in our own linguistically structured perception that there is no escape from it. They may well be right that the ultimate paradox of intellectual man is that he can understand atomic energy and cosmic space more easily than this enigma within himself.

To the extent, then, that we are able to travel without familiar mental luggage, we may perhaps cross the bridge about which I spoke and briefly escape the boundaries of our linguistic perception. We shall then find that while we use different terms for similar patterns or concepts in dealing with experience, the approach is comparable, for if, as Professor Eliade says (1960, pp. 17-18), religion begins where man's relation to the sacred is assumed by him in his entire being, and if it is an experience of existing in its totality, then the Hopi know religion in its essence. For the Hopi *hikwsi*, Breath Body, as the vital aspect of their being, is not confined within the mortal manifestation that is an individual Hopi, even during its sojourn in the Upperworld. It can be projected through thought, prayer, and dreams, and can thus, in one sense, interact with distant people and things. It is at once personal and universal; in some contexts it is a part of *'a'ne himu* (the Mighty Something). [Our informants,, when questioned about *'a'ne himu*, said in "certain ways of talking" this has "deep meaning" and that in this case, "it could mean all Hopi, past and present (tribe), or even be applied to one Hopi, but only to very extraordinary or sacred persons, things, or events." They were reluctant to discuss it and were annoyed at our questions.]

But the Hopi are not "embarrassed" by *hikwsi*, as we are by psyche. And the intensity factor, the action, and above all the thought with which Hopi religious concepts were implemented and the retained are radically different from those of intellectual man. Different, too, and perhaps most important in the "reality" of their dream experience, is their concept of existence as timeless in our sense, for they do not measure time as a linear band stretching behind and ahead of them. Rather, as Titiev (1944, Chap. 14) has stressed in his work on Hopi religion, the day and the year have duality, as do all aspects of being, including a duality of Spirit. When the sun shines in the Upperworld, it is dark in the Lowerworld; when it is summer, here it is winter there. When *hikwsi* occupies its human body, this duality lives in the Upperworld; after death the Breath Body goes alone to the Lowerworld, where it continues the same pattern of existence it knew in the Upperworld. But having merged with, or perhaps because it is now closer to, the Mighty Something, it can work more effectively for the welfare of the tribe, both past and present, in its dual capacity of Kachina and Clouds. The universe for the Hopi may be described, then, as divided into the Upperworld, which we all know through objective experience, and the Lowerworld, which we have called a vast and inexhaustible reservoir of universal being, of male- and femaleness, and of Spirit, the Mighty Something that every Hopi knows through his *hikwsi*, his own Breath Body. Its existence is confirmed in every ceremony, of which it is invariably a part; in fact, without the Lowerworld, the Hopi in the Upperworld would be helpless in their environment. This reservoir of being, however, imposes heavy responsibilities upon the living Hopi, for the *hikwsis* of living and dead Hopi must unite in, or with, the Mighty Something—which is accomplished through the unity of thought involved in their central religious concept of the Good Heart—so that the available potential

of their spiritual reservoir can be fully realized.

As Kennard (1937) has said, the abundant literature describing Hopi ritual has concentrated so much on the magical devices that produce automatic results, that the psychological concomitants have been largely neglected. Ceremonies may be observed and accurately recorded, but both concepts and subjective experience are frequently impossible to translate from one language into another, even in the rare instances where the sacred may be discussed without fear or embarrassment, and with no sense of betrayal in talking to those of another faith.[8] The average Christian, no less than the average Hopi, would find it difficult or impossible to describe to an anthropologist either the concepts of Christianity, or the subjective experience involved in his religion, even in his own language. This seems an obvious truism, but precisely because our intellectual tool *is* language we sometimes assume that conceptual thought is absent rather than untranslatable or withheld.

Whorf (1941, 1956) has attempted to correct this tendency toward ethnocentric bias, and to hurdle the inarticulate barrier that stands between the student of Hopi and understanding, by contrasting certain aspects of our linguistically conceived universe with that of the Hopi. He describes our two cosmic forms as "static, three-dimensional, infinite space and kinetic, one-dimensional time." As with our concept of the psyche, we also objectivize time, and divide it into measurable parts; and we conceive of space as measurable in light-years of time. We thus tend to "feel" about and to verbalize these cosmic "somethings" as a reality comparable to objects which we can hold in our hands, although we also speak of time and space as infinite, which has nonmeasurable and even nonknowable implications.

But the Hopi have no linguistic terms for what we call time; no past, present, or future tenses of verbs; nor do they have a term for space as we know it. Whorf divides the Hopi macrocosm into two entities, which he calls *objective* or *manifested,* and *subjective* or *manifesting.* "The objective or manifested comprise all that is or has been accessible to the senses," including the "historical physical universe, in fact, with no attempt to distinguish between the present and past. . . ." (1956, p. 59). It excludes, however, all that we call future. We see, then, that for the Hopi the *objective* or *manifested*—that which we call the past and present—is already fulfilled, although it continues to influence being, through an accumulation of what one Hopi tried to express to us as "power or force, or maybe just what you might call conscience." For the Hopi, and particularly as it influences their behavior, "time" seems to be that aspect of being which is the knife-edge of now as it is in the process of becoming both "past" and "future." Viewed thus, we have no present either, but our linguistic habits make us feel as if we had.

The Hopi are well aware of the difference between our concept of space and time and their own. With regard to space, one Hopi informant said: "Close your eyes and tell me what you see from Hopi House at the Grand Canyon." With enthusiasm I described the brilliantly colored walls of the canyon, the trail that winds over the edge of it reappearing and crossing a lower mesa, and so on. He smiled and said: "I see the colored walls too, and I know what you mean all right, but your words are wrong.

The trail does not cross, nor disappear, nor do anything. It is only where the mesa has been changed by feet. The trail is still there even when you do not see it, because *I can see all of it.* My feet have walked on the trail all the way down. And another thing, did you go to the Grand Canyon when you described it?" I said, "No, of course I didn't!" His answer to that was, "Part of you was there or part of it was here." Then with a broader smile: "It is easier for me to move you than to move any part of the Grand Canyon."

Similarly, the Hopi are aware of the burden that our concept of time imposes on us. They call us "hurry-up people," and say, "You are running around in circles trying to get nowhere in particular in a hurry." Another said, "You are running down a long road trying to catch up with something but it always keeps ahead of you." For people for whom time is an unceasing process in which everything is predetermined, rather than something that, through measurement, regulates behavior, our approach to time naturally seems demented. They further say, "When you ask a *bahana* [White] if he is hungry or sleepy he looks at his watch; you wear your God on your wrists."

And we can now understand that this Hopi feeling of timelessness in our sense, of the continuity, or more exactly the coexistence of events (the *manifesting* and *manifested*) through time, and the nonrestrictive aspects of their concept of space, give a validity to Hopi dream experience which we, with our linguistically circumscribed concepts of time and space, cannot know. For neither time nor space exists in dreams. Dream action for all men unites past and future in the present, and in dreams space is absent.

It is the cosmic entity of the *subjective* or *manifesting* that each Hopi, in spite of his studied calm, stands in his human condition, face to face with the Mighty Something, and is obliged to interact with it, both awake and asleep. It is *here* that he experiences religion in its essence, seldom if ever in exaltation, for Hopi religion contains no quality of ecstasy, either priestly or secular; but certainly a Hopi here experiences what Eliade calls a total revelation of reality, which regulates every aspect of life, both physical and mental, through the Hopian Good Heart. For this subjective or manifesting aspect of Hopi being—this knife-edge of now which is at once the past and the future—includes not only action but all that we call mental, everything that exists in the mind, that the Hopi speak of as the heart. The need that is prayer may be transferred from the heart by means of *hikwsi*—the Breath Body—to a prayer object with the same effect as spoken prayer. It is no more necessary to speak one's prayer than it is possible to hide a "bad" heart (Kennard 1937, p. 492).

We thus see that, for the Hopi, thought is not merely energy expended through electrical impulses, either turned inward upon self, or dissipated into the surrounding atmosphere; instead thought is a form of energy that acts upon anything with which it comes in contact, either in waking life or in sleep, and this desiring-praying energy may be said not only to be "organized" in ritual, but it must at the same time be "organized" in each Hopi's heart, for each Hopi is responsible to and for everyone in the community; even one heart burdened with malice, worry, or doubt, although it might not be visible to a mortal observer, could defeat the entire community's interaction with life-giving forces. In such a situation, since the Hopian concept of a Good Heart was impossible of attainment, and since one can tolerate only a certain amount of guilt, there was a great game of blame shifting among the Hopi and this added a further burden of guilt through constant gossip and suspicion. This concept of a good heart, in conscious contradistinction to a bad heart (*kahopi:* not Hopi and therefore not good), has been recorded by every observer of the Hopi since the early days of White contact, and is of greatest importance, not only in understanding Hopi philosophy but as the major factor in their deep sense of cultural continuity and their resistance to change. A good heart included conformity to all rules of Hopi good conduct, both external and internal; it was a positive thing. If a Hopi did not keep a good heart, he, or his children, might fall ill and die, or the ceremonies—and thus the vital crops —might fail, for, as has been said, only those with good hearts were effective in prayer. Doubt was *kahopi;* and through reiteration and drama, the dreamlike Lowerworld with its spirit inhabitants became as "real" as the Upperworld.

WATER SERPENT BELIEFS AND RITUALS

In order to relate the dreams given above to concepts provided by Hopi culture, and accepted as reality by the people, we now turn briefly to the religious background of the dreams in which Palulukon appears. Space requires belief and ceremony be shorn of their dramatic beauty, separated from the entity of related parts through which all these are united into a religion, and be merely summarized. Unfortunately, this is comparable to describing an abstract painting by referring to a fragment torn from it, and the Hopi justifiably resent such desecration of the tapestry of their lives.

It must therefore be stressed that neither the Palulukon ceremony, which is one of the number of winter night *kiva* (ceremonial chamber) dances in the Kachina cycle, nor the famous Snake Dance, which is performed in August in the village plazas, is of special importance in the total ceremonial cycle. Rather, each has its part in a related whole, and although both are particularly spectacular—and thus have a rich potential yield for imagery—they are chosen here only because their themes are easily identifiable in Hopi dreams, and *not* because mythical snakes occur more often than do other religious images. Rather they are scattered through Hopi dreams along with other dramatic characters.

Although the Water Serpent concept is widespread in American Indian culture, the Hopi, in particular, gave Palulukon a definite place in their ceremonial cycle. For them he was a flexible deity, at once a collective and a singular personage. As a specific deity he was spoken of as Palulukon who lives in the interior of the earth, controlling all the waters of the universe, including the large bodies of water on which we are floating. If displeased by the misconduct of humanity, particularly family, village, and tribal discord, and by sexual misconduct, he might turn over, thus causing earthquakes, landslides, and floods. The older Hopi were unanimous in saying that he is also asso-

ciated with agitated water, whirlpools, flooding waves, foaming water, and water bubbling up from the ground or bursting from cliff walls. Hopi tales about this serpent include some or all of the above items, and often the following as well: persons who go into the springs ceremonially, sometimes in punishment, sometimes voluntarily, sometimes turning into Water Serpents, sometimes returning in human form, but always carrying prayer objects to Palulukon. When any of these items are mentioned in a dream, particularly one in which intense affectual discomfort is reported, the Water Serpent is usually overtly or covertly present. The creature is also said to impregnate careless women, but in only one tale known to the writer does this happen, and there are no dreams reported where he does so. There are also female Palulukonti, as we shall find in the Palulukon ceremony. There is no doubt as to his general maleness, however, nor that he is a greater threat to women than to men (cf. La Barre 1962, p. 60).

Palulukon also supplies the life-giving sap to plants, and blood to animals, as well as water for all purposes, and in this sense, is all important to desert dwellers. Collectively—sometimes immense, and sometimes "just small"—he lives in his "house" in all springs, pools, and bodies of water. From these he is watching the affairs of men, judging not only their actions but the condition of their hearts.

It must be remembered in this connection that the same bodies of water that are inhabited by the conceptually collective Palulukonti are, by the same sort of extension, symbolic *sipapus*, which are entrances to what I have described as a reservoir of universal being; thus Kachinas and Clouds, which are also the Hopi dead, and other spirit people, as well as the Water Serpent, all have "houses" in these places of water, and it is evident from ceremony and tale that he can intercede effectively with these Cloud-Spirits-Dead to bring rain. Thus the Water Serpent, as deity of the fertilizing waters on the earth and a god of the Lowerworld, conceptualized by the Hopi as a place of germination, was normally á giver of life rather than a destroyer of life. But here, as in all facets of Hopi philosophy, the role that Palulukon might choose to play was the direct responsibility of the Hopi, individually and collectively. Prayer sticks, carrying, as we have seen, the powerful Breath-Spirit-Desiring-Prayer quality of the Hopian Good Heart, were made of this deity on all important ceremonial occasions. He was so sacred, in fact, that most of my informants were reluctant to discuss him, and Parsons reports that one of her informants refused to draw a picture of Palulukon for this reason (Parsons 1939, p. 186n.). If approached with reverence, however, and given prayer objects by persons with good hearts, he watched quietly, eventually disappearing with these into agitated water. Only those with bad hearts need fear Palulukon.

THE PALULUKON CEREMONY

The vital problem for the Hopi in their arid land was an uncertain water supply, and the outward expression of their deep need for the power available in their macrocosm was arranged in a cycle of ceremonies, the most impressive of which, at least among the exoteric rituals, were the Kachina dances mentioned above. These were colorful pageants in which meticulously trained dancers performed on winter evenings in underground ceremonial *kivas,* and often during the spring and summer in the village plazas from sunrise to sunset, with short intermissions for food and rest. Their bodies were ceremonially painted, and brilliant costumes were worn, along with beautifully carved and painted masks which identified the particular gods who were taking' part in the ceremony.

In the religious context, also, we must remember the intimate atmosphere that surrounded a Hopi child in the learning situation. Here children were taught that if *all* Hopi kept good hearts, the dancing gods would send rain. There was a holiday atmosphere throughout a village on dance days, but while each dance was being performed, there was the quiet of profound concentration. As the children grew older, carved likenesses of these gods, as well as other presents, were given to them by the gods themselves. These Kachina dolls were objects of instruction, and as a child grew in understanding, he could not fail to realize that the dancers were part of a religious ceremony of utmost importance in his world, that they were rain-bringing and thus life giving gods, as well as the focus of communal release from a drab workaday world. Of the winter *kiva* dances Kennard writes as follows:

The dance steps, the songs, and the Kachinas are the same that are used in the large dances in the plaza, but the effects are all intensified by the setting. Within that small enclosed space the gods seem to dominate. Nothing else matters. As a Hopi once remarked when we were watching a particularly colorful and vigorous dance, "You don't care about the outside world at all." The pounding of their feet on the floor reverberates, the song fills the *kiva* with music. The always pronounced rhythm becomes more pronounced. The flickering of the fire creates lighting effects impossible in a modern theatre as it flashes on silver bow guards, on shining black hair, on brightly painted mask, on glistening body paint. Each detail is accentuated for a moment and dropped into shadow again. The Kachinas turn and new colors, new feathers stand out for a moment and recede to mingle their individual beauty with that of the whole. For it is the whole line performing, the merging of so many details of costume, dance and song, in synchronous movement that creates such an effective performance. Their numbers seem doubled and trebled by the shadows on the walls and ceiling, which assume fantastic forms. (Kennard 1938, pp. 17-18)

It was during this series of night *kiva* dances, in this period of the year when freedom from fields meant freedom to unite worship and drama so richly on an inside stage, that the ceremony featuring Palulukon puppets was performed (cf. the following with Titiev 1944; Stephen 1936; Hough 1915). All observers agree that this ceremony is an intricate and magnificently staged drama. The Palulukonti "house" is an elaborately painted screen on which are depicted human and supernatural figures, among them Clouds, Corn, and Lightning—itself the acme of fertilization—and Snake, Sun, and Moon symbols. The Sun and Moon symbols are on hinged disks through which the Palulukonti are thrust during the dance. These effigies are cleverly constructed of a spine and a series of hoops, over which cured skin is tightly stretched and then painted. The serpents vary from one foot for the young Palulukonhoyas to four feet for the adults. the gourd heads have prominent eyes, and a horn of wood, white teeth, and a red leather tongue. The whole results in exceedingly realistic-looking serpents which are very flexible. There is always one large male and one large **female** serpent, the latter having

prominent seed-filled skin udders, and there are at least two young Palulukonhoyas.

On the night of the ceremony, while esoteric rites are being performed by the Kachinas at the village spring, villagers gather in the *Kiva* for the exoteric performance, and a fire is built in the fireplace. The return of the Kachinas carrying the serpent effigies from the spring is announced outside the *kiva* by the hoarse roar of gourd trumpets or drums, this being the voice of Palulukon. The Hopis say that the trumpeting during the course of the dance is the "voice of the water, or water talk." When the trumpet is first heard, the *Kiva* is darkened so that the scenery can be arranged. In preparation for the ceremony, members of the sponsoring *kiva* plant corn which is forced-grown in the *kiva*. On the night of the ceremony the young plants are arranged in small clay supports, which are invisible in the dimly lit *kiva,* and when the blankets are withdrawn from the front of the fireplace, the screen—which is described above—is in place, the field of growing corn is seen on what minutes before was a bare *kiva* floor, and small birds run back and forth on top of the screen. Then, as the songs of the Kachinas and the roar of the trumpet mingle and increase in volume, the Sun and Moon flaps suddenly spring open, and the Palulukonti, with fierce teeth and red tongue glinting in the firelight, come through them. The serpents struggle with one another and with the actors, they writhe and bite, until having emerged full length into the room, they finally bend down and "harvest" the corn in the stimulated field. At this point the central Serpent is seen to have udders, and she suckles the other serpents. Then, amid great excitement and a terrific sound of mingled "voice of the water," and Kachina voices, Hahai, the Mother of the Kachinas—and in this capacity also the ancestress of the Palulukonti —comes forward and presents her breasts to each of them, and each serpent goes through the motions of suckling from them.

After the performance the fire is again covered, so that the Kachinas may take the Palulukonti and the screen out of the *kiva* in darkness. The blankets are then removed from the fireplace and the "harvested corn" is given to the girls and women in the audience.

This *kiva* performance is deeply etched in the memory of all who have seen it, and for the Hopi, who know its sacred implications, and particularly for the uninitiated children, who, in the dimly lit *kiva* must certainly have believed that these were actually supernatural serpents, the impact of the entire ceremony must have been tremendous. And we again repeat that this was not an isolated, once-in-a-life-time experience, but something these older Hopi have experienced repeatedly from infancy.

SUMMARY

We can now return with greater understanding to the dreams reported above. We have suggested that dreams may be thought of as a triangular production: (1) the latent content that is said to appear in universal symbols, and represents material not accesible to consciousness; (2) the dreamer's personality organization, and his personal situation at the time of the dream; and (3) the relation of the dreams to cultural provision.

With reference to latent content and

universal symbols, we do not have the kind of data that can legitimately be used for depth analysis of specific dreams. We can, however, make certain general suggestions with regard to the symbolic implications of Palulukon. First, we have in Hopi individuals a strongly controlled ego structure, and throughout the society what we have called a culturally conditioned superego that was remarkably consistent among these older Hopi. As far as the writer has been able to determine through personal investigation and from the rich literature on the Hopi, there was strong overt control in *all* emotional situations: anger, physical aggression, joy—in fact, in everything except verbal aggression through gossip, and in sexual activity, but even here orgiastic group aspects that are present in many nonliterate groups were absent. Much evidence suggests that sexual activity early comes to be positively valued for reasons of intrigue, boasting, and joking, in addition to the physical act itself. Nor was sexual activity romanticized as it is in Western society. Rather sexuality was *assumed*, at both the personal and societal level, from childhood on, in a highly realistic and matter-of-fact fashion. In this situation sexual repression was a less serious problem than among ourselves and sexuality in dreams, as in waking life, was more directly expressed. Having separated sex from sin in all but certain specific categories, the Hopi have in one sense defanged the "snake."

We find, however, that Palulukon, as well as other fertility figures (for instance, Muingwa who grows heavy with seeds that grow on his body, and then thin when he shaves them off), remains a conscious sexual symbol in the culture, and as such is sometimes overt, or on the edge of awareness in

Hopi dreams. But Palulukon, along with other deities, objects to *all kahopi* behavior, including sexual misconduct, gossip, quarrels, and physical aggression. Thus we find that Palulukon, as a completely overt cultural concept, is taken over in individual dreams, as are other dramatic cultural characters, not in the sense of sought visions that are so frequently important in nonliterate cultures, but simply as everyday, culturally defined symbols that are applicable to personal situations in the dreamer's life situation at the time of the dream. When Palulukon appears in a Hopi dream, it indicates that the dreamer or his dream companions are *kahopi* and the dream usually indicates in what way this is so. Even though the dream may support the dreamer at the moment, we see that it is seldom completely satisfying, and Hopi rules about dream discussion thus start a frequently successful probing of the dreamer's situation. By contrast, in our culture, which does not stress dreaming, nor prescribe ways of dealing with dreams, nor define its symbols so plainly, an individual may awaken in fright from a dream in which he was in mortal danger from a snake, but unless he is psychoanalytically oriented, he is unlikely to connect the dream with transgression accomplished or desired.

The problem-solving dimensions of Hopi dreams, which have been discussed elsewhere (Eggan 1955), have great importance in a culture where ego is in the hands of a doubly reinforced superego—personal and societal. (It is not suggested that the larger but more diffuse society in which we live does not contribute to our own superegos; obviously it does, but by the very nature of its diffusion it cannot do so as effectively as does the closely knit and consistently conditioned Hopi society.) The personal factor, or state of being at the time of the dream, of course determines the specific use both of cultural and of personally invented symbols, as well as the use of culturally prescribed ways of dealing with the dream. We find that the Hopi Water Serpent is firmly imprinted upon Hopi minds through ceremony and tale, both as a possible punishing and a possible supportive agent. He may appear in dreams charged with guilt or fear, as in dreams 2 and 4 above, or in dreams that give ego-support through making the dreamer feel brave or good of heart and his enemies wicked, as in dream 3; occasionally he appears in dreams where the dreamer is somewhat humorously involved with his culturally constituted self.

If a man trespasses across a sacred cornmeal path (dream 1) he may pay the penalty imposed by the Snake Priests, who are known to have scorned this particular dreamer by refusing to utilize a socially recognized mechanism to initiate him into their society. The dreamer thus partially reassures his ego by going to Palulukon and proving in the dream that he is brave and good of heart, but he is not fully reassured; he awakens in fright after a narrow escape from lightning before he can report his success to them. In the second man's dream of trespass, his fear of *living* snakes is frankly admitted by running away from the Snake Priests and taking refuge with women so that the Snake Priests cannot capture him; and he indicates his laughing acceptance of sexuality as the possible result of such refuge by ending the dream in bed with two possessive women, but awakens with regret that it was only a dream. It is, after all, impossible for him to cross a sacred cornmeal path with complete disregard of its significance. This form of escape is as logical a solution for this dreamer as it would have been illogical for the first dreamer, who shows in many dreams that he is not sure of his welcome with women.

Again, if one approaches a sacred spring with selfish motives, or on unauthorized business, as indicated by the desire not to be seen (dream 2) one has reason to be afraid, and is vividly reminded of the questionable state of one's heart by being taken by Palulukon down through the water into the Lowerworld. Even in a dream where a nominal Christian sees Christ walking on a Water Serpent flood—in effect replacing the Palulukon of Hopi dreams—the dreamer is not reassured and he calls it an "awful dream." Christ evidently has not supplanted Palulukon effectively in his life. Nor does a second recently converted Christian (dream 9) find her new religion adequate protection against this *kiva* visitor of her childhood. Here a recent report by her grandmother of a Water Serpent in a specific spring, plus the dreamer's guilt over a current disgraceful affair with a clan relative—a brother of her companion in this dream—combine to produce a dream of sheer terror in which the snake is unquestionably a sexual symbol. This relationship is incestuous for a Hopi, even though Christian. And in addition, one does not ignore the warning of a strong old Hopi grandmother who is head of one's clan and who disapproves of the woman's shocking behavior. In dream 10, while in a spirit village, which is a dangerous situation in Hopi dreams, this same dreamer finds that her family, who exerted pressure to convert her to Christanity, has no protection from Palulukon. They are destroyed in the flood. Although Palulukon is not specifically mentioned in this dream, his attributes as given in the summary of beliefs regarding him, are present in it and in all the Christian dreams given. In this desert country, only Palulukon could cause a flood of such proportions.

As for the third aspect of the dream triangle, the cultural provisions, it is obvious that a cultural stress on dreams, and definite rules for dealing with them, must have important implications for an individual dreamer, if only because they emphasize recall and "confession" of the bad thoughts in a dream, a practice that results in a discussion of dreams and a tendency to further work out problems in them through "confession" of questionable behavior. That this practice contributes to secondary elaboration in frequently producing what is more properly termed a "dream story" than a dream cannot be denied; but it is almost always possible to distinguish clearly between the characteristically illogical dream and the culturally available associations with it (cf. Devereux 1957; Opler 1942; Wallace 1958; Hallowell 1948). Also the cultural elaborations chosen can usually be related to the known past and present problems of the dreamer, if one is familiar with both the dreamer and his culture. And it must be emphasized that the Hopi are perfectly well aware that any dream is an attempt by self (*hikwsi*) to make a statement about the dreamer's present situation and cultural integration. This is a conscious, culturally specific belief, otherwise dreams would not require specific treatment. A Hopi dreamer who wears his culture as easily as he wears his clothes, with satisfaction, with deep emotional commitment, or with humor, and is at the time of the dream more or less at peace with self, neither "begs" from his culture and its heroes, nor questions it in his dreams, as do the first male dreamer and the Christian dreamers above. Rather he simply experiences it as a continuation of his waking life, as does the second male dreamer discussed. But guilt, fear, and doubt make different demands upon self, upon cultural provisions, and upon dreams, and all these demands are clearly reflected in the manifest content of Hopi dreams.

We have long emphasized both the positive individual and social aspects of dreams as manipulated by the Hopi (Eggan 1949, 1952, 1955), and their pertinence in the study of Hopi society and culture. And while neither the conceptual nor the therapeutic utility of examining *kikwsi*-psyche in its many faceted parts can be questioned, the two are, after all, related wholes. For when a Hopi *hikwsi* searches through *dimoki*—the "bundle" of his dream thoughts—he finds it richly populated with cultural images that act as a rudder to push a demanding self back into the coercive tide of social process.

NOTES

1. My obligation to Hopi informant-friends cannot be adequately acknowledged because they wish to remain anonymous. I wish particularly to express my gratitude to Milton Singer, who is familiar with various fields that are relevant to this paper, and who has been kind enough to read several versions of it; Dr. Montague Ullman and Fred Eggan have also read preliminary drafts. It has been impossible, however, to incorporate many of the suggestions made by these readers. Fred and Alice Kabotie, close Hopi friends for several decades, have refused to act as "informants," but have tried to further my understanding of Hopi psychology.

2. Whorf (1956, p. 60) translates *'a'ne, himu as* "the Mighty Something"; cf. Voegelin and Voeglin (1957): *'a'ni*, "very or intensely so," and *himu*, "tribes or persons, things or belongings"; Stephen (1936, p. 1203): *'a'ni*, "very much, intense, powerful."

3. Cf. Devereux (1951) in which he demonstrates the use of dreams as a defense mechanism in "Wolf" Indian culture; see also Eggan (1955); French (1937); Wallace (1958); and further bibliography on this subject in Eggan (1961).

4. I do not agree, as is sometimes stated, that there is no direction connection between the two; it would seem that this conclusion depends upon what is meant by direct connection. Much evidence seems to indicate that there is a *conceptual* connection. The use of the same black paint—so sacred it can cause death if a young man touches it—in both ceremonies, the use of Palulukon figures on the Snake dancers' kilts, and the swelling and curing aspects among others of both Palulukon and live snakes indicate a connection among all aspects of the Sanke-spirit-substance (see Parsons 1939, I, 185n).

5. See Piers and Singer (1953, p. 6) where Dr. Piers defines "Super-Ego" as stemming from the internalization of the punishing, restrictive aspects of parental images, real or projected. Hopi society does not have a primary family in our sense, but extends relationships widely within the household and clan (children have man "mothers" around them from birth), so that punishment is more of a societal function than purely parental, as it is among ourselves (see Eggan 1956).

6. This is far from the situation workers have found among the Hopi. All investigators have recorded Hopi reluctance to discuss any esoteric aspect of ceremony or belief, although their ever present preoccupation with a Good Heart has been universally recorded. And it is not intended to imply, as the summary in this paper may seem to suggest, that each Hopi possesses a unified and articulate

body of philosophy. Such explicit codification depends upon written, rather than oral inheritance. But through ceremonies, tales, and dreams, as well as in the occasional discussions with Hopi where explanations of sacred concepts were attempted, a remarkably interconnected picture of Hopi philosophy has emerged, however illogical the components may seem to us.

REFERENCES

Asch, Solomon E.
    1952   *Social Psychology.* New York: Prentice-Hall.
Boss, Medard
    1958   *The Analysis of Dreams.* New York: Philosophical Library.
Devereux, George
    1951   *Reality and Dream: Psychotherapy of a Plains Indian.* New York: International Universities Press.
    1957   Dream learning and individual ritual differences in Mohave shamanism. *American Anthropologist* 59:1036-1045.
Eggan, Dorothy
    1949   The significance of dreams for anthropological research. *American Anthropologist* 51:177-198.
    1952   The manifest content of dreams: A challenge to social science. *American Anthropologist* 54:469-485.
    1955   The personal use of myth in dreams. *In* T. Sebeok (ed.), "Myth: A symposium." *Journal of American Folklore,* 68:445-453.
    1956   Instruction and affect in Hopi cultural continuity. *Southwestern Journal of Anthropology* 12:347-370.
    1961   Dream analysis. *In* B. Kaplan (ed.), *Studying Personality Cross-Culturally.* Evanston, Ill.: Row, Peterson.
Eliade, Mircea
    1960   *Myths, Dreams and Mysteries.* New York: Harper.
Fisher, Charles, and I. H. Paul
    1959   The effects of subliminal visual stimulation on images and dreams: A validation study. *Journal of American Psychoanalytic Association* 8 (1):35-83.
French, Thomas
    1937   Reality testing in dreams. *Psychoanalytic Quarterly* 6:62-77.
Hallowell, A. Irving
    1948   Acculturation processes and personality changes. *In* Kluckhohn and H. A. Murray (eds.), *Personality in Nature, Society and Culture.* New York: A. A. Knopf.
    1955   *Culture and Experience.* Philadelphia: University of Pennsylvania Press.
Hough, Walter
    1915   *The Hopi Indians.* Cedar Rapids, Iowa: Torch Press.
Kennard, Edward A.
    1937   Hopi reactions to death. *American Anthropologist* 39:491-496.
    1938   Introduction. *In* E. Earle and E. A. Kennard, *Hopi Kachinas.* New York: J. J. Augustin.
La Barre, Weston
    1962   *They Shall Take Up Serpents.* Minneapolis: University of Minnesota Press.
Murphy, Gardner
    1947   *Personality: A Biosocial Approach to Origins and Structure.* New York and London: Harper.
Opler, Marvin K.
    1942   Techniques in social analysis. *Journal of Social Psychology* 15:91-127.
Parsons, Elsie Clews
    1939   *Pueblo Indian Religion.* Chicago: University of Chicago Press.
Piers, Gerhart, and Milton B. Singer
    1953   *Shame and Guilt: A Psychoanalytic and a Cultural Study.* Springfield, Ill.: Charles C. Thomas.

Stephen, A. M.
1936   *Hopi Journal*. Elsie Clews Parsons, (ed.), New York: Columbia University Press.
Tauber, Edward S., and Maurice R. Green
1959   *Prelogical Experience*. New York: Basic Books.
Titiev, Mischa
1944   *Old Oraibi*. Papers of the Peabody Museum of American Archaeology and Ethnology 22 (1). Cambridge, Mass.: Harvard University Press.
Voegelin, Carl, and Florence Voegelin
1957   *Hopi Domains*. Indiana University Publications in Anthropology and Linguistics. Memoir 17. Bloomington, Ind.: Indiana University Press.
Wallace, Anthony F. C.
1958   Dreams and wishes of the soul. *American Anthropologist* 60:234-248.
Whorf, B. L.
1941   The relation of habitual thought to language. *In* L. Spier, A. Hallowell, and S. S. Newman, (eds.), *Language, Culture and Personality: Essays in Memory of Edward Sapir*. Menasha, Wisc.: Sapir Memorial Publication Fund.
1956   *Language, Thought and Reality: Selected Writings of Benjamin Lee Whorf*. J. B. Caroll, (ed.), Cambridge, Mass.: Technology Press; and New York: John Wiley and Sons.

15. TAHITI, SIN, AND THE QUESTION OF INTEGRATION BETWEEN PERSONALITY AND SOCIOCULTURAL SYSTEMS

ROBERT I. LEVY

Robert I. Levy, M.D., is Professor of Anthropology, University of California, San Diego. Reprinted from *The Psychoanalytic Study of Society*, Volume 5, Warner Muensterberger and Sidney Axelrad, editors, by permission of International Universities Press, Inc. Copyright © 1972, by International Universities Press, Inc.

[Editor's note: For a more comprehensive treatment of Tahitian personality, see *Tahitians: Mind and Experience in the Society Islands* by Robert I. Levy, University of Chicago Press, 1973.]

AMONG THE SEVERAL major contrasts that Westerners found between themselves and the savages they had begun to encounter in recent centuries of expansion, savages so useful to Europeans for the construction of identities and ideologies by opposition, was the contrast of self-control, of conscience. This was particularly true of Polynesia, one of the homes of the Noble Savage and site of much Puritan missionary activity. The romantic French explorer Bougainville (1771) found the Tahitians free of sexual shame:

Each day our people walked in the country, unarmed, alone or in small groups. The natives invited them to enter the houses and fed them there; but it was not a light snack to which the civility of the host is limited here. They offered them their daughters. The hut filled instantly with a curious crowd of men and women who made a circle around the guest and the young victim of duty to hospitality. The ground was covered with leaves and flowers, and musicians sang to the harmonies of the flute a hymn of joy. Venus is here the goddess of hospitality. Her worship does not admit of mysteries, and each joy is a celebration for the nation. They were surprised at the embarrassment that they witnessed. Our habits have tended to forbid that kind of publicity. (1771, p. 128).

The English nonconformist evangelical missionaries, intrigued by this apparent shamelessness combined with an evidently "gentle nature," moved avidly into the new mission field, made rapid conversions,[1] but were not satisfied. The wife of a missionary in the Cook Islands put the problem clearly in 1827, "I am far from considering the generality of them true Christians, as many who make a profession want the essentials, which are a sorrow for sin when committed and a hatred for it afterward" (Beaglehole 1957), p. 31).

The problems of motives and forms of self-control in non-Western peoples occupied anthropologists, particularly those working in culture and personality, in the 1930s and the following two decades. Much of this is summed up in *Shame and Guilt* by Piers and Singer (1953). An attempt was made to set up a dichotomy of "shame cultures" versus "guilt cultures" (shame and guilt being variously defined), according to whether social conformity was motivated or associated primarily with one or the other phenomenon. It became clear that the dichotomy was an attempt to set up simplified contrasting categories, following the missionary's wife, by starting from a Western ideal type and reifying its opposite. As the anthropologist Alfred Kroeber (1948) put it,

The reputedly independant and separate verdicts of Anglo-Saxon anthropologists on Asiatic, Oceanic, native American, and African cultures, that shame is a far more influential motivation in them than a sense of sin, does not really specifically characterize these cultures nearly so much as its opposite—conscious sinfulness—characterizes Anglo-Saxon and Protestant culture. (1948, p. 612).

The relationships between those sociocultural and psychological matters indicated by "shame" and "guilt," either at the phenomenological or analytic levels, turned out to be anything but simple polar types (De Vos 1960; Piers and Singer 1953; Reider 1950; Weidman 1965).

As for sociocultural analysis, Singer summed up,

Whether, then, we consider the criterion of internal and external sanctions, or the cross-cultural psychometric data, or the psychoanalytic interpretations of cultures, we cannot find sufficient evidence to justify the theory that most cultures of the world are shame cultures. . . . What evidence there is, tends to support the conclusion that the sense of guilt *and* the sense of shame are found in most cultures, and that the quantitative distribution of these sanctions has little to do with the "progressive" or "backward" character of a culture. (Piers and Singer 1953, pp. 78-79).

Singer had noted that one problem in the shame culture/guilt culture contrast was that,

psychological characterizations and comparisons of cultures . . . are of low validity because they seek to isolate "pure" psychological categories. Their validity and fruitfulness will increase as they abandon this "psychologism," and develop instead characterizing constructs in which the emotional emphases of a culture are integrally related to cultural values, world view, overt behavior, and features of social organization. (Piers and Singer 1953, p. 18).

Using this psychocultural approach, I wish, in relation to observations on Tahitian behavior, to suggest the nature of a structural contrast which is, I believe, the basis for the intuition that conceiving of guilt cultures and shame cultures was somehow meaningful. The two concepts point to important features, but, I will argue, they are related to social action in a way other than as alternative motives for conformity in a two-member contrasting set. There have been ample criticisms of the inadequacy of the dichotomy; I will suggest an alternative.[2]

I spent 26 months during 1961-1964 studying various psychological and anthropological patterns in two Tahitian-speaking communities in French Polynesia.[3] One of these communities was a rural, relatively traditional village on the island of Huahine, with a mixed subsistence (horticultural and fishing) and market (copra and vanilla) economy, which I call "Piri," the other was a relatively urbanized enclave, "Roto," in Papeete, the territorial administrative center on the island of Tahiti.

CULTURAL ASPECTS OF TAHITIAN BEHAVIORAL CONTROLS: SHAME AND EMBARRASSMENT

In the course of semistructured psychodynamic interviews which I gave to some individuals in the communities, I approached the question of the conscious and doctrinal aspects of self-control. I asked the subjects of the interviews whether they were aware of impulses which they had and which they forbear acting on. Most said they did have such impulses, and listed them. I then asked them why they did not act. I will present some sample responses, translated from the tape-recorded interviews. My questions are in parentheses. Two key terms to be analyzed further, I will leave in Tahitian: *Ha'ama*,[4] which may be glossed shame/embarrassment, and *arofa* (related to the Hawaiian *aloha*),which may be glossed empathy/pity/compassion.

Marae, a humble, easygoing member of Piri's village society has just said that he does have thoughts which he doesn't act upon.

(What kinds of thoughts?) One example . . . there grows up the thought to go and steal. And afterwards . . . I think it out, "ah, do not do it. It is a bad thing to go and steal and be seen, and be locked up in prison. Ah, that is a bad thing, so stop." [He pauses for a moment, and then goes on.] Another example, you decide to go and seduce some woman. ["You" rather than "I," serves in Tahitian, as in English, as a distancing device.] You think about going, but there grows in you the response, "Don't, it is a fear-producing action." (Why?) If you are seen, her man [husband] would come and beat you up, or if not, he would beat up the woman and kill her. That is the way it is when bad thoughts arise. (Do you have other bad thoughts?) There are some thoughts . . . some bad thoughts that one thinks about doing but [one says to oneself] "Don't, it involves fear." (Why?) It is a matter of *ha'ama* if one is seen. (A *ha'ama* matter if seen?) Yes, [it is] a *ha'ama* thing if seen, bad behavior. (Yes . . .) But if one does good things, ah!, it is not a matter involving *ha'ama*.

(Now suppose that the thought to steal came to you, or the thought to try to go and seduce [someone else's] woman, and if you were very sure that you would not be seen . . .) [He interrupts] . . . one *would be seen.* (No, we are not talking about the way things are, but just supposing . . .) All right. (If you were absolutely certain that no

one could see you . . . if a sorcerer or angel said to you nobody could see you, what would you do?) About stealing? [He is stalling for time.] (Stealing, that sort of thing . . .) If the desire within me were strong, I would go and steal.

I then asked him what he would do if everyone had left the village for a day, and he asnwered, "I think I would go and steal." (And as to the woman?) "There would be times when the wish would grow, and I would indeed go and 'play around.' There would be no way [to stop it], I would think that I should not do it, but no, the thought would be powerful to go and lie with her."[5]

Sequences of this kind gave casual Western observers the impression that they were dealing with a psychopath, an individual with a weak conscience, but even this short sequence evidently indicates that this is too simplistic an inference.[6] The emotion stressed by Marae is fear. He is afraid of the consequences of his act, one of which is feeling ashamed. He stresses visibility for both the physical harm and trouble arising from an act, and for his shame feelings . . . that is, his behavior will become seen or known to other members of the community. In Tahitian, the same word, *'ite,* signifies both see and know. Invisibility does not provide an easy escape, for actions, he feels, will most likely be seen. Finally he says that without the "visibility controls" his actions would depend on the strength of his impulses.

Marae talked of his anxiety about gossip if he were to be seen. "If you were seen when you go to play around with some woman it is a very *ha'ama* thing when morning comes and people say, 'That man, he went to play around with some woman.' "

Probing for conscious guilt-type controls, I asked Marae whether there were things that he had done which he kept thinking about weeks or months after the event. He then told of a woman whom he had temporarily taken from her spouse. He had then broken with her. She left the village and went to a "far away" place with her former man. Marae then said, "It caused *arofa* afterwards. [As a feeling within Marae.] That man . . . it was an *arofa* causing thing . . . because he had been staying with his woman, they had been well together. And then I, I had to play around with this woman, I was bad." But he then added, "I had [earlier] stopped that affair. But then I started again, yes, I started again. After a long time it became seen/known. It was a very *ha'ama* matter. If it hadn't been seen/known I would not have stopped." *Arofa*, empathy and pity, is invoked. Then he shifted to statements of visibility, with its associated fear and shame. Although Marae stressed that only the chances of being seen stopped him, his statement about *arofa* implies that these controls prevent him from doing things which are bad even apart from immediate public opinion—things which hurt someone else, which through empathy cause feelings of pity.

Some other villagers added reasons for avoiding bad-doing. One man said that even if no one else saw you God can see you. That is the person who is looking at you. You know that God is up in the heaven looking at you. Therefore, you don't steal." The village pastor added that he carefully follows the rules of the Bible, and this protects him from wrong-doing. The stress throughout is on the external source of control.

Ha'ama represents a very salient complex in Tahitian conception and behavior. It represents a very good deal of native psychological and moral

analysis. People readily provide lists in answer to the question "What makes people feel *ha'ama*?" Here is an example, given by a man in Piri. (1) When young people in Piri first see a stranger, they feel *ha'ama*. (2) If he, the speaker, were to enter someone's house and did not know the person, he would feel *ha'ama* at first. (3) If he were to bring me into a friend's house unannounced, and if the house were in disorder the friend would feel *ha'ama*. He stopped at this point.

Marae, quoted above, has a list with six items on it. (1) If you have to go ask someone to give you or lend you something. (2) If you try to seduce a woman and she calls out or chases you away. (3) If you are walking along the village path all dressed up with a wreath of flowers on your head and perfumed with perfumed oil and people make fun of you. (4) If you have been drunk and the next day people recount what you have done. (5) If you sing, but have a bad voice. (6) [A blanket final item] If you do something bad.

These typical first presentations are generally not involved with evident moral behavior of the *good versus evil* type, but, with the exception of Marae's vague sixth item, with two sorts of *ha'ama* situations. The first has no moral tone in itself, the second has the moral tone proper/improper, or more accurately fitting/unfitting or illfittingly.

The first group, the nonmoral *ha'ama* occasions, are situations wherein an individual becomes involved with other people in an extraordinary, unfamiliar way. A stranger in one's house, entering into the house of a stranger, having a familiar person enter one's house when it is not properly arranged, even being seen when one is more dressed up and decorated than usual, seem to have some of these features. When the children in a household in which I was working had begun to feel comfortable with me, we would occasionally find ourselves together at a family festival at a table in a part of the house which was not usually used for eating. The children became embarrassed again. That is, in these cases the shift of the familiar frames and contexts of behavior produced *ha'ama*. This aspect of *ha'ama* is constantly related in Tahitian speech to the commonly used expression *matau*, which means to get used to or be acquainted with a person or situation. People were said to be *ha'ama* because they were not *matau* in a situation, and becoming *matau* was an explanation for the disappearance of the *ha'ama*. This *ha'ama*, embarrassment caused by violation of the familiar, tends to be morally neutral in relation to the acts or conditions which bring it about. Sensitivity to *ha'ama* is considered a desirable characterological quality. It is a key element in villagers' approving separation of themselves from "brash" Europeanized Tahitians. It is good that one can feel *ha'ama*. In the examples of states or acts producing *ha'ama* referred to below, the state or act is morally disapproved, while the sensitivity to disapproval is, at another level of evaluation, approved. But in these examples the situation producing *ha'ama* does not reflect negatively on the person who has the feeling. *Ha'ama* as discomfort caused by becoming visible in unusual ways can, in fact, inhibit acts which are generally recognized as good acts. For example, a twelve-year-old girl in Piri told me that she wanted to give a flower wreath to the schoolteacher when he was to leave for a vacation, but did not because the other children were not going to do the same thing, and she was afraid she would feel *ha'ama*.

The examples of *ha'ama* about a disorderly house, and Marae's remark about his nonbeautiful singing voice (most people in Piri sing beautifully) are examples of a second cluster of occasions for *ha'ama*—those situations in which the body, body actions, personal skills, and the state of certain objects which intimately belong to one, such as clothes and house, are not maintained or performing adequately. These are related intimately to the approval or disapproval by others as judges. Dirtiness and disorder are salient aspects of this aspect of *ha'ama*, both in themselves and as metaphors for other types of shameworthy behavior. There is a great stress on avoiding personal dirtiness of body or of clothes. Such dirtiness is not only a matter of great shame, but is considered most deviant;[7] dirtiness, in fact, would suggest deviance of psychotic dimensions.

The word for clean is *ma*. One expression for the act of cleaning somethings is *ha'ama*, to make clean. Whether this homonymous word gives any clue to the historical etymology of *ha'ama* as shame/embarrassment, is unclear, but it is a tempting speculation. Metaphoric terms related to dirtiness, disorder, and disgust (the latter with a strong tone of gastric rejection, the core meaning referring to a desire to vomit) were used to refer to moral *ha'ama* situations such as incest.

Dirtiness seems to be a core metaphor for this maintenance/performance group. But there are other subtypes, to which dirtiness does not apply. Marae's inadequate singing voice is an example. Similarly, people sometimes say they feel *ha'ama* because of body defects. Adolescents with missing teeth cover their mouths when they laugh, and this was explained as being due to *ha'ama*. One elderly male said that he felt *ha'ama* as an adolescent because he was relatively puny. He put it, "In the time of youth, you had a little *ha'ama* because you were young and rather weak. You had *ha'ama* because people would say 'that person is a very weak person,' and you were ashamed."

Ha'ama is also related to sexual behaviors. Here the idea of *ha'ama*, both as a criticism and an affect, is particularly related to exposure of the genitalia. Whatever the complex of meanings and affects which might be involved with social disapproval of genital exposure, one strand of significance seems to involve dirtiness and contamination. Menstrual blood is believed to be magically contaminating. (Pre-Christian eating taboos involved sexually segregated eating, the violation of which was thought, according to some reports, to produce blindness in men. Blindness might have symbolized lack of clarity, of distinction, as well as castration.) There is a great deal of shame-sensitive concern among young adolescent boys about the lack of cleanliness of the penis (because of smegma) prior to the male supercision operation which follows puberty, and which has as one of its several themes the dirtiness of the head of the unsupercised penis.

Ha'ama is frequently invoked in criticism of incestual unions. This is in actual community experience mostly a question of incest in the extended family which is very much more common and distinct in much of its meaning from nuclear family incest. It is considered a matter involving *ha'ama*, disgust, and disorder. People frequently explain the cause of the impropriety of these extended family incestual unions as being that the relational designations of the people involved would become confused.

"Would she be his [classificatory] aunt or his wife?" "His son would be his own [classificatory] brother."

I have suggested that at first approach there are two groupings of situations in which *ha'ama* is felt or invoked. Both involve disorder. One cluster concerns the passive involvement of an individual in a situation which is not ordinary, familiar, and in order.[8] The other is more active, where a moral tone is introduced concerning adequacy in the presentation of self. This has a core of meanings around dirtiness and defect and questions of sexual propriety. A residual set, being ashamed because one is seen in an act which the community defines as bad, seems related because it has to do with competence and exposure. The act may be essentially shameful (dirtiness) or of another morally disapproved type (injuring someone), in which case the *ha'ama* is secondary. In this set of causes for *ha'ama*, it doesn't matter *why* the action is labeled as bad. It is sufficient that it is disapproved, that a violation takes place, and one has been shown to be incompetent.

The preceding paragraphs are related to the content of *ha'ama* situations. Some typical formal aspects were indicated. It is necessary to examine these further. I have noted the repeated stress on the relationship of *ha'ama* to the individual's perception that he has been observed. One man discussing causes of *ha'ama* put it, "If you are dirty or smell badly and hear someone comment on it, then it is a very *ha'ama* matter for you." In Marae's discussion of suppressed behavior he expresses a feeling of fear in anticipation of being seen in the performance of a disapproved act. His fear is connected with foresight, but his shame, in this sequence, would arise at the moment he realized that he had been seen. This is the external direction of shame-related behavioral controls which has been much emphasized.

Reports of the temporal extension of the feeling of shame in retrospect occur occasionally. "I felt ashamed the next morning, because somebody probably saw me while I was drunk." Most prospective statements however were like Marae's—including the sequence, "I had the impulse, I felt a sense of fear[9] that I might act on it and then experience *ha'ama* or some other punishment." In most cases *ha'ama* is related to the moment of feedback and to actual audiences, not imagined or internalized ones. If, however, *ha'ama* is limited to time, it is easily extendable in "actor space," from the self to people whom one feels identified with. People feel *ha'ama* for close friends, for their peer groups, for relatives, if the others are involved in something which would bring *ha'ama* to the self. The capacity to feel *ha'ama* for extensions of one-self varies with different individuals studied. Narcissistic and immature individuals (by both Tahitian and more general standards) had a narrow, sometimes self-limited sensitivity. Those more widely involved in village affairs, more trusted and respected, tended to have much wider *ha'ama* identifications. The fear of being shamed and the dysphoria of shame/embarassment when it is evoked are, judging by interviews and observations, strongly felt states and easily aroused.[10]

There are a number of cultural patterns which reduce the oppressiveness of *ha'ama* susceptibility. Essentially the controls are not intrusive; they are directed to surface presentations. Informants have no hesitation in listing impulses, for it is only the action which is involved with *ha'ama*

moral doctrine. Moral *ha'ama* is limited by an elaborated doctrine of "natural behaviors." Drinking, aspects of sexual behavior, adolescent shirking of household duties, may be matters of *ha'ama*, but they are also natural, part of the essence of a particular life stage, or of being human. They are matters which one will outgrow, which are qualities of one's family line, or made by God. Such deeply felt doctrines reduce both the use and the pain of the shaming.

Disapproval directed toward *ha'ama* action often tends to involve the idea of a context in which the behavior is wrong. The same behavior in a different setting may not be disapproved. People, for example, are generally expected to be freer in their drinking and sexual behavior when they visit the territorial capital. (A significant exception is in relation to seriously committed church members who are expected to live a more context-free mortality. An aspect of this is that they are related to a transvillage reference group of Protestant Communicants.)

Within the village there are restraints on looking, gossiping, and expressing curiosity. When people walked on the village path they carefully avoided looking at partially naked villagers who might be bathing in potential view of the path, or at people sitting in an outhouse, the door of which might have fallen off. Walkers carefully looked straight ahead.

If there were an argument on the path, "mature" people would pretend not to note, or would peek out secretly through a crack in their house, not showing themselves at the window. It was a matter of *ha'ama*, particularly for men (the highly functonal village gossips were mostly women) to show interest in squabbles. In potentially embarrassing exposed situations, people in a group avoided all eye contact. When a group of men, for example, were at a village political meeting which required them to play roles different from their everyday, ordinary life, although they joked and looked at each other before and after the formal part of the meeting, during the meeting itself when anybody talked no two people in the group met each other's eyes or looked at the speaker. Although gossip was an important part of shame control, the words designating gossip had a pejorative tone to them, and gossip was said to be a bad thing to do. Ideally, the behavior which would produce shame on becoming visible has to spontaneously force its way into visibility; people were not supposed to search out shameful acts. Such a searching out was in itself a *ha'ama* thing.

In spite of these restraints, community visibility and the resulting problem of privacy were ambivalently experienced. On the one hand, they were felt to be protective—they prevented one from doing bad things, to you. On the other hand, people who did leave the village for urban life expressed relief about being away from the village eye, although they might feel anxiety about the complementary dangers of city life, where other people were not restrained by village scrutiny. (In fact, town life was not dangerous; people away from village controls, were generally still cautious and gentle.)

CULTURAL ASPECTS OF TAHITIAN BEHAVIORAL CONTROLS: EMPATHY, ERROR, AND "SIN"

I have indicated that in a village sample of rural Tahitian culture, the affects shame/embarrassment have undergone considerable cultural definition and elaboration and are significant aspects of socially important behavioral control. In contrast, the affect of guilt is culturally played down to the point of conceptual invisibility. The Tahitian language has no word which signifies anything like a sense of guilt. Missionaries had to resort to awkward metaphors like "pain in the intestines" (the intestines are the locus of most emotions in Tahitian psychological theory), or "the burden of the intestines." The ordinary way of expressing what would seem to a Western observer to be, from the context, "guilt feelings" is the nonspecific term *pe'ape'a*, which indicates "trouble," either as an internal sensation, or in a social or interpersonal situation.

There is a term which contrasts with *ha'ama* in discussions of motives for self-control. It is a highly salient motivational explanatory principle. The terms is *arafa*, which, as noted, may be glossed empathy/pity/compassion. An informant in Roto, discussing conscious impulses on which he would not act, denied that his self control was a question of being seen and of *ha'ama:*

Whether people saw or did not see . . . if I really wanted to do it, I would do it. I am not afraid of people. It is not a matter of the person's talking about me. If I said to myself "Go and kill yourself," then I would go and kill myself. If [I decided] go and get money, I would go and get money . . . but I don't want to do such things because it is forbidden to me, I am prevented from doing them because of *arofa*. . . . (*Arofa* for whom?) *Arofa* for the person to whom I have done a bad thing, and *arofa* toward myself. I am jumping into a hole.

Others who deny that fear of being shamed is their main reason for caution emphasize their fear of violating the law—either French law or God's law—and being punished. Fear of punishment is related in the communities studied to a concept of impersonal, fairly clear, nonintrusive laws which punish you only when you violate their protected threshold. It is formally similar to the ancient attitudes about taboos and taboo violation. The concern is mostly about the avoidance of mistakes. (The Ten Commandments are called the ten "Do nots," and can be ritually manipulated.) *Arofa* also has an aspect of avoidance of mistake. By empathetically knowing which aspects of action will hurt someone else, by accepting the clues of compassion and pity, one can then avoid behavior which would produce harm, punishment, and inchoate guilt feelings.

The cultural forms of *arofa* and of fear of punishment are something else than *ha'ama*, than shame/embarrassment. But in quality they are still far from "a sorrow for sin when committed and a hatred for it afterwards," as understood by the Puritan missionaries. Although the missionaries did not find a term for guilt feeling, they did find terms which they thought mean "repent," and "sin." The word they used to translate "repent" was *tatarahapa*. *Tatara* means to untangle or unsnare. *Hapa* has the general sense of error. The term means literally to untangle oneself from the consequences of having made an error.

There have been some changes in the Tahitian language. In the first Tahitian dictionary compiled by missionaries in the early 19th century, some 60 years after the discovery of Tahiti by the West, *hapa* was one of three words given similar definition. *Hapa* was defined as "a deviation from a rule, a missing of a mark, an error, sin, or crime." *Hape* was defined as

"an error, a mistake, a sin." The third term, *hara*, was defined as "a sin, transgression, crime, or guilt,"[11] and also as "unequal, not hitting the mark, deviating from a line or rule." In contemporary Tahitian, *hape* refers in large part to minor mistakes (mostly technical, but including social ones), and *hara* to serious social transgressions which probably involve punishment. (The contemporary narrowing of reference of *hara*, the loss of its technical reference, is undoubtedly owing to Christian theological and biblical usage.) *Hapa* survives now mostly in compound terms such as *tatarahapa*. These words, with their implications of making an error or deviating from a mark, have as their complements in social discourse, words meaning (socially) proper which are also derived from physical correctness. Examples are *tano* which means to hit a target or mark, and *'afaro*, straight as a straight line.

Hara behavior is related to the idea of bad as a technical error and also to the notion of punishment. What are examples of *hara*, and how are they punished? The realm of *hara* has been taken over to a large degree by Calvinistic theology to deal with the Christian idea of sin. In pre-Christian Tahiti there were a number of punishable behaviors noted by the first Western observers. They included murder, sociosexual violations (adultery and incest), theft, failures in expected economic exchange, and violation of proper respect and deference behavior toward high authorities. There were a variety of punishments—deprivation of part or all of the offender's property; banishment; murder (one form of which was ritual sacrifice), carried out in some cases by the offended person who was protected by ideas of justice from further retaliation for his retaliatory act, in other cases by the tribal chief and other individuals[12] of high status.

When villagers were asked to list contemporary *hara*, the list depended to some degree on whether or not the individual was obsessively involved with the church. Thus, one elderly lady, very much involved in church activities, answered by listing selections from the Ten Commandments. She said these are the things you have to do to avoid going to hell. "You have to pay attention to the Law. . . . Do not steal, do not kill, do not thrash people, do not covet, do not commit adultery. . . . If you do this then your spirit will arrive [in heaven]. If not, then it will not." She stated she wasn't certain that she would avoid hell, but then she continues with confidence,

. . . if you pay careful attention, if you pay careful attention to His law. Do not do that thing, do not do that thing, do not do that thing, and continue like this until your end, you arrive in Heaven. If however you do not—even if you pay attention some times and there are other times when you do not pay attention to His Law—then you will go into the fire.

The need to pay continuous attention to not violating God's taboos as set forth in the Ten Commandments is common doctrine. It is all highly impersonal, mechanical, and legalistic, and neither repentance nor forgiveness —God's grace—is relevant. Again the stress, as in *ha'ama* behavior and in contrast to missionary doctrine, is on external behavior. Although there is much talk of New Testament Biblical doctrines about inner sincerity rather than external action as being relevant to salvation, this is a problematic doctrine for the traditional villagers (see Levy 1969c). Their idea of avoiding Christian sin has to do with avoidance of bad behavior, plus a ritualistic reading of the Bible.

Nonreligious lists usually stress hurting behavior. Asked to list ordinary, common *hara*, one man, for example, states: "Hitting someone, that is the most frequent *hara*." Asked what else, he says, "Killing someone." Pressed for others, he adds, "Insulting people." Some matters listed as causes for *ha'ama* are also listed as *hara*— particularly adultery and stealing. The consequence feared is village "trouble" or punishment by civic law. The ideas of hurt, of law, of punishment, are all associated with *hara* in its strongest moral aspect, as are technique and mistake in its performance aspect. The idea of *hara* also involves the idea of justice, the proper application of a law. Injury which would be accepted if merited is a *hara* if unmerited. "He hit me, but I did not know the reason. I had not done anything. Therefore it was a very bad thing."

The most general Tahitian terms for good, *maita'i*, and bad, *'ino*, have a wide range of uses. They apply to good and bad fish, good and bad craftsmanship, and personal skill. When they are applied as a moral evaluation they imply a dimension of good/evil. Destructive spirits are *'ino*, as a harmful and frightening man, a destructive hurricane, dangerous sharks. The semantic structure of the terms are complex, but in their sense of good/evil (as contrasted to good/ spoiled, nice/not nice, etc.) they are the usual evaluative terms applied to harmful or helpful behavior, as *ha'ama* is applied as an epithet to the behaviors described in the previous section.

PERSONALITY AND SOCIO-CULTURAL SYSTEMS, LEVELS OF INTEGRATION

In the preceding pages, starting with

some Tahitian answers to the question, "What keeps you from doing some of the things that you are aware that you would like to do?." I presented aspects of verbal response, and of associated actions and ideas. Some of what I presented is closely related to Tahitian conceptual association, for example the matters related to *ha'ama, arofa, hara, 'ino, maita'i;*[13] some is more covertly patterned. The data indicate that shame has a good deal to do with some behavior relating to self-control and the social evaluation of behavior in Tahiti, but by no means with all of it.

There seem to be two very general tendencies in the foregoing material, tendencies which are sometimes combined in statements about self-control. One involves shame, embarrassment, cleanliness, order, adequacy, fear of ridicule, fear of shame, orientation to the familiar, presentation of self. The other involves good/evil, harm, empathy, laws, justice, retaliation, social trouble, fear of punishment. This second group, which at first sight seems to involve guilt controls, has features which contrast with Western, particularly Calvinistic, expectations. With the partial exception of *arofa*, the emphasis is on being seen as a necessary element, on the externality of sanctions (physical consequences rather than painful guilt feelings), on avoiding evil rather than doing good, on action rather than intention as the evaluated element.

I propose a schema, which, I believe, organizes the data and indicates their contrast with Western forms. The schema has to do with the nature of the integration between individuals and sociocultural systems or sub-systems. It is important to note that I am not talking about private psychodynamics here. I will touch on such dynamics in regard, for example, to the status of private guilt feelings among Tahitians in the next section. I am concerned here with those forms which are most immediately associated with environing sociocultural dynamics.

The schema requires the introduction of some elementary system-theory jargon. I propose that the first group of phenomena involves the question of an individual's presentability, of his *entrance* into a cultural system of meanings and action. Is the unit (individual, behavior) fit to be an element in the system? I will refer to fitting into a system as *Level 0* integration. The other group involves behaviors which are related to maintaining the *variables* in a sociocultural system or systems, and will be referred to as *Level 1* integration. For the purpose of contrast with Western cultures we will also be concerned with *Level 2* integrative behavior, which does not characterize acceptable village Tahitian behavior. This is behavior related to changing the *parameters* of the sociocultural system or systems in which the individual operates. The idea of levels or "orders" has been developed in Bateson's work, deriving from concepts in cybernetic and communication theory.[14]

A quotation from Bateson will serve to illustrate levels of organization and the use of the words *variable* and *parameter:*

A house with a thermostatically controlled heating system is a simple self-corrective circuit. . . . A thermometer appropriately placed in the house is linked into the system to control a switch in such a way that when the temperature goes above a certain critical level the furnace is switched off. Similarly, when the temperatures falls below a certain level the furnace is switched on. But the system is also governed by another circumstance, namely, the setting of the critical temperatures. By changing the position of a dial the owner can alter the characteristics of the *system as a whole* by changing the critical temperatures at which the furnace will be turned on and shut off. Following Ashby [1956], I will reserve the word "variables" for those measurable circumstances which change from moment to moment as the house oscillates around some steady temperature, and shall reserve the word "parameters" for those characteristics of the system which are changed for example when the householder intervenes and changes the setting of the thermostat. I shall speak of the latter change as of a higher order than changes in the variables. (1958, p. 292)

With three levels of social behavior for individuals, entrance (Level 0), behavior bearing on maintenance of sociocultural variables within proper ranges (Level 1), and behavior bearing on shifting of sociocultural parameters (Level 2), we can define two types of sociocultural situation. In one the tendency is toward steady state, that is, in which the parameters of the system tend not to change, and where only *Level 0 and Level 1* considerations are salient. In the other there are tendencies toward growth, evolution, change, which alter the system itself. The first approximate rural Tahitian and most traditional societies, the second, some social segments of Western society.[15]

The meanings and the problems involved in the first two levels of person-sociocultural system integrations will be quite dissimilar in these two types of society. This will get us back, although in different terms, to the questions underlying the idea of "shame cultures" and "guilt cultures."

I will consider *Level 0* and *Level 1* integration in a steady-state tending society, and then ask what transformations might be expected if *Level 2* considerations become salient. The question for an individual at *Level 0* is: is one presentable in an on-going situation? Shame and embarrassment, with their stress on orderly orientation to familiar contexts, to the smooth presentation of self, to body cleanliness, to the fit into "culture" by controlling the disorder of precultural unsystematized sexuality and body function, are powerful affectual mediators of this kind of self-society integration. The idea of presentation must have reference to immediate feedback, to visibility, relating to the properness of fit into the immediate social situation. In Tahiti the smooth presentation of self involves powerful symbolic currents related to cleanliness, to stress on surface attractiveness, to making oneself palatable. The main way one fails here is by being unpresentable. One is then unfit, inadequate. This is in important contrast to failures at *Level 1* integration, where one is powerful, harmful, and bad, for at *Level 1* failure involves harm to others.

While questions of entrance require scanning of the immediate situation, related to a cluster of affects and ideas about immediate acceptability, the question of proper action in relation to larger system maintenance, *Level 1*, requires general information about the variable state of the sociocultural system and its fixed parameters or values. How much productive work should one do? How should one distribute various kinds of resources? How much deference, cooperation, criticism, affection, resistance are due various other people? To act, individuals must know what are the optima involved and where they are in relation to them. What is proper behavior, what should be done to make things go along properly, to avoid trouble? To the missionaries it seemed a kind of "good doing" which was pragmatic, shallow, trouble avoiding. This kind of successful integration did not involve self-realization, rising above the crowd, considerations of personal salvation.

Questions of law, of justice, of (in comparison to entrance considerations) relatively delayed feedback (e.g., a series of events culminating in trouble) enter here. Success equals a "good job," and "being a good citizen," failure equals a "poor job," and also the idea of harm. If an individual does not maintain system variables within proper ranges, it will result in having an effect on the situations of other people in the system. The harm can come from too much or too little of the proper behavior. Now this has something to do with one's fit into the system, and therefore there are still *Level 0* considerations, but now it has also to do with one's action in the system. The moral stress is on one's actions, not one's intentions. This latter will be added when *Level 2* considerations become important. Violence and physical injury are only one type of harmful behavior. Stealing, violation of orderly incest rules, *lèse majesté*, and underperformance (so that one's family, for example, goes hungry), are all harmful in relation to system maintenance.

Essential to this discussion is the status of guilt as an affect at this level in a steady-state soceity. It is *not* symmetrical with feelings of shame and embarrassment at *Level 0*, or the familiar usages of guilt at *Level 2*. In a steady-state society one should and can avoid major transgressions of the rules. The ideal is to have clearly marked and signalled boundaries within which one is free.[16] One activates the controls associated with the rules by behavior which approaches deviance, and feels their effect in the form of troubles caused, of disapproval from others, to covert feelings of guilt represented as "being troubled" or "feeling pity." But by attending to such clues, and because the rules with which they are involved are fairly clear, one can avoid a situationally determined sense of having sinned. One avoids guilt and can regulate one's life comfortably without becoming aware of guilt feelings. Shame is a *variable* control in relation to problems of *Level 0*, of presentation. The occurrence and intensity of shaming signals the presence and degree of deviance. At *Level 1* one has a variety of clues which provide variable controls against deviation, controls associated with conscious affects of fear and empathy. If these controls are breached in an individual and culturally pathological act, guilt will be mobilized, but it is a sign of breakdown of the ordinary controls, and represents a private and poorly understood experience. Knowledge of traditional laws, customs, taboos is protective. It keeps one from blundering into trouble.

The value of a steady-state is indicated in Tahiti in a number of ways. The transformed Calvinistic God represents it. God punishes people who become too proud, too ambitious, too innovative. He sends hurricanes into the world because Westerners have tried to get to the moon. To a considerable extent when things work out *better* than usual (in village affairs, in a family relationship, in fishing or farming) while a striving Westerner might be tempted to set a new and higher goal, the villagers would often consider it a matter of random good luck, a windfall—a kind of behavior which meant childishness or fatalism to missionary minds.

What happens when *Level 2* considerations—systematically changing parameters—become an important cultural consideration? There are individuals in Piri, and more in urban

Roto, who are striving, ambitious, future oriented; that is, they want to shift their group, or some subsystem of it, to new goals. They are "bad" within the terms of the steady-state ideal, and there are many external and internal sanctions which tend to suppress their striving behaviors. But what happens when such shifts become cultural goals, as in the West. Now the considerations relating to presentation, and to action keeping variables within the limits of steady-state must be violated. One must be able to ignore the short term balances and orientations related to shame and embarrassment, and some of the regulators—laws, taboos, disapprovals, trouble, as well as empathy and pity —of peaceful system maintenance. Not completely, because there is, confusingly, a mixture of steady-state processes, of presentations of self as immediately acceptable, which are still maintained. It is never clear at which point these considerations *should* be violated. The moral emphasis now shifts from acts to intentions and to reference to more transcendent values. For the consequences of the act cannot be judged solely by the ordinary and traditional concerns of hurt to others, nor of respect for traditional goals and limits expressed in law and custom. The paradigm for what is involved is Kierkegaard's discussion of the meaning of faith as expressed in Abraham's willingness to slay Isaac, to do what seems to be absurd evil in the service of some higher goal. The question now comes up as to whether such an act is somehow good in terms of some new reality. And it becomes important to know what it is that Abraham thinks he is doing. In such situations one must overcome embarrassment and shame constrictions; one must question the validity of clues

for immediate adjustive behavior; one must be rebellious; one must do harm in relation to some traditional system aspects. Now guilt comse to the fore, and the question becomes the authenticity of the feelings of guilt, feelings which are unavoidable. If I accept values of change I will violate old relationships; I will cause some suffering now for some future good. I will now *feel* guilty whatever I do, and must now decide which feelings of guilt are related to socially defined wrong—that is, are socially authentic —and which are unwarranted by social goals and realities and therefore neurotic, or otherwise invalid. The question of authenticity of guilt feelings helps give the tone to Calvinistic sin. That is, decisions are involved about authentic evil-doing in a context of pervasive feelings of sinfulness.

In an attempt to separate guilt feelings into socioculturally warranted and nonwarranted kinds, once the idea of original sin is rejected, the oedipal situation takes on a special meaning. The sense of guilt generated by participating in change involves rebellion and detachment from family definitions, relationships, and authorities. By stressing analysis and awareness of the oedipal situation rather than repression, some of the guilt of change, movement, individuation, seeking for new goals, can be located and defined as neurotic, as inauthentic, as invalid as a signal of wrongdoing. This is, I think, related to the historic importance of psychoanalysis in the West and explains the sociocultural reasons for the centrality of the analysis of the oedipal complex. Its concern with authentic versus neurotic guilt is meaningless in a steady-state society. A change oriented society would seem to entail guilt feelings in those who involve themselves in that change. These guilt feelings must be brought into awareness and exposed to some sort of systematic ordering. It is in this sense that Western societies are "guilt societies" in a way that Tahiti is not.

RELATED ASPECTS OF PERSONALITY: TAHITI

The preceding has suggested an analysis of behavioral controls bearing on individual-sociocultural system interaction made primarily in terms of sociocultural features. The question of the relationship of individual-sociocultural systematic interaction to the systematics of the psychological organization of various individuals in the community would be a next step in a psychologically oriented analysis. This relationship, it must be stressed, is an empirical problem. The nature of psychocultural integrations suggests underlying psychodynamic features, but without clues from specific studies of individual organization, assumptions as to deeper organization of personality based on more socially integrated aspects may lead to a kind of "wild analysis." It is not my purpose in this paper to attempt to describe in any complexity Tahitian personality as I understand it from my studies; I shall do that elsewhere. But I wish, albeit in a sketchy and condensed manner, to note some psychological matters related to the first part of the paper, and to some general questions traditionally associated with "shame" and "guilt."

The statement about the empirical nature of the relationships implies that various types of personality organization *may* support a specific sociocultural behavior. Among the individuals whom I studied were a few for whom behavior involving presentation of the self and behavior relating to respect

for balance and system maintenance were matters of accepting community values and ideals, rather than implications of more general organizational features of their personalities. These community values and ideals served as guides for defensive transformations of personal motives and meanings toward prevalent psychocultural forms. From the aspect of sociocultural dynamics these values served as redundant controls helping to insure adequate performance by individuals. Thus, men who seemed from contextual clues to be oriented to system change, that is, with deviant tendencies toward striving, future orientation, shifting the system to fit themselves rather than the inverse, acted as closely as possible after *ha'ama* models and explained their behavior in *ha'ama* terms. (Such men when their time arrives become agents for social change and may in kind of sudden discovery simplify the complexity of their psychological organization.)

But for most people the relation to entrance and maintenance seemed to be the expression of deeper aspects of their personalities, to be more "natural" behaviors.[17] Such people were cautious, gentle, sensitive to social contexts, and profoundly convinced of the impossibility of changing the eternal nature of things.[18] Such cautiousness and sensitivity to embarrassment pose a problem as to the correct "quantity" for an individual. Overcautious individuals were regarded as pathologically shy, and so labelled (*mamahu*).

Even the "normal" degree of timidity and caution provided recurrent problems when some aggressiveness was called for, as in establishing sexual relationships. Aspects of the culturally standardized experiences of male adolescence served to overcome youths' timidity in such areas. For example, entrance into male adolescence was associated with the operation of penile supercision. Major overt symbolic aspects of the rite emphasized the new cleanliness of the penis (there would be no more smegma), the freeing of the head of the penis, the effectiveness of traditional remedies for the effective healing of the cut, and the triviality of the cut itself. The message is presentability, unbinding, and phallic safety. (There were, as in all important *rites de passage,* other vital messages condensed into it, having to do, for example, with sexual identity and generational separation.) Some overcoming of caution and timidity is necessary for the minimal socially adventurous behavior required by community life, but one who had achieved a proper balance was still far from brash.[19]

Various aspects of Tahitian socialization techniques seem related to presentation and maintenance sensitivities and to the status of private guilt feelings in psychologically traditional individuals. Children between the ages of three to five become culturally defined as being no longer babies and are almost entirely pushed out of the close relationship with the mother which had prevailed until then into a diffuse caretaker network which may include older siblings, cousins, young aunts, and uncles. Parents are somewhat external to this system and mostly are concerned to regulate its abuses. The transition from a close and dependent relationship with mother to the care of older children and adolescents (principally girls) is often stressful for the child, as evidenced by alternating temper tantrums (which are usually ignored or, if too prolonged and disturbing, reacted to with anger) and apathetic behavior; but this period is then soon followed by the child's adjustment to the new conditions. It should be noted that the caretaker web does not usually provide a new "mother." It provides a group of people, *all* of whom exercise caretaking, frustrating, and punishing behavior.

Separation from mother seems to appear to the child to be produced by the system of others who come between the child and the mother, with the mother's approval. (Childhood is typically recalled as oppressive because of all the people one had to cope with.) Of importance is that nothing in the child's real behavior can cause a reversal of this withdrawal of maternal closeness at the culturally appropriate age. It is not *variably* contingent on moral worth, not used as punishment for error followed by return to closeness through mother's grace or the child's repentance. Whatever moral responsibility the child may imagine he has for the change, it is unconditional and unaffected by variations in his moral behavior. Furthermore, the system which frustrates him, which separates him from his mother, is so diffuse and redundant (if one sibling lets you "get away with something" the next oldest will pick up the error) that in contrast to the possibilities in the oedipal triangle, there is nothing he can do with it by force, charm, or trickery to undo its frustrations.[20]

This socialization system has an aspect which to some degree balances its oppressiveness. Although it is diffuse and difficult to manipulate, it tends to be nonintrusive. It does not punish a child unless he breaches fairly permissive boundaries of ordinary behavior. The child is, as it were, invisible to the system unless he becomes too annoying or refuses to do a task. But the tasks and prohibitions are generally well within the child's maturational possibilities. You can't change the system, but it will, except for occasional caprice of caretakers' moods, more or less let you alone if you do the simple (although often tiring) things that are necessary. These aspects of socialization present in their very structure a reality constituting an unalterable system, in which proper fit, maintenance, and adjustive behavior are in the nature of things.

Most informants stressed the protective aspects of shame sensitivity and of laws and rules. Protection was from external and internal danger: other people would be dangerous, and one would not be able to control oneself. The feeling of the danger of other people seems very much a projection. In comparison with other societies, Tahiti has had very little violence, crime, or destructive interpersonal behavior (see Levy 1969a).[21] It seems reasonable, and in agreement with material on the status of guilt in other shame-emphasizing societies, that guilt generated in the conditions described remains diffuse, primitive, unfocused. The residues of separation from mother cannot be worked through and given form either in later experiences of separation and forgiveness or in the course of concrete oedipal interactions. One is left with diffuse primitive guilt traces and fear of aggression, very far from any patterning as a control bearing on specific behaviors, and generally far from awareness. This may explain some of the motivation toward cautiousness. But one can be effectively cautious and effectively distance oneself from situation produced feelings of guilt, which, as I have suggested, is impossible for people involved in social change.

Although people are sensitive to being shamed, this does not imply (Piers has emphasized the distinction) that they are shame ridden. It may be noted that shaming and ridicule are sometimes directed toward children, but much less frequently than threats and hitting. They are applied in relation to a set of sphincter control expectations that seemed relaxed in comparison with various Western standards. Statements about sensitivity to embarrassment and shame are comparative in that they refer to Western expectations of form and quantity in these matters. Much of the contrast is probably due to Western attempts to modify, overcome and suppress these shame/embarrassment controls rather than something positive about the Tahitian situations. Erikson's much quoted statement (1950, p. 252) that, "Shame is an emotion insufficiently studied, because in our civilization it is so early and easily absorbed by guilt," is appropriate here. It seems plausible that much of the form of the shame and embarrassment sensitivities, particularly the aspects related to discomfort involving problems of comfortable fit into familiar contexts, involves phylogenetic dimensions which may be amplified or played down in various psychocultural contexts.

I have sketched these Tahitian forms to suggest some private aspects of Tahitian personality which have general psychodynamic implications and which are related to aspects of intersystemic integration presented in the first part of the paper.[22] The question of the similarity or difference in socialization, ontogenesis, and personality structure in societies with similar functional requirements is a problem for further study.[23]

NOTES

1. For a discussion of the transformations of meaning and emphasis of English Calvinistic Protestantism in Tahiti, see Levy, (1969c).

2. Attempts have been made to find contrasting features in sociocultural organization which might have been a more analytically satisfactory basis for shame/guilt impressions. Lebra (1970), in a paper on guilt and shame in Japanese culture, suggests that within any society guilt is related to social role relations involving reciprocity, and shame to role relationships involving asymmetry as well as to problems of status occupancy. The weightings of these two types of relationship in different cultures, their more generalized or more particularized qualities, would provide, she suggests, important sociocultural contrasts.

Weidman (1965) argues that whether the implicit and internalized normative controls of a culture or family are phrased principly in the form of "ought to," or "ought not to" constitutes an important contrast.

In *The Lonely Crowd* (1950, pp. 25-26), Riesman et al. suggested the three stage demographic typology—high growth potential, transitional growth, incipient population decline—with associated tendencies for behavioral controls which are respectively "traditional," "inner-directed," and "other-directed." They accepted the shame/guilt dichotomy for the first two of these types. Compliance among tradition-directed people involved "the fear of being shamed." The inner-directed person "has early incorporated a psychic gyroscope which is set going by his parents and can receive signals later on from other authorities who resemble his parents. . . . Getting off course . . . may lead to the feeling of guilt." The other-directed person internalizes "not a code of behavior but the elaborate equipment needed to attend to [social] messages. . . . As against guilt-and-shame controls, though of course these survive, one prime psychological lever of the other-directed person is a diffuse anxiety" (pp. 25-26).

3. The studies were supported by grants from the National Institute of Mental Health and the National Science Foundation. Other aspects of the work have been reported in various papers (Levy 1966, 1967, 1968a, 1968b, 1969a, 1969b, 1969c, 1971), and in a book, *Tahitians: Mind and Experience in the Society Islands.*

4. The glottal stop (') represents a vocal "catch" as in Hawai'i. The macron (-) indicates a long vowel.

5. The delicacies are direct translations from the Tahitian.

6. Although earlier studies such as Leighton and Kluckhohn's Navaho study *Children of the People* (1947) tended to contrast "shame" and "conscience," later treatments of the problem such as Spiro's *Children of the Kibbutz* (1958, p. 409) tended to consider *forms* of superego or conscience. Spiro talked of "guilt-oriented" and "shame-oriented" superegos, and remarked that "it must be emphasized that a shame—no less than a guilt-oriented superego constitutes a conscience."

7. A salient element in various people's anxiety related to their fantasies of what psychotic people were like was that they were dirty.

8. Not all kinds of disordered situations produce *ha'ama*. In a festival the disorder produces feelings of elation. It is the slight disorder of normal, on-going, everyday social frames and contexts which is involved. Disorder of certain familiar *physical* contexts may, and among the villagers frequently does, produce uncanny emotions.

9. There is a developed theory of fear, and a differentiated vocabulary analyzing types of fear in terms of qualities of associated feeling, supposed cause, and other features.

10. Some indication of the strength may be suggested by the fact that the standard way of chasing away ghosts and spirits is to swear at them and make them feel embarrassed and ashamed, thus causing them to flee. This also has something to do with the idea of the weakness of most spirits. Susceptibility to *ha'ama* is a valued aspect of the self, within limits, but it is associated also with a conscious sense of weakness.

11. That is, guilt as responsibility for a crime, etc.

12. The material on these offenses and sanctions was collated and analyzed by Douglas Oliver (in press).

13. The foregoing has indicated that these are semantically complex terms which involve different contrasts at different levels of meaning. Cf. Frake, 1961.

14. See the selected papers of Gregory Bateson (1971).

15. The shifting parameters may be random, change for change's sake, or more or less systematic. Logically, the parameter change may be constant or accelerated.

16. I have heard members of relatively traditional societies, such as Thailand, who had lived for long periods of time in the West refer to their greater feeling of personal freedom in their societies, which seemed more rigidly ordered to Westerners. It was the nonintrusive threshold rules which gave the room for personal freedom.

17. That is, for such people traditional cultural values have their formal support in personality structure. Studies of Polynesian (and the historically related Micronesian) personality, which seems to be remarkably similar throughout an enormous geographic area, indicate a marked conservation of psychological organization throughout historical time, an organization which has been resistant to change and maladaptive in contexts of modernization such as Hawaii (See Levy 1969d).

18. These characteristics seemed rather more marked in men than women. The socialization experiences to men and women differed in important dimensions. One might be able to make a case for the idea that in most cultures men carry the cultural specializations, have a burden of special socialization, and differ more, psychologically, from men in other cultures than women do from women. This may have some relation to Freud's puzzlements about European women's superegos.

19. Other community behaviors, including drinking, were involved in overcoming normal timidity (see Levy 1966). Too little characterological timidity seemed less of a problem than too much. Redundant controls involving, first, acceptance of behavioral norms, or, if not, then sanctions of disapproval directed to the "swollen up," or "high" individual, would still keep such an individual's behavior within tolerable limtis. If not, he might tend to leave the village for more modern urban life.

20. A number of implications of the socialization network are explored in Levy 1968a.

21. There has been an increase in violent behavior in Tahiti since my study was made, associated with new, stressful social conditions.

22. I have avoided touching on the shame/guilt :: ego ideal/superego question. That seems to have to do with questions of theoretical utility which are not relevant here. A note about identification may be in order. Unconscious identification would seem to be diffuse. Men seem to have strong feminine identifications, which are to some degree dynamically countered by certain cultural forms which help clarify sexual distinctions (Levy 1971). While a very few of the people studied recalled having had, as children, people whom they thought they might have resembled in one particular or another, no one reported having childhood or adolescent heroes, or models they wanted generally to mold themselves on. On the other hand, some people had conscious negative ideal models as children and adolescents . . . "I did not want to become like X." Whatever the relation of shame might be in a structural model to tensions between the ego and the ego ideal, it would seem that the Tahitian ego ideal in itself must have special features.

23. I wish to thank Melford Spiro, Roy D'Andrade, and Sam Nelken for valuable critical responses to an earlier draft of this paper.

REFERENCES

Ashby, W. R.
1956 *Introduction to Cybernetics.* New York: Wiley.

Bateson, G.
1958 *Naven*. Stanford: Stanford University Press.
1971 *Steps toward an Ecology of Mind*. San Francisco: Chandler.
Beaglehole, E.
1957 *Social Change in the South Pacific*. New York: Macmillan.
Bougainville, L. A.
1771 *Voyage Autour du Monde*. Paris: Club Des Libraires de France, 1958.
DeVos, G.
1960 The relation of guilt towards parents to achievement and arranged marriage among the Japanese. *Psychiatry* 23:287-301.
Erikson, E. H.
1950 *Childhood and Society*. New York: Norton.
Frake, C.
1961 The diagnosis of disease among the Subanun of Mindanao. *American Anthropologist* 63:113-32.
Kroeber, A. L.
1948 *Anthropology*. New York: Harcourt Brace.
Lebra, T. S.
1970 The social mechanism of guilt and shame: The Japanese case. Honolulu: University of Hawaii, Social Science Research Institute. Manuscript.
Leighton, D., and C. Kluckhohn
1947 *Children of the People*. Cambridge, MA: Harvard University Press.
Levy, R.
1966 Ma'ohi drinking patterns in the Society Islands. *Journal of the Polynesian Society* 75:304-20.
1967 Tahitian folk psychotherapy. *International Mental Health Research Newsletter, 9*.
1968a Child management structure and its implications in a Tahitian family. *In* E. Vogel and N. Bell (eds.), *A Modern Introduction to the Family*. New York: Free Press.
1968a Tahiti observed: Early European impressions of Tahitian personal style. *Journal of the Polynesian Society* 77: 33-42.
1969a On getting angry in the Society Islands. *In* W. Caudill and T. Lin (eds.), *Mental Health Research in Asia and the Pacific*. Honolulu: East West Center Press.
1969b Tahitian adoption as a psychological message. *In* V. Carroll (ed.), *Adoption in Eastern Oceania*. Honolulu: University of Hawaii Press.
1969c Personal forms and meanings in Tahitian Protestantism. *Journal de la Société des Océanistes* 25:125-36.
1969d *Personality Studies in Polynesia and Micronesia: Stability and Change*. Working papers No. 8. Honolulu: University of Hawaii, Social Science Research Institute.
1971 The community function of Tahitian male transvestitism. *Anthropological Quarterly* 44:12-21.
Oliver, D.
In press *Ancient Tahitian Society*. Honolulu: University of Hawaii Press.
Piers, G., and M. Singer
1953 *Shame and Guilt*. Springfield, IL: Thomas.
Reider, N.
1950 The sense of shame. *Samiska* 3.
Riesman, D., N. Glazer, and R. Denney
1950 *The Lonely Crowd*. New Haven: Yale University Press.
Spiro, M.
1958 *Children of the Kibbutz*. Cambridge, MA: Harvard University Press.
Weidman, H. H.
1965 *Shame and Guilt: A Reformulation of the Problem*. Birmingham: University of Alabama Medical Center, Dept. of Psychiatry. Manuscript.

16. AMAE: A KEY CONCEPT FOR UNDERSTANDING JAPANESE PERSONALITY STRUCTURE

L. TAKEO DOI

L. Takeo Doi, M.D., is Professor of Psychiatry, University of Tokyo. Reprinted with permission from *Japanese Culture: Its Development and Characteristics,* Robert J. Smith and Richard K. Beardsley, editors, Chicago, Aldine Publishing Company. Copyright © 1962 by Wenner-Gren Foundation for Anthropological Research, Inc.

I AM PARTICULARLY interested in the problem of personality and culture in modern Japan for two reasons. First, even though I was born and raised in Japan and had my basic medical training there, I have had further training in psychiatry and psychoanalysis in the United States, thus exposing myself for some time to a different culture from that of Japan. Second, I have had many opportunities of treating both Japanese and non-Japanese (mostly American) patients with psychotherapy. These experiences have led me to inquire into differences between Japanese and non-Japanese patients and also into the question of what is basic in Japanese character structure. In this paper I shall describe what I have found to be most characteristic in Japanese patients and then discuss its meaning in the context of Japanese culture.

The essence of what I am going to talk about is contained in one common Japanese word, *"amae."* Let me therefore, first of all, explain the meaning of this word. *Amae* is the noun form of *"amaeru,"* an intransitive verb that means "to depend and presume upon another's benevolence" (Doi 1956). This word has the same root as *amai,* an adjective that means "sweet." Thus *amaeru* has a distinct feeling of sweetness and is generally used to describe a child's attitude or behavior toward his parents, particularly his mother. But it can also be used to describe the relationship between two adults, such as the relationship between a husband and a wife or a master and a subordinate. I believe that there is no single word in English equivalent to *amaeru,* though this does not mean that the psychology of *amae* is totally alien to the people of English speaking countires. I shall come back to this problem after describing some of the clinical material through which I came to recognize the importance of what *amae* signifies.

It was in my attempt to understand what goes on between the therapist and patient that I first came across the all-powerful drive of the patient's *amae.* There is a diagnostic term in Japanese psychiatry, *shinkeishitsu,* which includes neurasthenia, anxiety neurosis, and obsessive neurosis. Morita, who first used *shinkeishitsu* as a diagnostic term, thought that these three types of neuroses had a basic symptom in common: *toraware,* which means "to be bound or caught," as by some intense preoccupation. He considered *toraware* to be closely related to hypochondriacal fear and thought that this fear sets in motion a reciprocal intensification of attention and sensation. In psychoanalytic work with neurotic patients of the *shin-*

keishitsu type I have also found *tora-ware* to be a basic symptom, but I have evolved a different formulation of its significance (see Doi 1958). I have observed that during the course of psychotherapy the patient's *tora-ware* can easily turn into hypersensitivity in his relationship with the therapist. This hypersensitivity is best described by the Japanese word *koda-wari*. *Kodawari* is the noun form of *kodawaru*, an intransitive verb meaning "to be sensitive to minor things," "to be inwardly disturbed over one's personal relationships." In the state of *kodawari* one feels that he is not accepted by others, which suggests that *kodawari* results from the unsatisfied desire to *amaeru*. Thus *toraware* can be traced back through *kodawari* to *amae*. In my observations the patient's *toraware* usually receded when he became aware of his *amae* toward the therapist, which he had been warding off consciously and unconsciously up to then.

At first I felt that if the patient became fully aware of his *amae,* he would thereupon be able to get rid of his neurosis. But I was wrong in this assumption and came to observe another set of clinical phenomena following the patient's recognition of his *amae* (see Doi 1960). Many patients confessed that they were then awakened to the fact that they had not "possessed their self," had not previously appreciated the importance of their existence, and had been really nothing apart from their all-important desire to *amaeru*. I took this as a step toward the emergence of a new consciousness of self, inasmuch as the patient could then at least realize his previous state of "no self."

There is another observation that I should like to mention here. It is about the nature of guilt feelings of Japanese patients (see Doi 1961).

The word *sumanai* is generally used to express guilt feelings, and this word is the negative form of *sumu,* which means "to end." *Sumanai* literally means that one has not done as he was supposed to do, thereby causing the other person trouble or harm. Thus, it expresses more a sense of unfulfilled obligation than a confession of guilt, though it is generally taken as an indication that one feels guilty. When neurotic patients say *sumanai,* I have observed that there lies, behind their use of the word, much hidden aggression engendered by frustration of their wish to *amaeru.* So it seems that in saying *sumanai* they are in fact expressing their hidden concern lest they fall from the grace of *amae* because of their aggression. I think that this analysis of *sumanai* would also apply in essence to the use of this word by the ordinary Japanese in everyday life, but in the case of the neurotic patient *sumanai* is said with greater ambivalence. In other words, more than showing his feeling or being obligated, he tends to create a sense of obligation in the person to whom he makes his apology, thus "forcing" that person eventually to cater to his wish.

I have explained three clinical observations all of which point to the importance of *amae* as a basic desire. As I said before, the state of *amae* originally refers to what a small child feels toward his mother. It is therefore not surprising that the desire to *amaeru* still influences one's adult years and that it becomes manifest in the therapeutic situation. Here we have a perfect example of transference in the psychoanalytic sense. But then is it not strange that *amaeru* is a unique Japanese word? Indeed, the Japanese find it hard to believe that there is no word for *amaeru* in European languages; a colleague once told me that he could not believe that the equivalent for such a seemingly universal phenomenon as *amae* did not exist in English or German, since, as he put it, "Even puppies do it, you know." Let me therefore illustrate the "Japaneseness" of the concept of *amaeru* by one striking incident. The mother of a Eurasian patient, a British woman who had been a long term resident of Japan, was discussing her daughter with me. She spoke to me in English, but she suddenly switched to Japanese, in order to tell me that her daughter did not *amaeru* much as a child. I asked her why she had suddenly switched to Japanese. She replied, after a pause, that there was no way to say *amaeru* in English.

I have mentioned two Japanese words that are closely related to the psychology of *amae: kodawaru,* which means "to be inwardly disturbed over one's personal relationships," and *sumanai,* which means "to feel guilty or obligated." Now I should like to mention a few more words that are also related to the psychology of *amae.* First, *amai,* which originally means "sweet," can be used figuratively to describe a person who is overly soft and benevolent toward others or, conversely, one who always expects to *amaeru* in his relationships with others. Second, *amanzuru,* which is derived from *amaeru,* describes the state of mind in which one acquiesces to whatever circumstances one happens to be in. Third, *tori-iru,* which means "to take in," describes the behavior of a person who skillfully maneuvers another into permitting him to *amaeru.* Fourth, *suneru* describes the behavior of a child or an adult who pouts and sulks because he feels he is not allowed to *amaeru* as much as he wants to, thus harboring in himself mental pain of a masochistic nature. Fifth, *higamu* describes

the behavior of a child or an adult who feels himself unfairly treated compared to others who are more favored, often suggesting the presence of a paranoid feeling. Sixth, *tereru* describes the behavior of a child or an adult who is ashamed of showing his intimate wish to *amaeru.* Seventh, *hinekureru* describes the behavior of a child or an adult who takes devious ways in his efforts to deny the wish to *amaeru.*

One could readily say that the behaviors or emotions described by all these Japanese words are not unknown to Westerners and that they appear quite frequently in the therapeutic situation with Western patients. But there remains the question I raised before: Why is there no word in English or in other European languages that is equivalent to *amaeru,* the most central element in all these emotions? To this, one might answer that the absence of a word like *amaeru* is no inconveniency, since it can be represented by a combination of words such as the "wish to be loved" or "dependency needs." That may be so, but does not this linguistic difference point to something deeper? Perhaps it reflects a basic psychological difference between Japan and the Western World. Before discussing this problem further, however, I would like to mention a theory of Michael Balint, a British psychoanalyst, which has much bearing on what I am talking about now.

In his psychoanalytic practice Balint observed that "in the final phase of the treatment patients begin to give expression to long-forgotten, infantile, instinctual wishes, and to demand their gratification from their environment" (Balint 1952). He called this infantile desire passive object love, since its primal aim is to be loved; he also called it primary love, since it is the foundation upon which later forms of love are built. I imagine that he must have wondered why such an important desire is not represented by one common word, for he points out the fact that "all European languages are so poor that they cannot distinguish between the two kinds of object-love, active and passive" (Balint 1952).

By now it must be clear that the primary love or passive object-love described by Balint is none other than the desire to *amaeru*. But then we have to draw the curious conclusion that the emotion of primary love is readily accessible to Japanese patients by way of the word *amaeru*, while to Western patients, according to Balint, it can become accessible only after a painstaking analysis. In my observations I have also noticed that the recognition of *amae* by Japanese patients does not signify the final phase of treatment, as it did in Balint's patients. I think that we have to try to solve this apparent contradiction very carefully, because therein lies, in my opinion, an important key to understanding the psychological differences between Japan and Western countries.

The reasoning behind Balint's observation that primary love appears in its pure form only in the final phase of treatment is as follows. The primary love of an infant is bound to be frustrated, leading to the formation of narcissism, as though he said to himself, "If the world does not love me enough, I have to love and gratify myself." Since such narcissism is part of the earliest and most primitive layer of the mind, it can be modified only in the last stage of treatment, at which time the long repressed urge to be loved can re-emerge in its pure state. Then what shall we say about the Japanese, to whom this primary desire

to be loved is always accessible? Does it mean that the Japanese have less narcissism? I think not. Rather I would say that the Japanese somehow continue to cherish the wish to be loved even after the formation of narcissism. It is as though the Japanese did not want to see the reality of their basic frustration. In other words, the Japanese, as does everybody else, do experience frustration of their primary love, as is well attested to by the existence of the rich vocabulary we have already encountered relating to the frustration of *amae*. But it seems that the Japanese never give up their basic desire to *amaeru*, thus mitigating the extent of violent emotions caused by its frustration.

In this connection I want to mention an interesting feature of the word *amaeru*. We do not say that an infant does *amaeru* until he is about one year old, thereby indicating that he is then conscious of his wish to *amaeru*, which in turn suggests the presence of a budding realization that his wish cannot always be gratified. Thus, from its inception, the wish to *amaeru* is accompanied by a secret fear that it may be frustrated.

If what I have been saying is true, then it must indicate that there is a social sanction in Japanese society for expressing the wish to *amaeru*. And it must be this social sanction that has encouraged in the Japanese language the development of the large vocabulary relating to *amaeru*. In other words, in Japanese society parental dependency is fostered, and this behavior pattern is even institutionalized into its social structure, whereas perhaps the opposite tendency prevails in Western societies. This seems to be confirmed by recent anthropological studies of Japanese society, notably that of Ruth Benedict, who said: "The arc of life in Japan is plotted in opposite fashion to that in the United States. It is a great U-curve with maximum freedom and indulgence allowed to babies and to the old. Restrictions are slowly increased after babyhood till having one's own way reaches a low just before and after marriage" (Benedict 1961). It is true that the restrictions Benedict spoke of do exist for adults in Japanese society, but it should be understood that these restrictions are never meant to be drastic so far as the basic desire to *amaeru* is cncerned. Rather, these restrictions are but channels through which that desire is to be duly gratified. That is why we can speak of parental dependency as being institutionalized in Japanese society. For instance, in marriage a husband does *amaeru* toward his wife, and vice versa. It is strongly present in all formal relationships, including those between teacher and student and between doctor and patient. Thus William Caudill (1961), in his observations on Japanese psychiatric hospitals, spoke of the mutual dependency he encountered in all relationships.

In this connection I cannot resist mentioning an episode that happened when I gave a talk on some characteristic Japanese words to a professional group in the United States. *Amaeru* was one of those words. After my talk one distinguished scholar asked me whether or not the feeling of *amaeru* is something like what Catholics feel toward their Holy Mother. Apparently he could not recognize the existence of such a feeling in the ordinary mother-child relationship. And if his response is representative of Americans, it would mean that in American society the feeling of *amaeru* can be indulged in perhaps only in the religious life, but here also very sparingly.

I would now like to mention a study by a Japanese scholar, Hajime Nakamura, professor of Indian philosophy at the University of Tokyo and an authority on comparative philosophy. In his major work. *Ways of Thinking of Eastern Peoples* (1960), he presents a penetrating analysis of thought patterns of Indians, Chinese, Japanese, and Tibetans on the basis of linguistic studies and observations on variations in Buddhist doctrine and practice in these four countries. What he says about the Japanese pattern of thought is parallel to what I have been saying here, though he reaches his conclusions from an entirely different source. He says that the Japanese way of thinking is greatly influenced by an emphasis on immediate personal relations and also that the Japanese have always been eager to adopt foreign cultural influences, but always within the framework of this emphasis on personal relations. To state this in psychoanalytic terms, the Japanese are always prepared to identify themselves with, or introject, an outside force, to the exclusion of other ways of coping with it. This character trait of the Japanese was touched upon by Benedict, too, when she said that "the Japanese have an ethic of alternatives" and "Japan's motivations are situational," referring particularly to the sudden complete turnabout of Japan following the defeat of the last war.

This leads, however, to the very interesting and important question of whether or not Japanese character structure has changed at all since the war. I think that Benedict was quite rght in assuming that Japan as a whole willingly submitted to unconditional surrender because it was the Emperor's order, that Japan wanted only to please the Emperor, even in her defeat. But it cannot be denied that things have been changing since then. For instance, the Emperor had to declare that he no longer wished to be considered sacred. Also the Japanese have been disillusioned to find that the paramount virtue of *chu,* that is, loyalty to the emperor, was taken advantage of by the ultra-nationalists, who completely failed them. With the decline of *chu* there was also a decline of *ko,* that is, of filial piety. In other words, the tradition of repaying one's *on,* that is, one's spiritual debts to an emperor and to one's parents, was greatly undermined. Thus there developed the moral chaos of present day Japan.

I think, however, that the nature of this chaos has a distinctly Japanese character and can best be understood by taking into account the psychology of *amae.* It seems that heretofore the stress upon the duty of repaying one's *on* to the emperor and to one's parents served the purpose of regulating the all too powerful desire of *amae.* Since the Japanese were deprived of this regulating force after the war, it was inevitable that their desire to *amaeru* was let loose, with its narcissistic element becoming more manifest. That perhaps explains why we now find in Japan so many examples of lack of social restraint. I wonder whether this recent tendency has also helped to increase the number of neurotics. I think it has, though we have no reliable statistics to confirm it. But I am quite certain that an analysis of the psychology of *amae* such as I am attempting here would not have been possible in prewar days, because *amae* was concealed behind the duty of repaying one's *on.* It certainly was not visible to the outside observer, even to one as acute as Ruth Benedict. I would like to give you one clinical example to illustrate this point.

One of my recent patients, who was a student of law, revealed to me one day his secret thoughts, saying, "I wish I had some person who would take the responsibility of assisting me." The remarkable thing about this confession was that the Japanese word that he used for "assist" was a special legal term *hohitsu,* which was formerly used only for the act of assisting the emperor with his task of governing the nation. In saying this, as the patient himself explained, he wanted, like the emperor, to appear to be responsible for his acts but to depend completely on his assistant, who would really carry the burden. He said this, not jokingly but, rather, with complete seriousness. It is obvious that this confession revealed his secret desire to *amaeru,* about which he spoke more clearly on another occasion. But what I would like to point out here is that in prewar days the patient could hardly have made such a confession, using a special term reserved only for the emperor. Of course, this is a special case, and the fact that the patient was a law student accounted for his use of such a technical term. Yet I think that this case illustrates the point that I want to make, that is, the more emphasis placed upon repaying one's *on,* the less clearly seen in one's desire to *amaeru.*

In this connection, let me say a few words about the nature of so-called "emperor worship," which served as the Japanese state religion in prewar days. It is true that the emperor was held sacred, but the element of taboo was greater than that of divinity. It is really tempting to apply what Freud said about taboo to the Japanese emperor worship. As a matter of fact, he did mention the Japanese emperor in his book on *Totem and Taboo,* but not from the viewpoint of what is being discussed here. I will not go into this subject any further now, except to add one more comment concerning the effect of elimination of the emperor taboo and its related system, apart from the already discussed release of the desire to *amaeru.* Some Japanese critics voiced the opinion that the tight thought control deriving from the emperor and the family system in prewar days stifled development of healthy selfhood, that one could assert himself in those days only by way of *suneru* and *higamu,* which are interestingly enough the very same Japanese words that I have described before as indicating frustration of *amae* (Maruyama 1960; Isono 1960). I agree that this opinion is generally true, but I do not believe that elimination of the emperor and family system alone can lead to development of healthy selfhood or personality. This is shown by many patients, who confess that they are awakened to the fact that they have "not had self" apart from the all powerful desire to *amaeru.* Then what or who can help them to obtain their "self"? This touches upon a very important problems of identity, which I will not attempt to discuss in detail. I can say only that the Japanese as a whole are still searching for something, something with which they can safely identify themselves, so that they can become whole, independent beings.

In closing I should like to make two additional remarks. First, it may seem that I am possibly idealizing the West in a way, since I have looked at the problem of personality and culture in modern Japan from the Western point of view. I do not deny that I have. In fact I could not help doing so, because Japanese culture did not produce any yardstick to judge itself critically. I really think that it is a fine thing for the West to have developed such a yardstick for critical analysis. And it seems inevitable that it involves a kind of idealization when the non-Westerners attempt to apply such a yardstick to themselves. I know, however, that in the psychoanalytic circles of Western countries idealization has a special meaning and is not something commendable. So they would certainly not call their use of the analytical method idealization. But I wonder whether they are entirely right in assuming that their use of the analytical method stands on its own without involving any idealization on their part.

Second, though I have stated that there is no exact equivalent to the word *amaeru* in all European languages, I do not say that *amaeru* is unique to the Japanese language. I have some information that the language of Korea and that of Ainu have a word of the same meaning. There seems to be some question about whether or not the Chinese language has such a word I am now most curious to know whether or not the Polynesian languages have a similar word I have a feeling that they may have. If they do, how would their psychology compare with that of the Japanese? It is my earnest hope that these questions will be answered by anthropological and psychological studies in the not too distant future.

REFERENCES

Balint, Michael
1952 *Primary Love and Psychoanalytic Technique*. London: Hogarth Press.
Benedict, Ruth
1961 *The Chrysanthemum and the Sword*. Boston: Houghton Mifflin Co.
Caudill, William
1961 Around the Clock Patient Care in Japanese Psychiatric Hospitals: The Role of the *tsukisoi*. *American Sociological Review* 26:204-214.
Doi, L. Takeo
1956 Japanese Language as an Expression of Japanese Psychology. *Western Speech* 20:90-96.
1958 Shinkeishitsu no seishinbyroi (Psychopathology of *shinkeishitsu*). *Psychiatria et Neurologia Japonica* 60:733-44.
1960 Jibun to amae no seishinbyori (Psychopathology of *jibun* and *amae*). *Psychiatria et Neurologia Japonica* 61:149-62.
1961 Sumanai to Ikenai (*Sumanai* and *Ikenai*)—Some Thoughts on Super-Ego. *Japanese Journal of Psychoanalysis* 8:4-7.
Isono, Fujiko
1960 Ie to Jigaishiki (Family and Self-consciousness). In *Kindai Nippon Shisoshi Koza* (History of Thought in Modern Japan), Vol. 6. Tokyo: Chikuma Shobo.
Maruyama, Masao
1960 *Chusei to Hangyaku* (Loyalty and Rebellion). In *Kindai Nippon Shisoshi Koza* (History of Thought in Modern Japan). Vol. 6. Tokyo: Chikuma Shobo.
Nakamura, Hajime
1960 *Ways of Thinking of Eastern peoples*. Japanese National Commission for UNESCO (comp.). Tokyo: Japanese Government Printing Bureau.

17. EXPRESSIVE SYMBOLISM IN WITCHCRAFT AND DELUSION: A COMPARATIVE STUDY

ANNE PARSONS

The late Anne Parsons was Research Anthropologist, Maclean Hospital, Boston. Reprinted with permission from *Belief, Magic and Anomie,* by Anne Parsons, New York: The Free Press, 1969. Copyright © Sociètè Internationale d'Ethnopsychologie.

WITCHCRAFT BELIEFS and delusions of persecution are two extreme examples of types of symbolism which must be understood in function of their value as representations of internal psychic reactions rather than as empirically valid representations of the external world.[1] Both express subjective motivation: they have in common the fact that they do so by means of a belief about the motives of a real or imaginary external agent. Prior to the theoretical advances in understanding of non-rational symbolic processes which have taken place in the last half century both in psychiatry, as represented by psychoanalytic theory, and in cultural anthropology, they were identified as "irrational" beliefs. But in spite of these advances, the tendency to assimilate the two forms has not disappeared. Within psychoanalytic theory the formation of delusions has been explained as a process of projection in which a threatening affect which has been denied by the conscious ego returns in the form of an external perception (Waelder 1951); by this means psychic equilibrium is re-established. Psychologically oriented anthropology has also had recourse to the concept of projection; consequently witchcraft beliefs have been considered as a mechanism which restores psychic equilibrium in the face of overwhelming anxieties or hostilities. Little detailed comparison has made, but, since both distort empirical reality in function of motivation, a basic similarity has frequently been affirmed. Whether from the standpoint of the assumption implicit to psychoanalysis that all of the primitive symbolic processes in which motivation is primary have something in common, or whether from the standpoint of the conviction of a number of anthropologists that the symbolism of non-literate societies is subject to interpretation on the basis of psychological principles common to our own society, it is the movement toward assimilation rather than a search for distinctive features which has been most prominent in recent decades.

But, as Lévi-Strauss has stated (1950), although there may be resemblances between the symbolic processes of the primitive, the abnormal (and the child), one should not lose sight of the fact that there are both children and abnormals in non-literate societies. In other words, we do not know whether or not these processes are equivalent, or if they are, in what specific respects, prior to a comparative analysis in which the variables are chosen from among all of the possible combinations provided by these three dimensions. The aim of this review is to further exchange between anthropologists and psychiatrists; our own interest lies in the area of symbolic content, and empirically, in that of the cross-cultural study of schizophrenia. Most important, we feel that comparative studies are lacking and badly needed at the present time. Consequently, we have decided to present a case history, chosen for the reason that the same manifest symbol can be viewed from either the psychoanalytic or the anthropological standpoint. The patient is a 37-year-old woman of Italian peasant origin hospitalized in the United States with a diagnosis of paranoid schizophrenia. Her symptoms include auditory hallucinations and withdrawal and passivity alternating with aggressive and self-destructive behavior, but of greatest interest to us in a delusion in which she sees herself as the victim of a spell effected by means of the evil eye, an idea which in itself is frequently found in Italian peasants even long after emigration to the United States. Focusing on a single symbolic construction which can be considered as either a delusion or a cultural belief, we hope by a sort of comparative analysis to be able to isolate some ways in which we think that the pathological specificity of the delusion is more striking than its resemblance to the same symbol as it might appear in a normal context.

More specifically, we have selected three more or less independent foci for organization of the case material. First, since it might be said that, given the correspondence in content with symbolism normal for the culture, it is impossible to characterize the case as pathological by the diagnostic criteria applicable to our own society, it is necessary to justify our initial assumption that the symbol is in fact delusional. However, on a rough empirical level the distinction appears to be less difficult to make than the assumptions of many anthropologists who have worked in the field of mental health would indicate. In this case, it requires nothing more than a conscious cross-cultural application of classical descriptive psychiatry; by stating the diagnostic indices used, the correspondence of the patient's behavior with that of other patients placed in the same category can be demonstrated. Reciprocally, we will also sum up the indices by which the patient's behavior differs from that of a normal person in her own milieu, thus justifying the appellation "pathological" in the latter as well as for the psychiatrist.

However, this first distinction is purely empirical and has to be made on the basis of the total behavior of the patient; it does not in itself provide any clues to a theoretical distinction between the psychic mechanisms involved in the formation of the respective beliefs. For this latter problem, we will have to restrict analysis to the symbol alone, comparing its structuring for the patient with that which would be found in a non-pathological believer in witchcraft. Here we have selected two foci of organization, namely the problem of relationships between symbol and the situation to which it refers, and, since both witchcraft beliefs and paranoid delusions (in some cases) involve personalized persecuting agents, the problem of agent choice.

The patient, Angelina Perella,[2] arrived in Boston, Massachusetts, with her husband and two of their eventual family of nine in 1921, toward the end of a wave of Italian immigration whose magnitude can be judged from the fact that in 1950 one out of every fifteen residents of the United States was born in Italy. The Perella family settled in a predominantly middle class suburb, where Mr. Perella became a garage worker. Thus superficially, they were considerably closer to assimilation with American culture than the large majority of first generation Italian-Americans among whom—or at least among the women—the phrase "going to America" was used to denote a trip from the Italian quarter to the central shopping district. Nevertheless, like most Italian women, Mrs. Perella showed little proficiency in English at the time of her hospitalization fourteen years after immigration, and was able to name three large cities in Italy but only one in the United States on the psychiatric examination.

She was born on June 19, 1898, in Piave, Province of Venice, as the second female child of nine live births. Her parents, both of whom were still living in Italy in 1935, were tenant farmers of marginal economic status. Angelina worked in a factory from the age of 14 to about 17, but did not work subsequently when the entire family was transported to Avellino, near Naples, where they lived for three years in a state barracks during the First World War. Avellino has sent many immigrants to the Boston area; it was here that Angelina met the man whom she married after a two-year courtship and with whom she emigrated at the age of 23.

We know nothing beyond the bare facts of Mrs. Perella's early life, since our knowledge of the case comes solely from hospital records. However, the husband's anamnesis was unusually complete, for he, to the contrary of his wife, spoke English fluently, and, moreover, was willing to reveal many intimate details, among which we find the fact that, to his knowledge, his wife had never evidenced any pleasure in sexual relationships, giving as a reason (although she gave birth to nine children) her fear of pregnancy. In addition, he felt that she tended to take her responsibilities as a mother too seriously, that otherwise she was a sociable personality, less inclined to worry than he, "practical rather than imaginative," but that over the years she withdrew more and more from social relationships, explicitly in order to care for the children. She was a nominal Catholic, but during the years prior to admission attended Mass rarely, since she felt it impossible to take all of the children. He considered her "unusually superstitious."

About June 1934, at which time the patient was pregnant for the ninth time, she became even more "superstitious." Between June and the September delivery, Mr. Perella spent a considerable sum of money in gratifying her whims, including the purchase of a live pig which he killed so that she could drink its blood. Six days after being delivered in a general hospital, the patient was visited by three neighbor women, including a Mrs. J. Later the same evening, she complained to her husband that Mrs. J. had bewitched her and that she had come under the influence of the evil eye. It is at this point that we can place the beginning of an acute psychosis. She began to complain of being hot and cold alternately and of feeling generally sick; her breast milk and her lochia dried up. No medical basis for these complaints was discovered, and 12 days *post partum* Mrs. Perella was returned to her home, diagnosed as homesick by the hospital staff.

On return, she found four of her children ill and was further convinced that malign influences were at work, that both she and the family were in danger, and that had she not returned from the hospital all of the children would have died. This and subsequent happenings over the next nine months were attributed to the spell cast by Mrs. J. who, according to the patient, was extremely jealous because of the many friends who paid visits and brought presents on the birth of her various children. When Mrs. J. paid a few calls, the patient did not directly accuse her of witchcraft; however, she was extremely disagreeable.

One month after delivery, the patient went to a fortune teller to have the spell lifted. Subsequently, her condition seems to have improved, until December when she developed a marked swelling and pain in her left arm which a little later gave place to the same affliction of the right member. This too was evidence of the evil eye cast by Mrs. J. During one visit to the fortune teller, Mrs. Perella was asked if Mrs. J. had taken anything from the house. Mr. Perella related on requests that Mrs. J. had taken and not yet returned two dresses belonging to one of the little girls. This was evidence that they had been used to work a charm on the little girl because she had become thin and did not seem to be in as good health as formerly. At the same time the patient began to talk about a dream that she had in the hospital following delivery in which the devil appeared, showed her a large knife, and told her that it was with this she would have to kill the child.

She was then informed by the fortune teller that there must be something blue in the house which caused her troubles. After considerable fretting and searching, she discovered an old American flag in the bottom of a trunk; she then rinsed the blue portion in cold water according to directions to obtain relief. Over this period she was extremely depressed,

often telling her husband that somebody would eventually kill him because he did not believe she had been bewitched. Between January and May 18, she improved somewhat while following the fortune teller's prescriptions. The latter date is that of her last visit to the fortune teller who informed her that she would soon find a tin can filled with money which they were to share. Mrs. Perella then began to act very mysteriously toward her husband, telling him that there was a great deal of money in the house. The morning of May 19, she got up at five o'clock and spent the entire day prowling about the house, opening cans, and insisting when she found no money that someone else had taken it. She became afraid that people had found out about the treasure, and, believing she had already found it, were going to kidnap her children and hold them for ransom. She kept the windows and doors locked, stated that the watchdog had been won over by thieves so that he would not bark, and showed an ever increasing restlessness. Her husband called a doctor who saw the patient several times over the next ten days and finally advised commitment to a mental hospital. Over this period she slept little and ate almost nothing. On May 30, Mrs. Perella was admitted to the Boston Psychopathic Hospital.

Most of the psychiatric observation we have covers the week of May 30 to June 7. As to her condition at that time, we may abstract from the hospital records:

On admission, the patient was overactive, overtalkative, and very resistive—requiring to be kept in seclusion for several days. She slept poorly but attended to her vegetative functions without prompting. . . . She exhibited no stereotypies or ritualisms . . (several days later) has quieted considerably and is a great deal more co-operative. Objectively, the patient seems to be bewildered and distressed . . . cries readily, is very suspicious of anything done for her in the hospital—physical and mental examinations, medications, etc. and constantly anticipates injury of some kind.

The psychiatrist qualified his mental status examination and felt himself unable to make more than a provisional estimate of the degree of cognitive disturbance due to the patient's difficulties with the English language. However, we can cite the following material as to thought content:

. . . it is quite clear that there has been inexplicable and sinister activity going on about her for some time. "People" call her crazy and say that many of the things in her house have been stolen (cf. information from husband), although actually they are prizes salvaged from the city dump by her children. Automobiles go round and round her house in the evening with their lights turned off apparently to prevent her from catching a glimpse of the occupant. Suspicious characters have been loitering around her grounds and flashing lights through the windows at night. "People" have been entering her house the past two or three weeks and turning everything upside down, disarranging her clothes, hiding one of a pair of shoes or a single stocking, so that she has great trouble in mating her wearing apparel. They have even gone so far as to heat her bed in some way, possibly by placing a fire under it so that she was unable to sleep and had to stay up most of the night. She at first denied ever having talked of the evil eye, but later stated that visitors at her home had repeatedly remarked that she had the evil eye . . . She at first denied searching for money about her house, saying that all her acquaintances did this but not she. Later she admitted that she looked for a cache but only in one room, while "other people" had ransacked her entire house. . . . During the course of the interview, she repeatedly twisted her hair into a knot at the back of her head, but had no hairpins with which to hold it in place. After a few moments of animated conversation, the chignon was loosened and the patient never tired of calling the examiner's attention to this as evidence that something was amiss.

Note vagueness of style and the use of the paranoid mechanism of denial and return in the form of a positive statement (to be discussed below) on occasions when the patient is confronted with her past behavior; she denies having talked of the evil eye, then states that "visitors in her house" accused her of having it. Likewise, she denies having searched for money, later states that she did in a particular instance, and that "other people" had done so. Note also the image of fire under the bed as a probable non-technological equivalent for the electricity image frequently found in paranoids.

The examining psychiatrist was not certain as to the presence of auditory hallucinations; however, on one occasion the patient stated that she was unable to answer a question because "head no feel a good, talk a talk a talk." This is a phrase frequently used by Italian patients to describe auditory hallucinations. In sum, although there may be some inaccuracies of detail due to the language barrier, the mental status information generally checks with that given by the husband and clearly substantiates the diagnosis of paranoid schizophrenia.

On June 7, the patient was withdrawn from the hospital by her husband against medical advice, as frequently happens in the case of first generation Italian patients for whom the value of family solidarity outweighs the commitment to specialized professional care. On June 12, she was readmitted in the following circumstances as described by Mr. Perella. She was considerably improved after the hospital stay, but a neighbor woman was called in during the day as a precautionary measure. On this date, the neighbor did not arrive on time and the patient was left alone with her three youngest children. As the patient later recounted to her husband, someone came to the door to ask the time, and as the kitchen clock was not working, she went upstairs to look for a timepiece. Once upstairs, she forgot the errand and (probably commanded by hallucinatory voices) took off all her clothes, rubbed her body with bathing alcohol and ignited it. She was next seen by the landlord, walking down the stairs in flames with a child under each arm. On June 22, she died in the hospital of severe burns.

The circumstances of her death are sufficient to place the patient outside the norms of her own culture. From the psychiatric standpoint, the following signs which determined the diagnosis can be briefly summarized; a) after the birth of her ninth child (with some forewarnings during pregnancy) the patient went through a distinct *personality change* in function of which: b) her behavior and ability to perform her normal role began to *disintegrate,* terminating in a state of *acute confusion* (from May 18 on); c) in the confused phase, rapid and apparently inconsistent *alternation of affects* (from cooperation to extreme suspicion, from passive withdrawal to overt aggression) were observed (as far as can be determined, the patient did not possess a consistently aggressive or suspicious personality before the change); d) it is highly probable that *auditory hallucinations* were present; e) in the confused state, the patient describes herself as the victim of a series of mysterious and indeterminate events

in the *vague style* characteristic of paranoids; f) after a period of improvement, the confusion returned suddenly and terminated in a *self-destructive act,* committed without determinable motive. All of these symptoms could be found in any psychiatric text as characteristic of paranoid schizophrenics.

From a biographical standpoint, three phases can be roughly delineated in the patient's married life (for lack of information, we exclude early life). The first extends up to the ninth pregnancy; it is characterized by a number of symptoms which can be called neurotic, that is, frigidity and compulsiveness as indicated both by overconscientiousness in care of the children and by her "unusually superstitious" nature.[3] But no gross pathology is observable in this period, and, although the presence of severe anxiety is indicated, the patient was able to function in her social role. By sharpest contrast, in the third period which follows failure of the magical attempts at self-cure, complete ego breakdown occurs; the patient is no longer able to function in her role and eventually destroys herself. Moreover, this period is characterized by total breakdown in symbolic functioning. To others, the patient is able to communicate only the impression of confusion—of vague mysterious events whose referents are undiscoverable to the non-specialist. That the cognitive structure of normal effective communication, as indicated by the use of language, was disrupted is probable.

However, the second and intermediate period which extends from the announcement that she has come under the influence of the evil eye until the breakdown of attempts at cure structured via this same symbol is more difficult to characterize; it is this period which will be the focus of our intensive analysis. After the fact, it is easy to spot indices of pathology during this period and presumably a skilled psychiatrist would have been able to spot them had he seen the patient at that time. But at first glance, it appears that the anthropological observer or the believer in the evil eye might not have found the means of distinguishing the belief from the normal for the very reason that the patient defines her situation in culturally formulated terms. Given her definition of the situation, she acts appropriately in seeking the fortune teller's aid in lifting the spell. Moreover, up to a point these means of cure are effective. It is only when they themselves are put in doubt, that is, when the patient constructs further paranoid agents who stole the money that she was to give to the fortune teller, that pathological thinking extends beyond all bounds.[4] But given the post-facto evidences of pathology, at least an attempt to isolate the pathological specificity of the thinking of this second period is legitimate; it is to this task that we can now turn.

To restate the question briefly, given that the symbols of this period correspond in content to the general cultural pattern, in what ways can they be distinguished both from the standpoint of their structuring in this case and from the theoretical point of view? In this formulation we will refer to Freud's Schreber case (1954) and to other articles in psychoanalysis and anthropology on the formation of the two types of belief. Throughout the discussion, we will make extensive reference to the works of Kluckhohn (1944) and Evans-Pritchard (1937) on witchcraft in Navaho and Zande societies respectively, while on delusion formation we will refer to Freud's Schreber case and to articles by Waelder (1951) and Tausk (1948). In addition it will be necessary to intersperse some empirical material or normal witchcraft beliefs in Italian society. Our foci of discussion are the following: first, what is the relationship between symbol and situation in each case; and second, how is the persecuting agent chosen?

Both Kluckhohn and Evans-Pritchard emphasize the function of witchcraft beliefs as an explanation of and as a means of channelling anxiety which results from random misfortunes which could not have been prevented by ordinary means of empirical or normative control. That the actually observed distribution of witchcraft beliefs according to evoking situation follows the pattern that would be expected from this assumption is clear in the data that they present: death and illness are by far the most prominent foci, while certain other categories of events seem outside the range of witchcraft. Among the latter, Evans-Pritchard presents the examples of the adulterer and the incompetent apprentice carpenter who breaks the wood; the actions of both are considered within the realm of human control whether technological or moral, while death and illness are not. Rather it is the witchcraft belief itself which provides the means of control whether in the form of preventive measures—amulets, incantations, etc.—or of post-facto rituals of exorcism or acts of vengeance against real agents supposed to be witches.

Not only does the distribution of beliefs follow a predictable pattern, but also the anxiety sources behind them can be discovered rather easily by the observer. When the Zande takes an anthropologist to visit a sick relative, the latter will agree as to the description of the symptoms and will understand the Zande's concern, although he will differ on explanation or prescription and although his greater understanding of illness may make the event seem less mysterious. Thus *although the witch herself is a non-empirical symbol, the situation in which she is evoked can be empirically located*. From this standpoint, witchcraft beliefs appear as elaborations which depart from commonly defined situations and whose result is *cognitively* to explain the situation by construction of a casual agent and by relating a number of discrete situations under a general category, and *expressively*, to alleviate the anxiety, concomitant to the situation in channelling it through a set of expectations and in furnishing the means for symbolic counteraction. Secondly there is a *reversible relationship between symbol and situation* in that the possessor of the symbol can himself return to the situation to which it refers, that is, explain it to an outsider.

But for the observer, the location of the source of anxiety behind paranoid symbols has proved much more difficult, and although considerable effort has been devoted to the problem, there is still some disagreement as to the interpretation of delusional symbols. The most striking characteristics of paranoid thinking are its vagueness and looseness of structure. If a Zande happened to say that his family was under a spell, one might ask him what he meant and receive the reply that his brother had just died suddenly; this event could only have been caused by witches. But the paranoid's situational referent would never be so clear; his circumlocutions might include some situ-

ational justification (as a secondary process) of the belief that he was being persecuted, but unless a "translation" from paranoid language can be obtained, one is never sure of the referent. Theoretically, this fact can be formulated in two ways: first, paranoid thinking is *irreversible*, that is, one cannot ask a paranoid what he meant; and two, paranoid symbolism lacks the dual character (*à deux faces*) of normal expressive symbolism which in fact is always partially cognitive, that is, refers simultaneously to an objective situation (cognitive referent) and to its effect on the subject (expressive referent).[5]

Given this lack of cognitive referents, only two possibilities are open in the interpretation of the delusional symbols: one can say that they refer to an abnormal subjective experience which is outside of the limits structured by normal communicative devices; or one can say that they express unconscious motivations and attempt to interpret them by genetic reconstruction as has been done by psychoanalysis.

Thus in summary fashion two provisional oppositions between witchcraft and paranoid symbolism can be stated: a) witchcraft symbolism refers to socially defined (and/or conscious) situations, while paranoid symbolism relates to purely subjective situations (or unconscious factors); and b) the relationship between symbol and situation is reversible and structured in the case of witchcraft beliefs and irreversible and unstructured in the case of paranoid delusions. Since the relationship is structured for witchcraft beliefs, it follows that there are appropriate situations in which they can be evoked; this point will serve as a basis for further discussion.

But some anthropologists may consider the assumption that witchcraft beliefs relate only to conscious anxieties as somewhat arbitrary; Kluckhohn in particular has emphasized their function as a means of expression for unconscious hostility. Nadel (1952) and Evans-Pritchard as well as Kluckhohn have demonstrated that there is a cross-cultural variation in the pattern of choice for those considered as witches and that the actual choices in a particular society can be explained in terms of the tensions inherent to the social structure. Witchcraft beliefs from this standpoint can be seen as expressing these tensions in a displaced form; in this sense one might speak of an unconscious determinant. However, this problem is more relevant to our second problem, that of agent choice, than to the first and can be left aside for the moment.

Actually if one attempts to evaluate the role of the unconscious in witchcraft beliefs from the standpoint of evoking situations, several questions to which presently available research does not furnish answers are raised: first, to what extent does the believer himself independently perceive a specific anxiety source relative to a given evocation of witches; second, can an anxiety source external to the subject (whether social or natural) always be located by the observer; third, what is the relationship between primary witchcraft belief as related to external situations and secondary anxiety due to fear of the witches themselves or anticipated consequences of witchcraft? In order to answer them, an isolation of levels of meaning would be necessary since the witchcraft symbol is presumably overdetermined. For example, the Italian mother who fears when her child is praised too highly by a stranger that

the evil eye may make him ill may on one level be channelling a conscious fear of illness and on another, expressing unconscious resentment of the praise; thus even if an external referent is present in all cases, the presence of additional unconscious elements is not excluded. However, for several reasons it seems best to leave aside this problem for the present paper, even at the risk of the accusation that we are eliminating the essential. Although other relationships are by no means excluded, the available data indicate a primary relationship between witchcraft beliefs and specific external anxiety-provoking events; it is this relationship that has been most clearly formulated in anthropological theory. It is also in this respect that the contrast with paranoid symbolism is most obvious; it thus serves as the best starting point in clarification of the differences. Secondly, starting from a theory of motivation in the cross-cultural interpretation of symbols always creates a certain risk that a culture-bound view will be imposed upon the data; starting from situations may eliminate some of this risk.

When we first examine the situation in which Mrs. Perella sees herself as the victim of the charm cast by Mrs. J., as she herself defines it, it is the similarities to culturally structured belief which are most apparent. An informant in Boston's Italian quarter has described the symptoms of the evil eye in much the same terms which, according to the description we possess, Mrs. Perella used: she felt generally sick, and alternately hot and cold, and had difficulties in nursing. Second, she attributed the children's illnesses to the charm; children are considered the most frequent victims of the evil eye in Italian culture. But we would nevertheless hesitate before overestimating the coincidence. Although, since the data are limited, it is necessary to use a certain amount of hypothetical reconstruction based on the assumption that the patient's thinking resembles that of other schizophrenics, some lines of distinction can be proposed which could be tested on other cases. First, it appears as if Mrs. Perella *first* complained that she was being bewitched and *then* began to complain of the physical symptoms usually attributed to the evil eye; moreover, no intermediate signs which indicate to her that she is in fact under a spell are evident. There is an apparent discrepancy in timing which means that the concept of witchcraft symbolism as an explanatory framework applicable to a specific category of events has to be discarded at the outset, for an explanation must follow and be appropriate to the event which it explains. Actually in most witchcraft cases, rites of divination are performed to find out whether or not witchcraft is involved and if so, who is responsible. Thus witchcraft is conceived of as a possible explanation and one which may be appropriate depending on an agreed-upon definition of the situation, while Mrs. Perella herself defines the situation before the application of any conventional means of interpretation.

In fact, of course, the sequence of events of a psychotic breakdown is not so simple, and a secondary report is bound to be highly selective in the direction of normal experience. From the literature on paranoid symbol formation (Freud 1954; Tausk 1948; Waelder 1951), we can suppose that Mrs. J's visit to the hospital provoked an impulse on the part of Mrs. Perella which was then rejected

from consciousness. Subsequently, she must have felt a sense of estrangement and a series of bizarre subjective symptoms inexplicable on the basis of existing expectations (i.e., not corresponding to the normal post-partum condition with which Mrs. Perella as the mother of nine would presumably have been familiar). The formation of the belief *both* explains and to the patient "is" the disease since she does not believe that she is ill independently of the charm.

But there is a common sense in which a belief can be maintained against opposition which has to be discarded in this case. Given the cultural difference, it is likely that Mrs. Perella might not understand the psychiatrist's definition of the situation as one of emotional conflict, or if she did, consider her own, that she was a victim of a charm, as superior in the light of her own cultural identification. However, it is the factor of timing which makes it possible to discard this interpretation; but we have first to state more clearly the psychoanalytic theory of the mechanism of projection in psychosis. According to Freud (1954) and Waelder (1951) a delusion of persecution (when an agent is involved) is the return, in the form of the belief that the agent is a persecutor, of feelings formerly attached to the latter. Thus Freud states that the proposition "I (a man) love x (a man)," one which is unacceptable to the ego, may be denied by reversal of subject-object relations and by *a transformation of affect into belief,* to give "x hates me." According to this formulation, it would appear that Mrs. Perella's belief about the charm is actually a *transformation of* an impulse felt towards Mrs. J. rather than a *belief about* the situation of illness. To the observer, this is seen in that the belief was formed at the moment when Mrs. J. paid her visit to the hospital and before the patient discusses her physical symptoms. These latter would have to be explained as further manifestations of the psychosis, either in the form of a description of actual sensations or in the form of a rationalization (secondary elaboration of the delusion) for the belief that she was being bewitched.

Thus although the communicable content of the symbol which the patient adopted does correspond to the normal precisely because she took over a common cultural representation (rather than a bizarre invention such as the influencing machine described by Victor Tausk 1948), its subjective content differs and is incommunicable except to those familiar with schizophrenic symptomatology. It is in this sense that Mrs. Perella's belief is culturally inappropriate. She does not interpret the situation as would normally be done; for example, by pouring oil upon water to determine from its spreading or failure to spread whether or not the evil eye is involved. Rather, she assumes immediately, and with a type of absolute conviction characteristic of paranoids, that it is.[6] In fact, the symbol refers to a different situation from the normal, and, as seen by the lack of the intermediate signs by which a social definition of the situation would be reached, the relationship between symbol and situation is unstructured (or better, structured by means of principles other than those of cultural belief systems whose laws must be sought in personality theory). Had she used such interpretative signs, she would have been able to communicate her belief to others, assuming they were of the same culture, who would have accepted (or rejected for predictable reasons) her definition of the situation. As it is, although these others recognized the words, they did not understand their meaning and called her "crazy."[7]

But it is precisely this communicability which characterizes cultural belief systems. A cultural belief system from one standpoint is a set of general categories, with fixed cognitive referents, possessed by all of the members of the community; specific and individual experiences can be referred to them and thus, via the return route from the general and communicable to the specific and individual, similar experiences are evoked on the part of others and understanding is reached. But in order that the categories remain stable— and consequently common to the community—specific steps by which one proceeds from a particular situation to the category are necessary.[8] Experiences can be referred to them and thus, via the return route, from the general and communicable to the specific and individual. Thus in the case of witchcraft, it is necessary that a set of criteria by which a particular event can be attributed to witchcraft be utilized; if this were not so, any event whatsoever could be so explained and the distinguishing capacity would vanish. A nonpathological deviant might change the meaning of the categories, but in most circumstances (where culture change is not involved), social correction mechanisms would operate against him: for example, a Zande might for personal reasons say that witches had induced him to commit adultery, but he would be laughed at because everybody knows "witches don't do that." Such correction mechanisms are notably inefficacious in the case of delusions.

In fact to say that such categories are both culturally and situationally appropriate is to state the same relationship in two ways, since cultural categories themselves carry with them some means of determining the range of situations to which they belong.[9] As such they contain a cognitive element by necessity and cannot be considered as pure expressive symbols as those of a schizophrenic might.

Another way of defining the lack of situational appropriateness of schizophrenic belief would be in turn of the "spread of meaning" by which psychiatrists have long characterized it. This can be seen in the case of Mrs. Perella when she attributes a series of apparently unrelated events to the charm cast by Mrs. J. without using independent criteria of relevance; it is as if the charm gave meaning to her entire life. The fact that she considers a single agent responsible for a series of events does not in itself place her beyond the limits of cultural symbolism: in all societies in which the witch exists as a stable social object, and in the case of certain stereotypes in our own society which have been explained in terms similar to witchcraft, the agent once defined as responsible may be evoked again with little reality testing. But again, we can isolate the difference by regarding the discrepancy of timing between the emergence of anxiety and the attribution of responsibility. Mrs. Perella does not, once she has blamed Mrs. J. for symptoms which she herself felt while in the hospital, forget the matter and *then* re-evoke Mrs. J. as agent after she discovers her children ill and again finds herself in an anxiety-provoking situation to which the same symbol might be appropriate. Rather the affect has spread to the point of eliminating distinctions between situations; the latter simply justify it secondarily. The selections inherent to a secondary report are in this case revealing; as her husband sees the situation, the patient felt herself continually under the spell and consequently found nothing unexpected in the further, and situationally unrelated, misfortunes. Moreover, she does not, as a neurotic might, simply exaggerate a given situation by fearing that the children might die of what was probably a minor illness. Rather she states it as a positive fact, via the paranoid mechanism of transformation of affect into belief, that the children *would have died* had she not returned from the hospital.

Second, in this particular case the delusion is not internally consistent, for she holds herself rather than Mrs. J. responsible. Rather the affective meaning of events has "spread" beyond the cognitive framework so that it is hostility or anxiety rather than situations which might provoke them which is constant; the malign influence of Mrs. J. reappears when one child is observed to have lost weight, but when Mr. Perella reveals his skepticism, the patient again shows inconsistency and states that "they" may kill him because he does not believe, not that Mrs. J. will react in some fashion. The constant element is that she sees her anxiety *as* reality via the mechanism of projection. In a sense it is for this reason that cognitive consistency lacks.

In concluding discussion of the first question, the following propositons can be stated as provisonally differentiating the two types of symbolism in regard to the structuring of relationships between symbol and situation. 1) Culturally defined witchcraft belief both provides an expressive form and fulfills a need for explanation by attributing a number of causally distinct (from the scientific standpoint) situations to a common agent; by this means consistency of action is assured in spite of the random arrival of misfortune and the resultant affects which might otherwise disorganize behavior; 2) in schizophrenic symbolism, on the other hand, the relationship to the immediate anxiety provoking situation is secondary; rather it is the presence of a negative affect which is constant and which itself creates the symbolic framework while the cognitive aspect of the latter may vary. Thus in the second case, the symbol is no longer a link between the individual and a given external reality, but rather creates a new and purely subjective reality by transformation of affect. One might speak of a reversal of relations between cognitive and culturally-structured) categories and affective processes as another way of stating the Freudian definition of psychosis as a dominance of id over ego processes.[10]

The second problem which we have to consider is that of the choice of agent. Anthropologists have made a number of hypotheses as to the bases of choice for witches (in those cases where they actually exist as social objects; in those where they do not, the same principles may be applied to the qualities which are attributed to them). As stated above, empirical observations indicate that the choice is predictable in function of tensions within the social structure; as a general rule one can say that witches are most frequently those persons against whom hostility is commonly felt, or representatives of those persons. Thus if the obligation to support the old is enforced but at the same time this obligation creates considerable economic strain, it is likely that old people will be frequently accused of witchcraft. But if the real object of hostility is one whose position within the social structure is such as to make direct expression of hostility too disrupitve, another object may be substituted by displacement; thus a man may accuse another in the next tribe of witchcraft when his own brother is the real source of tension. In other cases, it seems that witchcraft accusations act as a balancing mechanism which counteracts real power relations; for example, the rich are accused of witchcraft in a number of societies. This has a number of effects both in relieving some of the psychological pressure on the poor, in depreciating the value of wealth in a certain measure and consequently insuring against too great disparity, and in certain cases, it acts as a real sanction in that the rich know that if they do not donate sufficient sums to specified ceremonial occasions, they themselves may become victims of witchcraft (the assumed agent is frequently a potential victim). Although it will not fit all cases, the assumption has also been made and confirmed in some that those who deviate from the given social norms are among the most suspect. Thus in the concrete social structure, witchcraft accusations may act either negatively as a mechanism for the resolution of tension created by a given set of norms or positively as a sanction which reinforces these same norms.

However, on the level of symbolic processes which most concerns us here, it is the characteristics by which the witch is defined which is most important rather than the choice of real objects or the real effects of the belief on the psychosocial situation. In fact, witches are more often heard about than seen; anthropological research has had considerable difficulty in gathering accounts from the victims of witchcraft or from those actually so accused, although such do exist. It seems possible to account for a large percentage of witchcraft belief on a purely symbolic level; consequently it can be best analyzed not in the perspective of the choice of real object, but, like the images of Russians held by Americans who have never seen one, and vice versa, in terms of the composite characteristics of the image. Kluckhohn's data for the Navaho list a number of defining characteristics: witches are associated with night (they are feared only at night); with incest (it is necessary to commit incest to be initiated into a witch society); with animals (for the Navaho and many other societies, witches possess the capacity of taking animal guise), with death and with illegitimate possession of wealth (witches rob graves); and with out-groups (the neighboring Zuni are frequently accused of witchcraft). In sum, the witch is everything which the good Navaho who fears him is not. The latter identifies himself as a Navaho rather than a Zuni, as a man and not an animal, as one who works by day and sleeps by night, with his wife and not his sister, who obtains wealth by sheep-herding and cultivation and not by robbing, and finally, as someone who is alive and very much afraid of corpses. Each characteristic of the witch has its reciprocal in the positive characteristics by which the group (or individual) identifies itself.

A similar process of polarization has been described and analyzed by Moscovici (n.d.) for the formation of representations in propaganda. In this research, pairs of qualities of which the negative is attributed to the rejected opinion while the positive defines the group's own values were isolated: for example, Communist believers in dialectical materialism characterize psychoanalysis as idealistic, while for integrist Catholics it is mechanistic, in contexts in which it is opposed. In both cases, the rejected view is represented in terms contrary to the group's values. On the basis of the foregoing data on witchcraft imagery, we should like to apply the same principle: namely, that a series of negative qualities are structured around the witch in a relationship of reciprocal opposition to group identification. A further assumption which can be made is that the structuring of negative qualities in itself—because they are seen as oppositions—provides the basis for a structuring of positive qualities and consequently reinforces identification; it structures both external world and the subject's relation to it. In this sense, one can speak of "projection" but the process is quite different from that involved in the psychoanalytic theory of delusion formation; in delusions neither reciprocity nor the independence of subject and object is present.

Moreover, it follows that the witch must have a certain degree of stability as a social representation, for he is an element of a total symbolic structure, that is, the negative.

Our choice of the term "representation" rather than agent or object is intentional, but it raises a problem of levels of analysis which has been left implicit up to this point. For the witch-object is not necessarily constant; a person may be accused of witchcraft on one occasion and then forgotten, or, as is true in the case of the Italian evil eye belief, he is not always held morally responsible for his acts and is sometimes chosen on the basis of a randomly distributed characteristic, namely, the possession of heavy eyebrows. In considering witchcraft as a culture belief system, we have isolated it from what in terms of the general theory of action (Parsons, Shils, et al. 1951) would be called action processes in social or personality systems. Cultural forms, precisely because they are categories abstracted from concrete experience and exist only in consciousness, cut across the boundaries of personality and social structures. Thus with some justification, the Navaho definition of the witch can be interpreted in terms of a generalized representation of Navaho consciousness and in terms of the characteristics of the symbol alone. But pathological processes occur only in concrete personalities; consequently for the psychotic agent the problem is one of a real relationship to the object who becomes the persecutor (which may be formulated by a general theory of personality dynamics) or of particular associations which determined the substitution of a symbolic object for the real one. Holding this distinction in mind, we can turn to an analysis of Mrs. Perella's choice of persecutor.

Psychoanalytic theory furnishes several possibilities as to the basis of choice of agent. From Freud's paradigm of paranoid projection (stated above) we would assume that Mrs. Perella's delusion is a form of homosexual wishes. Consequently Mrs. J. was chosen because of a former homosexual attraction to her. In line with the increasing emphasis on the mother-child relationship in schizophrenia, one could equally well say that Mrs. J. represents the patient's mother: that in maintaining that Mrs.

J. is a witch, she is denying a previously stable attachment to the latter and perhaps her own feminine identification as well. The interesting fact that Mrs. J's surname is one that may also serve as a Christian name and is actually that of the patient's mother would support this interpretation; such associative bases of choice have been discovered in other cases. Moreover, Mrs. Perella's mother gave birth to nine children and she herself became ill during the ninth pregnancy. We do not possess sufficient information to make a valid dynamic interpretation, nor is it necessary for the present problem. The essential is that in spite of the theoretical indeterminacy which characterizes the present state of psychoanalytic research on schizophrenia, it is a generally recognized principle that the persecuting agent is a paranoid delusion is either a formerly loved object or a representative of such an object (see Freud 1949).

But in this respect the basis of choice is clearly different from that of the witch. In the case of either witchcraft symbolism or of the representations used in propaganda, the qualities of the object are those which for a given set of values are constantly negative; it is precisely this constancy which gives them the potentiality of structuring the world for a given culture and consequently of serving as expressive forms. But in the case of schizophrenia, which involves a breakdown of ego-functioning, that is, of cultural forms, the persecutor is or represents a formerly loved object. A transformation of love into hate is inherent to the mechanism of projection as it operates in psychosis; this transformation differentiates it from the ego-mechanisms which regulate the relationship between the two by structuring them in relation to the external world in a consistent fashion, although both may involve distortion of empirical reality. The difference between witchcraft beliefs and delusions could be summed up from both standpoints, that of choice of agent and that of relations between symbol and situation, in stating that the first structures relationships between subject and object by a process of polarization which divides the characteristics attributed to the self from those attributed to the (real or symbolic) object, while the delusion operates by a more direct *transformation* of subjective feeling into objective conviction which eliminates this very degree of independence.

However, the case for complete differentation of the two forms cannot be considered conclusive in all respects even in the light of presently available material. Several striking facts need more detailed consideration, among which are the similarity between the casual language of paranoids and that found in some of the descriptions of self-defined victims of witchcraft which have been collected. Both say frequently "they are doing such and such to me" in a form in which effects are directly and often impersonally seen to follow from the actions of external agents; in both the victim is unqualifiedly passive. In the area of means by which witches are thought to cause diseases, that is, the injection of objects into the victim, spraying of poisonous gases in the atmosphere, or the more general use of poison, there are crucial resemblances to paranoid symbolism. It might be possible to base research on the assumption that there is a progressive differentiation of function such that witchcraft beliefs have both a cultural-ego function in identification and serve as a more "primitive" means of expression, while in our own society the two functions are separated in propaganda (and other types of selective perception on the level of values) and mental illness respectively. Moreover, presumably a number of the self-defined victims of witchcraft must by our standards be mentally ill. A psychoanalyst has recently remarked to us that the first person to believe in witches might well have been a paranoid. If this statement were taken metaphorically rather than literally, it might serve to deepen our psychological understanding of witchcraft phenomena.

NOTES

1. This paper is based on research conducted under a grant given by the United States Public Health Service, Institutes of Mental Health, Bethesda, Md., to whom we are greatly indebted. We wish also to acknowledge Dr. Grete L. Bibring, Beth Israel Hospital, Boston, as sponsor of the project, and Dr. Harry C. Solomon, Superintendent of the Boston Psychopathic Hospital, for permission to publish data from the hospital files.

2. Angelina Perella is a pseudonym.

3. Of course since the source we possess is secondary, such a value loaded assertion has to be qualified. It may be that the patient actually was "more superstitious" than other Italian peasant women of the first generation, and consequently the presence of neurotic anxiety can be assumed. It may also be that she is simply "more superstitious" than her husband, who is a non-believer, would wish.

4. At this point, the case resembles one which has been collected by Benjamin and Lois Paul (unpublished field notes) in an Indian village in Guatamala. The patient maintained that an illness which had been intended for another person by witchcraft had been mistakenly given to her. Her *denial* of her own situation as culturally defined (others saw her illness as the direct result of witchcraft) is exactly equivalent to that found in the Western paranoid who feels he has been "railroaded" into the mental hospital by mistake since he is "really" not ill. Moreover, the Pauls' case felt that her persecutors were accusing her of having too much money; in the culture involved, possession of too much makes one susceptible to witchcraft.

5. See Parsons, Shils, *et. al.* (1951) for the theoretical distinction between cognitive and expressive assumed here.

6. Paranoids may call upon conventional means of verification for their assertions, but only as part of a process of secondary elaboration which rests on a prior conviction. In this paper, we refer only to the initial delution formation which accompanies an acute state, not to such systematizations more characteristic of chronic cases. Mrs. Perella's discovery that Mrs. J. had taken her child's dress as a means of effecting the charm falls in the latter category and as such both indicates a degree of systematization and is more closely integrated with cultural symbolism.

7. Of course the data from the second period do indicate that the content correspondence with cultural symbolism enabled the patient to "fool" others for a time and even to act effectively. But the husband's report indicates that he felt that "something was not quite right" although part of her behavior was understood. As a non-believer, he would have rejected the witchcraft explanation in any case, but had its utilization been normal, as a bi-cultural individual he would have understood it through his knowledge of the situations in which witchcraft beliefs are evoked.

8. Of course these criteria need not all be explicit. Although to the anthropologist, the events which a Zande explains as due to witchcraft may belong to the category "anxiety due to unpredictable causes," the Zande does not see it that way. Rather he will relate them on the basis of a particular feeling tone: the symbolized relation exists only in the witchcraft imagery.

9. In slightly different terms, cultural categories are reversible, i.e., if they are not understood, the speaker can either return to the situation to which they refer or substitute equivalent terms for those which did not communicate. A schizophrenic cannot substitute other terms at will; his delusion is both fixed and irreversible.

10. On the assumption that neurosis does not involve such a reversal of relations between affective and cognitive, one might question the current usage of the term "projection" as a neurotic mechanism; the latter is based on *selection* in function of affective factors rather than transformation and is not dissociated from cultural (or ego) symbolism. Neurotic perceptual distortion may be equivalent to witchcraft belief as discussed here.

REFERENCES

Evans-Pritchard, E. E.
1937 *Witchcraft, Oracles, and Magic among the Azande*. New York: Oxford University Press.
Freud, S.
1949 A case of paranoia running counter to the Psychoanalytical Theory of the Disease. In *Collected Papers*. Vol. II. London: Hogarth Press.
1954 Le Président Schreber. In *Cinq Psychoanalyses*. Paris: Presses Universitaires de France.
Kluckhohn, C. K.
1944 *Navaho Witchcraft*. Papers of the Peabody Museum of American Archaeology and Ethnology 22 (2). Cambridge, MA: Harvard University.
Levi-Strauss, C.
1950 Introduction a l'oeuvre de Marcel Mauss. *In* M. Mauss, *Sociologie et*

Anthropologie. Paris: Presses Universitaires de France.

1951 L'Efficacité symbolique. *Revue de l 'Histoire des Religions.*

Moscovici, S.

n.d. Logique et langage dans la propagande: quelques résultats. *Bulletin |de Psychologies* 8:7-8.

Nadel, S. F.

1952 Witchcraft in four African societies: An essay in comparison. *American Anthropologist* 54:18-29.

Parsons, T., E. Shils, et al.

1951 *Towards a General Theory of Action.* Cambridge, MA: Harvard University Press.

Tausk, V.

1948 On the origin of the influencing machine in schizophrenia. *In* R. Fliess (ed.), *The Psychoanalytic Reader.* Vol. I. New York: International Universities Press.

Waelder, R.

1951 On the structure of paranoid ideas; critical survey of various theories. *International Journal of Psychoanalysis* 32:167.

IV. ECOLOGY AND PERSONALITY

INDIVIDUALS MAY BE psychological products of their cultural environments, but what are the causes and consequences of this condition? How
does it fit in a larger view of human adaptation, one that includes individual
and group survival and that takes account of social and cultural evolution
past and present? These questions have not been ignored in culture and
personality theory and research (see LeVine 1973, Chap. 7). On the contrary, many pioneers in the field saw themselves as attempting to integrate
the perspectives of Darwin, Marx, and Freud. For example, Kardiner
(1939), in his collaboration with Linton, gave strong emphasis to economic factors as determining patterns of childhood experience which in
turn produced personality characteristics that found cultural expression;
Whiting and Child (1953) presented a similar paradigm. Barry, Child,
and Bacon (1959) showed that in a large sample of societies, aspects of
child training co-varied with subsistence economy, assuring survival through
the early inculcation of qualities required for occupational productivity.
It is only recently, however, that these suggestive and influential studies
have been followed up by behavioral and psychological investigations
of individuals who face different ecological demands. The results of
two such investigations appear in this section.

The two studies differ in content and method. The Munroes show
how a single demographic variable which can be thought as a general
population characteristic affects the immediate environment in which
infants are raised; their emphasis is on the means by which a macro-

social pattern is translated into an aspect of early psychological experience. Edgerton by contrast shows that economic differences globally characterized (pastoral versus farming) co-vary across groups with a number of personality indicators. The pattern of results presented in this excerpt and elsewhere in his book suggests a powerful effect of cultural mediation, such that knowing economy alone without the cultural affinities of the group would lead to inaccurate predictions about values and personality. In the rest of his book, which is one of the most important comparative personality studies done so far, many other interesting and sophisticated analyses are presented. The reader is referred to that volume for a fuller understanding of the contrasts involved. Edgerton's emphasis is on correlations between ecology and personality rather than the means by which the correspondences are produced in successive generations of individuals. Taken together, these studies point to a highly significant area of research, going beyond cultural values per se to link personality formation and function to ecological pressures on the population.

REFERENCES

Barry, H. H., I. L. Child, and M. K. Bacon
  1959 Relation of child training to subsistence economy. *American Anthropologist* 61:51-63.
Kardiner, Abram
  1939 *The Individual and His Society*. New York: Columbia University Press.
LeVine, Robert A.
  1973 *Culture, Behavior, and Personality*. Chicago: Aldine.
Whiting, John W. M. and Irvin L. Child
  1953 *Child Training and Personality*. New Haven: Yale University Press.

18. HOUSEHOLD DENSITY AND INFANT CARE IN AN EAST AFRICAN SOCIETY

RUTH H. MUNROE and ROBERT L. MUNROE

Ruth H. Munroe and Robert L. Munroe are Associate Professors of Anthropology, Pitzer College, Claremont, California. Reprinted with permission from *The Journal of Social Psychology* (1971) 83: 3-13.

SOCIALIZATION PRACTICES are treated in most studies as independent variables, with their hypothesized effects on child behavior and development as the primary focus.[1] In recent years, however, there has been interest in the possibility of accounting for socialization practices themselves. In this view, socialization is most likely to be influenced by environmental factors and basic sociocultural features, such as economic and social-structural institutions (Aberle 1961; Barry et al. 1959; Inkeles 1968; Minturn et al. 1964; B. Whiting 1963; Whiting and Whiting 1968; Whiting et al. 1966). One variable with high potentiality in this regard is household composition. In a cross-cultural study of 55 societies, Whiting found that infants are given indulgent care in societies which typically have an extended family residing in a single household. Societies with nuclear or mother-child households, on the other hand, are less likely to be indulgent to infants. The interpretation of the finding was that high indulgence tends to occur where there are "many hands to care for the infant" (1961, p. 358).

The main purpose of the present study was to explore the validity of the indulgence finding within a single society in which the number of caretakers varied sharply from one house-hold to another. The study was carried out among the Bantu-speaking Logoli people of western Kenya. The Logoli, numbering 100,000, occupy about 70 square miles in a well-watered highland area near Lake Victoria. The major subsistence activities are maize and millet cultivation, carried out primarily by adult females. The majority of adult males spend most of their time at wage-labor jobs away from the tribal area, but assist with horticulture or pursue independent economic activities when living at home.

Although many Logoli families are units within larger, extended family groupings, each nuclear family occupies its own house. Children of both sexes usually live in the house of their parents until adolescence, when they may sleep elsewhere but will continue to spend most waking hours in the household of their parents. Thus a household with an infant typically will contain the baby's mother, the siblings, and the father if he is not working elsewhere. It is unusual for a household to include more than one married female. Since children, as well as adults, act as caretakers of infants, the total household membership (excluding very young children) is an indicator of the number of persons potentially responsible for a baby.

A Logoli infant is given almost exclusive attention in the first months after birth. He is held most of his waking time and is breast fed on demand. As he gets older, less and less time is devoted to him until, at about age three, he is looking after himself most of the day. The mother has primary responsibility for the baby, and is careful to delegate the job of caretaking if she leaves the child at home in order to engage in an activity elsewhere. The back-carried infant, found in many parts of Africa, is seen but occasionally among the Logoli. The mother seldom takes the infant to the fields with her even when she is working close to home. The infant is often to be found in a cleared, yard-like work area in front of the house, a spot in which a good deal of the household activities take place.

The question of reliable observation of infant care raised certain problems. The original cross-cultural finding reported by Whiting (1961) was based on scales constructed by Bacon, Barry, and Child (1967) for use with ethnographic materials. The indulgence score took account of such complex factors as the consistency and degree of drive reduction, the immediacy of drive reduction and the absence of pain inflicted by caretakers. These categories, while perhaps optimal in theoretical terms, present problems for a within-society observational study with a more limited range of variation. A few simple aspects of infant care appeared most likely to satisfy both the need for establishing reliable observations and the need for valid indicators of indulgence. The elements of care most sharply focused upon were the amount of time infants were in physical contact with another person and the responsiveness of others to infant crying.

METHOD

SUBJECTS

The sample was comprised of 12 Logoli infants, seven male and five female, who resided in, or very near, a community already being studied. At the onset of the observations, the age range of the infants was from seven to 13 months. The large age difference resulted from limitations upon sample selection imposed by the within-community criterion. For a second set of observations, beginning when the same infants were between ten and 16 months of age, only ten of the original subjects were available (one had moved from the community, the other was sick during the entire observation period). Ages, often unattainable for older Logoli children, appeared to be quite accurate in this young sample. Sex of S was not related to the infant care measures.

By the conclusion of the second part of the study, all Ss were as yet unweaned but were being fed maize gruel and other solid foods in addition to breast feeding. Although Ss were learning to walk at the onset of the study, and almost all Ss could walk with some dexterity by the end of the study, all were still being held frequently throughout the two periods of observation.

Household membership size and composition for the sample infants appeared to be fairly typical of the Logoli community with the exception of one composition feature: the father was present in nine of the 12 sample households. In view of the absence of many adult males from the community, this sample includes an exceptionally high proportion of father-present homes. The household density, for each infant, was computed by including any individual over three years of age who was reported either to eat or sleep in the same household as the infant. In the total sample of 12 households, the membership ranged in size from two persons to ten, with a mean of 5.7 persons per household.

OBSERVATION SCHEDULES

Two periods of observation were conducted. The first, a modified time-sampling approach, was designed to yield data concerning the conditions of the infant's daily experiences. The second set of observations, designed primarily to yield data concerning the rapidity of response to the infant's crying, following an event-sampling model with running observations of the infant's position noted between the occurrences of crying behavior. The first set of observations was conducted by three relatively naive female Logoli assistants and one of the authors (RHM). The second set of observations was conducted by one male Logoli assistant, with training and postobservation reliability observations conducted by one of the authors (RLM).

The design for the first set of observations, originally planned as traditional time-sampling within an extended home visit (e.g., one observation per minute over a 15 minute period), was modified during the preobservation period. These early visits to the homes indicated that the interest expressed by the non-Logoli observer led to a "display" of the infant. Thus, as soon as the observers arrived at the home, the infant was picked up, readied for observation, and then brought somewhere close to the observers. Although this indicated that the Logoli mothers were highly

cooperative, it did not seem possible that this procedure would lead to data concerning the usual caretaking of the infant. The problem was overcome by a method which involved the observer in a quiet approach to the house, a mental recording of the people and activities immediately surrounding the infant, and, prior to actual approach and greeting, a recording of this information. The remainder of the items of interest—for example, the designated caretaker or the location of the mother—could be obtained after the observer had come closer to the infant and after greetings were exchanged. Thus the completed observations contained information on the location of the infant (in the house, in the yard outside the house, etc.), whether the infant was being held (and by whom), the location, activity, and proximity of persons within ten feet of the infant (all recorded as conditions existing when the infant was first visible to the observer), the identity, location, and activity of the designated caretaker and of the mother (if not included in the first notations), and, as a possible index of comfort, the cleanliness of the infant's eyes, nose, mouth, and hands.

The first set of observations included 14 such brief samplings, seven in the morning and seven in the afternoon, with no two observations being made during the same morning or afternoon. In order to approximate the usual balance of caretakers available, half of the observations were made on weekends or during school vacations and half during school hours.

In the second set of observations the primary emphasis was upon the infant's crying and responses to the crying. The observer followed an event-sampling method, with interspersed periods of notation of the location of the infant. This major focus upon a behavior of the baby made it possible to conduct observations over longer periods of time: the baby's crying behavior did not appear to be altered by the presence of an observer. When a cry occurred, the observer noted the number of seconds that elapsed from the beginning of the cry until the caretaker responded to the infant, the character of the response, and the time from the caretaker response to the cessation of the cry. If the infant began to cry within 60 seconds after the end of the cry, the observer recorded the new sequence as part of the same cry. An attempt was also made to judge the "cause" of each cry. The observer distinguished between "crying" (mouth open) and "fussing" (mouth closed), but the distinction was unrelated to other variables, and both sorts of vocalization have been retained as crying behavior in the analysis. During the intervals between the occurrences of crying behavior, the observer recorded the location of the infant, whether the infant was being held or not, and, if so, by whom.

The second set of observations included a total of four hours of observation of the infant during his waking time, two hours in the morning and two hours in the afternoon. The total time was spread over at least four sessions for each infant, with variable session length resulting mainly from infants' falling asleep.

Throughout the subsequent sections of this paper, the first set of observations will be referred to as Series 1 and will include those described above as a modified time-sampling approach. The second set of observations will be referred to as Series 2 and will include those described above as primarily an event-sampling approach. The data for holding are taken from observations in both Series 1 and Series 2; the data for crying and responsiveness to crying are taken from Series 2 observations; all other data are taken from Series 1 observations.

RELIABILITY

After an initial training period and an extensive set of pretrial observations it was established that reliability for categories in Series 1 observations was adequate (at least 80 percent agreement between observers). During the collection of the 168 observations, 17 reliability checks were conducted by one of the authors (RHM). Each Logoli observer was involved in at least one of these checks. Eleven of the 12 sample households were used. For all variables in Series 1 observations, the agreement between observers was high—94 percent to 100 percent, with an average of 99 percent agreement.

Reliability checks for Series 2 observations were conducted by one of the authors (RLM) with the Logoli observer in four sample households. The reliability checks were not carried out during any of the actual data collection sessions. Eighteen observations, each of ten minutes' duration, were conducted as the basis for determining the extent of agreement between the observers. With the exception of several judgments (to be discussed), the range of agreement as calculated by Spearman rank-order correlation coefficients was $+.80$ to $+.87$ with the average coefficient being $+.85$. The three variables on which reliability was low were the inferred causes of crying, types of response to crying, and the latency of response to crying. There was agreement on only 46 percent of the cries as to both the inferred cause and the response. Probably the major difficulty here was the Logoli observers' ability to pick up subtle cues missed by the outside observer. For this reason, the data on inferred cause and reaction to crying' probably are more reliable than the check indicates. Because such data are of interest, and because the major findings do not depend upon them, they have been retained in the analyses. The third variable with low reliability, latency of response to crying, was correlated $+.54$ ($p < .05$) for the two observers. The problem in this case seems to have resulted from the small range of reaction time to crying during the reliability check. Seventy-seven percent of the cries were responded to in ten seconds or less when both the Logoli observer and the outside observer were present, but during the actual long observations such quick reactions occurred on only 34 percent of the cries. The low reliability probably was due to the fact that household members were responding rapidly to the infant's crying when the outside observer was present, with the resulting reduced margin for error diminishing the degree of agreement between the observers. There is, of course, no method of demonstrating that this was the case. Despite this problem, the degree of agreement was at least significantly correlated, and the data on latency of response have been retained in the analysis.

RESULTS: HOUSEHOLD DENSITY AND INFANT CARE

All relationships have been computed with a rank statistic, Spear-

man's rho. Sample size is 12 for Series 1 observations, 10 for Series 2 observations. One-tailed tests have been used only for three cases in which specific predictions were made. In each case the prediction was that greater density would be associated with more indulgent treatment, that is to say, with more frequent holding, a smaller latency of response to crying, and keeping the infant cleaner.

For Series 1 observations, the correlation coefficient between number of household members and the proportion of observations in which the infant was being held is $+.55$ ($p < .05$). For Series 2 observations, the correlation between household membership size and the total time of infant holding is $+.76$ ($p < .01$). The two scores on amount of infant holding are correlated $+.72$.

A major problem with the finding on density and holding for the Series 1 observations is that age correlates with proportion of time the infant is held even more strongly (rho $= -.59$) than does household density. However, for Series 2 observations, the correlation of age with holding (rho $= -.48$, n.s.) is much weaker than the corresponding density holding correlation of $+.76$.[2]

The latency of response to crying is strongly related to household density (rho $= -.90$, $p < .0005$). The more persons living in the home, the quicker the response to the infant's cry. The relationship is not simply a function of the caretaker's responding more quickly because she is already holding the infant (as she would in fact be doing more frequently in a high density household). The correlation between density and latency of response to infant's crying when he is not being held is still strong, at $-.82$.

Given the fact that in a large household the infant is more frequently held and more quickly responded to when crying, it is of interest to know whether household density affects the amount of contact between the mother and the infant. Is the increased infant care in high density households due to a higher rate of care by the mother, by others, or by both? Surprising, it appears that in certain respects the mother has *less* to do with infant care in high membership households. Although the mother's holding of the baby is unaffected by density (for Series I observations, rho $= -.10$; for Series 2 observations, rho $= +.16$), she is less likely in large households to be the caretaker (rho $= -.65$, $p <$ .05) and is somewhat less likely to be within 10 feet of the baby (rho $= -.56$, $p < .10$). This apparent anomaly is resolved if Logoli economic and child-rearing activities are seen as part of a system of interdependencies. First, gardening and caretaking are seldom carried on simultaneously by any individual. The protocols show that the mother is gardening on almost one third of the observations for which she is not caretaking the infant, but that she is gardening on only one of 62 observations for which she is the caretaker. Second, the gardening activities are the primary responsibility of the mother. Given a large household membership, it would follow that the mother would spend more time in the fields in order to feed the family. (The correlation between household density and frequency of mother's gardening, while not significant, is fairly strong [rho $= +.41$].) It would also follow that if more time was spent in the field (and perhaps in other general household activities), then less time would be available to caretake the baby. And judging by

the evidence of actual caretaking, such is the case. The increased caretaking found in a large household is taken on by older siblings of the infant. A further piece of evidence indicating that the mother is less available to the infant in large households is found in the data on crying. There is a tendency for the mother in high density households to be a "cause" of the infant's crying (rho $= +.57$, $p <$ .10). The most frequent source of crying in this respect is the mother's leaving the scene. Thus the mother in the large household, far from being the source of increased infant care, is evidently busier and less available to her baby than the mother in the small household.

Correlations between household density and other aspects of infant care are as follows: pain as an inferred cause of crying, $-.06$; being put down as an inferred cause of crying, $+.48$; being left by caretaker as an inferred cause of crying, $-.49$; number of times cried, $-.05$; number of minutes cried, $-.04$; picking up infant as a response to its crying, $+.36$; "positive" response[3] to infant's crying, $+.60$ ($p <$ .10); caretaker within ten feet of infant, $+.50$; cleanliness of infant, $+.09$. Although none of the correlations is significant, some are strong enough to warrant further investigation.

DISCUSSION

For the Logoli infant, the mean level of caretaking and of close exposure to others is undoubtedly high in comparison to the level found in many Western societies. In the Series 1 observations, the infant was being held in 49 percent of the cases, and there were an average of 2.8 persons within ten feet of the infant per observation.[4] However, the general difference in levels does not imply that all categories of Logoli personnel are necessarily more involved with caretaking than are their counterparts in societies with lower levels. For example, the Logoli father and other adult males are responsible for very little of the care of the infant, and may participate much less, both in relative and absolute terms, than do comparable persons in some Western groups. On the other hand, the amount of sibling care is probably very much higher than is usually found in the West (Minturn et al. 1964). Thus the concept of a general level of care, though useful in many respects, should not be allowed to obscure important variability across social categories like kinship.

The findings have given general support to the expectation that household density would influence infant care. From other sources there is some additional supportive evidence. Relevant to the finding that the mother caretakes the infant less in a household with many children is a cross-cultural finding (Minturn et al. 1964) that the time mothers are rated to spend with infants is inversely related to the time that other children spend with infants. Also, a reanalysis of published data on the weaning of Zulu children in South Africa (Albino and Thompson 1956) indicates that the greater the number of people who reside in a home, the longer the infant will be breastfed (rank-order correlation coefficient between household membership and age of weaning $= +.57$, $p < .05$, $N = 13$, three cases excluded due to incomplete information). If prolonged breastfeeding can be interpreted as an aspect of positive care, then this relationship is consonant with the density-indulgence formulation. Although there is an apparent inconsistency between the indulgence implied in prolonged breastfeeding and the lower availability of the mother in large households, it may be that mothers in high density homes are to some extent compensating for their relative inaccessibility to the infant by a delay of weaning.

Household density is relevant to the theoretical issue of multiple caretakers and mother-infant attachment. Ainsworth's (1967) study of infants in Uganda includes data which can be used to assess the possible connection between household density and infant attachment behavior. A reanalysis of data presented by Ainsworth indicates that the rated level of mother-attachment among Ganda infants is inversely related to the number of persons in the home (rho $= -.49$, $p < .01$, $N = 27$, one case excluded due to incomplete information). The more people in the home, the less attached to the mother is the Ganda infant. Similar data from a study of American infants (Caldwell et al. 1963) indicated that higher emotional dependence upon the mother and more emotional interaction with the mother occurs among one-year-old infants who have been raised exclusively by the mother (as compared with infants raised by another female, as well as by their mothers). Although dependency and attachment may be quite different (Ainsworth 1969), both studies appear to indicate that some aspects of the infant-mother relationship are affected by the degree of exclusiveness of the mother's care and that this, in turn, is affected by the number of persons available to the infant.

Discussion of the potential effects of multiple caretakers has not been limited to infant behavior. Mead

(1928) has spoken of the diffuse nature of early relations in the large, extended household in Samoa as a potential antecedent of the shallow emotional ties she found among the adult Samoans. Both the large number of caretakers and the large number of persons typically found near the Logoli infants may constitute a situation comparable to that observed by Mead in Samoa. Though affective behavior was not rated in the study of the Logoli, it was noted casually that the high amount of care did not appear to be paralleled by an equally high amount of exchange of overt affectional responses. Whether the emotional intensity of Logoli relationships could be characterized as lower than in many other societies would be a matter to be determined by future research. In LeVine's (1963, 1973) view, a low level of affective intensity may receive sociocultural expression in the form of patterns of avoidance, segregated activities, and formal interaction even among family members. This possibility deserves further study.

Overall, the findings are consistent with the proposition that child-rearing practices are influenced by environmental and maintenance-system variables or, to use a general term, ecological variables. As Minturn, Lambert et al. have phrased it,

Most studies . . . have approached socializing practices as if the parents of the investigations were operating in terms of blueprints and curriculums . . . It now appears that the pressures impinging upon the growing child are much more in the nature of by-products of the horde of apparently irrelevant considerations that impinge upon the parents. These considerations of household composition, size of family, work load, etc., determine the time and energy that mothers have available to care for children. (1964, pp. 290-291)

Yet it is important to remember that the "blueprints" also have their effects. Cultural rather than ecological variables determine the fact that Logoli fathers do almost no holding or caretaking of infants. It is a cultural factor which leads the Logoli to designate a caretaker for the infant at almost all times, and it is a cultural factor which determines that the caretaker is rarely as much as 100 feet from the infant. Perhaps it is accurate to say that ecological variables can strongly influence behavior in many ways but that they are most likely to play a major determining role in areas—such as socialization—where the cultural plan is unspecific about numerous details.

SUMMARY

A cross-cultural relationship between household density and infant indulgence was investigated at the level of the individual household among 12 Logoli infants in East Africa. Time- and event-sampling observations were carried out. The findings (those statistically significant and those at the .10 level) are that the infant in the high density household is held more than the infant in the low density household, and is responded to more quickly and positively when he cries. On the other hand, in some respects the infant's mother is less accessible to him in the high density household: she is less often the baby's caretaker, is less often in close range (within ten feet), and is more likely to cause him to cry. The mother's lower availability was interpreted as probably due to the greater economic responsibilities she bears in a large household. The findings were taken as supportive of the view that socialization practices are influenced by ecological variables.

NOTES

1. The authors are indebted to the following for aid in various phases of the research: Printha Berry, John Biya, Josiah Embego, Myra Kagasi, Joyce Mmene, Maya Tsuji, Stella Vlastos, Beatrice Whiting, and John Whiting. The cooperation of the Kenya Ministry of Education, the local officials, and, most of all, the Logoli people, is gratefully acknowledged. The research was carried out in 1967 while the authors were members of the Child Development Research Unit (John Whiting, general director), University College, Nairobi, supported by the Carnegie Corporation of New York. The authors resided in the sample community for one year, collecting ethnographic data and conducting systematic interviews, observations, and testing sessions. Data analysis was supported by a grant from the National Institute of Mental Health (#MH-15876-01). The present report supersedes preliminary results given earlier (Munroe and Munroe 1967, 1968). Professor Robert Albert of Pitzer College generously read and commented upon an earlier version of this paper.

2. Kendall's tau, which can be generalized to a partial correlation coefficient, can be applied here. The uncontrolled tau between holding and household density is $+.60$, and that between holding and age, $-.29$. (The coefficients for tau and those for Spearman's rho are not numerically comparable, but the tests have equal power.) When partial correlation coefficients are calculated, holding and density (with age controlled) remain strong at $+.55$, whereas holding and age (with density controlled) fall to a very weak $-.12$.

3. "Positive" responses are defined as breastfeeding, picking up the infant, or talking or singing to him. Other responses to crying included no reaction, unusual responses, such as making noises (to divert the infant), and a few "negative" responses, such as shouting at or roughly shaking the baby.

4. Quantified descriptive data have been compiled on various aspects of Logoli infant care: namely, physical location of infants, crying behavior and responses to it, and caretaking and holding and their distribution along lines of residence, kinship, sex, and age. This information is available from the authors on request.

REFERENCES

Aberle, D. F.
    1961 Culture and socialization. *In* F. L. K. Hsu (ed.), *Psychological Anthropology*. Homewood, IL; Dorsey.
Ainsworth, M. D. S.
    1967 *Infancy in Uganda*. Baltimore: Johns Hopkins Press.
    1969 Object relations, dependency, and attachment: A theoretical review of the infant-mother relationship. *Child Development* 40: 969-1025.
Albino, R. C., and V. J. Thompson
    1956 The effects of sudden weaning on Zulu children. *British Journal of Medical Psychology* 29: 177-210.
Bacon, M. K., H. Barry, III, and I. Child
    1967 Definitions, ratings and bibliographic sources for child-training practices of 110 cultures. *In* C. S. Ford (ed.), *Cross-Cultural Approaches*. New Haven: HRAF Press.
Barry, H., III, I. L. Child, and M. K. Bacon
    1959 Relation of child training to subsistence economy. *American Anthropologist* 61: 51-63.
Caldwell, B. M., L. Hersher, et al.
    1963 Mother-infant interaction in monomatric and polymatric families. *American Orthopsychiatry* 33: 653-664.

Inkeles, A.
1968 Society, social structure, and child socialization. *In* J. A. Clausen (ed.), *Socialization and Society*. Boston: Little, Brown.
LeVine, R. A.
1963 Child rearing in sub-Saharan Africa. An interim report. *Bulletin of the Menninger Clinic* 27: 245-56.
1973 Patterns of personality in Africa. *Ethos* 1: 123-152.
Mead, M.
1928 *Coming of Age in Samoa*. New York: Morrow.
Minturn, L., W. W. Lambert, et al.
1964 *Mothers of Six Cultures: Antecedents of Child Rearing*. New York: Wiley.
Munroe, R. L., and R. H. Munroe
1967 Maintenance-system determinants of child development among the Logoli of Kenya. Paper presented at the American Anthropological Association Meeting.
1968 Space and numbers: Some ecological factors in culture and behavior. Paper presented to the East Africa Institute of Social Research Workshop in Social Psychology in Africa.
Whiting, B. (ed.)
1963 *Six Cultures: Studies of Child Rearing*. New York: Wiley.
Whiting, B. B., and J. W. M. Whiting
1968 Task assignment and personality: A consideration of the effect of herding on boys. Paper presented at the University of East Africa Social Sciences Conference, Dar es Salaam, Tanzania.
Whiting, J. W. M.
1961 Socialization process and personality. *In* F. L. K. Hsu (ed.), *Psychological Anthropology*. Homewood, IL: Dorsey.
Whiting, J. W. M., E. H. Chasdi, H. F. Antonovsky, and B. C. Ayres
1966 The learning of values. *In* E. Z. Vogt and E. M. Albert (eds.), *People of Rimrock: A Study of Values in Five Cultures*. Cambridge, MA: Harvard University Press.

19. PASTORAL-FARMING COMPARISONS

ROBERT B. EDGERTON

Robert B. Edgerton is Professor of Anthropology and Psychiatry, University of California, Los Angeles. Reprinted from *The Individual and Cultural Adaptation*, by Robert B. Edgerton, 1971. Originally published by the University of California Press; reprinted by permission of The Regents of the University of California.

[Editor's note: The author of the following selection conducted his psychological study as part of the UCLA Culture and Ecology Project which investigated four East African peoples: the Hehe of Tanzania, the Kamba and Pokot of Kenya, and the Sebei of Uganda. Each of these populations contains predominantly pastoral (cattle-herding) and predominantly agricultural subgroups. The Project involved intensive comparisons of geography, economy, and social structure as well as personality characteristics among these groups. Professor Edgerton mentions elsewhere in his book that the Hehe and Kamba are both Bantu-speaking peoples, while the Pokot and Sebei speak related Nilo-Hamitic languages and have cultural affinities that affected the pattern of results he presents. This comparative study is nevertheless the most intensive effort to utilize a "natural experiment" that we have had in social and psychological anthropology. Professor Edgerton's psychological study involved a lengthy test-interview battery administered to 505 men and women from all eight of the research sites.]

THIS CHAPTER PRESENTS a general review of the fundamental response differences between farmers and pastoralists. This comparison follows the original "four farming sites versus four pastoral sites" design of the research. To recapitulate for a moment, the design of the Culture and Ecology Project called for the controlled comparison of four societies, each of which contained the "same" internal differentiation into farming and pastoral sectors. Ideally, the four farming sectors would be highly similar as would the four pastoral sectors. It must be reiterated that the original design was not based upon the assumption that all four pastoral sites would be identical, nor that the four farming sites would be indistinguishable one from the other in their essential features, but it did anticipate a greater degree of similarity among related sites than was in fact found; ethnographic realities were difficult to mold to the requirements of our original comparative design. For example, while the four farming sites were relatively similar in their essential economic and physical environmental features, the four pastoral sites were relatively dissimilar, with only the Pokot pastoralists providing a satisfactorily close approximation to our hypothesized pastoral economic model.

Thus, even if the pastoral and farming models should prove to be entirely correct, it would be unreasonable on our part to expect completely consistent response differentials between the farmers and pastoralists in all four tribes. Furthermore, it would be naive to *confine* the analysis of the responses to this comparison of pastoral sites versus farming sites. These cautions notwithstanding, it is important to *begin* the analysis by looking for just such response differences, for it is basic to our inquiry to determine whether or not there are responses that do vary consistently between the farmers and pastoralists in all four societies. Of course, the inquiry should not stop at this point. Other inquiries must follow, and subsequent analyses of the same data will offer more varied and sophisticated perspectives upon the possible relationship between pastoralism or farming and evoked values, attitudes, and personality characteristics.

The responses presented in this chapter include all instances in which a response pattern differed between farmers and pastoralists in all four tribes. In addition, some findings that differed in three out of the four tribes are reported when they are of particular significance. As before, I avoid complicated statistical procedures. The findings are presented in as direct and straightforward a manner as possible, for here, without question, if meaningful differences exist, it should be a simple matter to locate and describe them. And no complex tests of statistical significance should be required to establish the importance of these differences. The findings are grouped into general categories. Each set of findings is discussed, but, in this context, extended reference is not made to the original hypotheses. These hypotheses are examined in detail in the final chapter where all the relevant findings can be brought together.

CATTLE VERSUS FARMING LAND

One of the most fundamental, and seemingly most obvious, questions in the interview concerned preferences for cattle as opposed to farming land. It was anticipated that, given a meaningful choice between the two, pastoralists would more often choose cattle and farmers would more often choose land. In theory, nothing could have been more simple. In fact, however, while responses did differ in the direction expected in all four tribes, the responses constituted a surprise, both in magnitude and in kind. Table 19.1 presents the responses to the question that most directly posed the choice between cattle and farming land.

In every one of the four societies, pastoralists said "cattle" more often than farmers did, but, obviously, the margin of difference is minute. For example, the Pokot pastoralists

TABLE 19.1

RESPONSES OF PASTORALISTS AND FARMERS TO THE QUESTION: WOULD YOU RATHER OWN GOOD FARMING LAND BUT NO CATTLE, OR GOOD CATTLE BUT NO FARMING LAND?

	Response	
Tribe	Land	Cattle
Hehe		
Farmers	59	5
Pastoralists	55	9
Kamba		
Farmers	56	5
Pastoralists	56	6
Pokot		
Farmers	14	51
Pastoralists	10	53
Sebei		
Farmers	59	2
Pastoralists	49	15

TABLE 19.2
MEAN NUMBER OF MENTIONS PER PERSON OF THE VALUATION OF CATTLE

Tribe	Farmers		Pastoralists	
	Mean number of mentions	Sample variance	Mean number of mentions	Sample variance
Hehe	3.93	1.59	6.19	4.45
Kamba	7.65	9.61	6.36	7.45
Pokot	12.15	37.33	12.93	27.46
Sebei	2.37	1.04	4.41	1.61

TABLE 19.3
ANALYSIS OF VARIANCE OF EFFECTS OF TRIBAL AFFILIATION AND ECONOMIC MODE UPON VALUATION OF CATTLE RESPONSES

Source	df	MS	F
Tribal affiliation (A)	3	2,041.36	178.58**
Economic mode (farmer/pastoralist) (B)	1	113.12	09.90*
A $\times$ B	3	233.72	30.45**
Error	496	11.43	

* P < .001
** P < .0005

responded as expected with an overwhelming preference for cattle. Surprisingly, however, the Pokot farmers expressed a preference for cattle that was almost equally strong. Conversely, in the other three tribes the choices were dominated by an emphasis upon land, even among pastoralists. Perhaps, however, the choice offered by this question was not a meaningful one, being too elementary in its all-or-nothing phrasing. What we appear to find are culturally relative emphases, with only the Pokot according cattle a primacy over land.

Other evidence, however, shows that pastoralists *did* more often express a valuation of cattle. Thus, when mean scores from the manifest content analysis category—all mentions of the desirability of cattle—were totaled, we found the distribution shown in Tables 19.2 and 19.3.

Only among the Kamba did farmers mention the desirability of cattle more often than did pastoralists. The repeated references by Kamba farmers to cattle may reflect frustrated or wishful desire, or they may indicate economic valuation, for cattle are a principal means of storing wealth acquired by farming, and the Kamba farmers have far more wealth to store than do the pastoralists. Indeed, the situation is admirably stated by this aforementioned, wistful comment of an elderly Kamba farmer who thought about the relative merits of cattle and land and then said, sadly but realistically: "Cattle are beautiful, but land is life." For the pastoralists in all tribes, cattle are no less beautiful, but they can also be life.

When mentions of land are tabulated, as in Tables 19.4 and 19.5, we find that, with the exception of the Hehe, farmers more often than pastoralists refer to land. The frequency of mention of land by pastoralists was no surprise; pastoralists may prefer

TABLE 19.4

MEAN NUMBER OF MENTIONS PER PERSON OF FARMING LAND

Tribe	Farmers		Pastoralists	
	Mean number of mentions	Sample variance	Mean number of mentions	Sample variance
Hehe	6.19	9.18	14.52	62.25
Kamba	12.76	10.37	10.24	36.48
Pokot	8.77	16.81	2.18	13.84
Sebei	8.60	76.04	8.13	89.49

TABLE 19.5

ANALYSIS OF VARIANCE OF EFFECTS OF TRIBAL AFFILIATION AND ECONOMIC MODE UPON MENTIONS OF FARMING LAND

Source	df	MS	F
Tribal affiliation (A)	3	877.44	187.56**
Economic mode (farmer/pastoralist)(B)	1	12.30	2.63*
A $\times$ B	3	1,257.86	268.88**
Error	496	4.68	

* $P < .05$
** $P < .0005$

cattle, but they also (except for the Pokot) value farming land, especially among the Hehe where cultivable land is in exceedingly short supply.

SOME RESPONSES THAT REFLECT THE PHYSICAL HABITAT

Although the influence of the physical environment upon the responses is often discernible, especially in the hot, dry, barren, and dangerous pastoral areas, it is seldom as directly related to the response differentials as it is in the few responses described in the paragraphs that follow.

For example, answers to the question, "What is the first useful task that a young girl is given?" corresponded very neatly to differences in the physical environment. Among the Kamba, Pokot, and Sebei, the farmers said that a young girl should be taught to farm; the pastoralists said that a young girl should be taught to fetch water. The differences here are quite marked, as shown in Table 19.6.

Hehe responses to the same ques-

TABLE 19.6

COMBINED KAMBA, POKOT, AND SEBEI RESPONSES TO THE QUESTION: WHAT IS THE FIRST USEFUL TASK THAT A YOUNG GIRL IS GIVEN?

Interview group	Response	
	Farm	Fetch water
Farmers	109	12
Pastoralists	20	55

Note: $x^2 = 82.76$, $P << .001$, df $= 1$

tion did not follow this pattern. Their answers mentioned grinding grain, doing housework, learning to obey adults, and cooking, not farming or fetching water. Although it is not clear why the Hehe farmers should not have mentioned farming, it is obvious why the Hehe pastoralists did not mention fetching water: they lived along the banks of a river, and water was readily at hand.

Another difference occurred when the question was: "What is the first useful task a boy is given?" In all four tribes the predominant response was "herd small animals [goats or calves]"; however, in all tribes the pastoralists replied, "herd small animals," more often than the farmers did (229 pastoralists to 188 farmers). The difference is not great, but it is present in each of the four tribes.

The final example reflects the relatively greater safety of living in the mountainous farming areas. Historically and to this day, life has been safer in the mountains of East Africa than it has been on the open plains below. In pre-British days, intertribal warfare made life on the plains perilous, and sometimes altogether impossible. And even in the 1960s, the pastoral areas of these four tribes were subject to occasional cattle raids in the course of which human life was sometimes lost. Life on the plains

was also in jeopardy from snakes and large animals such as lions, hyenas, and buffalo (the latter animal took several lives among the populations with which we worked during the course of this research). In addition, malaria was common on the plains, as were tsetse flies and several endemic diseases such as smallpox and viral meningitis, both of which reached epidemic proportions during the period of our research. In short, from disease, from animals, and from man, the threats to life are greater on the pastoral plains than they are in the highland farming areas. This is not to suggest that the farming areas are completely tranquil sanctuaries. Far from it. Farmers have their problems from disease, drought, and witchcraft; but, relatively speaking, in terms of objective threats to life and limb, living is more hazardous in the lowland plains.

When a content analysis of a concern for, or fear of, death is made, this relative emphasis is borne out. As seen in Tables 19.7 and 19.8, pastoralists in all four tribes mentioned a fear of death more often than their farming counterparts did. This relatively greater concern over death among pastoralists accords well with the realities of life in these environments.

TABLE 19.7
MEAN NUMBER OF MENTIONS PER PERSON OF A CONCERN WITH DEATH

Tribe	Farmers		Pastoralists	
	Mean number of mentions	*Sample variance*	*Mean number of mentions*	*Sample variance*
Hehe	12.86	28.52	15.55	62.25
Kamba	8.58	10.37	13.74	36.48
Pokot	14.18	16.81	15.40	13.84
Sebei	19.97	76.04	22.88	89.49

TABLE 19.8

ANALYSIS OF VARIANCE OF EFFECTS OF TRIBAL AFFILIATION AND ECONOMIC
MODE UPON MENTIONS OF CONCERN WITH DEATH

Source	df	MS	F
Tribal affiliation (A)	3	2,418.18	57.60*
Economic mode			
(farmer/pastoralist) (B)	1	1,130.22	27.00*
A × B	3	1,591.01	38.01*
Error	496	41.85	

* $P < .0005$

KINSHIP PREFERENCES

Another set of responses that differed between farmers and pastoralists concerns preferences for various categories of kinsmen. In the course of the interview, several questions were asked that posed explicit choices between various classes of kinsmen and nonkinsmen. Responses to several of the questions failed to discriminate between farmers and pastoralists. Other questions, however, did elicit contrasting response patterns. Thus, as is shown by Table 19.9, when faced with a choice between friends and kinsmen (who were not clansmen), pastoralists in all four tribes tended to choose kinsmen, whereas farmers tended to choose friends.

Although the differences in each of these tribes do not always reach statistical significance, they are always in

TABLE 19.9

RESPONSES OF PASTORALISTS AND FARMERS TO THE QUESTION: IS IT BETTER
TO HAVE MANY FRIENDS OR MANY KINSMEN (WHO ARE NOT CLANSMEN)?

Tribe	Response			Statistical difference
	Friends	Kinsmen	No answer*	
Hehe				
Farmers	17	44	0	$x^2 = 3.72$
Pastoralists	8	51	3	$P < .10$
				df = 1
Kamba				
Farmers	19	43	0	$x^2 = 1.77$
Pastoralists	13	51	0	$P < .20$
				df = 1
Pokot				
Farmers	42	23	0	$x^2 = 12.53$
Pastoralists	21	42	0	$P < .001$
				df = 1
Sebei				
Farmers	33	30	1	$x^2 = 1.76$
Pastoralists	26	38	0	$P < .20$
				df = 1

* Omitted in computation.

the same direction. That friends should have received greater preference in the farming areas was something of a surprise, although a partial explanation of this preference may be available, as we shall see in the course of subsequent discussions of this and other questions concerning the meaning of various kinship preferences.

A second, related difference involves a pastoralist emphasis upon the clan. Manifest content analysis of the number of times the clan was mentioned in a positive context (as distinguished from a neutral or derogatory one) indicates that, among the Hehe, Pokot, and Sebei, pastoralists mentioned the clan 25 percent more often than farmers did. Among the Kamba, the number of mentions of the clan among farmers and pastoralists was approximately equal. This same pattern was found in the answers to the following question: "Is it better to have many friends or many clansmen?" Again, the pastoralists more often chose clansmen, particularly among the Pokot. There appears to be a plausible explanation for this pastoral emphasis upon the clan; namely, that when clansmen are fewer in number because they are more widely dispersed, their importance in economic exchanges, particularly in bridewealth cattle exchanges, increases. This explanation was suggested by ethnographic and follow-up interviews in several sites. It should be recalled that both dispersion of clansmen and the importance of bridewealth cattle exchange is greater in pastoral areas. We might also suggest that among farmers everyday interaction focuses upon one's neighbors, those nonkinsmen who live nearby. Among pastoralists, it tends to focus upon kinsmen in extended families. In addition, among pastoralists the clan appears to possess important juridical functions, whereas these powers are often lost to some form of community-wide legal action among farmers.

Contrary to our expectations, preferences concerning age-mates did *not* differ between pastoralists and farmers. Neither when the choice was between friends and age-mates, nor when it was between clansmen and age-mates, was there any consistent pattern of response that distinguished farmers from pastoralists. The prevailing evaluation of age-mates (in all sites where they existed) was ambivalent. Mention of age-mates was as much negative as it was positive, and many respondents expressed both negative and positive feelings at the same time. This finding did not support our expectation that age-mates would be more important among pastoralists, but it may accurately reflect the diminishing importance of age-grades in present-day East Africa.

RESPECT FOR AUTHORITY

Farmers and pastoralists differed prominently in their expressed attitudes toward authority. Pastoralists were more given to express respect for authority, and not simply in the quantitative sense of mentioning respect for authority somewhat more often than did the farmers. A qualitative difference was also involved. Pastoralists expressed a sincere and deferential respect for the authority of various persons; in contrast, farmers expressed contempt, ridicule, or disrespect for the same categories of persons. An overall indicator of this difference can be seen in the content analysis category "respect for authority." When all instances in which respect for, or obedience to, a person

TABLE 19.10
MEAN NUMBER OF MENTIONS PER PERSON OF RESPECT FOR AUTHORITY

| Tribe | Farmers | | Pastoralists | |
	Mean number of mentions	Sample variance	Mean number of mentions	Sample variance
Hehe	3.47	1.71	5.94	4.58
Kamba	4.25	2.79	5.74	3.92
Pokot	4.86	4.84	5.12	4.54
Sebei	4.63	5.81	7.03	12.82

TABLE 19.11
ANALYSIS OF VARIANCE OF EFFECTS OF TRIBAL AFFILIATION AND ECONOMIC MODE UPON MENTIONS OF RESPECT FOR AUTHORITY

Source	df	MS	F
Tribal affiliation (A)	3	64.51	12.51*
Economic mode (farmer/pastoralist) (B)	1	732.19	141.94*
A × B	3	492.78	95.53*
Error	496	5.16	

* $P < .0005$

in a position of authority (e.g., father, chief, elder) were counted, the results were as shown in Tables 19.10 and 19.11.

Obviously, in all four tribes the pastoralists expressed respect for authority more often than did the farmers, and in three of the four tribes (Hehe, Kamba, and Sebei), the magnitude of difference is substantial. When only traditional authority is considered (fathers, elders, prophets, etc.) and chiefs are excluded, this differential becomes still larger, in-creasing the number of respectful mentions by pastoralists over farmers to more than two to one. Conversely, the farmers in all four tribes expressed at least three times as many disre-spectful or contemptuous mentions of authority as did the pastoralists. These responses are shown in Tables 19.12 and 19.13. As before, when the pas-toralists were disrespectful, it was usually toward nontraditional author-ity, principally the chiefs. The farmers were equally disrespectful toward everyone in authority.

TABLE 19.12
MEAN NUMBER OF MENTIONS PER PERSON OF DISRESPECT FOR AUTHORITY

| Tribe | Farmers | | Pastoralists | |
	Mean number of mentions	Sample variance	Mean number of mentions	Sample variance
Hehe	4.12	4.33	0.42	0.029
Kamba	3.17	2.62	0.29	0.012
Pokot	4.20	1.25	0.16	0.006
Sebei	3.32	1.19	1.03	0.176

TABLE 19.13
ANALYSIS OF VARIANCE OF EFFECTS OF TRIBAL AFFILIATION AND ECONOMIC
MODE UPON MENTIONS OF DISRESPECT FOR AUTHORITY

Source	df	MS	F
Tribal affiliation (A)	3	75.22	63.49*
Economic mode (farmer/pastoralist) (B)	1	1,312.51	1,107.81*
A × B	3	1,771.67	958.80*
Error	496	1.18	

* $P < .0005$

Three questions elicited clear pastoral-farming differences in attitudes toward authority: (1) "Under what circumstances can a younger brother tell an older brother that he is wrong?" (2) "Under what circumstances can a young adult tell a *mzee* ['elderly man'] that he is wrong?" (3) "Should a man always obey his father without argument?" In each instance, pastoralists expressed much greater respect for the senior person than the farmers did. For example, Table 19.14 lists the responses to the first of these three questions.

The differences between farmers and pastoralists are substantial, with the pastoralists expressing respect for the older brother more often than the farmers. Neither this difference, nor the differences in response to questions about the *mzee* or the father, is

TABLE 19.14
RESPONSES TO THE QUESTION: UNDER WHAT CIRCUMSTANCES CAN A
YOUNGER BROTHER TELL AN OLDER BROTHER THAT HE IS WRONG?

Tribe	Response			Statistical difference
	Never (or only if he is very wrong)	Whenever he is wrong	No answer*	
Hehe				$x^2 = 8.24$
Farmers	16	45	0	$P < .01$
Pastoralists	31	29	2	df = 1
Kamba				$x^2 = 45.53$
Farmers	4	58	0	$P << .001$
Pastoralists	41	23	0	df = 1
Pokot				$x^2 = 24.94$
Farmers	31	34	0	$P < .001$
Pastoralists	56	7	0	df = 1
Sebei				$x^2 = 25.27$
Farmers	30	33	1	$P < .001$
Pastoralists	57	7	0	df = 1

* Omitted in computation.

merely a product of greater acculturative disorganization in the lives of the farmers. On the contrary, it appears to represent a basic and perhaps long-standing difference between pastoralists and farmers in these four tribes. To clarify this difference, I should add that respect on the part of the pastoralists is backed by realities of economic existence in the protection, management, and accumulation of herds that may make the competence of older brothers and the wisdom of older men more important. And, of course, where cattle inheritance is so essential, respect for one's father is vital, for he holds these cattle as security against any sign of disrespect.

It may well be that these findings reflect the pastoralists' commitment to gerontocracy, not their respect for authority per se. In any event, it is clear that the findings do not relate directly to our hypothesis that formalized office would more often be found among farmers, whereas the pastoralists would more often give respect to achieved status. The findings discussed here are much more related to seniority than to these matters. Although ethnographic findings tend to support our anticipations about formal office and achieved status, the interview unfortunately did not elicit responses that bore directly upon these questions.

AGGRESSION

Several of the findings relate to aggression, and they all point to the same distinction between farmers and pastoralists: when the pastoralists spoke of aggressive action, they more often spoke of direct aggression; the farmers, on the contrary, were more likely to mention an indirect method of aggression. An indication of this difference is seen in the content analysis category "direct aggression." When all mentions of direct verbal or physical aggression were totaled, the results were as shown in Tables 19.15 and 19.16.

TABLE 19.15
MEAN NUMBER OF MENTIONS PER PERSON OF DIRECT AGGRESSION

Tribe	Farmers		Pastoralists	
	Mean number of mentions	Sample variance	Mean number of mentions	Sample variance
Hehe	23.64	31.92	32.13	77.26
Kamba	21.64	23.23	26.95	21.25
Pokot	24.21	61.31	28.56	45.56
Sebei	17.50	38.56	19.46	26.11

TABLE 19.16
ANALYSIS OF VARIANCE OF EFFECT OF TRIBAL AFFILIATION AND ECONOMIC MODE UPON MENTIONS OF DIRECT AGGRESSION

Source	df	MS	F
Tribal affiliation (A)	3	2,250.34	55.35*
Economic mode (farmer/pastoralist) (B)	1	3,184.75	78.33*
A × B	3	4,435.27	109.54*
Error	496	40.66	

* P < .0005

TABLE 19.17
MEAN NUMBER OF MENTIONS PER PERSON OF THE NEED
FOR PERSONAL SELF-CONTROL

Tribe	Farmers		Pastoralists	
	Mean number of mentions	Sample variance	Mean number of mentions	Sample variance
Hehe	15.91	44.76	16.47	38.94
Kamba	9.06	16.56	11.33	29.16
Pokot	6.66	8.12	8.42	11.29
Sebei	5.91	5.43	6.17	10.11

TABLE 19.18
ANALYSIS OF VARIANCE OF EFFECT OF TRIBAL AFFILIATION AND ECONOMIC
MODE UPON MENTIONS OF NEED FOR PERSONAL SELF-CONTROL

Source	df	MS	F
Tribal affiliation (A)	3	2,523.65	123.85**
Economic mode (farmer/pastoralist) (B)	1	185.25	9.09*
A× B	3	281.19	13.80**
Error	496	20.38	

* $P < .001$
** $P < .0005$

Although the differences between farmers and pastoralists were not great, pastoralists did express more direct aggression in every one of the four tribes. Consistent with this difference, pastoralists more often gave expression to a need for self-control. By self-control is meant an internal, psychological restraint rather than a social-institutional form of external constraint. When all mentions of a need for personal self-control were tabulated, the results were as shown in Tables 19.17 and 19.18. The differ-

ences between farmers and pastoralists that are presented in these tables correspond well to those concerning direct aggression: the greater the expression of direct aggression, the greater the expressed concern with self-control.

On the other hand, the control mechanisms most often mentioned by farmers were social. When all mentions of the need for various persons to cooperate together, and to conform to custom in order to prevent the outbreak of conflict, were tabulated

TABLE 19.19
MEAN NUMBER OF MENTIONS PER PERSON OF THE DESIRE TO AVOID CONFLICT

Tribe	Farmers		Pastoralists	
	Mean number of mentions	Sample variance	Mean number of mentions	Sample variance
Hehe	2.85	0.76	2.44	0.38
Kamba	2.87	0.59	3.08	1.17
Pokot	2.98	0.85	1.60	0.21
Sebei	1.98	0.36	1.51	0.14

TABLE 19.20
ANALYSIS OF VARIANCE OF EFFECTS OF TRIBAL AFFILIATION AND ECONOMIC
MODE UPON MENTIONS OF THE DESIRE TO AVOID CONFLICT

Source	df	MS	F
Tribal affiliation (A)	3	45.67	81.72*
Economic mode			
(farmer/pastoralist) (B)	1	33.09	59.21*
A × B	3	58.19	104.13*
Error	496	0.56	

* P < .0005

(Tables 19.19 and 19.20), the farmers took the lead. The one exception to the pattern of greater farming concern with social rather than personal control was the Kamba. As we shall now see, the Kamba continued to provide the exception to the rule that farmers more often expressed indirect aggression.

The following three instances illustrate differing aspects of the farming preference for indirect, rather than direct, means of aggression. First, farmers more often said that an insult had occurred, but they did *not* refer to direct confrontations in which one person openly insulted another. Instead, they made refernce to oblique insults, saying that an act of omission gave insult, that an overheard remark was offensive, or that one person "intended" to insult another. When pastoralists mentioned insults, they typically referred to a direct verbal affront of one person by another in a face-to-face situation. Table 19.21 totals all mentions of insults of both kinds. The analysis of variance of the effect of tribal affiliations and economic mode upon these mentions is presented in Table 19.22.

Thus we see that not only were the

TABLE 19.21
MEAN NUMBER OF MENTIONS PER PERSON OF INSULTS

Tribe	Farmers		Pastoralists	
	Mean number of mentions	Sample variance	Mean number of mentions	Sample variance
Hehe	20.19	62.25	17.71	51.70
Kamba	6.67	4.45	7.77	9.86
Pokot	8.18	13.32	4.86	2.96
Sebei	6.60	4.28	4.15	6.25

TABLE 19.22
ANALYSIS OF VARIANCE OF EFFECT OF TRIBAL AFFILIATION AND ECONOMIC
MODE UPON MENTIONS OF INSULTS

Source	df	MS	F
Tribal affiliation (A)	3	5,056.62	265.07*
Economic mode			
(farmer/pastoralist) (B)	1	402.60	21.10*
A × B	3	661.48	34.67*
Error	496	19.08	

* P < .0005

TABLE 19.23
MEAN NUMBER OF MENTIONS PER PERSON OF HATRED

Tribe	Farmers		Pastoralists	
	Mean number of mentions	Sample variance	Mean number of mentions	Sample variance
Hehe	12.47	29.27	11.05	15.68
Kamba	10.03	11.49	13.01	29.38
Pokot	9.26	17.47	5.06	4.24
Sebei	9.59	13.47	6.25	20.98

TABLE 19.24
ANALYSIS OF VARIANCE OF EFFECT OF TRIBAL AFFILIATION AND ECONOMIC MODE UPON MENTIONS OF HATRED

Source	df	MS	F
Tribal affiliation (A)	3	687.96	38.78**
Economic mode (farmer/pastoralist) (B)	1	140.82	7.94*
A × B	3	707.45	39.88**
Error	496	17.74	

* P < .001
** P < .0005

insults different in kind (the farmers' insults were indirect, the pastoralists' were direct), but the farmers (except for the Kamba) mentioned insults more often. The same pattern held for expressions of hatred. In tabulating mentions of hatred, every instance was counted in which it was said that one person hated, or wished serious harm or misfortune to, another, without mention of actual verbal or physical aggression. The results are shown in Tables 19.23 and 19.24.

The farmers not only mentioned hatred more often than the pastoralists did, they also mentioned witchcraft more often. In much of Africa, witchcraft is perhaps the most common, and is certainly the most feared, form of indirect aggression. When all mentions of witchcraft (for these purposes it was not distinguished from sorcery) were counted, the results were as seen in Tables 19.25 and 19.26.

Except for the consistently divergent Kamba, the farmers gave considerably

TABLE 19.25
MEAN NUMBER OF MENTIONS PER PERSON OF WITCHCRAFT

Tribe	Farmers		Pastoralists	
	Mean number of mentions	Sample variance	Mean number of mentions	Sample variance
Hehe	5.87	4.88	2.57	0.828
Kamba	0.50	0.008	7.16	1.66
Pokot	1.62	0.16	0.95	0.036
Sebei	1.88	0.31	1.01	0.063

TABLE 19.26
ANALYSIS OF VARIANCE OF EFFECT OF TRIBAL AFFILIATION AND ECONOMIC
MODE UPON MENTIONS OF WITCHCRAFT

Source	df	MS	F
Tribal affiliation (A)	3	310.46	318.13*
Economic mode			
(farmer/pastoralist) (B)	1	26.11	26.75*
A × B	3	619.19	634.48*
Error	496	0.976	

* P < .0005

TABLE 19.27
FARMER VERSUS PASTORALIST RESPONSES TO VALUES PICTURE 7:
WOMAN WATCHED BY MAN

Tribe	Response			Statistical difference
	No sex mentioned	Sex mentioned	No answer*	
Hehe				
Farmers	35	25	1	x^2 = 16.29
Pastoralists	13	46	3	P < .001
				df = 1
Kamba				
Farmers	15	40	7	x^2 = 18.82
Pastoralists	0	60	4	P < .001
				df = 1
Pokot				
Farmers	22	30	13	x^2 = 4.00
Pastoralists	15	46	2	P < .05
				df = 1
Sebei				
Farmers	45	19	0	x^2 = 5.74
Pastoralists	29	30	5	P < .02
				df = 1

* Omitted in computation.

greater evidence of a concern with witchcraft. All of these points about direct and indirect aggression are discussed in more detail in Edgerton (1971). It is sufficient here to note that in three of the four tribes differences in aggression between farmers and pastoralists are impressively consistent, and these differences are in the direction that we had expected. The anomaly of the Kamba is considered further in subsequent chapters.

SEXUALITY

Another set of findings suggests that there was a heightening of sexuality among pastoralists. The first example comes from the responses to values picture 7, depicting an attractive woman carrying water as she walks along a secluded path. In this picture, a man is crouching behind a bush and watching the woman as

TABLE 19.28
FARMER VERSUS PASTORALIST RESPONSES TO VALUES PICTURE 8:
MAN AND WOMAN TOGETHER INSIDE A HOUSE

Tribe	Response			Statistical difference
	No adultery mentioned	Adultery mentioned	No answer*	
Hehe				$x^2 = 15.93$
Farmers	20	39	2	P < .001
Pastoralists	3	57	2	df = 1
Kamba				$x^2 = 83.86$
Farmers	52	10	0	P << .001
Pastoralists	1	59	4	df = 1
Pokot				$x^2 = 42.14$
Farmers	35	21	9	P << .001
Pastoralists	3	55	5	df = 1
Sebei				$x^2 = 16.86$
Farmers	55	9	0	P < .001
Pastoralists	30	28	6	df = 1

* Omitted in computation.

she approaches him. Although the picture could have been interpreted as a sexual liaison, or as impending rape, it could as easily have been given a nonsexual interpretation. The responses are listed in Table 19.27. There is nothing in the picture itself to account for this marked difference in response between farmers and pastoralists. Neither was there anything in the next values picture to account for the differential response pattern

that it elicited. Values picture 8 depicted the inside of a house in which a man and woman were together in what could easily have been interpreted as a sexual embrace. The responses elicited by this scene are shown in Table 19.28.

Both of these values pictures evoked marked quantitative differences in response between farmers and pastoralists: the pastoralists mentioned sex and adultery far more

TABLE 19.29
MEAN NUMBER OF MENTIONS PER PERSON OF ADULTERY

Tribe	Farmers		Pastoralists	
	Mean number of mentions	Sample variance	Mean number of mentions	Sample variance
Hehe	1.83	0.240	4.11	2.624
Kamba	0.46	0.012	2.08	0.533
Pokot	0.90	0.058	1.34	0.162
Sebei	1.54	0.36	1.76	0.281

often than the farmers did.[1] In addition, the content analysis confirmed the relatively greater pastoral emphasis upon adultery. Tables 19.29 and 19.30 give the results of the content analysis of all mentions of adultery. It is not merely that the pastoralists in all four tribes more often mentioned adultery, for such a differential might mean only that the pastoralists, who own more cattle and value them more, were more fearful that, in being apprehended in adultery, they would lose their cattle through legal fines. More than mere frequency of mention is involved. The pastoralists emphasized their mentions of adultery and they enjoyed describing adulterous activities.

And so it was with all mention of sexual conduct. When sex was mentioned, there was a profound qualitative difference between the farming and pastoral responses. The pastoralists more often delighted in seeing sex; they reveled in it, exclaimed about it, grinned and chortled at the very thought of it, and, in short, thoroughly enjoyed themselves. When the pastoralists saw adultery, they did so with a vigorous "Aha!" quality; they were emotionally involved and often acted out their excitement with vivid gestures and facial expressions. In contrast, even when the farmers mentioned sex or adultery, they rarely (except for the Pokot!) invested their

responses about either one with any visible emotion. Indeed, they were quite matter-of-fact.

Mention must also be made of two additional differential responses to sexuality. When asked about the proper sexual conduct for unmarried males and females, farmers and pastoralists responded differently. Farmers tended to be very permissive for both males and females, saying that it was permissible for both sexes to have sexual relations before marriage. Pastoralists, on the other hand, tended to encourage male sexuality by saying that boys "needed" to have sexual experience, but at the same time they more often said that female premarital sexual relations were decidedly improper. It was admitted that girls engaged in sexual relations before marriage, but such actions were deplored. Men and women agreed upon this view. Thus, while it was clear that sexuality was accorded high value among the pastoralists, it was also indicated that this should be a male-oriented sexuality before marriage, becoming equally shared by males and females only after marriage.

PSYCHOSIS

When the respondents were asked to describe the behavior of a psychotic person, an interesting and entirely

TABLE 19.30

ANALYSIS OF VARIANCE OF EFFECTS OF TRIBAL AFFILIATION AND ECONOMIC MODE UPON MENTIONS OF ADULTERY

Source	df	MS	F
Tribal affiliation (A)	3	89.28	159.60*
Economic mode (farmer/pastoralist) (B)	1	163.75	292.72*
A × B	3	246.23	440.17*
Error	496	0.559	

* P < .0005

TABLE 19.31
FARMER VERSUS PASTORALIST RESPONSES TO THE QUESTION:
HOW DOES A PSYCHOTIC PERSON BEHAVE?

Tribe	Response			Statistical difference
	Socially disturbing	Socially benign	No answer*	
Hehe				$x^2 = 12.44$
Farmers	22	39	0	P $<$ .001
Pastoralists	5	52	5	df $= 1$
Kamba				$x^2 = 1.53$
Farmers	32	20	0	P $<$ .30
Pastoralists	26	38	0	df $= 1$
Pokot				$x^2 = 22.82$
Farmers	47	9	9	P $<$ .001
Pastoralists	19	30	14	df $= 1$
Sebei				$x^2 = 1.94$
Farmers	21	42	1	P $<$ .20
Pastoralists	13	46	5	df $= 1$

* Omitted in computation.

unanticipated difference between farmers and pastoralists emerged. The farmers were more inclined than the pastoralists to describe psychotics in terms of socially disruptive conduct. The results are shown in Table 19.31.

Although the differences were large in only two of the four tribes (the Hehe and the Pokot), the differences are in the same direction in all four tribes. Because the details of the methods by which this question and others concerning psychosis were asked and analyzed are described in another publication (Edgerton 1966), considerations of methodology will not be gone into here. The essential point that needs to be repeated is this: all respondents were referring to the same term for a psychotic (the Swahili term, *wazimu*), a term that was used and understood in all tribes.

The findings presented in Table 19.31 indicate that farmers tended to think of psychotic behavior as socially disturbing, while the pastoralists thought of it as relatively benign. It should be noted that these differentials were only seen in response to this, the first, question about psychosis. Two additional questions were asked: "How else do psychotics behave?" and, "Can you tell me about a specific psychotic person whom you have seen?" When the answers to these questions were examined, the pastoral-farming response difference disappeared. That is, when pastoralists and farmers gave their initial, their tip-of-the-tongue, impressions, they differed in the degree to which they described psychotics as dangerous, disturbing people; but when they were asked a second and third time to describe psychotic behavior, their answers no longer differed. I would conclude that there is no reason to believe that the psychotic behavior itself actually differed between pastoral and farming areas, but only that farmers and pastoralists were selective in their memory or feelings about such behavior. This interpretation is supported by other data concerning conceptions of psychosis in these four tribes (Edgerton 1966).

This response differential is difficult to interpret. I would have expected just the opposite of what was found, with pastoralists having the lower tolerance for psychotic deviance. Apparently, however, it is the farmers who have less tolerance, perhaps because of the vulnerability of their crops to theft by psychotics, perhaps because of their fear of physical assault. Both are common reasons given for fear of psychotics.

The six remaining categories are relatively minor in emphasis, representing but one or two response differentials, rather than a set of related responses. As before, each of these categories is described and discussed separately.

MILITARY PROWESS

Values picture 3 presented a scene in which a number of spear-waving warriors were rushing toward some cattle being protected by nothing more than a few small boys. As shown in Table 19.32, the responses to this scene indicated that there was a somewhat greater confidence in the outcome among pastoralists. Even though the differences are small, they are consistently in the direction of a greater sense of military prowess

TABLE 19.32
FARMER VERSUS PASTORALIST RESPONSES TO VALUES PICTURE 3:
ENEMY WARRIORS STEALING CATTLE

Tribe	Response			Statistical difference
	Enemy will steal cattle and escape	Enemy will be repulsed or pursued and killed	No answer or Don't know	
Hehe				
Farmers	53	4	4	$x^2 = 6.57$
Pastoralists	52	10	0	$P < .05$
				$df = 2$
Kamba				
Farmers	61	0	1	$x^2 = 17.36$
Pastoralists	46	5	13	$P < .001$
				$df = 2$
Pokot				
Farmers	19	13	33	$x^2 = 2.20$
Pastoralists	19	19	25	$P < .50$
				$df = 2$
Sebei				
Farmers	40	10	14	$x^2 = 5.31$
Pastoralists	27	16	21	$P < .10$
				$df = 2$

among pastoralists. And, here, as before, simple inspection of the table is a better guide than any test of statistical significance. Throughout the protocols, farmers in their mountain sanctuaries spoke grandiosely about their courage and skill in military affairs, but whenever the rhetoric was cast aside, as I believe it was in the responses shown in Table 19.32, pastoralists more often displayed quiet confidence in their military skills.

SUICIDE

Beliefs concerning suicide also differed between pastoralists and farmers. Pastoralists tended to say that women were more likely than men to kill themselves. This difference in response obtained in all four tribes, although it was large only among the Kamba and the Pokot.

When asked why men and women killed themselves, respondents in all four tribes agreed that men killed themselves because of poverty or quarrels with their wives or children, or because they were bewitched by a wife, a·son, or an enemy. Women were said to kill themselves because of grief over the death of a child, because they were forced to marry a man whom they detested, or because their husband's protective magic had punished them for an act of adultery. Thus we see that the reasons for male suicide were problems that were common among farmers, while the reasons for female suicide were problems that were more characteristic of the pastoralists. Consequently, the reasons men and women were said to kill themselves fit well with the problems of everyday life in farming and pastoral areas, with men more subject to suicide risk in farming areas, and

women more subject to this risk in pastoral areas. Unfortunately, I have no data that indicate the actual incidence of suicide in any of the tribal areas.

DIVINATION

As is evident from the content analysis data shown in Tables 19.33 and 19.34 there was a greater mention of divinatory practice among pastoralists than there was among farmers. We originally hypothesized that this difference would exist because of the greater individuation and uncertainty of pastoral life. Not only are there, in our view, more situations in which a pastoralist (we are speaking here principally of men) must make an explicit choice between alternatives, but there are also more in which he must do so without the guidance of routine, or tradition, or the counsel of his fellows. When these choices involve the imponderables of weather, enemy raiders, and wild animals among other things, recourse to divination seems a reasonable means by which an individual can reduce uncertainty. The data presented in Tables 19.33 and 19.34 suggest that pastoralists are indeed more involved with divination than are farmers. The ethnographic and follow-up data suggests that the data shown in the tables are probably an underestimate of the degree to which pastoralists are involved with divination. In fact, the interview was not well constructed for the elicitation of divination, and the mention of divination (even more so than most variables) can be taken only as a relative, not an absolute, indication of the importance of divination in the lives of these eight populations.

TABLE 19.33
MEAN NUMBER OF MENTIONS PER PERSON OF DIVINATION

Tribe	Farmers		Pastoralists	
	Mean number of mentions	Sample variance	Mean number of mentions	Sample variance
Hehe	0.00	0.00	0.49	0.026
Kamba	1.04	0.073	1.69	1.08
Pokot	0.22	0.002	1.59	1.25
Sebei	0.06,	0.0001	1.82	1.06

TABLE 19.34
ANALYSIS OF VARIANCE OF EFFECTS OF TRIBAL AFFILIATION AND ECONOMIC MODE UPON MENTIONS OF DIVINATION

Source	df	MS	F
Tribal affiliation (A)	3	49.37	112.14*
Economic mode (farmer/pastoralist) (B)	1	143.58	323.91*
A × B	3	102.10	231.93*
Error	496	0.440	

* $P < .0005$

AFFECTION

Not only was there a heightening of sexuality among the pastoralists, there was a greater expression of nonsexual affection as well. As used here, affection is defined as nonsexual. It includes expressions of love, tenderness toward a child, a strong positive emotional attachment to another person, and the like. All mentions of such expressions are tabulated in Tables 19.35 and 19.36.

Although the pastoralists have a reputation for brutality in many parts of East Africa and this reputation appears to be deserved, they also gave a freer expression to affection. Indeed, it may well be that they are more willing, and perhaps more able, than farmers to express affect of all kinds, positive as well as negative.

DEPRESSION

If pastoralists were more given to the expression of positive affect, so were they more likely to express depression. In all four tribes, pastoralists more often expressed gloom, de-

TABLE 19.35
MEAN NUMBER OF MENTIONS PER PERSON OF AFFECTION

Tribe	Farmers		Pastoralists	
	Mean number of mentions	Sample variance	Mean number of mentions	Sample variance
Hehe	2.36	0.672	5.14	1.99
Kamba	0.80	0.677	1.85	0.436
Pokot	6.60	7.34	9.20	16.00
Sebei	1.90	0.884	2.78	1.90

TABLE 19.36

ANALYSIS OF VARIANCE OF EFFECT OF TRIBAL AFFILIATION AND ECONOMIC
MODE UPON MENTIONS OF AFFECTION

Source	df	MS	F
Tribal affiliation (A)	3	1,052.79	285.79*
Economic mode (farmer/pastoralist) (B)	1	420.81	114.23*
A × B	3	591.83	160.66*
Error	496	3.68	

* $P < .0005$

spair, pessimism, and a strongly depressive feeling tone. In tabulating mentions of depression, expressions of fear of death were not counted, for, as has already been indicated, the pastoralists were also more involved than the farmers with such fears. Tables 19.37 and 19.38 are a tabulation and analysis of these depressive responses.

The nature of this depression among pastoralists was varied and included grief over the loss of a loved one, sadness over advancing age, a sense of despair over bad fortune, and, quite often, a concern with im-

potence. Frequently, however, it was a generalized sadness or hopelessness, one without a specific referent or antecedent. Here, I should note only that this differential was entirely unexpected. We had not anticipated that depression would differentiate farmers and pastoralists at all, much less that it would characterize pastoralists.

INDEPENDENCE

This final difference between pastoralists and farmers is one of the

TABLE 19.37

MEAN NUMBER OF MENTIONS PER PERSON OF DEPRESSION

Tribe	Farmers		Pastoralists	
	Mean number of mentions	Sample variance	Mean number of mentions	Sample variance
Hehe	0.99	0.084	1.44	0.25
Kamba	1.35	0.221	1.83	0.462
Pokot	2.01	1.23	2.87	1.61
Sebei	0.98	0.185	1.54	0.578

TABLE 19.38

ANALYSIS OF VARIANCE OF EFFECTS OF TRIBAL AFFILIATION AND ECONOMIC
MODE UPON MENTIONS OF DEPRESSION

Source	df	MS	F
Tribal affiliation (A)	3	40.60	69.65*
Economic mode (farmer/pastoralist) (B)	1	43.49	74.60*
A × B	3	59.39	101.88*
Error	496	0.583	

* $P < .0005$

TABLE 19.39

MEAN NUMBER OF MENTIONS PER PERSON OF INDEPENDENT ACTION

Tribe	Farmers		Pastoralists	
	Mean number of mentions	Sample variance	Mean number of mentions	Sample variance
Hehe	1.80	0.774	2.71	2.02
Kamba	1.23	0.423	3.00	1.35
Pokot	2.58	1.416	3.05	1.72
Sebei	1.55	0.548	2.36	1.12

TABLE 19.40

ANALYSIS OF VARIANCE OF EFFECT OF TRIBAL AFFILIATION AND ECONOMIC MODE UPON MENTIONS OF INDEPENDENT ACTION

Source	df	MS	F
Tribal affiliation (A)	3	38.41	32.79*
Economic mode (farmer/pastoralist) (B)	1	123.48	105.39*
A × B	3	174.28	148.76*
Error	496	1.17	

* $P < .0005$

most important, for, perhaps more than any other, it serves to characterize pastoral values and personality. This difference concerns independent action. When the number of mentions of an individual's explicitly taking independent action was tabulated, the distribution shown in Tables 19.39 and 19.40 resulted.

We had predicted that independence of action would typify pastoralism, and Tables 19.39 and 19.40 make it obvious that there was a greater number of such mentions among pastoralists in all tribes. What is more, when all mentions of instances in which independent action is valued—that is, when it was highly praised or said to be desirable—were tabulated (Tables 19.41 and 19.42) the differences were still more impressive.

Thus, when the valuation of independent action was considered, the pastoral response remained high, but the farming response decreased markedly. It would appear that independence of action is a pastoral trait, par excellence, and so it should be in an environment where individuals must make many decisions regarding

TABLE 19.41

MEAN NUMBER OF MENTIONS PER PERSON OF THE VALUATION OF INDEPENDENT ACTION

Tribe	Farmers		Pastoralists	
	Mean number of mentions	Sample variance	Mean number of mentions	Sample variance
Hehe	0.43	0.005	2.40	1.96
Kamba	0.46	0.014	2.78	2.46
Pokot	1.02	0.078	2.99	1.88
Sebei	0.81	0.026	1.94	1.08

TABLE 19.42

ANALYSIS OF VARIANCE OF EFFECTS OF TRIBAL AFFILIATION AND ECONOMIC
MODE UPON MENTIONS OF VALUATION OF INDEPENDENT ACTION

Source	df	MS	F
Tribal affiliation (A)	3	10.49	11.16*
Economic mode			
(farmer/pastoralist) (B)	1	430.07	457.54*
A × B	3	581.76	618.92*
Error	496	0.94	

* P < .0005

themselves and their herds, usually without recourse to tradition, or group consultation, and, what is more, without delay. In a world where man and his animals are vulnerable to so many threats, life without independent decisions, rapidly made and carried out, would be fragile indeed.

CONCLUSION

Each one of the categories that was described so briefly here could have been the subject of an extended analysis. Indeed, each one would have been, were a final understanding of the issues at hand to be attempted in this chapter. Such an understanding was not intended, however, for this chapter is no more than an introduction to the basic differences in response among all four pastoral sites and all four farming sites.

In conclusion to this introductory appraisal we must ask how succesful the original comparative design was. How many basic differences could have been expected, and how many were, in fact, found? Such an appraisal is more difficult than it sounds, because not every question in the interview was expected to produce pastoral-farming differences; nevertheless, some evaluations are possible. For example, the 85 questions that were asked in the interview were re-

duced to 66 coded sets of answers. Of these 66, about 20 percent showed differences between pastoralists and farmers in all four tribes. When it is considered that some of the 66 questions were general-purpose probes rather than specific questions to which we had anticipated differential response, the findings become increasingly positive. Thus, if we eliminate the 20 or so questions that were intended to be general probes, then some 40 questions remain for which we had anticipated response differences. Of these, over 30 percent showed differences between pastoralists and farmers in all four tribes.

In addition to these questions, there were nine values pictures. Each one of these was directly intended to evoke differences between pastoralists and farmers. Of the nine pictures, three (or 33 percent) showed differences between pastoralists and farmers in all four of the tribes. Finally, there were 31 content analysis categories, all but a few of which were expected to reflect pastoral-farming differences. Ten of these (over 30 percent) showed differences between pastoralists and farmers in all four tribes (another five showed differences in three of the four tribes).

What can we conclude concerning the probabilities that these pastoral-farming differentia were no more than the product of chance? First, it seems highly unlikely that chance would have directed so many of these response differentials to conform to our expectations based upon the pastoral and farming models. Most of these differentials *were* anticipated. What is more, although I am reluctant to invoke strict probabilistic formulas, in this instance, it may be useful to do so. If we convert the farming-pastoral differences into a binary (yes-no) set, such as that in a coin flip, then the probability that the pastoral sites will differ from the farming sites in all four tribes on any given question is one in sixteen. By this criterion, all the findings—from the 66 questions, from the 31 content analyses, and from the nine values pictures—could be expected to have occurred by chance less than one time in one thousand.

I think we must conclude that there are differences between the responses of farmers and pastoralists which could merit further investigation.

NOTES

1. The Pokot version of values picture 8 was, as mentioned, drawn in error so that the man was identified by his mudpack as being unmarried. This fact may have influenced the Pokot pastoralists to see the scene as adultery, for the actors could not be seen as a married couple. However, the Pokot farmers, who are also familiar with the symbolism of the mudpack, did not see the scene as adultery, so the insignia of the mudpack may not have influenced response to any great degree.

REFERENCES

Edgerton, Robert B.
   1966   Conceptions of psychosis in four East African societies. *American Anthropologist* 68: 408-425.
   1971   *The Individual and Cultural Adaptation.* Berkeley: University of California Press.

V. MOTIVES IN SOCIAL PERFORMANCE: THE INFLUENCE OF PERSONALITY ON INSTITUTIONAL PROCESS

THE PRECEDING PARTS of this book are primarily concerned with the influence of social and cultural factors on personality. As Spiro (1972) has pointed out, however, a major task of culture and personality research is to show how personality influences the operation of social and cultural systems. Theories have provided plausible models of how such influence might occur, but much of the evidence produced to demonstrate this influence has been subjected to alternative explanations—some of them plausible in themselves. One difficulty is that the most convincing evidence would be historical, showing the process by which institutional patterns were changed by individuals with certain personality dispositions. The collection of such evidence requires going beyond ordinary anthropological field work and cross-cultural comparison in search of a series of comparable data on one population over a substantial length of time, but available data lack reliable personality assessments. The situation is far from hopeless, however, as the readings in this section indicate.

These readings cover several different types of institutions: kinship and marriage, religion, and law. They exemplify my view (LeVine 1973, pp. 85-91) that all institutions offer multiple possibilities for conformity and that the individual's selection of one option over another is partly motivated by personality dispositions. This process of selection and its sources are most observable when individual choice is itself institutionalized or at least granted some legitimacy under existing social conditions. The ethnographer is then able to investigate why some individuals choose certain mates rather than others, choose a specialized religious role, or decide to initiate a lawsuit of a certain type under certain conditions. He can then aggregate cases, as Wolf, Lee, and Gibbs have, and give us statistics suggesting the personality background for decisions of social significance that we can well imagine to have an aggregate effect on the operation of social institutions. This is still some distance from proving the effect, but it is progress toward that goal.

Beidelman's study represents a different strategy: to analyze an institutional form in terms of the psychologically meaningful symbols it appears to embody. Here again, the institutional form is seen as offering multiple potentialities for symbolic arrangement, and the psychological interpretation is based on the content of the arrangement actually chosen from among the possibilities. In contrast with the other studies in this section, however, Beidelman's presents no evidence on individual choice patterns; he implicitly asks us to view Nuer ritual as the product of an evolutionary process in which Nuer individuals must have drawn upon the metaphorical resources of their unconscious mental processes to fashion the symbolic forms that were eventually institutionalized.

REFERENCES

LeVine, Robert A.
   1973 *Culture, Behavior, and Personality*. Chicago: Aldine.
Spiro, Melford E.
   1972 An overview and suggested reorientation, *In* F. L. K. Hsu (ed.),
   Psychological Anthropology, 2nd edition. Cambridge, MA: Schenkman.

20. CHILDHOOD ASSOCIATION AND SEXUAL ATTRACTION: A FURTHER TEST OF THE WESTERMARCK HYPOTHESIS

ARTHUR P. WOLF

Arthur P. Wolf is Associate Professor of Anthropology, Stanford University. Reproduced by permission of the American Anthropological Association from the *American Anthropologist* 72 (3), 1970.

IN THE VIEW OF most social theorists, the incest taboo is imposed on man for the sake of society. It is generally agreed that this taboo is necessary, but many reasons have been given to explain why. Edward Westermarck's (1922) suggestion to the contrary was widely criticized by his contemporaries and rarely receives favorable mention in more recent discussions of the subject. Not much more than supposition was needed to convict Westermarck of folly. With the exception of questionable evidence presented by psychoanalysts, the case against his hypothesis rests on Sir James Frazer's insistence that "the law only forbids men to do what their instincts incline them to do" (1910, vol. 4, p. 97). This criticism was quoted, as Westermarck himself wryly noted, "with much appreciation by Dr. Freud" (1922, vol. 2, p. 203) and is obviously the source of Leslie White's claim that "Westermarck's thesis . . . is not in accord with the facts in the first place and would still be inadequate if it were. Propinquity does not annihilate sexual desire, and if it did there would be no need for stringent prohibitions" (1948, p. 420).

The reason for this ready acceptance of Frazer's critique of Westermarck is obvious. In explaining the incest taboo as the social means of achieving the advantages of mating and marrying outside of the family, anthropologists have had to assume that men are naturally inclined to mate and marry within the family. If intimate childhood association were sufficient to preclude sexual interest, as Westermarck hypothesized, the incest taboo would not be necessary to obtain the biological advantages of out-breeding. Mankind would not have been faced with those momentous choices pictured so vividly by White and Claude Lévi-Strauss. They would not have had to choose "between biological families living in juxtaposition and endeavoring to remain closed, self-perpetuating units, overridden by their fears, hatreds, and ignorances, and the systematic establishment, through the incest prohibition, of links of intermarriage between them," the condition of "a true human society" (Lévi-Strauss 1960, p. 278). The tide that has run so long against Westermarck is drawn by the assumption that "the emergence of human society required some suppression, rather than a direct expression, of man's primate nature" (Sahlins 1960, p. 77).

This tide has at last begun to turn. We now know that the social life of

subhuman primates is not characterized by "selfishness, indiscriminate
sexuality, dominance and brute competition" (Sahlins 1960, p. 86). The
chimpanzees observed in the Yerkes
Laboratories emerge in purposive cooperation and often evince "a capacity
—or weakness—for developing a non-
destructive interest in others" (Hebb
and Thompson 1968, p. 744). Recent
field studies of Japanese and rhesus
macaques show that the young males
of the species do not commonly
choose to mate with their mothers
(Imanishi 1961; Kaufman 1965; Tokuda 1961-1962; Sade 1968). The
purpose of this paper is to provide
another example challenging the view
that man's behavior in society is
largely a creation of society. The data
reported continue but do not conclude
an argument initiated in an article
published in this journal in 1966.
They do not explain the incest taboo
and do not tell us why childhood
association and sexual attraction are
antithetical; they only suggest that
there is "a remarkable absence of
erotic feelings between persons living
very closely together from childhood"
(Westermarck 1922, vol. 2, p. vi).

The locale of my first study was
a small Chinese village in northern
Taiwan. It is situated near the town
of Shulin on the west bank of the
Tamsui River. Twelve miles upstream,
on the edge of the central mountain
range, is an old riverport known as
Sanhsia, the commercial center of the
area included in my second study.
The native residents of both communities are Hokkien-speaking Chinese whose ancestors migrated to
Taiwan from southern Fukien in the
17th and 18th centuries. Because of
their common origins and frequent
intermarriage, the people of the entire
area, from Shulin at one end of the

valley to Sanhsia at the other, support the same institutions and share
similar expectations about the nature
of family life. There is therefore no
need to repeat here the background
information provided in my two previous papers. I simply remind the
reader that customary law in this area
of China recognizes two distinct forms
of virilocal marriage. One I term the
major form of marriage: the bride
enters her husband's home as a young
adult, often not meeting the groom
until the day of the wedding. The
other I call the minor form of marriage: the bride is taken into her
future husband's household in infancy
or early childhood and raised as a
member of his family. These two
forms of marriage provide a unique
opportunity to test the Westermarck
hypothesis. The major form of marriage forges a conjugal bond between
strangers; the minor form unites a
couple whose experience of one another is as intimate as brother and
sister.

In comparing reactions to these two
forms of marriage we must always
keep in mind the changes that have
overcome this area of Taiwan in
recent years. When Taiwan was ceded
to Japan in 1895 as one consequence
of the first Sino-Japanese War, life
along the southern edges of the Taipei
basin was as conservative as anywhere
in China. Camphor and tea from the
hills around Shulin and Sanhsia were
poled down the Tamsui River to Taipei, where they were shipped to foreign markets, but the foreigners and
the influences they brought to China
did not move upstream into the rural
areas of the basin. The early years
of the Japanese occupation did little
to change this pattern. Although the
new colonial government quickly extended police control into the villages

and registered the land and the population, these changes did not challenge the authority of Chinese custom or create pressure for change. The full impact of the Japanese presence did not reach the rural areas until twenty years later when the government completed an improved transportation network and established schools in the villages and rural towns. Until that time people living outside of the city earned their livelihoods in agriculture or by means of small family businesses; they now sought employment in the coal mines opened along the edge of the basin and in new industries like the Hsulin winery. A few of the more fortunate graduated from local schools and then sought further education and employment in the city.

It was not long before these new opportunities began to have an effect on family life. Young married couples continued to live with their parents, as they do even today, but the internal structure of the family changed. Whereas young people had previously deferred to their parents in all important decisions, including decisions about their own marriages, they now began to demand more of a voice in family affairs, particularly the right to some influence in the choice of husbands and wives. The basis of their demand was economic. If a young man's parents tried to force him into an unsatisfactory marriage, he could leave the family and support himself by a job in the mines or in the city. The threat of desertion was usually enough to make the parents acquiesce. While the changes brought about by the Japanese occupation freed young people from a dependence on their parents, it did not free the parents from a dependence on their children. The new government did not offer pensions or open homes for the aged.

Without children to support him in his old age a man was no better off in 1930 than he would have been in 1830.

One of the first consequences of this change of authority in the family was a sharp decline in the frequency of the minor form of marriage. In the first two decades of this century the minor form of marriage accounted for nearly half of all virilocal marriages; by the end of the Japanese occupation the proportion of minor marriages had dropped to less than ten percent of the total. This change was not a result of parents deciding that the minor form of marriage was no longer so advantageous as it had once been, but was rather a direct result of emancipated young people refusing to marry a childhood associate. This is evident in the fact that the frequency of this form of marriage began to decline a decade before the rate of female adoption (Wolf 1966, p. 886). Parents continued to adopt girls to raise as wives for their sons until it became apparent that young people could no longer be forced to consummate these arrangements. Even today a few families raise girls in the hope of somehow persuading a son to marry in the minor fashion. They are always disappointed. One old man who had adopted a wife for his favorite grandson told me that he wanted them to marry "because that girl has always been very good to me, but I don't know whether they will or not. You just can't tell young people what to do anymore."

Were degree of childhood association the only difference between the two forms of marriage, this refusal of young people to marry a childhood associate would go a long way toward proving Westermarck's contention.

But unfortunately this is not the only difference between the two forms of marriage. As I have pointed out in previous papers, the major form of marriage has advantages that might incline young people to prefer it to the minor form (1966, pp. 887-888; 1968, pp. 866-867). It is the right and proper way to marry, the prestigious way to take a wife, and it provides the new couple with a dowry and the advantages of dependable affinal ties. Anthropologists who are inclined to look for sociological explanations will immediately see that young people's dislike of the minor form of marriage may be motivated by practical rather than personal concerns. They may be seeking prestige and practical advantage rather than trying to avoid sexual intercourse with a childhood associate.

This explanation of the decline of the minor form of marriage sounds reasonable, probably because prestige and practical advantage are such common goals of human behavior. When I first encountered the problem, it did not occur to me to look for any other explanation, but talking to people about their attitude toward the minor form of marriage convinced me that this was a mistake. Chinese villagers, regardless of education, are articulate, socially sophisticated people; they understand many of the intricacies of their own society and are capable of verbalizing their insights. They can discuss at length the advantages and disadvantages of marrying a mother's brother's daughter and are well aware of the sociological consequences of the major and minor forms of marriage (Wolf 1968, p. 871). They enjoy talking about the social calculations involved in deciding the appropriate value of wedding and funeral gifts. If young people objected to the minor form of marriage

because it is less prestigeful and entails certain practical disadvantages, I think they would say so. But of the many people I have talked to, not one has given me these reasons for not wanting to marry in this fashion. Asked why they do not want to marry a childhood associate, most informants blush and become inarticulate. All they say is that "it's embarrassing" or "uninteresting" or "difficult because people who are raised together know one another's hearts too well." They obviously are not thinking of the relative prestige of the two forms of marriage, the size of the dowry, or the value of affinal alliances.

These reactions give me confidence in the Westermarck hypothesis, but they will not do as proof of the hypothesis. The evidence rests too heavily on my impressions of the people I am studying. A better way of determining the relative importance of personal and practical concerns is to compare the conjugal relationships created by the two forms of marriage. If the resistance to the minor form of marriage is motivated by practical considerations, a couple raised together should be no less satisfied with one another than those who first meet as young adults. They may resent having their best interests sacrificed by their parents, but this is not likely to disrupt permanently their relations as husband and wife. If, on the other hand, the source of the resistance is a sexual aversion rooted in childhood association, it should persist and permanently mar the conjugal relationship. Couples raised together should be less intimate and more prone to marital discord than those brought together by the major form of marriage.

The problem becomes one of assessing the quality of the marital relationship. The ideal measure would be frequency of sexual intercourse and degree of sexual satisfacton, but it is difficult to obtain that kind of information in any society and next to impossible in China. Willing as they are to talk about the money a relative wastes on prostitutes and winehouse girls or the possibility that a neighbor is not his son's genitor, few Chinese will discuss the sexual act itself, and I doubt that any would be willing to talk about his experience with his own spouse. There is no point in even asking. Because the Chinese kinship system views the parent-child relationship as pivotal, the conjugal relationship is ideally distant and unemotional. Husband and wife must avoid displaying any sign of personal intimacy outside of the privacy of their own bedroom. Under these conditions couples who enjoyed the most blissful of relations would probably deny any interest in one another.

The only alternative is to look for the effects of marital dissatisfaction on other aspects of behavior. In my first study I made use of village gossip to identify men who commonly seek the company of prostitutes or neglect their wives in favor of mistresses. As one would expect if childhood association promotes sexual aversion, the majority of these men had married in the minor fashion (Wolf 1966, pp. 889-890). The problem I faced in returning to Taiwan last year was how to replicate this finding with a larger sample. Although I have since had occasion to doubt the wisdom of my choice, I decided to rely on the information available in the household registration records. Initiated by the Japanese at the turn of the century and maintained by the present Chinese government, these remarkable records contain a complete history of the composition of every family on the island. I made two predictions that

could be tested by an examination of these materials. Assuming a weakening of the conjugal bond as a result of sexual aversion, I predicted a higher divorce rate among minor marriages than among major marriages. And assuming a tendency for couples subject to an aversion to avoid sexual relations for long periods of time, I also predicted a lower birth rate.

By the time this test of the hypothesis was formulated, I was already living in Sanhsia and had made the acquaintance of the officials in charge of the local household registration office. I therefore decided to use these records for a preliminary test and chose for this purpose two of the districts into which Sanhsia Chen is divided. The two districts are located at the foot of the central mountain range on opposite sides of one of the tributaries of the Tamsui River. The district on one side of the stream includes four small hamlets, each clustered about a lineage hall; the district on the opposite side contains one large village with a number of small shops and a new temple. The majority of the men of both districts are descended from the ancestors enshrined in one or another of the four lineage halls; all but a few earn their livings as farmers, coal miners, laborers, or through a small family business. The differences between the wealthiest families and the poorest are too slight to support elaborate social distinctions. A local saying has it that the wealthy mix sweet potatoes with their rice while the poor mix rice with their sweet potatoes.

To avoid the complicating effects of social change I limited my sample to marriages contracted between 1900 and 1925. Since birth rates on Taiwan were rising at the same time that the frequency of minor marriages was declining, inclusion of marriages recorded after 1925 would produce an entirely spurious correlation between form of marriage and birth rates. There is also a danger that social change intensified the dissatisfaction of young people forced to marry a childhood associate. Those parents who insisted on the minor form of marriage after some had capitulated probably had to use exceptional means to see the arrangements consummated. If we included in our sample marriages contracted during the transitional period, the result would likely be a spuriously high rate of divorce among the minor marriages. As the reader can see by examining the information given in Table 20.1, the present sample avoids both these pitfalls. The relative frequency of major and minor marriages remains constant throughout the 25-year period. Any differences we find between the two forms of marriage cannot be traced to rising birth rates or the resentment of young people who were allowed no choice in marriage after choice had become a possibility. The absence of a decline in the proportion of minor marriages argues that parents managed to preserve their traditional authority until sometime after 1925.

I also decided to limit my sample to marriages contracted by the end of the bride's 25th year. Since all second marriages are necessarily of the major

TABLE 20.2
MARRIED WOMEN BY TYPE OF
MARRIAGE AND AGE AT MARRIAGE

Age at marriage	Minor marriage	Major marriage	Total by age at marriage
13	1	2	3
14	7	4	11
15	27	11	38
16	23	20	43
17	31	34	65
18	18	26	44
19	11	24	35
20	6	16	22
21	3	9	12
22	5	9	14
23		7	7
24		4	4
25		5	5
Totals	132	171	303
Average age	16.8 years	18.4 years	17.8 years

form, this was done to keep the ages of the two halves of my sample roughly comparable. Even with this limitation the average age of women married in the major fashion is nearly two years older than the average age of those married in the minor fashion. Since this difference could affect both birth and divorce rates, it is important to note that these effects work against rather than for the hypothesis. If we find that minor marriages produce more divorces and fewer children, it is clearly not a consequence of the bride's youth. Women who marry earlier have more time to get a divorce and more time to bear children. This effect of the earlier age at which minor marriages are contracted may be offset by the bride's being too young to bear children and too much of a child to consider divorce. The important point is that the evidence presented in Table 20.2 suggests that there is little danger of our accepting

TABLE 20.1
MARRIED WOMEN BY TYPE OF
MARRIAGE AND YEAR OF MARRIAGE

Year of marriage	Minor marriage	Major marriage	Total by year
1900-1905	26	38	64
1906-1910	17	31	48
1911-1915	22	34	56
1916-1920	29	34	63
1921-1925	38	34	72
Totals	132	171	303

the Westermarck hypothesis for the wrong reason.

The data reported in this paper were compiled for me by clerks in the household registration office. I spent my own time conducting a general ethnographic survey but naturally took advantage of every opportunity to inquire about reactions to the minor form of marriage. The stories and anecdotes I was given confirm the impressions formed during my first field study. There are at least five men in the town of Sanhsia who live with mistresses and are reputed to visit their wives and children only at the New Year. All five married a childhood associate. The most interesting aspect of these cases is the apparent lack of jealousy on the part of the two men whose wives responded to this treatment by taking lovers. Whereas the average Chinese husband would be outraged by a wife's infidelity, their neighbors claim that these two men "just don't care what their wives do." In one case the husband and his mistress and the wife and her lover live next door to one another in the same compound without any apparent friction. Perhaps the aversion that precludes interest in one another also precludes jealousy.

Consummation of a marriage of the minor type usually takes place on the eve of the lunar New Year. After locking up their doors and windows to exclude the malignant influences of a dying season, the family sits down to a large meal. It is usually at this meal that the head of the family tells his son and daughter that they are henceforth husband and wife. Whenever the opportunity offered, I asked my informants to describe the couple's reaction. One old man told me that he had to stand outside of the door of their room with a stick to keep the newlyweds from running away; an-

other man's adopted daughter did run away to her natal family and refused to return until her father beat her; a third informant who had arranged minor marriages for both of his sons described their reactions this way: "I had to threaten them with my cane to make them go in there, and then I had to stand there with my cane to make them stay." These are exceptional rather than typical cases, but as evidence they carry a special weight. Most of the people I talked to had heard of at least one instance of a father's beating his son and adopted daughter to make them occupy the same bedroom. When I asked whether thay had ever heard of this happening in the case of a major marriage, they just laughed.

But the new information I collected in the course of these interviews was not all encouraging. While it did confirm my confidence in the Westermarck hypothesis, it also raised doubts about my choice of a test of the hypothesis. Women whose husbands desert them to live with a mistress often take lovers or seek occasional sexual satisfaction with a neighbor. The problem is that the children are almost always registered as the husband's offspring. Even when the wife is loyal to a husband who prefers another woman, the registered children are not always the wife's progeny. One of the men who is reputed to visit home only once a year has registered three of his mistress's children as his wife's. A real difference in the number of children produced by the two kinds of marriage may be concealed by a combinaton of extramarital relations and falsification of the household registers.

My doubts about the test I had proposed were further aroused just by living again in a Chinese community. In the central room of every house, arranged on shelves generation by generation, are the family's ancestral tablets, mute but forceful reminders of every man's duty to perpetuate a line of descent. There must be heirs and descendants to inherit the family property and carry on the rites of ancestor worship. If there are no heirs to inherit, the work of many lifetimes is wasted; without descendants, the deceased members of the line are doomed to wander the world as hungry, homeless ghosts. Westermarck urged his readers to "not forget that a lack of desire, and even a positive feeling of aversion, may in certain circumstances be overcome" (1922, vol. 2, p. 201). He appears to have been thinking of situations in which there is no other opportunity for sexual gratification, but obviously the Chinese concern with perpetuating a line of descent would have the same effect. This concern may overcome and thereby conceal an aversion aroused by intimate childhood association.

There is also cause to worry about my use of divorce rates as a measure of marital dissatisfaction. No matter how dissatisfied a young couple may be with one another, for whatever reason, they cannot obtain a divorce easily. Divorce, like marriage, is under parental authority. Parents have the right to forbid a divorce that is not in the best interests of the family, and they also have the right to divorce a son's wife, with or without his consent. Because a major marriage requires payment of a brideprice and expensive wedding feasts, it is rare for parents to initiate divorce proceedings. But it is not uncommon for parents to use their authority to prevent a divorce. By threatening to desert the family or by actually running away for a few months, young people sometimes persuade their parents to allow

them to separate, but more often than not parental authority prevails. I know of a number of marriages in both Shulin and Sanhsia that would have ended in divorce if the couple's parents had not objected.

The role parents play with respect to divorce is relevant because it may introduce a bias against the Westermarck hypothesis. For reasons I have already discussed in detail elsewhere, a girl who is raised by her husband's family makes a better daughter-in-law than a girl who joins the family as a young adult (Wolf 1968, pp. 868-870). This is one of the reasons so many families choose to raise their sons' wives. Thus there is a possibility that parents will exert more pressure to preserve a minor marriage than a major one. The relative frequency with which the two forms of marriage end in divorce may not reflect relative marital satisfaction. Although the girl's early arrival in the minor form of marriage may preclude a close relationship with her husband, the problem may not be evident in divorce rates because of the girl's more satisfactory relationship with her husband's parents. Divorce may even be more common in the major form of marriage, not because of weaker conjugal ties, but because the husband's parents are more likely to be dissatisfied with their daughter-in-law.

These questions about the validity of my measures point up an important ambiguity in Westermarck's thesis. If the result of intimate childhood association is something as strong as "a positive aversion," the consequences of such association might be evident in birth and divorce rates despite contaminating circumstances. But if the consequences are only a mild distaste, as Westermarck suggests when he speaks of "an indifference," the effects of childhood association may be masked by other factors. My problem was to decide what conclusion to reach if the information from the household registers did not bear out my predictions. I could not argue that the failure to find any difference between the two forms of marriage indicates a mild aversion, but neither could I conclude that Westermarck's hypothesis is mistaken. The information I was collecting while the household registration data were being compiled argues that the minor form of marriage does create marital dissatisfaction and sexual avoidance.

I was beginning to look for another way to test the hypothesis when a young man who is known in the area as a petty racketeer and a confidence man asked me for a job. Because of his ties with people on whom my welcome in the community depended, I could not refuse his proposal, but at first I was at a loss as to how to make use of his talents. He suggested the answer when he told me a long, humorous story about his father's many escapades with prostitutes and winehouse girls. Here was a man who was charming, articulate, and completely without inhibition. He commanded respect because of his connections with important people, but his own reputation would not prevent free and easy conversation. Perhaps he could get people to talk about the adulterous affairs of their friends and neighbors. Our goal would be to identify those women who commonly sought sexual gratification outside of marriage. This would give me another way of testing the Westermarck hypothesis and would also allow me to correct some of the errors in the household registers.

After discussing the project with several of my friends and informal advisors, I decided to concentrate our attention on two men, one in each of the two districts from which my sample was drawn. These men are old enough to have known all of the women in the sample in their youth and are attuned to local gossip because they are often called upon to act as mediators and go-betweens. In outlining the nature of the project to my new assistant, who had had previous dealings of one kind or another with both men, I emphasized the need to explain the "scientific" nature of our interest. To credit my assistant's good manners, he listened politely; to credit his good sense, he ignored everything I said. He was a much better field-worker than I will ever be. His first step was to invite one of our potential informants to my house for dinner. After we had eaten and toasted one another repeatedly, he initiated a joking conversation about prostitution and adultery. He always began by pointing out how common they are in the United States and Western Europe, illustrating his point with any table or chart that happened to be lying handy on my desk. "Look," he would say, pointing to an appropriate number in a table reporting crude death rates for selected prefectures, "this is the United States. More than a third of all the women in the United States sleep with other men. And look at this; this is France. In France almost all the women have lovers." At the end of this spiel came a question: "What about around here? Does this kind of thing ever happen here?" By this time our informant was usually impatient to contribute his favorite stories to the conversation; if he wasn't, or if he was still discreet about mentioning names, my assistant went on to his own family tree, explaining with gusto his own origin. "You know my father isn't really my father; he lived with another woman and my mother lived with a man from Yingke. And my grandmother was the same way." The result was that by the next time we got together, our informant was talking freely about the sex lives of his friends and relatives. We asked three questions about each woman in our sample: "Do you know this woman? Have you ever heard of her sleeping with other men? Do you think all her children are her husband's offspring?"

The reader will wonder about the accuracy of gossip concerning events that took place fifty years ago. I have no way of knowing how accurate it is, but I do not think the time factor is important. In the small communities in which my subjects and informants live, what people say about one another is not easily forgotten. In this world gossip is more than malicious talk; it is a part of a person's social identity, no more likely to be forgotten than the person himself. The gossip may be partially mistaken, consisting more of accusation than of fact, but even this does not disqualify it as evidence. There is no stereotype of women who marry in the minor fashion that contrasts their sexual behavior with that of women who marry in the major fashion. Whatever error occurs in the answers we were given is random with respect to the hypothesis we are testing. If we do not find the predicted difference between the two forms of marriage, it may be because the error is great or because the hypothesis is wrong. But if we do find the predicted difference, it can be taken as evidence. Critics may be able to account for the difference in another way, but they cannot discount it. Random error does not produce significant differences.

We can now turn to the results of these various attempts to test the Westermarck hypothesis. Consider first the prediction that the minor form of marriage will end in divorce more often than the major form of marriage. As can be seen in the information reported in Table 20.3, my worries about the use of this measure of marital dissatisfaction were unfounded. There are clear and striking differences between the two forms of marriage. The one case in which a major marriage ended in divorce is one of those rare exceptions that does not detract from the rule. The woman in question had worked in Taipei as a prostitute for several years before her marriage. According to one of the couple's former neighbors, her husband was forced to divorce her "because she kept going back to work."

Table 20.3 also reports eight cases of permanent separation. This is part of the information collected by means of my unsolicited but invaluable assistant. We discovered two marriages that ended when the wife ran away to live with another man, another terminated by the wife's taking up a life of prostitution, and five others in which the husband permanently deserted his wife. Two of these five men ran away with local girls and are now living in mainland China. Although none of those marriages is registered as having ended in divorce, they can be taken as equivalent to divorce for our purposes. That seven of the eight

TABLE 20.3

NUMBER AND PERCENT OF MARRIAGES
ENDING IN DIVORCE OR SEPARATION

	Minor marriage	Major marriage
Total number of marriages	132	171
Number ending in divorce	25	1
Number of permanent separations	7	1
Percent ending in divorce or separation	24.2	1.2

are minor marriages makes the evidence in favor of the Westermarck hypothesis overwhelming. Perhaps these couples felt the same as the Somerset Maugham character who couldn't imagine Byron's taking interest in his sister. "Of course she was only his half-sister, but just as habit kills love I should have thought habit would prevent its arising. When two persons have known one another all their lives and lived together in close contact I can't imagine how or why that sudden spark should flash that results in love" (Maugham 1934, pp. 787-788).

Of the 303 women in my sample, 286 were known to one or the other of my two informants. They claim that 60 of these women had sexual relations with other men while their husbands were alive. Some of those affairs were brief and involved only one other man, but for some of the women adultery was a way of life. One is said to have slept with "more than a hundred different men." "They used to come here all the way from Yingke and Sanhsia to sleep with that woman." Another woman "couldn't see men at home because her parents-in-law were very strict, but if you gave her ten cents she'd meet you anywhere you wanted." The most interesting case is that of a girl who avoided sexual relations with her "brother" by feeding him a potion concocted with juice extracted from pomegranate roots. This is said to have made the husband impotent. "After that she slept with dozens of other men. I don't know what was so different about that woman's bones; she just couldn't do without a man."

The relative frequency of adultery in the two forms of marriage is reported in Table 20.4. The sharp difference between the two strongly suggests a need for extramarital sexual

TABLE 20.4
NUMBER AND PERCENT OF MARRIED WOMEN INVOLVED IN ADULTERY*

	Minor marriage	Major marriage
Total number of women	127	159
Number involved in adultery	42	18
Percent involved in adultery	33.1	11.3

* Five minor marriages and twelve major marriages were dropped for lack of information.

gratification on the part of women who marry a childhood associate. That this is due to a distaste for sexual relations with their husbands is evident in my informants' characterization of the conjugal relationship. About a third of the way through the interviews one of the informants insisted that a couple's four children were all the offspring of one or another of the wife's several lovers. When I asked him how he could be so sure, he answered, "Because she has never slept with her husband." After this I was careful to inquire about each woman's relations with her husband as well as her relations with other men. By the time the interviews were completed, twelve couples had been identified as having never engaged in sexual intercourse despite years of marriage. All twelve couples had been raised together. My informants say the reason for this remarkable abstinence is embarrassment, but this is obviously only a euphemism for some more intense emotion. The example of those couples who meet for the first time on the day of their wedding argues that people can be embarrassed without being inhibited.

Although it is not at all unlikely that adultery is a common cause of divorce, the fact is that the 26 registered divorces in our sample include only six of the 60 cases of adultery. This is important because it says that our two tests of the Westermarck hypothesis are independent. The hypothesis is confirmed not only by the two tests but also by two independent sets of data. The significance of this can be seen in Table 20.5, which combines the two sets of data into one overall measure of marital dissatisfaction. We now find evidence of dissatisfaction in nearly half of all the minor marriages as against only ten percent of the major marriages. The reader will not need statistical assurances to convince him that a difference of this magnitude is not likely to be due to chance.

TABLE 20.5
NUMBER AND PERCENT OF MARRIAGES ENDING IN DIVORCE AND/OR INVOLVING ADULTERY BY WIFE

	Minor marriage	Major marriage
Total number of marriages	132	171
Number involving divorce and/or adultery	61	18
Percent involving divorce and/or adultery	46.2	10.5

By the time the data from the household registers were complete, I had all but given up the idea of using birth rates as a measure of conjugal sexuality. The Chinese concern with perpetuating a line of descent, the errors in the household registers, and the simple fact that birth rates are, at best, only a crude index of frequency of sexual intercourse had all combined to discourage me. One could only hope to find the predicted relationship if couples raised together avoided one another for periods of a year or more at a time. But again my pessimism was unfounded. Contrary to my ex-

pectations, but in line with my prediction, minor marriages do produce fewer children, far fewer than major marriages. The evidence is reported in Table 20.6. The intervals in this table are calculated separately for each woman; the first interval begins at the date of marriage. When a marriage is terminated by death or divorce the case is dropped from this and all subsequent intervals. If, for example, a woman marries and bears two children in the first five years, these two children are included in the average of the first interval. If the woman then bears a third child in the sixth year of marriage but gets a divorce in the seventh year, this child and the case are not included in the averages of the remaining intervals. The method is imperfect, but it is the best that can be managed with a small sample.

The averages reported in Table 20.6 are based on the number of registered births. We have seen that some of these children are really the offspring of a mistress or children whose registered father is not their genitor. The information provided by my two informants allows us to correct at least the more obvious of these errors. We can discount children who were conceived while the husband was living with another woman in another part of the island, children who are

TABLE 20.6
AVERAGE NUMBER OF CHILDREN AS TAKEN FROM HOUSEHOLD REGISTRATION RECORDS

Years of marriage (in five-year intervals)	Minor marriage	Major marriage
1st	1.27	1.81
2nd	1.19	1.62
3rd	1.12	1.54
4th	1.06	1.23
5th	0.54	0.75

known to be the progeny of one of the husband's mistresses, and the children of women who are said to have never slept with their husbands. The corrected averages, shown in Table 20.7, provide striking, indeed surprising, confirmation of the assumptions made in my original prediction. Throughout the first 25 years of marriage, minor marriages produce 30 percent fewer children than major marriages.

By now all but the most skeptical readers will be willing to concede the existence of substantial differences between the conjugal relationships created by the major and minor forms of marriage. But they will ask, with good reason, whether there are other differences between the two forms of marriage that could produce these results. We must at least consider the fact that the girl who marries in the minor fashion is adopted. Although demographers have not as yet identified psychological factors that affect fertility, this is not to say they do not exist (Noyes and Chapnick 1964). Perhaps the trauma of adoption decreases a woman's chances of bearing children. The experience of being raised as an adopted daughter may also be relevant. Adopted daughters are often mistreated by their foster parents and are always expected to carry a heavier burden of household labors than the family's own daughters (Wolf 1968, p. 871). Women who were raised as adopted daughters claim that they did not eat as well as the family's own children. This experience might also affect their ability to bear children and could even make it more difficult for them to adjust to marriage.

Because the desire to economize is one reason for choosing to raise a son's wife, minor marriages are probably more common among the poor than among the wealthy. Women who marry a childhood associate may be less fertile because they have to work harder on a less satisfactory diet. And if families choosing the major and minor forms of marriage do differ in wealth, they may also represent different strata of the society. While social status cannot vary greatly in communities composed largely of farmers and laborers, there may be some variation, a difference between what some Americans call "good families" and "poor families." Perhaps divorce and adultery are more common among minor marriages because of the kind of family that chooses this type of marriage. The very fact that they choose to raise a son's wife indicates that these families are somewhat less concerned about prestige and public opinion than many of their neighbors.

There are reasonable replies to all of these objections, but fortunately my case does not have to rest on reason alone. The women in the sample who married in the major fashion include 42 who were raised as adopted daughters. A few of them came from families who decided against the minor marriage after having made the necessary arrangements. The majority are women whose intended husbands died before they were old enough to marry. Their foster par-

TABLE 20.7
AVERAGE NUMBER OF CHILDREN AS CORRECTED BY INFORMANTS

Years of marriage (in five-year intervals)	Minor marriage	Major marriage
1st	1.06	1.74
2nd	1.01	1.55
3rd	0.97	1.51
4th	0.94	1.21
5th	0.49	0.75

ents then had no choice but to allow them to marry out in the major fashion. Because the Chinese always look for a daughter-in-law among families of approximately the same social status, we can safely assume that these 42 major marriages are drawn from the same social strata as the minor marriages in the sample. And since all of these women were raised as adopted daughters, a comparison of the two is the ideal way to test for the effects of social status and the experience of adoption. The only difference between them is that one group of women married childhood associates while the other married strangers met for the first time the day of the wedding.

Consider first the evidence on divorce and adultery. The one major marriage that ended in divorce did involve a woman raised as an adopted daughter, but this is an exceptional exception. The reader will remember that the woman was a prostitute before marriage. Her neighbors claim she became a prostitute to avoid marrying her foster brother. That marital dissatisfaction is not often the lot of adopted daughters who marry in the major fashion is evident in

TABLE 20.8
NUMBER AND PERCENT OF MARRIAGES BY ADOPTED DAUGHTERS ENDING IN DIVORCE AND/OR INVOLVING ADULTERY BY WIFE

	Minor marriage	Major marriage
Total number of marriages	132	42
Number ending in divorce	25	1
Number ending in adultery	42	4
Percent involving divorce and/or adultery	46.2	9.5

TABLE 20.9
AVERAGE NUMBER OF CHILDREN BY ADOPTED DAUGHTERS AS TAKEN FROM HOUSEHOLD REGISTRATION RECORDS

Years of marriage (in five-year intervals)	Minor marriage	Major marriage
1st	1.27	1.78
2nd	1.19	1.77
3rd	1.12	1.76
4th	1.06	1.31
5th	0.54	0.90

Table 20.8. The likelihood of divorce or adultery among these women is only a fifth of what it is among adopted daughters who married a childhood associate. This is almost exactly the magnitude of the difference we found in comparing all major and minor marriages.

Major marriages involving an adopted daughter also produce more children than minor marriages. Table 20.9 reports the average number of registered children for the two groups; Table 20.10 includes the corrections made by my two informants. Again the difference between adopted daughters who marry in the major and minor fashions is almost exactly the same as the difference between all major and minor marriages. Although adopted daughters do experience trauma and deprivation and may represent a lower stratum of society, this is not the reason they bear fewer children, divorce their husbands, and sleep with other men. There is no evidence of unusual marital dissatisfaction as long as they marry a stranger; problems arise only when they are forced to marry a childhood associate.

This paper begins a story that is still years away from its concluding paragraphs. When I found the results of my first search of the household

TABLE 20.10

AVERAGE NUMBER OF CHILDREN BY
ADOPTED DAUGHTERS AS CORRECTED
BY INFORMANTS

Years of marriage (in five-year intervals)	Minor marriage	Major marriage
1st	1.06	1.73
2nd	1.01	1.73
3rd	0.97	1.76
4th	0.94	1.31
5th	0.49	0.90

registers so encouraging, I decided to copy the complete records for Shulin Chen and Sanhsia Chen, an area with a present population of approximately 80,000 persons. An analysis of these records will take at least five years and perhaps as long as ten. The goal of this project is to retest the propositions presented in this paper and at the same time to specify the vague term "intimate and prolonged childhood association." The household registers tell us when the parties to a minor marriage are brought into association and also the composition of the family in which they are raised. My hope is that this variation in the degree and quality of the association will allow me to isolate the conditions that produce lower birth rates and higher divorce rates. Raised like brother and sister, the parties to a minor marriage may come to think of themselves as brother and sister. They may be reluctant to marry because brother and sister never marry.

Identifying the precise conditions that make some couples more averse to marrying than other will eliminate this alternative explanation and allow a more general formulation of the Westermarck hypothesis.

I began this paper by quoting questions raised by Westermarck's critics. It is appropriate to conclude by noting his response. When Frazer and then Freud criticized Westermarck for failing to recognize that the incest taboo is necessary, the law itself being sufficient evidence of man's inclination to commit the forbidden act, he replied: "The law expresses the general feelings of the community and punishes acts that shock them; but it does not tell us whether an inclination to commit the forbidden act is felt by many or by few" (1922, vol. 2, pp. 203-204). Whether the feelings expressed by the incest taboo reflect an uncomplicated aversion, as Westermarck believed, or an anxiety created in reaction to strong desire, as Freud suggested on one occasion, or some other emotional consequence of family life remains to be determined. The only conclusion justified by the data presented in this paper is that there is some aspect of childhood association sufficient to preclude or inhibit sexual desire. This suggests that the taboo is not a response to the needs of the social order, instituted to suppress private motives, but that it is instead an expression of these motives, a formal statement of the feelings of the community, socially unnecessary but psychologically inevitable.

REFERENCES

Frazer, Sir James
   1910 *Totemism and Exogamy.* 4 Vols. London: Macmillan.
Hebb, D. O., and W. R. Thompson
   1968 The social significance of animal studies. *In* G. Lindzey and E. Aronson

(eds.), *The Handbook of Social Psychology*. 5 Vols. Reading, Massachusetts: Addison-Wesley.

Imanishi, K.
1961 The origin of the human family—a primatological approach. *Japanese Journal of Ethnology* 25: 119-130.

Kaufman, J. H.
1965 A three-year study of mating behavior in a free-ranging band of rhesus monkeys. *Ecology* 46: 500-512.

Lévi-Strauss, Claude
1960 The family. *In* L., Shapiro (ed.), *Man, Culture and Society*. New York: Oxford University Press.

Maugham, W. Somerset
1934 The book bag. *In East and West: The Collected Short Stories of W. Somerset Maugham*. Garden City: Garden City Publishing Company.

Noyes, Robert W., and Eleanor M. Chapnick
1964 Literature on psychology and infertility: A critical analysis. *Fertility and Sterility* 15: 543-556.

Sade, Donald Stone
1968 Inhibition of son-mother mating among free-ranging rhesus monkeys. *Science and Psychoanalysis* 12: 18-38.

Sahlins, Marshall
1960 The origin of society. *Scientific American* 203: 76-89.

Tokuda, K.
1961-62 A study on the sexual behavior in the Japanese monkey troop. *Primates* 3: 1-40.

Westermarck, Edward
1922 *The History of Human Marriage*. 3 Vols. London: Macmillan.

White, Leslie A.
1948 The definition and prohibition of incest. *American Anthropologist* 50: 416-435.

Wolf, Arthur P.
1966 Childhood association, sexual attraction, and the incest taboo: A Chinese case. *American Anthropologist* 68: 883-898.
1968 Adopt a daughter-in-law, marry a sister: A Chinese solution to the problem of the incest taboo. *American Anthropologist* 70: 864-874.

21. SPIRIT POSSESSION AMONG THE ZULU

S. G. LEE

The late S. G. Lee was Professor of Psychology, University of Leicester, England. Reprinted from *Spirit Mediumship and Society in Africa,* edited by John Beattie and John Middleton, by permission of Africana Publishing Company, a Division of Holmes & Meier Publishers, Ltd., and of Routledge and Kegan Paul, Ltd. Copyright © 1968, S. G. Lee.

I

THE FIRST HAND DATA cited in this paper were obtained between 1951 and 1957 when I was investigating the incidence, nosology, and etiology of fits of screaming, so common among Zulu women that it is a relatively ordinary event to hear a young woman crying out *"hayi, hayi, hayi"* or uttering yelping grunts for hours, days, or even weeks. Locally the usual explanation of this behavior is in terms of the effects of love magic, and no state of possession is involved. But in the course of my research I found myself concerned, peripherally, but in both a therapeutic and investigatory capacity, with many sufferers from different kinds of possession. In addition, when I investigated the "cryers" (persons claiming a history of the screaming) and contrasted them with a control group of women with no such record, quantitative differences appeared between the criterion groups' responses to questionnaires, a Thematic Apperception Test, etc. (Lee 1950, 1954, 1958, 1961), which threw light on the type of personality associated with possession, and some of this evidence is cited below. Its oblique nature is a direct reflection of my original intention to concentrate upon the modern crying disorder and not to carry out an intensive investigation of spirit possession.

However, various forms of supposed spirit possession are to be found among the Zulu and these still play an important part in the behavior of many people, both those possessed (henceforth, for brevity, I will treat the conceit of possession as reality) and others who are affected by the dicta and supposed powers of spirit-mediums. While demarcation lines between types of possession are sometimes blurred by confusion in their naming, classification can usefully be attempted by asking the following questions:

(i) How long is the history of any type of possession, or of any cult activities associated therewith?

(ii) How stereotyped are the symptoms or any rituals associated with the state?

(iii) What therapies are called into play to diagnose, develop, or end the possession?

(iv) What kinds of spirits are involved?

(v) Are any overt social purposes served by the possession and its consequences? What are the social functions of any associated cult activity?

All these questions can be considered, roughly, as social in their emphases, but we have also to deal with another set of criterion questions, pertaining to the individual sufferer, which are essentially of psychological interest.

(vi) What purposes, if any, in terms of both conscious and unconscious

387

wishes, are served by possession for the individual subject?

(vii) What kinds of people become possessed in the various ways? Here we must consider not only such objective variables as sex, age, or marital state, but also possible personality characteristics.

(viii) How is possession related, in the tribal frame of reference, to other disorders of individuals which are not attributed to spirit possession?

(ix) What light can Western psychopathology throw on the nosology and etiology of possession and associated states?

(x) What, if any, is the relationship between the social epidemiology of possession and the individual characteristics of sufferers?

All these questions form the background of the account that follows. If we apply our first set of social questions to the Zulu data we can see clearly the states of possession fall into two distinct main classes. The first of these, *ukuthwasa* possession, has been the more investigated by anthropologists and will be discussed in detail in Part II of this essay. For the present it is useful to note that it has a long history (as long, indeed, as recorded Zulu history itself), that it is rigid and invariant in its form, its symptoms (both physical and behavioral), its treatment within the canon of local medical practice, and in the rituals and social behavior consequent upon both the initial stages and continuation of the possession, although on occasion the full sequence of the latter does not ensue, because of deliberate therapeutic intervention. Ancestor spirits are involved and the usual result of a complete possession is that the person involved becomes an *isangoma* diviner (plural *izangoma*), possessed of diagnostic and thaumaturgic power, and a figure of some consequence in the society. A modern modification of this cult, closely related to it in terms of questions (iii), (iv), and (v) above, is found in the appropriation of many of its elements by the syncretist, nominally Christian, separatist churches, especially the Zionist forms of religion (cf. Sundkler 1961), and this is discussed in Part III below.

The other main class of possession is much more amorphous in its characteristics. Here we have the states of, typically, *amandiki, amandawe, amabutho* and *izizwe* possession. These conditions have been very little studied, though the Junods' accounts (1927, 1934) of *Ndjao* (*amandiki*) possession among the Thonga is a relatively full description of an essentially similar condition. My own material here is almost purely descriptive, of little explanatory value, and it is for this reason that it has been included in the first part of this paper—bread and butter before cake.

These possessions are of relatively recent origin, the first reports appearing about 1910, and there is great difficulty in establishing an adequate nomenclature, ascriptions and spelling varying from district to district. Sometimes the states are confused with each other, or with pathology attributed to sorcery, and symptoms of the various kinds of possession show great variation from individual to individual. The one common factor is that the naming and subjective etiology of the states follow closely social change, particularly in culture contact situations.

Let us take some of the available accounts in a rough chronological order. According to *The Collector* (1911), *amandiki* and *amandawu* possession are practically identical, though each cult possesses its own "language" (usually a distorted form of Zulu).

Amandawu (frequently the same word is used for both possession and possessed) have powers of divination whereas *amandiki* have none. The word *amandiki* means a spirit, and one of *The Collector's* informants claimed to have been entered by the spirit of the Zulu King Tshaka. By oral tradition both types of possession are claimed to have originated north of the Pongola river, in Swaziland or Thongaland, and the *amandiki* claimed originally to have been dispatched on a messianic mission by a woman, uSiqungana. "They came into Zululand after Dinizulu's return from overseas" (shortly after the disastrous Bambatha rebellion against White rule). The *amandiki* bark like dogs, speaking with strange tongues, and move around the country collecting money from their relatives and doing much dancing. The *amandiki* spirits, unlike the ancestor spirits of the *isangoma* diviner, never appear in visible form. They cry out (cf. "cryers" above) and belch like *izangoma*, and some informants claim that the possessing spirits are ancestors.

Asmus (1939) however, claims that:

The *amandiki* are a kind of prophet and diviner, as well as being doctors of medicine, and are mostly women. They imagine themselves to be possessed by spirits which are, however, different from the *amadhlozi* (ancestral spirits) . . . . They dance and belch deeply and often, and then begin to divine. . . .

The *amandawo,* itinerant doctors, are seized by a power called *ubundawo.* . . . From time to time they have seizures like epileptics. They also belch deeply and roar. They have no dealings with the *amadhlozi.* . . . (my translation).

Asmus mentions the custom of present-giving to *amandiki* and claims that, for purposes of gain, they spread their condition by the use of medicines. Here we can see a possible

motive but there are also individual personality factors involved for in these cases "which are of more recent times, we see a kind of obsessed hysterical person."

Sundkler is worth quoting in more detail:

A modern form of ancestor-possession is the *amandiki* or *amandawe* possession. The phenomena connected with this have been scientifically described as far as the Vandau, the Venda and the Lovedu are concerned. Quite recently—about 1910—they appeared in Zululand. It is characteristic that the two most serious epidemics in recent times among the Zulu —"influenza" in 1919-20 and malaria in 1933—were among the causes of the rapid spread of this form of possession. Like the *izizwe* hysteria, the *amandawe* possession is directed at curing some illness, and initiation into the cult is regarded as a healing agency, for it is believed to be therapeutic. As with *idlozi* possession [ordinarily *ukuthwasa*], dancing is an important feature of the more modern cult. However, whereas the *isangoma* novice is most often of a hysterical constitution, and the symptoms of the initiation (*ukwethwasa*) are quite violent, the initiates of *amandawe* possession are relatively quiet. An *amandawe* doctor is called to heal the patient. This is done by rites and dances designed to cause one of the patient's ancestral spirits to materialize. The initiate goes through many days of an exhausting dance, until at last the spirit enters her. It speaks through the initiate and expresses itself in a reputedly foreign tongue, as, for instance, a so-called "Indian" or "Thonga" language. In actual fact it may be only a series of meaningless sounds, which are thought by the audience to be some foreign language. Sometimes two or even as many as seven different ancestral spirits may take up their abode in the person concerned and speak in different languages. (Sundkler 1961, p. 23)

Of *izizwe* Sundkler writes: "The best parallel to tongues which people in Northern Zululand know of is the so-called *izizwe* or *amabutho.* When a person is ill the Zulu doctor [herbalist] may treat him in the following way. He gives his patient a mixture to smoke which when inhaled will drive away the illness or rather replace the illness by something the Zulu call 'soldiers' (amabutho)" (Sundkler 1961, pp. 248-49). This treatment is used for some cases of psychological disturbance and the treated person will speak in "foreign" tongues appropriate to the medicine administered.

Bryant, in an early account (1911), mentions the northern origin of the states, their epidemic nature, the possessing spirit akin to the ancestral types (idlozi and umlozikana or whistling familiar spirit), and attributes the symptoms and actions of sufferers to epilepsy and hysteria. The epileptic hypothesis is of interest, as epilepsy is common in the area, but it is equally distributed between men and women, unlike the possessions, which are almost always found in females. The Zulu have a clear idea of major epileptic seizures and while fits might be explained in terms of possession and might initiate behavior disorders they are not, in my opinion, a major contributor to the incidence of any of the disorders discussed in this essay.

My own informants confirmed some of the above accounts and, in older women, there is less confusion with other states. These latter denied that sorcery was in any way responsible for amandiki and said that it was caused solely by "the spirits of the dead." One claimed to have been treated with her sisters, prophylactically, during the 1933 malaria epidemic, and thus spared the possession which attacked her cousins. Izizwe was stated to result as an integral part of cures, particularly when the patient was threatened with impending "crying"—"I did not actually cry out, because the herbalist caused me to have izizwe. These cause one to speak out like amandiki, but one's bodily movements are different. Amandiki sit like men while, in izizwe, you just move your body in a shaking rhythmic manner." Izizwe is not regarded as always accompanied by physical distress, unlike most other forms, though psychological disturbance is often part of the syndrome.

Another informant claimed that she had suffered from amandawe possession but had had it converted into ukuthwasa by an isangoma diviner, as the former condition, unless treated, could lead to death.

In summary, much more intensive investigation of these states is needed and their nosology and etiology are far from clear. However, they do seem to bear a very close resemblance to the Dancing Manias of the Middle Ages (Hecker 1844), in their symptoms, their "infectiousness," and in the itinerant activities of the cults. At times of national disaster they tend to occur in an explosively epidemic form and then to persist, sporadically, in individual cases. They are new disorders, less indigenous to the Zulu than to neighboring tribes, and have probably been acquired from contact with other more northerly peoples. I have come across too few cases for the evidence to be of statistical value but, essentially, these possessions are highly individual phenomena, lacking the stable socially recognized framework of either ukuthwasa or Zionist possession.

In izizwe the person possessed has no diagnostic or therapeutic powers and indeed the contribution of all these "foreign" states to the medical practices of the Zulu is very small. To hazard a guess: the personalities of the women involved are probably not dissimilar to those of possessed Zionist converts—possession in both cases is neither as violent in its effects, both physical and psychological, nor as long lasting, as *ukuthwasa*. Possession by spirits speaking foreign tongues is of interest, particularly as English and Indian are tending to supplant the more traditional Swazi or Thonga. Indians are not allowed to settle in Zululand, yet in the fantasies of Zulu psychotics suffering delusions of persecution it is not uncommon to find Indians as the maleficent figures. We may well have here, at a very deep level, a reflection of new culture contact stresses, worthy of more intensive investigation.

II

The word *ukuthwasa* means a "coming out" or "emergence," as of the appearance of the new moon or the reappearance of a planet or constellation. In the case of "a new *umNgoma* emerging from his initiation and starting practice" (Bryant 1906), this coming out is the end result of possession by ancestor spirits—ideas of rebirth as a new person are involved and indeed the behavior and symbolic acts attributed to the possessed person resemble greatly certain universal birth symbols postulated by Freud (1954).

In most cases of *ukuthwasa* possession three distinct stages can be found: initial symptoms of considerable change in both physical and mental functioning; treatment, either to "seal off" the spirit or spirits or to "open the ways" of the victim for the ancestors; and, finally, if the second of these courses is pursued, the emergence of the possessed person as a fully qualified member of the *isangoma* cult. That these processes are relatively invariant will be seen from the following ethnographic accounts,

the first being that of an *ukuthwasa* experience described in 1951. The informant was a married woman aged 30 who had been in full practice as a diviner for some 18 months when she was interviewed by my research assistant, C. Mthembu. She was highly regarded in the area as a "smeller-out" of sorcerers.

I had been sick for over six months. I chiefly suffered from pains in the sides. The *izangoma* had been consulted. They said the spirits of my ancestors were angry about some unbecoming behavior that was taking place at home, so that they were stabbing me (sharp pain in the sides). A goat was killed to propitiate them. This had no effect. A young ox was killed. I thought I was recovering after this. I could even sit up by myself. I could walk with the help of a stick. Two weeks later it came on me again, now worse than before. I was already a bag of bones. I had a very deep sleep after going several nights without. I dreamt that I saw my grandfathers and great-grandfathers [in real life she had seen a grandfather, but no great-grandfather]. I felt afraid and bowed myself down. My grandfather called me and told me: "We are your ancestors. We have long tried to make your people understand (by illness) that we want you to be our house—to speak for us. We have decided to come ourselves as we see you in danger of death. Wake up. Dress. Go out quietly, and as soon as you are outside the *umuzi* [homestead], run fast before your absence is discovered. We shall then guide you where we want you to go." I woke up. It was a dream. Yet to my surprise I felt my bones strong. I felt I could walk, bag of bones as I was. I dressed quickly and slipped out of the hut. When I was out of the *umuzi* I ran. I made my unknown journey towards the east. It must have been midnight, as I reached my destination at dawn [the actual distance was 20 miles]. I came to a big *umuzi*. I felt something like a voice saying, "Go there." I went into one of the huts—a very big one. In it I found a number of *izangoma* sitting. Some were grinding medicines and others were smelling burnt skins and herbs. I went straight to the chief *isangoma* sitting right at the back of the hut. She simply looked at me without saying a single word. I suffered much consternation. Without asking me any questions she jumped up, howled, and began to dance. After this she burnt some medicine on burning embers and made me smell it. It made me dizzy and I felt a shiver go through my body and my heart became painful (i.e. "I felt sad and anxious"). Then I began to cry. I cried and cried until, after a time, I was ordered to follow immediately. We went with the chief *isangoma* into the *dongas* [eroded gullies] nearby. There I was given some emetic. We then returned home. Every morning this was done until one night the spirits of my ancestors came to me and told me to rest assured that they were with me. My home people could not trace me until three weeks had passed. I stayed for months in that *umuzi,* being initiated. We used to go out with the chief *isangoma* to gatherings of the *izangoma.* After a short time I felt that I could smell things out. At meetings of the *izangoma* people hid things here and there. I could not follow the thing until I pulled it out from where it was hidden. I did not *'bula'* [divine] at great meetings connected with sicknesses, and *abathakathi* [sorcerers] smelling out— as I was not yet a full professional. I did not do so until six months after, when I was to be sent home to be given presents by my people [presents are said to be given to the spirits and not to the *işangoma*]. The giving of presents is called *'ukubunga'.* This was a great ceremony, as all the local *izangoma* assembled at my home and danced through the whole night. I was brought in after dusk. Since I had arrived at the *umuzi* of the chief *isangoma,* I had been painted all over with ochre. It was in the morning of the following day that I went up with the others to the river to bathe. An ox and three goats were killed for the spirits. After the feast I was left at home and could work out my own cases.

This is a very typical modern account of the possession and training of an *isangoma,* through it is fairly common for the neophyte to be isolated for some months in a hut, and some of the odd subjective experiences of trainee diviners may be due to this form of sensory deprivation (cf. Bexton, Heron and Scott 1954; Hebb 1958, etc.). Space precludes the citing of earlier ethnographic evidence in full but three early accounts are worth quoting at some length:

(1) Fynn (1950, pp. 274-75), writing about 1833:

This species of witchcraft is professed by men and women which appears not to be a choice, nor could it be accomplished by choice, but as they state, commences with a fit of sickness in which case, as is general with all sick, they kill a cow, praying for a recovery from the spirits of their forefathers. They are then attacked with a delirium during which they dream dreams and run wild in the river or woods during which time the spirits appear to them with a song composed for his or her use which is the one sung by them on all occasions when called on.

He or she then plucks some plants from the riverside, part of which is eaten and the rest tied about the neck when he recovers from the trance which with the first sickness has been brought on him by the spirits of his forefathers with the intention that he should follow the profession of *inyanga.*
. . . On his return he is addressed with the same respect that is given to a chief. . . . Having previously prepared his dress for the event [divination of the whereabouts of a concealed object], he then puts it on, differing in persons as fancy may dictate. Some the blown entrails of a bullock tied round the neck and breast, on others immense numbers of gallbladders blown. Others, pieces of hides about their necks. . . .

(2) Shooter (1857, p. 191):

The seer's office, which may be filled by a female, is hereditary. It is, however (to quote the words of Mr. Fynn) "a principle understood throughout every tribe in Kafir-land that none of the children of a prophet can succeed their parent in that profession. It is believed that the requisite discernment and power are denied to them, but may frequently appear in their descendants of the second generation." Symptoms supposed to indicate an individual's coming inspiration are mental depression, a disposition to retire from his accustomed society, severe fits of an epileptic nature, severe and numerous dreams . . . . The neophyte talks about his marvellous visions, and "commences running, shrieking, plunging into water, and performing wonderful feats, until his friends say he is mad; and he speaks and acts like one under the influence of a super-natural being." He then catches live snakes (probably harmless ones) and hangs them about his neck. Thus arrayed he goes to a prophet; and presenting him with a goat, seeks to be instructed in the mysteries of the profession.

Shooter goes on to give a detailed description of such a case of possession in the father of one of his servants. An attempt was made to check the onset of possession, but this was only temporarily successful and the symptoms returned of dreams of wild animals, manic fugues, emaciation, glaring eyes and a snake draped around the victim's neck. He claimed possession by male ancestors, had visions of a boaconstrictor which was captured by his people on his instructions, and wandered among rivers. But there are compensations for the discomforts of possessions. "A prophet of reputation possesses very great influence. The people reverence him not only because he is believed to enjoy the peculiar favour of the spirits; but because he enjoys the tremendous power of charging a person with so-called 'witchcraft' " (Shooter 1857, p. 195).

(3) Callaway (1870, pp. 259-60):

The condition of a man who is about to be an *inyanga* is this: At first he is apparently robust, but in process of time he begins to be delicate, not having any real disease, but being very delicate. He begins to be particular about food, and abstains from some kinds, and requests his friends not to give him that food, because it makes him ill. He

habitually avoids certain kinds of food, choosing what he likes, and he does not eat much of that: and he is continually complaining of pains in different parts of his body. And he tells them that he has dreamt that he was being carried away by a river. He dreams of many things, and his body is muddled (*dungeka*—stirred up or made turbid—like a river) and he becomes a house of dreams constantly of many things, and on awaking says to his friends "My body is muddled today. I dreamt many men were killing me; I escaped I know not how. And on waking one part of my body felt different from other parts; it was no longer alike all over." At last the man is very ill, and they go to the diviners to enquire. The diviners do not at once see that he is about to have a soft head. (Note: a soft head, that is, impressible; diviners are said to have soft heads). . . .

So the man may be ill two years without getting better; perhaps even longer than that. He may leave the house for a few days, and the people begin to think he will get well. But no, he is confined to the house again. This continues until his hair falls off. And his body is dry and scurfy; and he does not like to anoint himself. People wonder at the progress of the disease. But his head gives signs of what is about to happen. He shows that he is about to be a diviner by yawning again and again, and by sneezing again and again. And men say "No! Truly it seems as though this man was about to be possessed by a spirit." This is also apparent from his being very fond of snuff; not allowing any long time to pass without taking some. . . .

Callaway goes on to describe further symptoms, including the shedding of tears, crying aloud, and the composing of the special song—"In this state of things they daily expect his death; he is now but skin and bones, and they think that tomorrow's sun will not leave him alive. . . ." The possessed person sleeps badly, leaps around, disturbing others, and he sings constantly. "At length another ancient *inyanga* [diviner] is pointed out to him [that is, by the *itongo* (ancestral spirit) in a dream]. At night whilst asleep he is commanded by the *itongo*, who says to him, 'Go to so-and-so, go to him, and he will churn for you emetic *ubulawo* [medicine], that you may be an *inyanga* altogether.' Then he is quiet for a few days, having gone to the *inyanga* to have ubulawo churned for him; and he comes back quite a different man, being now cleaned, and an *inyanga* indeed."

Of more modern descriptions, probably the most comprehensive are to be found in the accounts given by Bryant (1917), *The Collector* (1911), Asmus (1939), and Kohler (1941). *The Collector* gives a clear account of initial symptoms of *ukuthwasa*, the commonest signs being excessive belching and yawning and "having a certain creeping or nervous sensation, especially in the region of the shoulders." In the "sealing off" of ancestral spirits river symbolism recurs. If a woman is affected it is particularly difficult for the diviner consulted to find out whether the possessing spirits are those of her husband's or her own ancestors. Any determined spirit can prevail against the husband's efforts to have his wife closed to its influence. More than one spirit may be involved in the possession but there is always a leading spirit and the initial symptoms of possession will be the same as those which accompanied the death of the ancestor who has this role. (In my own experience all possessing spirits have been male, though Kohler reports spirits of both sexes as causal among the Bhaca.) Finally, *The Collector* states that the crying fits (*umbayiso*)—see below— rarely precede the *ukuthwasa* state. When this does happen the subject is regarded as lucky, as she will escape the more serious consequences to her health of possession, and will simply cry out and go into a fugue state, finding herself at the dwelling place of her senior training diviner.

Asmus (1939) shows, as do the other writers cited, that becoming an *isangoma* cannot be achieved through any apprenticeship, unlike the situation with herbalists (*izinyanga zokwelapha*) in Zulu society, and stresses that the calling is open to any person of whatever sex, age, or status. His account is precise and describes the placing of the crossed strips of magical goatskin over the shoulders of the novice, the plaiting of the hair into separate strings, and "amongst other things he is ordered [by the spirits] to fetch a snake from a deep pool. He runs to the stream and throws himself into the water. The people, who come running, see him emerge from the river painted all over with different colored clay—the work of the ancestor spirits—which they have performed down there in the depths of the waters. Around the neck of the *isangoma* coils a python, or perhaps a mamba, one of the deadly snakes to be found here" [my translation].

I feel that there may be some symbolic connection here between the python theme so common in accounts of *ukuthwasa* and the fact that the *inkata*, the central and most important sacred object of the Zulu (see Asmus 1939), was covered in the skin of a python. In most accounts the power-giving snake is a female python— an intriguing parallel with the delphic pythoness of the ancient world.

Asmus also suggests that heightened states of sensibility may well be engendered by the rigorous training of *izangoma* and, from my own field work, I think that this is very probable. Bryant (1917), found that 90 per cent of all diviners, in the early part of this century, were married women (this is still the case). An even higher proportion of all diviners used the "twenty questions" method of divination: [to every statement made by the diviner the surrounding people, including the petitioner, answer "we agree". Sometimes the diviner requires them to clap their hands or beat two sticks together as they give the response. Slight nuances of emphasis in response are picked up by the diviner who thus arrives at a satisfactory diagnosis. The procedure bears a remarkable resemblance to that devised by the Russian psychologist, Luria (1932), to accompany the use of word association tests]. The remainder, through the *ukuthwasa* process and training are much the same, divined directly, the spirits speaking in a high whistling tone through the possessed medium.

Finally, from one of my own informants, it emerged that *ukuthwasa* could be deliberately induced as a therapeutic procedure:

I have never had the crying ailment, but I had *ukuthwasa*. My forehead used to ache. Then my heart would ache. I had many dreams. This happened after I was married and had three children. There are two main causes of *ukuthwasa*: first, if you are continually bewitched (ensorcelled) with earth from the graves of your ancestors, you may get ill even to the extent of dying. If you are treated in good time this may be converted to *ukuthwasa*. Second, it may happen that you are born with the spirits of your ancestors. These cause you to *thwasa* and they are always benevolent towards you. You may have the crying ailment, but this is not a necessary condition.

So much then for the ethnography of *ukuthwasa* possession. Again and again we find: physical symptoms which include avoidance of food and consequent emaciation, behavioral symptoms of fugue states, belching and yawning; and psychological events which include hallucinations and the dreaming of stereotyped dreams of rivers, snakes, etc. All these coincide with the Zulu social expectation and are built into the local explanations in terms of the behests of the possessing ancestor spirits. Women are the chief sufferers and the whole *izangoma* cult is female centered, male neophytes being transvestite and copying the ways of women. Social power is gained by the possessed person whose "ways are clear." The great stereotyping of the processes is very evident and, psychologically, it is odd that there has not been more distortion, by the errors intrinsic to serial reproduction (Bartlett 1932), through the centuries of the cult's existence. Doubtless the closed society and "apostolic succession" of the *izangoma* contribute to this invariance.

Why do certain people become possessed? Certain very simple explanations have been offered by social anthropologists in terms of stresses in the social order and the acquisition of greater status through possession, while psychiatrists have tended to regard the state as simply the culturally colored manifestation, in behavior, of psychopathological states well known to Western medicine, frequently of a hereditary character. Of the first group Gluckman (1950), Hoernle (1937), Sundkler (1961), Kuper (1947), and Ashton (1943) (the last two of these were dealing with essentially similar states among the Swazi and Sotho, respectively) are, to all intents and purposes, agreed that "to become diviners is for pagan Zulu women the only socially recognized way of escape from an impossible situation in family life; it is also the only way an outstanding woman can win general social prestige" (Gluckman 1950).

Ashton's Sotho informants themselves stressed the gainful nature, in psychological terms, of ancestor possession and becoming a diviner, and thus accounted for the seven to one preponderance of women diviners.

Their possessions, they say, "are a reaction to neglect or to the dullness of women's lives; by becoming the center of these ritual dances, and by forcing their relatives to give them occasional feasts, they hope to attract attention and to liven their existence. Women, they say, have duller lives than men, and being as they are the passive element in social and sexual relations, they are more liable to neglect; consequently they are more attracted to this institution than men. This is a plausible theory, but one which I have not sufficient data to prove" (Ashton, 1943, p. 32).

A very different type of explanation is offered by Laubscher (1937, p. 229), working with predominantly Thembu patients in a mental hospital, who plumps firmly for the essentially biogenetic and psychotic nature of the phenomena:

The psychopathological antecedents in the forebears and relatives of the hospital patients are clearly in evidence in these family histories and support the inference that *ukuthwasa,* as it is popularly conceived, as well as *ukupambana* [stuporous states], are recognized psychopathological conditions well known to psychiatry. The hereditary bases of the biogenetic psychoses are thus further multiplied in this culture by the custom of second and third cousin marriage.

Incidentally, as Zulu do not marry close kin, the last sentence would not hold for them and weak strains should, theoretically, be "bred out." Laubscher's argument runs, in effect: biogenetic psychoses run in families —the relatives or friends of patients in my mental hospital state that *ukuthwasa* has appeared among the relatives of patients—therefore *ukuthwasa* states are biogenetic psychoses. Not only is the logic faulty but Laubscher's "facts" were derived from a brief postal questionnaire to relatives or friends of patients whose replies might, in the extended polygynous family system, refer to individuals from a reference group of scores of "relatives" and, in the absence of any control groups, little real proof of his hypothesis is adduced. It is not my intention to argue that there is no hereditary factor in *ukuthwasa* possession, but simply that any one to one equation, either in nosology or etiology, with Western patterns of psychosis, is a gross oversimplification.

However, later in the same volume, we find: "It is possible that the psychotics of the past have left their impressions on the memory of the race and these impressions have ultimately become the recognized form of behaviour and belief for most of those claiming mediumistic powers." The psychological implications of this statement are not clear and any such Lamarckian or Jungian hypothesis is not, at present, testable.

Far more useful, at this stage, are the possibilities considered by Hammond-Tooke (1962) to explain *ukuthwasa* among the Bhaca.

(a) Possibly sufferers are neurotic and neurosis initiates the possession.

(b) Possibly the initial illness is organic and the traditional interpretation in terms of *ukuthwasa* is sufficient to lead to the rest of the process.

(c) Possibly such female functions as menstruation, pregnancy and the menopause may contribute to the high female incidence.

(d) Possibly a strong minded and intelligent woman may find freedom from her common roles and the restraints of her husband.

(c) Possibly, since Hammond-Tooke found female diviners to be well-integrated individuals, intelligent and friendly, as against male diviners who appeared "psychopathic," moody, and probably homosexual, the causes might operate differentially between the sexes.

All these seem to me to be highly probable, in the light of my own research, and useful in that both social and individual causes are envisaged.

My own research was directed at elucidating the crying fits mentioned above. Three separate investigations were carried out, using questionnaires, interviews, and a form of the Thematic Apperception Test, designed specifically for the culture and the salient points of the investigation. Half of each of three large samples of Zulu women were found to report a history of the crying—a new disorder of this century. The crying is accompanied by an intense subjective feeling of fear, localized between the shoulder-blades, and a common precipitating cause is a feeling of pent-up anger. All women reporting having suffered from the crying will be called "cryers" throughout the rest of this essay; all others with no such history, "controls." For each of these categories definite and enduring patterns of personality were found. A woman who has cried once shares a great many characteristics with a woman with a lifetime of it, which she does not share with controls.

This topic is essentially peripheral to that of possession. Nevertheless, as I was investigating a "Bantu Disorder" (in Western terms, often possession or other psychogenic disorder; cf. Lee 1950), against the background of a mission hospital in the Nqutu district of Zululand, it was inevitable that I should come into contact with the *izangoma* cult. Among my patients I had women with *ukuthwasa*, as well as others with other types of possession, and eventually it was common for patients with a wide range of behavioral disorders to be referred to me by the local *izangoma* they had consulted.

Within this context, then, I wish to examine certain of the statements and hypotheses that have been set down by previous enquirers in this field.

(1) POSSESSION IS MOST COMMONLY FOUND IN WOMEN.

In my experience *ukuthwasa* is almost entirely confined to women, though males are occasionally encountered. The latter are almost certainly of homosexual bent and are usually younger and unmarried at the initiation of their possession. I recall the news of the marriage of one male *isangoma* being greeted with Rabelaisian comment throughout the district. The possessed male will probably be trained by a female diviner, will adopt female dress and will speak in high-pitched tones. I found severe anxiety neurosis in roughly five per cent of all males of a hospital population, over two years, and in many of these cases the homosexual nature of their dreams was very clear (usually the dreamer was passive and being attacked, sexually or aggressively, by another male, sometimes his own male ancestors) (Lee 1958). In general, I would agree with Hammond-Tooke that grosser pathology is to be expected in cases of male *ukuthwasa*.

In an extensive survey, based on 416 women and 148 men, I found a much higher incidence of "Bantu disease" among women, roughly 15 percent of women claiming a history of minor possession, as against some five percent of men. Disease attributed to sorcery was equally distributed, 17 percent and 18 percent, between women and men respectively. One specifically male disorder reported by

Kohler (1941), *iqondo*, was rare in the area, found in about one male in a hundred, and, in any case, has none of the attributes of possession. Similarly, in dreaming, women showed, significant statistically, a much higher reported incidence of unpleasant dreams (Lee 1958), so that, psychologically they would appear to be the sex more prone to overt behavioral disorder—the more vulnerable group. These rough figures should be cautiously regarded as the ages of the samples differed between the sexes. Although the sample was representative of the district, many more women appeared in the 21-30 age group. This is a function of the migrant labor situation, most of the men of working age being away in the towns.

Incidentally, the possibility that tertiary syphilis was causal in these psychopathological states was not confirmed, for positive Wassermann reactions were equally distributed between the sexes and though Bantu disease was slightly more common among the 24 women with syphilis than in women free from the disease, no such relationship showed itself among the men. It would seem more likely that this slight tendency among women is not directly due to any causal role of syphilis (although this may contribute to infertility—frequently a precipitating cause of breakdown), but rather to the fact that a disordered sex life may lead to both venereal infection and neurosis (Lee 1954).

(2) DOES UKUTHWASA POSSESSION RUN IN FAMILIES? IF SO, IS THE INCIDENCE GENETICALLY OR SOCIALLY DETERMINED?

Here my evidence is essentially oblique, as I have not specifically studied the family relationships of *izangoma*.

Results showed the cryers were no more prone to *ukuthwasa* possession than were the controls, the ethnographic evidence implying a relative immunity for cryers (*The Collector* 1911; cf. also Nadel 1946). As I found that the crying attacks were not so much hysterical as a very direct discharge of anxiety (Lee 1954, 1961), with possible beneficial cathartic effects, this view may well be tenable, despite the fact that nearly all diviners are women and the crying fits are found in 50 percent of women as against ten percent of men.

But I had asked the question: "have any of your blood relatives had *ukuthwasa*?" and the cryers, themselves possibly protected against *ukuthwasa* by their own condition or "crying personality," showed many more such relationships than the controls:

	YES	NO	
Cryers	21	18	p= < .01
Controls	26	46	

A rather neat control situation exists here. In Zululand there is another kind of medical practitioner, whose training involves no unusual psychological experience. This is the herbalist, essentially a therapist rather than a diagnostician. In relationship to herbalists there were no significant differences between my criterion groups.

	YES	NO	
Cryers	21	17	p=.41
Controls	32	36	

In a recent predictive study, not yet published, of a random sample of 200 Zulu women, a rather similar result appeared in that, although cryers were significantly more often related to both diviners and herbalists than were controls, *within* the crying group relationship to diviners was far more frequently found than relationship to herbalists. Space precludes any detailed discussion of the actual relationships established in this predictive study, but nearly all relatives cited as *ukuthwasa* sufferers were female, and the majority—from earlier generations—were related to the subjects through their fathers. Both cryers and controls reported, in a number of instances, sisters and half-sisters as *ukuthwasa* cases. One subject who had herself had *ukuthwasa* reported that her mother had also done so; another *isangoma* reported that her daughter had *ukuthwasa,* and these instances do not bear out Shooter's hypothesis (1857).

In both these studies we have the 'indigenousness' of the situation controlled. Both types of practitioners are equally ancient and traditional. Yet the cryers are related, at a high level of statistical significance, to a psychopathological group from whose symptoms they are themselves relatively immune. In these circumstances it is unlikely that mere "social infection" or imitation is responsible. A genetic weakness, capable of manifesting itself in either of the two ways, is much the more likely explanation, and Linton's (1956) hypothesis: "data regarding mental disorders in other societies tend to suggest that there is a definite, though often not easily detectable, foundation in the organic realm for whatever psychiatric illnesses may become manifest on the behavioral levels," receives partial confirmation.

(3) GIVEN THAT THERE IS A HEREDITARY ELEMENT IN UKUTHWASA, WHICH MIGHT INDEED HAVE BEEN SUSPECTED FROM THE ACCOUNTS CITED EARLIER, ARE WE DEALING WITH FRANK "ORGANIC" PSYCHOSIS COMMON IN THE WEST? (cf. Laubscher, 1937)

Several facts seem to me to be against this explanation: (a) The *isangoma* diviner is a highly efficient person, intelligent and alert, and a remarkably high rate of spontaneous remission of psychosis would be needed to account for the emergence of such people from, say, a schizophrenically withdrawn condition. (b) In my research I found that visual and auditory hallucinations were very common among Zulu women. Over 20 percent of women reported a history thereof. None of these showed any signs of psychosis, though many were anxiety cases. Hallucinations (common in *ukuthwasa*) do not carry the grave prognosis that they would in our society. Visions of the ancestors, angels, or babies are legitimate expectations within the belief systems of this society as, indeed, is the dreaming of certain stereotyped dreams (Lee 1958). (c) The symptoms that I have observed as preceding or accompanying the *ukuthwasa* state are usually those of an anxiety state, sometimes those of conversion hysteria. One of my patients, admitted to hospital with hysterical paraplegia, first persuaded me to "seal off" her dreams with barbiturates (in a double blind trial with these I found that their efficacy was roughly half attributable to the tablets, half to suggestion!) then to "reopen her ways" with *nux vomica.* Eventually she became possessed by the spirit of her paternal grandfather, a very potent personage as he had been killed at the battle of Isandhlwana in 1879. She was then trained by a senior diviner, a process which included six months' isolation in a hut, and set up a lucrative practice in my backyard. A fairly typical case, certainly not psychotic. (d) It is unnecessary to call in psychosis in hereditary disorder. A hereditary lability of autonomic function would be sufficient cause to explain most of the symptoms (cf. Jost and Sontag 1944). (e) Severe neurosis would seem to be a more apt description of the state. A severe anxiety state is here followed by *anorexia nervosa* and the symptoms may be precipitated or exacerbated by *post partum* disturbance or glandular dysfunction. One additional fact which may be of significance is the excessive yawning of *ukuthwasa*. In my own work it appeared that cryers shared this action with diviners, being much more prone to yawning attacks than were the controls. It is possible that we have to consider here ensuing hyperventilation tetany as contributory to both the physical and behavioral anomalies of both syndromes (cf. Wallace 1961, in his treatment of "Arctic Hysteria").

(4) CAN THE "ANOREXIA NERVOSA" HYPOTHESIS SERVE TO CLARIFY THE ETIOLOGY OF UKUTHWASA?

Let us first examine Western accounts of *anorexia* and follow this with some examination of the social and psychological position of the Zulu women.

Mayer-Gross et al. (1955, pp. 138-39) state:

This *(anorexia nervosa)* is a condition almost confined to women in the years of adolescence and early adult life, although it also occurs rarely in young men. . . . The *constitutional factors* in etiology are important. The patient will have shown signs in earlier years of hysterical tendencies, sometimes also minor obsessional traits, and there may be a family history of psychopathy or nervous illness. . . . *Physically* the patient is invariably thin and sometimes has lost so much weight that the skin seems to be lying loosely over bones only just beneath the surface. . . . The skin itself is dry and papery, without normal suppleness or elasticity. . . . There is amenorrhoea [common among Zulu women]. . . . Psychogenic factors also

play an important part. The illness nearly always arises out of a *conflict situation,* e.g. an engagement to marry which the patient secretly does not feel willing to carry out, impaired relations with the parents. . . .

The *anorexia* is profound. The patient has *no desire for food* of any kind, and most foods, especially the more nutritious, are regarded with repulsion. . . . Despite her physically reduced state, the patient nearly always shows a remarkable degree of *energy, alertness and initiative.* . . . She herself does not feel ill, and her *anorexia* is hardly so much a symptom to her as a guiding principle of her life. . . . There is no depression, nor any symptom of a schizophrenic kind; and it is hardly possible to mistake the condition for a psychotic state (italics in original).

Here we have a description almost identical with that of the condition of a diviner (the emaciation, scurfiness of the skin, etc.). While it does not help us with the underlying etiology of the *anorexia* (applying it to the Zulu) some hints may emerge from the causes cited. The family history is present in both disorders, and conflict situations, for the Zulu women, abound (Lee 1950, 1954, 1958, 1961).

Consider, also, the Freudian background to anorexia offered by Saul 1944, p. 274):

In these cases it has been found that certain impulses which are rejected by the rest of the personality as intolerable because of guilt and shame are so closely associated with eating that food cannot be taken. In many cases these rejected impulses are of a sexual nature, for example, unconscious wishes to fellatio or cunnilingus or wishes for pregnancy. . . . In other cases not libidinal but aggressive impulses are in the foreground —grasping, envious, attacking desires. These are unconscious and are associated with biting and eating, which are inhibited because of guilt and shame.

Whatever the validity of such largely untestable "depth" hypotheses, the purely descriptive fit is a close one, and it may be profitable to examine in greater detail the stresses inevitable in the life of Zulu women and some of their reactions to them. Anthropological implication is often that *ukuthwasa* is almost a matter of deliberate choice by the possessed person. But it is dreaded. I have had to try to treat women in hospitals and health centers who felt themselves threatened by impending ancestral possession and who were desperately seeking any way to avoid it. I asked 114 women: "Do you think that diviners have a profitable life?" and "Would you like to be one?" Only six thought the life profitable, though in purely economic terms I found that the average Zulu tended to have consulted *izangoma* on at least two occasions in his or her life. Nobody wished to be a diviner—"No. Possession by the ancestors is an unpleasant life."

So that the choice whether to become a diviner, if there is a psychological choice involved, is almost certainly at an unconscious level. It seems to me likely that the basis of the condition is neurosis and that the degree of conscious willingness to become a diviner varies inversely with the severity of the neurosis. The relatively healthy, active and intelligent woman may indeed gain authority and prestige from the process and be able to enact a more male role, all formal authority and religious observance being entirely the prerogative of Zulu men; and she is the less likely to fear the condition the more she resents, consciously, any stresses or deprivations in her everyday existence. (It is noteworthy that all *izangoma* reported by my informants continued living with their husbands after their initiation, so that their independence is psychological rather than spatial.) On the other hand, the neurotic will be pushed, willy nilly, into *ukuthwasa*

by her neurosis and, in her case, predisposition will be more important than immediately exciting causes attributable to socially induced stress.

There is a possible parallel to be drawn here with the *nomkumbulmana* ceremony, where male and female roles are reversed for one day, which anthropologists (cf. Gluckman 1954) tend to take as a catharsis of the tensions of Zulu women's subservient roles. In investigating crying I had to try to assess the chief conflict and stress situations of their life. Initially I had expected that the new disorder of crying would be linked with rapid social change, the absence of migrant labor husbands, and so forth. In this I was disappointed. The crying tended to take place when their husbands were at home (Lee 1961), and nightmares of a sexual nature were more common in women with nonmigrant husbands. Sex in marriage—as contrasted with premarital sexual activity —was not enjoyed and often dreaded. Conflicts existed between lack of children and poverty, and in the confusion of goals at menopause (Lee 1958). The cryers were apparently affected more by rather *less* dislodgment from their traditional rut than had been experienced by the controls. Their goals, while often Western in nature, could not be achieved because they were the less trained group. They had new aims but no means to secure them.

But the cryers seem comparatively immune to *ukuthwasa*. How is one to explain the fact that many women, despite Government ban, still suffer *ukuthwasa* and become diviners when they may well (in terms of crying at least) come from the "healthier" half of the population of Zulu women?

Of my two groups I asked three other questions. First: "What time of your life was the most happy?" Here it appeared that preadolescence or very early adolescence was regarded as the happiest time of life. Attitudes to marriage were commonly negative —"Before I married"; "When I was nine years old I was healthy and had no worries." The bearing of children had, however, been the happiest time to some 15 percent of informants.

This last was reflected in the answers to the second question: "If you had your choice, what would you like best in the whole world?" The cryers tended to want babies, as did many of the controls. Health and money were also desired, but cryers wished much more often for traditionally feminine gratifications, passively, while controls wished for independent success: "To get a job and earn my own living;" "A business stand near a town;" "To be a Western doctor;" "To get a job as an industrial worker." This ambitious group was far the more out looking and adventurous and it would not be surprising, in personality terms, if diviners were drawn from their ranks. On the other hand, one cryer did wish to become "a Zionist diviner and healer" (see below).

This greater "masculinity of wish" (on the part of the controls) appeared in answer to the third question: "Have you ever wished that you were a man?" "If so, when?" More than half the cryers had wished to be male, as against just over a quarter of the controls, but for very different reasons. The former wished to avoid the painful lot of women: "Always, I would not suffer childlessness;" "When I meet difficulties, I would be able to stand them better," "When annoyed, I would be able to fight." The latter's motives were far more activist: "When I see my brothers failing to control the home well, I would do better;" "Always, being an intelligent woman, I could improve the living of my family;" "When worried, I would be independent." In the first instances, we have male powers desired to *avoid*; in the second we have a courting of experience, largely the prerogative of males.

So the passivity of cryers probably precludes their making a success, in psychological terms, of *ukuthwasa*, and it *is* the more active and "masculine" half of Zulu women who will be motivated to the status accruing to the diviner—though more modern outlets may be available to any highly trained in Western skills. To quote Gluckman (1954), "The symbol of a successful initiation was the right to carry a shield and spear, those badges of manhood." Today the equivalent might well be the owning of a small business, but such outlets, through Government legislation, are usually closed to rural Zulu women.

Further confirmation of the more active attitude of the controls was gained, obliquely, by the use of a Thematic Apperception Test picture stimulus depicting an *isangoma* stirring her medicines. All subjects showed a considerable knowledge of the practices of the cult, but only two out of 84 subjects described her as happy. There was considerable difference between the groups in the full descriptions of the actions of the diviner in the picture. The cryers tended to see her merely as stirring emetic or making medicine to clear her ways, the controls on the other hand introduced clients into their stories, and showed themselves as the group more capable of envisaging constructive action and dominance in a social situation of divination.

From all this we have, obliquely, possible evidence of statistical links between *ukuthwasa* and individual personality, but there are also some general anecdotal considerations worth taking into account, if the early condition in *ukuthwasa* is regarded as *anorexia nervosa* (cf. Saul 1944). We have seen that conflict is common concerning sex and aggression, that masculinity of role is desired, and we have aggressive and phallic symbols recurring in the state of *ukuthwasa*. Also, meat and beer, masculine prerogatives in everyday life and rarely available to premenopausal women, are freely enjoyed by *izangoma*. Husbands who have been bitten by their wives are often admitted to hospital. These last two sentences seem slightly dissociated, until one reflects that the Zulu language is filled with "oral" terms. Hundreds of words in Zulu refer to the feel of substances in the mouth (Bryant 1906; Doke and Vilakazi 1948); apprehension of outside stimuli is, in linguistic terms, predominantly oral rather than visual or tactile, and a possible corollary is given by the fact that the hundreds of words for "oral aggression" (backbiting, slander, vilification, etc.) greatly outnumber the mere handful of words connected with physical aggression. This in a warrior nation. A possible connection may exist between this facet of the culture and the fact that the most serious and important form of possession is accompanied by disturbances in eating.

But all this is largely speculation and needs empirical verification. All that can legitimately be claimed at present is that it might be possible, along these lines, to illuminate the psychological background of ancestral possession.

III

I wish now to examine a modern modification of *ukuthwasa* possession, brought about by the conflicts of cultures, but probably fulfilling much the same purposes, both social and psychological.

This arises within the framework of the so-called separatist churches, of which over two thousand exist in South Africa. These are break-aways from orthodox Christianity and, roughly speaking, may be divided into two types, "Ethiopian" (more consciously nationalistic and adapted to modern culture contact conditions), and the "Zionist" type of sect, in which Christian tenets have been adapted to indigenous patterns of thought. There is no space to discuss either these syncretist sects or the possessions found therein in great detail, but a very good and full account can be found in Sundkler (1961).

In the Zionist churches possession is apt to be ascribed to the presence of *umoya*, possibly best translated as "spirit" which—in my experience—is a transmutation of a collective ancestral spirit, although it is, naturally enough, within these nominally Christian sects, linked with ideas of the Holy Spirit of Christianity. To cite one of Sundkler's informants, a Zionist prayer woman: "The diviners [*izangoma*] defile the Christian faith, claiming that they too have the Holy Spirit." Patients of mine who claimed, as good Zionists, to dream often of *ingelosi*, angels, on being pressed further, described these angels as ancestors wearing long white robes and, occasionally, wings!

So that despite all the Christian trappings and symbols involved, what we have here is essentially the old divination cult in a new form. The dreams of those possessed by The Spirit are very similar in content to *ukuthwasa* cases, water and snake symbols abounding, and the dress of the future diviner will be influenced by dreamed instructions. The crooks or staves carried by Zionist women may well be the counterpart of the spear and gnu's tail of the *izangoma*. Briefly, other parallels exist in the sacred dancing of Zionists, immersion in pools, either in baptismal or other rites (though pools are regarded as being inhabited by essentially maleficent monsters—cf. Sundkler 1961), belching is common as an accompaniment to "speaking with tongues" and prophesying by the Zionist diviner. Divination tends to be by direct speech of The Spirit, though "amen" can serve the same purpose as "we agree" when the audience's participation is required. Food taboos operate, pork and stimulants often being prescribed. Diagnoses of the causes of illness, a most important function in both cults because of the prevailing ill health of the people, are likely to be couched in terms of sorcery, but therapy in the separatist churches would never consist in the replacement of The Spirit by foreign spirits such as *amandiki* or *izizme*, as these latter are regarded as of the devil. Ancestral visitation is regarded as morally tolerable for it can suffer an easy change into angelic influence or "The Spirit" and, as in the older cult, misfortune is readily ascribed by the Zionist diviner to the displeasure of the ancestral shades. I have come across several cases of *izangoma* who have become respected Zionist practitioners.

Generally, Zionist possession and divination cult activities would seem to be the less strenuous form, both physically and psychologically. There

is seldom serious illness involved and I have found no record of sensory deprivation during training— the emphasis lies rather on baptismal rites and purification. Drumming in church services tends to be less protracted, and as a result dissociation is not so extreme, and cataleptic states —often found among *izangoma*—are rare. Separatist ritual and belief are much less stereotyped and great local variation can be found within an area ten miles square.

It should not be thought, however, that all women who join the separatist Churches will become diviners therein. In the crying study cited above, 38 out of one hundred and fourteen women had belonged to a Bantu church— sometimes to more than one, as fission and segmentation are very common in these sects—but of these only four had talked with tongues, and five claimed to have had *Umoya*, "The Spirit." There was a slight tendency, not statistically significant, for the Bantu churches to be found more among the denominations claimed by cryers than among the controls, but reports of any possession by "The Spirit" were evenly distributed between the two groups.

However, we can again look for any association between *ukuthwasa* and membership of separatist churches, in genetic terms. In the later predictive study, which included a random sample of 176 Zulu women, the following figures emerged:

Question: Have any of your blood relatives had *ukuthwasa*?

Controls (no history of crying: N:88)

Denomination:	YES	NO
Western Churches	12 ,	38
Separatist sects (including Zionists)	8	11
(Zionists	5	2)
Pagans	10	9

Cryers (a history of the
crying fits: N:88)

Western Churches	23	27
Separatist sects (including		
Zionists)	11	5
(Zionists	6	3)
Pagans	14	8

While again it is obvious that cryers are more likely to be related to sufferers from *ukuthwasa* than are the controls, irrespective of religious affiliation, it appears that *within* both groups, cryers and controls, the members of separatist churches, particularly the Zionists, tend to be related to *ukuthwasa* cases. It would seem to be a most tenable hypothesis that any genetic weakness, giving a predisposition to neurotic disorder, may be accommodated by at least three types of behavioral reaction: (1) *ukuthwasa* and becoming a diviner (if the subject is of an active and aggressive personality), (2) crying out (if the subject is "feminine" and passive), and (3) joining one of the Zionist-types sects (possibly for women of an intermediate position as regards these personality characteristics).

Just as practically all cryers and *izangoma* are female, so there is a great preponderance of women within the Zionist sects. Traditionally minded chiefs often complain, "These damned Zionists steal our women," and with good cause. Becoming a Zionist gives a Zulu woman considerably more independence—whether or not she becomes a diviner she can hold authority, preach, and be respected in her own right. Should she become a diviner she is not isolated in her practice as is the *isangoma*, but will be sustained by the presence and support of her congregation. She will not have had to endure the stringent suffering and training of the older cult and she will not be under the same economic pressure to produce results—only token payments are made to *izangoma* for unsuccessful divination. (Equally she is not as likely to make as much money for her own use.) In effect, the Zionist diviner's burden is the lighter.

However, it seems very likely that, in motivational terms, *ukuthwasa* and Zionist possession have many common elements—membership of both cults, in different ways, tending to act as a therapy for both constitutional neurosis and immediate social deprivation. In both cases the guilts aroused by the omnipresent ancestors can be coped with and assuaged. In both cults—indeed in all the syndromes that we have discussed—the unconscious life of the individual woman may shape, formally, her actions in her society.

REFERENCES

Ashton, E. H.
1943 *Medicine, Magic and Sorcery among the Southern Sotho.* Communications from the School of African Studies, No. 10. Cape Town: University of Cape Town.
Asmus, G.
1939 *Die Zulu, Welt und Weltbild eines bauerlichen Negerstammes.* Essen: Essener Verlagsanstalt.
Bartlett, F. C.
1932 *Remembering.* Cambridge: Cambridge University Press.
Bexton, W. H., W. Heron, and T. H. Scott
1954 Effects of decreased variation in the sensory environment. *Journal of Canadian Psychology* 8.

Bryant, A. T.
1906 *Zulu-English Dictionary*. Pinetown: Marianhill Mission Press.
1911 Zulu medicine and medicine men. *Annals of the Natal Museum* 2.
1917 The Zulu cult of the dead. *Man* 95.

Callaway, Conon
1870 *The Religious System of the Amazulu*. Springvale: John A. Blair.

Collector, The
1911 Pinetown: Marianhill Mission Press.

Doke, C. M., and B. W. Vilakazi
1948 *Zulu-English Dictionary*. Johannesburg: Witwatersrand University Press.

Freud, S.
1954 *The Interpretation of Dreams*. London: Allen and Unwin.

Fynn, H. F.
1950 *The Diary of Henry Francis Fynn*. D. McK. Malcolm, ed. Pietermaritzburg: Shuter and Shooter.

Gluckman, M.
1950 Kinship and marriage among the Lozi of Northern Rhodesia and the Zulu of Natal. *In* A. R. Radcliffe-Brown and D. Forde (eds.), *African Systems of Kinship and Marriage*. London: Oxford University Press.
1954 *Rituals of rebellion in South-east Africa*. Manchester: Manchester University Press.

Hammond-Tooke, W.
1962 *Bhaca Society*. Cape Town: Oxford University Press.

Hebb, D. O.
1958 *A Textbook of Psychology*. Philadelphia: Saunders.

Hecker, J. F. C.
1844 *Epidemics of the Middle Ages*. London: G. Woodfall and Sons.

Hoernle, Mrs. A.
1937 Social organization. *In* I. Schapera (ed.), *The Bantu-Speaking Tribes of South Africa*. London: Routledge.

Jost, H., and L. W. Sontag
1944 The genetic factor in autonomic nervous-system function. *Psychosomatic Medicine* 6.

Junod, H. A.
1927 *The Life of a South African Tribe*. London: Macmillan.

Junod, H. Ph.
1934 Les cas de possession et l'exorcisme chez les Vandau. *Africa* 7: 270-299.

Kohler, M.
1941 *The Izangoma Diviners*. Ethnological Publications, 9. Pretoria: Department of Native Affairs.

Kuper, H.
1947 *An African Aristocracy*. London: Oxford University Press.

Laubscher, B. J. F.
1937 *Sex, Custom, and Psychopathology*. London: Routledge.

Lee, S. G.
1950 Some Zulu concepts of psychogenic disorder. *Journal of Social Research* 1.
1954 A study of crying hysteria and dreaming in Zulu women. Ph.D. thesis, University of London.
1958 Social influences in Zulu dreaming. *Journal of Social Psychology* 47: 265-283.
1961 *Stress and Adaptation*. Leicester: Leicester University Press.

Linton, R.
1956 *Culture and Mental Disorders*. Springfield: Thomas.

Luria, A. R.
1932 *The Nature of Human Conflicts, or Emotions, Conflict and Will*. New York: Liveright.

Mayer-Gross, W., E. Slater, and M. Roth
1955 *Clinical Psychiatry*. London: Cassell.

Nadel, S. F.
1946   A study of shamanism in the Nuba mountains. *Journal of the Royal Anthropological Institute* 76: 25-37.

Saul, L. J.
1944   Physiological effects of emotional tension. *In* J. McV. Hunt (ed.), *Personality and the Behaviour Disorders*. New York: Ronald Press.

Shooter, J.
1857   *The Kafirs of Natal and Zulu Country*. London: Stanford.

Sundkler, B.
1961   *Bantu Prophets in South Africa,* 2nd Edition. London: Oxford University Press.

Wallace, A. F. C.
1961   Mental illness, biology and culture. *In* F. L. K. Hsu (ed.), *Psychological Anthropology*. Homewood: Dorsey Press.

22. THE OX AND NUER SACRIFICE: SOME FREUDIAN HYPOTHESES ABOUT NUER SYMBOLISM

T. O. BEIDELMAN

T. O. Beidelman is Professor of Anthropology, New York University. Reprinted with permission from *Man* (1966) 1 (n.s.): 453-467.

IN THIS PAPER[1] I try to account for the fact that Nuer usually must use neutered animals, preferably oxen, in their sacrifices. In doing so I consider certain salient features of Nuer sexual symbolism, showing certain parallels between Nuer symbolic categories and certain Nuer social categories. I suggest that the ambiguous, medial aspects of certain Nuer symbolic motifs coincide with certain ambiguities in their social relations. The power of these symbols and the important social ambiguities with which they seem to correspond may relate to the problem of socializing sexual drives within Nuer society. This neo-Freudian aspect of my analysis cannot be proved conclusively from the material at hand, but the discussion points out certain importance features of Nuer symbolism and Nuer social relations not previously discussed and which must eventually be accounted for if we are to understand Nuer society. Future research may sustain or disprove my points, but, in any case, the issues raised require explanation. The literature on the Nuer is perhaps the most detailed for any African society, and the analytical framework in which Professor Evans-Pritchard has presented these data has had profound theoretical influence on subsequent social anthropological research. For these reasons further examination of important structural questions about

Nuer society has a value far beyond the confines of Nilotic or African ethnography.

Writing of the identification of Nuer men with their oxen, Evans-Pritchard states:

We may ask why the identification is with oxen and not with bulls. It might be expected that a man who is himself a *tut,* a bull, not only in the general sense of "male," but also in a common metaphor of speech derived expressly from cattle, would take his name from a bull rather than an ox. The commonsense answer is that Nuer castrate all but a very few of their bulls, so that there would not be enough entire animals to go round, and this may be the right explanation. Even if it is not, or is not a sufficient explanation, we must here take it as given that the equation is between man and ox. (1956, p. 254)

Evans-Pritchard makes the identification between Nuer and their cattle one of the central points in his interpretation of Nuer sacrifice (1956, pp. 261-2); yet, there the prominence of oxen rather than bulls can hardly be explained in the commonsense terms of the prevalence of oxen over bulls, for we learn that "a male victim must be a neuter. If it is not, it is castrated before the rites begin" (1956, p. 202).

On a few particular sacrificial occasions bulls or cows, rather than oxen, are prescribed, but these are exceptions to the rule and may be fitted within a pattern relating a beast's sexuality to its sacrificial function. The symbolic identification by Nuer men with both oxen and bulls is a crucial aspect of Nuer religious thought. A search for the explanation takes one to the heart of Nuer philosophy.

The general facts about the Nuer are so well known that I provide no background information here. However, in the next two sections I outline a few basic aspects of Nuer thought and social structure which relate directly to the problems at hand.

THE NATURE OF NUER RITUAL

THE DUALISTIC ASPECT OF NUER SACRIFICE

The most fundamental distinction in Nuer thought is between immaterial Spirit (*kwoth*) and the material world of its Creation (*cak*) (1956, pp. 124-5). The order in the material world was set by Spirit, and the world's activity is due to animation by forms of Spirit; the customary order of Nuer society derives its moral rightness from its accord with Spirit. Spirit and Creation should be consistent and are interrelated with one another. In the mythical past the world of Spirit and the world of Creation became separated.[2] Although these two spheres are now normally separated, there is contact between them. Rain, lightning, human and livestock sickness, droughts, death, unusual phenomena, are all manifestations of Spirit's intrusion into the sphere of Creation. Sometimes such manifestation is the result of disturbance within the moral order of Creation itself, as by bad acts or bad intentions on the part of men. Men should observe these orderly divisions in their activities. Evans-Pritchard translates the verb *thek* as "respect," but it clearly refers to the observation of the differences and correspondences between the various categories of things and acts within Creation (cf. 1949c; 1956, pp 64-5, 79, 129, 177-83, 241, 291; 1936a). Failure to observe rules, to keep within the categories and divisions of prescribed behavior, leads to a temporary but highly dangerous confusion of the normal separation between Spirit and man (cf. my discussion of *thek*, Beidelman 1968). By symbolically reemphasizing these categories and by sacrificing to Spirit, Nuer believe that such sins are rectified, Spirit reseparated from Creation, and order restored. On other occasions Spirit may manifest itself on earth for no reason known to men: lightning strikes a person dead; sickness infects persons or livestock; twins or monorchids are born. In these cases, Spirit must be re-separated from the sphere below since its manifestation brings dangerous disorder to those categories by which Creation runs its normal course.

All such intrusive manifestation of Spirit bear the attributes of dirt, matter out of place. Nuer religious rites remove this dirt by re-separating these two spheres of categories. Conversely, Nuer prophets and certain other persons with unusual spiritual gifts obtain these powers through assuming "dirty," aberrant characteristics normally separated and whose confused combination is seen by Nuer as a sign of Spirit's presence.

In all societies religious rites involve some symbolic communication between the spheres of man and the supernatural. This often involves vehicles which embody attributes normally kept separated. In our own society the ambiguous symbolic attributes of Christ (man/god), Mary (mother/virgin) and the eucharistic feast are examples of this. In Nuer society oxen, and objects substituted for oxen, are vehicles for such mediation and synthesis, being male yet not partaking of active sexuality. They combine opposed attributes which give them a character betwixt-and-between Spirit and Creation, of neither and of both. Such ritual involves a paradox: it establishes contact between two spheres so that these may be better separated. The sacrifice or consecration to Spirit is thought to efface the unusual disorder caused by Spirit's intrusion outside its normal bounds and to turn Spirit back, reestablishing the orderly categorization of the world which separates Spirit and its Creation (cf. 1954; 1956, chap. 8).

SOME GENERAL ASPECTS OF NUER DUALISTIC SYMBOLISM

In Nuer ritual certain physical qualities such as direction, temperature, texture, color, sex, and so forth are assigned symbolic moral significance. For example, Nuer associate the right arm with strength and order; it is the spear arm, the hand for auspicious acts. Nuer speak of "right-handed peace" (1956, p. 235), lay corpses on their right sides so they may walk aright and bring good (Huffman 1931, p. 53). Conversely, the left is associated with weakness and misfortune; it is the side associated with graves (Evans-Pritchard 1949b, p. 57); the left side of purgative sacrificial objects is thrown away, sometimes into the bush. A full account of the vocabulary and grammar of Nuer symbolism would require a long paper in itself (cf. 1953; 1956, chap. 9). The main point here is that such physical attributes have acquired symbolic ritual ends. The social and ultimately psychological bases for such symbolic processes are too complex to be discussed here (cf. Beidelman 1964; 1966; 1968).

There are, however, two general points I wish to present here in relation to such symbolism: for Nuer it seems that moral man is an amalgam of two asymmetric, complementary sets of attributes (cf. 1953). It is not simply that a Nuer adult can, if he wishes, represent favorable and unfavorable, strong and weak, clean and polluting attributes by his active spear arm and his incapacitated left. Rather, because he himself contains both such sets of attributes, he embodies the alternatives which define moral conduct in a society.[3] Only adult Nuer men embody such a contrast, manifested in certain asymmetrical symbolic qualities, and only such men partake wholly of the moral acts of ritual and authority expressed in feud, mortuary rites, and property exchange. If women occasionally approach this status, it is only when sterility makes them somehow resemble men. In the symbolic motifs attached to a Nuer man, both his socially ideal self and his actual, flawed, private self are merged and yet distinguished. These are merged in one body, yet distinguished through the asymmetric categorization associated with his right and left, as well as through his appreciation of the differences between ideal norms and expedient behavior. Those attributes associated with the right, the ideal, are also associated with the spear, an extension separable from the body, just as a man's social self, embodied in his name and social reputation, has an independence and perpetuity partly outside himself and his personal conduct.

NUER SOCIETY AND THE DIVISIVE NATURE OF WOMEN

Nuer society may be divided into two groups: a) adult men with moral and jural authority; and b) children and women, who lack such authority and have a more passive status in domestic groups (1936b, p. 234). Adult men are ranked by age. In large part such rank corresponds to real power and formal authority, so that it is only with age that a man may succeed in accumulating sufficient cattle and children to become a leader, a founder of a settlement.

Some of the complexity in the social analysis of Nuer society derives from the discrepancies between certain Nuer ideals about social relations and actual Nuer practices. This contrast is particularly sharp between patrilineal relations in which ritual and political actions are expressed and kin relations (cognatic and affinal) in which ordinary domestic life is set:

For it is very apparent that there are two kinship configurations of persons among the Nuer; the ones consisting of their domestic interrelations have a relatively low degree of consistency and durability compared with the legal and, in our sense of the word, structural, interrelations. (1945, p. 65)

The underlying agnatic principle is therefore in glaring contrast to social actualities. But the actualities are always changing and passing while the principle endures. (1945, p. 64)

Traceable cognatic kin relations are *mar*; agnatic relations between groups which can no longer trace actual genealogical connexions but which maintain enduring political relations termed *buth* (1940, p. 193). Individual Nuer men struggle to increase their domestic groups, to gain followers and found their own settlements.

In time, successful men, especially if they belong to aristocratic clans, may become ancestors to lineage segments occupying a particular area; their names are memorialized as reference points in the articulation of political groups after death, their hectic personal machinations in the field of domestic kinship (*mar*) will then have been transformed into permanent political agnatic statuses (*buth*). "A man's memorial is not in some monument but in his sons" (1956, p. 162). "This is the only form of immortality Nuer are interested in. They are not interested in the survival of the individual as a ghost, but in the survival of the social personality in the name" (1956, p. 163). Nuer institutions of the levirate, ghost-marriage and even woman-woman marriage rest on such values (1956, p. 162). Perpetuation of the social self is often, though not invariably, in terms of these ideal symbolic extensions of the person, such as ox-names and spear-names (1953, p. 14-5; 1956, p. 62). At marriages, blood feud settlements, mortuary rites, adoption of Dinka clients, and in battle, agnatic groups are considered as exclusive corporate groups, and spear-names of such *buth* groups are emphasized. Then it is the general aspect of Spirit (*kwoth*) rather than its less absolute refractions, such as ancestral ghosts, that provides the moral reference (1956, p. 1962; 1953, p. 14). The interplay of ideal and real factors is revealed in Nuer domestic groups, especially in the contrast within three sets of relations: a) ideal and actual agnatic relations between men; b) husband-wife relations; c) paternal-maternal kin relations.

I consider these sets of relations briefly to indicate certain aspects of sexuality which seem to account, to Nuer, for their failures to live up to their moral ideals. All of these relate to certain ambiguous aspects of women's sexuality and men's relations toward women.

IDEAL AND ACTUAL AGNATIC RELATIONS BETWEEN MEN

Nuer can fit all local persons into one kinship scheme of cognatic (*mar*) and affinal relations (1951a, pp. 173-4); the inevitable differentiations in loyalty and property within ordinary relations are also expressed along lines of inclusion and exclusion of kin by preference and obligation. The patrilineal extended family, the most important Nuer social unit, partakes of both the ideal aspects of agnatic relations (*buth*) and the divisive, individualistic aspects of separate Nuer households (1950, pp. 39-41). Such groups of men are divided by women; uterine brothers are far more loyal to each other than to their half-brothers and ortho-cousins (1950, p. 42). Such potentially divided agnates engage in extravagant obscenity, often of an aggressive, homosexual nature possibly related to the preoccupations with uterine-based conflicts (1951a, pp. 160-1).[4] The term for ideal agnatic ties (*buth*) means "to share" (1956, p. 287), whereas the term for more divisive kin ties (*mar*) appears to refer to "mother," namely, the one who divides agnates (1934, p. 29). This may be why a lineage selects its master of ceremonies, *gwan buthni* (owner of *buth*), from a collateral lineage, a person not so likely to let uterine biases affect agnatic solidarity (1934, pp. 32-3; 1956, pp. 34, 287-8).

HUSBAND-WIFE RELATIONS

Nuer family relations seem rich in latent hostility between men and women (1950, p. 32). Evans-Pritch-ard remarks that his own experiences among Nuer suggested tranquil marital relations, yet he notes:

Nuer have told me that there is what we would call a latent hostility between husband and wife, and indeed between man and woman. They say that when a man has begotten several children by his wife he wants her to die, and may even pray for this to happen, for he does not want to die before her and another man to cohabit with her, rule in his home, use his cattle, and perhaps illtreat his children and rob them of their birthright. Men say also that women in their hearts wish for their husbands' deaths, and when a youth marries, his mother is said to warn him that when he visits his bride she may crouch to the right of the doorway to force him to enter to the left of it, which is the side of death. If she does this, he must order her to the other side. Nuer men also say that women have bad mouths and that evil comes out of them, and they account for this by a story which relates that the mouths of women used to be, before God changed their position, where their vaginas are now; and they say that women are sensual and fickle, God having at their request, as another story relates, cut their hearts in two so that one half might be added to the male organ to give them greater pleasure in coitus. There are other stories which suggest a deep-lying hostility toward women. (1950, p. 32; cf, 1951a, p. 133)[5]

A legendary bad wife brought the mosquitoes that torment humans (1938, p. 39) and some think women brought death.[6] There are no data on a woman's relations with her sons' wives, but one tale suggests conflict between such women over the sexuality and resources of the son-husband (Crazzolara 1933, pp. 212-8).

MATERNAL AND PATERNAL KIN

Were space to permit, oppositions of agnatic to uterine loyalties and values could be demonstrated by the terminology of Nuer households (Evans-Pritchard 1950, pp. 22-3); by Nuer comments on the conflicting loyalties of maternal and paternal kin (1950, p. 38; 1951a, pp. 139-40); by the contrast between the curses of maternal and paternal kin (1949d, p. 288; 1951a, pp. 164-5, 168) and, revealingly, in Nuer notions of incest, in which relations connected in some way with one's mother and her kin are far more heinous than any involving only agnates (1951a, p. 37; 1949a, pp. 91-2). Ironically, too, uterine agnates are pointed out as more loyal and dependable than non-uterine, collateral agnates (1950, p. 42).

These negative, divisive attributes of women are consistent with the sexual interpretation I advance for the symbolism of Nuer oxen and the Nuer fighting spear.

THE SPEAR AND MAN'S SEXUALITY

Evans-Pritchard describes the spear as an extension of the right hand and all it stands for: "It is a projection of the self, so when a man hurls his spear he cries out 'my hand' or the name of the ox with which he is identified" (1953, p. 4).

For the Nuer also the right arm stands for what is strong, virile, and vital and consequently for masculinity and hence for the paternal kin and the lineage. . . . The left side symbolizes evil as well as feminity, and there is here a double association, for the female principle is also associated with evil directly, as it were, and not merely through the convergence of feminity and evil in the concept of the left side. (1953, p. 5)

The fighting spear (*mut*) and an ox are the two significant objects given a Nuer youth after his intiation, when he emerges as an adult man. Ox-names and spear-names are used interchangeably. Attributes of male adulthood are concentrated in these two symbolic objects. With adulthood a Nuer man takes on moral responsibilities for his acts. These moral qualities are meaningful in terms of the social groups to which he belongs: his family, settlement, lineage and clan. The moral man subordinates some of his individual personal desires and aims to the interests of the members of these larger units. The spear is brandished at all important occasions at which the corporate lineage is involved; spear-names and ox-names should be shouted out then (1949a, pp. 86-7; 1953, pp. 15-6; 1956, p. 162). Evans-Pritchard suggests that the spear is the object symbolizing the clan because of these associations with war and sacrifice (1953, p. 17). This may be true, but I think it is only part of the explanation. The spear's function in effecting aggression and death in war and sacrifice and, symbolically, in shaving at certain rites (where a death from one status and birth into another is achieved), relates to its being a medial object of sexual significance. The term *mut* (fighting spear) also refers to ritual shaving (1953, p. 4), and the *mut nyier* (shaving of maidenhood) is the ceremony transferring the girl to the groom's group (1951a, p. 71). Nuer castrate with spears (1940, p. 33) and cut their oxen's horns with them (1940, p. 38).[7] The gift of a spear to a newly initiated youth conveys a new sacramental relation between him and cattle in which the spear as the instrument of death allows him to mediate with Spirit (1953, p. 11).

In Nuer rituals, phrases, and folklore, the spear has very obvious sexual connotations (Crazzolara 1953,

p. 17; Fergusson 1924, p. 112; Evans-Pritchard 1949a, p. 87; Stigand 1919, p. 225).[8] These aggressive sexual qualities are especially prominent in certain ceremonies between a man and his wife's kin (Evans-Pritchard 1951a, pp. 65, 72; 1948b, pp. 34-5; Jackson 1923, p. 105). In these ceremonies between affines the spear serves as a kind of symbolic, socialized penis[9] in which certain dangerous, medial aspects of masculine sexuality are expressed within ideal, moral limits. These aspects of a Nuer man's sexuality account for the fact that though Nuer men ordinarily go about undressed, a Nuer must cover his genitals in the presence of his affines (Huffman 1931, p. 37; Evans-Pritchard 1948a, pp. 3-4; 1949c, p. 74; Howell 1954, p. 89, 93; Fischer 1964). Elsewhere I discuss in detail the problem of Nuer nakedness and its relation to Nuer notions of sexuality and affinity (Beidelman 1968).

Among Nuer, as in all societies, sexuality is a source of powerful conflicts and ideological ambiguities. The negative aspects of such acts seem to be embodied in, to be projected onto, women; we have seen that even the size of the penis is of negative feminine origin. Nuer men express their own sexuality and "libidinous" impulses in terms of their affections toward women. The household which a man forms with a wife is the means by which he produces heirs, but that same woman serves to separate her sons from those he has produced by other wives; furthermore, a husband's loyalties toward his own extended households (defined by wives and their sons) often threaten to separate him from his other agnates. In their roles as wives and mothers, Nuer women are essential to perpetuating agnatic groups, but the sexual and maternal affections they generate in men often run counter to the ideal moral norms of a man's agnatic group. And it is men's own sexuality which makes them a part of such conflicts. A man's phallic sexuality is expressed sometimes in the aggressive, subordinating spear, sometimes in the motif of the quarrelsome bull (see below), sometimes in the association of the negative aspects of sexuality with its feminine goal. Ironically, it is by marriage and sexual union that the most powerful divisions in Nuer society threaten to occur. The resultant domestic group creates new loyalties which threaten the natal loyalties of the spouses involved; and with children it sets up divisions between husband and wife over the issue of paramountcy of agnatic or domestic loyalties. It is the symbolic recognition of these new configurations that accounts for the peculiar sexual and alimentary prohibitions (for Nuer, alimentation and sexuality are closely related, cf. Beidelman 1968) and other regulations associated with a first-born child.[10]

THE PARALLELS BETWEEN CATTLE AND HUMANS

There is a highly developed symbolic relation between Nuer and their cattle: they go through somewhat similar stages of development and, just as Nuer fall into social categories, such as children, women, adult men, influential adults (usually men), so, too, cattle fall into categories of calves, cows, oxen, and bulls. Consideration of the notions behind such parallels and the uses of different beasts in various rites and activities provides insight as to why oxen are required in Nuer sacrifice.

Evans-Pritchard has remarked that for the Nuer "Their social idiom is a bovine idiom" (1937, p. 214) and that their herds express all their significant social relations (1937, pp. 212-3). Livestock are the media by which men express their relations to one another. They are also the substance from which Nuer fashion the model for their relations.

Cattle express both the ideal and also the actual modes and relations by which Nuer see their world. They serve as the agents by which these two systems (which they embody) are resolved:

When, therefore, we seek to estimate what their cattle are to Nuer and how they see them, we have to recognize that they are the means by which men can enter into communication with God, that they are, as Father Crazzolara puts it, "the link between the perceptible and the transcendental." (1956, p. 271)

When Nuer give their cattle in sacrifice they are very much, and in a very intimate way, giving part of themselves. (1956, p. 279)

I consider each of the Nuer categories of cattle in turn: cows, bulls, and oxen.[11]

a) *Cows*: Nuer seem to equate cows with women. Nuer girls sometimes take ox-names from the bullcalves of the cows they milk, but these have negligible use (1956, p. 250; 1937, p. 213; 1960, p. 223). Nuer women take names from the cows they milk (1960, p. 223; 1956, p. 250). Women may receive only cows as their share of any bridewealth payments (1951a, pp. 75-6). Women and children are the only persons normally allowed to milk cows, but women must avoid livestock during their menstrual periods or after they have given birth. Then they may not milk nor even drink milk (Jackson 1923, p. 95; Huffman 1931, p. 57). Like women for lineages, cows are the essential means by which herds are perpetuated, and, of course, women and cattle are the two objects exchanged to establish domestic households. Cows provide the symbol for the continuity of an agnatic group, and honorific titles of clans and lineages refer to cows and not to bulls or oxen (Evans-Pritchard 1956, pp. 59-60).[12] Yet, these same herds are a source of conflicts which lead men to fail at times to meet various social ideals: "Cattle destroy people" (1938, p. 40). Nuer express this negative aspect of sexuality in terms of the quarrelling of bulls, which is said to account for agnatic cleavages (1950, p. 258).

One of the most important ways by which adult men are distinguished from uninitiated boys is that men may not milk cows. This task is reserved for boys and women. At initiation, when they are undergoing a transition to their new status, such youths are called hornless cattle (*cotni*), that is, neither cattle nor non-cattle, a term also apparently used for bald old men (Kiggen 1948, p. 63). It is said that initiates avoid all cattle

. . . though the fact that they drink milk suggests that the interdiction really concerns their relations to the oxen rather than to cattle in general, just as the interdiction on women drinking milk during their periods concerns their relations to cows and not to cattle in general. (Evans-Pritchard 1956, p. 255)

Nor are such new initiates allowed contact with pregnant women or their husbands (1936, pp. 234, 241; 1956, p. 256; Huffman 1931, p. 32). Dances held at such times are called *ruash* (a bull-calf between the time it is weaned and the time it is made an ox) (Evans-Pritchard 1956, p. 256). The acts and terms of such initiation involve considerable cattle imagery (1956, pp. 255-6). In these various prohibitions relating men and women to oxen and cows, the most important principle is a sharp division between adult men/women and boys and oxen/cows. At other periods a person is excluded from his bovine correspondent, as when menstruating women avoid cows and new initiates avoid oxen; this is because such persons are then "monstrous" beings betwixt any proper social category. (I discuss this in detail in Beidelman 1968)

b) *Bulls*: To Nuer, the whole bull embodies certain attributes of manliness and vitality which are admirable but, in a certain sense, not entirely moral. The term *tut* (bull) appears related to *tute*, to impregnate (Kiggen 1948, p. 302). It embodies the aggressive, ambitious aspects of each man's character which leads him to try to dominate others, to separate him from his agnates in order to found his own group which he may control (Evans-Pritchard 1950, p. 23; 1940, p. 179; 1951a, pp. 27-8). It is only "bulls" who, as men of authority, usually sacrifice oxen (1956, p. 287). Such qualities provide the impetus by which individual Nuer fulfill their individual ambitions within their social scheme; they are the modes by which Nuer groups expand and flourish, at the expense of Dinka or other Nuer tribal groups. Uterine brothers are bound together through the same herd and therefore it is not as likely that each is able to become prominent in his own right. But paternal half-uncles, paternal half-brothers, and paternal ortho-cousins are "bulls". Nuer say, "There is no incest among bulls" (1951a, p. 37).[13] They express this in terms of such men not sharing a common mother; common solidarity around a mother and the herd allotted to her household and derived from her daughters overrides all other potential kin loyalties or competition.

Nuer take pride in the violence of their bulls which seems to parallel the violent bravery of men:

Nuer say that if they do not castrate most of the bull calves the cows will get no peace and there would be continual fighting in the kraals and commotion in the byres. When a bull is old and can no longer stand up against a younger bull, he grazes by himself and not with the herd. Nuer do not discourage bulls from fighting. They scrape their horns with the shell of a giant land snail so that they will be sharp for fighting, for it is "manly" for a bull to fight. Bull fights are often cited in traditions as the cause of fission in a kinship group and of the migrations that result from it. (1937, pp. 229-30)

The awesome vitality of bulls may lie behind the expression *tut kwoth*, greatness (bull) of god (Kiggen 1948, p. 302).

c) *Oxen*: With his first owned ox, *thak gareda*, "ox of my cutting" (initiation), a Nuer youth takes on a moral status. He then continues to have some *dil thak*, favorite ox, all his life (1956, pp. 251-2).[14] "He makes tassels to hang from one of its horns,[15] and he loves to see it toss the tassels in the air with a swing of the neck" (1956, p. 251). He provides his ox with a bell, and he enjoys rubbing and cleaning his ox and leaping after it as it is led around his byre by a herdboy. Henceforward, the man has a *cot thak*, an ox-name:

A man shouts out the name of the favourite ox *(thak mec)* from which he has taken his name when he spears a man in war or an animal or fish in hunting. Also young men of about the same age call out their ox-names (with many embellishments) to one another at dances, often after a bout of duelling with clubs; and two lines of youths stand opposite each other and shower ox-names on one another preparatory to a spectacular jump into the air in unison. (1960, p. 223)

Such names are only used among men

of the same or near age-sets, for they are said to have egalitarian, solidary implications; it would be inappropriate to use such terms between men of different rank and authority (1960, p. 258), namely, persons involved in a "bull subordinate herd" relationship. If such a special ox dies, or if a Nuer secures another which he admires more, he may replace it, for "it is not the ox of initiation itself with which there is 'identification' but ox, the idea of oxen" (1956, p. 254).

Ox-names are essentially the names of men, males who have passed through the rite of initiation to manhood. Boys may take ox-names in play but only in imitation of their elders. Likewise, maidens may take ox-names, from bull calves of the cows they milk, but they are mainly used only between girls themselves and in the nature of a game, copying their brothers; and the names are short-lived. Married women use cow-names among themselves, but, here again, this is similitude, and it has none of the significance of the ox-names of men. Perhaps also here again the distinction between the copy-names of boys, girls, and women and those taken by men may be important because of its logical relations, which concerns our present discussion, to the fact that men, and not boys or women, are the sacrificial agents. The two sides of the standard equation are the human male and bovine male, man and ox. (1956, p. 250)

In this sense, only initiated men are jural persons. Sterile women sometimes approach masculine roles as magical experts and curers and as "husbands" to women; rarely they are even "bulls" and camp leaders.[16] Rarely, a woman may even be a prophet, but only if she is a barren, old woman who consequently resembles a man (1956, p. 307). Similarly, a sterile cow may be substituted at a sacrifice in place of an ox (1937, p. 214).

Nuer themselves often draw such parallels between cattle and men: I have already noted how ambitious and influential men are compared to bulls and how young initiates are compared to developing oxen. Nuer steers (never bulls or cows) often have their horns cut to be trained into shape:

It is remarkable also that Nuer compare to the initiation of youths the cutting *(ngat)* of the horns of favourite oxen (they are entire animals at the time) so that they will grow against the cut at fancy angles, generally in a curve across the muzzle *(magut)*. They say that the operation, which is performed before castration, is the *gar,* the cutting of the marks of manhood, on the young bulls. If the operation has not already been carried out before a father presents a young bull to his son at initiation it is likely to be one of the young man's first acts in the period immediately following his own initiation. I have noted earlier how soon after their initiation youths, if they can procure the metal, fasten bracelets up their left arms so tightly as to render them, for the time of their wearing, incapable of use, and that they also render useless the left horns of their favourite oxen by deforming them. (1956, pp. 256-7)

In initiation of cattle, a bull's sexuality and associated bellicosity have been subordinated in terms defined by society; in the initiation of men, the immature, nonjural youth is transformed into a jural man whose sexuality and desires are ideally subordinated to the ranking and discrimination of the moral order.[17]

Symbolic castration is expressed in the parallel between cattle and human initiation and mutilation; it is also expressed in Nuer emphasis upon the cutting of the ox's scrotum as the most important act defining agnatic kinship, and the equating of such moral bonds with sexual prohibitions; "A man who has cut the scrotum of your beast, if he has sexual relations with your daughter, he will die" (1940, p. 222). Such cutting, too, is more generally delegated to the man representing the lineage as a corporate group and embodies the moral obligations which unite its members (1956, pp. 288-9).

There is a Nuer tale which nicely suggests this equation of sexual submission to social, moral values. A social man (with cattle) links himself with an asocial man (of the bush); this social transformation is confirmed with the masturbatory castration and slaughter of a bull:

There is a myth accounting for a special ritual relationship between the Gaagwong lineage of the Gaat Gam Kiir clan and the Lek clan. Lek was a man who possessed no cattle but who lived in a hole he had excavated from an ant-hill. He used to kill elephants, buffalos, and other animals and lived on their flesh. Gaagwong, who possessed cattle, went to visit Lek one day and said to him, "Why do you live like this? Why don't you come and live with me at my home and lead the life of a man?" For a long time Lek refused to go home with Gaagwong but after receiving a promise that Gaagwong would not kill him he consented to go home with him. When they reached home Gaagwong gave Lek a male calf over which Lek proceeded to utter a conditional curse in the Nuer manner. He said, "Now we are related since I have come to live in your home. Our sons and daughters shall never intermarry and if a son of yours seizes the hand of a daughter of mine, or a son of mine seizes the hand of a daughter of yours, then both shall die." After making this invocation Lek said that he would slay the calf with a spear but Gaagwong said, "No, let us slay it with our hands." So Lek seized its penis and pulled and waggled it so that it urinated till there was no more urine left in the body. Then he continued to pull its penis till it urinated blood and died. (1935, p. 36)

Today, men of these same two clans are thought to suffer a castrating ulcer if they come into sexual contact with one another (Soule 1932, pp. 14-5). Sexuality embodies the ambiguity of human actions, their vital-

ity, but also their tendency toward morbid conflict. This is not important in the case of most women, who are outside the jural, ritual sphere, but it is crucial in defining the moral conduct of men. Removal or isolation of sexuality achieves, at least in terms of certain intellectual models, a temporary ordering and a clear expression of the moral dichotomy by which social ideals are framed. Desexualization may be seen as providing medial or synthetic objects between the ideal and actual spheres of existence. Such objects serve as basic models of the ideal ordering of a world subordinated to the moral concepts envisioned within a society. With these ideas in mind, perhaps the Nuer choice of sacrificial beast may now make more sense:

The sacrificial animal *par excellence* is an ox, and in important social ceremonies, such as weddings and those held for settlement of feuds, the victim must be an ox. Oxen are also sacrificed in times of general calamity, sometimes when people are dangerously ill, and occasionally to spirits. A barren cow may take the place of an ox. Bulls are only sacrificed in one of the rites closing a blood-feud, and occasionally, though only old beasts, in honour of a dead father. Except in these instances a male victim must be a neuter. If it is not, it is castrated before the rites begin. Fertile cows are only sacrificed at mortuary ceremonies, and then only for senior persons, as a tribute to their position in the community. It does not matter what is the colour of the victim, though in certain sacrifices there is a preference for beasts with certain markings. . .

However, Nuer have not large herds and could not afford to slaughter oxen on every occasion of sacrifice, so, except on such occasions as the slaughter of an ox is obligatory, they generally use wethers and castrated he-goats as surrogates. (1956, p. 202)

In hard times even a cucumber may substitute for an ox, but it is the idea of "ox" that Nuer have in mind (cf.

1951b, pp. 112-3; 1937, p. 214; Howell 1954, pp. 46-8).

Oxen or surrogate-oxen are sacrificed on occasions when members of Nuer groups convene to re-establish the moral order of things and conduct which, by some event, have been shown to be out of joint, or when they seek to clarify such order at a time of change in persons' social statuses. The neutered beast embodies moral, asymmetric order. Whole beasts are slain not to re-establish any such order but, rather, as acts of termination of certain statuses or existences, such as the death of a prominent individual, a "bull." The termination of a blood feud, in a sense, corresponds in part to such a mortuary rite in that the perturbed ghost of the slain man is laid and no longer figures in the world of his kin (now that blood-wealth will be used to secure a ghost-wife for that person). These aspects of a Nuer which are expunged from the memories of his group should be embodied in his bullness, in his desire for influence and authority. With his social death, this bullness is transformed into less morally ambiguous attributes, as embodied in an ox-name.

In this essay I have concentrated upon the sexual significance of the Nuer spear and ox. However, certain other objects associated with the ox also seem to have important ritual significance, for example manure ash, cattle horns and skulls, cattle tails, ox urine, and the caul or blood of sacrificial beasts.[18]

CONCLUSIONS

The preceding discussion suggests basic symbolic sexual implications in the Nuer choice of oxen as the primary objects for sacrifice. The moral nature of an ox, in terms of the asymmetrically ordered attributes embodied in it, is irreversibly achieved by castration. This symbolic aspect of castration requires explanation; this may be found through examining those aspects of sexuality which Nuer seem to relate to the ambiguous character of men's viable energy, leading them to act and yet also accounting for the failure of their acts to conform perfectly to the ideal models of society. These conflicts are also manifested in Nuer attitudes about nakedness in the presence of affines (Beidelman 1968). For Nuer, individuality with its libidinous sexual connotations is epitomized in the bull, whose sexuality is associated with ambition and divisive self-interest. Freud's comment on the symbolic efficacy of inhibited sexuality comes to mind with reference to Nuer notions of bulls and oxen:

Those sexual instincts which are inhibited in their aims have a great functional advantage over those which are uninhibited. Since they are not capable of really complete satisfaction, they are especially adapted to create permanent ties; while those instincts which are directly sexual incur a loss of energy each time they are satisfied, and must wait to be renewed by a fresh accumulation of sexual libido, so that meanwhile the objects may have been changed. The inhibited instincts are capable of any degree of admixture with the uninhibited; they can be transformed back into them, just as they arose out of them. (Freud 1960, p. 91)

Thus, for Nuer, the parallels are as in Table 22.1. The extraordinary attachment and sentiment which Nuer men express toward their spears and oxen conform to Freud's remarks:

Psychoanalysis, which illuminates the depths of mental life, has no difficulty in showing that the sexual ties of the earliest years of childhood also persist, though repressed and unconscious. It gives us courage to assert that wherever

TABLE 22.1

inhibited sexuality	uninhibited sexuality
social constraint and sharing	greed and uterine divisions
oxen	bulls
ideal, solidary groups (age-sets, agnatic society)	specific, actual attachments (lineage segments, settlements, families)
corporate, ordered, enduring relations	divisive, capricious, transient relations
homogeneous, ideal society (figured in terms of ancestral relations)	heterogeneous, actual society (in terms of present groups of living kin)
ox-names and spear-names and reference to clans	bull reputations and reference to offspring
asymmetric socialization of attributes (as neutered beast, altered horns and arms)	opposed, libidinous attributes (as a bull in a herd, as fertile cows, unaltered arms of boys and women, unaltered horns of bulls and cows)
ritual relations	mundane life

we come across an affectionate feeling it is successor to a complete "sensual" object-tie with the person in question or rather that person's prototype (or *imago*). (Freud 1960, p. 91)

Here the repressed feelings relate to men's uterine and domestic connections, an association which explains the otherwise puzzling association of spear-names and ox-names with the names of mothers' sisters (Evans-Pritchard 1951a, p. 167).

Evans-Pritchard makes the identification of Nuer oxen with Nuer men a crucial feature of his analysis of Nuer philosophy; this identification has an even closer, more complex parallel than his brilliant interpretation suggests. He draws no parallels between the castration of Nuer oxen and the moral subordination of Nuer male sexuality to social values. Indeed, sexuality has never entered his exposition of the Nuer, though I suggest that sexuality is at the very core of Nuer moral ideas.

The sacrifice of oxen may be considered in terms of two interrelated sets of socio-sexual symbols, the spear and the ox, both modes expressing certain symbolized attributes of the Nuer man. The ambiguity' of a Nuer man's sexuality manifests itself in both the hastate and bovine idioms.

The spear, as a socialized penis, represents the aggressive, superordinating aspects of the penis, the subjection of women to the demands of the agnatic group. Furthermore, it is the vehicle of death and it is only through the transformation by death that the ideal aspects of agnatic values are attained. This appears both in the common solidarities expressed in terms of warfare and feud (with the concomitant sanctions of ghostly curse), and in the transformation of cognatic (*mar*) to agnatic (*buth*) relations, memorialized in ox-names and spear-names of oneself as a pivotal ancestor in a segmentary political framework.

The ox is the socialized bovine male; it bears the weight, power and dignity of masculinity, but the negative aspects of bullness are removed. The individual libidinous aspects of Nuer are expressed in the concept of a bull (*tut*) which dominates its herd of cows and their calves, and for Nuer "bull" is the synonym for the powerful man responsible for intra-agnatic conflict, intrigue and division centering on uterine loyalties. Only with the extinction of such urges do men live wholly consistent to their agnatic ideals, and only in death is such an attainment possible. The castration of the ox with a spear creates such a living symbol of a social ideal, a kind of bovine monster betwixt-and-between the ideal of Spirit 'and the sexual actuality of Creation. In the spearing of an ox a Nuer expresses a kind of transfiguration, through immolation, of his sexual self and an anticipation of his own transformation, through death, into the agnatic ideal person which his own living domestic, sexual self cannot wholly be and, indeed, cannot wholly accept. This is not to suggest that Nuer consider agnatic ideals the only important values in their society. It is their recognition of their deep personal commitment to domestic values which conflict with these ideals that leads them to focus ritual upon the ambiguous tensions these cross-cutting values produce. The values of agnation are more inclusive and enduring than domesticity, but Nuer seem to recognize that these are less compelling in everyday life. Sexuality and death are combined in one complex ritual act which attempts to express some lasting meaning to the social inhibitions surrounding these forces of transformation. In this sense the death of an ox is both a symbolic model to Nuer men of the social processes of their society and also a kind of pledge to Spirit that Nuer remain aware of moral order, even though they cannot and do not wish to conform to it entirely in all stages of their everyday lives.

NOTES

1. This paper is the outcome of lectures on the Nuer given at Harvard University. Inevitably such analyses become critiques of the work of Professor Evans-Pritchard, the most distinguished anthropologist alive today. It is a tribute to the range and richness of his findings that one may use his own superbly detailed data to provide alternative or supplementary explanations. I present this paper with the deepest admiration for his work which is a measure of breadth and excellence attained by few in the history of the discipline.

The leisure and facilities for writing this paper were provided through the Center for Advanced Study in the Behavioral Sciences, the National Institute of Mental Health, and Duke University. I should like to thank Professor John Middleton, Dr. Rodney Needham, Dr. Terence Turner, and Professor Victor Turner for comments on various drafts of this paper. All the references are to Evans-Pritchard's publications unless stated otherwise.

2. Evans-Pritchard suggests that one account of this division is probably of Dinka origin, yet this seems to accord with Nuer thought. Death resulted from the separation of heaven and earth, due to the bad acts of hyena and durra-bird, two negatively regarded, medial creatures, the former allegedly bisexual and eating human dead, the latter a very destructive creature of the bush which consumes man's grain rather than feed in the wild (1956, p. 10).

3. The parallel is imperfect, but it may help the reader to compare this to Christian thinking about the soul and body, both amalgamated in one human being and yet accounting for certain discrepancies between ideal and actions.

4. Such homosexual obscenities have been suggested by some psychologists to relate to conflicts in identification and loyalties toward the two parents, a situation suggested for the Nuer.

5. Compare this to a Masai tale (Beidelman 1965).

6. A Nuer tale which Evans-Pritchard suggests originated with Dinka presents a woman as the source of death. The motif of transformation is a river (a similar motif in other Nuer tales) and the medial woman is barren or divorced (1956, pp. 20-1).

7. Evans-Pritchard reports that Nuer sharpen horns with snail shells (1937, pp. 229-30), but in the more serious operation of training ox horns, a spear is utilized.

8. In another Nuer tale, early man speared the mother of buffalo and cow: the two offspring sought revenge in different yet complementary ways, cow in man's settlements and buffalo in the bush. May one see the spear here as an agent in the division of creation into society and bush? (1965, pp. 268-9).

9. It is not clear whether Nuer attach any important attributes to the different parts of the genitals, such as a distinction between the prepuce and glans which is important in some African societies. Kiggen records *tang cul,* haft of the penis, vis. prepuce *(tang,* haft, as a spear haft, *tang mut);* he also records this same term as meaning glans (1948, pp. 67, 221, 289). We lack information to clarify this, but such terms do illustrate the hastate vocabulary of Nuer terms for the penis. Nuer seem to draw a parallel between the penis and the spear, as I suggested above. Evans-Pritchard states that young Nuer lengthen the prepuce up to half the penis' length (1947, p. 116) and that Nuer claim this is to prevent the prepuce tearing during coitus. Whatever the reason, we see from photos that Nuer prepuces often appear very long (1956, plate 12). Yet, what are we to make of the circumcised Nuer (1951, plate 4)? Nuer are said to circumcise to prevent a castrating disease caused by sexual contact between certain clans which should be separated (Soule 1932, pp. 14-5). No useful information is available regarding terms for the scrotum.

10. The recognition of this ambiguous (divisive yet creative) aspect of sexuality, often symbolized by the genitals, is the subject of brilliant analysis by Leach (1961, pp. 125-32) and Lévi-Strauss (1963, pp. 150-4). Such concepts are extremely widespread, perhaps universal, and one must recall the very famous example among Old Testament Jews (cf. Gray 1925, pp. 33-6).

11. In terms of the problem of distinguishing various concepts about livestock, much earlier published material on the Nuer is difficult to analyze since writers do not carefully distinguish between various types of cattle. Nuer usage hardly simplifies this matter since Nuer, like speakers of English, often refer to any bovine beast as a cow *(yang)* (1937, p. 235; Westerman 1912, p. 114). Nuer sometimes refer to a sacrificial ox *(thak)* as a cow *(yang)* (1956, p. 247).

12. Elsewhere, Evans-Pritchard seems to suggest that such names may refer to oxen as well as cows (1933, pp. 36-7). Cows are not dedicated to God but only to spirits, since dedication to God implies eventual sacrifice (1956, pp. 41-2). This may parallel the relation of spirits to divisions within various units of Nuer society, whereas God seems associated with more ideal unitary aspects.

13. But there is adultery; is this related to the custom of an accused adulterer swearing his innocence as he holds the testicles of a stud bull or ram? (Jackson 1923, pp. 105-6).

14. *dil,* pure, true, perfect, aristocratic.

15. In Evans-Pritchard 1940, plate 4, we have the only photo I know of a Nuer ox with tassels; it has a pair, one on each horn. Both horns of this ox curve downward, cf. below. The term *dhur* refers to the tips of cattle tails, to the tassel put on cattle horns, and to the tassels put on youths' heads (Kiggen 1948, p. 93).

16. In two of the three Nuer settlements which Evans-Pritchard discusses in detail, women reside who approach socially being men (1945, pp. 31-2; 1951a, pp. 17-8).

17. Durkheim parallels Freud in his analysis of institutionalized pain as a subordination of the inhibited self to the social morality (Durkheim 1934, pp. 312-7).

18. Such facts as the following suggest that certain bovine motifs merit further analysis: a) *ashes:* the spirit *biel* as associated with cattle ashes (Howell 1953, p. 86); and, in general, ashes from cattle dung are essential to most sacrifices (1954, pp. 1, 8). If no sacrificial object is handy, manure-ash may suffice (Crazzolara 1953, p. 75). Such ashes also incorporate a child into a lineage (1951a, p. 73; cf. Beidelman 1968). Ash rubbing does not accompany a mortuary or lightning-spirit averting ceremony, perhaps because the new statuses of such dead, as individuals, are outside Nuer life (1951a, p. 262). Instead, wood ash, rather than manure ash, may be thrown in the air to ward off a lightning-spirit (1951a, p. 56). In thunderstorms Nuer throw manure ash out of doors (Crazzolara 1953,

p. 94). The use of cattle ashes as an item of grooming by Nuer men may also have some symbolic implications since this is not done by women (1937, p. 236). b) *Cattle bones:* the horns and skull of a sacrificial beast are hung over the byre entry (Crazzolara 1953, p. 80), though we do not learn why. The horns of an ox slain to open blood-wealth payments are stuck in an earth heap (1934, p. 4). c) *Cattle tails:* the removal of tails from beasts has some unclear significance: if oxen's tails are cut off, such oxen are rendered useless for anything except slaughter (Stigand 1919, p. 176); before Nuer can drink milk of a cow which has borne a calf, they must cut off the tip of the calf's tail, the owner must spit on this and this tip is thrown over the cow's back (1937, p. 23), and the final cow sacrificed at the termination of a feud has its tail cut, (Jackson 1923, p. 103; cf. Beidelman 1966, for a comparison). d) *Body contents:* caul and blood from sacrificial beasts also seem to take on special incorporating attributes (1934, p. 51; 1956, p. 214; Crazzolara 1953, p. 80). e) *Cattle urine:* such urine serves many purposes for Nuer, but only ox urine is normally used in preparing daily food (1937, p. 221). I have found no practical, rational explanation of this since the hormones absent from ox urine do not seem to possess any pronounced chemical or taste properties which would justify this.

REFERENCES

Beidelman, T. O.
    1964 Pig *(guluwe):* An essay on Ngulu sexual symbolism and ceremony. *Southwestern Journal of Anthropology* 20: 59-92.
    1965 A Masai text. *Man* 65: 191.
    1966 Swazi royal ritual. *Africa* 36: 373-405.
    1968 Some Nuer notions of nakedness, nudity and sexuality. *Africa* 38: 113-132.
Crazzolara, J. P.
    1933 *Outlines of a Nuer Grammar* (Anthropos linguist. Bibl. 13). Mödling bei Wien: Anthropos Institut.
    1953 *Zur Gesellschaft und Religion der Nueer* (Stud. Inst. Anthropos. 5). Mödling bei Wien: Institut Anthropos.
Durkheim, E.
    1934 *The Elementary Forms of Religious Life.* London: Allen and Unwin.
Evans-Pritchard, E. E.
    1933 The Nuer: Tribe and clan 1-4. *Sudan Notes and Records* 16: 1-53.
    1934 The Nuer: Tribe and clan 5-7. *Sudan Notes and Records* 17: 1-57.
    1935 The Nuer: Tribe and clan 7-9. *Sudan Notes and Records* 18: 37-87.
    1936a Customs and beliefs relating to twins among the Nilotic Nuer. *Uganda Journal* 3: 230-238.
    1936b The Nuer: Age sets. *Sudan Notes and Records* 19: 233-71.
    1937 Economic life of the Nuer. *Sudan Notes and Records* 20: 209-45.
    1938 Economic life of the Nuer. *Sudan Notes and Records* 21: 31-77.
    1940 *The Nuer.* Oxford: Clarendon Press.
    1945 *Some Aspects of Marriage and the Family among the Nuer.* Lusaka: Rhodes-Livingstone Institute.
    1947 A note on courtship among the Nuer. *Sudan Notes and Records* 28: 115-126.
    1948a A note on affinity relationships among the Nuer. *Man* 48: 3-5.
    1948b Nuer marriage ceremonies. *Africa* 18: 29-40.
    1949a Nuer rules of exogamy and incest. *In* M. Fortes (ed.), *Social Structure.* London: Cambridge University Press.
    1949b Burial and mortuary rites of the Nuer. *African Affairs* 48: 56-63.
    1949c Two Nuer ritual concepts. *Man* 49: 74-76.
    1949d Nuer curses and ghostly vengeance. *Africa* 19: 288-292.
    1950 The Nuer family. *Sudan Notes and Records* 31: 21-42.
    1951a *Kinship and Marriage among the Nuer.* Oxford: Clarendon Press.
    1951b Some features and forms of Nuer sacrifices. *Africa* 21: 112-21.

1953 Nuer spear symbolism. *Anthropological Quarterly* 26: 1-19.
1954 The meaning of sacrifice among the Nuer. *Journal of the Royal Anthropological Institute* 84; 21-33.
1956 *Nuer Religion.* Oxford: Clarendon Press.
1960 Nuer modes of address. *In* D. Hymes (ed.), *Language in Culture and Society.* New York: Harper and Row.
Fergusson, V.
1924 Nuer beast tales. *Sudan Notes and Records* 7: 107-112.
Fischer, H.
1964 The clothes of the naked Nuer. *Int. Arch. Ethnogr.* 50: 60-71.
Freud, S.
1960 *Group Psychology and the Analysis of the Ego.* New York: Bantam Books.
Gray, G. B.
1925 *Sacrifices in the Old Testament.* Oxford: Clarendon Press.
Howell, P.
1953 Some observations on "earthly spirits" among the Nuer. *Man* 53: 85-88.
1954 *A Manual of Nuer Law.* London: Oxford University Press.
Huffman, R.
1931 *Nuer Customs and Folk-lore.* London: Oxford University Press.
Jackson, H.
1923 The Nuer of the Upper Nile Province, Khartoum. *Sudan Notes and Records* 6: 59-107.
Kiggen, J.
1948 *Nuer-English Dictionary.* London: St. Joseph's Society for Foreign Missions.
Leach, E.
1961 *Rethinking Anthropology.* London: Athlone Press.
Levi-Strauss, C.
1963 *Structural Anthropology.* New York: Basic Books.
Soule, C. B.
1932 *Some Nuer Diseases and Their Remedies* 1: 2. Nasir: American Mission.
Stigand, C.
1919 The story of Kir and the white spear. *Sudan Notes and Records* 2: 224-226.
Westermann, D.
1912 The Nuer language. *Mitt. Semin. Orient. Sprache* 15: 84-141.

23. LAW AND PERSONALITY: SIGNPOSTS FOR A NEW DIRECTION

JAMES L. GIBBS, JR.

James L. Gibbs, Jr., is Professor of Anthropology, Stanford University. Reprinted with permission from *Law in Culture and Society*, Laura Nader, editor, Chicago, Aldine Publishing Company. Copyright © 1969, by Wenner-Gren Foundation for Anthropological Research, Inc.

IN NADER'S REVIEW of the anthropology of law she correctly notes that in the ethnography of law "the tendency has been to treat the legal system as an institution virtually independent and isolated from the other institutions of society" (Nader 1965, p. 17). This is not the only oversight of the legal anthropologists. They have treated the legal system in isolation from the personalities of the members of society also. The magnitude of our blindness is indicated by the fact that even Nader (1965, p. 23) in formulating questions that point to new directions in the ethnography of law exhorts us to ask: "What are the manifest and latent jobs of the law and how are they related to the *social structure?*" (italics added). Bohannan (1965, p. 41), too, in answering his own question, "What should we and our students be doing?" makes the same omission.

If we rephrase Nader's question to read: "What are the manifest and latent jobs of the law and how are they related to social structure *and to personality dispositions?*" we bring the frame of reference of psychological anthropology to the study of legal systems. This step forces us to ask other new questions, and answering them will require us to refine our old methods as well as to develop new ones. This assumption was anticipated in a paper of Spiro's in which he cautioned that the functions of social systems should be explained more "by reference to their capacity for the gratification and frustration of personality needs (cf. Cohen 1966)" (Spiro 1961, p. 472).

The first part of this paper is a review of selected literature on law and personality. Next is a call for more research on law and personality. Some data from my own field research in this area conclude the paper.

STUDIES OF LAW AND PERSONALITY

The considerable body of research on the relationship between law and personality is scattered in the literature of such diverse disciplines as psychology (general, clinical, criminal, social, and legal); sociology (the sociology of law, and the sociology of deviance); anthropology (social anthropology —especially ethnolaw—and psychological anthropology); law itself (notably jurisprudence); and such related fields as psychiatry and social work. Obviously a complete review of this extensive literature is out of place here, but a rough mapping of the field can be sketched and some illustrative studies pointed out as landmarks.

Research relating law and personality is rarely global or holistic in scope, but usually posits a link between some particular aspect of "law" on the one hand and a specific aspect of personality on the other.[1] It then proceeds to examine this link. In broadest terms, the law-personality links that have been studied can be grouped into the following general categories that reflect fundamental dimensions of conflict. They are: (1) the psychic sources and functions of the breach of norms (including the societal incidence of the breach of certain norms); (2) the psychic sources and functions of institutionalized procedures for dealing with the breach of norms; and (3) the results of institutionalized counteraction to breach of norms.[2] Some studies representative of each of the categories are cited below.

THE BREACH OF NORMS

A series of studies of Western societies have noted that different social classes and ethnic groups show characteristic but different patterns of crime. For example, Kardiner and Ovesey's (1951) classic study of the American Negro sees drunkenness, one of the most common offenses committed by that group, as having roots in the ethnic personality.[3] Drinking in this subculture functions as an escape from the psychic pain of a societally instilled low self-image.

Winick, Gerver, and Blumberg (1961, p. 129) deal with the phenomenon of judges who breach norms of their profession by issuing what are "deviant" decisions. They state that "inconsistency between social class background and judicial attainment may have resulted in some unusual decisions and opinions." Implicit in this view is the assumption that this inconsistency results in certain intrapsychic tensions that are resolved by issuing a particular type of decision. Parsons (1962, p. 65), classifying deviant behavior among lawyers, notes that excessive formalism stems in part from the fact that "the legal profession probably has at least its share, if not more, of 'compulsive personalities.'"

Berndt's (1962) controversial study of law in the Eastern Highlands of New Guinea characterizes the ethnic personality of the Highlanders as showing admiration for and focus on power, strength, and physical force, as well as a fusion of aggression with sexuality. Some of the breaches in that culture, such as necrophilia and cannibalistic incorporation of sexual organs, are not only memorable for the reader, but patently rooted in Highland ethnic personality dispositions.

A germinal cross-cultural study by Bacon, Child, and Barry (1963) documents a similar hypothesis. The authors find a correlation between lack of strong male identity in men (and a derived defensiveness against a feminine identity) and a high incidence of theft and personal crime. Poggie (n.d.) shows that in Tepoztlán the high crime rate, which is rooted in weak male identity, is perpetuated by the role in socialization of the dominant male personality type.

Wife-beating and the wife's reporting to the authorities of the assaulting husband are both deviant acts in our society, part of a related syndrome studied by Snell and his associates (1964). They found that such behavior occurs in families where both the husband and wife have a need for role reversal; she, for punishment for her usual hostile, castrating activity directed toward her husband; he, for asserting his masculine identity, about which he has great anxiety. The beating goes unreported for years until an older son reaches adolescence and intervenes in his parents' fighting, an act that his physical size and re-activated Oedipal position makes potentially dangerous.

These and similar studies indicate that one level of explanation of the types of breach committed is a psychological one.

THE COUNTERING OF BREACH

The largest body of personality-law studies deals with the relationship between personality and institutionalized social control procedures for dealing with the breach of norms. One focus of research is the degree to which the decisions of judges in Western societies are reached by forming a personality-influenced, intuitive, overall impression of the case and its issues. Several studies have shown that the sentencing behavior for an identical offense varies from judge to judge (Winick et al. 1961, pp. 134-135). As early as 1923 it was suggested (Haines 1923) that personality factors are responsible for this variation, a conclusion supported by some of the autobiographical writings of judges who discuss the way in which they reach decisions (Winick et al. 1961, pp. 132-135). Thus the citation of precedents and legal reasoning rationalizes what is a more private, psychically colored process. This position is summarized well by Cowan (1962, p. 109), who refers to law as "a system for organizing and systematizing *feeling* judgments" (italics added).

The customary behavior (rather than deviant acts noted above) of the attorney in the dispute-settling process, like that of the judge, also has some psychic roots. Winick et al. (1961, p. 137) imply that there is some self-selection of trial lawyers in terms of their interest in the adversary system

with its focus on conflict and differences. The same authors (1961) and lawyer-turned-sociologist Riesman (1962, p. 37) note that attorneys have a strong component of egotism, which is satisfied in the "exhibitionism" of the courtroom (and for judges, in the fact that opinions are signed rather than anonymous [Winick et al. 1961]). It is obvious that there are also psychological bases for the self-selection of other lawmen such as policemen, jailers, and wardens (Frenkel-Brunswick 1954).[4]

There has been a good deal of recent research on jury processes in the United States, although most of it has been sociological rather than psychological. However, Winick (1961) reviews a series of psychological studies and cites those with findings directly relevant to understanding what he terms the "psychology of the jury." The studies, drawn from many fields of psychology, deal with the processes of projection, displacement, ability to make accurate judgments, recall, suggestibility, decision-making, and so on.

An anthropological study that relates personality dispositions to institutionalized reactions to breach is the study of New Guinea Eastern Highlanders mentioned earlier (Berndt 1962). The accepted forms of self-help to which the Highlanders turn to counter a breach of norms are markedly violent in flavor; warfare, suicide, sorcery, sexual assault, and cannibalism. Berndt sees this development as connected with the ethnic personality trends centering on physical force, aggression, and the fusion of sex and aggression. He also indicates (1962, p. 325) that those who render judgment in the informal courts of the Highlanders often mete out violent punishment, and that it "gives emotional satisfaction not only to the person administering the punishment but also to the complainant and the spectators." It is clear that Berndt is speaking of something other than Durkheim's (1933) concept of repression when he notes (1962, p. 312) that: "There is some reason to believe that if the punishment is not too severe it may also be suffered with some degree of *excitement* if not *pleasure* by the victim" (italics added). A case in point is the use of forced copulation as a way of shaming guilty adulterers, an action that, the field worker notes (1962, p. 336), expresses violence as well as providing indirect sexual stimulation to the Highlander judges, litigants, and spectators.

Hoebel (1954, p. 316), in discussing law among the tribes of the American Northwest Coast, cites Crane's (1951, p. 144) observation that "the big stick which is relied on in this control system [is] not physical punishment, but social attacks upon the extremely vulnerable egos of the members of the group." Further consequences of the ethnic personality's sensitivity to shaming are noted by Hoebel (1954, p. 316), who adds: "this same vulnerability leads to wanton killing and strains the legal machinery to the utmost."

Gibbs (1963a), in an analysis of the Kpelle moot as a forum for the settlement of marital disputes, states that it functions as successfully as it does because it stimulates and capitalizes on certain psychic responses in exactly the same manner as does group therapy in Western society.

In a comparative study of preferred modes of dispute settlement among the Gusii and the Nuer, LeVine (1960) observes that the Nuer prefer to settle disputes by a resort to physical force, whereas the Gusii, whose culture is similar in many ways, prefer to utilize the courts. The hypothesis offered to explain this discrepancy is that there is an underlying difference in ethnic personality and in related child-training patterns. The Gusii ethnic personality is characterized by an avoidance of the direct expression of aggression, and socialization patterns include an authoritarian concentration of power in the hands of the father. Among the Nuer the ethnic personality is one that values the direct expression of aggression, and socialization patterns involve an egalitarian locus and use of power.

More broadly cross-cultural studies also offer insight into certain features of the dispute settlement processes. Roberts (1965, pp. 205-206) in his exploratory cross-cultural study of oaths and autonomic ordeals finds that oaths are found primarily in societies where adults show anxiety about responsibility, a personality disposition that is rooted in the stress on responsibility training in the child-socialization procedures of those societies. Autonomic ordeals, on the other hand, are found in societies where adult anxiety centers more on obedience because of cultural stress on obedience training in socialization practices. Beatrice Whiting (1965), in a study that draws upon the concepts of Bacon, Child, and Barry (1963) mentioned earlier, seeks psychological roots for certain types of assault and concludes that a high incidence of certain types of physical violence can be interpreted as an expression in the adult male personality of "masculine protest" as a reaction against identification with women in infancy.

If we include judicial concepts as a significant aspect of the institutionalized procedures dealing with breach, as Bohannan (1957) rightly urges us to do, we should also cite Cohen's (1964) cross-cultural study, which relates the concept of liability to initiation rites and puberty. He finds that the presence of "several" (individual) liability for a wrong correlates with the presence of a sense of identity focused on the nuclear family, whereas the presence of "joint" (shared) liability is associated with a sense of identity focused on the wider kin group.

The studies that have been reviewed, diverse as they are, remind us that psychological hypotheses provide one order of explanation for a cultural preference for one mode of institutionalized reaction to breach as opposed to another. Similarly, psychological factors may also explain the existence of certain procedural features of social-control mechanisms.

RESULTS OF INSTITUTIONALIZED COUNTERACTION

Some writers have reminded us that the result of counteraction is not always the restoration of equilibrium. The counteraction may not end the deviance of the offender but may lead to a cycle of progressive alienation that may result in the commission of progressively graver offenses (Parsons 1951). Legal anthropologists have not systematically studied this "failure" of social control. However, Whitaker (n.d.) uses the Parsonian paradigm in discussing the effect of being convicted upon defendants in Chiapas courts. Noting that the convicted litigant may undergo an "identity struggle," she asks, "does the acceptance of the identity, wrong-doer, alienate the defendant and push him into a position where he will commit further deviant acts?"

A PLEA

The purpose in citing the research reviewed above is not to suggest that the psychological explanation is the only order of explanation we should seek in ethnolaw; it should be apparent to any behavioral scientist that psychological and socio-cultural explanations are not mutually exclusive. Nor is it my purpose to imply that the studies cited are without flaws. Many of them, for example, set forth "psychological" explanations without having measured the relevant personality variables in the individual with valid psychological indices (cf. Inkeles and Levinson 1954). Others ignore alternative explanations or confuse cause and effect. In the case of the cross-cultural studies, one can raise the usual questions about the completeness and comparability of the data.

I have soft-pedaled critical comment because legal anthropologists have almost completely neglected the contribution of such studies. Unless we believe that what has been cynically referred to as "gastronomic jurisprudence" is relevant only to our own society, we must ask more often than we have the question raised in the introduction to this paper: "What are the manifest and latent law jobs of the law, and how are they related to social structure and to personality dispositions?"

Even brief contemplation of the rephrased question germinates some profitable hunches. For example, where a litigant—whether he is Kapauku, Lozi, Arusha, or whatever—has a choice of settlement modes for harmonizing his dispute, to what extent will his choice among the alternatives reflect psychic as well as social structural factors? Further, a question is raised when Hoebel's (1964) work on the correlation between features of the law and societal subsistence levels is placed alongside Bacon, Child, and Barry's (1963) demonstration that there are different personality patterns associated with the basic societal subsistence modes. It must be decided to what extent Hoebel's "trends of the law" are rooted in psychic as well as economic and social features. Suggestive in this regard is Liberty's (n.d.) hypothesis that holds for the Cheyenne: "in societies where male model personality is disintegrating, or showing radical stress or adjustment to change, the 'trend of the law' (with increase of public over private law and kin-dominated dispute settlement . . .) may halt or reverse."

A NEW TREND

There are two portents of an awakening anthropological interest in law and personality. Nader (1965, p. 12) singles out as indicative of a new trend the publication of two cross-cultural law papers by anthropologists (Roberts 1965, Whiting 1965) that bring the Human Relations Area Files cross-cultural approach to bear on legal material. Perhaps it is not simply fortuitous that both these new-wave papers make use of psychologically oriented hypotheses.

An even more encouraging sign on the horizon is Swartz' (1966) study of the bases of political compliance among the Bena of Tanzania. In many ways his study is a model of the sort for which the present paper is calling. Swartz questions the Bena's obedience to the orders of their local political officials "even when doing so does not provide them immediate or direct gratification" (1966, p. 89). In particular, he is concerned with why the Bena take their disputes for settlement in adjudicatory hearings—barazas—by political leaders.

Swartz did measure personality variables in the individual, and from his analysis of motives concludes that among the Bena distrust and dependency are fused in a search for security. Bena seek aid and succor from their fellows in both specific and diffuse ways and yet do not trust each other to provide the expected support. Moreover, they are reluctant to express even indirect hostility because they are fearful of return counter-hostility. Even within the nuclear family the three common Bena goals of getting aid and succor, avoiding distrust, and escaping hostility are difficult to achieve because of the relative absence of community of interests.

Why, then, do the Bena turn to the courts? Swartz suggests that the baraza satisfies Bena dependency needs by insuring that one's kinsmen do as "they ought to do." Thus, even though they may not do so out of kin loyalty, they will do so because of the external control of the court. The courts also reduce the fear of hostility from others because they are believed to short-circuit the process of retaliation and counter-retaliation. The baraza gets disputants to forswear their grievances, to eschew hostile counteractions, and to re-establish harmonious relations.

Swartz' analysis indicates that the Bena's motives for agreeable, winning behavior are harnessed in the procedures of the baraza so that the parties are likely to tell the truth and to come to agreement on the facts and the appropriate solution. As Swartz puts it: "the disputants are motivated not only to participate in [the adjudications] but to participate in such a way as to increase the likelihood of their success." He adds: "Successful adjudication does not remove the distrust and conflict from within the community, nor does it obviate the fear of others' hostility. However, the adjudication removes these desiderata from being the individual's unaided concern and brings them out where they can be subjected to broad social pressures. When they succeed, the adjudications do not ensure complete harmony, cooperation, or freedom from fear, but they provide a *social* mechanism that ameliorates the failure of attainment of these goals on a strictly *interpersonal* basis" (1966, pp. 104-105; italics added). In Swartz' view a key aspect of the *baraza* is the fact that the Bena feel it is objective, allowing a solution to emerge rather than imposing one. Swartz, like the Bena, seems to feel that the *baraza* is objective, and he traces this objectivity to the way in which the hearings capitalize on and manipulate the dispositions of the most common Bena needs. In any case, Bena *barazas* are strikingly consensual in flavor and show a basic mechanism markedly parallel to what I describe as underlying the Kpelle moot (Gibbs 1963b).

Finally, it should be noted, Swartz concludes that the dispute-settling process of the *baraza* bestows legitimacy upon the political official who represents and organizes the process (1966, p. 108).

Swartz is concerned *primarily* with the political consequences of the Bena adjudicatory process and sees the adjudicator's role more as political than as legal. Nevertheless, his study is an important contribution to the ethnography of law because he is concerned explicitly with the psychological as well as the structural factors that shape legal procedures.

LAW AND PERSONALITY AMONG THE KPELLE

Partly in response to my own plea, I am in the midst of a long-term study of law and personality among the Kpelle of Liberia that incorporates the basic assumptions of the present paper.[5] Some preliminary findings follow.

THE KPELLE: AN ETHNOGRAPHIC SKETCH

The Kpelle are a Mande-speaking, patrilineal group of some 300,000 rice cultivators who live in central Liberia and the adjoining regions of the Republic of Guinea. In contrast to many African societies, strong corporate patrilineages are absent among the Kpelle. The relatively minor role of descent groups is explained partially by the presence of secret societies—notably the tribal fraternity, the Poro Society, and its sister organization, the Sande Society for women. The functions of these exotic societies, strongly diagnostic of the culture area of which the Kpelle are a part, have been much discussed in the anthropological literature. Among these functions are political ones (cf. Little 1965-1966). Other political functions inhere in the secular political structure, which is centralized. Although there is no single king or paramount chief, there are a series of paramount chiefs of the same level of authority, each of whom is superordinate over district chiefs and town chiefs. The Kpelle form of political organization can be termed the polycephalous associational state.

The structure of the formal Kpelle legal system parallels that of political organization. In Liberia the highest court of a tribal authority and the highest tribal court chartered by the government is that of a paramount chief. A district chief's court is also an official court. Disputes may be settled in these official courts or in unofficial courts, such as those of town chiefs or quarter (clan-barrio) elders.

Parallel to and overlapping that legal structure is another system of courts that was added in 1964, with the introduction of the Liberian county system to the interior regions of the country (previously administered by a type of indirect rule). The newer courts are those of the justices of the peace, magistrates, county commissioners, county superintendents, and the circuit courts of appeals. In some areas paramount chiefs hold appointments as justices of the peace, thereby creating a fusion of the two court systems at the lowest levels. Thus, Kpelle litigants have a whole series of courts to which they may carry their grievances. In addition to this, disputes are settled informally by associational grouping such as church councils or cooperative work groups as well as by the secret societies.

The systematic study of Kpelle personality is the aim of a forthcoming phase of the present research. Until it is completed, it is useful to draw a highly tentative outline of some of the features of Kpelle ethnic character based, faute de mieux, on inferences from cultural data. The Kpelle ethnic character includes the following traits: deference to authority, dependency, lack of ability to cooperate easily with other people, detachment, autonomy, preference for indirect forms for expressing aggression, male feelings of inadequacy vis-a-vis women, practical orientation, self-concept centering on work, instrumental orientation, manipulativeness, secretiveness, and suspiciousness.

THE LEGAL DATA

This section of the paper is based on data collected during two field periods. The first field period, seventeen months in 1957-1958, provided a description of Kpelle social organization and the Kpelle legal system. The second field period, which involved a more narrow problem orientation (the relationship between law and personality) covered twelve months in 1965-1966. Specifically it contributed additional quantitative depth for the analysis of Kpelle disputes. To provide this depth, a case inventory was completed for courts in Fokwele, Panta Chiefdom (the primary research site) and Gbarnga (the chiefdom's county seat). The complete case inventory includes elemental data on 1,967 cases. In addition, a census survey of Fokwele provides data on 999 other cases in the form of self-reports.

Although the case inventory currently undergoing analysis contains an impressive number of instances, the data on the cases are disappointingly uneven because of the nature of record keeping in Kpelle courts. Most often there is no record at all, the only documentary evidence that a hearing took place being the presence at a writ of summons or subpoena. Decisions are often not recorded. Similarly, when a recorded decision indicates, for example, that damages are to be paid at a later, specified date, there is often no recorded follow-through. Except in higher courts, there is usually no indication whether a case was heard de novo or on appeal. Ethnic affiliation, age, sex, and home town of litigants are not recorded, although some of these attributes can often be inferred either from knowledge of the culture or from the internal evidence of the case or from both. The implication for the present research of this pattern of record keeping is that, even with a large sample of cases with which to work, it is sometimes impossible to glean enough cases with comparable, complete data from which indices can be constructed to quantitatively test hypotheses of the sort listed below.

Fortunately, however, the large body of varyingly complete cases in the case inventory and the self-report inventory are supplemented by other cases for which there are more complete data in the form of tape-recorded case transcripts or informants' accounts. All these sources of legal data are utilized in the analysis and discussion below.

THE PRELIMINARY HYPOTHESES

The 1963 research proposal for the 1965-1966 law and personality study included the following hypotheses, which were tested in the field period.

1. The Kpelle preference for the indirect expression of aggression will be reflected in: (a) failure to fulfill a commitment as a common offense; and (b) a tendency to sue a person for a reason other than that revealed in court.

2. A high incidence of disputes about rights over women is rooted, not only in structural factors (cf. Gibbs 1963b), but also in male feelings of inadequacy vis-a-vis women.

3. Authoritarian submission will be reflected in a tendency to acquiesce in a judge's decision in the courtroom; but, when out of authority's view, to appeal the case.

4. Ordeals and conditional oaths will be resorted to when there is an absence of proof or conflicting testimony that there is no more "rational" way of resolving. But conditional oaths will be resorted to also when the offense is one which, analytically viewed, is an attack on self-identity as defined by the Kpelle.

5. Individuals whose personalities show a high level of hostility or blocked aggression will tend to be involved in litigation repeatedly; further, they will be more likely to appeal cases they have lost in the first hearing.

FREQUENCY OF DISPUTE TYPES IN KPELLE LAW

The analysis of the case inventory described above is still in process, but a picture of the frequency of various types of disputes can be obtained from the census survey of Fokwele conducted in 1965-1966. Household heads were asked to report the number of times they and each adult member of their household had been involved in disputes that were aired either in a court or in a moot (house palaver). They were also asked to describe very briefly each of the disputes reported. A frequency distribution for the disputes reported appears in Table 23.1.[6]

Some explanation of the case categories included in Table 23.1 and the way in which they were devised will make the subsequent analysis more meaningful. The census-survey protocols were given a content analysis, and an extensive classification of dispute types was constructed. Each of the self-reported cases was assigned to as narrow and specific a category as possible. The general, more inclusive categories that appear in Table 23.1 and the narrow, specific categories were derived from the actual universe of reported cases. Thus, both the detailed taxonomy and the general categories into which it is divided emerge from the data rather than being imposed upon it. As will be noted below, where categories were not clear, specific dispute types were categorized as the Kpelle categorize them, making the heuristic scheme

used here both emic and etic. However, the broader Kpelle categories turn out to be rather congruent with those from the common law.

The content of each of the twelve general categories of dispute types will be briefly noted.

Rights Over Women (*"woman palaver"*). The first category refers to certain types of sexual, marital, and personal wrongs, such as adultery or allegations of adultery, divorce, refusal of sexual access by the wife, and non-fulfillment of specific wifely duties. It

TABLE 23.1
FREQUENCY OF DISPUTE TYPES IN KPELLE COURTS AND MOOTS

	Courts		Moots		Total		Rank Order
	n	*%*	*n*	*%*	*n*	*%*	
1. Rights over women ("women palaver")	253	53.4	168	32.1	421	42.2	1
2. Derivative rights over women	. . .	. . .	17	3.2	17	1.7	11
3. Other conjugal disputes	9	1.9	146	27.9	155	15.5	2
4. Derivative conjugal:	0	0.0	40	8.0	40	4.0	7
(a) Co-wives	(0)	(0.0)	(35)	(7.0)	(35)	(3.5)	
(b) Affines	(0)	(0.0)	(5)	(1.0)	(5)	(.5)	
5. Discord in family of orientation	1	.2	28	5.4	29	2.9	10
6. Supernatural assaults	. . .	. . .	2	.4	2	.2	12
7. Other wrongs against the person	40	8.4	16	3.1	56	5.6	5
8. Nonperformance of an obligation:	70	14.8	10	1.9	80	8.0	4
(a) Debt	(36)	(7.6)	(6)	(1.1)	(42)	(4.2)	
(b) Other "breach of contract"	(13)	(2.7)	(4)	(.8)	(17)	(1.7)	
(c) Failure to fulfill an obligation to government	(21)	(4.4)	(. . .)	(. . .)	(21)	(2.1)	
9. Using or transferring the property of others without permission	20	4.2	13	2.5	33	3.3	8
10. Other property disputes	22	4.6	8	1.5	30	3.0	9
11. Other	39	8.0	47	9.0	86	8.6	6
12. Incomplete, nonclassifiable	21	4.4	29	5.5	50	5.0	3
Totals	475	99.9*	524	100.2*	999	100.0	

* Percentages do not total 100% because of rounding to tenths.

includes cases of improper marriage (for example, when the alleged wrong is the improper transfer of bride-wealth), and cases where a woman's guardian is sued to determine if bride-wealth has been paid for her. Beating or verbal abuse of the husband by the wife is classed here rather than in the third category because this method fits the Kpelle way of thinking. In such a case a woman is violating her duty to be overtly submissive *to* her husband, not asserting a right to be assertive over him. The case will be viewed as stemming from a fault of the woman rather than from a lack in the man.

Derivative Rights Over Women. The second category refers to disputes that do not involve the operation of the marriage itself but are closely related to its formation. Generally the disputes raise issues that are not specific enough to be taken to court or that are not amenable to traditional legal sanctions. Thus, cases in this category are heard only in moots (house palavers). Such issues as the moot is expected to air include whether a person should marry, whom a particular person should marry, or how bridewealth should be raised. There are relatively few of these cases, and an argument could be made for grouping them with the first category, "rights over women."

Other Conjugal Disputes. The classification of other conjugal disputes refers to arguments that, if we used a more Western oriented, etic approach, we would categorize as *"man* palaver," since they involve wrongs against women committed by men: the husband's refusal to consort with his wife, nonsupport by the husband, nonfulfillment of other specific husbandly duties, beating or verbal abuse of the wife. Because of the androcentric bias that characterizes Kpelle treatment of spouses' rights over each other, these cases are aired largely in moots.

Derivative Conjugal. The fourth category subsumes disputes that center on a marriage but do not involve a husband-wife pair but other parties to a marriage—either co-wives or a spouse and his or her affines. Thus, it includes discord between co-wives centering on accusations of jealousy or verbal abuse and in-law problems involving either spouse's mother.[7]

Discord in the Family of Orientation. This is a grouping that includes wrongs such as nonsupport by a parent and beatings or verbal abuse by a parent or member of the nuclear family other than a spouse or co-wife. This category is used in order to distinguish marital discord (categories 1 through 4) from other types of family discord.

Supernatural Assault. This minute rubric covers cases of accusation of sorcery or witchcraft. Because of the difficulty of proof there is no doubt that there are more allegations mentally phrased than are ever actually articulated in moots or courts.

Other Wrongs Against the Person. This category refers to various types of assault against the person that are not directly or derivatively marital: beating or verbal abuse by peripheral kinsmen or nonkinsmen, other physical assaults, and actual or attempted homicide.

Nonperformance of an obligation. This includes three subcategories. The first, *debt*, contains cases in which the offense is nonpayment of a monetary obligation. Cases in the second subcategory, *other breach of contract,* involve nonfulfillment of a specific or implied contract—for example, where a person has agreed to thatch a roof in return for a payment he has received and yet refuses to provide the service or to return the payment. Also included here are cases in which a court has ordered a payment, such as adultery damages or return of bridewealth, and the order has been ignored. By including this last type of case here we follow Kpelle thinking, which stresses the unmet obligation to the other party rather than the obligation to the court. *Failure to fulfill an obligation to government* is the last subcategory. This may consist of non-payment of hut tax, refusal to perform public works duty, or contempt of court for ignoring a summons or failure to appear in court as a bondsman or witness.

Using or Transferring the Property of Others Without Permission. The ninth category includes such wrongs as borrowing and not returning property and misappropriation of funds or goods (including embezzlement).

Other Property Disputes is a category that includes cases of misappropriation of land, of livestock's damaging crops, and of theft. The number of cases is smaller than one would expect from a middle-level horticultural society in Sub-Saharan Africa.

Other. There is a residual category for cases that fit nowhere else and are primarily singular, so that they cannot be combined into additional significant rubrics.

Incomplete and Nonclassifiable cases are those for which the interviewer's report of the informant's accounting of a case is too incomplete or too ambiguous for classification.

TESTING THE HYPOTHESES

Judicial Implications of Indirect Expression of Aggression. The self-reported cases from Fokwele and a review of the larger case inventory indicate that the judicial results of the indirect expression of aggression were more wide-ranging than predicted in the original first hypothesis. It suggested that the Kpelle dislike of expressing aggression directly, as in physical assault, will be reflected in failure to fulfill a commitment as a common offense and a tendency to sue a person for a reason other than that given in court.

At first glance the incidence of non-performance of an obligation tallied in Table 23.1 seems small. But the rank order of frequency is fourth, and it is the most frequent single category of breach apart from woman palaver and other conjugal disputes.[8] This finding confirms the first condition of the hypothesis. A review of some actual cases reveals the underlying causal relationships.

The Case of the Delinquent Market-woman. In a typical case heard before a justice of the peace, the defendant, Kɔtu,[9] was a woman who had borrowed six dollars[10] from the male plaintiff, Zo Gbelai, in order to engage in petty trade. After four months she had failed to make a report of the earnings, as she had promised, or to return any of the capital. Her backer sued in order to recover his investment and a portion of her profits.

A lender always makes a loan in the presence of witnesses, inasmuch as Kpelle society is basically non-literate, making the use of promissory notes cumbersome. Thus the borrower is almost certain to lose his case if the dispute is taken to court because the lender's witnesses confirm the existence of the obligation. He then has to repay the loan as well as the courts costs.

Why does a litigant allow himself to be placed in a position so disadvantageous from the point of view of the economics involved? The hypothesis suggests that it is because of the somewhat ulterior (and largely unconscious) motivation of the defendant. David Aberle (personal communication) has suggested an alternative explanation: that in a culture making the transition from a subsistence economy to a cash economy individuals commonly perform acts that seem highly uneconomic simply because they are undergoing a type of monetary socialization.

Aberle's suggestion is plausible, and it and the present hypothesis are not mutually exclusive. However, a look at further Kpelle cases heightens the feeling that another factor beside economic motives or monetary inexperience is involved. This idea is suggested initially by the fact that often very small sums of money are at stake.

The Case of the Indebted Fisheater. Dennis Flumo sued Yakpawolo before a justice of the peace. The words of the complaint on the writ speak for themselves: "That defendant Yakpawolo of Gbarnga is justly indebted to him in the sum of $0.36 for two tins of fish, notwithstanding plaintiff has made repeated demands for payment, defendant has failed so to do. Plaintiff prays for redress."

In one case a father sued a son for failure to provide services in return for expenses the father had incurred on the son's behalf. In Kpelle society, as in our own, to sue a kinsman is unusual. There such a case would normally be heard in a moot, if at all.

Finally, it should be pointed out that the failure to fulfill an obligation takes forms other than reneging on a debt, notably failure to perform a service. For example, a typical case involved a man who agreed to make some doors for $16.00, accepted $15.40 in payment, and failed to construct the doors or to return the payment.

The cases cited above supply some of the connotations implicit in the rubric "failure to fulfill an obligation" —connotations that gave rise to the hypothesis. In the case of the father who sued his son, it is clear that something other than the actual tangible obligation must have been involved. Similarly, in the Case of the Indebted Fisheater, the loser had to pay not only the debt of 36 cents, but also court costs of at least $8.50. I suggest that the defendant did not renege on paying the 36 cents for lack of money or for lack of skill in the handling of money. For whatever reason, he wished to cause the shopkeeper some difficulty, even though it would hurt him in his own pocketbook. Then, too, the shopkeeper must have had more than his 36 cents in mind when he went to the trouble of instituting suit. On one level, many cases of this sort represent Kpelle instrumentality, the attempt to get more from the other person than he gets from you. If someone will let a friend forfeit on repaying an obligation without pressing him, that is the debtor's good fortune, and a Kpelle does not expect to meet an obligation until he is asked to do so or even until he is pressed by the person to whom he is obligated. On another level, we see the failure to honor a commitment as serving to express aggression indirectly, as is most apparent in those cases in which a person fails to meet an obligation even after being pressed repeatedly.

Finally, the two needs are not mutually exclusive. The high incidence of reneging may simultaneously gratify both needs widespread in the Kpelle population: the need to manipulate others to one's own end and the need to channel aggression obliquely.

The hypothesis suggests that suing a person for a reason other than the one stated in the complaint and allegations is another manner in which Kpelle express aggression indirectly.

The Case of the Defaulting Workman. In the case of Flumo Zao (plaintiff) versus Sua Kweli (defendant), heard before a district chief, this dimension emerges baldly in the words of the writ of summons: "That you, Sua Kweli, have failed to repair Pl. Flumo Zao's house and you have his wife." In this instance both the overt and more covert grievance are listed. However, more characteristic is the following case to which the hypothesis applies, where the covert grievance does not emerge.

The Case of the Vengeful Shopkeeper. Tokolong Dolo (plaintiff) sued Wua Lopu (defendant) before a justice of the peace in an "action of debt for the sum of 50 cents being value for a tin of carbide which [you]• have failed absolutely to pay for." However, the case was more complicated than these words of the plaintiff's formal complaint indicated.

My inquiries into the background of the case indicated that Wua had bought the 50 cents can of carbide from Tokolong Dolo's small shop on credit. Wua is the *koti* for the quarter in which he and Tokolong live. The *koti* is the tribal authority responsible for seeing that the members of the quarter carry out their primary obligations to the central government—paying taxes and reporting periodically for the public labor in lieu of taxes which the Kpelle often refer to as "government work."

Wua in his capacity as *koti* has exempted Tokolong from public works duty because he operates a shop for which he pays a license fee to the government. Tokolong's father, Nang Ba, was also exempted because of his extreme old age. Because of these exemptions the *koti* had granted him and his father, Tokolong did not press Wua Lopu for payment of the 50 cents.

One day a small detachment of soldiers came to town, and it was Wua's quarter's turn to lodge and feed them. Everyone in the quarter, except Tokolong's father, had gone to his farm. Wua told the soldiers that the old man was obligated to feed them because he and his son were exempted from other public works duty. But the old man had no food and the soldiers beat him.

When Tokolong came home from the farm, the old man told him what had happened. Tokolong said, "I won't sue Wua for letting them beat you. But he has owed me 50 cents for a long time, and I haven't bothered him about it. So I will sue him for the 50 cents."

In the court hearing Tokolong never even mentioned that beating of his father. Wua admitted that correctness of the debt charge, and agreed to pay the 50 cents, court costs, and expenses.

This case is a very clear-cut example of use of a cover grievance in bringing suit. Suing for other than the stated reason is reflected in a concomitant descriptive attribute characteristic of the configuration of Kpelle dispute settlement—frequent long delays between the time of the alleged wrong and the time of filing suit. Such a delay is often a cue to the fact that a long-smoldering grievance has been revived to serve as the means for countering a more recent act committed by the offending party. Normally the cue can be verified only for those cases for which the researcher has more than the court records as a source of information and can obtain a more complete account of events.

The syndrome of failure to state the actual reason for bringing suit is often also reflected in cases thrown out of court for "suing without sufficient reason."

Other manifestations of the indirect expression of aggression that appear in the configuration of dispute settlements are: (a) failure to honor a promise to a litigant to appear as a witness on his behalf; (b) a plaintiff's suing and subsequently failing to appear in court for the trial; (c) verbal aggression (called "abuse" by the Kpelle) and supernatural aggression; (d) adulterous actions directed at the wives of another man. These manifestations were not predicted by the original hypothesis but emerged from analysis of case incidences summarized in Table 23.1.

Examination of some additional cases sheds light on the subhypothesis that actions directed at another man's wife can be a vehicle for the expression of aggression or hostilty. Adultery and divorce cases, lumped by the Kpelle as "woman palaver," most often reveal a flavor of desire for the woman combined with hostility directed against the husband.

The Case of the Amorous Herbalist. Mulruba (plaintiff) sued Surong Tei (defendant). Mulruba's wife, Nowai, had a headache for a week, and she asked him to take her to the clinic for treatment. He demurred, saying that he would make medicine for her himself. He then left, saying that he had to go to his farm but that he would see about the medicine when he returned.

Surong Tei was a friend of Mulruba's and, according to local gossip, the lover of Mulruba's wife. Surong Tei saw Nowai looking unwell and asked what the trouble was. She told him, and he suggested that she accompany him to the bush, where he would show her a leaf for preparing medicine for her headache.

While they were gone, Mulruba returned and people told him that his wife had gone into the bush with his friend. When the couple returned, Mulruba asked Surong Tei why he had taken Nowai into the bush without his permission. He added that this action confirmed the tale that Surong Tei and Nowai were lovers and that, accordingly, he would sue Surong Tei.

Mulruba sued for damages in a complaint holding "that you the above defendant have administered medicine on [sic] the plaintiff's wife without telling him, which was very illegal." Surong Tei was found guilty and fined 25 dollars. The case was treated by the justice of the peace as a criminal matter, the fine being paid to the government.

In analyzing the case, it is important to know that the Kpelle feel that normally a man and woman who are not husband and wife should not go to the bush together, even if they are brother and sister. If they do, the assumption is that they have engaged in sexual intercourse. This explains Mulruba's reasoning and consequent acton. In addition, Surong Tei assumed a role that is expressly allocated to the husband—that of providing medicine for an ill wife. Thus his actions were doubly demeaning of Mulruba.

I have argued elsewhere (Gibbs 1963b) that the status of Kpelle men is highly dependent on the economic contribution of their wives, especially in polygynous households. Thus, when one man acts to seduce another man's wife, he is attacking not only that man's self-identity as a sexually and conjugally adequate person, but also his means to high status and therefore his psychic security. In short, Kpelle men use actions toward women not only as a means of asserting power over women, but also as a way of communicating their negative feelings and power needs toward their fellow males.

Examination of the frequency distribution of dispute types and of some individual disputes indicates that the first preliminary hypothesis can be extended. It can be rephrased as follows. Among the Kpelle the need to discharge aggression or hostility is reflected judicially in a relatively high incidence of the following type of offenses: (a) failure to fulfill a commitment; (b) tendency to sue for a manifest stated grievance rather than the covert one that actually troubles the plaintiff; (c) woman palaver, much of which begins with adulterous actions directed at the wife of another man. Aggression may also be discharged through offenses with a relatively low frequency, such as verbal aggression and supernatural assault.

In Llewellyn and Hoebel's (1941) terms, the preference for the indirect expression of aggression provides the Kpelle legal system with much of its "law work"—in particular with a substantial percentage of its disputes. To be sure, structural as well as psychological factors are at work. Thus the question can be raised concerning the structural factors producing the recurring strains that are resolved by this patterned discharge of aggression in courts and moots. I have done this for woman palaver in a previous paper (Gibbs 1963b).

This type of hypothesis is similar to the one advanced by LeVine (1960). As noted in the review of the literature above, he explained the difference in the overall incidence of litigation among the Nuer and the Gusii in terms of a differential preference for the direct expression of aggression.

The present study indicates that the judicial implications of modes of discharging aggression are more sweeping than the LeVine study suggests. More results from different styles of expressing aggression than merely a preference for litigation as opposed to other types of dispute settlement. These styles even affect the types of wrongs that most commonly occur and, as we shall see, the procedural steps used to adjust those wrongs.

PSYCHOLOGICAL ROOTS OF WOMAN PALAVER

The Kpelle themselves say, "The only palaver we have in this land is woman palaver." Table 23.1 indicates that this assertion is not much of an exaggeration. As noted in the discussion of the first hypothesis, the adulterous acts Kpelle men direct at other men's wives suggest a need for power over women, for power over other men, and for directing hostility against other men. The second hypothesis holds that this need for power is partly an expression of male feelings of inadequacy vis-a-vis women.

Actions such as those of Surong Tei, the defendant in the case cited above, often result ultimately in divorce and the woman's remarriage to the lover. Analytically, this pattern of alienation of affections followed by remarriage can be viewed as wife-stealing. If so, then theft—broadly conceived—becomes one of the most common offenses among the Kpelle. This fits Bacon, Child, and Barry's (1963) suggestion that theft by males is sometimes a defense against a feminine identity. In support of this interpretation, it should be recalled that we have already observed that Kpelle men do owe much of their status to women; thus they have a not-too-latent envy of women as powerful figures and, correspondingly, some uncertainty about their identity as males. Thus hypothesis two builds upon my own earlier analysis of Kpelle marital instability and the thinking of the Whiting-Human Relations Area Files school to suggest that there are psychological as well as structural roots for the incidence of disputes over women among the Kpelle.

The Case of the Sensitive Husband.
George Keller, a Kpelle evangelist, sued
Tia, a Bassa tribesman, for "abusing"
his wife. The case was heard before a
justice of the peace. Tia lived with a
fellow tribesman who, like himself, was
a sawyer. Keller's wife, Nyeei Puu, used
to visit the wife of Tia's landlord, who
was her friend. She would often see
Tia there and jokingly started to call
him "Big Head" because of his physical
appearance. He, appraising her appearance, in turn began to call her "Big
Behind."

One day, when Nyeei Puu was on the
way to the bush with another man, she
passed Tia washing his clothes in the
creek. She greeted him: "Good morning,
Big Head." He returned her salute in the
usual fashion, saying, "Good morning,
Big Behind." However, because Nyeei
Puu was with someone else, she became
worried that her companion would mis-
understand their joking and report her
to her husband as being too familiar
with another man. She therefore acted
insulted, claiming Tia had greeted her
by saying, "Good morning, Big Ass."
She reported her version of the incident
to her husband when he came home
that night.

The next morning Keller went to Tia's
house to ask if his wife's account was
true. However, Tia and his landlord had
already gone into the bush to saw.
Therefore Keller went immediately to
the justice of the peace and filed suit
against Tia.

When the case was heard, it came
out that Nyeei Puu and Tia had established a kind of joking relationship
and that they always used the same
nicknames in addressing each other.
Moreover, the man who had accompanied Nyeei Puu on the morning in
question testified that he had heard Tia
address Nyeei Puu by the inoffensive
term, "Big Behind."

The court stated that Keller should
have checked with Tia before bringing
suit. It found in Tia's favor and ordered
Keller to pay court costs and incidental
expenses. Tia wanted to file a counter-
suit for defamation of character, but
the court dissuaded him.

Nyeei Puu's discomfort and consequent shame at the creek indicates that
she was fully aware of the explosive
potential of male-female interaction in
Kpelleland. She also anticipated her
husband's concern with face, which
led to his precipitous suit. He shows
to a higher degree what is common
to many Kpelle men—nagging uncertainty about his ability to uphold
his masculine authority and prestige.

Further evidence of male feelings of
inadequacy vis-a-vis women emerges
in a sequence analysis of what occurs
in Kpelle divorce cases.

The Case of the Sojourning Wife. In
this case, heard before a paramount
chief, Nyema (the plaintiff) sued her
mother, Gopuu, requesting that the old
lady return the bridewealth that had
been paid for her because she no longer
wished to live with her husband. This
was therefore a suit for divorce and the
"real" defendant was Nyema's husband,
Kwi Kwili.

When Nyema was asked why her
mother—who for purposes of the suit
acted as her guardian in place in her
deceased father—should return her
bridewealth, she replied in the manner
customary for Kpelle wives seeking
divorce: "I do not want my husband's
home anymore." To substantiate her
charge, she recounted the history of her
marriage as first wife to Kwi Kwili, a
classificatory father's sister's son. Kwi
Kwili, in turn, gave his chronicle of
their marriage. A crucial element in the
dissension between them was the fact
that after their marriage Kwi Kwili inherited some additional wives from his
deceased father who, at the time of his
death, was living in Guinea. There was
jealousy between Nyema and the new
wives. Quite some time after that, Nyema's father had died in another chiefdom and she went to the funeral and
stayed, remaining away from her husband for a year and a half. She came
back to institute suit for divorce.

Nyema made her allegations against
Kwi Kwili in the following order:

1. A child of hers had died because
of her husband's mother's witchcraft.

2. Her husband had not supported her
because he failed to clear a rice farm
for her.

3. He had disrespected her by not
going to offer condolences whenever any
of her relatives died.

4. He had not shown appreciation for

special wifely acts: (a) treating his ill-nesses, (b) helping him to acquire money to offer the chief in lieu of hav-ing to perform public works duty, (c) showing more concern and considera-tion than her co-wives.

5. Her husband "overlooked" her, did not treat her with kindness or gratitude.

The key allegations seemed to be the witchcraft charge and the nonsupport charge, because each was repeated. But when questioned by her husband at the beginning of his testimony, Nyema indi-cated that she was not leaving him be-cause of the child's death but because of the nonsupport.

Kwi Kwili made the following allega-tions of his own:

1. Nyema was guilty of promiscuous behavior, notably the taking of frequent lovers.

2. She objected to his inheriting addi-tional wives.

3. When he did accept his inheritance of plural wives, Nyema, as the headwife, treated the co-wives badly, causing dis-sension in his household.

4. By staying away so long, she had deserted him.

Finally, Kwi Kwili countered his wife's primary allegation by referring to two of his own. He stated that the reason why he had not cleared a farm for her was that she was living elsewhere and forming liaisons with another man or men.

At the beginning of the case the chief established that Nyema wanted to leave Kwi Kwili "because of his ways." He then questioned her.

Chief: All right! Nyema, it reaches you. What did this person [the husband] do to you?

Nyema: The thing he did to me . . . when a person is in a home her child should live. And when a person is in a home, someone should work for her.

Thus a veiled accusation of a child's death by alleged witchcraft opened her allegations, which continued for many minutes. She catalogued the additional complaints noted above. Finally the chief, a bit exasperated and weary, turned to her and spoke:

Chief: The thing that you are saying, say it to the point. What are you saying? Say it to the point.

Nyema: This person they gave me to —when I have a child, his mother eats it. [She has restated—more baldly—the

witchcraft accusation with which she opened her allegations.]

Chief: Who is that who eats human beings?

Nyema: This person's [indicates her husband, Kwi Kwili] mother. This is one of his mothers sitting here. When they are doing like that to you in a home, can you stay there?

Chief (to spectator): Man, you who are sitting like that, if you lift up your head, that piece of stick will hit your head. What did you come to look for?

Man: No. [Meaning: I didn't come to look for anything special.] I just came to sit and listen to the case for a while.

Chief: You are sitting in a bad place. You will strike your head and hurt it. [Turning to Nyema] Are you through?

Nyema: There [In all I have said] is why I say: I don't want him. [It is] Because I took him from death and he overlooks me. He is just behaving like that to me.

Even though Nyema ranked nonsup-suport as her major allegation, it was clear that the child's death was also a great concern to her. It is equally clear that the chief was not anxious to probe into the matter and found a subtle way to avoid it by distracting Nyema, who was prone to ramble in testifying. We cannot be certain of whether or not the chief's gambit was conscious or uncon-scious. The effect was the same in either case.

The paramount chief granted the di-vorce, holding Nyema at fault, and he ordered Nyema and her mother to re-turn Kwi Kwili's bridewealth and to pay damages. This is the usual pattern in Kpelle divorce actions. The person who brings suit for divorce is felt to be at fault, and the plaintiff in divorce cases is almost always a woman.[11]

Although fault seems presumed in a Kpelle divorce case, it must be proven. It is in the pattern of proof that we find some psychological ramifications. In the case of the sojourning wife the only allegation of Nyema's investigated by the chief was that of nonsupport. In finding her at fault he accepted Kwi Kwili's counterallegation that he had not farmed with her because she had deserted him. The chief did not delve into Nyema's plea that she waited in vain at her deceased father's house, expecting Kwi Kwili to send for her. In effect the chief said that inasmuch as Nyema's primary reason for holding her husband at fault had been vitiated, she herself was at fault and the divorce would be granted on the grounds that she no longer wanted to live with her husband. There was no attempt to see whether she could substantiate any of her other reasons for holding her husband at fault—even the fairly serious charge of witchcraft. Even in delving into the nonsupport charge, the chief questioned Nyema in such a way that it was all but impossible for her to win her point. At a point early in Kwi Kwili's testimony, when the chief interrupts him to question Nyema, the transcript reads:

Chief (to Nyema): *Nee* Nyema, during the *whole time* you were in this man's hand, didn't he make any rice farm for you? [Emphasis added]
Nyema: When we were at Zowa, his mother and I used to make rice farms. He used to go to Firestone [Plantation] and we made swamp [rice] farms. But he used to just up and go across the river. . . . Then I told his mother that "I will be with you here, making farms for you."
Chief (to Nyema): *Mama,* did you say this person has not made *any* farms for you? [Emphasis added]
Nyema: I said that he used to make farms for me. But since we crossed the river, he has not made farms for me nor built a house for me.
Chief: And since you two came here?
Nyema: It was just recently that they told him that if he didn't come back across the river, his women will no longer be his. This is why he came here.
Chief: Since he came here, has he made any farm for you?
Nyema: I told you that I was at our home.

Chief: Go and sit down. That is just what they said about you.

By rephrasing Nyema's question to make it seem that she was holding that Kwi Kwili had *never* made a rice farm for her, it made it easy for Kwi Kwili to disprove her allegation simply by showing that he had farmed with her at some point in their marriage. Moreover, the chief led Nyema to the point of repeating that she had lived at her father's home for a long period of time, thereby setting the stage for Kwi Kwili's subsequent allegations of promiscuity and desertion. Thus the chief used his investigatory initiative to act somewhat as a prosecutor.

The incomplete investigation of the wife's allegations can be explained in two ways. The first is a judicial explanation. A Kpelle woman sues for divorce because she no longer wishes to stay with her husband. The chief hearing the case has only to determine that this is indeed so and to find a single basis for allocating fault. Having done so, he need proceed no further. Thus, as I have indicated elsewhere (Gibbs 1962), Kpelle divorce cases take on something of the cut and dried flavor of Monday morning drunkenness cases in American municipal courts. Finally, having assigned blame, the Kpelle judge determines the bridewealth to be returned.

However, there is a second, psychological, interpretation, based on the fact that the incompleteness of investigation operates to the woman's disadvantage. The chief, seeking out a single ground for allocating fault, usually airs the one most likely to show the woman at fault, not the one or two that have contributed most to the bad feelings between the litigants. This selective manner of focusing on allegations is a way in which Kpelle chiefs not only handle divorce cases with dispatch, but also express male control and dominance. Although chiefs can see fault on both sides in the divorce cases they hear, Kpelle conventions with regard to the handling of divorce cases require a unilateral ascription of blame. Thus, regardless of his actions toward his wife, the husband is almost always declared the winner and to his wife is ascribed the fault. The divorce court is one arena in which a Kpelle man— either litigant or spectator—can find counterbalance for feelings of inadequacy vis-a-vis women.

The judicial and psychological explanations are not mutually exclusive but complementary. The incidence of woman palaver—including divorce— is rooted in both structural and psychic factors, as was noted earlier. The treatment of divorce cases is patterned by the hardened nature of the estrangement, which demands severance of the union. But logically the biased investigation of allegations and assignment of blame could equally well go against the husband. However, if such were the case, additional psychic tensions would be created for Kpelle men. On the other hand, the androcentric bias in the investigation of allegations and assignment of fault serves to alleviate Kpelle men's feelings of inadequacy vis-a-vis women. Thus we see the law functioning, not only to settle disputes, but also to gratify the personality needs of litigants.

Qualitative case analysis suggests confirmation of the second preliminary hypothesis in its original form: A high incdence of disputes about rights over women is rooted not only in structural factors, but also in male feelings of inadequacy vis-a-vis women.

JUDICIAL IMPLICATIONS OF AUTHORITARIAN SUBMISSION

The Kpelle tendency to submit to authority figures and their stress on autonomy in interpersonal relations sometimes combine to produce a type of passive resistance to the decisions of judicial figures. Some of this resistance is predicted by the third preliminary hypothesis. This syndrome emerges very clearly in the Case of the Contemptuous Debtor, in which a justice of the peace sued the defendant, an acculturated Kpelle named James Reeves, for contempt of court in a debt case. The words of the summons were: "that you were sued in the above court and writ of summons issued; you failed to appear; two (2) consecutive letters were sent to you as friend but you never care to appear."

The Case of the Acquiescent Farmer. A more complicated case, also heard before a justice of the peace, involved Labla Kweli as plaintiff and Kiamu Pee and Goma Tokpa as co-defendants. All three litigants lived in the same quarter of their town. Kiamu Pee was entrusted with a steer owned by a Malinke from a nearby town. Goma Tokpa was also entrusted with a steer, in this case one owned by the paramount chief. The two steers went to the farm of Labla Kweli and ate much of the knee-high rice crop. Labla reported as much to the two caretakers, each of whom replied that he was not the owner of the beast and that Labla would have to sue the owners. The cattle went to the farm a second time and consumed the balance of the crop; Labla then sued both caretakers. Both owners of the cattle, the Malinke and the paramount chief, also appeared in court, although they were not named as co-defendants in the summons.

Although not named as a co-defendant, once in court the Malinke was held responsible for the acts of his steer and was ordered to pay $150—the value of the rice crop—and incidental fees."

In the pleadings Labla asked $150 from Goma Tokpa and the paramount chief. The paramount chief who appeared with Goma Tokpa admitted that the second beast was his and that it had destroyed the rice crop. He stated that he (the paramount chief), Goma Tokpa, and Labla were all related, implying that Labla could not sue him and Goma Tokpa because he would, in effect, be suing himself. Labla and the court accepted this argument.

The paramount chief then paid the court costs and gave Labla $20, saying that because the steer was Labla's, too, he should drop the matter. Labla agreed, saying that inasmuch as he was a co-owner of the beast, he would accept only $10 from the paramount chief.

The paramount chief stressed a kinship link that, under other circumstances, might be ignored. Because of Labla's submissiveness, the Malinke, as an alien in the chiefdom, bore more than an equitable share of the damages.

In this case Labla's deference to the paramount chief was open and apparent. However, informants reported that one reason the suit was filed in the first place—even though the paramount chief was a shadow defendant—was that the people of the town in which the three litigants lived were angry with the paramount chief. In fact, they filed a formal complaint against him with the county superintendent about the same time. Thus, as in some previous cases, we also see in this case the indirect expression of a grievance, suing for both overt and covert reasons. However, Labla's timorousness robbed the community of a complete victory in their covert goal.

Examination of the census survey figures of frequency of types of disputes and selected individual cases suggests a modification of the third preliminary hypothesis, to read: Authoritarian submission and stress on individual autonomy combine to produce a type of passive resistance to some aspects of the judicial process. This takes the form of litigants ignoring summonses and subpoenas and/or ignoring court decisions in which they have concurred before the court.

FUNCTIONS OF CONDITIONAL OATHS

The fourth of the original hypotheses suggests that the use of conditional oaths is found not just where there is an absence of other means of proof, but also where the issues in the case take on marked psychological salience.

This is found most commonly in cases of woman palaver in which a man's wife is leaving him. Before returning the brideprice and thus severing the union, the man who is being divorced will ask the court to have the woman swear a conditional oath that she has revealed all the names of any lovers she has had. The primary reason for this action is that the husband wishes to avail himself of the right to collect adultery damages from each of these men—a right that he will lose as soon as the divorce is effected. However, it seems probable that a second reason is that the husband can "get back" at those men who have attacked him by consorting with his wife.

The association of the use of conditional oaths and psychological salience emerges most dramatically in a type of case that is relatively rare in Kpelle courts—when the wrong is what can best be termed supernatural assault.

The Case of the Menacing Blacksmith. Yakpawolo Gbanga and Sumo live in the same quarter of their town, where Sumo is the quarter blacksmith. Yakpawolo is crippled by a disease which caused both of his lower legs to swell so greatly that he cannot walk. One day when Yakpawolo was in Sumo's blacksmith's shed, Sumo told him that the reason he was crippled was that he (Sumo) had once obtained a sheep and made a sacrifice using Yakpawolo's name.

Yakpawolo sued Sumo before the district chief, demanding that Sumo indicate why he had sorcerized him. At first Sumo denied having made the statement, but there were several witnesses to the incident who testified otherwise. The court found Sumo guilty and ordered him to bring a sheep to sacrifice to clear the bad feelings. In handing down his decision, the chief explained: "then the spirits of the old people [the] ancestors would leave them, . . . otherwise they would continually be in trouble." Since Sumo did not have a sheep, he brought a white dog instead, white being the color Kpelle associate with having "good heart" toward others. Yakpawolo refused to accept the suggestion of the sacrifice, saying that what he desired was to know why Sumo had directed a sacrifice against him. The district chief suggested that they should kill and eat the dog and that Sumo should drink the dog's blood and swear on it that he had not made a sacrifice against Yakpawolo.

Yakpawolo still refused to accept the court's decision and appealed the case to the paramount chief's court, where it was heard the following day. The paramount chief also found Sumo guilty and offered him two alternatives. One was that first suggested by the district chief, that Sumo swear his innocence on the blood of the dog; the other, that he swear it on *kafu*.[12] This time Yakpawolo accepted the court's decision, and Sumo swore his innocence on *kafu*.

This case illustrates both functions of the use of conditional oaths. First, for the tension of grievances to be dissipated at all, it was necessary for the court to use the conditional oath to find out whether or not the alleged act of sorcery had taken place. By swearing the oath, Sumo said in effect that he had been lying when he told Yakpawolo that he had performed sorcery against him. It was then necessary for the effects of the admitted wrong, malicious lying, to be reduced. This second result was also achieved by the use of the conditional oath. It served the second function of allaying anxieties aroused in Yakpawolo by Sumo's boast. Sumo's swearing on *kafu* assured Yakpawolo that the blacksmith's feelings against him were not so hostile that they had led him to perform sorcery, although the false boast was itself an antagonistic act, albeit of lesser magnitude.

In effect Yakpawolo asked the court to require Sumo to issue a supernaturally buttressed denial of sorcery, a form of redress that was rooted in his own psychic needs, his desire to institute the process of repression (or even denial) of what he had heard that painful day in the blacksmith's shed. Because Sumo's denial was cast in the potentially boomeranging form of a conditional oath, Yakpawolo found it all the more believable and all the more soothing. However, this interpretation must not be over-extended. Yakpawolo was not ruled completely by his anxieties, for he admitted that he had appealed the case partly because he hoped that the paramount chief would require Sumo to pay him $100 to use for medical treatment!

Qualitative case analysis suggests a slight revision of the fourth preliminary hypothesis. It can be stated as follows: Ordeals or conditional oaths will be resorted to when there is an absence of proof or conflicting testimony that there is no more "rational" way of resolving. But conditional oaths will be resorted to also when the offense is one that is psychologically very disturbing to the wronged party's psychic equilibrium. Usually this wrong will be one that is, in Kpelle terms, an assault on the wronged party's self-identity. However, the incomplete nature of Kpelle court records makes it impossible to test the revised hypothesis quantitatively.

PERSONALITY DISPOSITIONS AND
INCIDENCE OF LEGAL INVOLVEMENT

The data suggest modification of the fifth original hypothesis, which states that people with a high degree of blocked aggression show a greater frequency of involvement with the law. It is more accurate to predict that persons with a high frequency of involvement in litigation may be deviant psychologically. Of course, some instances of frequent appearance in court can be explained by structural factors. Thus, shopkeepers in Kpelleland—whether they be Kpelle, Malinke, Lebanese, or Americo-Liberian—are more likely to be involved in suits for debt than other people. Other instances of frequent appearance in court yield to a more psychological explanation.

The Case of the Bellicose Suitor. This pattern is illustrated by the case of Dolo Gbia (plaintiff) versus Kiakula (defendant). Dolo Gbia had Kiakula working on his farm, and he noticed that Kiakula had a sexual interest in his wife, Nyeme. Dolo Gbia then offered the woman to Kiakula as his consort, and Kiakula thus became his client.[13] After six months the woman and Kiakula terminated their relationship by mutual agreement. Kiakula then directed his attention to Dolo Gbia's and Nyeme's daughter. The daughter spurned his advances, saying that she could not have an affair with her mother's former lover because she now thought of him "as a father." This angered Kiakula, who assaulted the girl. He was sued by Dolo Gbia before a justice of the peace, found guilty, fined, and ordered not to return to his home town for three months but to work on the farm of the justice of the peace instead. However, Kiakula

violated this injunction, and before the three months were up he returned to his home town and assaulted the girl again, threatening to beat her to death. This time he was arrested and tried at the county seat, where he was jailed for a month.

The court clerk who was my informant with reference to this case observed that Kiakula, a man with a withered arm, was "always in trouble." It is probable that the withered arm affected Kiakula's sense of adequacy and consequently led him to assert himself in ways that brought him into conflict with the law. The nature of Kiakula's offense and the repetition of it both lend support for this type of hypothesis.

Until the next phases of the research are completed, it is not possible to test quantitatively the correlation between high involvement in litigation and psychological deviance predicted by the preliminary hypothesis because of the absence of "hard" personality data. However, qualitative examination of some cases and substantial personal knowledge of many individuals in the culture yield subjective support for the fifth preliminary hypothesis.

The preliminary hypothesis, which was phrased in too narrow terms, can be modified to read as follows: With a few statable exceptions (such as merchants, chiefs), persons with a high frequency of involvement in litigation or who are frequent appellants are likely to be psychologically deviant.

This type of psychologically oriented hypothesis does not preclude a complementary sociological (or structural) one. Frequent involvement in litigation may be reflective of a person's status attributes, such as occupation (trader) or rank, wealth, and responsibility (chief).

THE REVISED HYPOTHESES

The preliminary hypotheses can now be stated in less tentative form, as dictated by the preceding analysis. Among the Kpelle:

1. The need to discharge aggression or hostility is reflected judicially in a relatively high incidence of the following types of offenses: (a) failure to fulfill a commitment; (b) tendency to sue for a manifest stated grievance rather than the covert one that actually troubles the plaintiff; (c) woman palaver, much of which begins with adulterous actions directed at the wife of another man.

2. A high incidence of disputes about rights over women is rooted not only in structural factors, but also in male feelings of inadequacy vis-a-vis women.

3. Authoritarian submission plus stress on individual autonomy combine to produce a type of passive resistance to some aspects of the judicial process. This takes the form of litigants' ignoring summonses and subpoenas and/or ignoring court decisions in which they have concurred before the court.

4. Ordeals or conditional oaths will be resorted to when there is an absence of proof or conflicting testimony for which there is no more "rational" resolution. But conditional oaths will be resorted to also when the offense is one which psychologically is very disturbing of the wronged party's psychic equilibrium. Usually this wrong will be one that is, in Kpelle terms, an assault on the wronged party's self-identity.

5. With a few statable exceptions (such as merchants, chiefs), persons: with a high frequency of involvement in litigation or who are frequent appellants are likely to be psychologically deviant.

AN ANALYTICAL NOTE: INDIVIDUAL DIFFERENCES AND GROUP TRENDS

The careful reader will observe that all these hypotheses can be phrased and investigated from either of two viewpoints: one is that of individuals' differences; the other, that of group trends. For example, as phrased, the fifth hypothesis suggests that when Litigant A appeals his lost case and Litigant B does not, we may explain this in terms of differences in their two personalities; that A has more blocked aggression, which he discharges through being litigious. On the other hand, we may derive figures both for the level of blocked aggression and the incidence of appeals from lower courts characteristic of the group as a whole. If both are high, we say that the high incidence of appeals may reflect a personality trait that is characteristic of the *group*. To be sure, one would not wish to overlook other factors that contribute to the frequency of appeals, such as what our society calls "judicial error" or simple uncertainty as to what the law (in the sense of rule) is. Obviously these various independent variables must be weighed differently when explaining the separate appeal frequencies of particular offenses. Thus, in cases involving new laws, a high incidence of appeals is likely to reflect uncertainty about the law and judicial error; in cases involving old laws, it is more likely to reflect a widespread psychodynamic factor.

This distinction between the "individual" and "group" approach is seen in beautiful simplicity with regard to the second hypothesis, which explains the incidence of disputes in rights over women. The approach espoused here is not so much concerned about why particular Kpelle men get involved in adultery or divorce cases or both as it is with why 44 percent of all self-reported litigation in the town in which I have done most of my field work involves rights over women or marital problems. The concern is with the impact such "group" incidences has on both the procedures and the substance of the law.

The present study is oriented to the "group" point of view for several reasons. First, the aim is to examine and explain the regularities of Kpelle law. Second, most of the presently available personality assessment techniques lend themselves more readily to discerning recurring traits than to validly isolating differences (particularly when used in nonliterate societies). Third, the concern is not with explaining the particular behavior of particular individuals in particular litigation situations, for neither our assessment techniques nor our predictive models are yet sufficiently sophisticated to do this.

A review of the literature scattered across several behavioral science disciplines reveals numerous studies that relate personality variables to particular aspects of law and social control. However, these studies have had little impact on the mainstream of work in the ethnography of law of nonliterate and peasant societies. Research in this area has concentrated primarily on dispute settlement, particularly the judicial process. Even when anthropologists (who form the majority of scholars working in the subdiscipline) analyze the relationship between personality and law, they have explored the relationship between personality and a single aspect of law rather than attempting to relate it to the profile of major descriptive attributes characteristic of a single legal system.

The writer's on-going study of law and personality among the Kpelle is broader in scope than preceding studies in that it traces connections between personality variables and several dominant features of the judicial system.

Notes

1. My thinking in this area has benefited from the contributions of the student members of a graduate seminar on Law and Personality that I taught at the University of Minnesota in the spring of 1965. They were: Rachel Bonney, Margot Liberty, John Poggie, Katherine Salter, and Gretel Whitaker. I would also like to acknowledge the comments and criticisms of my fellow participants at the Wenner-Gren symposium on the ethnography of law in August 1966 for which an earlier version of this paper was prepared. In particular I would like to express thanks to Sally Falk Moore, the discussant for the paper.

2. It should be noted that there is no significant body of research literature on the psychic sources and functions of norms, a fourth dimension of social control.

3. I define "ethnic personality" as those recurring basic personality dimensions that are most characteristic of a culture or community. This definition is meant to parallel the term "national character" but stresses the presence of more than one representative "character." Ethnic personality is multimodal, not unimodal.

4. Frenkel-Brunswik (1954, pp. 232-233) notes that in a study of ethnocentrism in children she found "variations of the authoritarian personality syndrome to be

related to parental occupation." In a fleeting comment she states that salesmen, policemen, firemen, and their families are more likely to be found among authoritarians and that choosing to be a policeman "may reveal identification with authority and aggression and poor adjustment to work *per se.*" A rather thorough bibliographical search fails to reveal any other studies that deal with the relationship between authoritarian personality variables and legal occupations, a surprising gap in research foci.

5. The field research reported here has been supported by several bodies whose support I acknowledge with gratitude. The 1957-1958 field period was carried out while I held a Ford Foundation Foreign Area Fellowship, and it was also supported by a grant from the Laboratory of Social Relations of Harvard University. Initial analysis was done while I held a predoctoral fellowship from the National Science Foundation; further analysis was made possible by a Faculty Summer Research Grant from the University of Minnesota. The 1965-1966 field period and subsequent analysis has been supported by the National Science Foundation. I would also like to acknowledge the assistance of the Center for International Studies of Stanford University.

The research design was drawn up in 1963-1964 while I was the holder of a postdoctoral fellowship from the Social Science Research Council for training in methods of personality assessment; the Council's support is gratefully acknowledged. During that year I learned much from the staff of the Departments of Psychiatry and Psychology at the Hennepin County General Hospital, Minneapolis, Minnesota, and from the faculty members of the Department of Psychology and the Institute of Child Development at the University of Minnesota.

Both periods of field work were facilitated by the cooperation of the Liberian Government. I would also like to thank all those individual Liberians who have contributed to the research effort. Space precludes my mentioning all of them here, but I would particularly like to thank my primary field assistants: Lewis T. Currens, John Kellemu, and John Wealar. I am grateful to Daniel Pearlman of the Peace Corps and University of Liberia Law School and his students, who helped to compile the case inventory of Kpelle disputes, and also to Cuttington College for numerous courtesies and for student clerical assistance. I also owe appreciation to the United States Peace Corps and to many individual Americans too numerous to mention here.

I extend my appreciation to my Stanford research assistants, Peter Dolan and Patrick O'Grady, who have carried out their assignments with diligence, enthusiasm, and high competence. The first version of this paper was typed in Liberia by Mrs. Bonita Estes; the present one, by Mrs. Millie Dunn and Mrs. Anne Gamble.

6. Table 23.1 represents self-reported cases collected, as noted, in a census survey of Fokwele. There is evidence that respondents did not report all the cases in which they had ever been involved, especially house palavers. However, there is no evidence that the under-reporting was not random or that some kinds of cases were reported more than others.

7. Fathers-in-law do not pose a major problem to families of the next descending generation.

8. The rank remains fourth even when the subcategory "failure to fulfill obligation to government" is excluded.

9. Pseudonyms are used in all the cases presented here to preserve the anonymity of the litigants, although all cases are a matter of public record.

10. American currency is used in Liberia as legal tender, although there are some specially minted Liberian coins. Thus monetary figures used in the cases are actual dollar figures.

11. The guilty party pays damages fixed by statute at $100, and if it is the wife, as it most often is, the refunded bridewealth her guardian repays on her behalf is fixed by statute at a minimum of $40. The man retains filiation of the children regardless of whether he is held at fault. If the man is held at fault, he forfeits bridewealth and has to pay damages. No bridewealth is deducted for children born to the woman, regardless of where fault is assigned.

12. *Kafu* is a colorless liquid kept in a stoppered whiskey or wine bottle and is believed to have supernatural potency. In taking it a witness swears that, "if I bear

false witness . . . then the *sale* [medicine] should kill me." It is believed that a person who breaks such an oath will be "caught" by the *kafu*. His stomach will swell and he will die, or some other illness will eventually strike.

13. This is a type of union which I referred to as "male concubinage" (Gibbs 1965). A man who does not have the means of obtaining a marriage payment will go to a wealthy man and ask to be given one of the wealthy man's wives as a consort. The woman remains the legal wife of the *tɔnuu* (patron) but the *lɔɔ pɔlɔɔng* (client) cohabits with her in a house provided by the patron-husband. Although the patron gives up sexual access to his wife, he retains the right to collect any adultery damages that may be incurred by her actions, and children born to her and the client legally belong to the patron. The client and the woman work on the farm of the patron, and they may also work a farm of their own. In a formal sense the client gains little more than sexual access to the woman.

REFERENCES

Bacon, M. K., I. L. Child, and H. Barry III
  1963   A cross-cultural study of correlates of crime. *Journal of Abnormal and Social Psychology* 66: 291-300.
Berndt, Ronald M.
  1962   *Excess and Restraint: Social Control among a New Guinea Mountain People*. Chicago: University of Chicago Press.
Bohannan, Paul
  1957   *Justice and Judgment among the Tiv of Nigeria*. London: Oxford University Press.
  1965   The differing realms of the law. *American Anthropologist* 67 (6): 33-42.
Cohen, Yehudi A.
  1964   *The Transition from Childhood to Adolescence: Cross-Cultural Studies of Initiation Ceremonies, Legal Systems and Incest Taboos*. Chicago: Aldine.
  1966   On alternative views of the individual in culture and personality studies. *American Anthropologist* 68 (2): 355-361.
Cowan, Thomas A.
  1962   What law can do for social science. *In* W. M. Evan (ed.), *Law and Sociology: Exploratory Essays*. New York: Free Press.
Crane, W. C.
  1951   Kwakiutl, Haida and Tsimshian: A study in social control. Ms., University of Utah Library.
Durkheim, Emile
  1933   *On the Division of Labor in Society*. New York: Macmillan.
Frenkel-Brunswik, E.
  1954   Further explorations by a contributor to the Authoritarian Personality. *In* R. Christie and M. Jahoda (eds.), *Studies in the Scope and Method of the Authoritarian Personality*. New York: Free Press.
Gibbs, James L., Jr.
  1962   Poro values and courtroom procedures in a Kpelle chiefdom. *Southwestern Journal of Anthropology* 18: 341-350.
  1963a Marital instability among the Kpelle: Towards a theory of epainogamy. *American Anthropologist* 65 (3): 552-573.
  1963b The Kpelle moot: A therapeutic model for the informal settlement of disputes. *Africa* 33: 1-11.
  1965   The Kpelle of Liberia. *In* J. L. Gibbs, Jr., (ed.), *Peoples of Africa*. New York: Holt, Rinehart and Winston.
Haines, Charles G.
  1923   General observations on the effect of personal, political and economic influences in the decisions of judges. *Illinois Law Review* 17 (1): 96-116.
Hoebel, E. Adamson
  1954   *The Law of Primitive Man*. Cambridge: Harvard University Press.

Inkeles, A., and D. J. Levinson
  1954 National character: The study of modal personality and socio-cultural systems. *In* G. Lindzey (ed.), *The Handbook of Social Psychology*, Volume II. Cambridge, MA: Addison-Wesley.
Kardiner, A., and L. Ovesey
  1951 *The Mark of Oppression: Explorations in the Personality of the American Negro*. New York: Norton.
LeVine, Robert A.
  1960 The internalization of political values in stateless societies. *Human Organization* 19: 51-58.
Liberty, Margot
  n.d. Law and personality in acculturation: The Cheyenne Indians. Paper presented in a seminar on law and personality at the University of Minnesota, spring 1965; mimeo.
Little, Kenneth
  1965-66 The political functions of the Poro. *Africa* 35: 349-365; 36: 62-72.
Llewellyn, K., and E. Adamson Hoebel
  1941 *The Cheyenne Way*. Norman: University of Oklahoma Press.
Nader, Laura
  1965 The anthropological study of law. *American Anthropologist* 67 (6): 3-32.
Parsons, Talcott
  1951 *The Social System*. New York: Free Press.
  1962 The law and social control. *In* W. M. Evan (ed.), *Law and Sociology: Exploratory Essays*. New York: Free Press.
Poggie, John J., Jr.
  n.d. The intergenerational perpetuation of crime in Tepoztlan. Paper presented in a seminar in law and personality at the University of Minnesota, spring 1965; ms.
Riesman, David
  1962 Law and sociology: Recruitment, training and colleagueship. *In* W. M. Evan (ed.), *Law and Sociology: Exploratory Essays*. New York: Free Press.
Roberts, John M.
  1965 Oaths, autonomic ordeals, and power. *American Anthropologist* 67 (6): 186-212.
Snell, J. E., R. J. Rosenwald, and A. Robey
  1964 The wifebeater's wife: A study of family interaction. *Archives of General Psychiatry* 11 (2): 107-112.
Spiro, Melford
  1961 An overview and suggested reorientation. *In* F. Hsu (ed.), *Psychological Anthropology*. Homewood, IL: Dorsey Press.
Swartz, Marc J.
  1966 Bases for political compliance in Bena villages. *In* M. J. Swartz, V. W. Turner, and A. Tuden (eds.), *Political Anthropology*. Chicago: Aldine.
Whitaker, Gretel H.
  n.d. Law and personality: An outline of perspectives and an analysis of their relationship in Chiapas. Paper presented in a seminar on law and personality at University of Minnesota, spring 1965; mimeo.
Whiting, Beatrice B.
  1965 Sex identity conflict and physical violence: A comparative study. *American Anthropologist* 67 (8): 123-140.
Winick, Charles
  1961 The psychology of juries. *In* H. Toch (ed.), *Legal and Criminal Psychology*. New York: Holt, Rinehart and Winston.
Winick, Charles, I. Gerver, and A. Blumberg
  1961 The psychology of judges. *In* H. Toch (ed.), *Legal and Criminal Psychology*. New York: Holt, Rinehart and Winston.

INDEX

CULTURE AND PERSONALITY: CONTEMPORARY READINGS

ROBERT A. LEVINE, EDITOR

Publisher / Alexander J. Morin
Production Editor / Georganne E. Marsh
Production Manager / Mitzi Carole Trout

Designed by Aldine Staff
Composed by Production Type, Inc., Dallas, Texas
Printed by Printing Headquarters, Inc.,
Arlington Heights, Illinois
Bound by The Engdahl Company, Elmhurst, Illinois